Jaiva-dharma

The Universal Religion

By Srila Bhaktivinoda Thakura

Translated by Kuśakratha Dāsa
Edited by Pūrṇaprajña Dāsa

RAS BIHARI LAL & SONS
RBL&S
VRINDAVAN

The Universal Religion

Jaiva-dharma

By Srila Bhaktivinoda Thakura

ISBN 81-8403-014-2
Published By: Rasbihari Lal & Sons.
Loi Bazar, Vrindaban-281121 (U.P.) India.
Phone: 91-565-2442570
Fax: 91-565-2443970
E-mail: brijwasi2001@hotmail.com
Our Other Division Brijwasi Exports

Our Other Publications

Govinda Lilamrata
Sri Gaudiya Kanthahara
Dhamali (By Gadadhar Prana)
Sri Gopal Sahasra Nama
Sri Krsna Astottara Satnama
Sri Radha Sahasra-Nama- Stotra
The Life of Ramanujacarya
Namamrta Samudra
Narottama Vilasa
Sri Prem Bhakti Chandrika
Lessons From The Ayurveda
Sanskrit Gramar
Caitanya Candramrtam
Garuda Purana
Life of Madhavacharya
Padama Purana
Skand Purana
Sri Narad Puran
Braja-Vilasa Stavah
Mukta Caritra (The Perl Story)
Sri Manah Siksa
Sri Sri Dana Keli Cintamanih
A Handbook of Vaisnava Songs & Practices
A Vaisnava Harmonium and Singing Method (With 2 tape)
Practical Mrdanga Lessons (With One Tape)
Food for Peace (Cook Book)
Astakala Lila Padavali
Lalit Madhava
Mathura Mahatmaya
Sri Krsna Caitanya Divya Sahasra-Nama
Sri Radha Krsna Ganoddesa Dipika
Vidagdha Madhava
Hari Bhaktivilas Vol. 1-5
Sri Krsna Lila Stava
Sri Sikastaka

Ujjvala-Nilamani
The Mahabharat
The Songs of Lochan Dasa Thakura
Harivamsa Purana: Vol. 1-3
Sri Narad Pancaratra: Vol. 1-2
Srimad Bhagavadgita
The Glories of Ekadasi
From Nothingness to Personhood
Narasimha Avatar
The Four Principal of Freedam
The Heart of Devotion
The Life and Times of Lord Caitanya
The Lives of Vaishnava Saints
The Six Goswamies of Vrindavan
Vedic Archeology & Assorted Essays
Sri Gopala Tapani Upanisad
Sri Krsna Bhavanamrta Mahakavya
Sri Prem Samput
The Bhakti Trilogy
Sri Caitanya Bhagavata - Complete Edition
Sri Vrndavana Mahimamrta - only 17th Chapter.
Sri Vrndavana Mahimamrta - Complete Edition
Garga Samhita
Bhakti Ratnakara
Sri Krsna Karnamrta
Jagannatha Vallabha Nataka
Camatkara Candrika
Sri Vrajariti Cintamani
Sri Caitanya Carita Mahakavya
Vaisnava Saints
Bhagavad Gita by Bhaktivinoda Thakura
Sri Uddhava-Sandesa & Sri Hamsaduta
Sri Krisna's Names In Bhagavad Gita
Bhavishya Purana

Dedicated to

His Divine Grace

A.C. Bhaktivedanta Swami Prabhupāda

founder - ācārya

International Society

for Krishna Consciousness

Table of Contents

Introduction - 12

Chapter One: - 19
The soul's eternal and temporary natures.

Chapter Two: - 31
The soul's eternal nature is pure and everlasting.

Chapter Three: - 43
The soul's temporary duties are imperfect, horrible, contaminated, and short-lived.

Chapter Four: - 61
Another name for the eternal religion is the Vaiṣṇava religion.

Chapter Five: - 77
Vaidhī-bhakti—the eternal religion. It is not temporary.

Chapter Six: - 95
Eternal religion and the differences of caste.

Chapter Seven: - 117
Eternal duties, household life, and the material world.

Chapter Eight: - 141
Eternal religion and ordinary activities.

Chapter Nine: - 165
Eternal religion and modern science-civilization.

Chapter Ten: - 183
Eternal religion and history.

Chapter Eleven: - 199
Eternal religion and byūt-parasta, or Deity worship.

Chapter Twelve: - 211
Eternal religion and devotional service in practice

Chapter Thirteen: - 227
Eternal religion and sambandha, abhidheya and prayojana (Evidence and truth)

Chapter Fourteen: - 245
Eternal religion and sambandha, abhidheya, and prayojana (The Lord's potencies)

Chapter Fifteen: - 263
Eternal religion and sambandha, abhidheya and prayojana (The individual spirit souls)

Chapter Sixteen: - 279
Eternal religion and sambandha, abhidheya, and prayojana (The individual souls swallowed by māyā)

Chapter Seventeen: - 293
Eternal religion and sambandha, abhidheya, and prayojana
(The souls free from māyā's prison)

Chapter Eighteen: - 311
Eternal religion and sambandha, abhidheya and prayojana
(Simultaneous oneness and difference)

Chapter Nineteen: - 329
Eternal religion and sambandha, abhidheya, and prayojana
(Abhidheya)

Chapter Twenty: - 347
Eternal religion and sambandha, abhidheya and prayojana
(Abhidheya: Vaidha-sādhana-bhakti)

Chapter Twenty-one: - 369
Eternal religion and sambandha, abhidheya and prayojana
(Abhidheya: rāgānuga-sādhana-bhakti)

Chapter Twenty-two: - 385
Eternal religion and sambandha, abhidheya and prayojana
(The discussion of prayojana begins)

Chapter Twenty-three: - - - - - - - - - - - - - - - - - - 399
Eternal religion and sambandha, abhidheya and prayojana
(The discussion of the holy name begins)

Chapter Twenty-four: - 411
Eternal religion and sambandha, abhidheya, and prayojana (Offenses to the holy name)

Chapter Twenty-five: - 423
Eternal religion and sambandha, abhidheya, and prayojana (Offenses to the holy name)

Chapter Twenty-six: - 435
The discussion of rasa begins

Chapter Twenty-seven: - 445
Further consideration of the rasas

Chapter Twenty-eight: - 453
Further consideration of the rasas, part two

Chapter Twenty-nine: - 465
Further consideration of the rasas, part three

Chapter Thirty: - 477
Further consideration of the rasas, part four

Chapter Thirty-one: - 487
Mādhurya-rasa, part one

Chapter Thirty-two: - 503
Mādhurya-rasa, part two

Chapter Thirty-three: - 519
Mādhurya-rasa, part three

Chapter Thirty-four: - 537
Mādhurya-rasa, part four

Chapter Thirty-five: - 551
Mādhurya-rasa, part five

Chapter Thirty-six: - 565
Mādhurya-rasa, part six

Chapter Thirty-seven: - 583
Śṛṅgāra-rasa (Mādhurya-rasa)

Chapter Thirty-eight: - 593
Śṛṅgāra-rasa, part two

Chapter Thirty-nine: - 605
Entering the Lord's pastimes

Chapter Forty: - 615
The greatest good fortune

Introduction

Jaiva Dharma is a Vaiṣṇava novel written in Bengali prose. Most of the book is very philosophical, consisting of dialogue of questions and answers between the characters of the book. The book is primarily based on two books of Śrīla Rupa Gosvami— Bhakti-rasamrta-sindhu and Ujjvala-nilamani. These two books are accepted as the most important and authoritative books on rasa-tattva. Śrīla Bhaktivinoda Ṭhākura has taken the essential understanding of these books and presented it in an easy-to-read story format. Simply by reading Jaiva Dharma, the serious student of bhakti can understand the intricacies of the soul's eternal relationship with the Absolute Truth, the Supreme Personality of Godhead, Śrī Kṛṣṇa.

The precise meaning of Jaiva Dharma is given in the book itself, as follows: The activity of such pure souls is called bhakti (devotional service). Hari-bhakti (devotional service to Lord Hari) is also called by the names suddha-Vaiṣṇava-dharma (pure Vaiṣṇava religion), nitya-dharma (eternal religion), jaiva dharma (duty of the individual souls), bhāgavata-dharma (religion of worshiping the Supreme Personality of Godhead), paramārtha-dharma (way to attain the final goal of life), and para-dharma (highest religion).

Śrīla Bhaktivinoda Ṭhākura must be recognized as the devotee who totally revitalized the movement of Śrī Caitanya Mahāprabhu. Although the Ṭhākura is especially noted for his having re-discovered the site of Lord Caitanya's birth, in fact, he practically re-discovered and re-established Lord Caitanya's movement, which was obscured by the cultural and religious chauvinism of the ruling British, and discredited by the perverse and useless activities of a number of sahajiyā sects and other groups with motivated, concocted philosophies.

It is often pointed out that it was he who made the prediction that the day would soon come when devotees from around the world would congregate at Śrīdhāma Māyāpur, chanting the holy names of the Lord. In his youth, Śrīla Bhaktivinoda Ṭhākura took an interest in Western philosophy and literature, and only gradually came to the path of pure devotional service to the Lord. This is mirrored in Jaiva Dharma, which embodies the mood of the staunch preacher of Kṛṣṇa consciousness.

The main character throughout the first half of the book is Śrī Prema dāsa Bābājī, who is known as a paramahaṁsa, or a topmost swan-like devotee of the Lord who has transcended all external forms of religiosity. He is always overwhelmed with pure ecstatic love, and his personal worship of the Lord cannot be understood by an ordinary person. One day, the bābājī is approached by a sannyāsī who is himself very well-versed in the revealed scriptures but has concluded that the impersonal conception of the Absolute is supreme. The sannyāsī asks many questions, and the bābājī gives the conclusive answers, thereby convincing the him of the supremacy of the personal theism of the Vaiṣṇavas.

Other characters gradually make their appearance in the novel, and various philosophical discussions take place. This is a very thorough book, touching on practically every major topic of devotional life, and Śrīla Bhaktivinoda Ṭhākura has quoted profuse scriptural passages to support his conclusions.

Finally, the last fifteen chapters of Jaiva Dharma discuss the subject of transcendental rasa very elaborately. Two sincere devotees named Vijaya-kumāra and Vrajanātha approach Prema dāsa Bābājī with many questions, and together they discuss the nature of ecstatic symptoms, transcendental emotions, and affection for the Lord in the relationships of neutrality, servitude, friendship, parenthood, and conjugal love. Vijaya-kumāra, who wishes to be further instructed in the conjugal mellow, is directed by Premadāsa Bābājī to proceed to Jagannātha Purī and receive the audience of Gopāla-guru Gosvāmī, a disciple of Svarūpa Dāmodara Gosvāmī. From him he learns about Kṛṣṇa's role as the Supreme Hero, Rādhā's role as the Supreme Heroine, descriptions of

Rādhā's girlfriends, stimulants for ecstatic love, the Lord's pastimes conducted throughout eight periods of the day, varieties of enjoyments shared by the Divine Couple, and so on.

The book ends with a description of how the two devotees, Vrajanātha and Vijaya-kumāra attain the ultimate goal of life by taking the teachings of their spiritual master to heart. Vrajanātha remained on the banks of the Gaṅgā in Śrīdhāma Māyāpura, and Vijaya-kumāra stayed in a secluded cottage near the Jagannātha Purī seashore.

As to be expected, Kuśakratha Prabhu has given us a very clear, concise, readable, and poetic description of the topics that he most relished. Jaiva Dharma is a very complex philosophical work but Kuśakratha Prabhu has presented it in a way that one can relish it without becoming exhausted by the complexities.

Pūrṇaprajña Dāsa

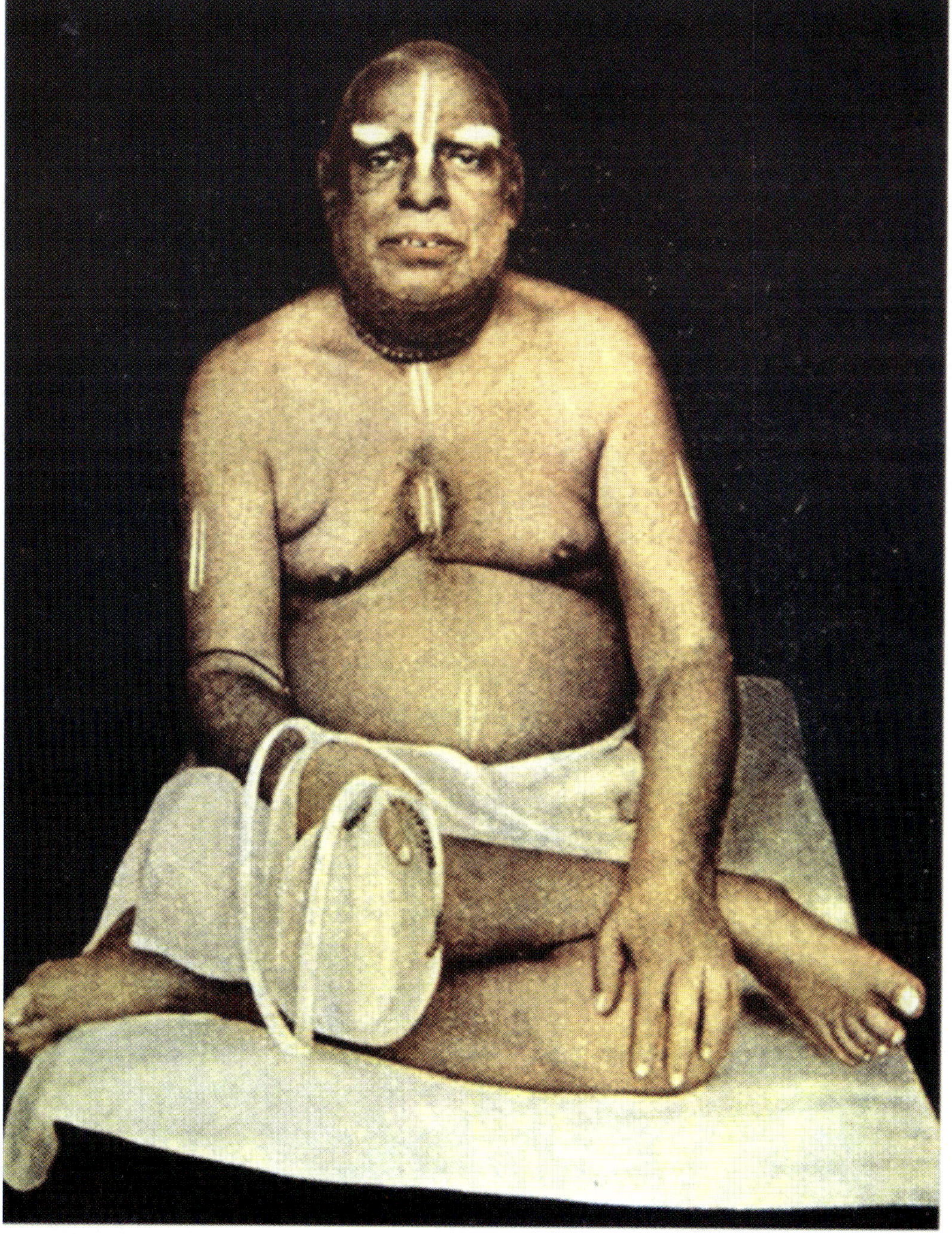

Srila Bhaktivinoda Thakura, the autor of the "Jaiva-Dharma"

A.C. Bhaktivedanta Swami Prabhupāda
founder - ācārya International Society for Krishna Consciousness

Who is the Supreme Lord? Who is the individual spirit soul? What is the material world? (Page 387)

Like the qualities of Śrī Kṛṣṇa, the qualities of Vṛndāvana's queen, Rādhā, are limitless and cannot truly be counted or listed in full... (Page 522)

Chapter One

The soul's eternal and temporary natures.

Of all earthly realms, Jambūdvīpa is the best. Of all places in Jambūdvīpa, Bhārata-varṣa is the best. Of all places in Bhārata-varṣa, Gauḍa-deśa is the best. Of all places in Gauḍa-deśa, Śrī Navadvīpa-maṇḍala is the best. In one part of Śrī Navadvīpa-maṇḍala, on the Gaṅgā's shore, the beautiful village of Śrī Godruma is splendidly manifested eternally. In ancient times, many *bhajanānandī* devotees made their homes in the gardens of Śrī Godruma.

In that place, in a cottage of vines, a *surabhī* cow once worshiped Lord Gaurasundara, the Supreme Personality of Godhead. Not far from that place was a *bhajana-kuṭira* named Pradyumna-kuñja. In that *bhajana-kuṭira*, which was thick with vines, a *parāmahāṁsa bābājī*, who was an initiated disciple of the Supreme Lord's personal associate, Pradyumna Brahmacārī, always stayed, rapt in the bliss of worshiping the Lord (*bhajanānanda*).

Aware that Śrī Godruma is not different from Śrī Nanda-grāma in Vṛndāvana, Śrī Prema-dāsa Bābājī, who was learned in all the scriptures, had taken shelter in that holy place. Every day, he chanted Lord Hari's holy names two hundred thousand times. Every day, he offered hundreds and hundreds of *daṇḍavat* obeisances to all the Vaiṣṇavas. He maintained his life by *mādhukarī* begging at the homes of the cowherd people there. He strictly followed the rules of a saintly life.

When he had finished all his spiritual duties, he would not waste his time with gossip. Rather, he would read, with tears in his eyes, the *Prema-vivarta* of Lord Gaurasundara's dear associate, Jagadānanda Paṇḍita. At those times the devotees in that forest grove would listen with love and devotion. And why not? The book *Prema-vivarta* is full of the sweet mellows (*rasas*) of devotional service. Also, this *bābājī* read it so sweetly that hearing its words at once extinguished whatever remained of the poisonous fire of material desires in the hearts of the devotees.

One afternoon, when he had finished the chanting of all his rounds, the *parāmahāṁsa bābājī* sat down in his *mādhavī*-vine covered cottage and read from *prema-vivarta* and as he read, he became plunged in the ocean of devotional love. At that moment, an austere *sannyāsī* approached him and again and again offered *daṇḍavat* obeisances at his feet.

Plunged in devotional bliss, the *bābājī* was for a moment unaware of external events. Finally seeing the *sannyāsī* prostrate before him, the *bābājī*, who was more humble than a blade of grass, at once bowed down to greet him. Saying, "O Lord Caitanya, O Lord Nityānanda, please be merciful upon me, a fallen soul," the *bābājī* began to weep.

Then, the *sannyāsī* said to the saintly *bābājī*, "O master, I am very lowly and fallen. Why, imitating my actions, do you mock me in this way?" Then, taking the dust of the *bābājī*'s feet, the *sannyāsī* sat down before him.

Giving the *sannyāsī* a tree bark sitting place, and then sitting beside him, the *bābājī*, his words choked with spiritual love, said, "O master, I am a fallen soul. How may I serve you?"

Setting down his *kamaṇḍalu*, the regal *sannyāsī* respectfully folded his hands and said, "O master, I am very unfortunate. I studied the *saṅkhyā*, *pātañjala*, *nyāya*, *vaiśeṣika*, *pūrva-mīmāṁsā*, and *uttarā-mīmāṁsā* philosophies. I studied the *Vedānta*, *Upaniṣads*, and many other scriptures also. I traveled on pilgrimage to Vārāṇasī and many other holy places. I spent much time debating with others the meaning of the scriptures."

"It is twelve years now since I accepted a *sannyāsī* daṇḍa from Śrīla Saccidānanda Sarasvatīpada. After I accepted the *daṇḍa*, I spent my time always traveling to all the holy places. Wherever I went in Bhārata-varṣa, I always associated with the *sannyāsī* followers of Śaṅkarācārya. Passing through the stages of *kuṭīcaka*, *bahūdaka*, and *haṁsa*, after a few days, I attained the stage of *parāmahāṁsa*. Then, I stayed always at Vārāṇasī."

"Observing a vow of silence, I took shelter of the sayings *ahaṁ brahmāsmi* (I am Brahman), *prajñānaṁ brahmā* (Brahman is consciousness), and *tat tvaṁ asi* (You are that), which Śaṅkara declares are the *mahā-vākyas* (most important statements of the scriptures)."

"Then, one day, a saintly Vaiṣṇava, singing songs about Lord Hari's pastimes came before me. Opening my eyes wide, I gazed at him. He was bathed by the tears flowing from his eyes, and the hairs of his body stood erect in ecstasy. In a choked voice he chanted, 'Śrī Kṛṣṇa Caitanya! Prabhu Nityānanda!' Again and again he danced with faltering steps. Sometimes he fell to the ground.

"As I gazed at him and heard his song, my heart became filled with love, a love I have no power to describe. Even though I became filled with love,

I followed the rules of *parāmahāṁsa* life and I did not speak a word to him."

"I am pathetic, my rules of *parāmahāṁsa* life are pathetic, and my so-called good fortune is also pathetic. Why did I not speak to him?"

"Since that day, my heart has been irresistibly drawn to the lotus feet of Śrī Caitanya. I became very agitated. I spent many days searching for that Vaiṣṇava, but I did not see him anywhere."

"When I saw that Vaiṣṇava and heard the holy names from his mouth, I became filled with a pure and sacred bliss. Before that time, I did not know that such a bliss existed anywhere. I did not think it was possible for a human being to experience such bliss."

"After some days of thinking, I decided that it would be best for me to take shelter of the feet of a Vaiṣṇava. Then I left Vārāṇasī and went to Śrīdhāma Vṛndāvana."

"There I saw many Vaiṣṇavas. Every one of them was calling out the names, 'O Śrī Rūpa! O Śrī Sanātana! O Śrī Jīva Gosvāmī!' and lamenting. They were all meditating on Śrī Śrī Rādhā-Kṛṣṇa's pastimes and in voices choked with love, calling out the name of Navadvīpa."

"From that moment, I have yearned to see Navadvīpa. After a long journey from Śrī Vraja-dhāma, I arrived in Māyāpura a few days ago."

"In Māyāpura town I heard of your glories, so now I have come to take shelter of your lotus feet. Please be merciful to me, accept me as your servant, and give my story an ending that is good."

Weeping again and again, and humbly placing a blade of grass between his teeth, the saintly *parāmahāṁsa* said, "O saintly *sannyāsī*, I am very unfortunate. I fill my belly, I sleep, and I speak useless gossip. In this way, I have wasted my life."

"Now I pass my days in the place where Śrī Kṛṣṇa Caitanya enjoyed His pastimes. Still, I have no power to taste what is true love for Lord Kṛṣṇa."

"You are fortunate. Gazing at a Vaiṣṇava, for a moment, you tasted that love. You have received the mercy of Lord Kṛṣṇa Caitanya. If, when you taste pure spiritual love, you once remember this fallen person, my life will be a great success."

Speaking again and again in this way, the saintly *bābājī* tightly embraced the saintly *sannyāsī* and bathed him with the tears flowing from his eyes. Touched by a Vaiṣṇava, the saintly *sannyāsī* felt an emotion he had never known before. He danced and wept. As he danced, he sang this verse: Glory to Śrī Kṛṣṇa Caitanya! Glory to Lord Nityānanda! Glory to my spiritual master, Śrī Prema-dāsa! Glory to the bliss of devotional service!

After a long time of chanting and dancing, the two of them talked about many things. Saintly Prema-dāsa Bābājī humbly said, "O great soul, please stay in this Pradyumna-kuñja for some days and purify me."

The saintly *sannyāsī* replied, "I place my body in the service of your lotus feet. What to speak of a few days, I will serve you to the end of my life. That is my wish."

The saintly *sannyāsī* was learned in all the scriptures. He knew well the spiritual benefit to be attained by staying in the spiritual master's home and studying under his guidance. Therefore, he very happily stayed for some says in that forest grove.

After some days, the *parāmahāṁsa bābājī* said, "O great soul, Śrī Pradyumna Brahmācārī Ṭhākura kindly keeps me at his lotus feet. Today, he is rapt in the worship of Lord Nṛsiṁha in the village of Deva-palli, in the outskirts of Navadvīpa-maṇḍala. When we have finished our *mādhukarī* begging for alms, let us go and see him.

The saintly *sannyāsī* replied, "As you order, so I shall do."

Crossing the Alakanandā River, the two of them came to Deva-palli, at two in the afternoon. Then, crossing the Sūryaṭīlā River, they saw the Supreme Lord's personal associate, Śrī Pradyumna Brahmācārī, in the temple of Lord Nṛsiṁha.

From a distance, the *parāmahāṁsa bābājī* offered *daṇḍavat* obeisances to his spiritual master. Melting with love for the Lord's devotees, the saintly Brahmācārī at once left the temple, with both hands lifted up the *parāmahāṁsa bābājī*, affectionately embraced him, and inquired about his welfare.

After a long talk about spiritual matters, the *parāmahāṁsa bābājī* introduced the saintly *sannyāsī*. The saintly Brahmācārī respectfully said, "You have attained a proper spiritual master. You should learn *Prema-vivarta* from Prema-dāsa. It is said (*Śrī Caitanya-caritāmṛta*, Madhya 8.128): "Whether one is a *brāhmaṇa*, *sannyāsī* or *śūdra*, regardless of what he is, he can become a spiritual master if he knows the science of Kṛṣṇa."

Then, the saintly *sannyāsī* humbly offered *daṇḍavat* obeisances to his *parāma-guru* (the spiritual master of his spiritual master) and said, "O master, You are a personal associate of Lord Caitanya. Your glance of mercy can purify hundreds of arrogant *sannyāsīs* like myself. Please be merciful to me."

The saintly *sannyāsī* was not experienced in the relationships among devotees. Still, he could see the relationship of the *guru* and *parāma-guru*, and he did act in the way a sincere disciple should to his spiritual master. Then, after seeing the *sandhyā-ārati*, the two of them returned to Śrī Godruma.

After some days had passed in this way, the saintly *sannyāsī* desired to learn the spiritual truth from the *parāmahāṁsa bābājī*. Except for his garments, the *sannyāsī* had become like the Vaiṣṇavas. Controlling his mind and senses, and filled with a host of virtues, he had full faith in the spiritual path. In addition to that, he was very humble and he now had faith in the transcendental pastimes of the Supreme Lord.

One morning, at sunrise, the *parāmahāṁsa bābājī* sat in his cottage of *mādhavī* vines and chanted his rounds on *tulasī* beads. As he remembered the Lord's pastimes of leaving Vṛndāvana, tears flowed again and again from his eyes. Now aware of his original spiritual form and forgetful of his external material body, he became engaged in a service appropriate for that time of morning. Approaching, the saintly *sannyāsī* could see that the *bābājī* was plunged in an ecstatic trance.

Staring at the *sannyāsī*, the *parāmahāṁsa bābājī* said, "O *gopī* friend, please silence that monkey, so he will not break the happy sleeping of our Rādhā-Govinda. If They waken, then our friend, Lalitā, will be unhappy and she will rebuke me. Look! Anaṅga-mañjarī is signaling that it be done. You are Ramaṇa-mañjarī. This is the service given to you. Please be careful and attentive."

Speaking again and again in this way, the *parāmahāṁsa bābājī* finally became unconscious. Now understanding his identity in the spiritual world, the saintly *sannyāsī* became engaged in those services.

The sun then rose and the beauty of dawn became manifest. The birds sang. Gentle breezes blew. The morning sunlight made the cottage of *mādhavī* vines very beautiful, beyond description.

The *parāmahāṁsa bābājī* was sitting on a seat made from banana bark. Gradually he regained external consciousness. Then he continued to chant the holy names. At that time, the saintly *sannyāsī* offered *daṇḍavat* obeisances to the feet of the *bābājī*, humbly sat down beside him, and said, "O master, this lowly person has a question. Please answer his question and make his burning life cool and happy again. Please sprinkle the nectar of Vraja on his heart, a heart burned by the fire of impersonalism."

The *bābājī* replied, "You are qualified to hear answers. Please ask your question, and I will reply as I am able."

The *sannyāsī* said, "O master, for many days I have heard about religion. I have asked many people about the truth of religion. Sad to say, their answers were not in harmony with each other. Therefore I ask: What is the true duty of the individual soul? Why do different teachers give different explanations of the truth of religion? If there is only one truth, why do the philosophers not agree in their opinions?"

Meditating on the lotus feet of Śrī Kṛṣṇa Caitanya Prabhu, the saintly *bābājī* replied, "O fortunate one, as far as my understanding allows, I will tell you the truth of religion. Please listen."

"The eternal nature of a thing is its eternal religion. The religion of something comes from its original identity. When Lord Kṛṣṇa desires to create something, He creates its original nature. That original nature is its eternal religion. However, when a thing comes into contact with other things, its nature may become changed. After some days, that changed state becomes firmly established and it seems to be the eternal nature of the thing. However, this changed nature is not in truth the real nature of the thing. These changed natures are called *nisarga*. I will give you an example of such a changed nature. Water has an original nature. The original nature of water is that it is liquid. However, in contact with certain circumstances, that nature becomes changed and the formerly liquid water may become solid ice. That is the changed nature of water, which seems to be its original nature. However, this changed nature is not eternal. It is always temporary. It is manifested for some reason, it remains for some time, and eventually it disappears of its own accord. On the other hand, the original nature of a thing is eternal. Even when the changed nature is manifested, the original nature remains, although it is dormant. In the course of time, when circumstances are favorable, the original nature is again openly manifested."

"The original nature of a thing is eternal. Its changed nature is temporary. One who knows the truth knows the difference between the eternal and temporary nature. One who does not know the truth thinks the temporary nature is eternal."

The saintly *sannyāsī* then asked, "You speak of a 'thing' (*vastu*). What does this word mean?"

The *parāmahāṁsa* replied, "The word *vastu* is derived from the verb *vas* (to exist) and the affix *tu*. Therefore, that which exists is called *vastu*."

"There are two kinds of *vastu*: Things that exist in reality and things that do not exist in reality. What exists in reality are spiritual truths and the spiritual goal of life. What does not exist in reality are material objects, material qualities, and the like. What exists in reality exists in truth. What does not exist in reality exists only in someone's mistaken belief."

"When a person believes something, it may be that what he believes is the truth, or it may be that it is only an illusion. In *Śrīmad-Bhāgavatam* (1.1.2) it is said:

'The highest truth is reality distinguished from illusion for the welfare of all.'

In this way, it is proved that the world of spirit is the true reality. The Supreme Personality of Godhead is the only reality. From Him, the many individual spirit souls, who are all His parts and parcels, are manifested, and from Him also the potency of illusion (*māyā*) is also manifested."

"Therefore the word 'thing' (*vastu*) may be applied to three things: 1. The Supreme Personality of Godhead, 2. The individual spirit souls, and 3. The illusory potency (*māyā*). These three things exist in reality. Knowledge of the relationships that exist between these three things is said to be pure knowledge."

"There are many different conceptions of the true natures of these three things. These conceptions tend to be full of errors. The *vaiśeṣika* philosophers, in their categorization of things and qualities, believe to be true many things that are not true."

"Things that exist in truth have specific attributes. These attributes determine their nature. The individual spirit souls exist in truth. The individual spirit souls have specific attributes that are eternal. These determine the natures of the individual souls."

The saintly *sannyāsī* then said, "O master, I yearn to understand this properly."

The saintly *bābājī* then said, "A devotee named Kṛṣṇadāsa Kavirāja, who has received the mercy of Lord Nityānanda, showed me a manuscript of a book he had written, a book named *Śrī Caitanya-caritāmṛta*. In that book (Madhya 20.108 and 117) Śrī Mahāprabhu gives this instruction: It is the living entity's constitutional position to be an eternal servant of Kṛṣṇa because he is the marginal energy of Kṛṣṇa and a manifestation that is simultaneously one and different from the Lord."

"Forgetting Kṛṣṇa, the living entity has been attracted by the external feature from time immemorial. Therefore, the illusory energy (*māyā*) gives him all kinds of misery in his material existence."

"Lord Kṛṣṇa is the totality of spiritual existence. He is like a sun from which many spiritual universes have come. The individual spirit souls are rays of light from that Kṛṣṇa-sun. There are many individual spirit souls."

"Someone may say, 'You say that the individual spirit souls are parts of Lord Kṛṣṇa. This means that when He is broken up to become the individual spirit souls, Kṛṣṇa ceases to exist. This is like a mountain that is broken up into many parts. When it is broken in this way, the mountain ceases to exist.'"

"To this I reply, 'You cannot speak in that way.' If my opponent then protests, 'Why not?' I reply: From Lord Kṛṣṇa limitless individual souls are manifested as His parts and parcels. Still, Lord Kṛṣṇa is not diminished even slightly because of that. In all the Vedas, it is said that the individual souls are like sparks emanating from the blazing fire of Lord Kṛṣṇa. However, none of these comparisons give a completely accurate picture of the real truth. The examples of the great fire and the spark, the sun and the rays of light, and the alchemist's stone and gold do not describe the entire situation. Therefore, rejecting these material analogies, one should look inside his heart and there he will understand the truth of the soul's nature."

"Lord Kṛṣṇa is the great spiritual being and the individual soul is the infinitesimal spiritual being. Lord Kṛṣṇa and the individual soul are one in the sense that they are both spiritual. However, Lord Kṛṣṇa is the complete whole and the individual souls are only parts of the whole. That is the difference between them."

"Lord Kṛṣṇa is the supreme master eternally, and the individual spirit soul is His servant eternally. In this way their natures are described."

"Lord Kṛṣṇa is the supreme attractive and the individual spirit soul is attracted to Him. Lord Kṛṣṇa is the supreme controller and the individual spirit soul is controlled by Him. Lord Kṛṣṇa sees all, and the individual spirit soul is observed by Him. Lord Kṛṣṇa is perfect and the individual spirit soul is poor and lowly. Lord Kṛṣṇa is all-powerful and the individual soul is powerless. Therefore, the eternal nature or religion of the individual soul is to be a faithful servant of Lord Kṛṣṇa eternally."

"Lord Kṛṣṇa is the master of limitless potencies. All these potencies are perfectly manifested in the spiritual world. For the manifestation of the individual souls, a particular potency, the *taṭasthā śakti*, is employed."

"The imperfect material universes are also manifested by one of the Lord's potencies. That is the same potency, called the *taṭasthā śakti*."

"This potency also acts instrumentally to create a world where spiritual beings and inanimate matter stay together in the same realm. In this way, it creates a kind of relationship between the spiritual world and the material world."

"Spirit, which is conscious and pure, and matter, which is inanimate, are opposites. Therefore, it is not really possible for the conscious spirit soul to have a relationship with unconscious and inanimate matter."

"The individual soul is a small particle of spirit. Nevertheless, one of the Supreme Lord's potencies makes some individual souls somehow have a relationship with matter. The potency that does this is called *taṭasthā śakti*."

"The place that exists between a river's water and the dry land is called *tata* (shore). Such a place touches both land and water. In that place between land and water, the attributes of both the land and water are manifested."

"The individual soul is spiritual. Nevertheless, the spiritual soul may be placed under the control of inanimate matter. Thus, the individual soul is not like the spiritual world, which never comes into contact with the material world. Nor is the individual soul like inanimate matter. In this sense, the individual soul is neither spirit nor matter. That is why it is true that the Supreme Personality of Godhead and the individual spirit souls are different beings eternally."

"The Supreme Personality of Godhead is the master of the illusory potency *māyā*. *Māyā* is under His control. On the other hand, the individual spirit soul may in some circumstances find himself under the control of *māyā*. Therefore, the Supreme Personality of Godhead, the individual spirit souls, and the illusory potency, *māyā*, are three distinct entities eternally."

"That the Supreme Personality of Godhead is the eternal root of all existence is confirmed by the following words of the *Vedas* (*Kaṭha Upaniṣad* 2.2.13 and *Sevatasvatara Upaniṣad* 6.13): The Supreme Lord is eternal and the living beings are eternal. Thus, the individual spirit soul is a servant of Lord Kṛṣṇa eternally. The spirit soul is manifested from the Lord's *taṭasthā śakti*. For this it may be concluded that the individual spirit soul is simultaneously one and different from the Supreme Personality of Godhead."

"The individual soul may sometimes find himself under the control of the illusory potency, *māyā*, but the Supreme Personality of Godhead is always the controller of *māyā*. In this way, the individual spirit soul and the Supreme Personality of Godhead are different eternally."

"The individual soul is spiritual in nature and the Supreme Personality of Godhead is also spiritual in nature. Thus, the individual soul is one of the potencies of the Supreme Personality of Godhead. On the other hand, because he is part and parcel of Him, the individual soul is also not different from the Supreme Personality of Godhead eternally. If the individual soul and the Supreme Personality of Godhead are simultaneously one and different eternally, then the eternal difference between them is most important."

"The eternal nature and duty of the individual soul is service to the Supreme Personality of Godhead. If he forgets this duty, the individual soul comes under *māyā*'s control. Then, the soul stays away from Lord Kṛṣṇa. That staying away from Lord Kṛṣṇa means that the soul enters the material world."

"It is not possible to give an historical account describing when, in time, the soul first fell into the material world. That is why it is said *anādi-bahirmukha*(the living entity has been attracted by the external feature from time immemorial). This staying away from Kṛṣṇa and the time of entering *māyā*'s world are both different from the soul's eternal nature. They are perversions of it."

"It is because he is in contact with *māyā* and under her control that the soul's temporary nature and temporary duties are manifested. The eternal nature of the soul is one, unchanged, and completely faultless. The temporary natures, created by contact with the material world, are of great variety."

After speaking these words, the saintly *parāmahāṁsa bābājī* stopped and began to chant the names of Lord Hari. After hearing this description of the truth, the saintly *sannyāsī* offered *daṇḍavat* obeisances and said, "O master, today I will think over all that you have said. If I have any questions, tomorrow I will place them before your lotus feet."

Chapter Two

The soul's eternal nature is pure and everlasting.

The next morning, saintly Premadāsa Bābājī was plunged in the ecstasies of Vraja. Although the saintly *sannyāsī* wished to place some questions before him, there was no opportunity. Then, in the afternoon, when they had finished their *mādhukarī* begging of alms, they both entered the cottage of *mādhavī* and *mālatī* vines. The saintly *parāmahāṁsa bābājī* then kindly said, "O best of devotees, now that you have heard my explanation of the true nature of the soul, what is your conclusion?"

Happy to hear these words, the saintly *sannyāsī* asked, "O master, if the individual spirit soul is by nature only atomic in size, how is it possible that his eternal nature is pure and perfect? If the soul is created at a certain point in time, then the soul's nature is also created at that time. If this is true, how can the soul's nature be eternally existing in past, present and future?"

Hearing this question, the *parāmahāṁsa bābājī* meditated on the lotus feet of Lord Caitanya, smiled, and then replied, "O noble-hearted one, even though he is atomic in size, the soul is nevertheless perfect, pure, and eternal. His being atomic is only in relation to his substance. The Supreme Personality of Godhead, Lord Kṛṣṇacandra, is alone great in substance. The multitude of individual souls are His limitless atomic parts. Although the fire itself is not broken up into parts, many tiny sparks come from it. In the same way, Lord Kṛṣṇa, the supreme conscious being, is not divided into parts, but still a great multitude of individual spirit souls are manifested from Him. As each spark has all the power of fire, so each individual soul has all the powers of consciousness. As each spark has all the burning powers of fire, and can, in the right circumstances, start a fire that will burn down the entire material universe, so each individual soul has the ability to fall in love with Lord Kṛṣṇacandra. He has the ability to be plunged in an ocean of love for Lord Kṛṣṇa. As long as he is not in touch with his original nature, the consciousness and atomic soul cannot manifest its natural powers. In truth, the nature of the soul is considered in terms of the soul's perception of others. Thinking, 'What is the soul's eternal nature?' one should carefully search for the truth. The soul's eternal nature is love. Therefore, the soul is not unconscious or inanimate. It is different from unconscious matter. The soul's nature is to be conscious. The soul's nature is to love. In its pure state, love is identical with devotional service to Lord Kṛṣṇa.

Therefore love, manifested as devotional service to Lord Kṛṣṇa, is the original nature of the individual soul."

The individual soul may be situated in two states of existence: 1. The soul's pure state and 2. The soul's state of material bondage. In the pure state, the individual soul is manifested as pure spirit only, free of any contact with inanimate matter. In his pure state, the soul is still atomic, and for this reason, it is possible that he may change his state of existence. Because Lord Kṛṣṇa is the supreme consciousness, He never changes His state of existence. In truth, Lord Kṛṣṇa is supreme, perfect, pure, and eternal. In the conditioned state, the individual spirit soul is pathetic, broken, and impure. In his original state, the soul is great, unbroken, pure, and eternal. When the individual soul is in his pure state, his pure nature is manifested. But when the individual soul is in contact with the illusory potency, *māyā*, the soul's pure state is not manifested. Then, his original nature is perverted and he is impure. Then, he does not take shelter of Lord Kṛṣṇa. Then, he is tormented by happinesses and sufferings. When he forgets the service of Lord Kṛṣṇa, the soul finds himself situated in the material world of repeated birth and death."

"As long as he remains pure, the individual soul retains his original nature and understands that he is a servant of Lord Kṛṣṇa. However, when he comes into contact with the illusory potency, *māyā*, the soul becomes impure. In that condition, the understanding of Lord Kṛṣṇa's service is diminished. Thus, the soul accepts many different material bodies, one after another. When he is in contact with the illusory potency, *māyā*, the individual soul is covered by a body of gross and subtle material elements. First, the soul identifies himself with the subtle material body. Second, he identifies himself with the gross material body. Third, he identifies himself as the subtle and gross bodies mixed together. In this way, the soul's conception of his identity becomes changed. In his pure state, the individual soul is an unalloyed devotee of Lord Kṛṣṇa."

"When he identifies himself as the subtle material body, the soul thinks of himself as the enjoyer of the fruits of his work. In this way, his conception of himself as a servant of Lord Kṛṣṇa becomes covered over by his misidentification of himself as the subtle material body."

"When he identifies himself as the gross material body, the soul thinks,

'I am a *brāhmaṇa,*' 'I am a king,' 'I am poor,' 'I am unhappy,' 'I am defeated by disease and grief,' 'I am a wife,' 'I am a husband,' and so on. Thus the soul's misidentification with the gross material body is manifested in a great variety of ways."

"When the soul thus has a false conception of his identity, his original nature becomes perverted. The original nature of the pure soul is pure love. That pure love appears in the subtle material body in a perverted way as material pleasure, suffering, lust, and hatred. That pure love is seen in the gross material body in an even more perverted way as material eating, drinking, and a host of other so-called pleasures derived from contact with inanimate matter. In this way, you can see that the soul's eternal nature is manifested only when the soul is in his pure state of existence. When the soul is situated in material bondage, only the soul's temporary nature is manifested. Thus, the eternal nature of the soul is that the soul is perfect, pure, and eternal. The temporary nature of the soul I will describe in more detail on another day."

"In the scripture, *Śrīmad-Bhāgavatam,* pure devotional service to Lord Viṣṇu is described. That devotional service is the eternal activity of the individual soul. Three different conceptions of the soul's nature are described in the material world. They are: 1. The eternal nature, 2. The temporary nature and 3. The nature that contradicts the eternal nature."

"The conception that rejects the existence of the Supreme Personality of Godhead and the eternal soul is the third of these. The conception that accepts the existence of the Supreme Personality of Godhead and declares that one should employ temporary, material means to win His mercy, is the second of these—the conception of the soul's temporary nature. The conception that declares that by employing the activities of spiritual love one should strive to attain direct service to Lord Kṛṣṇa is the first of these—the conception of the soul's eternal nature."

"The conception of the soul's eternal nature may be described differently in different countries, among different peoples, and in different languages, but these descriptions all refer to the same eternal nature of the soul. Still, the Vaiṣṇava religion followed in India is the original form, the prototype, of all these conceptions of the soul's eternal nature. And the form of the Vaiṣṇava religion that Lord Caitanya, the son of Śacī and the Lord of our hearts, taught the world is the purest form of the Vaiṣṇava religion, the form that the great souls filled with the bliss of pure spiritual love accept and follow."

At this point, the saintly *sannyāsī* folded his hands and said, "O master, at every moment I see that what was taught by Lord Caitanya, the son of Śacī, is the best form of the pure Vaiṣṇava religion. I also see that the theory of impersonal monism taught by Śaṅkarācārya is very wretched and horrible."

"Still, a thought has risen in my mind, a thought I will not accept unless it is first placed before your lotus feet. It is this: Is the state of deep ecstatic spiritual love revealed by Lord Caitanya really different from the state of merging into the impersonal Supreme?"

When he heard the name, "Śaṅkarācārya," the *parāmahāṁsa bābājī* at once offered *daṇḍavat* obeisances. Then, he spoke the following words: "O noble-hearted friend, one should always think: 'Śaṅkarācārya is Lord Śiva himself.' Śaṅkarācārya is actually the spiritual master of all the Vaiṣṇavas. That is why Lord Caitanya Mahāprabhu honors him with the title, *ācārya*. Śaṅkarācārya is a perfect Vaiṣṇava."

"When Śaṅkarācārya appeared in Bhārata-varṣa, there was great need for a *guṇa-avatāra* of the Lord. The voidist philosophy of Buddha had already practically destroyed the teachings of the *Vedas* and the duties of *varṇāśrama-dharma*. Voidist Buddhism even denied the existence of the Supreme Personality of Godhead. Although it did hint at the existence of the individual soul, Buddhism denied the soul's true eternal nature. At that time, the *brāhmaṇas* had practically become Buddhists, and had practically abandoned the religion of the *Vedas*."

"At that time, extraordinarily powerful Lord Śiva descended as Śaṅkarācārya to this world, re-established the authority of the *Vedas*, and transformed voidist Buddhism into the philosophy of Vedic impersonalism. For succeeding in this extraordinary work, the world will be long indebted to Śaṅkarācārya."

"Every work in this world may be considered in two ways. Some work is useful in the context of a certain period of time, and other work is useful for all time. Śaṅkarācārya performed work that was very important for that particular period in history."

"From his efforts, many good results came. Śrī Rāmānujācārya and Śrī Madhvācārya built the palace of pure Vaiṣṇava religion on the walls and foundation created by Śrī Śaṅkarācārya. Therefore, Śaṅkarācārya is a great friend of the Vaiṣṇava religion. He is one of its founding teachers. The benefit created by Śaṅkarācārya's teaching is now enjoyed, without any effort on their part by the Vaiṣṇavas."

"Individual souls still in the grips of material bondage urgently need to understand their relationship with the Supreme Personality of Godhead. The individual soul is different from and superior to the gross and subtle material bodies in the material universes. The Vaiṣṇavas and Śaṅkarācārya agree on this point. They do not disagree on the spiritual nature of the individual soul."

"Liberation is defined as becoming free from the material world. Both agree on this also. Up to the stage of liberation, Śaṅkarācārya and the Vaiṣṇavas agree on many points."

"By worshipping Lord Hari, one purifies his heart and attains liberation. Śaṅkarācārya teaches this also. However, about the state of existence that is superior to impersonal liberation, Śaṅkarācārya is silent. Śaṅkarācārya knew well that if the individual soul employed the worship of Lord Hari as the way to proceed on the path of liberation, the soul would begin to taste the pleasures of devotional service and would eventually become a pure devotee of Lord Hari. It is for this reason that Śaṅkarācārya, after showing the true path, did not reveal anything more about the secrets of Vaiṣṇava religion."

"Those who carefully study all his commentaries can see that this was Śaṅkarācārya's hidden intention. It is only those who waste time merely circling the outskirts of Śaṅkarācārya's teachings who stay far away from the Vaiṣṇava religion. Being one with the Supreme Lord and attaining love for Him are, in one sense, the same thing. However, those who narrowly define oneness with the Lord claim that it is different from love for the Lord."

"Consider, for a moment, the meaning of the word 'love'. The thing that attracts one spiritual entity to another spiritual entity is called 'love.' If the two spiritual entities are not in truth different from each other, they cannot love each other."

"All spiritual entities are naturally attracted to the supreme spiritual entity, Lord Kṛṣṇacandra. That attraction is called *Kṛṣṇa-prema*, or love for Lord Kṛṣṇa." Lord Kṛṣṇacandra and the individual spirit souls are eternally distinct spiritual entities. Therefore, the love they bear for each other is an eternal fact."

"Three things exist eternally: 1. The enjoyer, 2. The enjoyed, and 3. The way enjoyment is obtained. If the person who enjoys by loving another is identical with the object of his enjoyment, or love, then the love he feels can never be eternal."

"If oneness is defined as the spiritual living entity's pure state, where he is free from any contact with matter, then oneness and spiritual love are identical."

"However, the present day *paṇḍita* followers of Śaṅkarācārya are not content to accept such a definition. Instead, they undertake a great struggle to prove that the *Vedas* teach the existence of ultimately only one spiritual entity, an entity who transforms Himself into everything that exists. Such a view kills the eternal existence of love. The Vaiṣṇavas have conclusively proved that this view contradicts the true teachings of the *Vedas*."

"Śaṅkarācārya affirmed that the pure spiritual state is one of perfect oneness. However, his present-day followers do not understand the hidden meaning of his words. Thus they gradually ascribed to him a position not truly his own. They declare the various stages of pure spiritual love to be products of the illusory potency, *māyā*. It is for this reason that their theory is called Māyāvāda. It is the lowest and most horrible of all theories in the world."

"The Māyāvāda philosophers refuse to accept the existence of more than one spiritual entity. They refuse to accept the existence of spiritual love. They say that the supreme spirit (Brahman) stays aloof from matter only as long as He remains one and undivided. They say that when He assumes any form of His own, or the forms of the many individual souls, He is in the grips of illusion (*māyā*). Thus, they think that the eternal, pure, and spiritual form of the Supreme Personality of Godhead is a manifestation of the illusory potency, *māyā*. They think the separate existence of the individual spirit souls to be an illusion created by *māyā*."

"Thinking that spiritual love and its manifestations are all products of the illusory potency, *māyā*, they affirm that meditation on the oneness of everything is the only thing beyond *māyā*'s touch. Thus, these bewildered fellows' idea of oneness is not at all the same as spiritual love."

"However, the spiritual love Lord Caitanya tasted in His pastimes and taught to the world is completely beyond the touch of the illusory potency, *māyā*. That love is the highest fruit of pure spiritual oneness."

"*Mahābhāva* is a specific transformation of that pure spiritual love. It is a very intense form of the bliss of pure love for Lord Kṛṣṇa. In it, the confidential relationship between the lover and the beloved reaches an intensity never known before. On the other hand, the Māyāvāda philosophy is shallow and unimportant. It can never understand that exalted love."

Then, the saintly *sannyāsī* respectfully said, "O master, my heart is filled with conviction that the Māyāvāda theory is shallow and unimportant. Any doubt I had about that is now thrown far away, by your mercy. Still, I myself wear the garments of a Māyāvadī *sannyāsī*. Now, I yearn to rid myself of them."

The saintly *bābājī* replied, "O great soul, I do not teach that one should like or hate any particular kind of garments. When one's heart is purified, his garments will also become pure. When a person gives great respect to his outward garments, it shows that he does not give great attention to the condition of his heart."

"In my opinion, one should first purify his heart. Then he may adopt the external activities and garments of a saintly person without committing an offense. In your heart, become a sincere follower of Śrī Kṛṣṇa Caitanya.

Then you will naturally desire to accept the external things that are appropriate for that following. Let that be the way you act. Always remember these words of Lord Caitanya Mahāprabhu (*Śrī Caitanya-caritāmṛta*, Madhya 16.238-239): You should not make yourself a show bottle devotee and become a false renunciant. For the time being, enjoy the material world in a befitting way and not become attached to it."

"Śrī Caitanya Mahāprabhu continued: Within your heart, you should keep yourself very faithful but externally, you may behave like an ordinary man. Thus Kṛṣṇa will soon be very pleased and deliver you from the clutches of *māyā*."

Understanding, the saintly *sannyāsī* did not say anything more about changing his garments. Folding his hands, he said, "O master, I am your disciple and I have taken shelter at your lotus feet. Whatever instruction you give, I will place on my head without argument. By hearing your words, I have understood that pure love for Lord Kṛṣṇa is the only Vaiṣṇava religion. That love is the eternal religion of the soul. That religion is perfect, pure and natural. How should I regard the other religions in the various countries of the world?"

The saintly *bābājī* replied, "O great soul, religion is one. It is not two, and it is not many. There is only one religion for the soul. That religion is called the Vaiṣṇava religion. There is no reason why religion should be different for different languages, countries, and peoples. The religion of the soul may be called by different names, but it is not possible that there can be different religions. The religion of the soul is the pure love the atomic spiritual entity bears for the supreme spiritual entity. Because of differing material conceptions, some spirit souls have distorted that original religion and given it a variety of different shapes. The pure and original form of the soul's religion is the Vaiṣṇava religion. Other so-called religions are merely distorted forms of the Vaiṣṇava religion. Other religions are pure to the degree that they are like the Vaiṣṇava religion."

"Some days ago, in Śrī Vraja-dhāma, I placed this same question before the feet of Śrīla Sanātana Gosvāmī, who is a personal associate of Lord Caitanya. 'In the religion of the Yavanas, there is a word 'esk'. Does this word mean pure spiritual love, or does it not.' That was my question. The saintly Gosvāmī is learned in all scriptures and he is especially learned in the language of the Yavanas. In that language, his learning has no limit. Śrīla Rūpa Gosvāmī, Śrīla Jīva Gosvāmī, and many other learned scholars were also present in that assembly. Saintly Śrīla Sanātana Gosvāmī kindly replied in these words: 'Yes, the word 'esk' means love. When the Yavanas worship God, they use the word 'esk'. However 'esk' is often used to mean material love also. Examples of this may be seen in the history of Layala Manjanu and the writings of Hafiz. The Yavana *ācāryas* could not understand the true meaning of spiritual life. When they write of 'esk,' they mean love in terms of either the gross or subtle material bodies. However, they could not distinguish between material love and pure spiritual love, and they could not understand pure love for Lord Kṛṣṇa. I have not seen an accurate description of spiritual love in any of the books of the Yavana teachers. I have seen them only in the books describing the Vaiṣṇava religion. The Yavana teachers use the word '*ru*' to describe the pure individual soul. However, they could not understand the soul in truth. They used the word '*ru*' to describe the conditioned souls bound by *māyā*. That was all they could understand. I have not seen a description of pure love for Lord Kṛṣṇa in any but the Vaiṣṇava religion. Generally speaking, pure love for Lord Kṛṣṇa is described only in the books of Vaiṣṇava religion. Pure love for Lord Kṛṣṇa is described in these words of *Śrīmad-Bhāgavatam* (1.1.2): Completely rejecting all religious activities which are materially motivated, this *Bhāgavata Purāṇa* propounds the highest truth. I am confident that before Śrī Kṛṣṇa Caitanya came to this world, no one had given a complete description of pure love for Lord Kṛṣṇa. If you have faith in my words, then you may accept this conclusion.'"

"After hearing these instructions, again and again, I offered *daṇḍavat* obeisances to Śrīla Sanātana Gosvāmī."

At that time, the saintly *sannyāsī* offered *daṇḍavat* obeisances. The *parāmahāṁsa bābājī* the said, "O great devotee, now I will answer your second question: Please listen with an attentive mind. The words 'the creation of the individual soul' or 'the fashioning of the individual soul' are all manifested by the illusory potency, *māyā*. They are material words that describe inanimate material things. The three divisions of time are: 1. Past, 2. Present and 3. Future. These divisions refer to material time, time within the realm of the illusory potency, *māyā*. In the spiritual world, the present exists eternally. In the spiritual world, the past and future do not exist. Lord Kṛṣṇa and the individual spirit soul exist in that eternal present. In this way, the individual soul is eternal and his original nature, which is his pure love for Lord Kṛṣṇa, is also eternal. Talk of the individual soul's being 'created' or 'fashioned' is a misconception, mistakenly imposing the time patterns of the inanimate material world on a spiritual entity."

"The atomic individual soul is spiritual and eternal. He existed before his entrance into the material world. Because in the spiritual world there is no past or future, whatever exists there exists in an eternal present. Therefore, the soul and its nature are both eternal. They exist in that eternal present. I am only describing this in words. Your understanding will depend on your ability to understand the pure spiritual world. I can only give a hint here. In spiritual trance, you will be able to see all this directly. The logic and argument of this material world will not help you to understand it. Your ability to directly perceive the spiritual world beyond the realm of matter will depend on how much you can loosen the shackles of material bondage. In the beginning, you will see your own pure spiritual form. By again and again chanting the spiritual and holy names of Lord Hari, you will come to understand the nature of the soul. By practicing *aṣṭāṅga-yoga* or following the path of the impersonalists you will not be able to see the pure spiritual nature. By directly serving Lord Kṛṣṇa you will be able to understand the eternal nature of the soul. Therefore you should chant the holy names of Lord Hari always and with enthusiasm. Only by chanting the names of Lord Hari will you make advancement in spiritual life. Again and again chanting the holy name of Lord Hari for some days, you will eventually attain love for the holy name, a kind of love you had never known before. Accompanying that love will be direct perception of the spiritual world. Of all the different activities of devotional service, chanting the holy names of Lord Hari is the most important and the most quickly effective. In Kṛṣṇadāsa Kavirāja's delightful books (*Śrī Caitanya-caritāmṛta*, Antya 4.70-71) Lord Caitanya Mahāprabhu teaches:

"Among the ways of executing devotional service, the nine prescribed methods are the best, for these processes have great potency to deliver Kṛṣṇa and ecstatic love for Him."

"Of the nine processes of devotional service, the most important is to always chant the holy name of the Lord. If one does so, avoiding the ten kinds of offenses, one very easily obtains the most valuable love of Godhead."

"O great soul, if you now ask, 'Who is a Vaiṣṇava?' I give this reply: A person who without offense chants the holy names of Lord Kṛṣṇa is a Vaiṣṇava. The Vaiṣṇavas are again divided into three groups: 1. *kaniṣṭha* (neophyte), 2. *madhyama* (intermediate), and 3. *uttama* (advanced). One who from time to time chants the holy names of Lord Kṛṣṇa is a neophyte devotee. One who always chants the holy names of Lord Kṛṣṇa is an intermediate devotee. A person the sight of whose face causes others to chant the holy names of Kṛṣṇa is an advanced devotee. Lord Caitanya Mahāprabhu has taught us that one should not use any other criterion to determine who is a Vaiṣṇava."

Diving into the nectar of these teachings, the saintly *sannyāsī* began to chant:

Hare Kṛṣṇa Hare Kṛṣṇa, Kṛṣṇa Kṛṣṇa Hare Hare, Hare Rāma Hare Rāma, Rāma Rāma Hare Hare. Singing these holy names, he danced again and again. From that day forward, he found great pleasure in chanting the holy names of Lord Hari. Offering *daṇḍavat* obeisances to his spiritual master's lotus feet, he said, "O master, please be merciful to this fallen person."

Chapter Three

The soul's temporary duties are imperfect, horrible, contaminated and short-lived

Staying on a small hill in Godruma forest and looking to the north, the saintly *sannyāsī* spent the whole day and three hours of the night chanting the holy names of Lord Hari. Then, the full moon rose and filled Navadvīpa-maṇḍala with a wonderful splendor and beauty. The *sannyāsī* placed his glance on Śrī Māyāpura, which was not very far away.

The saintly *sannyāsī* said, "Ah! Now I can see the wonderfully blissful spiritual abode. The Gaṅgā shore is splendid, garlanded with light from many great jeweled palaces, temples, and archways. In many places, tumultuous chanting of Lord Hari's holy names fills the sky. Hundreds of devotees playing *vīnās* chant and dance like Nārada Muni."

"In one place, Lord Śiva, the master of the demigods, manifests a white form. Playing a *ḍamaru* drum, he chants, "O Caitanya, O maintainer of the universes, please be merciful to me!" Wildly dancing again and again, he finally falls to the ground."

"In another place, four-faced Brahmā lectures on the *Vedas* to an assembly of sages. He quotes and then purely explains these words (*Śvetāśvatara Upaniṣad* 3.12): The Supreme Personality of Godhead is Mahāprabhu, who disseminates transcendental enlightenment. Just to be in touch with Him is to be correct with the indestructible *brahmajyoti*."

"In another place, Indra and the demigods jump and chant: "Glory to Lord Gauracandra! Glory to Lord Nityānanda! The birds on the branches chirp: "Caitanya! Nityānanda!"

"Everyone is intoxicated by drinking the nectar of Lord Caitanya's holy names. From the gardens in the four directions come sweet humming sounds. Intoxicated by drinking the nectar of Lord Caitanya's holy names, Prakṛti-devī (the goddess of the material nature) fills every place with beauty and splendor. Ah! Now that I see Śrī Māyāpura, what can I not see? What do I see now?"

Remembering his spiritual master, he said, "O master, now I understand. It is by your mercy that I am able to see the spiritual Māyāpura. From this day, I will stay in the association of Lord Caitanya's devotees. Now that I have seen the spiritual Māyāpura, I will wear *tulasī* beads, *tilaka*, and the writing of the holy names. This I will do."

Saying this again and again, the saintly *sannyāsī* fell unconscious for a moment. After a moment, he became conscious again. However, he could no longer see the wonderful spiritual vision he saw before. Weeping again and again, the saintly *sannyāsī* said, "I am very unfortunate. By my spiritual master's mercy, I was able for a moment to see the holy abode of Śrī Navadvīpa."

The next day, the saintly *sannyāsī* threw his *ekadaṇḍa* in the water, placed *tulasī* beads around his neck, wore Vaiṣṇava *tilaka* on his forehead, chanted "Hari! Hari!" and danced. Seeing his wonderful new garments and demeanor, and remarking how fortunate he had become, the residents of Godruma offered *daṇḍavat* obeisances to him. Embarrassed, the saintly *sannyāsī* said, "It is by the Vaiṣṇavas' mercy that I am now dressed like a Vaiṣṇava. However, there is still a danger for me. Again and again, I heard from my spiritual master's mouth these words (Śrī *Śikṣāṣṭaka* 3, *Śrī Caitanya-caritāmṛta*, Antya 20.21):"

"One who thinks himself lower than the grass, who is more tolerant than a tree, and who does not expect personal honor, but is always prepared to give all respects to others, can very easily always chant the holy name of the Lord."

Then he remembered his Vaiṣṇava spiritual master. He thought, "I should offer my obeisances to him." Again and again thinking in this way, he approached the *parāmahāṁsa bābājī* and offered *daṇḍavat* obeisances to him.

Sitting in his cottage of *mādhavī* vines, the saintly *bābājī* was chanting the holy names of Lord Hari again and again. Seeing that the saintly *sannyāsī* had completely changed his garments and was chanting the holy names with spiritual love, the *bābājī* again and again bathed his disciple with the tears flowing from his eyes. Embracing him, the *bābājī* said, "O Vaiṣṇava dāsa, by today touching your perfectly auspicious body, my life is now a great success."

When he heard these words, the saintly *sannyāsī* at once threw far away his previous name. Now he accepted the name Vaiṣṇava dāsa. From that day on, the saintly *sannyāsī* began a new life. He threw far away his Māyāvadī *sannyāsī* garments and arrogant *sannyāsī* name. In the afternoon, many residents of Śrī Pradyumna-kuñja, Śrī Godruma, and Śrī Madhyadvīpa came to see the saintly *parāmahāṁsa bābājī*. They all sat in a circle around the saintly *parāmahāṁsa bābājī*. They all chanted the holy names of Lord Hari on *tulasī* beads. Some chanted, "O Gaurāṅga-Nityānanda," others chanted, "O Advaita, husband of Sītā!," others chanted "Glory to the son of Śacī!" Chanting again and again, their eyes became filled with tears. All the Vaiṣṇavas conversed about spiritual matters. All the assembled Vaiṣṇavas circumambulated the *tulasī* plant and offered *daṇḍavat* obeisances to the assembled Vaiṣṇavas. Then, Vaiṣṇava dāsa circumambulated the *tulasī* plant and rolled about in the dust that had touched the Vaiṣṇavas' feet. The saintly Vaiṣṇavas said, "This is not the same *sannyāsī*. Now his form is wonderful."

Rolling on the ground before the Vaiṣṇavas, Vaiṣṇava dāsa said, "Today I have attained the dust of the Vaiṣṇavas' feet. Now my life is a success.

By my spiritual master's mercy, I have learned the truth. Without the dust of the Vaiṣṇava's feet, my future is not good. The dust of the Vaiṣṇava's feet, the nectarean water that has washed the Vaiṣṇavas' feet, and the nectarean food touched by the Vaiṣṇavas' lips are three medicines to cure the disease of repeated birth and death. When he is cured of the disease of repeated birth and death, a person enjoys great pleasure. O Vaiṣṇavas, formerly I was very proud of my great learning, but today there is no pride in my heart. I was born in a *brāhmaṇa* family, I studied all the scriptures, and I entered the *sannyāsa āśrama*. In this way, my pride reached the highest point. When I was first attracted to the Vaiṣṇava religion, the seed of humbleness was planted in my heart. Gradually, by your mercy, I have thrown far away the pride felt for my birth, learning, and *sannyāsa*. Now in my heart I know that I am only a small soul, a soul without any shelter. Without taking shelter of the Vaiṣṇava's feet, for me there is no hope. My status as a *brāhmaṇa*, my learning, and my *sannyāsa* were actually making me degraded: leading me lower and lower. Therefore, I truly make this request at your feet: Please accept me as your servant."

Hearing Vaiṣṇava dāsa's humble words, the Vaiṣṇavas said, "O best of the devotees, we are very eager to attain the dust from the feet of Vaiṣṇavas like Vaiṣṇava dāsa. Please be merciful and make our lives successful by giving us the dust of your feet. You have attained the mercy of a saintly *parāmahāṁsa bābājī*. Please give us your association and purify us. Devotional service is attained by one who associates with devotees like yourself. This is confirmed by the following words of *Bṛhan-nāradīya Purāṇa*:"

"Devotional service is attained by associating with devotees. The association of devotees is attained by past pious deeds."

"Therefore it is because in the past we performed many devotional pious deeds that we have obtained your association. Because we have attained your association, we may now hope to attain true devotional service."

Saintly Vaiṣṇava dāsa thus stayed among the devotees as they humbly offered obeisances to each other and conversed about devotional service. He looked splendid and glorious as in his hands he held new beads for chanting the holy names of Lord Hari.

That day, a fortunate person came to that group of Vaiṣṇavas. Since childhood, he was able to read and write the language of the Yavanas. He imitated the activities of the Mohammedan kings and in their country, he counted himself one amongst them. His home was in Śāntipura. He was born in a *brāhmaṇa* family. He associated with many wealthy men. For many days, he enjoyed all worldly pleasures, but they did not make him happy. At the end, he turned to religion and began chanting the holy names of Lord Hari. When he was a child, he had studied *rāgas* and *rāginis* from a Delhi classical music teacher. He would employ this knowledge in melodiously singing the holy names of Lord Hari. Gradually, he became famous as a singer and musician in Vaiṣṇava circles, and his sweet singing was in great demand. After some days, he began to understand the pleasures that reside in the Lord's holy names with the Vaiṣṇavas there. He stayed at a Vaiṣṇava's *āśrama*. Accompanied by this Vaiṣṇava, he came to the cottage of *mālatī* and *mādhavī* vines in Pradyumna-kuñja. Hearing from Vaiṣṇava dāsa of the Vaiṣṇavas' saintliness and humbleness, some doubts still remained in his mind. With boldness and eloquence, he placed a question before the assembled Vaiṣṇavas.

He asked, "In *Manu-saṁhitā* and the other *dharma-śāstras*, it is said that the *brāhmaṇas* are the best caste. In those scriptures are described the *brāhmaṇa's* regular duties, which begin with chanting the Gāyatrī *mantra*. If these are the regular activities of the best caste, then why are the duties of the Vaiṣṇavas different?"

The Vaiṣṇavas did not reply. Afraid to dispute with this *brāhmaṇa* logician, they gave no answer. After the asker of the question had sung the holy names of Lord Hari, the Vaiṣṇavas finally said, "The saintly *parāmahāṁsa bābājī* will answer your question. His reply will make us happy."

Hearing the order of the assembled Vaiṣṇavas, the saintly *parāmahāṁsa bābājī* offered *daṇḍavat* obeisances and said, "O saintly devotees, if you wish, Śrī Vaiṣṇava dāsa, the best of devotees, will give the proper answer."

Everyone was happy with this proposal. Hearing his spiritual master's words and reflecting on his own good fortune, Śrī Vaiṣṇava dāsa said, "I am very fallen, and I do not possess anything of any value. Therefore, it is not right that I speak very much in the assembly of the saintly and wise. However, the spiritual master's order should always be respectfully carried on one's head. I have drunk the nectar of truth, nectarean words that flowed from my spiritual master's mouth. Therefore, I will repeat what I can remember of his words. That I will do."

After speaking these words, Vaiṣṇava dāsa placed on all his limbs the dust from the feet of the saintly *parāmahāṁsa bābājī*. Then, offering *daṇḍavat* obeisances, Vaiṣṇava dāsa spoke the following words:

"The original form of the Supreme is the supremely blissful Supreme Person (*bhagavān*). The impersonal Brahman is the effulgence of His transcendental body, and the all-pervading Supersoul is His expansion. Śrī Kṛṣṇa Caitanya, who is the abode of all glory, and all pastimes, taught this to us. The *Manu-saṁhitā* and other *dharma-śāstras*, which are supplements to the original *Vedas* and which explain what should and should not be done, should be followed by the entire world. The religious activities of human beings are of two kinds: 1. *vaidhī* (spiritual rules and regulations to be followed), and 2. *rāgānuga* (spiritual activities to which one is naturally attracted and which one performs even without being impelled to do so by the rules of the scriptures). When he is under the control of the illusory potency, *māyā*, the human being must perform *vaidhī* spiritual activities. When he is freed from *māyā*'s grip, the human being need not perform *vaidhī* spiritual activities. Then, his spiritual activities are *rāgānuga*. Engagement in *rāgānuga* spiritual activities is the pure state of the individual spirit soul, a state that is naturally pure, spiritual, and free from matter. By Lord Kṛṣṇa's wish, the pure spirit soul may become free from the grip of matter. However, as long as that is not Lord Kṛṣṇa's wish, the soul remains thrust into the calamity that is life in the material world. As long as he is thrust into the calamity of material life, the soul cannot truthfully become liberated from the grip of matter simply by his own endeavors. When he is truthfully liberated from the grip of matter, the pure soul naturally engages in *rāgātmikā* spiritual activities."

"The spiritual activities of the people of Vraja are *rāgātmikā*. When the soul still resides in the calamity that is the material world, these activities are *rāgānuga*. As long as he engages in *rāgānuga* spiritual activities, the soul in the material world is happy. As long as he does not engage in *rāgānuga* spiritual activities, the soul in the material world is attracted to the illusions of *māyā*. Attracted to *māyā*, the soul becomes bewildered, so that he is not attracted to pure spirit. 'It is 'I' and 'It is mine' are the two conceptions *māyā* thrusts upon the soul. The soul then thinks, 'I am this body' and 'everything in relation to the body is mine.' In this condition, the soul loves persons who bring pleasure to his material body and hates persons who thwart the bringing of pleasure to his material body. Thus, the bewildered soul becomes a slave of love and hatred."

"The bewildered soul thinks others are either his friends or his enemies in three ways: 1. *saririla* (in relation to material bodies) 2. *samājika* (in relation to society and social groups), and 3. *naitika* (in the context of ideas). One who unlawfully desires gold and women will find himself a slave to pleasures and pains. That condition of life is called *saṁsāra* (the world of repeated birth and death). One who is attached to the world of *saṁsāra* is subject to birth, death, karmic reactions, and a variety of living conditions, some high and some low. Thus the souls bound by material illusion wander here and there in the material worlds. However, the souls attracted to spirit do not experience these troubles. Those who are attracted to spirit attain their eternal spiritual nature. Those who forget they are by nature small particles of spirit fall down into the experience of material life. Staying in the material world, they suffer many misfortunes, although they think they do not suffer misfortunes at all."

"For the souls bound by *māyā*, the activities of *rāgātmikā* are far away and the activities of *rāgānuga* are not accepted. It is only by the mercy of a devotee of the Lord that the activities of *rāgānuga* may arise within a conditioned soul's heart. The activities of *rāgānuga* are rare and difficult to attain. The residents of the material world have been cheated of them."

"However, the Supreme Personality of Godhead is all-knowing and full of mercy. He sees that the souls imprisoned by *māyā* have been cheated by their spiritual activities. How will these souls attain auspiciousness? By what means will the souls bewildered by *māyā* remember Lord Kṛṣṇa? The answer is that by associating with saintly devotees, the soul is able to understand that he is in reality a servant of Lord Kṛṣṇa. The rules of ordinary piety do not enjoin that one associate with saintly devotees. How then does one associate with devotees, or what makes one desire to associate with devotees? The association of devotees does not generally happen when one follows the path of rules and regulations (*vidhi-mārga*). That is not the way one comes to associate with devotees. It is from the merciful glance of the Supreme Personality of Godhead that the scriptures are created. Born from the mercy of the Supreme Personality of Godhead, the sun of the scriptures rises in the sky of the devotee's heart. In this way, the rules of piety are manifested."

"In the beginning is the *Vedas*. One part of the *Vedas* teaches fruitive work, another part transcendental knowledge, and another part loving devotional service. The individual souls bewildered by *māyā* are situated in different states of existence. Some are very bewildered, some are a little enlightened, and some are very enlightened. In this way, the conditioned souls have different kinds of intelligence. The *Vedas* teach all these classes of souls. Although one may consider that the souls have an infinite variety of natures, still, they are grouped into three broad categories: 1. Those qualified to perform fruitive work (*karma*), 2. Those eligible for transcendental knowledge (*jñāna*), and 3. Those eligible to engage in loving devotional service (*prema*) to the Supreme Lord. The *Vedas* thus describe these three categories of eligibility."

"The *Vedas'* description of what should be done and should not be done by these three classes of living entities constitute *vaidhī-dharma* (the rules of religion). When one actively performs misdeeds—that is called *vaidhī-pravṛtti*. Those who do not follow the rules of *vaidhī* commit sinful acts. Therefore, living entities should always avoid actions that violate these rules and regulations. Those who are outside the jurisdiction of the *Vedas* are called by the name *mleccha*, and by other names also. The conclusion, then, is that three classes of living entities are qualified to follow the *Vedas*."

"For their benefit, the great sages have written many books to supplement the hymns of the *Vedas*. Manu and twenty other sages thus wrote the *dharma-śāstras* to benefit the persons eligible to perform pious fruitive work (*karma*). Different philosophers wrote books of logic and philosophy to benefit the persons eligible for philosophical speculation (*jñāna*). The great devotees wrote the *Purāṇas* and pure *Tantras* to teach the persons eligible to engage in devotional service (*bhakti*), and to guide their actions. This is the nature of all the Vedic literatures. The philosophy of *Mīmāṁsaka* is not seen anywhere in the original scriptures. Every point that the followers of *Mīmāṁsaka* claim shows the superiority of their idea is easily thrown into a dark hole of counter-arguments and doubts. In all the scriptures, the *uttarā-mīmāṁsā* (*Vedānta*) philosophy is most clearly shown in *Bhagavad-gītā*. The teaching of *karma* that ignores *jñāna* is an atheistic kind of *karma* and that teaching should be rejected. In the same way, the teaching of *karma* and *jñāna* that ignores *bhakti* is atheistic *karma* and *jñāna*. There are only three kinds of *yoga*: *karma-yoga*, *jñāna-yoga*, and *bhakti-yoga*. That is the Vaiṣṇava description of the *Vedas*' teachings."

"The individual soul bewildered by *māyā* first takes shelter of fruitive work (*karma*). Then, he takes shelter of *karma-yoga*. At the end, when he comes to the conclusion of *karma-yoga* and *jñān- yoga*, he takes shelter of *bhakti-yoga*. The soul bewildered by *māyā* does not ascend only one step in the staircase. Ascending only one step of the staircase, he cannot enter the temple of devotional service."

"What is taking shelter of fruitive work (*karma*)? Fruitive work is the activity performed by the body and mind while one is alive in the body. Fruitive work is of two kinds: 1. auspicious, and 2. inauspicious. By performing inauspicious work, one attains an inauspicious result. Inauspicious work is called either *pāpa* (sin) or vi*karma* (evil work). When one does not perform auspicious work, that is called *akarma*. Both of these are bad. Auspicious work is good. Work is of three kinds: 1. *nitya* (regular), 2. *naimittika* (occasional) and 3. *kāmya* (desired). *Kāmya* work, where the desire for personal benefit is very prominent, should be avoided. *Nitya* and *naimittika* work, on the other hand, is work prescribed by scripture. Considering what should and should not be done, the scriptures explain what is *nitya*, *naimittika* and *kāmya* work. *Akarma* (failure to do auspicious work) and vi*karma* (inauspicious work) are not the same as *karma* (auspicious work). When one avoids *kāmya* work, then his work is *nitya* or *naimittika*. When that brings auspiciousness to the body, the mind, other people or humanity at large, is called *nitya* work. Everyone should perform *nitya* work. When work prompted by a temporary circumstance is like *nitya* work in this way, it is called *naimittika* work. Chanting Gāyatrī, offering obeisances, and cleanliness are activities that maintain one's body and the welfare of society at large. So also do honest dealings and protection of those who should be protected. All these are *nitya* work. Duties to one's deceased parents, other such duties, and atonement of sins are all *naimittika* work."

"*Nitya* and *naimittika* work bring good to the world. Therefore, the great sages order that such auspicious work be performed. Considering the different natures of the human beings, they thus describe what is called the *varṇāśrama* system. According to their natural tendency for work, human beings are thus divided into four classes: 1. *brāhmaṇa*, 2. *kṣatriya*, 3. *vaiśya*, and 4. *śūdra*. In this material world, there are also four other divisions, called *āśramas*. The four *āśramas* are: 1. *gṛhastha*, 2. *brahmācārī*, 3. *vānaprastha* and 4. *sannyāsī*. Those who are fond of performing *akarma* and vikarma work are called *antyaja* (the lowest) and *nirāsrama* (outside the *āsrama* system). The different *varṇas* (classes) are determined according to 1. birth, 2. nature, 3. work and 4 qualities. Whenever the *varṇas* are determined by birth, the meaning of the *varṇāśrama* system is lost. The different *āśramas* are determined according to these states: 1. Being married, 2. Not being married, and 3. The renunciation of association with women. Those who are married are in the *gṛhastha āsrama*. Those who are not married are in the *brahmācārī āsrama*. Those who have renounced association with women are in the *vānaprastha* and *sannyāsa āśramas*. Of all the *āśramas*, the *sannyāsa āsrama* is the best. Of all the *varṇas*, the *brāhmaṇa varṇa* is the best. This is all described in the crest jewel of all scriptures, *Śrīmad-Bhāgavatam* (11.17.15-21) in the following words: The various occupational and social division of human society appeared according to inferior and superior natures manifest in the situation of the individual's birth."

"Peacefulness, self-control, austerity, cleanliness, satisfaction, tolerance, simple straightforwardness, devotion to Me, mercy, and truthfulness are the natural qualities of the *brāhmaṇas*."

"Dynamic power, bodily strength, determination, heroism, tolerance, generosity, great endeavor, steadiness, devotion to the *brāhmaṇas*, and leadership are the natural qualities of the *kṣatriyas*."

"Faith in Vedic civilization, dedication to charity, freedom from hypocrisy, service to the *brāhmaṇas*, and perpetually desiring to accumulate more money are the natural qualities of the *vaiśyas*."

"Service without duplicity to the *brāhmaṇas*, cows, demigods, and other worshipable personalities, and complete satisfaction with whatever income is obtained by such service, are the natural qualities of *śūdras*."

"Dirtiness, dishonesty, thievery, faithlessness, useless quarrel, lust, anger, and hankering constitute the nature of those in the lowest position, outside the *varṇāśrama* system."

"Non-violence, truthfulness, honesty, desire for the happiness and the welfare of all others, and freedom from lust, anger, and greed constitute duties for all members of society."

"In the assembly of the wise, everyone can understand the meaning of the scriptures. Therefore, I shall not give any comment on these words. I will only say this: The duties of *varṇa* and *āsrama* are the root of following the scriptures' rules and regulations (*vaidha*). A country is impious to the degree it does not follow *varṇāśrama*."

"Now, let us consider: How are the words *nitya* (eternal) and *naimittika* (temporary) used here with the word *karma*? If we consider the deep meaning of the scriptures, we will see that these two words do not refer to the supreme spiritual goal of life. The terms are used in connection with ordinary or material meaning."

"Words like *nitya-karma*, *nitya-tattva*, and *nitya-sattva* may be applied only to the soul's pure spiritual position. They cannot be used to refer to anything else. Therefore, when the word *nitya* is used to modify the word *karma*, that *nitya karma*, seemingly of the material world, indirectly refers to the eternal spiritual reality. The *karma* of the material world is never eternal. When *karma* is employed in *karma-yoga*, *karma-yoga* leads to the search for *jñāna* (knowledge) and that search leads to *bhakti* (devotional service), then that *karma* and *jñāna* may be called *nitya* because they lead to something that actually is *nitya*."

"Therefore a *brāhmaṇa's* chanting of the Gāyatrī *mantra* is called a *nitya karma* because, even though it is an activity in relation to the material body, it does have an oblique reference to the path of devotional service. Therefore, these things may be called *nitya*, even though in themselves they are not really *nitya*. Such a usage is called *upacāra* (a figure of speech)."

"The word *nitya karma* can be applied truthfully only to *Kṛṣṇa-prema* (pure love for Lord Kṛṣṇa). The word *nitya karma* can be applied truthfully only to the realm of the spirit. When the activities of this material world are used for advancement in spiritual life, those activities may be called *nitya karma*. There is nothing wrong with that usage. However, one who sees the truth does not call these activities *nitya* (eternal). He prefers to call them *naimittika* (temporary). It is not really true that the words *nitya karma* and *naimittika karma* may refer to materialistic activities."

"In truth, the eternal nature of the soul is purely spiritual. The religion that describes the pure soul is the real eternal religion. All other religions are temporary. *Varṇāśrama dharma*, *aṣṭāṅga-yoga*, *saṅkhyā*, and austerities are all temporary. If an individual spirit soul is not bound by *māyā*, there is no need for him to follow any of these paths. These temporary religions are meant only for souls bewildered by *māyā*. All these religions are intended for certain specific circumstances. Therefore, the truth is that they are all temporary."

"The *brāhmaṇas* are the best of the social classes. The *brāhmaṇa's* duty is to chant the Gāyatrī *mantra*, and the *sannyāsī's* duty is to renounce other duties. However, all these duties are temporary. All these duties are praised by the *dharma-śāstras*, and they are good for some spiritual aspirants. Still, they are not in any way equal to the eternal duties of the soul. *Śrīmad-Bhāgavatam* (7.9.10) explains:

If a *brāhmaṇa* has all twelve of the brahminical qualifications (as they are stated in the book called *Sanat-sujāta*) but is not a devotee and is averse to the lotus feet of the Lord, he is certainly lower than a devotee who is a dog-eater but who has dedicated everything—mind, words, activities, wealth and life—to the Supreme Lord. Such a devotee is better than such a *brāhmaṇa* because the devotee can purify his whole family, whereas the so-called *brāhmaṇa* in a position of false prestige cannot purify even himself."

"The twelve brahminical qualifications are: 1. truthfulness, 2. self-control, 3. austerity, 4. freedom from envy, 5. modesty, 6. tolerance, 7. freedom from malice, 8. sacrifice, 9. charity, 10 steadiness, 11. hearing the *Vedas*, and 12. observing vows. A *brāhmaṇa* who possesses these twelve qualities should be honored by everyone in the world. However, if a *brāhmaṇa* has all these qualities, but has no devotion for Lord Kṛṣṇa, then that *brāhmaṇa* is degraded. Even a devotee who is a dog-eater is better than such a *brāhmaṇa*. The meaning here is that the dog-eater referred to is a person who has taken birth in a dog-eater family but by association with saintly persons, becomes purified (*saṁskāra*), and because of that purification, engages in the eternal spiritual activities of the soul. The *brāhmaṇa* referred to here is a person who has taken birth in a *brāhmaṇa* family but is averse to the eternal activities of the soul, and prefers to perform temporary, material activities in their stead. Than such a *brāhmaṇa*, such a dog-eater is better."

"Human beings in the material world are of two kinds: 1. The intelligent, and 2. The unintelligent. The material world is filled with unintelligent human beings. Intelligent human beings are rare. Among such unintelligent persons, the *brāhmaṇas* are the best and thus the duties of the *brāhmaṇas*, such as their chanting of the Gāyatrī *mantra*, are the best of these kinds of duties. 'Intelligent person' is a synonym for the word 'Vaiṣṇava.' The activities of the Vaiṣṇavas and the activities of unintelligent persons are inevitably very different. However, the teachings of the Vaiṣṇavas and the teachings of the unintelligent followers of the *smṛti-śāstra* (the so-called *smārtas*) are not really opposed to each other. The teachings of the scriptures are always in harmony with each other. Intelligent persons accept the scriptures as their friends. They do not think that the different duties described in the scriptures have different purposes in the end. The duties prescribed in the scriptures for unqualified persons are indeed different from the duties prescribed for the intelligent. Still, these different activities have the same purpose at their root. For the unintelligent, the scriptures prescribe temporary duties as most appropriate. However, temporary duties are all imperfect, horrible, contaminated, and short-lived."

"These temporary duties are not the same as directly spiritual duties. Temporary duties may be accepted when they follow the spiritual path. Then they help one to attain the spiritual nature. When the means does not lead to the goal, the means should be rejected. Therefore, the means is not complete in itself. It is merely a part, a separated fragment of what will be the final goal. Therefore, temporary duties are not complete. For example, a *brāhmaṇa*'s chanting Gāyatrī, like his other duties as well, is subjected to various rules, and is meant to be performed only at certain specified times. All these duties are not manifested from the soul's natural spiritual activities. However, after many days of following such rules, a person may become purified by associating with saintly Vaiṣṇavas. Then, he develops a liking for the spiritual holy name of Lord Hari. At that time, he does not continue other activities, such as the chanting of Gāyatrī. Chanting the holy name of Lord Hari is the perfect spiritual activity."

"The chanting of Gāyatrī and other such activities are only various means to attain the goal, which is the chanting of Lord Hari's holy name. Therefore, these activities are not the final perfection. Saintly persons teach that these temporary duties, while honorable in themselves, are still imperfect, horrible, contaminated, and short-lived. The spiritual truth is the final goal. Because they bring one into contact with matter and materialists, temporary duties are horrible for the individual souls. Temporary duties are essentially material. Temporary duties bring with them many irrelevant results. The individual soul naturally attains these results. Even though he does not wish these petty results, he cannot escape them."

"For example, that a *brāhmaṇa* worships the Supreme Personality of Godhead is good. However, a *brāhmaṇa* tends to think, 'I am *brāhmaṇa*. Other souls are inferior to me.' Such a falsely proud *brāhmaṇa* finds that his worship of the Lord brings a horrible result. Mystic powers obtained by practicing *aṣṭāṅga-yoga* also bring horrible results. They are very inauspicious for the individual souls. Material sense gratification and impersonal liberation are the two unavoidable friends of temporary duties. Only if he can cheat these two will the individual soul attain his root spiritual nature. Therefore, temporary duties are very horrible for the individual soul. Temporary duties are short-lived.

The soul's temporary duties are not performed in all situations and all times. For example: a *brāhmaṇa*'s nature, a *kṣatriya*'s nature, and other such natures also, are manifested because of a particular cause. When the cause ceases to be, these natures vanish. A person may in one birth be a *brāhmaṇa*, and in the next birth an outcaste. Therefore, the duties of the *brāhmaṇa* caste are temporary. They are not the original duties of the soul. Therefore, in reference to temporary duties, the phrase 'own duty' is only a figure of speech. That is why in every birth, a soul's 'own duty' changes. However, in none of these births does the soul's eternal duty ever change. This eternal duty is the soul's true 'own duty'. Temporary duties are all short-lived."

"If one asks, 'What are the duties of the Vaiṣṇavas?,' then I answer: The Vaiṣṇavas' duties are the eternal duties of the soul. When he is liberated from the world of matter, the Vaiṣṇava soul attains his pure spiritual body and with that body, he engages in devotional activities that express his spiritual love for Lord Kṛṣṇa. When he resides in the material world, a person who is intelligent respectfully accepts all that advances his spiritual life and rejects all that hinders it. He does not blindly follow the orders and prohibitions of the scriptures. When the scriptures encourage devotion to Lord Hari, then such a person happily accepts those teachings. When the scriptures' teachings do not encourage devotion, he does not dishonor those teachings. In the same way, a Vaiṣṇava also honors or rejects the prohibitions taught in the scriptures. A Vaiṣṇava is the best person in the world. A Vaiṣṇava is the friend of everyone in the world. A Vaiṣṇava is the auspiciousness of the world. In this way, I have humbly said all I wish to say to this assembly of Vaiṣṇavas. May the Vaiṣṇavas wash away all my faults and mistakes."

After speaking these words, Vaiṣṇava dāsa offered *daṇḍavat* obeisances to the Vaiṣṇava assembly and then sat down to one side. The Vaiṣṇavas' eyes were filled with tears. With one voice, the Vaiṣṇavas called out, "Well done! Well done!" The four directions of Godruma forest echoed with, "Well done! Well done!"

The *brāhmaṇa* singer who had first asked the question could see deep truth in many of the speaker's arguments. Although he still had some doubts, the seed of faith in the Vaiṣṇava religion had been very firmly planted in his mind. With folded hands, he said, "O great souls, I was not a Vaiṣṇava. Again and again hearing Lord Hari's holy names, I have now become a Vaiṣṇava. If you are merciful and teach me a little more, all my doubts will go far away."

Then, Śrī Prema dāsa, the saintly *parāmahāṁsa bābājī*, mercifully said, "Stay with Śrīmān Vaiṣṇava dāsa. He is learned in all the scriptures. At Vārāṇasī, he deeply studied *Vedānta-sūtra* and accepted *sannyāsa*. By the limitless mercy of Śrī Kṛṣṇa Caitanya, who is the Lord of our lives, he was attracted to Śrī Navadvīpa. He knows all the truths of the Vaiṣṇava religion. Deep love for Lord Hari's holy names has taken its birth within him."

The questioner was a pious man named Śrī Kālidāsa Lāhirī. Hearing the saintly *bābājī*'s words, in his heart, he accepted Vaiṣṇava dāsa as his spiritual master. In his mind, he thought, "This person was born in a *brāhmaṇa* family and he accepted *sannyāsa*. Therefore, he is fit to teach a *brāhmaṇa*. Also, I see that he has deeply entered the truths of Vaiṣṇava religion. From him I will learn much about the Vaiṣṇava religion."

Thinking in this way, Lāhirī Mahāśaya offered *daṇḍavat* obeisances at Śrī Vaiṣṇava's feet and said, "O great soul, please be merciful to me." Offering *daṇḍavat* obeisances to him, Vaiṣṇava dāsa replied, "If you are merciful to me, then I have attained my wish."

With sunset approaching, everyone returned to their own places. Lāhirī Mahāśaya's home was in a secluded part of the village. It was in a grove. In the middle was a cottage of *mādhavī* vines and a platform of *tulasī-devī*. There were two rooms, one on each side. The yard was hedged with *cita* bushes. With a *baela* tree, *nim* tree, and some other trees bearing fruits and flowers, the place was charming. The proprietor of that grove was named Mādhava dāsa Bābājī. At first, the *bābājī* had been a good soul but by bad association, he had fallen away from the Vaiṣṇava religion. Because of improper association with a woman, his devotional practices were now dwarfed. Pushed by poverty, he could not live happily. He begged in many places and rented out one of his rooms. Lāhirī Mahāśaya was now staying in that room.

In the middle of the night, Lāhirī Mahāśaya's sleep was broken. Again and again, he thought of what Vaiṣṇava dāsa Bābājī had said. Then he heard a sound in the courtyard. Coming outside, in the courtyard, he saw Mādhava dāsa talking with the woman. Seeing him, the woman disappeared. Embarrassed before Lāhirī Mahāśaya, Mādhava dāsa stood motionless.

Lāhirī Mahāśaya said, "Bābājī, what's wrong?"

Tears in his eyes, Mādhava dāṣa replied, "O my misfortune! What more can I say? What was I in the past? What am I now? How much faith the saintly *parāmahāṁsa bābājī* had in me! Now I am ashamed even to come near him."

Lāhirī Mahāśaya said, "If you tell me clearly, I can understand."

Mādhava dāsa said, "The woman you saw was my married wife in my former *āsrama*. A few days after I accepted a life of renunciation, she came to Śrī Śāntipura and lived in a cottage she built by the Gaṅgā's shore. Many days passed in that way. Walking by the Gaṅgā's shore at Śrī Śāntipura, I saw her and said, 'Why did you leave your home?' She told me, 'Material life is not good. Now that I am robbed of your feet, I will stay at a holy place and beg alms.' Not saying anything more, I slowly returned to Śrī Godruma. At Śrī Godruma, I eventually stayed at a Ṣaḍ-gopa's house. Every day, at some place or other, I would see her. The more I tried to avoid her, the more she tried to come near me. Now she stays at an *āsrama*. She comes late at night and tries to ruin me. Now I am infamous everywhere. Because I now associate with her, my devotional service has become dwarfed. I am a cinder that blackens the family of Śrī Kṛṣṇa Caitanya's servants. Since the time of Chota Haridāsa's punishment, I am the one now deserving of punishment. Being merciful, the *bābājīs* of Śrī Godruma have not yet punished me, but they do not trust me."

Hearing these words, Lāhirī Mahāśaya said, "Take care, O Mādhava dāsa Bābājī". After speaking these words, he entered the house. The *bābājī* sat on his own seat.

Lāhirī Mahāśaya could not sleep. Again and again he thought, "Mādhava dāsa Bābājī has fallen down. He is like one who eats his own vomit. I should not stay in this house. Why not? Even if I do not fall down by associating with him, I will be criticized by others. Not trusting me, the pure Vaiṣṇavas will not teach me."

At sunrise, he went to Pradyumna-kuñja, properly greeted Śrī Vaiṣṇava dāsa and asked for a place to stay. When Vaiṣṇava dāsa informed the saintly *parāmahāṁsa bābājī* of this request, the *bābājī* said he could stay in a cottage on one side of the forest. Lāhirī Mahāśaya stayed in that cottage and arranged to get *prasādam* at the home of a nearby *brāhmaṇa*.

Chapter Four

Another name for the eternal religion is the Vaiṣṇava religion.

The cottage of Lāhirī Mahāśaya and the cottage of Śrī Vaiṣṇava dāsa stood side by side. Nearby were some mango and *kāṅṭhāla* trees. Some betel plants gracefully enclosed the place on four sides. In the courtyard was a large circular terrace. The terrace had been there since the days when Pradyumna Brahmācārī lived there. Many days since then the Vaiṣṇavas came to call that place "Surabhī's Terrace" and became accustomed to circumambulate it and offer *daṇḍavat* obeisances.

It was shortly after dusk. Sitting on a leaf-seat in his cottage, Śrī Vaiṣṇava dāsa chanted the holy names of Lord Hari. It was the dark fortnight. The night was gradually becoming dark. A flickering lamp burned in Lāhirī Mahāśaya's cottage. Seeing a snake at his doorway, Lāhirī Mahāśaya quickly trimmed the lamp and took up a stick to kill the snake, but when he came outside with his lamp, he did not see the snake. Then Lāhirī Mahāśaya said to Vaiṣṇava dāsa, "Take care. A snake has entered your cottage." Vaiṣṇava dāsa replied, "Why do you worry about a snake? Come. Enter my cottage without fear." Lāhirī Mahāśaya entered the cottage and sat on the leaf seat. Still, his mind was agitated about the snake. He said "O noble-hearted one, Śāntipura is very good in this way. It is a city and there is no fear of snakes or other dangers. In Nadiya there is always fear of snakes, especially in Godruma and the other forest places. It is hard for a gentleman to live in those places."

Śrī Vaiṣṇava dāsa Bābājī replied, "O Lāhirī Mahāśaya, it is foolish to let the mind be agitated over these things. You must have heard the story of Mahārāja Parīkṣit in the *Śrīmad-Bhāgavatam*. Giving up all fear of snakes, with an unagitated mind, he heard nectarean descriptions of Lord Hari from the mouth of Śrīla Śukadeva Gosvāmī. In this way, he attained transcendental bliss. No snake can kill a man's spiritual body. The spiritual body is bitten only by the snake of separation from hearing the nectarean topics of the Supreme Lord. The material body is not eternal. Some day you must give it up. One may do everything to maintain his material body but still, whenever Lord Kṛṣṇa wills, that material body will certainly collapse, and one will not be able to protect it. If the time of one's death has not yet come, one may even sleep beside a snake, but the snake will not harm him. Therefore one who gives up fear of snakes or other dangers may be called a true Vaiṣṇava. If it is afraid of every danger, the mind will always be restless. How can a restless mind always think of Lord Hari's lotus feet? Therefore, one should abandon all fear of snakes and all attempts, born from that fear, to kill snakes."

Becoming a little faithful, Lāhirī Mahāśaya said, "O saintly one, your good words have made my heart fearless. I know that only a person with a noble heart is qualified to attain the final goal of life. The great souls who stay in mountain caves and worship the Lord there are never afraid of wild animals. On the contrary, it is because they fear the association of materialistic persons that they voluntarily live in the forest, surrounded by wild animals."

The saintly *bābājī* then said, "When Bhakti-devī (the goddess of devotional service) appears in someone's heart, that heart naturally becomes exalted. The whole world loves such a person. Saints and ruffians alike—everyone loves a devotee of the Lord. Therefore, every human being should become a Vaiṣṇava."

Hearing this, Lāhirī Mahāśaya said, "You have given me great faith in the eternal religion. The Vaiṣṇava religion is very close to the eternal religion. That is my belief. I am not convinced that the Vaiṣṇava religion is completely identical with the eternal religion. Therefore, I ask you to tell me what you think of all this."

Vaiṣṇava dāsa Bābājī then said: "In this material world, two different religions are called by the name of the Vaiṣṇava religion. One is the pure Vaiṣṇava religion and the other is the contaminated Vaiṣṇava religion. The pure Vaiṣṇava religion is one, although it is divided into four, according to the different *rasas*. Thus, there is the Vaiṣṇava religion in servitorship (*dāsya*), the Vaiṣṇava religion in friendship (*sākhya*), the Vaiṣṇava religion in parental love (*vātsalya*), and the Vaiṣṇava religion in conjugal love (*mādhurya*). Still, the pure Vaiṣṇava religion is one. It is not many. 'The eternal religion' and 'the transcendental religion' are merely other names for the Vaiṣṇava religion."

"The *Śruti śāstra* declares: By understanding the Supreme, one comes to understand everything. These words refer to the Vaiṣṇava religion. This truth will gradually be revealed to you."

"The contaminated Vaiṣṇava religion is of two kinds: 1. Vaiṣṇava religion contaminated by fruitive work (*karma*) and 2. Vaiṣṇava religion contaminated by the impersonalist fallacy (*jñāna*). The activities of the Vaiṣṇava religion as conceived by the *smārta paṇḍitas* are the Vaiṣṇava religion contaminated by fruitive work. Although it includes initiation into chanting a Viṣṇu *mantra*, this conception of the Vaiṣṇava religion belittles the all-pervading Supreme Personality of Godhead and makes Him subordinate to fruitive work. According to these people, even though He is the master of all the demigods, Lord Viṣṇu is merely a part of the process of *karma* and is Himself subject to the laws of *karma*. Thus, *karma* is not subordinate to the will of Viṣṇu, but Viṣṇu is subordinate to the will of *karma*. According to them, all worship and spiritual practices are merely various aspects of fruitive work, and therefore nothing is higher than fruitive work. This form of Vaiṣṇava religion according to the conception of the Mīmāṁsaka philosophers has existed for many days. In India, many follow this idea, and they claim to be Vaiṣṇavas. They do not accept the pure Vaiṣṇavas to be Vaiṣṇavas at all. Such is the misfortune of the followers of Mīmāṁsaka."

"Vaiṣṇava religion contaminated by impersonal philosophy is also prevalent in India. According to the impersonalists, in order to attain the qualityless impersonal Brahman, one should worship Sūrya, Gaṇeśa, Śakti, Śiva, or Viṣṇu. When one attains perfect knowledge, he can discard the form that he had worshipped. Then, at the end, he attains the qualityless impersonal Brahman. Accepting these ideas, many persons dishonor the pure Vaiṣṇava religion. The worship of Lord Viṣṇu is included in the impersonalists' worship of five Deities (Sūrya, Gaṇeśa, Śakti, Śiva, or Viṣṇu, as described above), and that worship includes initiation, Deity worship, and the other aspects of devotion to Lord Viṣṇu. Sometimes it may even include the worship of Śrī Śrī Rādhā-Kṛṣṇa. Still, this is not the pure Vaiṣṇava religion."

"The pure Vaiṣṇava religion is different from these kinds of contaminated Vaiṣṇava religion. It is the true Vaiṣṇava religion. Because of the defects of Kali-yuga, many people do not understand what is the pure Vaiṣṇava religion. They think these varieties of contaminated Vaiṣṇava religion are the true Vaiṣṇava religion.

The worshippers of the Paramātmā (Supersoul) wish to meet the Supersoul. Desiring to enter a mystic trance and there meet the Supersoul, they engage in *kriya-yoga*, *karma-yoga*, or *aṣṭāṅga-yoga*. According to these people, initiation into chanting Viṣṇu *mantras*, worship of Lord Viṣṇu, meditating on Lord Viṣṇu, and other kinds of devotional service, are all various aspects of *karma-yoga*. Among these people, Vaiṣṇava religion contaminated by fruitive work is manifested."

"*Śrīmad-Bhāgavatam* explains that the most fortunate persons are attracted to pure devotional service, service to the pure form of the Supreme Personality of Godhead. Such persons engage in Deity worship and the other activities of devotional service. These activities of devotional service are not subordinate aspects of *kriya-yoga*, *karma yoga*, or the speculations of the impersonalists. Rather, they are aspects of pure devotional service. These activities are the pure Vaiṣṇava religion."

"*Śrīmad-Bhāgavatam* (1.1.1) explains: Learned transcendentalists who know the Absolute Truth call this non-dual substance Brahman, Paramātmā, or Bhagavān. One should see in this way. The Supreme Personality of Godhead, who is not different from either the Paramātmā or the impersonal Brahman, is the final manifestation of the Supreme. The Supreme Personality of Godhead is Lord Viṣṇu, who is the supreme pure. Individual spirit souls that become His followers are also pure. The activity of such pure souls is called *bhakti* (devotional service). *Hari-bhakti* (devotional service to Lord Hari) is also called by the names *suddha-Vaiṣṇava-dharma* (pure Vaiṣṇava religion), *nitya-dharma* (eternal religion), *jaiva dharma* (duty of the individual souls), *bhāgavata-dharma* (religion of worshiping the Supreme Personality of Godhead), *paramārtha-dharma* (way to attain the final goal of life), and *para-dharma* (highest religion)."

"Religions that strive to attain the Paramātmā and the impersonal Brahman are all temporary religions. A material motive pushes one to seek the impersonal Brahman. Therefore, the religion of the impersonal Brahman is materially motivated and temporary, and is not eternal. The individual soul trapped in the material world is eager to escape his material bondage. To escape this material bondage, the soul searches for the impersonal Brahman. In this way, he takes shelter of a religion that is both temporary and materially motivated. Therefore, the religion of seeking the impersonal Brahman is not eternal. Seeking the happiness of rapt meditation (*samādhi*), a soul may take shelter of the religion of seeking the Paramātmā. Thus, seeking a more subtle kind of material pleasure, he follows a temporary religion based on a material motive. Therefore, the religion of seeking the Paramātmā is not eternal. The religion of serving the Supreme Personality of Godhead is alone eternal."

Hearing these words, Lāhirī Mahāśaya said, "Please describe to me the pure Vaiṣṇava religion. I am advanced in years. I take shelter of your feet. Please be merciful and accept me. I have heard it said that a person previously initiated and instructed by an unworthy person should find a worthy teacher and accept initiation and instruction from him. For some days, I have heard your good instructions and now I have faith in the Vaiṣṇava religion. Please be merciful. Teach me the Vaiṣṇava religion and, when your teaching is concluded, initiate me and purify me.

A little embarrassed, the saintly *bābājī* said, "Saintly brother, I will teach you as far as I am able, but I am not qualified to be an initiating spiritual master. However that may be, you should now learn about the pure Vaiṣṇava religion."

"Śrī Kṛṣṇa Caitanya Mahāprabhu, who is the original spiritual master of the entire world, teaches that there are three basic truths in the Vaiṣṇava religion. They are: 1. *sambandha* (the relationship of the Supreme Personality of Godhead and the individual soul), 2. *abhidheya* (the activities in that relationship), and 3. *prayojana* (the final goal, which is pure love for the Supreme Personality of Godhead). One who understands these three truths can act properly. He is a pure Vaiṣṇava, or a pure devotee of the Lord."

"Within *sambandha* are three distinct truths: 1. The material world, or the illusory potency, *māyā*, 2. The individual soul, or the subordinate living entity, and 3. The Supreme Personality of Godhead, who is one and unrivaled, the master of all powers, all-attractive, the abode of all opulence and sweetness, and the only shelter of both the individual spirit souls and the illusory potency, *māyā*. Although He is the only shelter of both the individual spirit souls and the illusory potency, *māyā*, He is always supremely independent, and His transcendental form is both sublimely handsome and eternal."

"The impersonal Brahman effulgence is merely a distant reflection of the splendor of His limbs. With His potency of transcendental power (*aisi śakti*) He manifests the material universes and places the individual souls within them. Then, He expands to become the Supersoul. As the Supersoul, He enters the material universes. In this way, He is the supreme controller. When He manifests His feature of supreme opulence, He is Lord Nārāyaṇa in the spiritual sky. When He manifests His feature of supreme sweetness, He is Lord Kṛṣṇacandra, the *gopīs'* beloved in Goloka Vṛndāvana. His different forms and pastimes are all limitless and eternal. No person or thing is His equal. Nothing is superior to Him. All His forms and pastimes are manifested by his *para śakti* (transcendental potency)."

"Of His many transcendental potencies, three are especially known to the individual souls. One of these potencies is called the *cit* potency. Employing this potency, the Supreme Personality of Godhead enjoys all His transcendental pastimes. Another of these potencies is called the *jīva* potency, or marginal potency. By this potency, limitless individual souls are manifested and maintained. The third potency is called the *māyā* potency. By this potency, all material things, material time, and material activities are manifested."

"The Supreme Personality of Godhead has a relationship with the individual spirit souls. The material energy and the individual spirit souls both have relationships with the Supreme Personality of Godhead. The Supreme Personality of Godhead and the individual souls both have relationships with the material energy. These different relationships are called *sambandha. Sambandha* is understood when one understands these different relationships. Without first understanding these relationships, it is not possible for anyone to become a pure Vaiṣṇava."

Lāhirī Mahāśaya said, "From the Vaiṣṇavas themselves, I have heard that Vaiṣṇavas surrender to their emotions and therefore, they have no need for knowledge. What kind of statement is that? I myself, up to this time, have chanted the holy names of Lord Hari only to attain a certain feeling. I did not strive to understand any relationships."

The *bābājī* said, "A Vaiṣṇava's feelings of ecstatic love are the final result of his devotional service. However, such love must be pure. Those who think that this ecstatic emotion culminates in oneness with the impersonal Brahman cannot have actions and ecstatic emotions that are pure. Their pure ecstatic emotions are all an empty show. A single drop of pure ecstatic love fulfills all the desires of the spirit soul. However, when that emotion is contaminated by impersonalism, the only result is trouble and calamity for the spirit soul. The devotional emotional displays of one who, in his heart, thinks he is not different from the impersonal Brahman are merely a trick to cheat the innocent people. Therefore, pure Vaiṣṇavas must thoroughly understand these relationships."

Faithful Lāhirī Mahāśaya then said, "Is there something higher than the impersonal Brahman? If the Supreme Personality of Godhead is the origin of the impersonal Brahman, then why do the philosophers not leave the impersonal Brahman and worship the Supreme Personality of Godhead instead?"

The saintly *bābājī* laughed and said, "Brahmā, the four Kumāras, Śukadeva Gosvāmī, Nārada, Śiva, and all other truly great philosophers took shelter of the Supreme Personality of Godhead's lotus feet."

Lāhirī Mahāśaya said, "If the Supreme Personality of Godhead has a form situated within space, then that form must also be limited in spatial terms. How, then can the spatially limited form of the Supreme Personality of Godhead be the resting place of the all-pervading, spatially limitless impersonal Brahman?"

The *bābājī* replied, "Even in the material world, the element, ether, is also all-pervading and spatially limitless. Why then should the impersonal Brahman be considered so glorious, merely because it is all-pervading and spatially limitless? From the splendor of His transcendental limbs, the Supreme Personality of Godhead manifests the all-pervading, spatially limitless impersonal Brahman, and at the same time, His transcendental form is spatially limited, situated in a specific place. Who has seen anyone like Him? Because no one is like Him, and because He has no rival, the Supreme Personality of Godhead is superior to the impersonal Brahman. His form is wonderfully attractive. In His transcendental form, all-pervasiveness, omniscience, omnipotence, the greatest mercy, and the greatest bliss are gloriously manifest in their completeness. Is this form good? What virtue does it not have? What power does it not have? Is an amorphous, all-pervading, unknowable something good?"

"The truth is that the impersonal Brahman is the qualityless aspect of the Supreme Personality of Godhead. Personality and impersonality exist side by side in the handsome form of the Supreme Personality of Godhead. The impersonal Brahman is merely one aspect of the Supreme Personality of Godhead. This formless, changeless, qualityless, unknowable, immeasurable feature of the Lord is liked by short-sighted persons. However, those who see everything do not like any feature but the original and complete form of the Lord. The Vaiṣṇavas cannot place their faith in the formless impersonal Brahman, for to do so would block their eternal nature and also block their pure love for Lord Kṛṣṇa. The Supreme Personality of Godhead, Lord Kṛṣṇa, is the resting place of both features: the qualityless Brahman and the quality-filled Supreme Person. He is an ocean of transcendental bliss and therefore He is attractive to all pure spirit souls."

Lāhirī: Kṛṣṇa was born, performed activities, and then left His body at death. How is it possible that His form is eternal?

Bābājī: Śrī Kṛṣṇa's form is eternal and full of knowledge and bliss. His birth, activities, and so-called death are not material.

Lāhirī: Why do the *Mahābhārata* and other scriptures describe Him in that way?

Bābājī: The eternal Absolute Truth is beyond description. Pure souls see Lord Kṛṣṇa's form and pastimes. These persons then describe these both with words. Those words are like ordinary historical accounts of material persons. Those who know the true meaning of the *Mahābhārata* and the other scriptures understand Lord Kṛṣṇa's pastimes and other features in one way, and the unintelligent materialists understand Lord Kṛṣṇa's pastimes and other features in a very different way.

Lāhirī: When one meditates on Lord Kṛṣṇa's form, in one's heart naturally arises the idea of a form limited by both time and space. What other way is there to think of Lord Kṛṣṇa's form?

Bābājī: Thinking is an activity of the mind. As long as the mind is not purified and spiritualized, the mind's activity of thinking and meditating cannot be spiritual in its nature. When it develops a devotional attitude, the mind gradually becomes spiritualized. Then the mind's activity of thinking and meditating is inevitably spiritual in nature. When the Vaiṣṇava devotees, who delight in devotional service, chant the holy names of Lord Hari, the material world has no power to touch them. They are spiritualized. Residing in the spiritual world, they meditate on Lord Kṛṣṇa's daily activities. In this way they attain the bliss of confidential service to the Lord.

Lāhirī: Please be merciful and give that spiritual understanding to me.

Bābājī: When you give up all material arguments and doubts, and when you chant the holy names day after day, then after a few days, genuine spiritual understanding will rise in your heart. As long as those material arguments remain, your mind will stay in the shackles of material understanding. When you taste the nectar of the holy name, the material shackles will become loosened. Then, the spiritual world will be gloriously manifested in your heart.

Lāhirī: Please be merciful and tell me about that. That I desire.

Bābājī: The mind and words cannot understand it. Only when one attains the bliss of spiritual life can one understand it. Give up all your arguments and for a few days chant the holy names of Lord Hari. Then all your doubts will go far away. Then you will no longer ask any question of anyone.

Lāhirī: I know that a person who has faith in Lord Kṛṣṇa and tastes the nectar of His holy names attains the highest of all goals. I have well understood the relationship of the Lord and the individual soul. I will take shelter of the Lord's holy names.

Bābājī: That is the best of all. Understand well your relationship with the Lord and you will directly see the spiritual truth.

Lāhirī: I understand the truth of the Supreme Personality of Godhead. The Supreme Personality of Godhead is the ultimate form of the Supreme. The impersonal Brahman and the Supersoul are subordinate to Him. He is all-pervading. In the spiritual world, He manifests His wonderful form. He is a person, He is eternal and full of knowledge and bliss, and He is the master of all potencies. Even though He is the master of all potencies, He is always overcome with bliss in the company of His *hlādinī śakti* (pleasure potency). Now please tell me about the individual spirit souls.

Bābājī: Among the limitless potencies of Śrī Kṛṣṇa, one is called *taṭasthā śakti*. Positioned between the spiritual and material, this potency can reside in either of them. This potency is also called *jīva-tattva* (the individual spirit souls). The individual souls are tiny particles of spirit. Because they are tiny particles, they may attain bondage in the material world. However, because they are pure spirit, they may also reside eternally in the supremely blissful spiritual world. The individual souls are of two kinds: 1. Souls who reside in the spiritual world, and 2. Souls in bondage who reside in the material world. Souls in bondage in the material world are of two kinds: 1. intelligent and 2. unintelligent. Birds, beasts and human beings who do not strive to attain the supreme spiritual goal are the unintelligent materially bound souls. Human beings who follow the path of the Vaiṣṇava religion are intelligent. Those who are not Vaiṣṇavas do not actively strive for the real goal of life. Therefore, the scriptures declare the service to Vaiṣṇavas and association with Vaiṣṇavas are the best of all activities. Intelligent human beings who have faith in the scriptures and chant the holy names of Lord Hari naturally associate with Vaiṣṇavas. Those who are not intelligent do not have faith in the scriptures and do not chant the holy names of Lord Kṛṣṇa. Even though they may serve the Deity form of Lord Kṛṣṇa according to the rules passed down through the disciplic succession, in their hearts, such unintelligent persons do not properly honor Vaiṣṇavas.

Lāhirī: Now I understand the truth about Lord Kṛṣṇa and the truth about the individual spirit souls. Now please tell me the truth about the illusory potency, *māyā*.

Bābājī: *Māyā* is matter. *Māyā* is one of the potencies of Lord Kṛṣṇa. *Māyā* is also called *apara śakti* (material potency) and *bahiranga śakti* (external potency). As a shadow stays far away from light, so *māyā* stays far away from Lord Kṛṣṇa and His devotees. *Māyā* manifested the fourteen material worlds, earth, water, fire, air, ether, mind, intelligence, and false ego, which makes one think 'I am this material body.' The gross and subtle material bodies of the bound souls are manifested by *māyā*. When a soul attains liberation, his spiritual body is cleansed of *māyā*'s influence. To the extent he is tightly bound by *māyā*, to that extent the soul is far away from Lord Kṛṣṇa. To the extent the soul is free of *māyā*'s influence, to that extent the soul is able to see Lord Kṛṣṇa face-to-face. The material universe, which is a place of sense pleasures for the bound souls has sprouted from Lord Kṛṣṇa's will. The spirit souls do not stay forever in the material world. The material world is only a prison for the spirit souls

Lāhirī: O master, now please tell me of the eternal relationship that exists between *māyā*, the individual soul, and Lord Kṛṣṇa.

Bābājī: The tiny spirit soul is an eternal servant of Lord Kṛṣṇa. The world of *māyā* is the souls' prison. By associating with devotees and chanting the holy names, the soul attains Lord Kṛṣṇa's mercy. Then, restored to his original spiritual form, the soul tastes the nectar of direct service to Lord Kṛṣṇa in the spiritual world. These are the confidential relationships between these three. Without understanding this, how can anyone engage in devotional service?

Lāhirī: If one should carefully attain this knowledge, must one become a great scholar before becoming a Vaiṣṇava?

Bābājī: A Vaiṣṇava need not study different languages, nor become a great scholar. To throw far away the bewilderment presented by *māyā*, what the soul must do is take shelter of the lotus feet of a bona-fide Vaiṣṇava spiritual master. By the spiritual master's words of instruction, and by the disciple's own spiritual activities, the disciple comes to understand the truth of these relationships. This is called *dīkṣā* (initiation) and *śikṣā* (instruction).

Lāhirī: What does one do after initiation and instruction?

Bābājī: Living a moral life, one should serve Lord Kṛṣṇa. This is called *abhidheya*. Because it is clearly described in the *Vedas* and all other scriptures, Lord Caitanya Mahāprabhu called this activity *abhidheya*.

Lāhirī (with tears in his eyes): O spiritual master, I take shelter of your lotus feet. By hearing the honey of your words, I now understand my relationship with Lord Kṛṣṇa. By your mercy, all my previous ideas of caste, knowledge, and spiritual instruction are thrown far away. Now please mercifully instruct me about *abhidheya*.

Bābājī: There need be no more worry. Now that you are humble, Śrī Kṛṣṇa Caitanya will certainly be merciful to you. Association with devotees is the only cure for souls bound in the material world. The bona fide spiritual master mercifully teaches one how to serve Lord Kṛṣṇa. By engaging in devotional service, one gradually attains the goal of life. Thus devotional service is called *abhidheya*.

Lāhirī: Please tell me: How does one serve Lord Hari?

Bābājī: Devotional service to Lord Hari is called *bhakti*. *Bhakti* has three stages: 1. *sādhana* (devotional service in practice), 2. *bhāva* (ecstasy) and 3. *prema* (pure love). The beginning stage is *sādhana*. By again and again performing *sādhana*, *bhāva* is manifested. When *bhāva* becomes perfect, it is called *prema*.

Lāhirī: What are the different kinds of *sādhana* and how are they performed? Please teach me that.

Bābājī: In his book *Śrī Hari-bhakti-rasāmṛta-sindhu*, Śrīla Rūpa Gosvāmī has elaborately described all this. I will give a brief summary. There are nine kinds of *sādhana*. In *Śrīmad-Bhāgavatam* (7.5.23) it is said:

"Hearing and chanting about the transcendental holy name, form, qualities, paraphernalia, and pastimes of Lord Viṣṇu, remembering them, serving the lotus feet of the Lord, offering the Lord respectful worship with sixteen types of paraphernalia, offering prayers to the Lord, becoming His servant, considering the Lord one's best friend, and surrendering everything unto Him (in other words serving Him with the body, mind and words)—these nine processes are accepted as pure devotional service."

Thus, in *Śrīmad-Bhāgavatam* it is written that the nine kinds of *sādhana-bhakti* are: 1. Hearing and chanting about the transcendental holy name, form, qualities, paraphernalia, and pastimes of Lord Viṣṇu, 2. Remembering them, 3. Serving the lotus feet of the Lord, 4. Offering the Lord respectful worship with sixteen types of paraphernalia, 5. Offering prayers to the Lord, 6. Becoming His servant, 7. Considering the Lord one's best friend, and 8. Surrendering everything unto Him. Describing the different limbs and sub-limbs that are parts of these, Śrīla Rūpa Gosvāmī describes 64 different kinds of *sādhana bhakti*. While considering these points, another topic needs to be explained. *Sādhana bhakti* is of two kinds: 1. *vaidhī* (according to rules and regulations), and 2. *rāgānuga* (spontaneous). In *vaidhī bhakti* one engages in the nine kinds of activities previously described. In *rāgānuga-bhakti* one engages in the activities of *sādhana bhakti*, but one becomes a follower of the people of Vraja, and in one's mind one sees Lord Kṛṣṇa as they do. One should engage in the kind of *sādhana bhakti* for which he is qualified.

Lāhirī: How does one know he is qualified for one or the other of these kinds of *sādhana bhakti*?

Bābājī: A faithful person who follows the rules and regulations is qualified. In the beginning, his spiritual master teaches him *vaidhī sādhana-bhakti*. Then, when the disciple becomes qualified, the spiritual master teaches him how to worship the Lord by following the path of *rāgānuga-bhakti*.

Lāhirī: How does a person know he has become qualified for this?

Bābājī: One who has not yet experienced in his heart the love that characterizes *rāgānuga-bhakti*, and who instead wishes to serve the Lord according to the rules and regulations described in the scriptures, is qualified to engage in *vaidhī bhakti*. One who does not wish to be ruled by the scriptures' rules and regulations in his devotional service to Lord Hari, and in whose heart a spontaneous love for Lord Hari's devotional service has become manifested, is qualified to engage in *rāgānuga-bhakti*.

Lāhirī: O master, please tell me for which one I am qualified. I cannot understand these explanations of who is qualified for what. I do not know whether I should engage in *vaidhī* or *rāgānuga bhakti*.

Bābājī: If you examine your heart, you will understand where you are qualified. In your heart, do you see the idea that it is not possible to engage in devotional service to Lord Hari without following the scriptures' teachings?

Lāhirī: In my mind is the idea that *sādhana-bhakti* following the scriptures teachings brings the best result. But now in my mind I also think that devotional service to Lord Hari is a great ocean of nectar, and by engaging in devotional service, I will gradually be able to taste that nectar.

Bābājī: You can now see that the scriptures' rules and regulations are the ruler of your mind. Therefore, you should engage in *vaidhī bhakti*. Gradually, the spiritual love that is *rāgānuga bhakti* will manifest in your heart.

Hearing these words, Lāhirī Mahāśaya, his eyes now filled with tears, touched the *bābājī*'s lotus feet and said, "Please be merciful and engage me as I am qualified. I am not able to understand my own qualifications." The saintly *bābājī* then embraced him and made him sit down again.

Lāhirī: Please clearly order me, and I will thus engage in devotional service.

Bābājī: You should chant the holy names of Lord Hari. Taking shelter of the holy names is the most powerful of all kinds of devotional service. The name of the Lord and the Lord Himself are not different. By offenselessly chanting the holy names, one quickly attains all spiritual perfections. Therefore, with great faith, you should chant the holy names. By again and again chanting the holy names, one engages in all nine kinds of devotional service. By chanting the holy names aloud, one engages in *śravaṇam* (hearing) and *kīrtanaṁ* (chanting).

As one chants the holy names, one will naturally remember (*smaraṇaṁ*) the pastimes of Lord Hari, and in one's mind, one will serve His lotus feet (*pāda-sevanam*), worship Him (*arcanaṁ*), offer obeisances to Him (*vandanam*), serve Him (*dāsyam*), think of Him as a friend (*sākhyam*), and surrender everything to Him (*ātma-nivedanam*). In this way, one engages in all nine activities of devotional service.

Lāhirī: My heart is very eager to receive the holy names. O master, please be merciful. Please don't delay any further.

Bābājī: O great soul, without committing offenses, you should always chant this *mantra*: *Hare Kṛṣṇa Hare Kṛṣṇa, Kṛṣṇa Kṛṣṇa Hare Hare, Hare Rāma Hare Rāma, Rāma Rāma Hare Hare.*

As he chanted these words again and again, the saintly *bābājī* placed in Lāhirī Mahāśaya's hands a string of *tulasī* beads. Weeping, Lāhirī Mahāśaya again and again chanted the holy names on these beads. He said, "O master, I cannot express the happiness I feel today."

Overcome with happiness, Lāhirī fell unconscious at the *bābājī*'s feet. The saintly *bābājī* carefully picked him up. After a long time, Lāhirī Mahāśaya said, "Today I am fortunate. Never before have I been so happy."

Bābājī: O great soul, you are fortunate, for you have faithfully accepted the holy names. Thus you have made me fortunate also.

From that day, Lāhirī Mahāśaya chanted the holy names on those beads. Without fear, he stayed in his cottage and chanted the holy names. Some days passed in this way. Lāhirī Mahāśaya wore the twelve *tilaka* marks. He did not eat anything but Kṛṣṇa *prasādam*. Every day, he chanted two lakhs of the holy names of Lord Hari. He would always offer *daṇḍavat* obeisances to the *parāmahāṁsa bābājī* before attending to other duties. He always served his spiritual master. He was not attracted to useless gossip or non-devotional music. He was not the same Lāhirī Mahāśaya. Now he was a Vaiṣṇava.

One day, he offered *daṇḍavat* obeisances to saintly Vaiṣṇava dāsa Bābājī and asked, "O master, what is the final spiritual goal (*prayojana*)?"

Bābājī: Pure love for Lord Kṛṣṇa (*Kṛṣṇa-prema*) is the final spiritual goal for the individual soul. Again and again performing the duties of *sādhana-bhakti*, one attains the state of *bhāva* (ecstasy). When *bhāva* becomes complete and reaches its perfection, it is called *prema* (pure spiritual love). That is the individual soul's eternal nature, his eternal wealth, his highest goal. The absence of this love is the greatest calamity. It means bondage in the material world. It means the attempt to enjoy with the material senses. Nothing is higher or better than this spiritual love (*prema*). Lord Kṛṣṇa Himself is controlled by this love alone. This love is purely spiritual. It is filled with the most intense spiritual bliss.

Lāhirī (weeping again and again): Will I ever be qualified to attain this spiritual love?

Bābājī (embracing him): Look, and in a few days your *sādhana-bhakti* will become *bhāva bhakti*. A few days after that, Lord Kṛṣṇa will certainly be merciful to you.

Overcome with joy to hear this, Lāhirī Mahāśaya said, "Ah, aside from the spiritual master, nothing is important. My spiritual master has mercifully rescued me from the blind well of material sense gratification."

Chapter Five

Vaidhī-bhakti — the eternal religion. It is not temporary.

Jaiva-dharma

Lāhirī Mahāśaya had a large family in his home in Śāntipura. His two sons were famous scholars. One was named Candranātha, who was 35 years old. He was a landowner (*zamindar*) and he looked after all the household affairs. He was learned in the medical texts. He didn't trouble himself much with religion. Still, he was honored in *brāhmaṇa* society. He took care of the servants, maids, doorkeepers, and others, and he looked after the household affairs. The second son was named Devīdāsa. From childhood, he eagerly studied the *Nyāya-śāstra* and *Smṛti-śāstra*. He had his own school with ten or fifteen students. He bore the title Vidyāratna (the jewel of knowledge).

One day, in Śāntipura, there was a rumor that Kālidāsa Lāhirī had become a Vaiṣṇava ascetic. The rumor was everywhere: at the bathing *ghāṭas*, in the marketplace, and on the streets. Some said that he was now a senile old man. Indeed, on that day, the general opinion was that he had become senile. Some said, "Perhaps he was struck with some disease. He is a *brāhmaṇa* by birth. His sons and wife and family obey him. What suffering led him to renounce the world?"

Some said, "Such is the sad end of those who run here and there advertising their love for religion."

Some educated persons said, "Kālidāsa Lāhirī is a very pious man. Although everything this world has to offer is in his possession, in his old age, he has become attracted to the holy names of Lord Hari."

In these ways, they talked. Hearing all these rumors, someone repeated them to Devīdāsa Vidyāratna Mahāśaya.

Rapt in thought, Vidyāratna approached his elder brother and said, "Brother, I think our father is in great trouble. His body is in good health. He is staying at Godruma in Nadīyā. But, he has fallen into bad association. We cannot be blind to the rumors in the village."

Candranātha replied, "O brother, I have also heard some of these rumors. The fame of our house is very great. Still, when I hear these rumors about father, I can no longer hold my head high. We have always held the family of Advaita Prabhu in low esteem. But, what has now happened in our own house? Let us go home, consult with our saintly mother, and do what we can."

Devīdāsa and Candranātha sat on the veranda of their home. A *brāhmaṇa* widow served them their meal. Their mother sat with them, arranging for the meal. Candranātha said, "Mother, have you heard any news about father?"

The saintly mother replied, "Why? Is his health good? He is in Navadvīpa now. He is mad after the holy names of Lord Hari. Why don't you bring him back here?"

Devīdāsa said, "Mother, his health is good. But I have heard that other things are not good. If we bring him home, our reputation will be ruined."

Then, the saintly mother asked, "How can it be? The other day at the Gaṅgā's shore I talked about many things with the daughter-in-law of one of the big Gosvāmīs. She said to me, 'Your husband is very fortunate. The Vaiṣṇavas honor him.'"

Devīdāsa said, "He is not honored in our social circles. Now that he is old in years, will he stay at home and allow us to serve him? No. He eats the remnants left by men who wear loincloths. He has defiled our exalted family. O wicked age of Kali! Our father has seen and heard so much! What has happened to his intelligence now?"

The saintly mother said, "Bring him here and keep him hidden until you can bring him to his senses."

Candranātha said, "What else can we do? Accompanied by two or three men, Devī should go to Godruma and secretly bring father back."

Devīdasa said, "You know very well that father, thinking me an atheist, does not have a very good opinion of me. If I cannot even talk with him, there should be something else I can do."

Devīdāsa's maternal cousin, Sambhunātha, was liked by their father. Indeed, Sambhunātha stayed with him and served him for many days. So it was settled that the two of them, Devīdāsa and Sambhunātha, were to go to Godruma. A servant was sent in advance to arrange their stay in some *brāhmaṇa*'s home.

The next day, Sambhunātha and Devīdāsa finished their meal and set out for Godruma. Arriving, they descended from their palanquins and gave the bearers permission to depart. At their new place, they would have one *brāhmaṇa* cook and two servants.

At sunset, Devīdāsa and Sambhunātha peacefully walked about Pradyumna-kuñja. They saw Lāhirī Mahāśaya sitting on a leaf-seat in Śrī Surabhī's courtyard. His eyes closed, he was chanting the holy names of Lord Hari on his beads. His limbs were glorious with the twelve *tilaka* marks. Quietly entering the courtyard, Sambhunātha and Devīdāsa offered *daṇḍavat* obeisances to the feet of Lāhirī Mahāśaya. Startled, Lāhirī Mahāśaya opened his eyes and said, "Sambhu, why have you come? What is in your mind, that you have come here? Devī, is all well with you?'

The two of them humbly said, "Because you have blessed us, all is well."

Lāhirī Mahāśaya asked, "Will you take your meal here?"

The two answered, "We are already guests at someone's house. You need not worry for us."

At that moment, the sound of Lord Hari's holy names came from Śrī Prema dāsa's cottage of *mādhavī* and *mālatī* vines. Then, Śrī Vaiṣṇava dāsa came from his cottage and asked Lāhirī Mahāśaya, "Why does the sound of Lord Hari's holy names come from the *parāmahāṁs bābājī*'s cottage?"

Lāhirī Mahāśaya and Vaiṣṇava dāsa went there. There, they saw many Vaiṣṇavas chanting the holy names of Lord Hari and circumambulating the saintly *bābājī*. The two of them joined in these activities. Then, everyone offered *daṇḍavat* obeisances to the saintly *parāmahāṁsa bābājī*. Everyone sat down. Devīdāsa and Sambhunātha also sat down to one side. They were like two ducks surrounded by a flock of swans.

One of the Vaiṣṇavas said, "We come from the town of Kattwa. Our primary reason to come here is to see Śrī Navadvīpa and Śrī Māyāpura, and to attain the dust of the *parāmahāṁsa bābājī*'s lotus feet. Embarrassed, the *parāmahāṁsa bābājī* said, "I am a fallen sinner. You have come here to purify me. After a short time, it became obvious that these Vaiṣṇavas are very expert in singing the glories of Lord Hari. In a moment, *mṛdaṅga* and *karatālas* were brought. Reading from a paper, an elderly Vaiṣṇava sang these words:

"O Śrī Kṛṣṇa Caitanyacandra! O Prabhu Nityānanda! O Gadādhara! O Advaitacandra! O devotees of Lord Gaura!"

"O Vaiṣṇava Ṭhākura, O shoreless ocean of mercy, please be merciful to me, a fallen sinner."

"Master, please be merciful and deliver me, a person mad with pride in my birth, learning, and wealth."

"Please purify me of the desire for gold, women, and fame. That is my prayer.

"O servant of Lord Kṛṣṇa, please be merciful and give me attraction for the holy name, mercy to the living entities, and happy association with the Vaiṣṇavas."

"The shade of your lotus feet is my only hope. Whether I live or die, you are my only shelter."

When these verses came to an end, Lāhirī Mahāśaya sang a prayer he had himself composed:

"I was in the grip of illusion. I had fallen into the ocean of birth and death. You were merciful to me. You gave me the shade of your lotus feet. You rescued me."

"Please hear me! O saintly Vaiṣṇava, please hear me! Now I surrender to your lotus feet. Please throw my sufferings far away."

"Pride of caste is hell. Material learning is ignorance. Please purify me and place me before Lord Nityānanda's lotus feet. Please extinguish the fire that burns within me."

"Please be merciful and place on my tongue the holy names of the Divine Couple. Kālidāsa prays: Please place Śrī Śrī Rādhā-Śyāmā in my heart."

Hearing this song, everyone became wild with happiness. Together, they stood up. Again and again they sang. Again and again singing the words "Please place Śrī Śrī Rādhā-Śyāmā in my heart," they danced wildly. Again and again dancing, some Vaiṣṇava become overwhelmed with spiritual love and fell unconscious.

Something unprecedented then happened, something that when he saw it made Devīdāsa think, "Father is now plunged in meditation on the Absolute. It will be difficult to take him home again."

The meeting broke up in the middle of the night. After saying their farewells, everyone returned to their own places. After bidding farewell to Lāhirī Mahāśaya, Devīdāsa and Sambhunātha returned to their host's home.

The next day, after they had finished their meal, Devī and Sambhu entered Lāhirī Mahāśaya's cottage. After offering *daṇḍavat* obeisances, Devīdāsa

Vidyāratna placed the following request before Lāhirī Mahāśaya: "This is my request: Please reside in Śāntipura. In this place, there are many troubles and inconveniences. All of us will happily serve you at home. If you order, we will arrange a solitary room for you to stay there."

Lāhirī Mahāśaya replied, "It is not a bad idea. Still, in Śāntipura, I will not be able to associate with devotees as I do here. Devī, you know that the people of Śāntipura are atheists and delight in criticizing others. It is not a happy place for anyone to live. True, there are many *brāhmaṇas* there, but their intelligence is warped by association with weavers. The three characteristics of Śāntipura's people are fine garments, pompous words, and blasphemy of Vaiṣṇavas. That is why the descendants of Advaita Prabhu suffer there. By bad association, even many of them have also turned against Lord Mahāprabhu. Therefore, please arrange that I may stay here in Godruma. That is my desire."

Devīdāsa said, "Father, what you say is true. Still, why need you have any contact with Śāntipura's people? In your own private room, you can chant Gāyatrī and perform your other religious duties. In this way, you may pass your days. A *brāhmaṇa* has eternal duties and eternal religions rituals. Great souls like yourself should always be absorbed in these duties."

Lāhirī Mahāśaya said, "Son, those days are no more. Now that I have stayed for some months with the devotees, and have heard the teachings of my spiritual master, my view of life is completely changed. What you call eternal duties I call temporary duties. Devotional service to Lord Hari is the soul's only eternal duty. Chanting Gāyatrī and other like duties are all temporary."

Devīdāsa replied, "Father, I do not see that duty in any scripture. Is chanting Gāyatrī not the worship of Lord Hari? If chanting Gāyatrī is the worship of Lord Hari, then it is an eternal religious duty. How is chanting Gāyatrī different from hearing and chanting about Lord Hari and the other activities of *vaidhī-bhakti*?"

Lāhirī Mahāśaya said, "Child, chanting Gāyatrī and other *karma-kanda* activities are very different from *vaidhī-bhakti*. Chanting Gāyatrī and other *karma-kanda* activities are performed with a desire to attain impersonal liberation. However hearing and chanting about Lord Hari and the other activities of *vaidhī-bhakti* are not performed with any material motive. When, in the scriptures, such results are seen to come from the devotional activities that begin with hearing and chanting the glories of Lord Hari, that is so only for the purpose of attracting the materialists. Devotional service to Lord Hari brings only one result—devotional service to Lord Hari. It brings no other result. The primary result attained by *vaidhī-bhakti* is that one becomes attracted to serve Lord Hari."

Devīdāsa said, "Father, then it is true that some secondary results also come from devotional service to Lord Hari."

Lāhirī Mahāśaya: For different kinds of neophyte devotees there are secondary results. Still, a true Vaiṣṇava engages in *sādhana-bhakti* so that he may some day attain the perfection of devotional service. They who are not true devotees perform *sādhana-bhakti* to attain two goals: 1. material sense gratification, and 2. impersonal liberation. Externally, one cannot see a difference in the activities of true Vaiṣṇavas and pretenders but internally, at the root, there is a difference of faith. The worship of Lord Hari performed by a person who thinks that worship is a material fruitive activity may bring purity of mind, impersonal liberation, cure of diseases, or other material results. Still, the worship of Lord Hari performed by a person who thinks that worship is spiritual devotional service brings attraction to Lord Kṛṣṇa's holy names as its only result. For the materialists, observance of the Ekādaśī vow destroys sins. For the devotees, observance of the Ekādaśī vow increases devotion to Lord Hari. You can see the difference here. The subtle difference of *sādhana-bhakti* performed by those who think it a material activity and those who think it is spiritual devotional service can be understood only by the mercy of the Supreme Personality of Godhead. The materialists are caught up in the secondary results. The devotees attain the primary result. All secondary results may be grouped into two categories: 1. material sense gratification, and 2. impersonal liberation.

Devīdāsa: Then why do the scriptures praise these secondary results?

Lāhirī Mahāśaya: Two kinds of human beings inhabit the material world: 1. the intelligent and 2. the unintelligent. The unintelligent will not perform any spiritual activity unless they see an immediate material benefit comes from it. For such persons, the scriptures praise the secondary results of devotional service. However, it is not the purpose of the scriptures that such persons shall remain always content with these secondary results. The idea is that, after a short time, and by the mercy of the Lord's devotees, such persons will become attracted to the primary result.

Devīdāsa: Are Raghunandana and the other authors of *smṛti-śāstra* then unintelligent?

Lāhirī Mahāśaya: No. They themselves seek the primary result. Still, the code of actions they prescribe is meant for the unintelligent.

Devīdāsa: In some scriptures, we see only the secondary results are described and there is no mention of this primary result. What is the reason for that?

Lāhirī Mahāśaya: The scriptures are of three kinds, according to the three classes of human beings eligible to receive them. For human beings in the mode of goodness, there are scriptures in the mode of goodness. For human beings in the mode of passion, there are scriptures in the mode of passion. For human beings in the mode of ignorance, there are scriptures in the mode of ignorance.

Devīdāsa: In which of these scriptures should one place his faith? How can a person in the lower stages become elevated?

Lāhirī Mahāśaya: Persons with different kinds of qualifications have different kinds of faith. Those who are in the mode of ignorance have faith in the scriptures of the mode of ignorance. Those who are in the mode of passion have faith in the scriptures of the mode of passion. They who are in the mode of goodness have faith in the scriptures of the mode of goodness. Thus, a person believes the conclusions of the scripture in which, according to the modes, he naturally has faith. By faithfully performing the duties for which he is qualified, and by associating with saintly devotees, one becomes elevated in this birth. Thus elevated, a person attains faith in the scriptures meant for elevated persons. The authors of the scriptures are perfectly learned and not at all bewildered. They composed the scriptures in such a way that by faithfully performing his own duties, a person may be gradually elevated. That is why the different scriptures describe many different kinds of duties. Faith in the scriptures is the source of all auspiciousness. *Bhagavad-gītā* describes all the different conclusions of the different scriptures and at the end it clearly describes the final conclusion of all scriptures.

Devīdāsa: Since boyhood, I have studied many scriptures, but today, by your mercy, I can understand the wonderful purpose of them all.

Lāhirī Mahāśaya: In *Śrīmad-Bhāgavatam* (11.8.10) it is written: "Just as a honeybee takes nectar from all flowers, big and small, an intelligent human being should take the essence from all religious scriptures." Son, I used to call you an atheist. Now I do not speak ill of anyone. Anyone who faithfully performs the prescribed duties that suit his nature should not be criticized. In fact, everyone acts according to their nature and all will be gradually elevated at the proper time. You are learned in books of logic and fruitive action. Therefore, you are not to blame if your words follow those ideas.

Devīdāsa: I know some things, but I am not learned in the Vaiṣṇava religion. I used to think that the Vaiṣṇavas are fanatics who insisted on interpreting the scriptures in their own way. But now that I heard your explanation, I know that among the Vaiṣṇavas, there are learned persons who know the true meaning of the scriptures. From what great soul have you learned all this about the scriptures?

Lāhirī Mahāśaya: Son, recently I have been instructed by a staunch Vaiṣṇava. In the next cottage my spiritual master worships the Lord. He has taught me the meanings of all the scriptures. He is the person I have described to you. If you approach his lotus feet, you may ask him about devotional service. Come, you and I will visit him.

After speaking these words, Lāhirī Mahāśaya took Devīdāsa Vidyāratna to the cottage of Śrī Vaiṣṇava dāsa. Leaving him there, Lāhirī went to his own cottage, sat down, and chanted the holy names.

Śrī Vaiṣṇava dāsa: Child, have you studied the scriptures?

Devīdāsa: I studied the *nyāya-śāstras* from *Muktipāda* to *Siddhānta-kusumāñjali*, and I also studied the *smṛti-śāstras*.

Śrī Vaiṣṇava dāsa: Did you study many scriptures diligently? What was your conclusion after diligently studying them?

Devīdāsa: The conclusion is given in the words, "With great trouble one should renounce everything and attain impersonal liberation." Therefore the conclusion of the scriptures is that one should struggle by every available means to attain impersonal liberation. Thinking in this way, while faithfully executing my prescribed duties, I have sought impersonal liberation.

Śrī Vaiṣṇava dāsa: At one time I also studied all books and, like you, I also yearned to attain impersonal liberation.

Devīdāsa: Why did you abandon the desire for impersonal liberation?

Śrī Vaiṣṇava dāsa: Child, tell me: What is the nature of impersonal liberation?

Devīdāsa: In the opinion of the *nyāya-śāstras*, Brahman and the individual soul are eternally distinct. How then is it possible to renounce everything and attain impersonal liberation? According to this system, it is clearly not possible. According to the *Vedānta* philosophy, however, liberation is defined as understanding that the individual soul and the Supreme are not really different from each other. According to this system, impersonal liberation is clearly possible.

Śrī Vaiṣṇava dāsa: Child, for fifteen years I studied Śaṅkara's interpretation of *Vedānta* and after that, I accepted *sannyāsa*. In many ways, I struggled to attain impersonal liberation. For many days I meditated on what Śaṅkara considered the four most important statements of the *Vedas*. Afterward, thinking them all foolish, I rejected what I had read.

Devīdāsa: Why did you think those books were foolish?

Śrī Vaiṣṇava dāsa: Child, a person should examine his own heart. How can others do it for him? How can others understand his heart?

Devīdāsa could see that Śrī Vaiṣṇava dāsa was honest, intelligent, and very learned. Devīdāsa had never studied *Vedānta*. In his heart, he thought, "If he is merciful to me, I can learn *Vedānta* from him." Thinking in this way, he said, "Am I qualified to study *Vedānta*?"

Śrī Vaiṣṇava dāsa: You know Sanskrit well, so you may easily study *Vedānta*.

Devīdāsa: If you feel merciful to me, then please teach it to me. I would learn it from you.

Śrī Vaiṣṇava dāsa: These are my words: I am a penniless servant of the Vaiṣṇavas. Because I attained the mercy of a saintly *parāmahāṁsa bābājī*, I stay here and always chant the holy names of Lord Hari. I have very little opportunity to teach anyone *Vedānta*. Also, I have heard that Śrīla Rūpa Gosvāmī, who is the spiritual master of the entire world, has forbidden the Vaiṣṇavas to hear or explain Śaṅkara's *Śārīraka-bhāṣya* commentary on *Vedānta*. Therefore, now I will neither study nor teach Śaṅkara's commentary. Lord Caitanya Mahāprabhu, who is the son of Śacī-devī and the spiritual master of all living entities, taught the right commentary of *Vedānta-sūtra* to Śrī Sārvabhauma Bhaṭṭācārya. His commentary is recorded in the notebooks of many Vaiṣṇavas. If you make a copy of that commentary, then perhaps I can help you. Go to Kāñcana-pallī and you may get a copy of that commentary from the home of Śrīmān Kavikarṇapūra.

Devīdāsa: I will try. You are a great scholar of *Vedānta*. You have spoken honestly with me. Why should I not study the Vaiṣṇava commentary on *Vedānta*?

Śrī Vaiṣṇava dāsa: In the past I have studied and taught Śaṅkara's commentary. There is also Śrī Rāmānujācārya's *Śrī-bhāṣya* and many other commentaries also. The Bengali Vaiṣṇavas have the commentary that Lord Caitanya Mahāprabhu gave to Śrī Gopīnatha Ācārya. I have not seen any commentary better than that. No one can dispute the Supreme Personality of Godhead's own explanations of the *Vedānta-sūtras*. Commentaries on the *Vedānta-sūtras* should include many quotations from the *Upaniṣads*. If one simply writes what he thinks, and does not support his arguments with quotations from the *Upaniṣads*, learned persons will not accept his commentary.

Happy at heart to hear these words, Devīdāsa Vidyāratna offered *daṇḍavat* obeisances to Śrī Vaiṣṇava dāsa. Then Devīdāsa entered his father's cottage and told him all that had been said. Filled with happiness, his father said, "Devī, you have studied and taught many books. Now you should research the eternal nature of the soul."

Devīdāsa: Father, I had earnestly hoped to bring you away from Śrī Godruma. That is why I came here. Please be merciful. Come back just once and fulfill everyone's desires. Especially my saintly mother yearns to see your feet just one more time.

Lāhirī Mahāśaya: I have taken shelter of the Vaiṣṇavas' lotus feet. I have made a solemn vow that I shall never return home, for even a visit would obstruct my devotional life. In the past, you have all worshipped Lord Viṣṇu. You may all visit me.

Devīdāsa: Father, what kind of answer is that? At our home, we are all servants of the Supreme Personality of Godhead. We do not dishonor the holy names of Lord Hari. I am always ready to serve a Vaiṣṇava guest! Are we not Vaiṣṇavas?

Lāhirī Mahāśaya: If you think your activities are the same as the Vaiṣṇavas' activities, then you are not a Vaiṣṇava.

Devīdāsa: Father, why am I not a Vaiṣṇava?

Lāhirī Mahāśaya: A Vaiṣṇava renounces temporary material duties and takes shelter of his eternal spiritual duty.

Devīdāsa: Still, I have a doubt. You have given a very good analysis of the scriptures. The Vaiṣṇavas' activities of hearing (*śravaṇa*), chanting (*kīrtana*), remembering (*smaraṇa*), serving the lotus feet (*pāda-sevana*), worship (*arcanā*), obeisances (*vandana*), carrying out the orders (*dāsya*), friendship (*sākhya*), and surrendering everything (*ātma-nivedana*) are activities mixed with materialism. Are they not all impelled by material motives? I think you are unreasonably attached to these things. Worshipping the Deity of the Lord, fasting, and worshiping the Lord by offering Him material things are all material activities. How can they be eternal?

Lāhirī Mahāśaya: Son, I have thought about these things for many days. Please think about this carefully. There are two classes of human beings: 1. Those who are interested in this material world, the here and now, and 2. Those who are interested in the highest goal of life. The materialists are interested only in material happiness, material fame, and material exalted status.

Human beings who are interested in the highest goal of life are divided into three classes: 1. The devotees of the Supreme Personality of Godhead, 2. Those who are attached to impersonal speculation, and 3. Those who desire mystic powers.

Those who desire mystic powers are eager to attain the results offered by the *karma-kanda* section of the *Vedas*. By performing these *karma-kanda* activities, they attain extraordinary powers. By performing *yajñas* and *yoga*, one can attain these powers. They think that the Supreme Personality of Godhead is obliged to give them the results of their *karma-kanda* activities.

The next group is those who are attached to impersonal speculation. By cultivating impersonal knowledge, such persons strive to become the Supreme. Some of them say the Supreme Personality of Godhead exists, and others say He does not exist. Some of them say the Supreme Personality of Godhead is merely an imagination and that by worshiping this imaginary God, one gradually attains impersonal knowledge. Others among them say that one must use the worship of the Supreme Personality of Godhead as a tool to attain impersonal knowledge. Then, when one attains impersonal knowledge, the tool of worship should be thrown away. According to them, when one attains the result of worshiping the Supreme Personality of Godhead, that worship becomes transformed into impersonal knowledge. In their opinion, neither the Supreme Personality of Godhead nor the worship of the Supreme Personality of Godhead is eternal.

The third class of human beings who are interested in the highest goal of life is the devotees of the Supreme Personality of Godhead. Indeed, the devotees are the true seekers of the highest goal of life. In the opinion of the devotees, there is one Supreme Personality of Godhead, who has neither beginning nor end. Employing His potencies, He manifests the individual spirit souls and the material world. The individual spirit souls are all His servants. Eternal service to the Lord is the soul's eternal duty and eternal nature. On his own power, the individual soul is not able to do anything. By performing materialistic activities (*karma*), the individual soul cannot attain any result that is eternal. However, by obeying and serving the Supreme Personality of Godhead, the individual soul can, by the Lord's mercy, attain the fulfillment of all his desires.

The previous two classes of human beings are called: 1. *karma-kāṇḍī* (those who perform material pious deeds), and 2. *jñāna-kāṇḍī* (impersonalists). The third class is called *īśā-bhakta* (devotees of the Supreme Personality of

Godhead). The *karma-kāṇḍīs* and *jñāna-kāṇḍīs* are proud to call themselves seekers after the highest spiritual goal. However, the truth is that they are materialists. They are materialists because whatever pious deeds they perform are all pushed by personal, material motives.

The present day worshippers of Śiva, Durgā, Gaṇeśa, and Sūrya are all followers of the *jñāna-kāṇḍa*. When such persons engage in the devotional activities that begin with hearing and chanting, their goal is to attain impersonal liberation and become one with the Supreme.

Those who do not have material sense gratification or impersonal liberation as their goal when they perform the devotional activities that begin with hearing and chanting are devotees of Lord Viṣṇu. They worship the Deity form of Lord Viṣṇu. The form of the Supreme Personality of Godhead is eternal, spiritual, and all-powerful. If the Supreme Personality of Godhead were not the highest object of worship, then it may be said that the worship of Him is temporary, and not eternal.

Son, the service you offer to the Deity form of the Supreme Personality of Godhead will not bring you the highest spiritual benefit. Why not? Because you do not think the Lord's form is eternal. Therefore, you are not a devotee of the Lord. Do you understand the difference between worship that is eternal and worship that is temporary and pushed by material motives?

Devīdāsa: Yes. If one does not think that the form of the Supreme Personality of Godhead is eternal, then one's worship of the Lord is not eternal worship. But why can one not employ a temporary kind of worship to seek the eternal truth?

Lāhirī Mahāśaya: You cannot say that the worship you perform is eternal worship. The worship the Vaiṣṇavas perform is eternal. The form of the Lord is eternal, their worship of that form is eternal, and all in relation to them are eternal. Therefore the Vaiṣṇava religion is eternal.

Devīdāsa: The Deity form of the Lord is a statue made by a human being. How can such a form be eternal?

Lāhirī Mahāśaya: The Deity form worshipped by the Vaiṣṇavas is not like that. First, the Supreme Personality of Godhead is not formless, like the impersonal Brahman. The form of the Supreme Personality of Godhead is all powerful, eternal, and filled with knowledge and bliss. That is the Lord's form that should be worshiped. In the beginning, the Lord's form is manifested within the individual spirit soul. Thus, the Lord's form appears in the living entity's heart. When *bhakti-yoga* (devotional service) is manifested in the heart, then the Lord's form also appears there. When a devotee sees in his heart the spiritual form of the Supreme Personality of Godhead, the devotee knows that this is the same form manifested externally as the Deity. The impersonalists do not worship the form of the Supreme Lord in this way. They think the Deity is a statue made of material elements, a statue that while it is being worshipped is imagined to be the same as the impersonal Supreme. However, the truth is that the Deity form the Lord is not at all a statue made of material elements. In this way, the impersonalists and the devotees have very different conceptions of the worship of the Deity of the Lord. By the mercy of a bona fide master, one may accept Vaiṣṇava initiation. Then, one is able to directly see that the Deity of the Lord is not a statue made of material elements.

Devīdāsa: I see that. The Vaiṣṇavas are not fanatics. They see very subtle things. The worship of the Deity form of the Lord and the worship of a material statue are very different indeed. However, I do not see any difference in the external actions of these two kinds of worship. The difference is in the spiritual faith of the worshiper. I will think about this subject for a few more days. Father, I have one big doubt. As far as I am able to understand, the impersonalists' worship of the Lord is merely a form of cheating and trickery. At a later time. I will place this question before your feet.

After speaking these words, Devīdāsa Vidyāratna went with Sambhunātha to their host's house, where they spent the remainder of the afternoon. Still, they did not find an opportunity to talk among themselves. Everyone at that house found all their happiness in singing the holy names of Lord Hari.

The next afternoon, they all went to the *parāmahāṁsa bābājī*'s terrace. There, Devīdāsa Vidyāratna, Sambhunātha, and Lāhirī Mahāśaya stayed close together. At that time, the *kazi* of *brāhmaṇa-puṣkariṇī* also came there. Seeing the *kazi*, the Vaiṣṇavas respectfully stood up. Happily greeting the Vaiṣṇavas, the Kazi entered the terrace.

The *parāmahāṁsa bābājī* said to him, "We are now fortunate, for a descendant of the Canda Kazi who received the mercy of Lord Caitanya Mahāprabhu has come to visit us. Please give your mercy to us."

The Kazi then said, "It is by the mercy of Lord Caitanya Mahāprabhu that I have received the mercy of the Vaiṣṇavas. Lord Caitanya is the master of my life. I do not do anything without first offering my *daṇḍavat* obeisances to Him."

Lāhirī Mahāśaya was fluent in the language of the Muslims. He had studied the Koran, and also many books of the Sufis. To the Kazi, he addressed this question: "What is your idea of liberation?"

The Kazi replied, "Where you use the word *jīva* (individual spirit soul), we use the word *ru*. The *ru* has two states of existence: 1. *ru-mujarradi* and 2. *ru-tarkibi*. What you call *cit* (spirit) we call *mujarra'*. What you call *acit* (matter) we call *jisam*. The spiritual world (*mujarrad*) is beyond material time. The material world (*jisam*) is subject to time's control. The *tarkibi-ru*, or *baddha-jīva* (conditioned soul), is filled with material desires. His mind is filled with material ideas. The *mujarrad-ru* (liberated soul) is pure and free from these contaminations. A person who says, '*alam misal*' (I am spirit) is able to become a *mujarradi-ru* (liberated soul). By the gradual development of *esk* (spiritual love) the *ru* (soul) becomes purified. A great saint goes to the abode of God. He does not stay in the material world. In that spiritual world, he is the servant and God is the master. The soul and God have that relationship eternally. The attainment of that pure relationship with God is called liberation. The Sufis explain the Koran in that way, but not everyone is able to understand this explanation. By the mercy of Lord Caitanya Mahāprabhu, Canda Kazi understood this and taught this to me. In that way, I know that you are all pure devotees of the Lord.

Lāhirī Mahāśaya: What is the teaching that is at the root of the Koran?

Kazi: There are many teachings in the Koran. I cannot single out a particular kind of worship to tell you. However, the purpose of life is to worship God. When they see the supremely blissful Supreme God, all people become plunged into transcendental bliss. Lord Caitanya has explained in this way.

Lāhirī Mahāśaya: How does the Koran describe the form of God?

Kazi: The Koran says that God has no form. However, Lord Caitanya told the Canda Kazi that the meaning of these words of the Koran is that God has no material form. The Koran does not mean to say that God does not have a spiritual form. The prophet himself saw the form of God, which is filled with transcendental love. He also described all the *rasas*, but only in a concealed way.

Lāhirī Mahāśaya: What do the Sufis say?

Kazi: Their philosophy is *anal hak*, which means "I am God." In this way, the philosophy of the Vedic impersonalists and the Muslim Sufis is the same.

Lāhirī Mahāśaya: Are you a Sufi?

Kazi: No. I am a pure devotee. I have surrendered my life to Lord Caitanya.

Thus talking about many things, the saintly Kazi and the Vaiṣṇavas treated each other with great respect. Finally, the meeting ended with a great chanting of the holy names of Lord Hari.

Chapter Six

Eternal religion and the differences of caste.

Devīdāsa Vidyāratna was a teacher. For many days, he had complete faith that the *brāhmaṇas* were the best of all castes. He thought, "None but the *brāhmaṇas* could understand the spiritual goal of life. Without first taking birth in a *brāhmaṇa* family, no one can attain liberation. It is by birth that one becomes a *brāhmaṇa*."

When he heard the conversation the Vaiṣṇavas had with Canda Kazi's descendant, he became very disgusted. He could not enter into an understanding of the truths explained by the saintly Kazi. In his mind, he thought, "The Yavana caste certainly acts strangely. No one can understand the meaning of what they say. Ah well, father could read Persian and Arabic. He has spent many days studying religion. But, why does he respect the Yavanas so? In that assembly, why did Vaiṣṇava dāsa and the *parāmahāṁsa bābājī* show so much respect to a Yavana, whose contaminating touch makes one take a bath?"

That night he said, "Śambhu, with the fire of logic, I will burn the philosophy of the offenders into ashes. It was in Navadvīpa that Sārvabhauma and Śiromaṇi discussed the *nyāya-śāstra*. It was in Navadvīpa that Raghunātha churned the twenty eight truths from the *smṛti-śāstras*. How can Hindus and Yavanas mingle together in this same Navadvīpa? Perhaps the teachers of Navadvīpa do not understand how they should act. In one or two days, this Vidyāratna will do something to set this situation right."

Nine hours had passed. Covered by the malice of clouds, the sun had not yet been able to glance upon the earth. At dawn, it rained with thudding sounds of "dipdip." During the twelfth half-hour, Devī and Śambhu ate *kicharī*. The Vaiṣṇavas were delayed in their *mādhukarī* begging for alms. By the time the third three-hour watch had passed, all the Vaiṣṇavas had honored *prasādam*. Now, they stayed in one part of the *mālatī* and *mādhavī* vine terrace and chanted the holy names on their beads. The *parāmahāṁsa bābājī*, Vaiṣṇava dāsa, Paṇḍita Ananta dāsa, who had just come from Nṛsiṁha-palli, Lāhirī Mahāśaya, and Yādava dāsa from Kuliyā were happily chanting the holy names on their *tulasī* beads. At that time, Vidyāratna Mahāśaya, Caturbhuja Pādaratna from Samudrāgara, Cintāmaṇi Nyāyaratna from Vārāṇasī, Kālidāsa Vasaspati from Pūrvasthalī, and the famous Paṇḍita Kṛṣṇa Cuḍāmaṇi all came there. The Vaiṣṇavas very respectfully offered sitting places to their *brāhmaṇa paṇḍita* guests.

The *parāmahāṁsa bābājī* said, "It is said that a day overcast with clouds is a bad day indeed. However, for us it has become a good day, for many learned *paṇḍitas* who live in holy places have mercifully placed the dust of their feet in my cottage."

Because they were naturally humbler than a blade of grass, the Vaiṣṇavas, saying, "We offer our respectful obeisances to the *brāhmaṇas*," bowed down to offer their respects. Thinking themselves to be very learned and important, the *brāhmaṇas* responded by offering blessings. Vidyāratna had invited them there for a great debate. Because they were all younger than him, the *brāhmaṇas* bowed down before Lāhirī Mahāśaya. Because he now understood the real truth, Lāhirī Mahāśaya at once reciprocated by bowing down before the *brāhmaṇas*.

Among these *paṇḍitas*, Kṛṣṇa-Cuḍāmaṇi was the most eloquent. In Vārāṇasī, Mithilā, and many other places, he had defeated many *paṇḍitas* with the great power of his logic. He was short, splendidly dark, and grave. His eyes glistened like two stars. It was he who began the discussion with the Vaiṣṇavas.

He said, "Saying amongst ourselves, 'Today we shall see the Vaiṣṇavas,' we have now come here. We do not think everything you do is very good, but still we think your single-pointed devotional service is very good indeed. The Supreme Personality of Godhead Himself has said (*Bhagavad-gītā* 9.30): Even if one commits the most abominable actions, if he is engaged in devotional service, he is to be considered saintly because he is properly situated."

"We offer our respectful obeisances to these words of *Bhagavad-gītā*. Therefore, I have come here to see many saintly persons. However, we have another purpose also. It is this: On the pretext of devotional service, you associate with Yavanas. I want to talk with you about that. One of you expert in debate should now please step forward."

Hearing Cuḍāmaṇi's words, the Vaiṣṇavas became unhappy. The saintly *parāmahāṁsa bābājī* said, "I am a fool. What do I know of debates? As great saints have acted in a saintly way, so we also try to act. You please repeat the teachings of the scriptures and we will listen in silence."

Cuḍāmaṇi said, "What kind of talk is this? If the Hindus do not understand the scriptures, then the whole world will perish. You will act in a way that violates the scriptures and then you will claim you are following the great saints. What is this? Of what saints do you speak? If they are persons who follow the scriptures and teach the message of the scriptures, then they are saints indeed. But if the people follow anyone and everyone, calling them all great saints, and if they defend their actions by quoting the words *mahājano yena gataḥ sa panthā* (one should accept whatever progressive path the *mahājanas* advocate), then how can there be any auspiciousness in this world?"

Hearing Cuḍāmaṇi's words, the Vaiṣṇavas assembled in one of the cottages to decide what should be done. They came to this conclusion: When great saints are criticized, the Vaiṣṇavas should, if they are able, defend them in debate. The *parāmahāṁsa bābājī* did not participate in this discussion. Although the Paṇḍita Ananta dāsa Bābājī had seen the farther shore of the *nyāya-śāstra*, everyone decided that Vaiṣṇava dāsa should argue in the debate. Everyone could understand that Devīdāsa Vidyāratna was the real cause of all this trouble.

Staying among them, Lāhirī Mahāśaya openly said, "Devī is very proud. His mind became agitated when he saw us associating with the saintly Kazi. That is why he has brought all these *paṇḍitas*."

Taking the dust of the *parāmahāṁsa bābājī*'s lotus feet, Vaiṣṇava dāsa said, "I carry the Vaiṣṇavas' command upon my head. Today all my scholarship will be successful."

By then all the clouds had gone. A sitting place was arranged in the grove of *mālatī* and *mādhavī* vines. On one side were the *brāhmaṇa paṇḍitas* and on the other were all the Vaiṣṇavas. All the Vaiṣṇava *paṇḍitas* from Śrī Godruma and Madhyadvīpa came. Many *brāhmaṇas* and students from nearby also joined the meeting. It was not a small meeting. On one side were a hundred *brāhmaṇa paṇḍitas* and on the other were two hundred Vaiṣṇavas. Ordered by the Vaiṣṇavas, Vaiṣṇava dāsa Bābājī peacefully sat in front. Then, something wonderful happened. When they saw it, the Vaiṣṇavas happily shouted out the holy name of Lord Hari. The wonderful event was this: a cluster of *mālatī* flowers spontaneously fell on Vaiṣṇava dāsa's head. The Vaiṣṇavas said, "This is a sign of Lord Caitanya Mahāprabhu's mercy."

On the other side Kṛṣṇa-Cuḍāmaṇi turned up his nose and said, "You may think that, but flowers will not do. The tree is known by its fruit."

Without showing any pride, Vaiṣṇava dāsa declared, "Today's meeting in Navadvīpa is just like a meeting in Vārāṇasī. This is a source of great joy. Although I live in Bengal, I stayed for a long time in Vārāṇasī. There, I studied and I also spoke in many meetings. Therefore, I am not accustomed to speak in Bengali. I wish that for today's meeting, the questions and answers shall be in Sanskrit."

Although Cuḍāmaṇi had labored greatly in his scripture study, aside from memorizing some verses, he could not speak Sanskrit. Taken aback by Vaiṣṇava dāsa's proposal, he said, "Why? For a meeting in Bengal, it is best to speak the Bengali language. I am not like the *paṇḍitas* in the western provinces. I cannot speak Sanskrit."

Hearing this, everyone could understand the Cuḍāmaṇi was becoming afraid to debate with Vaiṣṇava dāsa. Speaking together with one voice, everyone requested Vaiṣṇava dāsa Bābājī to speak in Bengali, and he agreed.

To start the debate, Cuḍāmaṇi asked, "Is caste eternal? Are the Yavanas and the Hindus different castes? Does a Hindu fall down by associating with Yavanas?"

Vaiṣṇava dāsa answered, "In the *nyāya-śāstra* it is said that caste is eternal. However, the true difference is not seen among human beings born in different countries in different situations. The real differences are birth as a cow, or a goat, or a human being. These are real differences."

Then Cuḍāmaṇi said, "Yes. What you say is true. Still, are the Hindus and the Yavanas in different castes?"

Vaiṣṇava dāsa replied, "Yes. In one sense, there is a difference of caste, but that caste distinction is not eternal. The human race is one. Differences of language, country, garments, caste, and the like are only imaginary differences."

Cuḍāmaṇi: Are human beings different according to the differences of their birth? If this is not so then is the difference between a Hindu and a Yavana only the difference of their clothing and other external things?

Vaiṣṇava dāsa: According to his past *karma*, the soul accepts a higher or lower birth. The differences of caste are considered according to how human beings are qualified to perform different kinds of work. The four castes are *brāhmaṇa, kṣatriya, vaiśya* and *śūdra.* All others are outcastes.

Cuḍāmaṇi: Are the Yavanas not outcastes?

Vaiṣṇava dāsa: Yes. In the conclusion of the scriptures, they are outcastes. They are outside the four castes.

Cuḍāmaṇi: If this is so, then how can a Yavana become a Vaiṣṇava, and how can a pious Vaiṣṇava associate with a Yavana?

Vaiṣṇava dāsa: One who engages in pure devotional service is a Vaiṣṇava. Simply by being human one is qualified to be a Vaiṣṇava. Because they have taken a low birth, the Yavanas may not be qualified to perform the duties of the different castes. Nevertheless, they are perfectly qualified to engage in all the activities of devotional service. One who does not understand the subtle differences of the *karma-kanda, jñāna-kanda,* and *bhakti-kanda* parts of the *Vedas* cannot be said to be truly learned in the scriptures.

Cuḍāmaṇi: Good. By acting rightly one becomes pure in heart. When the heart is purified, one is qualified to understand transcendental knowledge. Among those who have attained transcendental knowledge, some are impersonalists and some are Vaiṣṇavas, who believe in spiritual variety. In the beginning of spiritual life, one must perform pious deeds (*karma*). If one's pious deeds have attained their completion, one can become a Vaiṣṇava. However, the Muslims are not qualified to perform pious deeds. Therefore, how can they ever become qualified to engage in devotional service?

Vaiṣṇava dāsa: Even outcastes can become qualified to engage in devotional service. This is accepted by all the scriptures. In the *Bhagavad-gītā* (9.32) it is written: O son of Pṛthā, those who take shelter in Me, though they be of lower birth—women, *vaiśyas* (merchants), as well as *śūdras* (workers) approach the supreme destination. Here, the word *asraya* means, " to engage in devotional service." Also, in the *Kāśī-khaṇḍa* it is said: Whether a *brāhmaṇa, kṣatriya, vaiśya, śūdra,* or outcaste, a person is most exalted if he engages in devotional service to Lord Viṣṇu. In the *Nārada Purāṇa* it is also said: O king, a dog-eater who is devoted to Lord Viṣṇu is better than a *brāhmaṇa.* A *sannyāsī* who is not devoted to Lord Viṣṇu is also inferior to such a dog-eater devotee.

Cuḍāmaṇi: There are many scriptural quotes like that. How should these quotes be understood? That we must see. How can the defect that is attained by birth be removed by any means other than another birth?

Vaiṣṇava dāsa: The defect of a low birth comes from *prarabdha-karma* (past *karma* that has begun to bear fruit). When one chants the holy names of the Supreme Personality of Godhead, those karmic reactions are thrown far away. In *Śrīmad-Bhāgavatam* (6.16.44) it is said: Merely by hearing the holy name of Your Lordship only once, even *caṇḍālas*, men of the lowest class, are freed from all material contamination.

It is also said (*Śrīmad-Bhāgavatam* 6.2.46): Therefore, one who desires freedom from material bondage should adopt the process of chanting and glorifying the name, fame, form, and pastimes of the Supreme Personality of Godhead, at whose lotus feet all the holy places stand. One cannot derive the proper benefit from other methods, such as pious atonement, speculative knowledge, and meditation in mystic *yoga*, because even after following such methods, one takes to fruitive activities again, unable to control his mind, which is contaminated by the base qualities of nature, namely passion and ignorance.

It is also said (*Śrīmad-Bhāgavatam* 3.33.7): Oh, how glorious are those whose tongues are chanting Your holy name! Even if born in the families of dog-eaters, such persons are worshipable. Persons who chant the holy name of Your Lordship must have executed all kinds of austerities and fire sacrifices and achieved all the good manners of the Āryans. To be chanting the holy name of Your Lordship, they must have bathed at holy places of pilgrimage, studied the *Vedas*, and fulfilled everything required.

Cuḍāmaṇi: Why is it, then, that an outcaste who chants the holy name of Lord Hari is not qualified to perform *yajñas* and other rituals?

Vaiṣṇava dāsa: To perform *yajñas* and other rituals, one needs to take birth in a *brāhmaṇa*'s home. A person who takes birth in a *brāhmaṇa*'s home is qualified to perform Vedic rituals after he has received the sacred thread, so an outcaste who has become purified by chanting Lord Hari's holy name but who has not taken birth in a *brāhmaṇa*'s home cannot perform *yajñas* and other rituals. However, the various activities of devotional service are immeasurably better than the performance of Vedic *yajñas*.

Cuḍāmaṇi: What kind of conclusion is that? That a person not qualified for an ordinary thing can be qualified for an exalted thing! What is the clear proof for that?

Vaiṣṇava dāsa: Human activities are of two kinds: 1. material and 2. spiritual. Even after becoming qualified, one may not necessarily be able to perform certain material activities. For example, a person born in a Yavana family may become purified and, spiritual speaking, may become a genuine *brāhmaṇa*. Still, according to the material conception, he is still not qualified to marry a *brāhmaṇa*'s daughter.

Cuḍāmaṇi: Why not? What is wrong with that?

Vaiṣṇava dāsa: It is wrong to violate social custom. Those who are proud of their material activities do not break social custom, and those who are qualified to make spiritual advancement do not break social custom either.

Cuḍāmaṇi: How does one become qualified to perform material activities? How does one become qualified to perform devotional service?

Vaiṣṇava dāsa: One's nature, birth, and other things qualify one to engage in material activities. Faith in the truth qualifies one to perform devotional service.

Cuḍāmaṇi: Without overwhelming me with *Vedānta* vocabulary, please clearly tell me: What are the natures needed to perform the different kinds of duties?

Vaiṣṇava dāsa: Some qualities in a *brāhmaṇa*'s nature are: 1. peacefulness, 2. self-control, 3. austerity, 4. purity, 5. satisfaction, 6. tolerance, 7. honesty, 8. devotion to the Supreme Personality of Godhead, 9. mercy, and 10. truthfulness. Some of the qualities in a *kṣatriya*'s nature are: 1. power, 2. strength, 3. determination, 4. heroism, 5. tolerance, 6. generosity, 7. perseverance, 8. gravity, 9. service to the *brāhmaṇas*, and 10. leadership. Some of the qualities in a *vaiśya*'s nature are: 1. religiousness, 2. charity, 3. faith, 4. humbleness, and 5. eagerness to become wealthy. Some of the qualities in a *śūdra*'s nature are: 1. service to the *brāhmaṇas*, cows and demigods, and 2. being satisfied with whatever is one's situation in life. Some of the qualities in an outcaste's nature are: 1. impurity, 2. untruthfulness, 3. theft, 4. atheism, 5. senseless quarreling, 6. lust, 7. anger, and 8. desire for material sense gratification. The scriptures teach that the different castes are determined by seeing the qualities. To determine the castes by birth alone is the materialistic practice of modern times.

A person's natural inclinations and natural ability to learn different skills are to some extent determined by birth. Thus, one's nature makes him qualified to perform specific duties. The nature of many people is determined by their birth. From childhood, they manifest certain specific tendencies. In this way, it is seen that one's nature is determined by his birth. However, birth is not the only factor determining one's nature and one's fitness to perform certain kinds of work. There are many other factors also. For this reason the scriptures affirm that in determining a person's fitness for a certain kind of work, one should examine his nature and qualities.

Cuḍāmaṇi: What did you mean when you said the words, "faith in the truth?"

Vaiṣṇava dāsa: When a person has in his heart sincere faith and trust in the Supreme Personality of Godhead—that is called faith. When a person is materialistic, has an impure heart, in his heart has a false conception of the Supreme Personality of Godhead, and is selfish, proud, and eager for fame—his faith is called "insincere." Some saintly persons say that "sincere faith" means "faith that follows the scriptures' teachings." This kind of sincere faith makes one qualified to engage in devotional service.

Cuḍāmaṇi: Various persons may possess this "faith that follows the scriptures' teachings," but they are not necessarily all exalted great souls. Are such persons qualified to engage in devotional service?

Vaiṣṇava dāsa: A person's nature makes him qualified to perform specific duties, but it does not necessarily qualify him to engage in devotional service. Please look at the explanation written in this page of *Śrīmad-Bhāgavatam* (11.20.27-30 and 32-33): Having awakened faith in the narrations of My glories, being disgusted with all material activities, knowing that all sense gratification leads to misery, but still being unable to renounce all sense enjoyment, My devotee should remain happy and worship Me with great faith and conviction. Even though he is sometimes engaged in sense enjoyment, My devotee knows that all sense gratification leads to a miserable result, and he sincerely repents such activities. When an intelligent person engages constantly in worshiping Me through loving devotional service, as described by Me, his heart becomes firmly situated in Me. Thus, all material desires within the heart are destroyed.

The knot in the heart is pierced, all misgivings are cut to pieces, and the chain of fruitive actions is terminated when I am seen as the Supreme Personality of Godhead. Everything that can be achieved by fruitive activities, penance, knowledge, detachment, mystic *yoga*, charity, religious duties, and all other means of perfecting life is easily achieved by My devotee through loving service unto Me. If, somehow or other, My devotee desires promotion to heaven, liberation, or residence in My abode, he easily achieves such benedictions.

In this way, faith in devotional service develops.

Cuḍāmaṇi: What if I have no respect for *Śrīmad-Bhāgavatam*?

Vaiṣṇava dāsa: *Śrīmad-Bhāgavatam* teaches the conclusion of all the scriptures. The scriptures are one. If you do not respect *Śrīmad-Bhāgavatam*, then you insult all the other scriptures. I do not need to show evidence from many scriptures. Does everyone accept *Bhagavad-gītā*? Think about that. When you first spoke, from your mouth came a verse from *Bhagavad-gītā*, a verse that contains the teachings of all the scriptures.

In the *Gītā* (9.30-32) it is said: Even if one commits the most abominable actions, if he is engaged in devotional service, he is to be considered saintly because he is properly situated. He quickly becomes righteous and attains lasting peace. O son of Kuntī, declare it boldly that My devotee never perishes. O son of Pṛthā, those who take shelter in Me, though they be of lower birth—women, *vaiśyas* (merchants), as well as *śūdras* (workers), approach the supreme destination.

These verses mean that a person who has faith in the Lord alone (*ananya-bhāk*), and who engages in the activities of devotional service, which begin with hearing and chanting Lord Hari's holy names, and the descriptions of Lord Hari, renounces all impious deeds, which are naturally sources of misery. He renounces materialistic activities and he is considered saintly. In this way, he follows the glorious spiritual path. One path is the path of *karma-kanda*, which begins with the duties of *varṇāśrama*. A second path is the path of *jñāna-kanda*, which begins with speculative knowledge and renunciation. The third path is to stay among the devotees and have faith in the holy name of Lord Hari and the descriptions of Lord Hari. Sometimes these three paths are considered *yogas*. In this way, they are called *karma-yoga*, *jñāna-yoga* and *bhakti-yoga*. Some people practice these different *yogas*. Thus, they are called *karma-yogī* or *jñāna-yogī*. Among all these *yogīs*, the *bhakti-yogī* is the best, for in *bhakti-yoga* one attains limitless auspiciousness. At the end of the first six-chapter section of *Bhagavad-gītā* (6.47), one may see the following conclusion: And of all *yogīs*, he who abides in Me with great faith, worshipping Me in transcendental loving service, is most intimately united with Me in *yoga* and is the highest of all.

One must properly understand the meaning of *Bhagavad-gītā* (9.31). This verse means that a person who faithfully engages in devotional service quickly casts far away all faults in his character and activities. A person who engages in devotional service to the Supreme Personality of Godhead becomes pious, for the Supreme Personality of Godhead is Himself the root of all piety. The Supreme Personality of Godhead Himself is conquered by devotional service. When the Supreme Personality of Godhead stays in a person's heart, the bondage of *māyā* is at once thrown far away. Such a person need not adopt any other process to become free from *māyā*. Whether he performs material pious deeds or not, a devotee's heart is naturally filled with piety and saintliness. Lust is then thrown far away, and in its stead, peacefulness enters his heart. The Supreme Lord Himself promises: My devotee will never perish. The *karmī* or *jñānī* may fall into bad company, but My sincere devotee will never fall into bad company, for he always has Me as his companion. Therefore he will never fall down. Whether born in a sinful family or a *brāhmaṇa* family, a devotee always has the supreme goal of life in the palm of his hand.

Cuḍāmaṇi: Look, my scriptures say the qualification that comes from birth is the best. I was born in a *brāhmaṇa*'s home. By chanting the Gāyatrī *mantra* and performing other like duties, I will gradually attain transcendental knowledge and at the end, I must attain liberation. How does faith arise? I do not know. I see that the *Gītā* and *Bhāgavatam* teach that faith leads to devotional service. Please explain what the soul must do to attain that faith.

Vaiṣṇava dāsa: Faith is part of the soul's eternal nature. The duties of *varṇāśrama* and other like duties arise when the soul's temporary nature is manifested. That is the conclusion of all the scriptures. In the *Chāndogya Upaniṣad* (7.19.1) it is said: A person who has faith can understand. A person who has no faith cannot understand. A person who has faith can understand.

Therefore one should ask about faith. "O master, I wish to know about faith."

Some philosophers define the word "faith" as "trust in the words of the *Vedas* and the spiritual master." That is not a wrong definition. However, it is not very clear. In my *sampradāya*, "faith" is defined in these words (*Āmnāya-sūtra*57): Faith is a specific activity performed in the heart. It makes one desire to engage in devotional service. It is different from the other means of spiritual advancement.

By associating with devotees and repeatedly hearing from them, a person becomes convinced in his heart that ordinary pious deeds (*karma*), impersonal speculation (*jñāna*), and the gymnastics of *yoga* will not help him reach the eternal destination, and that destination cannot be attained by any means other than sincerely taking shelter of Lord Hari's lotus feet. When one thinks in this way, he naturally attains faith in the words of the Vedas and the spiritual master. The nature of this faith is described in these words (*Āmnāya-sūtra*58): Faith is characterized by taking shelter of the Lord and surrendering unto Him.

Thus it is seen that taking shelter of the Lord and surrendering unto Him is the external symptom of faith. This surrender and taking shelter are described in these words (*Śrī Hari-bhakti-vilāsa* 11.417): The six divisions of surrender are the acceptance of those things favorable to devotional service, the rejection of unfavorable things, the conviction that Kṛṣṇa will give protection, the acceptance of the Lord as one's guardian or master, full self-surrender, and humility.

Thus, one makes the following vow: "I will do whatever is favorable for pure devotional service, and I will reject whatever is not favorable for it. The Supreme Personality of Godhead is my protector. By being active in impersonal speculation (*jñāna*), *yoga*, and other such activities, I cannot attain anything of value. I cannot protect myself. I will serve the Lord as far as I am able, and He will protect me. In this way, I will be protected. Who am I? I am His property. Whatever He wishes, that I will do. In this way, I will offer myself to Him. I own nothing. I am poor and lowly."

In this way, one understands his lowly position. When this vow, along with trust, confidence that the Lord will give protection, complete self-surrender, and humility are manifested in the heart, that is called "faith." When this faith is manifested in the heart, one is qualified to engage in devotional service. This faith is the first step to becoming pure and eternally liberated. This faith is part of the soul's eternal nature. All spiritual paths that differ from this faith are temporary in their nature.

Cuḍāmaṇi: I understand that much. But how is this faith attained? You have not told me that. If faith is created by pious deeds, then my argument is stronger, for one who does not perform the pious duties and rituals of *varṇāśrama* cannot attain faith. The Yavanas do not perform these pious *varṇāśrama* duties, so how can they become qualified to engage in devotional service?

Vaiṣṇava dāsa: It is true that faith is created by pious deeds, for the *Nārada Purāṇa* declares: Devotional service is attained by associating with devotees. The association of devotees is attained by past pious deeds.

Pious deeds are of two kinds: 1. eternal, and 2. temporary. The pious deeds that bring association with devotees and devotional service are called eternal pious deeds. The pious deeds that bring material sense gratification and impersonal liberation are called temporary pious deeds. The pious deeds that bring eternal results are called eternal pious deeds. The pious deeds that bring temporary results are called temporary pious deeds. All kinds of material sense gratification are clearly temporary in their nature. They are not eternal. Many think that impersonal liberation is eternal, but such persons do not understand the real nature of impersonal liberation. The individual soul is pure, eternal, and unchanging. The individual soul imprisoned in the material world of illusions is in his temporary nature. When his prison shackles are cut and he is released, that moment is called "liberation." The act of becoming liberated from the prison occurs in a single moment. Therefore, the act of becoming liberated is not in itself eternal. There is the moment of liberation, and that moment comes to an end. When the soul's temporary nature is destroyed, the result is liberation. When liberation does not occur, then the temporary state is manifested. Attraction to Lord Hari's lotus feet never comes to an end. That attraction is part of the soul's eternal nature. No impartial person will claim that these aspects of the soul's nature are temporary in nature. So-called devotional service that ends when liberation is attained is temporary in nature. That so-called devotion is actually a specific kind of material activity. However, the devotional service that exists before, during, and after liberation is eternal. It is the eternal nature and duty of the soul. Liberation is merely a less important by-product of that devotional service.

In the *Muṇḍaka Upaniṣad* (1.2.12) it is said: Seeing the true nature of the higher worlds attained by pious *karma*, a *brāhmaṇa* does not desire them. To learn transcendental subject matter, one must approach the spiritual master. In doing so, he should carry fuel to burn in sacrifice. The symptom of such a spiritual master is that he is expert in understanding the Vedic conclusion and therefore, he constantly engages in the service of the Supreme Personality of Godhead.

Pious fruitive work (*karma*), impersonal speculation (*jñāna*) and *yoga* are all temporary pious deeds. Association with devotees and the performance of activities that lead to devotional service are eternal pious deeds. A person who for many previous births has performed such eternal pious deeds attains faith. A person who performs temporary pious deeds may attain many different results, but faith in pure devotional service is not one of them.

Cuḍāmaṇi: Please clearly describe association with devotees and the performance of activities that lead to devotional service. What kind of pious deeds are these?

Vaiṣṇava dāsa: Conversing with a pure devotee, serving him, and hearing his explanations—all these I call association with devotees. Chanting the holy names in towns and cities in the company of other devotees, and other like activities, are all activities of devotional service. Giving charity and performing *yoga*, when connected to devotional service, are activities that lead to devotional service. In the scriptures it is said that cleaning the temple of Lord Hari, offering a lamp to Tulasī-devī, fasting on Ekādaśī, and other such activities, are activities of devotional service. Even if they are performed without pure faith, or even if they are performed accidentally, these pious activities still increase one's devotion for the Lord. When these pious deeds gradually become powerful, after many births, they lead to pure faith in the association of devotees and the performance of pure devotional service. The word *vastu-śakti* means that everything has a certain innate power. The activities of devotional service have the power to increase one's love and devotion for the Lord. Even if they are performed without faith, or even if they are performed with contempt, they still bring good results, and so what to speak of when they are performed with faith.

In the *Prabhāsa-khaṇḍa* it is said: Kṛṣṇa's name is the sweetest of sweet things, the most auspicious of auspicious things, the transcendental fruit of the vine of all Vedic literature. O best of the Bhṛgus, chanted even once, either with faith or contempt, it delivers the chanter.

Thus, these pious deeds that increase one's devotion for the Lord are all eternal pious deeds. As these pious deeds gradually become powerful, they lead to faith in the association of devotees and the performance of pure devotional service. Because of his past temporary misdeeds, a person may take birth in a Yavana's home, and because of past eternal pious deeds, he may also attain faith in pure devotional service. What is surprising about that?

Cuḍāmaṇi: I say that if a person has performed even a small number of the pious deeds that lead to devotional service, then his other deeds must all be pious deeds also. One who is born as a Yavana cannot possibly have performed only pious deeds and therefore, it is not possible that in the past he performed the pious deeds that lead to devotional service.

Vaiṣṇava dāsa: One should not have such a belief. Eternal pious deeds and temporary pious deeds are independent of each other. One does not need the other to exist. It is said that a hunter who was filled with many sins and misdeeds by accident fasted and kept an all-night vigil on a day sacred to Lord Śiva, and because of performing this eternal pious deed, he attained devotion to Lord Hari. It is said in (*Śrīmad-Bhāgavatam* 11.13.16): *Vaiṣṇavānāṁ yathā śambhuḥ*. (Lord Śiva is the foremost Vaiṣṇava). Because of these words, I accept that Lord Śiva is supremely worshipable, and a great Vaiṣṇava. Therefore, by observing his holy day, one can certainly attain devotion to Lord Hari.

Cuḍāmaṇi: Then you say it is possible to perform eternal pious deeds accidentally?

Vaiṣṇava dāsa: All is an accident. Even the path of *karma* is like that. It was by accident that the individual soul first fell into the cycle of *karma*. What was that chance accident? The followers of *karma-mīmāṁsā* claim that *karma* has no beginning but the truth is that there is a root from which *karma* has grown. The individual soul's aversion to the Supreme Personality of Godhead is the accident that is the root of *karma*. As that is believed to be an accident, so eternal pious deeds may also be believed to be chance accidents.

In the *Śvetāśvatara Upaniṣad* (4.6-7) it is said: Although the two birds are on the same tree, the eating bird is fully engrossed with anxiety and moroseness as the enjoyer of the fruits of the tree. But, if in some way or other he turns his face to his friend, who is the Lord, and knows His glories, at once the suffering bird becomes free of all anxieties.

In *Śrīmad-Bhāgavatam* (10.51.53 and 3.25.22) it is said: O my Lord! O infallible Supreme Person! When a person wandering throughout the universes becomes eligible for liberation from material existence, he gets an opportunity to associate with devotees. When he associates with devotees, his attraction for You is awakened. You are the Supreme Personality of Godhead, the highest goal of the supreme devotees and the Lord of the universe. The spiritually powerful message of Godhead can be properly discussed only in the society of devotees, and it is greatly pleasing to hear in that association. If one hears from devotees, the way of transcendental experience quickly opens and gradually, one attains firm faith that in due course develops into attraction and devotion.

Cuḍāmaṇi: In your opinion, is there no difference between a Hindu and a Yavana?

Vaiṣṇava dāsa: There are two kinds of difference: 1. spiritual and 2. material. Spiritually, Hindus and Yavanas are not different. However, materially there is a difference.

Cuḍāmaṇi: Why do you speak with the pompous words of the *Vedānta*? What is the material difference between the Hindus and Yavanas?

Vaiṣṇava dāsa: I speak of material social customs. According to the material idea, a Yavana is untouchable. Thus, in the materialists' idea, one should neither touch nor associate with a Yavana. Thus, a Hindu touched by a Yavana must at once bathe with water. Also, a Hindu should not accept food or other things from a Yavana. Because it is attained by committing sinful deeds, a Yavana's body is horrible and should be avoided. Therefore it is untouchable.

Cuḍāmaṇi: If this is so, then how can the Hindus and Yavanas be the same spiritually? Please clearly explain.

Vaiṣṇava dāsa: The scriptures declare: O best of the Bhṛgus, the holy name of Lord Kṛṣṇa delivers the chanter.

These words mean that the Yavanas and everyone else can attain the supreme spiritual goal of life by chanting the holy name of Lord Kṛṣṇa. In this way, the Hindus and Yavanas may become equals. A human being who does not perform eternal pious deeds, like chanting Lord Kṛṣṇa's name, is declared by the scriptures to be *dvi-pāda-paśu* (an animal pretending to be a human being). This is because such a person has no faith in the holy name of Lord Kṛṣṇa. Although such a person may have taken birth as a human being, he is not really human. In truth, he is an animal.

The *Mahābhārata* explains: O king, a person whose past pious deeds are small cannot have faith in Lord Govinda, the remnants of food offered to Him, His holy name, or His devotees.

Eternal pious deeds, which purify the soul, are called "great pious deeds." Temporary pious deeds, which are performed without spiritual faith, are called "small pious deeds." The remnants of food offered to Lord Kṛṣṇa, Lord Kṛṣṇa, Lord Kṛṣṇa's holy name, and the pure Vaiṣṇavas—these four are spiritual. They reveal the spiritual truth.

Cuḍāmaṇi (with a smile): What kind of talk is this? This is just the Vaiṣṇavas' fanatic dogma. How can rice, dal, and curry be spiritual? There is nothing that you will not claim.

Vaiṣṇava dāsa: Do what you like, but please do not criticize the Vaiṣṇavas. That is my request. In a debate, only the various arguments should be considered. Why do you need to verbally attack the Vaiṣṇavas? The remnants of foods offered to the Lord are beyond the touch of the material world. One should not eat food that is not thus offered to the Lord, for eating the remnants of food offered to the Lord illumines the way to the spiritual world and drives away all that is foolish and material.

Therefore *Śrī Īśopaniṣad* (*Mantra* 1) explains: Everything animate or inanimate that is within the universe is controlled and owned by the Lord. One should therefore accept only those things necessary for himself, which are set aside as his quota, and one should not accept other things, knowing well to whom they belong.

Whatever exists in the material universe has a relationship with the potency of the Supreme Personality of Godhead. A person who sees that everything has a relationship with the Lord's potency will not attempt to enjoy the things of this external material world. If a spiritually conscious soul accepts only what he must to maintain his material body in this world, and if he understands that everything is the Supreme Personality of Godhead's mercy, then he will not fall down. That is the way a person eager to attain the spiritual world will act. Therefore, the remnants of food offered to Lord Kṛṣṇa are called *mahā-prasāda* (great mercy). Still, you are not attracted to these spiritual things—that is your misfortune.

Cuḍāmaṇi: Let's change the subject. Let's consider ordinary material things: How should one behave with Yavanas?

Vaiṣṇava dāsa: As long as a person is a Yavana, we should ignore him. However, if by performing eternal pious deeds, the Yavana becomes a Vaiṣṇava, then I will not use the word "Yavana" to refer to him.

The scriptures declare (*Padma Purāṇa* and *Itihāsa-samuccaya*): He goes to hell who thinks in terms of his birth and caste, and who thus sees a Vaiṣṇava as a *śūdra*, a barbarian, or an outcaste.

The Supreme Personality of Godhead said: A scholar learned in the four *Vedas* is not truly dear to Me. An outcaste who has become My devotee is truly dear to Me. To him, gifts should be given. From him, blessings should be accepted. He should be worshiped as much as I."

Cuḍāmaṇi: I understand. If this is so, then why cannot a Vaiṣṇava householder marry his daughter to a Yavana Vaiṣṇava, or why cannot he himself marry the daughter of a Yavana Vaiṣṇava?

Vaiṣṇava dāsa: In ordinary material understanding, when a person is born in a Yavana family, he remains a Yavana until his death. However, in the spiritual understanding, when he engages in devotional service, he is a Yavana no longer. Ten kinds of ordinary social rites are described in the *Smṛti-śāstra*. Marriage is one of them. If a householder Vaiṣṇava is a Hindu, then he has a status within the four castes and it is proper that he should marry within his own caste, for in ordinary material dealings, it is best to accept the temporary duties assigned to the four castes. One does not become a Vaiṣṇava merely by rejecting the duties of the four castes. A true Vaiṣṇava is one who does whatever is favorable for devotional service. If a person becomes spiritually advanced, and thus qualified to ignore or renounce the duties of the four castes, then he may do so. Then he may renounce all duties of the four castes. If the duties of the four castes are not favorable for one's devotional service, then they may be easily rejected. If association with the Yavanas is not favorable for devotional service, then a faithful Yavana Vaiṣṇava should reject their association. What is the difference between a Hindu Vaiṣṇava who properly rejects the duties of the four castes, and a Yavana Vaiṣṇava who rejects association with Yavanas? Both have rejected what is material and inferior. Spiritually, they are brothers. However, this may not be true for a householder Vaiṣṇava. Even though his associates and duties may not always be favorable for his advancement in devotional service, he should not renounce them prematurely. He may renounce them only when he is properly qualified. However, when his attachment to devotional service becomes very strong, he will naturally renounce unfavorable association and duties.

In *Śrīmad-Bhāgavatam* (11.11.32) the Supreme Personality of Godhead explains: Understanding these virtues and faults I have described, a sincere devotee renounces all ordinary material duties and worships Me alone. Such a devotee is the best of all.

In the concluding statements of *Bhagavad-gītā* (18.66), the Supreme Personality of Godhead declares: Abandon all varieties of religion and just surrender unto Me. I shall deliver you from all sinful reactions. Do not fear.

In *Śrīmad-Bhāgavatam* (4.29.54) it is said: When a person is fully engaged in devotional service, he is favored by the Lord, who bestows His causeless mercy. At such a time, the awakened devotee gives up all material activities and ritualistic performances mentioned in the *Vedas*.

Cuḍāmaṇi: If a Yavana becomes a sincere Vaiṣṇava, can you take food, drink, and other things with him?

Vaiṣṇava dāsa: *Sannyāsī* Vaiṣṇavas may take *mahā-prasāda* with them. Householder Vaiṣṇavas who are materialistic may not be so inclined. However, there is no rule forbidding one from even taking the remnants of food left by any other Vaiṣṇava. Indeed, one should take their remnants.

Cuḍāmaṇi: Why is it, then, that in Vaiṣṇava temples, Yavana Vaiṣṇavas are not allowed to touch the Deities?

Vaiṣṇava dāsa: It is an offense to call a Vaiṣṇava born in a Yavana family a "Yavana Vaiṣṇava." Simply by being a Vaiṣṇava, he is qualified to serve Lord Kṛṣṇa. If a householder Vaiṣṇava engaged in serving the Deity of the Lord is, in the opinion of materialistic persons, outside the caste rules of *varṇāśrama dharma*, the Vaiṣṇava is at fault only from the point of view of persons eager to follow material customs. Still, a *sannyāsī* Vaiṣṇava should not worship the Deity, for if he worships the Deity, then his status as a person beyond the caste system becomes ruined. Instead, in his heart, he should worship Lord Kṛṣṇa, the beloved of Śrī Rādhā.

Cuḍāmaṇi: I understand. Now please tell what you think about the *brāhmaṇas*.

Vaiṣṇava dāsa: *Brāhmaṇas* are of two kinds: 1. *brāhmaṇas* by nature and 2. *brāhmaṇas* only by birth. Those who are *brāhmaṇas* by nature are mostly Vaiṣṇavas. Serious thinkers from every philosophical camp will honor such a *brāhmaṇa*. Those who are *brāhmaṇas* by birth are honored because of ordinary social customs.

That the Vaiṣṇavas should be honored as the genuine *brāhmaṇas* is confirmed by the following words of scripture (*Śrīmad-Bhāgavatam* 7.9.10): If a *brāhmaṇa* has all twelve of the brahminical qualifications (as they are stated in the book called *Sanat-sujāta*) but is not a devotee and is averse to the lotus feet of the Lord, he is certainly lower than a devotee who is a dog-eater but who has dedicated everything—mind, words, activities, wealth, and life—to the Supreme Lord. Such a devotee is better than such a *brāhmaṇa*, because the devotee can purify his whole family, whereas the so-called *brāhmaṇa* in a position of false prestige cannot purify even himself.

Cuḍāmaṇi: The *śūdras* are not allowed to study the *Vedas*. If a *śūdra* becomes a Vaiṣṇava, would he not then be allowed to study the *Vedas*?

Vaiṣṇava dāsa: Regardless of the caste in which he was born, a pure Vaiṣṇava becomes a *brāhmaṇa* according to spiritual calculations. The *Vedas* are divided into two parts: 1. The *Vedas* describing ordinary rituals and duties and 2. The *Vedas* describing the spiritual truth. Those who are *brāhmaṇas* because of social custom are allowed to study the *Vedas* describing ordinary rituals and duties, and those who are *brāhmaṇas* according to spiritual calculations are allowed to study the *Vedas* that describes the spiritual truth. Regardless of the caste in which he was born, a pure Vaiṣṇava is perfectly qualified to study and teach the *Vedas* that describes the spiritual truth.

This is described in the following words of *Bṛhad-āraṇyaka Upaniṣad* (4.4.21): A wise *brāhmaṇa* should study the part of the *Veda* that describes the Supreme Personality of Godhead.

It is also said (*Bṛhad-āraṇyaka Upaniṣad* 3.8.10): He is a miserly man who does not solve the problems of life as a human, and who thus quits this world like the cats and dogs, without understanding the science of self-realization. He is a *brāhmaṇa* who does solve the problems of life as a human and who quits this world knowing the truth of the eternal Supreme Personality of Godhead.

Those who are *brāhmaṇas* because of social custom are described in these words of *Manu-saṁhitā* (2.168): A *brāhmaṇa* who does not study the Vedic literatures, and who instead laboriously studies many other books about material things becomes at once, in this life, and along with his entire family, a *śūdra*."

The qualification of a person entitled to study the *Veda* that describes the spiritual truth is stated in these words (*Śvetāśvatara Upaniṣad* 6.23): Only unto those great souls who have implicit faith in both the Lord and the spiritual master are all the imports of Vedic knowledge automatically revealed.

The word *para bhakti* here means, "pure devotional service." I cannot say more on this subject. Please understand it as far as you are able. The summary conclusion of all this is: A person who has faith in pure devotional service is qualified to study the part of the *Vedas* describing spiritual truth, and a person who has attained pure devotional service is qualified to teach the part of the *Vedas* describing spiritual truth.

Cuḍāmaṇi: Is your conclusion, then, that the part of the *Vedas* describing spiritual truth teaches only the Vaiṣṇava religion and does not teach any other religion?

Vaiṣṇava dāsa: There is only one religion. There is no such thing as two religions. That one religion is called, "the eternal religion," or "the Vaiṣṇava religion." Other religions are temporary. They serve as steps leading up to the Vaiṣṇava religion.

In the Eleventh Canto (*Śrīmad-Bhāgavatam* 11.14.3), the Supreme Personality of Godhead explains: By the influence of time, the transcendental soul of Vedic knowledge was lost at the time of annihilation. Therefore, when the subsequent creation took place, I spoke the Vedic knowledge to Brahmā, because I Myself am the religious principles enunciated in the *Vedas*.

The *Kaṭha Upaniṣad* (1.2.15 and 1.3.9) explains: All the *Vedas* describe the abode of the Supreme Personality of Godhead. Now I will briefly describe that abode to you. The realm of Lord Viṣṇu is the supreme spiritual abode.

When the discussion had reached this point, the faces of Devī Vidyāratna and his associates had become pale and withered. The great *paṇḍita* teachers were completely demoralized. It was now five o'clock. Everyone said, "Let us end the meeting now."

Everyone agreed, and the meeting ended. With one voice, the *brāhmaṇa paṇḍitas* praised the learning of Vaiṣṇava dāsa. Chanting the holy names of Lord Hari as they went, the Vaiṣṇavas returned to their homes.

Chapter Seven

Eternal duties,
household life and
the material world.

On the bank of the River Sarasvatī was an ancient merchant town named Saptagrāma. Since a long time, a thousand merchants and bankers have lived there. By the mercy of Lord Nityānanda, since the time of Śrī Uddhāraṇa Datta, these merchants have enthusiastically chanted the holy names of Lord Hari. Fearing that much money would be spent, a merchant named Caṇḍī dāsa would not join the people of the town in chanting the holy names of Lord Hari. By living very frugally, he had accumulated a lot of money. His wife, Damāyānti, who had contracted this nature from her husband, would not give due respect to Vaiṣṇavas or guests.

In their youth, this merchant couple had four sons and two daughters. Marrying off first one and then the other daughter, the couple carefully kept their great wealth to give to their sons. When Vaiṣṇavas never visit a home, the children naturally do not become very kind or generous. These qualities become stunted. As the children grew up, they became more and more selfish. Eager to get their inheritance, they yearned for their parents' deaths.

The unhappiness of the merchant couple knew no bounds. One by one, the sons were also married. Imbibing their husband's nature, the daughters-in-law also began to wish that their husband's parents would die. When they became able, the sons divided their father's wealth and set themselves up as merchants.

One day, Caṇḍī dāsa called together his sons and said, "Look. By living frugally since childhood, I have accumulated some wealth for your sake. For all this time, your mother and I have not eaten good food or dressed in nice clothing. Now we are growing old and you should take care of us. That is your duty. However, I see that you are not inclined to take care of us, and that has made me very sad. I have some wealth hidden away and I will give it to whomever amongst you acts like a good son."

Hearing these words, the sons and their wives became silent. Meeting in another place, they all decided that the best thing would be to send their father and mother far away and then take the hidden money, for there was no saying to whom the old man would wrongly give it. All were sure that the wealth was hidden in the father's bedroom.

The father's eldest son was name Nārī-caraṇa. One morning, he said to his father, "Father, you and mother should go and see Śrīdhāma Navadvīpa. In that way, your human life will be successful. I have heard that in the age of Kali, no holy place is as sacred and auspicious like Navadvīpa. To travel to Navadvīpa is neither difficult nor expensive. If you cannot walk, for two *panas*, a boat can take you there. If you wish, a Vaiṣṇava lady is willing to accompany you there.

Caṇḍī dāsa consulted with his wife, Damāyānti. She was very happy and said, "Your words the other day brought our sons to their senses. We are not so weak that we cannot walk. Passing through Kālnā and Śāntipura, let us go to Śrīdhāma Navadvīpa."

Noting an auspicious day, the two began their pilgrimage. Walking and walking, on the next day, they came to Ambikā. Staying there at a merchant's place, they cooked and ate their meal. A man from Saptagrāma came there and told them, "Your sons broke into your room and took all your belongings. They will not allow you to return home. They have taken all your hidden wealth."

Upon hearing this, Caṇḍī dāsa and his wife lamented greatly. On that day, they would not eat. They wept and wept. The Vaiṣṇava lady accompanying them said, "Don't be attached to your home. Continue traveling. Renounce the world. Meet the Vaiṣṇavas. They for whom you have done so much have now become your enemies. Now you cannot return home. Continue traveling. You can stay in Navadvīpa. By begging, you can eat. All will be well."

Hearing of what their sons and daughters-in-law had done, Caṇḍī dāsa and his wife said again and again, "We will not return home. It is better that we give up our lives. That would be best."

After that, they stayed at the home of a Vaiṣṇava in Ambikā-grāma. After two or four days, they went to see Śāntipura and then they went to Navadvīpa. There, they stayed in Māyāpura, in the home of a relative who was a merchant. They stayed for two or four days and then went to see the seven villages of Navadvīpa, and, on the other side of the Gaṅgā, the seven villages of Kuliyā-grāma. After a few days, love for their sons and daughters-in-law again arose in their hearts.

Caṇḍī dāsa said, "Come. Let us go to Saptagrāma. Will not our sons love us even a little?"

Then, the Vaiṣṇava lady who was accompanying them said, "Have you no shame? They will kill you."

Hearing this, the old couple became afraid. They said to her, "O saintly Vaiṣṇava, please return to your home. We will live alone. We will approach a saintly person, learn from him, and live by begging."

The Vaiṣṇava lady left. The merchant couple gave up all hope of returning home. They considered building a new home in the Chakari Catta neighborhood of Kuliyā-grāma. After begging from many good people, they were able to build a cottage. In sacred Kuliyā-grāma, past offenses are all forgiven. When a person lives there, his past offenses are thrown far away. That is what is said about that place.

One day, Caṇḍī dāsa said, "O mother of Hari, why do you continue like this? Don't say anything more about your sons. Don't even think of them. In our past lives, we must have committed many, many offenses. That is why we took birth in the homes of merchants. Because of that low birth, we became misers and refused to serve Vaiṣṇavas and guests. If here we can make a little money, we should use it to serve guests. Then, our next birth will be good. I have set my mind to open a grocery store."

After a few days of striving in that way, Caṇḍī dāsa finally opened a small store. Every day he earned a small profit. After eating a full meal, every day the husband and wife fed a guest. Caṇḍī dāsa lived better than he did before.

Caṇḍī dāsa was a little educated. In his spare moments at the store, he would read Guṇarāja Khan's book *Śrī Kṛṣṇa-vijaya*. He was honest in buying and selling, and he would serve guests. In this way, five or six months passed. When they learned his story, the people of Kuliyā-grāma began to have faith in Caṇḍī dāsa.

It was in that neighborhood that Yādava dāsa lived. Yādava dāsa was a household Vaiṣṇava. He would read *Śrī Caitanya-maṅgala*. Sometimes, Caṇḍī dāsa would listen to him reading. Yādava dāsa and his wife liked to serve the Vaiṣṇavas. Seeing them, Caṇḍī dāsa and his wife also came to like serving the Vaiṣṇavas.

One day, Caṇḍī dāsa asked Yādava dāsa, "What is the material world?"

Yādava dāsa replied, "On the other shore of the Gaṅgā, on the island of Godruma, live many learned Vaiṣṇavas. Go there. Ask them this question. I go there sometimes and in that way, I learn many things. Nowadays the Vaiṣṇava *paṇḍitas* in Śrī Godruma are better scripture scholars than even the *brāhmaṇa paṇḍitas*. Yesterday, an assembly of *brāhmaṇa paṇḍitas* were defeated in debate by Śrī Vaiṣṇava dāsa Bābājī. He will give a good answer to your question."

That afternoon, Yādava dāsa and Caṇḍī dāsa crossed the Gaṅgā. Damāyānti was now accustomed to serve the Vaiṣṇavas. The miserliness in her heart had lessened. She said, "I will go with you to Śrī Godruma."

Yādava dāsa said, "The Vaiṣṇavas there are not householders. They are renunciants. I think they will not be happy to have you in their midst."

Damāyānti said, "I will offer *daṇḍavat* obeisances from afar. I will not enter the middle of the grove. I am an old lady. They will not be angry with me."

Then, Yādava dāsa said, "The custom is that women may not go there. It is better that you merely wait nearby and accompany us when we return."

At nine in the morning, the three of them crossed the Gaṅgā and approached Pradyumna-kuñja. At the entrance to the forest grove, Damāyānti offered *daṇḍavat* obeisances and sat down under an old banyan tree. Yādava dāsa and Caṇḍī dāsa entered the forest grove and devotedly offered *daṇḍavat* obeisances to the Vaiṣṇavas sitting in the place of *mādhavī* and *mālatī* vines.

The *parāmahāṁsa bābājī* was sitting there. On his four sides were Śrī Vaiṣṇava dāsa, Lāhirī Mahāśaya, Ananta dāsa Bābājī, and many others. Yādava dāsa approached and sat down. Caṇḍī dāsa sat beside him.

Saintly Ananta dāsa Bābājī asked, "Who is the new man?"

Yādava dāsa repeated all of Caṇḍī dāsa's story. Ananta dāsa bābājī smiled and said, "Yes. That is what is called 'the material world.' He who knows the true nature of this world is wise. He who is trapped in the cycle of birth and death in this world is truly an object of pity."

Caṇḍī dāsa's heart gradually became purified. One who performs eternal pious deeds attains auspiciousness. Honoring the Vaiṣṇavas and reading and hearing the Vaiṣṇava scriptures were the beginning of Caṇḍī dāsa's eternal pious deeds. By performing these pious deeds again and again, he became pure in heart and attained sincere faith in pure devotional service. When he heard Ananta dāsa's words, Caṇḍī dāsa, his heart now beginning to melt, said, "Today

I make this request: Please be merciful and tell me clearly: What is the material world?"

Śrī Ananta dāsa: Caṇḍī dāsa, your question is very serious. I wish that either the *parāmahāṁsa bābājī* or Śrī Vaiṣṇava dāsa Bābājī would give the answer.

The *parāmahāṁsa bābājī*: This is a serious question. Śrī Ananta dāsa Bābājī is qualified to give the answer. Today we will all listen to the instruction he gives.

Ananta dāsa: I must obey your order. I will speak as far as I have understanding. I will begin by remembering the lotus feet of my spiritual master, Śrīla Pradyumna Brahmācārī, who is an exalted personal associate of the Supreme Personality of Godhead.

The individual spirit soul has two states of existence: 1. The liberated state, and 2. The state of bondage in the prison of the material world. An individual soul who is a pure devotee of Lord Kṛṣṇa is not bound by the illusory potency, *māyā*. By Lord Kṛṣṇa's mercy, such a soul is liberated from the material world of *māyā*. He is a liberated soul. His state of existence is the liberated state. On the other hand, a soul who tries to avoid Lord Kṛṣṇa falls into the gaping mouth of the illusory potency, *māyā*. Such a soul is imprisoned in the material world. His state of existence is residence in the material world.

A soul liberated from *māyā* is always conscious of his original spiritual identity. His whole life is service to Lord Kṛṣṇa. Such a soul does not reside in the material world. He resides in one of the pure spiritual worlds. Goloka, Vaikuṇṭha, and Vṛndāvana are the names of some of these pure spiritual worlds. The souls free from *māyā* are limitless in number. They cannot be counted.

The souls bound in *māyā*'s prison are also limitless in number. They cannot be counted either. A soul averse to Lord Kṛṣṇa is bound by Lord Kṛṣṇa's shadow potency, *māyā*, who binds that soul with ropes of goodness, passion, and ignorance. Because of the difference of these three ropes, the imprisoned souls are placed in many different states of existence. The variety of those states is astonishing. Those who think for a moment will see this astonishing variety. These souls manifest an astonishing variety of material bodies, an astonishing variety of states of existence, an astonishing variety of forms, an astonishing variety of natures, an astonishing variety of residences, and an astonishing variety of movements.

When he first enters the material world, the soul is covered by a new sense of identity. In his pure state of existence, the soul thinks, "I am a servant of Lord Kṛṣṇa." However, in the state of material bondage, the soul thinks, "I am a human being," "I am a demigod," "I am an animal," "I am a king," "I am a *brāhmaṇa*," "I am an outcaste," "I am suffering," "I am hungry," "I am insulted," "I am generous," "I am a husband," "I am a wife," "I am a father," "I am a son," "I am an enemy," "I am a friend," "I am learned," "I am handsome," "I am wealthy," "I am poor," "I am happy," "I am sad," "I am strong," and "I am weak," In this way, the soul may have different conceptions of his identity. This is called false-ego. There is also another thing called false possessiveness. In the grip of false possessiveness, the soul thinks, "This is my house," "This is my thing," "This is my wealth," "This is my body," "This is my son and my daughter," "This is my wife," "This is my husband," "This is my father," "This is my mother," "This is my caste into which I was born," "This is my power," "This is my form," "This is my virtue," "This is my knowledge," "This is my renunciation," "This is my wisdom," "This is my activity," "This is my good fortune," and "These are my servants and dependents." In this way, the souls uses the word "my" in many different ways. This great variety of "I" and "Mine" are called the material world.

Yādava dāsa: I see how there are many kinds of "I" and "Mine" in the state of material bondage. But, is there no "I" and "Mine" in the liberated state?

Ananta dāsa: In the liberated state, the "I" and "Mine" are all spiritual and free of fault. In the liberated state, there is manifested the soul's original spiritual identity, which was originally created by Lord Kṛṣṇa. Because of these different spiritual identities, in the spiritual world, there are varieties of "I". Although all souls there are Lord Kṛṣṇa's servants, they have a great variety of spiritual relationships with the Lord. All the different relationships manifest the idea of "Mine."

Yādava dāsa: If this is so, then what is the fault in the great variety of "I" and "Mine" manifest among the souls bound in the material world?

Ananta dāsa: The fault is this: In the soul's pure state, the ideas of "I" and "Mine" are based on reality. However, when the soul resides in the material world, these ideas of "I" and "Mine" are artificial impositions. They are not real. They are illusions. In the material world, they are all temporary, unnatural, and the sources of fleeting pleasures and pains.

Yādava dāsa: Then, is the material world an illusion?

Ananta dāsa: The material world is not an illusion. By Lord Kṛṣṇa's will, it is reality. However, a soul who enters this world has many illusory conceptions of "I" and "Mine." Those false conceptions are illusions. The Māyāvādīs, who are all offenders, claim that this world is an illusion.

Yādava dāsa: Why do we have illusory material relationships?

Ananta dāsa: The individual soul is a tiny particle of spirit. The first situation of the soul is on the boundary line that separates the spiritual and material worlds. In that condition, the souls that do not forget their original relationship with Lord Kṛṣṇa come under the control of the spiritual potency and are drawn into the spiritual world. Becoming eternal associates of Lord Kṛṣṇa, they enjoy the bliss of serving Him directly. The souls who are averse to Lord Kṛṣṇa and who wish to enjoy the pleasures offered by *māyā* are drawn into the world of *māyā*. That is why we now reside in the material world. When we enter the material world, we forget our true spiritual identity. Then, we think, "I am the enjoyer of *māyā*." Then, *māyā* encircles us with a great variety of false identities.

Yādava dāsa: Why then, although we endeavor to attain it, we do not succeed in regaining the consciousness of our original spiritual identity?

Ananta dāsa: Those endeavors are of two kinds: 1. appropriate, and 2. inappropriate. Appropriate endeavors inevitably throw far away all material illusions about our identity. On the other hand, how can one succeed if his endeavors are not appropriate?

Yādava dāsa: What are inappropriate endeavors? Please tell me.

Ananta dāsa: When a soul purifies his heart by performing the duties of *karma-kanda*, takes shelter of the impersonal Brahman, and thinks, "Now I will become free of *māyā*," his endeavors are all inappropriate. When a soul tries to attain spiritual perfection by performing *aṣṭāṅga-yoga* and entering a trance of *samādhi*, his endeavor also is inappropriate. There are many other kinds of inappropriate endeavor also.

Yādava dāsa: Why are these endeavors not appropriate?

Ananta dāsa: They are not appropriate because many obstacles stop one from attaining the desired results by practicing them, and because there is only the most slender chance that one will succeed by practicing them. We were thrust into this material world because we committed an offense. We will not be able to throw away our material condition of life without first attaining the mercy of that person we offended. Without His mercy, we will not attain our original pure state.

Yādava dāsa: What are the appropriate means?

Ananta dāsa: Association with devotees and surrender. Association with devotees is described in these words of *Śrīmad-Bhāgavatam* (11.2.30): Therefore, O completely sinless ones, I ask you to kindly tell me what the supreme good is. After all, even half a minute's association with pure devotees within this world of birth and death is a priceless treasure for any man.

If you ask, "How can the souls in this material world attain the supreme good," then I say, "If one has a moment's association with the devotees of the Lord, then one will attain the supreme good." The Supreme Personality of Godhead describes surrender in these words of *Bhagavad-gītā* (7.14): This divine energy of Mine, consisting of the three modes of material nature, is difficult to overcome. But those who have surrendered unto Me can easily cross beyond it.

Here, the Lord says, "My divine *māyā* potency consists of the three material modes of goodness, passion and ignorance. By his own endeavor, a human being cannot cross beyond this *māyā*. Therefore, this *māyā* is very difficult to overcome. However, a person who surrenders unto Me and takes shelter of Me can cross beyond this *māyā*."

Caṇḍī dāsa: O saintly one, I am not able to understand all these explanations very well. This much I understand: I am originally a pure being. Forgetting Kṛṣṇa, I have fallen into *māyā*. I am bound in the prison of the material world. By Lord Kṛṣṇa's mercy, I may be released. If I do not attain Lord Kṛṣṇa's mercy, I will stay in this condition.

Ananta dāsa: Yes. Now you accept this much. Your teacher, Yādava dāsa, knows all these truths, and you have learned them from him. In the book Śrī *Prema-vivarta*, Śrī Jagadānanda, who is a close associate of the Supreme

Personality of Godhead, has said: The individual soul is a tiny particle of spirit, and Lord Kṛṣṇa is a great sun of spirit. The liberated soul always gazes at Lord Kṛṣṇa. The liberated soul always worships Lord Kṛṣṇa. As soon as one becomes inimical to Kṛṣṇa and desires sense gratification, he is immediately struck down by the illusory energy of the Lord.

When a living entity is conditioned by material nature, he is exactly like a person haunted by a ghost. Forgetting the words, "In my perfect state, I am servant of Kṛṣṇa," he serves *māyā* for a long time. Sometimes he is a king. Sometimes he is a citizen. Sometimes he is a *brāhmaṇa*. Sometimes he is a *śūdra*. Sometimes he is sad. Sometimes he is happy. Sometimes he is a tiny insect. Sometimes he is in Svargaloka. Sometimes he is in the earthly realms. Sometimes he is in hell. Sometimes he is a demigod. Sometimes he is a demon. Sometimes he is a servant. Sometimes he is a master. Thus, he wanders in the material worlds. When he attains the association of devotees, he can understand the truth about himself. When he understands the truth about himself he no longer wishes to stay in the material world. Then, he laments, "Why did I serve *māyā* for so long?" He weeps and cries out, "O Kṛṣṇa, I am Your servant. By leaving Your lotus feet, I lost everything." When the soul once cries for Kṛṣṇa in this way, Lord Kṛṣṇa becomes merciful and helps him leave the material world. Then, the soul turns away from *māyā*. Again and again worshipping Kṛṣṇa, the soul attains Kṛṣṇa's lotus feet. Kṛṣṇa then places that soul under the protection of His internal potency. *Māyā* then loses her power. *Māyā* no longer attracts that soul. This is attained by associating with devotees and chanting the holy names of Lord Kṛṣṇa. There is no other way to escape the material world of birth and death.

Yādava dāsa: O saintly *bābājī*, you speak of association with devotees, but devotees also live in the material world. They also suffer in the material world. How is it possible that they can deliver other souls?

Ananta dāsa: Devotees live in the material world. Still, the material world that is their home is very different from the material world that is home to the souls bewildered by *māyā*. Looking at them from the outside, they seem to be in the same world. But within, they are very different. There are always some devotees in the material world. Still, the non-devotees do not choose to associate with them. The association of devotees is rarely attained.

The souls devoured by *māyā* may be divided into two groups: 1. Those who, mad to enjoy the tiny pleasures of *māyā*, worship the material world, and 2. The intelligent souls who, not attracted to the pleasures of *māyā*, hope to attain better pleasures. In this way, the residents of the material world are divided into two groups: 1. the unintelligent, and 2. the intelligent. Some call these two groups: 1. Those who desire material sense gratification, and 2. Those who desire liberation. The phrase, "those who desire liberation," does not refer to the impersonalists. It means, "those who, burned by the flames of the world of repeated birth and death, seek to understand their true spiritual identity. The Vedic literatures call such persons, "those who desire liberation." When such persons renounce the desire to attain impersonal liberation and instead engage in worshiping and serving the Supreme Personality of Godhead, their worship is called pure devotional service.

The scriptures do not order that one should renounce the desire for liberation. Rather, the moment he understands the truth of Lord Kṛṣṇa and the individual spirit soul, the person desiring liberation becomes at once liberated.

This is explained in the following words of *Śrīmad-Bhāgavatam* (6.14.3-5): In this material world, there are as many living entities as atoms. Among these living entities, a very few are human beings and among them, few are interested in following religious principles. O best of *brāhmaṇas*, Śukadeva Gosvāmī, out of many persons who follow religious principles, only a few desire liberation from the material world. Among many thousands who desire liberation, one may actually achieve liberation, giving up material attachment to society, friendship, love, country, home, wife, and children. And, among many thousands of such liberated persons, one who can understand the true meaning of liberation is very rare. O great sage, among many millions who are liberated and perfect in knowledge of liberation, one may be a devotee of Lord Nityānanda, or Kṛṣṇa. Such devotees, who are fully peaceful, are extremely rare.

As the number of grains of sand in the world cannot be counted, so also the conditioned souls are countless. Among these souls, a small number seek eternal auspiciousness. Most are interested in material sense gratification. Of those who seek the highest spiritual good, most are interested in liberation, which means to escape the material world. Of thousands and thousands of souls seeking liberation, few attain the perfection of truth and actually become liberated. Of millions and millions of liberated souls, few become peaceful devotees of Lord Nārāyaṇa. A devotee of Lord Nārāyaṇa is very rare. A devotee of Lord Kṛṣṇa is even rarer. Even though they may live in the material world, the devotees of Lord Kṛṣṇa experience a life that is different from the life of the materialists. The devotees of Lord Kṛṣṇa experience two conditions of existence.

Yādava dāsa: You have said that there are four kinds of intelligent persons. What are their different statements of existence, and what is association with devotees?

Ananta dāsa: There are four kinds of intelligent persons: 1. Those who are the beginning stage of being intelligent, 2. Those who desire to attain liberation, 3. Those who are liberated, and 4. Those who have attained perfection, or in other words, the devotees of the Lord. For persons at the beginning states of being intelligent, association with persons who desire liberation is good. The liberated souls may be divided into two groups: 1. Liberated souls who taste the nectar of the spiritual mellows, and 2. The Māyāvādīs, who falsely imagine that they are not different from the Supreme. These Māyāvādīs are considered offenders. All classes of people are forbidden to associate with them.

In the Tenth Canto (*Śrīmad-Bhāgavatam* 10.2.31) it is said: O lotus-eyed one, those who think they are liberated in this life but do not render devotional service to You must be of impure intelligence. Although they accept severe austerities and penances and rise to the spiritual position, to impersonal Brahman realization, they fall down again because they neglect to worship Your lotus feet.

The fourth kind of intelligent people, the devotees, are divided into two groups: 1. Those who worship the Lord in His feature of opulence, and 2. Those who worship the Lord in His feature of sweetness. Association with such devotees is beneficial in every way. Especially if one takes shelter of a devotee who is attached to the Lord's feature in sweetness, the nectar of pure devotional service rises within his heart.

Yādava dāsa: You have said that there are two kinds of devotees. Please describe them more clearly, so even unintelligent persons like me can understand.

Ananta dāsa: The devotees are of two kinds: 1. Householder devotees, and 2. Devotees who have renounced householder life.

Yādava dāsa: What is the situation of a householder devotee in the material world? Please explain this.

Ananta dāsa: The word "householder" does not mean, "one who builds a house." Rather, the word means, "a person who accepts a wife and stays with her in a house." A devotee in this situation is called a householder devotee. A soul bound in the prison of the illusory potency, *māyā*, enters the material world through the doors of the five knowledge-acquiring senses. Through the door of the eyes he sees forms and colors. Through the door of the ears he hears sounds. Through the door of the nose he smells fragrances. Through the door of the skin he touches. Through the door of the tongue he tastes. Entering the material world through these five doors, the soul becomes attached to the world. As he becomes attached to the material world, the soul goes farther and farther from Śrī Kṛṣṇa, the Lord of the heart. That is why the material world is called "the external world."

Those who are mad after enjoying the material world are called hedonists. The householder devotees of the Lord are not eager to please their senses. Therefore, they are not like the hedonists. For a householder devotee, his wife is the maidservant of Lord Kṛṣṇa. His sons and daughters are also the servants of Lord Kṛṣṇa. When, with his eyes, he sees the Deity form of Lord Kṛṣṇa, or the form of things related to Lord Kṛṣṇa, the householder devotee becomes happy. When, with his ears, he hears the topics of Lord Kṛṣṇa, or the biographies of the great devotees, the householder devotee becomes happy. When, with his nose, he smells the *tulasī* leaves and fragrances offered to Lord Kṛṣṇa, the householder devotee becomes filled with bliss. With his tongue, the householder devotee tastes the holy names of Lord Kṛṣṇa, and the remnants of food offered to Lord Kṛṣṇa. When, with his skin, he touches the feet of the Lord's devotees, the householder devotee becomes happy. His hopes, actions, desires, hospitality, and service to the Deity are all used in the service of Lord Kṛṣṇa. His entire life is a great festival of 1. Mercy to others, 2. The holy name of Lord Kṛṣṇa, and 3. Service toVaiṣṇavas.

In this way, a devotee householder remains aloof from hedonism. In the age of Kali, it is very appropriate that the individual souls become householder Vaiṣṇavas. In that way, there is no fear that they will fall down. Also, by following this path, one may attain the full perfection of devotional service. Many self-realized Vaiṣṇava spiritual masters are householders. Their children are also pure devotees. In this way, association with householder devotees of the Lord is especially beneficial to the souls in this world.

Yādava dāsa: Householder Vaiṣṇavas are naturally under the control of the *smārta paṇḍitas*. If the Vaiṣṇavas try to be independent of them, there is trouble. In this situation, how is it possible to engage in pure devotional service?

Ananta dāsa: For marrying off sons and daughters, for performing funeral rites, and for a few others rituals, it may be necessary to engage *smārta paṇḍitas*. Still, there is no need to engage them for the spiritual activities that are most dear to the heart. Look, for maintaining the material body, all are dependent on others. Even those who proudly think themselves independent are in truth still dependent on others. When one suffers from disease, he must take medicine. When one is hungry, he must eat food. To ward off the cold, one must accept clothing. Because of the sun, rain, and other difficulties, one must build a house. For these and many other things, one needs to maintain his material body, and so one must depend on others.

To be independent is merely, as far as possible, to limit these situations of depending on others. The truth is, however, that no one can be completely independent and still maintain his material body. Still, to be independent as far as possible is good and helpful for devotional service. If one observes all these previously described rituals in relation to Lord Kṛṣṇa, then there is no fault in observing them. For example, if marriage is accepted not only to beget good children and worship the Prajapati, but also to engage one's wife and family in devotional service to Lord Kṛṣṇa, then household life is favorable for devotional service. Let the materialists, the Vedic priests, and others say what they will—one still attains the spiritual benefit of these devotional activities.

On the *śrāddha* day, one should first worship Lord Kṛṣṇa, offer the remnants of that offering as *pinda* to his ancestors, and then feed the *brāhmaṇa* Vaiṣṇavas. These activities are favorable for a householder's devotional service.

Thus, these *smārta* rituals may be performed in the context of devotional service.

Ordinary activities should be done with a sense of detachment and renunciation. Spiritual activities should be performed in the association of devotees. Then, one will not be at fault. Look. Most of Lord Caitanya Mahāprabhu's personal associates were householder devotees. Since time immemorial, many great *rājarṣis* (saintly kings) and *devarṣis* (divine sages) were householder devotees. Dhruva Mahārāja, Prahlada Mahārāja, the Pāndavas, and many others were all householders. Householder devotees of the Lord are worshiped by all in the world.

Yādava dāsa: If householder devotees are so worshipable and qualified to attain all spiritual love, then why do some devotees renounce householder life?

Ananta dāsa: Among the householder devotees, for some it is appropriate to renounce household life. However, in the material world, the number of these devotees is very small and association with them is very rare.

Yādava dāsa: What makes a man qualified to renounce household life?

Ananta dāsa: Human beings have two kinds of activities: 1. External activities, and 2. Internal activities. In the language of the *Vedas*, these activities are called *parāk* and *pratyak*. When a pure spirit soul forgets his original spiritual form, misidentifies himself as a subtle material body (of mind, intelligence, and false ego), and exits through the doors of the material senses, he becomes attracted to the external world of material sense objects. These are called "external activities." When the direction is reversed, and the soul goes from the material sense objects to the mind and then to the original form of the soul, these are called "internal activities."

As long as the desire to perform external activities is strong, one should stay in the association of devotees, and without offense perform these external activities with the idea that this material world is Lord Kṛṣṇa's property. By thus taking shelter of devotional service to Lord Kṛṣṇa, in a very short time, the external direction of one's activities becomes reversed and one's activities are then directed inward. When one is thus fully engaged in internal spiritual activities, he becomes qualified to renounce household life. If one tries to renounce household life before one reaches that stage, then there is the danger that he will fall down. Household life is then a school where one gains experience and learns the true nature of the spirit soul. When the education is complete, one may leave the school.

Yādava dāsa: What are the symptoms of a devotee qualified to renounce household life?

Ananta dāsa: The first symptom is that 1. One is not enthusiastic to associate with women. Other symptoms are: 2. Mercy to all living entities, 3. Considering that activities to accumulate money are not very important, 4. Endeavoring to attain a home and clothing only when they are genuinely needed, 5. Faith in Lord Kṛṣṇa, 6. Love and devotion for Lord Kṛṣṇa, 7. Considering that it is not good to associate with worldly people, 8. Thinking praise and criticism are the same, 9. Aversion to material activities, and 10. Not being concerned whether one lives or dies.

These symptoms are described in the following words of the scriptures (*Śrīmad-Bhāgavatam* 11.2.45, 3.25.22 and 11.2.55): A person advanced in devotional service sees within everything the soul of all souls, the Supreme Personality of Godhead, Śrī Kṛṣṇa. Consequently, he always sees the form of the Supreme Personality of Godhead as the cause of all causes and understands that all things are situated in Him. Such a *sādhu* engages in staunch devotional service to the Lord without deviation. For the sake of the Lord, he renounces all other connections, such as family relationships and friendly acquaintances within the world.

Hari, the Supreme Personality of Godhead, who destroys everything inauspicious for His devotees, does not leave the hearts of His devotees, even if they remember Him and chant about Him inattentively. This is because the rope of love always binds the Lord within the devotees' hearts. Such devotees should be accepted as most elevated.

When these qualities manifest in a householder devotee, that devotee finds himself unable to continue with his household duties. At that time, he renounces household life. Such a renounced devotee is rare. Association with such a devotee brings great good fortune.

Yādava dāsa: Nowadays, I see that some young men renounce household life, accept the garments of a renunciant, build a temple, and serve the Lord. As time passes, they eventually fall into evil association with women, but they do not give up chanting the holy names of Lord Hari. To maintain the temple, they beg alms at different places. Are such devotees householders or renunciants?

Ananta dāsa: You ask many questions at once. Can I reply in a single answer? Being young or old has no bearing on renunciation. By purification in past lives or in this life, a young man may become qualified to renounce household life. From his very birth, Śukadeva Gosvāmī was qualified for renunciation. One should see if the qualification is genuinely there. It should not be artificial. If he is genuinely renounced, there is no harm in a young man accepting the renounced order.

Yādava dāsa: What is genuine renunciation and what is artificial renunciation?

Ananta dāsa: Genuine renunciation is strong. It does not break in any situation. Artificial renunciation is based on the desire to be honored by others. This kind of renunciation is marked by cheating and impiety. Thinking, "A devotee who renounces household life is worshiped and respected," and hoping to be worshiped in this way, a man artificially renounces the world. Such renunciation brings no benefit. Rather, it is the source of great inauspiciousness. As soon as he attains his end and he accepts the order of renunciation, his qualifications disappear. From that moment, his true wickedness is manifested.

Yādava dāsa: When a devotee renounces family life, should he accept the garments of a renunciant?

Ananta dāsa: When he has definitely thrown far away the desire for household life, a devotee may live in the forest (as a renunciant) or he may live at home (as a householder). In either situation, he remains a renounced soul, who has nothing to do with the material world. Such a great devotee purifies the entire world. Among these renounced souls, some accept the external signs of the renounced order and wear the *kaupīna* and *kantha*. At the time of accepting the *kaupīna* and *kantha*, they take a firm vow of renunciation in the presence of other renounced Vaiṣṇavas. This is called, "entering the renounced *āsrama*," or "accepting the garments of a renunciant." If one accepts the garments of a renunciant, what is the harm? One who has thus renounced the world should not stay in contact with his relatives. He should stay away from them. He should not desire to enter either his home or that of others. A person who is genuinely renounced should be cautious in dealing with others. A person advanced in renunciation does not need to wear the garments of a renunciant. Still, for some persons wearing the garments of renunciation is useful.

It is said (*Śrīmad-Bhāgavatam* 4.29.45): When a person is fully engaged in devotional service, he is favored by the Lord, who bestows His causeless mercy. At such a time, the awakened devotee gives up all material activities and ritualistic performances mentioned in the *Vedas*.

Yādava dāsa: From whom should one accept the garments of a renunciant?

Ananta dāsa: One should accept the garments of a renunciant from a Vaiṣṇava who has renounced household life. A householder devotee has not experienced the ways of one who has renounced household life. Therefore, a householder devotee should not give initiation into the renounced *āsrama*.

The reason for this is written in these words of the scriptures (*Śrī Brahmā-vaivarta Purāṇa*): If one teaches a religious principle he does not himself follow, that teaching pushes the world closer to destruction.

Yādava dāsa: What thoughts arise in the mind of a spiritual master who is about to give initiation into the renounced *āsrama*?

Ananta dāsa: First, the spiritual master should see whether the disciple is qualified. Has this householder devotee been able, by engaging in devotional service, to control his mind and senses and act in a spiritual way? Is he free of the desire to associate with a woman? Has he uprooted the thirst for money and the desire to eat sumptuous food? The spiritual master will stay near the disciple and observe him for some days. When he knows for certain that the disciple is qualified, the spiritual master will initiate him into the renounced order. He will not initiate any disciple before knowing that he is qualified. If he gives an unqualified person initiation into the renounced order, the spiritual master himself will fall down.

Yādava dāsa: Now I see. Accepting the renounced order is not simply a matter of speaking words with one's mouth. It is very difficult. Pretenders who are not qualified to be spiritual masters are making it a common thing. Now is only the beginning. No one knows what will be the end.

Ananta dāsa: In order to keep this system pure, Lord Caitanya Mahāprabhu punished Chota Haridāsa, whose offense was very slight. The followers of Lord Caitanya should always remember the punishment of Chota Haridāsa.

Yādava dāsa: After accepting the order of renunciation, should one build a temple and worship the Deity of the Lord?

Ananta dāsa: No. A person who has accepted the renounced order should live by begging every day. In that way, he should maintain his life. He will not enter a situation of dealing with material affairs, as will come from building a temple. He will live in a secluded cottage, or in a temple managed by a householder. He will not do anything that requires money. He will always offenselessly chant the holy names of Lord Kṛṣṇa.

Yādava dāsa: What do you say about a renunciant who builds a temple and then lives like a householder?

Ananta dāsa: I say he is a person who eats his own vomit. First he vomits and then he eats what he has vomited.

Yādava dāsa: Is he not a Vaiṣṇava?

Ananta dāsa: He has become a materialist. He breaks the rules of scripture and the rules of being a Vaiṣṇava. Why should you associate with him? He has renounced the ways of pure devotional service and accepted the role of a cheater. How is he like the Vaiṣṇavas?

Yādava dāsa: If he has not given up chanting the holy names of Lord Hari, how can you say he has ceased to be a Vaiṣṇava?

Ananta dāsa: Chanting the holy names of Lord Hari and committing offenses to the holy name of Lord Hari are different things. When a person commits sin on the strength of chanting the holy name—that is an offense to the holy name. You should stay always very far away from offenses to the holy name.

Yādava dāsa: Should his household life not be called, "household life dedicated to Lord Kṛṣṇa?"

Ananta dāsa: It should not be called that. In household life dedicated to Lord Kṛṣṇa, there is no cheating or hypocrisy. That household life is completely honest and sincere. That household life is not based on an offense.

Yādava dāsa: Then, I suppose he is inferior to a regular householder devotee.

Ananta dāsa: He is not a devotee. How can you consider his status, high or low, among the devotees?

Yādava dāsa: How can he be rescued?

Ananta dāsa: When he gives up all his offenses, always chants the holy name, and sheds tears of repentance, he may be counted again among the devotees.

Yādava dāsa: O saintly *bābājī*, householder devotees live under the shelter of the *varṇāśrama* system. May a householder devotee leave the *varṇāśrama* system?

Ananta dāsa: Ah! The Vaiṣṇava religion is very broad and generous. Another name for the Vaiṣṇava religion is *jaiva-dharma* (the religion for all human beings). This means that every human being is qualified to join the Vaiṣṇava religion. Even outcastes may embrace the Vaiṣṇava religion and live as householders. For them, there is no *varṇāśrama*. Those who break the *varṇāśrama* rules of *sannyāsa* may, by associating with devotees, attain pure devotional service. Then they may be householder devotees. For them, there are no rules of *varṇāśrama*. Those who, because of their misdeeds, have left the *varṇāśrama* system may still, along with their children, take shelter of pure devotional service in the association of the devotees. Then they are householder devotees. But, they are not part of the *varṇāśrama* system. Householder devotees are of two kinds: 1. Those who follow the *varṇāśrama* system, and 2. Those who do not follow the *varṇāśrama* system.

Yādava dāsa: Of these two which is the best?

Ananta dāsa: He who has more devotion is the best. If neither has any devotion, then according to the material point of view, the follower of *varṇāśrama* is better because he is pious and the other is an outcaste. However, from the spiritual point of view, they are both degraded, for neither has any devotion.

Yādava dāsa: Is a householder devotee allowed to wear the garments of a renunciant?

Ananta dāsa: No, for he cheats himself, and he cheats the world also. Those are his two faults. If a householder wears a *kaupīna* and the other garments of a renunciant, then that householder mocks and insults the true renunciants.

Yādava dāsa: O saintly *bābājī*, do the scriptures describe how one should accept the garments of a renunciant?

Ananta dāsa: Not very specifically. People of every caste may become Vaiṣṇavas. However, in the opinion of the scriptures, none but the *brāhmaṇas* may accept *sannyāsa*.

In *Śrīmad-Bhāgavatam* (7.11.35), after describing the features of the different castes, Nārada Muni explains: If one shows the symptoms of being a *brāhmaṇa*, *kṣatriya*, *vaiśya*, or *śūdra*, as described above, even if he has appeared in a different class, he should be accepted according to those symptoms of classification.

This verse means, "A person's caste is determined by his personal characteristics, and they were previously described. Thus, the scriptures declare that a person born in a non-*brāhmaṇa* family should be considered a *brāhmaṇa* if he is seen to have the qualities of a *brāhmaṇa*, and that such a *brāhmaṇa* may become qualified to accept *sannyāsa*. This is the opinion of all the scriptures. From the spiritual point of view, this is proved. Still, those who look at things from the material point of view do not accept it.

Yādava dāsa: Caṇḍī dāsa, that certainly answered your question.

Caṇḍī dāsa: Of all the instructions that came from the saintly and honorable *bābājī*'s mouth, this much I understand: The individual soul is eternally the servant of Lord Kṛṣṇa. Forgetting Kṛṣṇa, the soul takes shelter of a material body and, pushed by *māyā*'s modes of nature, experiences material happiness and distress. The result of his material activities is that he must wear around his neck a garland of birth, old age, and death. Sometimes he is born in an exalted situation and sometimes in a lowly situation. He takes birth after birth, and in each birth, he has a new conception of who he is. As he stays in a fragile material body that may be torn apart at any moment, hunger, thirst, and other promptings push him to act in various ways. Unable to attain what he wishes, he is troubled in many ways in this world. His material body grows old and torments him in many ways. Again and again quarreling with wife and children, he is pushed so far that sometimes he even commits suicide. To get money, he sometimes commits many sins. He suffers punishment from the king, the insults of his neighbors, and a great variety of other troubles. He is separated from his loved ones, he loses his wealth, and he is robbed by thieves. Again and again, he suffers many troubles. When he grows old, his relatives refuse to care for him. This makes him suffer greatly. His old body is troubled by mucus, rheumatism, and host of other troubles. Finally he dies. Then, he is again pushed into a mother's womb. Still, as long as he is alive in that material body, lust, anger, greed, delusion, pride, and envy remain very powerful and they refuse to give any place to intelligence. That is life in the material world. Now I know the meaning of the phrase, "the material world." Again and again, I offer my *daṇḍavat* obeisances to the saintly *bābājī*. It is the Vaiṣṇavas who are the true spiritual teachers of the world. By the mercy of the Vaiṣṇavas, I have learned the truth about the material world.

After hearing the instructions of Ananta dāsa Bābājī, all the Vaiṣṇavas called out, "Well done!" and began to chant the holy names of Lord Hari. Gradually, may Vaiṣṇavas gathered there. Then, Lāhirī Mahāśaya sang a song he had written:

"Fallen into the horrible material world, a person suffers without end. Still, if he associates with devotees and worships Lord Hari, a person will make his sufferings come to an end."

"The heart burns in the fire of sense gratification. This fire burns more and more. Avoiding offenses, chant the holy names of Lord Kṛṣṇa. That will pour water on the fire."

"He who has taken shelter of the lotus feet of Lord Caitanya and Lord Nityānanda is my shelter in life and death. Thus says Kālidāsa."

As these words were sung, Caṇḍī dāsa began to dance with great joy. He happily rolled in the dust that had been touched by the Vaiṣṇava *bābājīs*' feet. He wept. Everyone said, "Caṇḍī dāsa has become very fortunate."

After some time, Yādava dāsa Bābājī said, "Come, Caṇḍī dāsa, now we must cross the river."

Caṇḍī dāsa joked, "If you carry me across, I will cross."

After offering *daṇḍavat* obeisances to Pradyumna-kuñja, the two of them left. There, they saw Damāyānti. Again and again offering *daṇḍavat* obeisances, she said, "Alas, Why did I take birth as a woman? If I had taken birth as a man, I could have easily entered this forest grove, seen the saintly devotees, touched the dust from their feet, and made my life a great success. Birth after birth, I will serve the Vaiṣṇavas in Śrī Navadvīpa. In that way, I will pass my days."

Then, Yādava dāsa said, "Ah! Godruma is a very sacred place. Simply by entering this place, a soul attains pure devotion. This Godruma is the pastime place of the master of our lives: Lord Caitanya, the son of Śacī. It is identical with holy Vṛndāvana, the village of cowherds.

Understanding this truth, Śrīla Prabodhānanda Sarasvatī wrote the following prayer (*Śrī Navadvīpa-śataka* 36): Fools, the path of the world and the *Vedas* will bring you only trouble! Give up everything and make yourself a leaf-hut in Śrī Godruma in Gauḍa-deśa!

The three of them crossed the Gaṅgā and returned to Kuliyā-grāma. From that day forward, Caṇḍī dāsa and his wife, Damāyānti, became wonderful Vaiṣṇavas. Understanding the truth about them, the illusory material world no longer touched them. Service to Vaiṣṇavas, continual chanting of the holy name of Lord Kṛṣṇa, and mercy to all living entities were the ornaments they wore. Glorious became that merchant couple! Glorious is the mercy of the Vaiṣṇavas! Glorious is the holy name of Lord Hari! Glorious is the land of Śrī Navadvīpa!

Chapter Eight

*Eternal religion
and
ordinary activities.*

One afternoon, after honoring *prasāda*, the Vaiṣṇavas of Śrī Godruma gathered in a secluded forest grove on the northeast side of Śrī Gaura Lake. There, Lāhirī Mahāśaya sang a song that awakened in them the ecstatic love of Vraja. He sang: How many pastimes did Lord Caitanya enjoy here with Advaita and the other devotees? Here He chanted the names of Lord Kṛṣṇa and danced. As Lord Kṛṣṇa rescued Kāliya, here our Lord rescued a crocodile.

When the song ended, the Vaiṣṇavas discussed the similar natures of Lord Kṛṣṇa's and Lord Caitanya's pastimes. Then, two or four Vaiṣṇavas from Barāgachi came there. They offered *daṇḍavat* obeisances, first to Gaura lake and then to the Vaiṣṇavas. The Vaiṣṇavas honored them and offered sitting places. In that secluded grove was an old banyan tree. Around its roots, the Vaiṣṇavas had built a stone platform. They all informed the visitors from Barāgachi that the tree was honored with the name Nitai-bata (Lord Nityānanda's banyan tree), for Lord Nityānanda liked to sit under it.

Sitting under Lord Nityānanda's banyan tree, the Vaiṣṇavas talked about spiritual life. Among the Vaiṣṇavas from Barāgachi was a youth who wanted to ask a question. He suddenly said, "I want to ask a question. Someone please answer it and make me happy."

In that secluded grove lived Hari dāsa Bābājī, who was a very learned scholar. He almost never left that place. He was almost a hundred years old. On some rare occasions, he would go to Pradyumna-kuñja and meet with the *parāmahāṁsa bābājī*. He had personally seen Lord Nityānanda sitting under that banyan tree. He had a desire. He wished that when he left his body it would be at that place. He said, "Son, now that the *parāmahāṁsa bābājī*'s associates have assembled here, why should you worry about the answer to your question?"

Then the Vaiṣṇava from Barāgachi asked his question. "The Vaiṣṇava religion is the eternal religion. How should a person who has taken shelter of the Vaiṣṇava religion act in relation to others. I wish to understand this very thoroughly."

Glancing for a moment at saintly Vaiṣṇava dāsa Bābājī, Hari dāsa Bābājī said, "O Vaiṣṇava dāsa, nowadays, no one in Bengal is learned and devoted like you. You should answer this question. You had the association of Śrīla Sarasvatī Gosvāmī and you were personally taught by the *parāmahāṁsa bābājī*. You are thus very fortunate. You have certainly attained the mercy of Lord Caitanya Mahāprabhu."

Saintly Vaiṣṇava dāsa Bābājī humbly said, "O great soul, you personally saw Lord Nityānanda, who is an incarnation of Lord Balarāma. In the assembly of many great souls you taught many students. Please be merciful and give some instruction to us. All the Vaiṣṇavas there begged Hari dāsa Bābājī to answer the question. The *bābājī* at last agreed.

After first offering *daṇḍavat* obeisances to Lord Nityānanda under that banyan tree, the saintly *bābājī* began to speak: Addressing them all as "servant of Lord Kṛṣṇa," I offer my obeisances to every soul in this material world. It is said (Śrī Caitanya-caritāmṛta, Adi 6.85): Some accept Him whereas others do not, yet everyone is Lord Kṛṣṇa's servant.

I place upon my head these words of the saintly devotees. Although every soul is by nature a perfect servant of Lord Kṛṣṇa, some souls, because of the ignorance of bewilderment, do not accept that they are His servant. They are one group. Other souls, however, do accept that they are His servants. They are another group. Thus, in this material world, the souls may be divided into two groups: 1. Those who turn away from Lord Kṛṣṇa, and 2. Those who are eager to approach Lord Kṛṣṇa.

In the material world, most of the souls prefer to turn away from Lord Kṛṣṇa. Many of these souls do not accept any religion. There is no need to say much about these persons. They have no idea of what should and what should not be done. For them, their own personal happiness is the be-all-and-end-all of their lives.

Persons who accept religion have an idea of what should be done. For their benefit, the great Vaiṣṇava, Manu, has written (Śrī *Manu-saṁhitā* 6.92): The ten features of religious life are: 1. patience, 2. forgiveness, 3. self-control, 4. honesty, 5. cleanliness, 6. sense control, 7. knowledge, 8. wisdom, 9. truthfulness and 10. freedom from anger.

Among these, six are features that benefit the performer. They are: 1. patience, 2. self-control, 3. cleanliness, 4. sense control, 5. knowledge, and 6. wisdom. The remaining four are done for the benefit of others. They are: 1. patience, 2. honesty, 3. truthfulness, and 4 freedom from anger. Devotional service to Lord Hari is not clearly mentioned in this list of ten features. These ten features of religious life are taught here for the benefit of ordinary people.

It cannot be said that by faithfully following the teaching of this verse, one will attain perfect auspiciousness, for *Śrī Viṣṇu-dharmottara Purāṇa* explains: To live for five days as a devotee of Lord Viṣṇu is far better than to live for a thousand *kalpas* as a person who has no devotion for Lord Kesava.

Those who are not devotees of Lord Kṛṣṇa cannot be said even to be human beings. Those who are not devotees are all counted as animals walking on two legs. It is said (*Śrīmad-Bhāgavatam* 2.3.19): Men who are like dogs, hogs, camels and asses praise those men who never listen to the transcendental pastimes of Lord Śrī Kṛṣṇa, the deliverer from evils.

Here, the question is not what these persons should or should not do. The question is only how should persons who have taken shelter of the path of devotional service act in relation to these persons. Of that I will speak. Those who have taken shelter of the path of devotional service may be divided into three groups: 1. *kaniṣṭha* (neophyte), 2. *madhyama* (intermediate), and 3. *uttama* (advanced).

Although he has taken shelter of the path of devotional service, a neophyte is not yet a true devotee. He is described in these words (*Śrīmad-Bhāgavatam* 11.2.47): A *prākṛta*, or materialistic devotee, does not purposefully study the *śāstra* and try to understand the actual standard of pure devotional service. Consequently, he does not show proper respect to advanced devotees. He may, however, follow the regulative principles learned from his spiritual master, or from his family who worships the Deity. He is to be considered on the material platform, although he is trying to advance in devotional service. Such a person is a *bhakta-prāya* (neophyte devotee), or *bhaktābhāsa*, for he is a little enlightened by Vaiṣṇava philosophy.

Thus, one who faithfully worships the Deity of the Lord but does not faithfully worship the Lord's devotees is a materialistic devotee (*prākṛta-bhakta*). The conclusion, then, is that faith is the seed of devotional service. To faithfully worship the Deity of the Lord is to engage in devotional service. Still, if one does not also worship the Lord's devotees, his worship is not pure devotional service. His worship is not devotional service in its complete form. His worship is merely stepping into the entrance of the house of devotional service.

The scriptures (*Śrīmad-Bhāgavatam* 10.84.13) explain: A human being who identifies this body made of three elements with the self, who considers the by-products of the body to be his kinsmen, who considers the land of his birth as worshipable, and who goes to a place of pilgrimage simply to take bath rather than meet men of transcendental knowledge there, is to be considered as an ass or a cow.

The meaning is this: Although, in the beginning, devotional service consists of worship of the Deity and nothing else, and although dry, materialistic logic is not recommended, for it crushes the heart into powder, it is nevertheless necessary that one understand that the Deity of the Lord and service to the Deity are pure and spiritual. All living entities in the material world are spiritual by nature. Among these living entities, those who are devotees of Lord Kṛṣṇa especially manifest their pure and spiritual nature. The devotee and Lord Kṛṣṇa are two different pure and spiritual identities. To understand their true spiritual natures, one must understand the relationships between the material world, the individual soul, and Lord Kṛṣṇa. A person who understands these relationships and simultaneously worships the Deity of Lord Kṛṣṇa and serves the Lord's devotees acts rightly. When one faithfully worships the spiritual truth in this way, it is said that he has "faith in the scriptures." A person who worships the Deity of the Lord but does not understand the relationships that exist between the various spiritual entities has only a materialistic kind of faith. Although he stands at the entrance of the house of devotional service, his service is not pure devotional service. That is the conclusion. A person thus standing at the entrance to the house of devotional service is described in these words of the scriptures: A person who has accepted a Vaiṣṇava initiation and who devotedly worships Lord Viṣṇu is said by the wise to be a Vaiṣṇava. All others are not Vaiṣṇavas.

Persons born in families who, generation after generation, are initiated by their family priest into the chanting of Viṣṇu *mantras* and who thus worship the Deity of the Lord with materialistic faith are neophyte (*kaniṣṭha*), or materialistic devotees. They are not pure devotees. Over them, the shadow of devotional service is strongly cast. However, the reflection of devotional service is not manifested in them, for the reflection of devotional service is counted among the offenses. Therefore, those who possess this reflection are not Vaiṣṇavas. However, from the shadow of devotional service may come a great good fortune, for such a neophyte devotee may gradually become an intermediate (*madhyama*) and eventually an advanced (*uttama*) devotee.

However that may be, persons at that stage of spiritual advancement are not yet pure devotees. They may worship the Deity of the Lord with material faith, and they may manifest the ten signs of piety in dealing with ordinary persons. Still, the scriptures' descriptions of the devotees' ways are not meant to describe them. To convert non-devotees into devotees is not in their power.

The ways of the intermediate (*madhyama*) devotees are described in these words (*Śrīmad-Bhāgavatam* 11.2.46): An intermediate, second-class devotee shows love for the Supreme Personality of Godhead, is friendly to all devotees, and is very merciful to neophytes and ignorant people. The intermediate devotee neglects those who are envious of devotional service.

The behavior described in this verse is the behavior of one who follows the eternal religion. Temporary or material activities are not described here. In a Vaiṣṇava's life, such behavior must be followed. Other kinds of behavior, as long as they do not contradict this behavior, may be adopted when necessary.

A Vaiṣṇava relates to four kinds of persons: 1. The Supreme Personality of Godhead, 2. The devotees who are surrendered to the Lord, 3. Innocent persons, and 4. Those who are enemies of devotional service. To these four kinds of persons, a Vaiṣṇava shows love, friendship, mercy, and neglect. To the Supreme Personality of Godhead he shows love, to the devotee he shows friendship, to the innocent people in general he shows mercy, and to persons filled with hate he shows neglect.

First he shows love to the Supreme Personality of Godhead. To Lord Kṛṣṇa, the Supreme Personality of Godhead, the master of all, he shows love (*prema*). The word *prema* means, "pure devotional service."

The characteristics of pure devotional service are described in these words (*Śrī Bhakti-rasāmṛta-sindhu*): One should render transcendental loving service to the Supreme Lord Kṛṣṇa favorably and without desire for material profit or gain through fruitive activities or philosophical speculation. That is called pure devotional service.

These words describe the devotional service of an intermediate (*madhyama*) Vaiṣṇava, service that reaches up to the stages of ecstasy (*bhāva*) and pure spiritual love (*prema*). By itself, without the addition of the qualities described here, worshiping the Deity of the Lord with faith is the activity of a neophyte devotee. This means that a neophyte devotee does not have the qualities of pure devotional service, which are: 1. Being without desire for material profit or gain through fruitive activities or philosophical speculation, and 2. Rendering transcendental loving service to the Supreme Lord Kṛṣṇa favorably. However, on the day that these qualities are manifested in his heart, such a person may be called an intermediate (*madhyama*) devotee. That is how a materialistic devotee becomes an intermediate devotee. As long as these qualities do not arise in his heart, he is a materialistic devotee. This means that he is considered only a shadow of a true devotee, or a shadow of a true Vaiṣṇava. Here, the word *kṛṣṇānuśīlanam* refers to spiritual love (*prema*). However, the word *ānukūlyena* refers to all four qualities of an intermediate devotee: 1. favorable love for Lord Kṛṣṇa, 2. friendship, 3. mercy, and 4. neglect.

The second of these qualities is that one is friendly to the devotees, who are surrendered to the Supreme Lord. Any person in whom pure devotional service is manifested is considered a devotee surrendered to the Supreme Personality of Godhead. Neophyte devotees are neither pure devotees, nor are they surrendered to the Lord. Their tendency is to disrespect the true pure devotees. Therefore, one should make friendship with intermediate and advanced devotees only. In answering a Kulina-grāma devotee's question, Śrī Caitanya Mahāprabhu described the neophyte, intermediate, and advanced devotees. He explained that the intermediate and advanced devotees are counted among the true Vaiṣṇavas, whereas the neophyte devotees, who do not know anything beyond worshiping the Deity, are not yet true Vaiṣṇavas.

The true holy name of the Lord does not appear on the mouths of such worshipers of the Deity. The name that appears on their mouths is only the shadow of Lord Kṛṣṇa's holy name (*chāyā nāmābhāsa*). Lord Caitanya Mahāprabhu ordered the intermediate (*madhyama*) householder devotees to serve all three classes of devotees, the three classes being: 1. A person on whose mouth the holy name of Lord is heard even only once, 2. A person on whose mouth the holy name of Lord Kṛṣṇa is heard always, and 3. A person the sight of whom inspires one to chant the holy name of Lord Kṛṣṇa. One should serve a Vaiṣṇava who chants only a shadow of Lord Kṛṣṇa's holy name. One should also serve a Vaiṣṇava who takes shelter of the pure holy name of Lord Kṛṣṇa.

As there are different kinds of Vaiṣṇavas, so there are different kinds of service to Vaiṣṇavas. The "making friendship" includes associating with Vaiṣṇavas, conversing with them, and serving them. The moment one sees a pure Vaiṣṇava, one should greet him, honor him, and offered both a sitting place and conversation. One must serve him in all these ways. One should never hate, envy, or insult him. One should not disrespect him if his body is ugly, or if he suffers from some disease.

The third of these qualities is that one is merciful to the innocent people in general. The phrase, "innocent people in general" means, "those who do not understand the spiritual truth," "those who are bewildered," and "those who are foolish." Persons who are not educated, have not entered into the theories of the Māyāvādīs and other offenders, have not learned how to hate the devotees and devotional service but, being overcome by powerful false ego and false possessiveness, do not yet have faith in the Supreme Personality of Godhead, are called, "the innocent people in general." Even if one is a great scholar, if he does not have faith in the Supreme Personality of Godhead, he is counted among the innocent people in general. Even though he has approached the entrance to the house of devotional service, a materialistic neophyte devotee may also be counted among the innocent people in general, for such a devotee has not yet attained pure devotional service and does not yet clearly understand his relationship with the Supreme Personality of Godhead.

When such a devotee understands his relationship with the Supreme Personality of Godhead, associates with pure devotees, and chants the holy name with purity, then his status as one of the "innocent people in general" is thrown far away and he attains the status of an intermediate (*madhyama*) Vaiṣṇava. For an intermediate devotee, it is absolutely essential that he be merciful to the innocent people in general. As far as possible, he should invite them to his home. Even that is not enough. He should show mercy to such persons by helping them to attain faith in pure devotional service and attraction for the pure holy name of the Lord. Because they are not learned in the scriptures, the innocent people in general may easily fall down because of association with wicked persons. Therefore, the intermediate devotee should mercifully give his association to the innocent people and gradually allow them to hear the glories of the holy names and the various teachings of the scriptures.

A diseased person cannot cure himself. He must be cured by a physician. If the patient sometimes speaks angrily or commits other such offenses, he is to be forgiven. In the same way, if an innocent person sometimes acts improperly, he is to be forgiven. This is called mercy. An innocent person may have many misconceptions. He may have faith in the *karma-kanda* portion of the *Vedas*, faith in various non-devotional philosophies, an inclination to worship the Deity of the Lord in order to attain various material desires, faith in *yoga* and other like paths, disinterest in associating with pure Vaiṣṇavas, or attachment to *varṇāśrama* and other such things. In this way, he may have many different kinds of misconceptions.

When, by good association, mercy, and spiritual instruction, he gradually gives up these misconceptions, the neophyte devotee quickly becomes an intermediate devotee. Then he is a pure devotee. His worship of the Deity form of Lord Hari was thus the foundation upon which he built the house of all spiritual auspiciousness. Of this there is no doubt. He does not make the mistake of trying to follow one of the myriad of competing philosophies. Because he does not make this mistake, he has a scent of true faith. When he worships the Deity of Lord Hari, a follower of the Māyāvadi philosophy, or other like philosophies, does not have even the slightest true faith in the Deity. Such a person is an offender.

It is for this reason that *Śrīmad-Bhāgavatam* (11.2.47) describes him with the phrase, *śraddhayehate* (he worships with faith). In their hearts, the followers of the Māyāvadi philosophy and other such philosophies think, "The supreme spirit has no form. The Deity form that we worship is merely the product of our imagination." How can such persons have faith in the Deity form of the Lord? In this way, the Māyāvadi's worship of the Deity and the most neophyte Vaiṣṇava's worship of the Deity, are very different. It is for this reason that, even though he does not have the various virtues of a Vaiṣṇava, because he is not a Māyāvadi, the neophyte is called a "materialistic Vaiṣṇava." In this way, he is considered a Vaiṣṇava.

By the mercy of saintly devotees, such a neophyte gradually becomes elevated. This is inevitable. Second class pure Vaiṣṇavas are inevitably merciful to them. Then, the neophyte devotee's worship of the Deity and chanting of Lord Hari's holy name do not remain shadows of the real thing. Quickly, they manifest their true spiritual nature.

The fourth of these qualities is that one neglects hateful persons. One should understand the different kinds of hateful persons. Envy is a synonym of hatred. Hatred is the opposite of love. The Supreme Personality of Godhead is the only true object of love. The opposite of love for Him is hatred of Him. This hatred is manifested in five ways: 1. To not believe in the existence of the Supreme Personality of Godhead. 2. To believe that the living entity himself has created God. 3. To not believe that God has a form. 4. To not believe that the individual souls are eternally subordinate to God. 5. To be merciless.

Persons contaminated by hatred do not have pure devotion. Neither do they have the materialistic devotion manifested by neophytes who worship the Deity. These five kinds of hatred brings with them, as a by product, attachment to material sense gratification. It is sometimes seen that the third and fourth of these kinds of hatred may bring one to austerities so severe that one kills himself in the process. This is seen in the lives of the Māyāvadi *sannyāsīs*. How should a pure devotee relate to all these hateful persons? A pure devotee should avoid them.

Avoiding them does not mean that one should renounce all ordinary dealings that one human being naturally has with another. It does not mean that if a hateful person falls into danger or want, one should not try to help him. A householder devotee has many relationships with others. By marriage, he has many relatives. By buying and selling various goods, he has many relationships. By owning property and protecting animals, he has many relationships. By acting to treat diseases and relieve others' sufferings, he has many relationships. The king and his subjects have many kinds of relationships.

Avoiding hateful persons does not mean suddenly renouncing all these different kinds of relationships. In ordinary material dealings, one may have relationships with such persons, but in spiritual activities, such persons should be shunned. As the result of past *karma*, a family member may be such a hateful person. Should such a person be cast out of the family? No. Without becoming attached, behave with that person as is expected in ordinary dealings, but do not share that person's ideas of spiritual life. In this way, one should avoid that person. Meeting for spiritual activities, conversing about spiritual activities, and helping and serving one another in spiritual life are the different kinds of spiritual association. To avoid such association is called, "neglect of hateful persons."

If he hears the praises the pure devotional service, or teachings about pure devotional service, a person who accepts the philosophy of hateful persons will only argue needlessly. In this way, neither he nor you will be benefited. Avoiding such barren debates, associate with him only in ordinary material things. If you say that you will consider such a hateful person among the innocent people in general and you will be merciful to him and thus benefit him, then I say you may very well harm him and yourself. If you must try to do good to him, then do it very carefully.

An intermediate (*madhyama*) pure devotee should act in these four ways. If such an intermediate devotee is reluctant to act in these ways, then he commits the fault of acting improperly, in a way he is not qualified to act. Thus, he avoids acting properly, in the ways he is qualified. This is a great fault, as the scriptures explain:

One who accepts the duties for which he is qualified is praiseworthy, and one who does not is subject to blame. That is the right conclusion.

Thus, an intermediate (*madhyama*) devotee should perform the activities of pure devotional service, follow the scriptures, love the Supreme Personality of Godhead, make friendship with pure devotees, be merciful to the innocent people in general, and neglect persons who hate the Supreme Personality of Godhead. Different degrees of advancement in devotional service on the part of one's devotee friends may elicit different degrees of friendship. Different degrees of sincerity on the part of innocent persons may elicit different degrees of mercy. Different degrees of hatred on the part of hateful persons may elicit different degrees of avoidance. Considering these differences, an intermediate devotee should behave, in his spiritual activities, differently with different persons. Material activities should be performed honestly, and they should be secondary to spiritual activities.

Then, Nityānanda dāsa from Barāgachi asked, "What are the material activities of these devotees you have described?"

Hari dāsa Bābājī replied, "Son, if you ask this question of me, then I cannot give a good explanation. I am an old man, my memory is short, my mind is not powerful, and I easily forget."

Hari dāsa was a very strict *bābājī*. No fault could ever be seen in him. Still, when this inappropriate question was asked, he gave this reply. When they heard his words, everyone was stunned.

After again bowing down before the banyan tree of Lord Nityānanda, Hari dāsa said, "When his love and devotion becomes intensified, then an intermediate (*madhyama*) devotee becomes an advanced (*uttama*) devotee. The qualities of an advanced devotee are written in these words of *Śrīmad-Bhāgavatam* (11.2.45): A person advanced in devotional service sees within everything the soul of all souls, the Supreme Personality of Godhead, Śrī Kṛṣṇa. Consequently, he always sees the form of the Supreme Personality of Godhead as the cause of all causes and understands that all things are situated in Him.

An advanced (*uttama*) Vaiṣṇava sees that the Supreme Personality of Godhead loves all souls, and that all souls love the Supreme Personality of Godhead. For an advanced devotee, there is no other love. Whatever other kind of love he may manifest in different situations is all but a transformation of that spiritual love. Look. Śrīla Śukadeva Gosvāmī is an advanced devotee. Still, he insulted Kaṁsa by calling him, "the vicious sinner of the Bhoja dynasty." However, that insult was really manifested from love. It was based on spiritual love and there was not any malice in it. When pure love becomes his entire life, then a person is called, "the best of devotees." In this state, the differing degrees of love, friendship, mercy, and neglect described before are no longer manifested. Now, everything is spiritual love. For such a person, there is no difference between neophyte, intermediate, and advanced devotees. Indeed, for him there is no difference between devotees and non-devotees. Such a state is very rarely attained.

A neophyte devotee does not serve Vaiṣṇavas, and an advanced devotee does not think that some persons are Vaiṣṇavas and others are not. Therefore, it is only the intermediate devotees who honor and serve Vaiṣṇavas. An intermediate devotee must serve the three kinds of Vaiṣṇavas: 1. He who once chants the holy name of Lord Kṛṣṇa, 2. He who always chants the holy name of Lord Kṛṣṇa, and 3. He who, simply by being seen, makes others chant the holy name of Lord Kṛṣṇa. Thus, Vaiṣṇavas should be served according to the degree of their advancement, whether they are a good Vaiṣṇava, a better Vaiṣṇava, or the best Vaiṣṇava. No one can judge who is a good Vaiṣṇava and who is an intermediate Vaiṣṇava. Only an advanced Vaiṣṇava can understand that. If an intermediate (*madhyama*) Vaiṣṇava tries to say this, he will commit an offense. Lord Caitanya Mahāprabhu hinted this in His instructions to the residents of Kulina-grāma. All intermediate devotees should honor that teaching more than even the *Vedas*. Someone may ask: What are the *Vedas*, or *Śruti*? The answer is given: The *Vedas* are the orders of the Supreme Personality of Godhead.

After speaking these words, Hari dāsa was silent for a moment. Then, the visitor from Barāgachi said, "May I ask a question?"

Hari dāsa Bābājī replied, "As you like."

Young Nityānanda dāsa asked, "Saintly *bābājī*, what kind of Vaiṣṇava am I? Am I a neophyte Vaiṣṇava, or an intermediate Vaiṣṇava? An advanced Vaiṣṇava I certainly am not."

Saintly Hari dāsa Bābājī smiled and said, "Can a person who accepts the name Nityānanda dāsa not be an advanced Vaiṣṇava? Our Nityānanda is very merciful. Even when He is beaten, He gives love in return. How can words properly glorify a person who chants Lord Nityānanda's name and becomes His servant.

Nityānanda dāsa: I would like to know truthfully what my position is.

Hari dāsa: Son, tell me all about yourself. If Lord Nityānanda gives me the power to say, I will tell you.

Nityānanda dāsa: I was born in a lowly family in a village on the bank of the Padmavatī. I was married at a young age. I did not learn how to be wicked. When my wife died, thoughts of renunciation came to my mind. In Barāgachi,

I saw many Vaiṣṇavas who had renounced family life. Everyone was respectful to them. Desiring to be honored like that, and inspired by the temporary feeling of renunciation my wife's death brought, I accepted the garments of a Vaiṣṇava renunciant. After some days, wickedness came into my mind. My Vaiṣṇava friend was a very good person. Now he stays in Vraja. He gave me good advice, protected me with his good association, and kept my mind pure. Now my mind no longer wants to leave the right path. It likes to chant one hundred thousand holy names every day. I understand that the Supreme Personality of Godhead and His holy name are not different. Both are perfectly spiritual. I observe Ekādaśī according to the scriptures, and I water *tulasī*. When the Vaiṣṇavas sing the holy names together, I join in the singing. I drink the nectarean water that has washed the Vaiṣṇava's feet. I read *Śrī Caitanya-maṅgala*. I do not desire opulent food and clothing. I do not like to hear gossip. When I see how the Vaiṣṇavas are filled with ecstatic love, I also become ecstatic and I roll in the dust that has touched their feet. In spite of all this, to a certain extent, I still desire fame. Now, please tell me: To what class of Vaiṣṇavas do I belong? How should I behave?

Showing a little smile, Hari dāsa Bābājī said to Vaiṣṇava dāsa, "You say. To what class of Vaiṣṇavas does Nityānanda dāsa belong?"

Vaiṣṇava dāsa: From what I have heard, he has left the neophyte stage and has become an intermediate devotee.

Hari dāsa: I also think that.

Nityānanda dāsa: Good. From the mouth of a great soul, I now know my true position. Please give your mercy to me so I may gradually become an advanced devotee.

Hari dāsa: When you first accepted the garments of a *sannyāsī*, you desired material fame. That inappropriate desire meant that you were still fallen. In spite of that, the mercy of the Vaiṣṇavas brought auspiciousness to you.

Nityānanda dāsa: I still have a slight desire for fame. In my mind, I think, "Bewildered by the tears in my eyes and many other symptoms of ecstatic love, the people will worship me."

Hari dāsa: You should struggle to renounce those thoughts. Don't keep thoughts like those. There is the danger that they will diminish your devotional service. If you allow them to diminish your devotion, you will again become a neophyte devotee. Even after lust, anger, and other vices have left, the desire for fame may stubbornly stay with a Vaiṣṇava. It does not go away very easily. A single drop of sincere love for the Lord is better than an elaborate pretense of that love.

Touching the dust of Hari dāsa Bābājī's feet, Nityānanda dāsa Bābājī said, "Please have mercy on me."

Hari dāsa at once embraced him and made him sit down. How wonderful is the result attained by a Vaiṣṇava's touch! Tears streamed from Nityānanda's dāsa's eyes. Taking a blade of grass between his teeth, he said, "I am very fallen and lowly. I am very fallen."

Hari dāsa Bābājī embraced him and wept. How wonderful it all was! Nityānanda dāsa had attained the true goal of life. After a short time, when all the symptoms of ecstatic love had subsided, in his heart, Nityānanda dāsa accepted Śrī Hari dāsa as his spiritual master. Then, Nityānanda dāsa asked a question.

Nityānanda dāsa: What are the primary and secondary features of a neophyte devotee's devotional service?

Hari dāsa: The two primary features of a neophyte devotee's devotional service are: 1. Faith that the Supreme Personality of Godhead's form is eternal, and 2. Worship of the Lord's Deity form. The secondary features of a neophyte devotee's devotional service are: 1. Hearing about the Lord, 2. Chanting the Lord's glories, 3. Remembering the Lord and 4. A host of other activities, beginning with offering obeisances to the Lord.

Nityānanda dāsa: Without having faith that the Lord's form is eternal, no one can be a Vaiṣṇava. Also, without worshipping the Deity form of the Lord according to the rules of worship, no one can be a Vaiṣṇava. I can understand why these two are the primary features. However, I do not understand why the other features are secondary.

Hari dāsa: A neophyte devotee does not understand the true nature of pure devotional service. Hearing and chanting the Lord's glories, as well as other such devotional activities, are all part and parcel of pure devotional service. However, a person who does not understand the true nature of devotional service does not think these are the primary activities of devotional service. Such a person considers these activities secondary. The three modes of material nature are: 1. goodness, 2. passion and 3. ignorance. When the performer takes shelter of these material modes, he considers these devotional activities to be secondary. When the performer is free from the influence of the material modes, he considers these activities, which begin with hearing and chanting the Lord's glories, to be the primary features of devotional service. When a person is thus free of the material modes, he is an intermediate (*madhyama*) devotee.

Nityānanda dāsa: A neophyte devotee is still contaminated by mental speculation, fruitive work, and non-devotional desires. Why is he still considered a devotee?

Hari dāsa: Faith is the root of devotional service. Anyone who has faith is qualified to engage in devotional service. A neophyte devotee stands at the entrance to the house of devotional service. Of that there is no doubt. The word, "faith" means "trust." Because he trusts that the form of the Lord is a reality, the neophyte devotee is qualified to engage in devotional service.

Nityānanda dāsa: When will such a person attain true devotion to the Lord?

Hari dāsa: When he becomes free from mental speculation and fruitive work, when he desires only to engage in unalloyed devotional service, when he understands that honoring a guest is different from honoring a devotee, and when he desires to serve the devotees, that service being very conducive to the attainment of true devotion, then he becomes an intermediate (*madhyama*) devotee, a pure devotee.

Nityānanda dāsa: Pure devotional service is manifested at the same time one attains knowledge of his relationship with the Lord. When does he attain knowledge of that relationship, knowledge that makes him eligible to engage in pure devotional service?

Hari dāsa: When he is no longer contaminated by Māyāvāda philosophy, then his awareness of his true relationship with the Lord and his engagement in pure devotional service are manifested simultaneously.

Nityānanda dāsa: How many days does that take?

Hari dāsa: A person who in the past performed many pious deeds will attain it quickly.

Nityānanda dāsa: What is the first result these past pious deeds bring?

Hari dāsa: Association with devotees.

Nityānanda dāsa: What result is gradually attained by associating with devotees?

Hari dāsa: *Śrīmad-Bhāgavatam* (3.25.25): In the association of pure devotees, discussion of the pastimes and activities of the Supreme Personality of Godhead is very pleasing and satisfying to the ear and the heart. By cultivating such knowledge, one gradually becomes advanced on the path of liberation, and thereafter he is free, and his attraction becomes fixed. Then real devotion and devotional service begin.

Thus, a person who, in the association of devotees, hears about Lord Hari, gradually attains faith and other virtues.

Nityānanda dāsa: How does one attain association with devotees?

Hari dāsa: I have already explained that. It is by past pious deeds. It is said (*Śrīmad-Bhāgavatam* 10.51.53): O my Lord! O infallible Supreme Person! When a person wandering throughout the universe becomes eligible for liberation from material existence, he gets an opportunity to associate with devotees. When he associates with devotees, his attraction for You is awakened. You are the Supreme Personality of Godhead, the highest goal of the supreme devotees and the Lord of the universe.

Nityānanda dāsa: If, in the association of devotes, a neophyte devotee worships the Deity of the Lord, can it be said that the neophyte devotee does not by that action also serve the devotees there?

Hari dāsa: By associating with devotees, one gradually attains faith in the Deity form of the Lord. However, one must worship the Supreme Personality of Godhead and also serve His devotees. As long as one does not have faith in both the Lord and His devotees, one will not attain true faith and one will not be qualified to engage in pure devotional service.

Nityānanda dāsa: Through what stages does a neophyte devotee pass as he makes spiritual advancement?

Hari dāsa: First, he has faith in the Deity, but he has not yet lost the desire for material things and non-devotional talk. Every day he worships the Deity. Devotees come to visit the temple where he worships the Deity. He honors the devotees as he would any visitors. The neophyte devotee sees the activities of these more advanced devotees. He hears them discussing the scriptures and the Vaiṣṇava philosophy. Thus, hearing and hearing and seeing and seeing, he develops respect for the good character of the more advanced devotees. Then, he himself gradually becomes purified. Gradually his interest in mental speculation and fruitive activities becomes less and less. Then, his heart becomes purified and the material desires in it are thrown far away. Hearing and hearing about Lord Hari's nature and activities, he becomes learned in the scriptures. Studying again and again the truth that Lord Hari is beyond the touch of the material modes of nature, Lord Hari's holy name is beyond the touch of the material modes of nature, and the devotional activities that begin with hearing and chanting the glories of Lord Hari are also beyond the touch of the material modes of nature, he gradually comes to understand the truth of his relationship with Lord Hari. When that understanding becomes perfect, he becomes an intermediate (*madhyama*) devotee of the Lord. Then, he spontaneously associates with and serves the devotees. Then he can understand that the devotees who have accepted a spiritual master are different from ordinary guests.

Nityānanda dāsa: Many neophyte devotees do not become advanced in this way. Why is that?

Hari dāsa: When his association with persons who hate devotional service is strong, he quickly loses the right to be a neophyte devotee. Then, his interest in mental speculation and fruitive actions becomes strong. Sometimes the neophyte devotee neither makes advancement nor falls away.

Nityānanda dāsa: When does that happen?

Hari dāsa: When the neophyte's association with devotees and persons who hate devotional service is of equal strength. Then it is seen that he neither advances, nor does he fall away.

Nityānanda dāsa: When does he definitely make advancement?

Hari dāsa: When his association with devotees is great and his association with persons who hate devotional service is small. Then, he makes swift advancement.

Nityānanda dāsa: What are the sins and virtues of the neophyte devotee?

Hari dāsa: In the beginning, a neophyte devotee may be much like the mental speculators (*jñānīs*) and fruitive workers (*karmīs*). However, as he makes advancement in devotional service, his sins and defects are thrown far away. Then, his desire to please the Supreme Personality of Godhead becomes strong.

Nityānanda dāsa: O master, I have understood the description of the neophyte devotees. Now, please describe to me the primary qualities of the intermediate (*madhyama*) devotees.

Hari dāsa: The primary qualities of the intermediate (*madhyama*) devotees are: 1. Unalloyed devotion to Lord Kṛṣṇa, 2. Friendship with persons who identify themselves as devotees, thinking, "Kṛṣṇa is my Lord," and visit holy places, 3. Mercy to the innocent persons who do not understand the truth, and 4. Neglect of persons who hate devotees. The primary activities of the intermediate devotees are these: 1. By understanding one's relationship with Lord Kṛṣṇa (*sambandha*) and 2. By engaging in devotional service (*abhidheya*) to Lord Kṛṣṇa, the intermediate devotee, 3. Attains the highest goal (*prayojana*), which is the perfection of love for Lord Kṛṣṇa. Without committing offenses, the intermediate devotee performs various kinds of devotional services in the association of other devotees, services that begin with the chanting of Lord Hari's holy name.

Nityānanda dāsa: What are the secondary qualities of an intermediate devotee?

Hari dāsa: The way an intermediate devotee lives his life is his secondary quality. He lives in such a way that he obeys Kṛṣṇa's will and serves Kṛṣṇa favorably.

Nityānanda dāsa: Is he not able to sin or commit offenses?

Hari dāsa: In the beginning, he may be a little prone to sin or offend but gradually, he throws these things far away. In the beginning, these faults may be present but in time, they become completely destroyed. They become like chickpeas crushed into powder. Thus an intermediate devotee's life is characterized by appropriate renunciation (*yukta-vairāgya*).

Nityānanda dāsa: Are philosophical speculation (*jñāna*), fruitive action (*karma*), and the desire for things outside the realm of devotional service not present even slightly in his life?

Hari dāsa: In the beginning, there may be the dim reflection of these things, but at the end, they are torn up by their roots. In the beginning, they may sometimes be visible, but in the course of time, they are never seen again.

Nityānanda dāsa: Do the intermediate devotees wish to continue living in the material world? If so, why?

Hari dāsa: They wish to continue living in the material world only so they may attain the perfect stage of pure devotional service. They do not wish to live in the material world for its own sake, nor do they not wish to attain liberation for its own sake.

Nityānanda dāsa: Why do they not wish for death? What happiness can they find in this dull and inert material body? By Lord Kṛṣṇa's mercy, will they not at once attain their original spiritual forms when they die?

Hari dāsa: They want whatever Kṛṣṇa wants. If Kṛṣṇa wishes that something happen, it will happen. They do not need to wish for anything independently.

Nityānanda dāsa: Now I understand the qualities of an intermediate (*madhyama*) devotee. What are the secondary qualities of an advanced (*uttama*) devotee?

Hari dāsa: His only secondary qualities are the actions he performs with his body, actions impelled by pure spiritual love (*prema*), free from the material modes (*nirguṇa*). Therefore, these actions cannot be seen as true secondary qualities.

Nityānanda dāsa: O master, a neophyte (*kaniṣṭha*) devotee does not renounce householder life, and an intermediate (*madhyama*) devotee may live either as a householder or a *sannyāsī*. Is it possible for an advanced (*uttama*) devotee to remain as a householder?

Hari dāsa: These conditions are present in all the stages of devotional service. It is not that simply by remaining as a householder or by accepting *sannyāsa* one becomes situated in a particular stage of advancement in devotional service. An advanced devotee may remain in householder life.

The residents of Vrajapura were all householders, yet they were all certainly advanced devotees. Many of Lord Mahāprabhu's personal associates were householders. They were also certainly advanced devotees. Rāmānanda Rāya is the first proof of that.

Nityānanda dāsa: O master, if an advanced devotee is a householder and an intermediate devotee is a *sannyāsī*, how should they act in regard to each other?

Hari dāsa: The less-advanced devotee should offer *daṇḍavat* obeisances to the more advanced devotee. This rule applies only to intermediate devotees. An advanced devotee is not very interested in things like offering obeisances. He sees the Supreme Lord present in the hearts of all living beings.

Nityānanda dāsa: Should many Vaiṣṇavas gather together to hold festivals and honor the Lord's *prasādam*?

Hari dāsa: Devotees often gather together. At these times, householders who are intermediate devotees like to offer *prasādam* to the other devotees. From the spiritual point of view, no one should object to this. However, it is not good to make a great pompous display of serving the Vaiṣṇavas. That is in the mode of passion. Otherwise, one should certainly offer *prasādam* to saintly Vaiṣṇavas. In that way, one honors the Vaiṣṇavas. If one wishes to serve the Vaiṣṇavas in this way, one should invite only pure Vaiṣṇavas.

Nityānanda dāsa: In my home place of Barāgachi, it is customary to honor the descendants of great Vaiṣṇavas. Householders who are neophyte devotees invite them to honor *prasādam*. Is this proper?

Hari dāsa: Are these descendants of great Vaiṣṇavas pure devotees?

Nityānanda dāsa: I don't see pure devotion in all of them. They say they are Vaiṣṇavas. Some wear the *kaupīna* of a *sannyāsī*.

Hari dāsa: How this custom started I cannot say. It is not right. This happens because a neophyte devotee does not have the power to understand who is truly an advanced Vaiṣṇava.

Nityānanda dāsa: Is it right to give special honor to the descendant of a great Vaiṣṇava?

Hari dāsa: A Vaiṣṇava should be honored. If the descendant of a great Vaiṣṇava is himself a pure Vaiṣṇava, then certainly he should be honored according to the level of his own advancement in devotional service.

Nityānanda dāsa: And, if the descendant of a great Vaiṣṇava is himself only an ordinary man?

Hari dāsa: Then, he should be counted among the ordinary men. He should not be honored or counted among the Vaiṣṇavas. Still, one should always remember Śrī Mahāprabhu's teaching (*Śikṣāṣṭaka* 3): One who thinks himself lower than the grass, who is more tolerant than a tree, and who does not expect personal honor but is always prepared to give all respects to others, can very easily always chant the holy name of the Lord.

This means that one should be humble and give appropriate honor to all other people. To a Vaiṣṇava, one should give the honor proper for a Vaiṣṇava. To one who is not a Vaiṣṇava, one should give the honor that one should give to every human being. A person who does not honor others is not qualified to chant the holy names of Lord Hari.

Nityānanda dāsa: What kind of humility is appropriate?

Hari dāsa: One should not proudly think, "I am a great *brāhmaṇa*," "I am wealthy," "I am a great scholar," "I am a great Vaiṣṇava, or" "I am a great *sannyāsī*." One should not aspire to be honored by others. One should not think, "I should be honored, for I am exalted in many ways." Instead, one should think, "I am very poor and fallen. I am lower than a blade of grass."

Nityānanda dāsa: From this, I can understand that without being humble and merciful, one cannot be a Vaiṣṇava.

Hari dāsa: That is true.

Nityānanda dāsa: Does the goddess of devotion (Bhakti-devī) require humbleness and mercy from the devotees?

Hari dāsa: Devotional service is independent. Devotional service is beautiful by itself. It does not need to be decorated by good qualities. Those two virtues, humility and mercy, are not separate from devotional service. They are spontaneously included with devotional service. A person who has devotion to the Lord is naturally humble. He naturally thinks, "I am a servant of Lord Kṛṣṇa. I am poverty-stricken. I do not have anything. Kṛṣṇa is my only treasure, my everything, the be-all and end-all of my life." When a person is situated in devotional service, his heart melts with love for Kṛṣṇa. Because such a person sees all other living beings as servants of Kṛṣṇa, his heart also melts with love for them. Thus, he has mercy on them. In this way, mercy is naturally included within devotional service. Forgiveness is situated between mercy and humility. In this way, one thinks, "I am poor and fallen, how can I be qualified to punish others?" When this thought joins with mercy, forgiveness is born. In this way, forgiveness is also naturally included within devotional service. Kṛṣṇa is eternal and real (*satya*), the individual spirit soul is eternal and real, the individual spirit soul's service to Lord Kṛṣṇa is also eternal and real, and the individual soul's temporary sojourn in the material world is also real. In this way, the relationship between the individual soul and Kṛṣṇa, a relationship that is manifested as devotional service, is eternal and real. Therefore, eternal spiritual reality, humility, mercy, and forgiveness are four things naturally included in devotional service.

Nityānanda dāsa: How should a Vaiṣṇava relate to persons of other religions?

Haridāsa: *Śrīmad-Bhāgavatam* (1.2.26) gives this explanation: Those who are serious about liberation are certainly non-envious, and they respect all. Yet they reject the horrible and ghastly forms of the demigods and worship only the all-blissful forms of Lord Viṣṇu and His plenary portions.

The Vaiṣṇava religion is the only religion. There is no other religion but that. The other religions that are present in this world are either steps of the staircase leading to the Vaiṣṇava religion, or else perverted reflections of the Vaiṣṇava religion. When other religions are steps leading to the Vaiṣṇava religion, these religions should be appropriately honored. When other religions are perverted reflections of the Vaiṣṇava religion, one should ignore them, and without malice or envy, place his thoughts on the truths of devotional service. In this way, one should avoid attacking other spiritual paths. When his auspicious day comes, the follower of another religion will naturally become a Vaiṣṇava. Of this there is no doubt.

Nityānanda dāsa: Then, one should not preach the Vaiṣṇava religion?

Hari dāsa: One should preach in every way possible. Our Lord Mahāprabhu has given us all the duty to preach the Vaiṣṇava religion. He said (*Śrī Caitanya-*

caritāmṛta, Adi-lila 7.92 and 9.36): My dear child, continue dancing, chanting, and performing *sankīrtana* in association with devotees. Furthermore, go out and preach the value of chanting Kṛṣṇa-nama, for by this process, you will be able to deliver all fallen souls. Therefore I order every man within this universe to accept this Kṛṣṇa consciousness movement and distribute it everywhere.

However, keep this in mind: Unworthy persons must first be made worthy before you give them many instructions about the holy name. In certain situations, one should remain silent. Do not give elaborate explanations in situations where your words become an obstacle to preaching.

Overwhelmed with love by hearing saintly Haridāsa Bābājī's sweet words, Nityānanda dāsa began to roll about on the ground in ecstasy. Then, all the assembled Vaiṣṇavas chanted the holy names of Lord Hari. They all offered *daṇḍavat* obeisances to the saintly *bābājī*. Then, that day's meeting in the secluded grove came to an end, and everyone returned to his own place.

Chapter Nine

Eternal religion and modern science-civilization.

Living among the Vaiṣṇavas in Godruma for three or four years, Lāhirī Mahāśaya became pure in heart. He always chanted the holy names of Lord Hari. He wore simple clothing. He had neither sandals nor wooden slippers. His pride of caste was now thrown far away. Whenever he saw a Vaiṣṇava, he would at once offer *daṇḍavat* obeisances and insist on taking the dust of that Vaiṣṇava's feet. He would search for pure Vaiṣṇavas and accept the remnants of their meals. Sometimes, his sons would visit. Understanding his situation, they would not propose that he return home. Everyone could see that Lāhirī Mahāśaya was a Vaiṣṇava *bābājī*. Following the conclusion accepted by the Vaiṣṇavas of Śrī Godruma, he understood that renunciation was needed within the heart, and the external trappings of renunciation were not important. Following the example of Śrīla Sanātana Gosvāmī, he would take one piece of cloth and divide it into four. Those would be his garments. He still wore a sacred thread around his neck. Sometimes, his sons would try to give him money. Saying, "I do not accept money from materialists," he would not take it. Once, Candraśekhara tried to give him a hundred coins to have a great festival for the Vaiṣṇavas. Remembering the example of Raghunātha dāsa Gosvāmī, Lāhirī Mahāśaya refused the money.

One day, the *parāmahāṁsa bābājī* said, "O Lāhirī Mahāśaya, you never act in any way improper for a Vaiṣṇava. Though I am the *sannyāsī*, you teach me what true renunciation is. If you accept a Vaiṣṇava name from me, then everything will be complete."

Lāhirī Mahāśaya replied, "You are my *parama-guru*. Whatever you wish, that will be done."

The saintly *bābājī* said, "You come from Śāntipura. Therefore, I will call you Advaita dāsa."

Offering *daṇḍavat* obeisances, Lāhirī Mahāśaya accepted the merciful gift of his new name. From that day forward, everyone called him Advaita dāsa, and the cottage where he performed devotional service they called Advaita-kuṭīra.

Advaita dāsa had a childhood friend named Digambara Caṭṭopādhyāya. Holding various high posts in the Mohammedan government, he had become wealthy. Attaining old age, he retired from his government post, returned to his home town of Kālnā, and tried to find Kālidāsa Lāhirī. He heard that Kālidāsa Lāhirī had gone to Śrī Godruma, accepted the name Advaita dāsa, and was always chanting the holy names of Lord Hari.

Digambara Caṭṭopādhyāya was a fanatical devotee of Goddess Durgā. His response to hearing a Vaiṣṇava's name was to cover his ears with his hands. Hearing that his old friend had become fallen in that way, he declared, "O Vāmana dāsa, arrange for a boat. I will go to Navadvīpa and rescue my unfortunate old friend, Kālidāsa. Quickly arranging for the boat, Vāmana dāsa returned and informed his master. Digambara Caṭṭopādhyāya was very intelligent. He was learned in the *Tantras*, and he was also learned in the ways of the Mohammedans. Arguing in Persian and Arabic, he could even defeat the best Mohammedan scholars. Arguing about the *Tantras*, he made the best *brāhmaṇa* scholars speechless. His name was well known in Delhi, Lucknow, and other places. In his leisure time, he had written a book titled *Tantra-sangraha* (An anthology from the *Tantras*). He was learned in many subjects and could discourse on many scripture passages.

Proudly grasping his *Tantra-sangraha*, Digambara stepped into the boat. After a six hour journey, the boat landed at Śrī Godruma. Staying in the boat, he sent an intelligent messenger to Śrī Advaita dāsa.

Śrī Advaita dāsa was sitting in his cottage and chanting the holy names of Lord Hari. Digambara Caṭṭopādhyāya's messenger approached and bowed down. Advaita dāsa asked him, "Who are you, and why have you come?"

The messenger replied, "I am sent by Śrī Digambara Caṭṭopādhyāya. He asks this question: 'O Kālidāsa, do you remember me, or have you forgotten?'"

Śrī Advaita dāsa replied, "Digambara? Where? My childhood friend! Do I have the power to forget him? Has he taken shelter of the Vaiṣṇava religion?"

The messenger said, "He is sitting in a boat by the landing place. I cannot say whether he has become a Vaiṣṇava."

Advaita dāsa said, "Why does he stay at the landing place? Why does he not come to my cottage?"

Hearing this, the messenger left. After an hour, Digambara Caṭṭopādhyāya appeared at Advaita-kuṭīra, with three or four gentlemen. Digambara always was generous at heart. When he saw his old friend, his heart became filled with joy. Singing some verses he himself had written, he embraced Advaita dāsa.

He sang: O Mother Kali, who in the three worlds knows all about Your transcendental pastimes? Sometimes You are a man, sometimes a woman, and sometimes a ferocious warrior. You become Brahmā and create the world. You become Śiva and destroy it. You become all-pervading Viṣṇu and protect everyone. You become Kṛṣṇa and play the flute in Vṛndāvana forest. You become Gaura and make all of Navadvīpa wild with the chanting of the holy names.

Advaita dāsa said, "My brother, come in. Come in."

Digambara sat on a leaf-seat. Tears of love glistened in his eyes. He said, "Dear brother Kālidāsa, where shall I go? Now you are a *sannyāsī* and you have given up duties and demigods. How hopeful I was when I first came from Punjab. Our boyhood friends: Pesa, Pagla, Khenda, Girisa, Ise Pagla, Dhana Māyāra, Kele Chutor, and Kanti Bhattacarji—all have died. Only you and I remain. I thought some days I would cross the Ganges and visit you at Śāntipura, and other days, I thought you would cross the Ganges and visit me at Ambikā. In the few days that remain for us, we would sing together and study the *Tantras* together. Alas, bad luck has struck my head. You have become a bullheaded fool, useless in this world and the next. Look at yourself. Tell me: How has this happened to You?"

Advaita dāsa could see that this person was very bad company. He began to think how he could escape the hands of his childhood friend. He said, "Brother Digambara, do you remember how one day, when we were playing *daṇḍaguli*, we gradually came to that old tamarind tree?"

Digambara: Yes, yes. I remember. That was near Gauridāsa Paṇḍita's house. The tamarind tree where Gaura- Nitāi used to sit.

Advaita: As we were playing, you said, "Don't touch that tamarind tree! Aunt Śacī's son used to sit here. If we touch this tree, we will become *sannyāsīs*."

Digambara: I remember. I could see that you liked the Vaiṣṇavas. I said, "You will fall into Gaurāṅga's trap."

Advaita: Brother, for a long time, I was like that. I was always just about to fall into that trap. Now I have fallen in.

Digambara: Catch hold of my hand and come out. It is not good to stay in a trap.

Advaita: Brother, I am very happy in this trap. I pray that I shall stay here forever. Just once, you should touch this trap and see what it is like.

Digambara: I have seen. In the beginning, it is happiness. But in the end, it is a hoax.

Advaita: Do you think the trap where you live will bring you happiness at the end? My mind says that it will not.

Digambara: Let us see. We are servants of Goddess Mahāvidya. In this life, we have happiness, and in the next life, we also have happiness. You think that you are happy, but I don't see that you are happy. In the end, there will be no end to your sufferings. Why does someone become a Vaiṣṇava? I cannot say. Look, we enjoy eating fish and meat and other things. We are happy. We are more civilized than you. We enjoy all the good things modern science provides. You have renounced all these good things. And in the end, for you, there will be no escape.

Advaita: Why, brother, will there be no escape for me?

Digambara: If Mother Nistāriṇī becomes averse, then even Brahmā, Viṣṇu, and Śiva cannot escape. Mother Nistāriṇī is the primordial power. She gives birth to Brahmā, Viṣṇu, and Śiva. By her power, she protects them. When the great mother wills, the great pot of the material universe will again enter her womb. Have you worshipped the mother, so she will have mercy on you?

Advaita: Is Mother Nistāriṇī conscious, or is she unconscious matter?

Digambara: She is consciousness personified. All her desires are at once fulfilled. It is by her wish that spirit was created.

Advaita: What is spirit, and what is matter.

Digambara: Vaiṣṇavas only worship. They know nothing of philosophy. Spirit and matter are like the two halves of a chick-pea. Unhusk it, and there are two halves. Leave the husk untouched, and there is one chick-pea. When consciousness and unconsciousness join and become one—that is called Brahman.

Advaita: Is your mother female or male?

Digambara: Sometimes she is male and sometimes female.

Advaita: Spirit and matter are like the two halves of a chick-pea. Which is the mother and which is the father?

Digambara: You are eager to know the truth? We know the truth very well. The truth is that matter is mother and spirit is father.

Advaita: Who are you?

Digambara: When I am bound by ropes of illusion, I am an individual soul. When those ropes are untied, I am Lord Sadā-ṣiva.

Advaita: You are spirit? You are not matter?"

Digambara: I am spirit. Mother is matter. When I am bound by illusion, she is my mother. When I am free of illusion, she is my wife.

Advaita: Now the truth is out! Now doubt is gone. Where did you get these truths?

Digambara: Brother, you are always saying, "Vaiṣṇava! Vaiṣṇava!" I am not like that. I have associated with many *sannyāsīs*, *brahmācārīs*, and *tantrik* saints. I have studied the *Tantras* day and night. That is how I have attained this knowledge. If you like, I can teach it to you.

Advaita: (thinking to himself) How horrible! How unfortunate! (aloud) Very good. Please explain one thing to me. What is civilization, and what is modern science?

Digambara: 1. To speak in such a way that pleases respectable people, 2. To wear clothing that pleases them, and 3. To eat food they like, to do things like them, and not to do anything to displease them. You do not do any of these three!

Advaita: How is that?

Digambara: You do not associate with others. You are very unsocial. The Vaiṣṇavas have never learned the art of flattering others with sweet words. When they see someone, they always tell him to chant the name of Hari. Can't they say something else? When people see your clothing, they refrain from inviting you to visit them. You wear a stupid tuft of hair on the top of your head and beads around your neck, and your own garment is a loin cloth! You only eat vegetables and roots! You are not civilized, even slightly.

Advaita: (thinking to himself) If I quarrel with him, he will go away. That would be good for me. (aloud) Does this kind of civilization make one's next life auspicious?

Digambara: It does not make the next life auspicious. If there is no civilization, how will society become uplifted? First society must be uplifted. When it is uplifted, then people may try to improve the next life.

Advaita: Brother, if you do not become angry, I could say something.

Digambara: You are my boyhood friend. I would give up my life for your sake. Why would I not peacefully tolerate a single statement of yours? We are civilized men. Even if we are angry, sweet words will stay on our mouths. The more we hide our true feelings, the more civilized we become.

Advaita: Human life is for only a few days. Still, it contains many troubles. In this very short life, one should sincerely worship Lord Hari. The civilization you talk about is only a way to cheat the soul. Therefore, I say that this civilization is only another word for cheating. When men walk on the path of truth, they are simple and honest. When men's actions are a collection of lies, their hearts are full of cunning, their deeds are sins, and their words are empty flattery. That is your civilization. True civilization is not like that. In true civilization, men are honest and sincere. Nowadays, people merely hide the wickedness in their hearts, and that hiding they call civilization. The true meaning of civilization is "honesty and goodness." What you call civilization is only cheating and wickedness.

Civilization that is sinless is found only among the Vaiṣṇavas. So-called civilization that is filled with sins is liked only by those who are not Vaiṣṇavas. The civilization you describe has nothing to do with the soul's eternal nature. If wearing fashionable clothes that please others is the true mark of civilization, then prostitutes are the most civilized. The purpose of clothing is only to cover the body. Clothing should be neat and clean, and free from unclean odors and other faults. Food should be pure and nutritious. There is nothing wrong with food like that. You think only that food should be palatable. You don't consider whether it is pure or not. Liquor and meat are naturally impure and unholy. A civilization that lives by enjoying them is only a collection of sins. What you call modern civilization is the civilization of Kali-yuga.

Digambara: Have you forgotten the very civilized society of the Muslim emperors? You should see how the people dress fashionably and speak politely in the Muslim emperor's court!

Advaita: That is only material politeness. What does a man lose if he is unaware of this exaggerated politeness? Brother, you spent too many days working for the Muslims. That is why you defend the Muslim ways. True civilization is when men are free from sins. Civilization that encourages sin is the civilization of Kali-yuga. That kind of civilization is only a pathetic joke.

Digambara: Look, the modern idea is humanism. Those who don't accept modern civilization aren't considered human. Fashionable clothing that makes women attractive and masks their imperfections are very popular nowadays.

Advaita: You should consider whether this is good or bad. I see that the people who advance this modern civilization are only clever opportunists. Partly because they are superstitious and partly because they like to conceal their own flaws, these people like this dishonest civilization. Will a wise man be happy in such a civilization? This civilization of rogues can be kept together only by meaningless words and by brute force.

Digambara: Some say that the people of the world are gradually becoming more educated. As they become more educated, they will become more civilized, and as the people become more civilized, the earth will gradually become Svargaloka.

Advaita: Those philosophers are smoking *ganja*. Anyone who believes those stories is rich in blind faith. Those who don't believe those stories are fortunate. There two kinds of knowledge: 1. spiritual, and 2. material. I don't think spiritual knowledge is increasing. In many places, spiritual knowledge is collapsing. I think it is material knowledge that is increasing. Does material knowledge touch the soul eternally? When material knowledge increases, then the heart becomes attracted to material things and has contempt for the spiritual truth. I agree that material knowledge is increasing, but from that knowledge comes a dishonest civilization. That civilization brings great misfortune to the soul.

Digambara: Why misfortune?

Advaita: As I said before, human life is very short. The soul is like a traveler briefly staying at an inn. He should use this short time to attain spiritual perfection. If the travelers are concerned only with how to be most comfortable at the inn, the time they should be spending on planning their journey is lost. As material knowledge increases, the time spent on spiritual things will decrease. I think that material knowledge should be accepted only as far as is needed in ordinary affairs. There is no need for more material knowledge or its lady friend, material civilization. For how many days will the benefits of this world last?

Digambara: I have fallen into the company of a fanatic *sannyāsī*. Is society not important?

Advaita: Different kinds of society bring different results. If one associates with Vaiṣṇavas, then there is a good result. If one associates with materialists, then the results are not good for the soul. Let us stop talking of this. What is material science?

Digambara: Many kinds of material sciences are described in the *Tantras*. Whatever knowledge, skill, and beauty are present in the material world are all described in material science. Military science, medicine, music, and astronomy are all examples of material sciences. The material nature is the first power (again I describe the spiritual truth!). She gave birth to the material world. From her it is manifested. By her power it is filled with wonderful variety. One by one, all forms come from her. One by one, all kinds of knowledge come from her. When a person understands this, Mother Nistāriṇī frees him from sin and he becomes liberated. The Vaiṣṇavas will not seek out Mother Nistāriṇī. However, we attain liberation by understanding these truths. Look, by the careful study of material knowledge, Plato, Aristotle, Socrates, the famous Hakim, and many other great souls in the Yavana countries have written many, many books.

Advaita: You said that the Vaiṣṇavas are not interested in science. That is not true. Why not? The Vaiṣṇavas are interested in the science of pure knowledge, which is described in these words of Śrīmad-Bhāgavatam's four nutshell verses (2.9.30): The Supreme Personality of Godhead said: Knowledge about Me as described in the scriptures is very confidential, and it has to be realized in conjunction with devotional service. The necessary paraphernalia for that process is being explained by Me. You may take it up carefully.

Pleased by Brahmā's devotional service, the Supreme Personality of Godhead gave him this instruction even before the material world was created. In this way, the Lord taught him the pure Vaiṣṇava religion. The Lord said, "O

Brahmā, knowledge about Me as described in the scriptures is very confidential, and it has to be realized in conjunction with devotional service. The necessary paraphernalia for that process is being explained by Me. You may take it up carefully."

O Digambara, there are two kinds of knowledge: 1. spiritual knowledge, and 2. material knowledge. Because it is attained through the material senses, material knowledge is very impure. Neither is it needed for spiritual advancement. It is needed only for the conditioned soul's life in the material world. Spiritual knowledge is called *śuddha-jñāna* (pure knowledge). That eternal knowledge is the foundation stone of the Vaiṣṇavas' temple of devotional service. Spiritual knowledge and material knowledge are very different. They are opposites.

You call material knowledge "science," but it is not science at all. You call medical knowledge and other kinds of material knowledge science, but it is spiritual knowledge, which is different from material knowledge, that should be called science. Knowledge and science are synonyms. Direct perception of the spiritual truth is called knowledge. When it eclipses material knowledge, pure spiritual knowledge is called science. Thus, these two are actually the same thing, called either knowledge or science in different circumstances. You call material knowledge science. The Vaiṣṇavas call the proper use of material knowledge science. Military skill, medicine, astronomy, chemistry, and all other kinds of material knowledge have no eternal relation to the soul. Therefore, they have no bearing at all on the soul's eternal activities and eternal duties. The Vaiṣṇavas do not criticize the materialists who perform Vedic rituals (*karma-kanda*) for material elevation. Why not? Indirectly, their attempts for material elevation help the spiritual advancement of the Vaiṣṇavas. You may call material knowledge material science. What is wrong with that? It is foolish to squabble over names.

Digambara: Well, if there were no progress in material knowledge, it would not be so easy for you to pass your life in devotional service. Therefore, you also should strive for material progress.

Advaita: Different people, with different desires, try in different ways, and the Supreme Controller gives each person the fruits of his actions.

Digambara: Why do people have different desires?

Advaita: Desires are created by past *karma*. One whose material desires are strong becomes learned in material things and expert in material work. What is produced in this way may help the Vaiṣṇavas in their service to Lord Kṛṣṇa. However, the Vaiṣṇavas themselves need not become expert in these different skills. Look, a carpenter may make a cart, and a householder Vaiṣṇava may use that cart to carry the Deity of the Lord. Bees may gather honey, and the devotees of the Lord may take the honey and employ it in the Lord's service. Not everyone in this world is interested in spiritual advancement. From their different desires, different kinds of work are manifested. Men are of different kinds, some exalted and others lowly. Those whose desires are lowly may work in different ways, and those whose desires are lofty may use the result of that work for good purposes. Pushed by these differences, the circle of the world turns. Materialistic men work in different ways, and what they produce may be helpful to the spiritualists, the Vaiṣṇavas. The materialists do not understand how they are helping the Vaiṣṇavas. Still, bewildered by Lord Viṣṇu's *māyā* potency, they act in that way. Thus, the entire world unknowingly serves the Vaiṣṇavas.

Digambara: What is the illusory potency of Lord Viṣṇu you mentioned?

Advaita: In the *Caṇḍī-mahātmya* of the *Markandeya Purāṇa* it is said: The entire world is bewildered by Lord Hari's *māyā* potency.

These words describe Lord Viṣṇu's *māyā* potency.

Digambara: Then, who is the goddess I know as Mother Nistāriṇī?

Advaita: She is Lord Viṣṇu's *māyā* potency.

Digambara: (opening his book about the *Tantras*) Look! Here it says, "My Mother is the form of spiritual consciousness. Her desires are at once fulfilled. She is beyond the touch of the three modes, but still She manifests the three modes."

Your *māyā* potency of Lord Viṣṇu is not beyond the three modes. How can you say that your *māyā* potency of Lord Viṣṇu is the same as my Mother? When I see how you Vaiṣṇavas are such closed-minded fanatics, it does not make me happy at all.

Advaita: Brother Digambara, please don't be angry. After so many days, you have seen me again. I want to make you happy. If I say, '"the *māyā* potency of Lord Viṣṇu," how have I become small-minded? Lord Viṣṇu is the all-knowing Supreme Personality of Godhead. All that exists is His potency. The word "potency" does not mean a substance. Rather, it means the quality that a substance possesses. Therefore, the statement that a potency is the root of all existence goes counter to the truth. A potency cannot exist apart from its substance. An original substance with a spiritual form must first be accepted. After all, the commentary on *Vedānta-sūtra* declares: The potency and the possessor of the potency are not different.

The meaning, then, is that the potency does not exist apart from its substance. The only true substance is the Supreme Personality of Godhead, the master of all potencies. The nature of the potency is either to be a quality of the Supreme Lord, or submissive to His will. When it is said that the potency has pure consciousness—that means that because the potency and the master of potencies are not different, therefore, like the master of potencies, the potency also has a form of spiritual consciousness, has desires that are at once fulfilled, and is beyond the touch of the three modes. It is not a mistake to say these things. Will and consciousness are qualities of the Supreme Personality of Godhead. By itself, the potency does not possess will but rather, it carries out the will of the Supreme.

For example, you have power, and by Your will, your potencies act. If you say that the power acted, then that means that the possessor of the power was actually behind the action. To say that the power acted is only to use a figure of speech. In truth, the Supreme Personality of Godhead has only one potency. When she performs spiritual actions, she is called the spiritual potency, and when she performs material actions, she is called the material potency, or *māyā*.

The *Vedas* (*Śvetāśvatara Upaniṣad* 6.8) explain: The potency of the Supreme is manifested in many different ways.

The potency that manifests the three modes is the material potency. She creates and destroys the material universes. Those are her duties. In the *Purāṇas* and *Tantras*, this potency is called by many names, such as *viṣṇu-māyā*, *mahā-māyā*, and *māyā*. She is also called, "the mother of Brahmā, Viṣṇu and Śiva," "the killer of Sumbha and Nisumbha," and other like names that describe her different activities. As long as he remains deeply enmeshed in material consciousness, the soul is under her power. When he attains pure spiritual knowledge, the soul can understand the nature of his original spiritual form. Then he is freed from the ropes of *māyā*. Then, he is under the power of the spiritual potency. Then he becomes happy.

Digambara: Are you under the power of one of these potencies, or are you not?

Advaita: Yes. We are also a potency. We are *jīva-śakti*, individual souls. When we become free from the ropes of the *māyā* potency, we are in the power of the spiritual potency.

Digambara: Then you are also a *śakta*, a worshipper of the potency.

Advaita: Yes. The Vaiṣṇavas are naturally *śaktas*. We are the servants of Śrī Rādhika, who is the spiritual potency. Under Her patronage, we worship and serve Lord Kṛṣṇa. Who is more of a *śakta* than us? I don't see any difference between the *śaktas* and the Vaiṣṇavas. Those who do not take shelter of the spiritual potency, but only take shelter of the material potency, *māyā*, may be *śaktas*, but they are not Vaiṣṇavas. They are materialists.

In the *Nārada-pañcarātra*, Goddess Durgā explains: O Kṛṣṇa, I am Rādhā, who stays on Your chest during the *rasa* dance in Vṛndāvana forest.

Thus, from Durgā-devī's words, we can understand that the Lord does not have two potencies. There is only one potency, who manifests Herself as the spiritual potency, Rādhika, and the material potency, *viṣṇu-māyā*. When the potency is free from the material modes, she is called the spiritual potency, and when she is within the sphere of the material modes, she is called the material potency.

Digambara: You said that you yourself are a potency, the *jīva-śakti*. What potency is that?

Advaita: In *Bhagavad-gītā* (7.4-5), the Supreme Personality of Godhead explains: Earth, water, fire, air, ether, mind, intelligence, and false ego—altogether these eight comprise My separated material energies. Besides this inferior energy, O mighty-armed Arjuna, there is a superior energy of Mine, which are all living entities who are struggling with material nature and are sustaining the universe.

Digambara, do you know the glory of *Bhagavad-gītā*? It is the best of all scriptures. It solves all the problems of life. It explains that the individual souls are superior to dull matter, and that they are one of the potencies of the Lord. The wise call the individual souls *taṭasthā-śakti* (marginal potency). The marginal potency is superior to dull matter and inferior to the Lord's *cit-śakti* (internal potency). Therefore, the individual spirit souls are one of the potencies of the Lord.

Digambara: Kālidāsa, have you seen this *Bhagavad-gītā*?

Advaita: Yes. I have read that book.

Digambara: What does it teach?

Advaita: Brother Digambara, men praise molasses only as long as they have not tasted sugar candy.

Digambara: My brother, you are a fanatic. *Devī-bhagavata* and *Devī-gītā* are honored by everyone. You Vaiṣṇavas alone have not heard of them.

Advaita: My brother, have you read *Devī-gītā*?

Digambara: No. Why should I lie? I tried to make a manuscript copy of it, but I was not able.

Advaita: How can I say that a particular book, which I have not read, is good or bad? Am I the fanatic, or are you?

Digambara: My brother, I am always afraid of you. You were always very talkative. As a Vaiṣṇava, you are even more talkative. Whatever I say, you refute.

Advaita: I am a fool. But I can see that there is no pure religion but the Vaiṣṇava religion. For a long time, you held a grudge against the Vaiṣṇavas. That is why you could not see that path that leads to your own auspiciousness.

Digambara: (a little angry) Is it? I do so much worship and devotion, and you say I cannot see the path to my own good! Have I been walking the wrong path all along? Look! Here is the *Tantra-sangraha*! How I labored on it! Now that you are a Vaiṣṇava, you like to blaspheme modern science and modern civilization! What can I do to convince you? Go to civilized people and see whether they praise you or me!

Advaita: (thinks to himself) How good it will be when this very bad company runs away! (aloud) Very well! Brother, when you die, you will see how much benefit modern science and modern civilization have given you!

Digambara: Kālidāsa, you are being foolish. Is there anything after death? As long as you stay in this world, try to become famous among civilized men, and try to enjoy the five material pleasures. Enjoy. At the time of death, Mother Nistāriṇī will take you to a good place. She will protect you. Death will come at its own time. Why should you suffer before then? When you die, and the ingredients of your body mingle with the other ingredients of the world, where will you be? This world is an illusion. It is *māyā*, *yogamāyā*, and *mahā-māyā*. It is she who gives you pleasure here, and it is she who will give you liberation after death. Nothing exists but the potency. From the potency you have come. Into the potency you will enter at the end. Serve the potency! Just see the power in the knowledge she gives! Try to increase your own spiritual power! At the end, you will see that there is nothing but the spiritual potency!

What *ganja* did you smoke to dream up the fantastic story that an all-knowing personal God exists? Believing that story, you attained only suffering. In the next life, what benefit will you earn that I will not also get? I do not know. What is the use of believing in a personal God? Serve the potency! You will merge into the potency. In her, you will rest forever.

Advaita: My brother, you are very attached to the material potency. If an all-knowing personal God exists, what will be your fate after death? What is happiness? Happiness is peace of mind. Renouncing material pleasures, I have found peace and happiness inside my heart. If something good exists after death, I will attain it. You are not peaceful and happy. The more you enjoy, the more your thirst for evermore pleasure increases. You have never known real happiness. Again and again, you call out, "Pleasure! Pleasure!" One day, you will become plunged into an ocean of sufferings.

Digambara: Whatever will be, will be. Why do you shun the company of good people?

Advaita: I do not shun the company of good people. I already have their company. I only shun the wicked.

Digambara: Who are these wicked?

Advaita: Please don't become angry when you hear. I say this (*Śrīmad-Bhāgavatam* 4.30.33): Dear Lord, as long as we have to remain within this material world due to our material contamination and wander from one type of body to another and from one planet to another, we pray that we may associate with those who are engaged in discussing Your pastimes. We pray for this benediction, life after life, in different bodily forms and on different planets.

Again, in the Seventh Canto it is said: One should never associate with materialists and non-devotees. By their association, all is lost. By their association, one falls into the lower worlds.

In the *Kātyāyana-saṁhitā* it is said: Even if one is forced to live within a cage of iron, or in the midst of a blazing fire, he should accept this position rather than live with non-devotees, who are through and through against the supremacy of the Lord.

In the Third Canto, it is said (*Śrīmad-Bhāgavatam* 3.31.33-34): (By associating with unrighteous people, a person) becomes devoid of truthfulness, cleanliness, mercy, gravity, spiritual intelligence, shyness, austerity, fame, forgiveness, control of the mind, control of the senses, fortune, and all such opportunities. One should not associate with a coarse fool who is bereft of knowledge and self-realization, and who is no more than a dancing dog in the hands of a woman.

In the *Garuḍa Purāṇa* it is said: Even though one may have gone to the other side of all the *Vedas*, and even though one is well-versed in all the revealed scriptures, if one is not a devotee of the Supreme Lord, he must be considered the lowest of mankind.

In *Śrīmad-Bhāgavatam* (6.1.18) it is said: My dear king, as a pot containing liquor cannot be purified even if washed in the waters of many rivers, non-devotees cannot be purified by processes of atonement, even if they perform them very well.

In the *Skanda Purāṇa* it is said: A person who attacks, criticizes, or hates the Vaiṣṇavas, or who becomes angry with them, does not respectfully greet them, or is not pleased to see them, finds himself in the six hells.

Digambara, association with wicked people will never bring one any good. What will one gain by associating with them?

Digambara: What a fine fellow I have come to talk with! He thinks we are all wicked people! You stay with your pure Vaiṣṇavas! I am going home.

Advaita: (thinking to himself) It is almost done. Now I had best speak very sweetly to him. (aloud) Ah, now you must go home. You are my boyhood friend. I do not wish to see you go. If you are kind, then please stay. Stay for some time, take *prasādam*, and then go.

Digambara: Kālidāsa, you know very well that I eat only *haviṣya*, and I already had some *haviṣya* before I came here. I am glad to see you. I will come again if I find the time. I can't stay the night because I must follow the spiritual practices my guru gave me. For today, brother, I must go.

Advaita: Let us go then. I will walk with you to the boat.

Digambara: No. No. You do your own business. I have some friends with me.

After speaking these words, Digambara burst into a song glorifying Goddess Durgā and left. Advaita dāsa returned to his cottage and, without encountering any more interruptions, chanted the holy names of Lord Hari.

Chapter Ten

Eternal religion
and
history.

Jaiva-dharma

A doubt arose in the mind of Śrī Harihara Bhaṭṭācārya, a teacher who lived in Agradvīpa. He discussed it with some people, but his doubt would not go away. It troubled his mind more and more. One day, when he was in the village of Arkatila, he asked Śrī Caturbhuja Nyāyaratna, "O saintly Bhaṭṭācārya, please tell me: How old is the Vaiṣṇava religion?"

Harihara Bhaṭṭācārya is an initiated Vaiṣṇava and he worships Lord Kṛṣṇa in his home. Nyāyaratna Mahāśaya has pursued twenty years of laborious study. He was not interested in any religion. He did not like talking about religion. Only when Goddess Durgā was worshipped would he show a slight religious sentiment. Harihara's question made him think, "This Harihara must be a supporter of Vaiṣṇavism. He could get me in some trouble. It is best to keep trouble away."

Thinking in this way, Nyāyaratna Mahāśaya said, "What kind of question is this today? You have read many books. You even read the *Muktipāda*. Look, in the whole of *nyāya-śāstra*, there is no mention of the Vaiṣṇava religion. Why do you annoy me with this question?"

Harihara said, "O Bhaṭṭācārya Mahāśaya, I come from a Vaiṣṇava family and I am an initiated Vaiṣṇava. I never had any doubts about the Vaiṣṇava religion. You know Tarka-Cuḍāmaṇi of Vikramapura. Wishing to uproot the Vaiṣṇava religion, he preaches against it in many places in this country, and others also. In this way, he has earned a lot of money. In a gathering of mostly Durgā worshipers, he said the Vaiṣṇava religion is modern in its origins and has no substance or reality. He said only low-class people call themselves Vaiṣṇavas and upper class people have no respect for the Vaiṣṇava religion. When I heard this *paṇḍita's* conclusion, at first I was pained at heart, but then, as I thought it over, I could see that before Prabhu Caitanyadeva there was no Vaiṣṇavism in Bengal. At that time, almost everyone performed worship by chanting Durgā *mantras*. Some few of us worshiped by chanting Vaiṣṇava *mantras*, but all of those Vaiṣṇavas wanted in the end to attain impersonal liberation and become Brahman. All those Vaisvas were *pañcopāsakas*. However, after Prabhu Caitanyadeva, Vaiṣṇavism assumed a new form. Now, Vaiṣṇavas cannot bear to hear the words *mukti* and Brahman. What is their understanding of devotional service? I do not have the power to say. There is a saying: "The followers of a one-eyed guru will be led astray." I see these Vaiṣṇavas are like that. My question is: "Did this kind of Vaiṣṇavism exist before, or was it only invented after the time of Caitanyadeva?"

Nyāyaratna Mahāśaya could see that Harihara's mentality was unusual. In other words, Harihara was not an orthodox Vaiṣṇava. When this thought entered his mind, his face blossomed with happiness. He said, "Harihara, you are a good scholar of *nyāya-śāstra*. I agree with your idea. Nowadays, a new kind of Vaiṣṇavism has come. I am afraid to say anything against it. It is the Kali-yuga! We should be a little careful. Many rich and respectable gentlemen have accepted Caitanya's philosophy. They have no faith in us. They think that we are the enemies. I think that in a few days, our business will collapse. The *suvarṇa-vaṇiks* and other mercantile people have taken to talking about the scriptures. They have brought great trouble to us. Look, for a long time, the *brāhmaṇas* had so arranged things that no other caste could read the scriptures. Even the *kāyasthas*, who were next below the *brāhmaṇas*, could not chant the sacred syllable *oṁ*. All followed what we said but nowadays, all these Vaiṣṇavas are discussing the spiritual truth. They have completely defeated us. Since the time of Nimāi Paṇḍita, the *brāhmaṇa* religion has practically disappeared."

"O Harihara, Tarka-Cuḍāmaṇi spoke the truth. Considering what they have seen or heard, others may say what they like about him. I say he has spoken well. When I hear the words of these Vaiṣṇava fools, my whole body burns with anger. They even say that Śaṅkarācārya's books are false, and his words are all *māyā*. They say that Lord Viṣṇu ordered him to speak a pack of lies. And then on top of that, they say that the Vaiṣṇava religion had no beginning. The Vaiṣṇava religion is barely a hundred years old! And now, it has no beginning. As the saying goes: The fools find an innocent man, make him into a scapegoat, and attack him again and again."

"Let them say what they like. Navadvīpa was as good in the past, just as it is bad at present. Nowadays, a few Vaiṣṇavas who live at Barāgachi in Navadvīpa see the ideas of the entire world as foolish. Some two or three scholars amongst them have turned the whole country upside-down. The ideas that castes are rigidly fixed, that the whole world is an illusion, and that one should worship Goddess Durgā have all been crushed by them. Look. Nowadays, there are not even many *śrāddha* ceremonies. What will happen to the professional *brāhmaṇas*?"

Then, Harihara said, "O Bhaṭṭācārya Mahāśaya, is there no remedy? In Māyāpura, there are still five or six big, big *brāhmaṇa* scholars. Then, on the other side of the Ganges, there are many scholars of *Smṛti* and *Nyāya*. Why do they not join forces and attack Gadigacha?"

Nyāyaratna said, "Yes! If they band together, the *brāhmaṇa* scholars can do it! Of course, the *brāhmaṇa* scholars tend to fight among themselves. They like to fight, and they pretend that fighting among themselves is part of the job of being a scholar. I heard that some followers of Kṛṣṇa-Cuḍāmaṇi went to Gadigacha for a debate and came back defeated. Now, they won't even come out of their classrooms. Some have said that."

Harihara said, "O Bhaṭṭācārya Mahāśaya, you are our teacher. You are the teacher of many great scholars. By studying your commentaries on *nyāya-śāstra*, many have learned the art of tricking others by juggling words. Please go and defeat the Vaiṣṇava scholars once and for all. The Vaiṣṇava religion is a modern concoction. It is not the teaching of the *Vedas*. Please go and prove these truths. Then our *pañcopāsaka* worship, which is the teaching of all the previous authorities, will be saved."

In Caturbhuja Nyāyaratna's mind there was a fear. He was afraid that he would meet the same fate as Kṛṣṇa-Cuḍāmaṇi and others who had already been defeated by the Vaiṣṇavas. He said, "Harihara, I will go there in disguise. You go there also. Pose as a scholar, and kindle the fire of debate in Gadigacha."

Harihara said, "I must obey your order. Calling myself Mahādeva, on Monday I will cross the Ganges."

Monday came. Accompanied by Śrī Caturbhuja Nyāyaratna of Arkatila, the three scholars—Harihara, Kamalākānta, and Sadāśiva —crossed the Ganges. After a little more than ten hours of traveling along the Ganges, they finally arrived at Śrī Pradyumna-kuñja. Again and again calling out, "Haribol! Haribol!" like a small contingent of Durvāsa Munis, they entered the grove of *mādhavī* vines.

Advaita dāsa came out, greeted them, gave them sitting-places, and asked, "What order would you like to give to me?"

Harihara said, "We have come to discuss some things with the Vaiṣṇavas."

Advaita dāsa replied, "The Vaiṣṇavas of this place do not engage in debates. But if you sincerely have some questions, then that is all right. The other day, some scholars came, asked some questions, stirred up a great debate, and were left unhappy at the end. I will ask the saintly *parāmahāṁsa bābājī*, and then I will give you his answer."

After speaking these words, he entered the cottage of the *parāmahāṁsa bābājī*. After a moment, Advaita dāsa returned among them and began to arrange sitting places for everyone. Entering the beautiful grove, the saintly *parāmahāṁsa bābājī* offered *daṇḍavat* obeisances first to the *tulasī* plant and then to the *brāhmaṇa* guests.

He asked them, "O saintly ones, what order would you like to give to me?"

Then, the Nyāyaratna said, "I have two questions to ask. Please answer them."

Hearing this, the saintly *parāmahāṁsa bābājī* called for saintly Śrī Vaiṣṇava dāsa Bābājī. When the Vaiṣṇavas were all seated comfortably, Nyāyaratna Mahāśaya asked, "First consider, and then speak: Is the Vaiṣṇava religion ancient or modern?"

Following the saintly *parāmahāṁsa bābājī*'s wish, Vaiṣṇava dāsa spoke. He said, "The Vaiṣṇava religion is eternal. It has always existed."

Nyāyaratna: As I see it, there are two kinds of Vaiṣṇava religion. In one kind of Vaiṣṇava religion, it is accepted that the Supreme is the formless Brahman. However, no one can actually worship something that is formless. Therefore, one may imagine that the Supreme has a form, and by worshiping that imagined form, one gradually becomes pure in heart. When one becomes thus pure in heart, knowledge of the formless Brahman naturally arises within him. Thus, by worshiping the imaginary forms of Rādhā-Kṛṣṇa, Rāma, or Nṛsiṁha, one eventually attains knowledge of Brahman. Those who accept this philosophy worship the Deity of Viṣṇu and chant Viṣṇu *mantras*, considering themselves Vaiṣṇavas and counting themselves among the *pañcopāsakas*. Another kind of Vaiṣṇava religion affirms that Lord Viṣṇu, Lord Rāma, or Lord Kṛṣṇa have real forms that are eternal. Then, by worshiping these forms and chanting Their *mantras*, the devotee attains eternal knowledge of Them, and Their mercy also. This Śaṅkara is in error and his idea that the Supreme is formless is a pack of lies. Of these two kinds of Vaiṣṇava religion, which is eternal? Which of them always existed?

Vaiṣṇava dāsa: The second one you mentioned is the real Vaiṣṇava religion. It is eternal. The first one is Vaiṣṇava religion in name only. It is the enemy of the true Vaiṣṇava religion. It is not eternal. It is only a collection of lies.

Nyāyaratna: I can understand that in your opinion, the only true Vaiṣṇava religion is the philosophy of Caitanyadeva. Thus, the Vaiṣṇava religion does not mean only the worship of Rādhā-Kṛṣṇa, Rāma, and Nṛsiṁha, it means worshipping Rādhā-Kṛṣṇa and the other Deities according to the principles taught by Caitanya. Very good. However, how can you say that this kind of Vaiṣṇava religion is eternal?

Vaiṣṇava dāsa: The four *Vedas* teach this kind of Vaiṣṇava religion. All the *smṛti-śāstras* teach this kind of Vaiṣṇava religion. All the Vedic histories (*Itihāsas*) sing the glories of this kind of Vaiṣṇava religion.

Nyāyaratna dāsa: Caitanyadeva was born not even 150 years ago. From what I can see, He is the first teacher of this kind of religion. If this is so, how can this kind of religion be eternal?

Vaiṣṇava dāsa: As long as any souls ever existed, this kind of Vaiṣṇava philosophy existed also. The time when the individual souls first came into existence cannot be calculated according to material time. Actually, there never was a time when the individual souls first came into existence. As the individual souls are thus beginningless, so the Vaiṣṇava religion is also beginningless. Brahmā was the first individual soul to take birth in this universe. As soon as Brahmā was manifested, the words of the *Vedas*, which are the root of the Vaiṣṇava religion, were also manifested.

This is recorded in the four essential verses of *Śrīmad-Bhāgavatam* (2.9.33-36). This is also described in these words of *Muṇḍaka Upaniṣad* (1.1.1): Brahmā, who is the first demigod, the creator of the universe, and the protector of the worlds, spoke knowledge of the Supreme, the first of all kinds of knowledge, to his eldest son, Atharva.

This knowledge of the Supreme is also taught in these words of the *Ṛg Veda* (1.22.20): The lotus feet of Lord Viṣṇu are the supreme objective of all the demigods. These lotus feet of the Lord are as enlightening as the sun in the sky.

In the *Śvetāśvatara Upaniṣad* (5.4.) it is said: The glorious Supreme Personality of Godhead alone rules all creatures.

In the *Taittirīya Upaniṣad* (2.1.2) it is said: The Supreme Personality of Godhead is real, eternal, limitless, and all-knowing. One who understands the Supreme Lord residing in his heart goes to the spiritual world. There, He associates with the all-knowing Supreme Lord. There, all his desires are fulfilled.

Nyāyaratna: You say that the *Ṛg Veda* verse, *tad viṣṇoḥ paramaṁ padaṁ*, describes your kind of Vaiṣṇava religion, and not the Vaiṣṇava religion that follows the Māyāvāda theory of impersonalism. How can you claim that?

Vaiṣṇava dāsa: The Vaiṣṇava religion that is a part of impersonalism refuses to affirm that service to Lord Viṣṇu is eternal. That religion claims that by attaining spiritual knowledge, a person himself becomes the Supreme. However, in the *Kaṭha Upaniṣad* (1.2.23) it is said: The Supreme Lord is not attained by expert explanations, by vast intelligence, nor even by much hearing. He is attained only by one who He Himself chooses. To such a person He manifests His own form.

Service to the Lord and surrender to the Lord are the only true religion. By following that religion, one attains the Lord's mercy, and only then is one able to see the Lord's eternal form. By cultivating impersonal speculation, one will not attain that form of the Lord. By understanding these clear and unequivocal words of the *Vedas*, one can see that the pure Vaiṣṇava religion has its roots in the *Vedas*. The Vaiṣṇava religion that Śrīmān Mahāprabhu taught is the same religion that is taught in the *Vedas*. Of this there is no doubt.

Nyāyaratna: Does any Vedic passage affirm this idea that the worship of Kṛṣṇa, and not impersonal knowledge, is the highest attainment?

Vaiṣṇava dāsa: In the *Taittirīya Upaniṣad* (2.7.1) it is said: The Supreme Personality of Godhead is the reservoir of transcendental mellows.

In the *Chāndogya Upaniṣad* (8.13.1) it is said: To attain Lord Kṛṣṇa, I surrender to Śrī Rādhā. To attain Śrī Rādhā, I surrender to Lord Kṛṣṇa.

I can quote many Vedic passages proving that devotional service to Lord Kṛṣṇa is the highest attainment.

Nyāyaratna: Is the name Kṛṣṇa found in the *Vedas*?

Vaiṣṇava dāsa: Is not the word Śyāmā a name of Lord Kṛṣṇa? In the *Ṛg Veda* (1.22.164) it is said: Then I saw a cowherd boy who will never die.

This is only one of the many Vedic passages that describe Lord Kṛṣṇa, the son of a *gopa*.

Nyāyaratna: These are all strained and twisted interpretations of the Vedic passages.

Vaiṣṇava dāsa: If one studies the *Vedas* thoroughly, he will see that these are the right interpretations. We should understand the *Vedas* according to the explanations given by the ancient sages.

Nyāyaratna: Now please narrate the history of the Vaiṣṇava religion.

Vaiṣṇava dāsa: I have already said that when the first individual soul came into existence, the Vaiṣṇava religion came into existence with him. Therefore, the demigod, Brahmā, is the first Vaiṣṇava. Lord Śiva is also a Vaiṣṇava. The original Prajāpatis are all Vaiṣṇavas. Brahmā's mind-born son, Nārada Gosvāmī, is also a Vaiṣṇava. Can you not see that the Vaiṣṇava religion was present at the moment the material universe was created? The truth is that not everyone is beyond the influence of the material modes. Whoever is genuinely free of the material modes is a genuine Vaiṣṇava. The *Mahābhārata*, Ram*āyā*na, and *Purāṇas* are all histories of the Vedic civilization. You have already seen that the Vaiṣṇava religion was present at the moment the material universe was created.

When the scriptures describe the different demigods, human beings, and demons, there are descriptions of Prahlāda, Dhruva, and other Vaiṣṇavas from the very beginning. The Vedic histories have only recorded the names of some of the most famous. There's no saying how many hundreds of other great Vaiṣṇavas there were at the time of Prahlāda and Dhruva. Dhruva, Manu's sons, and Prahlāda, are all grandsons of Prajāpati Kaśyapa. Therefore, they lived at the very beginning of the universe. Of this there is no doubt. In the

Vedic histories, it is seen that the Vaiṣṇava religion was present at the very beginning of time. The kings of the *candra-vaṁśa* and *sūrya-vaṁśa*, as well as the great *munis* and *ṛṣis*, were all sincerely devoted to Lord Viṣṇu. These things are written in the descriptions of the three *yugas*: Satya, Tretā and Dvāpara. In the Kali-yuga, Śrī Rāmānuja, Śrī Madhvācārya, and Śrī Viṣṇu Swami in the south, and Śrī Nimbarka Swami in the west, brought many thousands to the pure Vaiṣṇava religion. By their mercy, perhaps half the people of Bhārata-varṣa crossed the ocean of *māyā* and found shelter at the lotus feet of the Supreme Lord. In Bengal, you may see Lord Śacīnandana, who is the master of our hearts. How many fallen souls did He deliver? When you look at all these great souls, you do not see the glory of the Vaiṣṇava religion!

Nyāyaratna: Yes. But what kind of Vaiṣṇavas are Prahlada and the others? What do you say?

Vaiṣṇava dāsa: One must study the scriptures thoroughly. Rejecting the impersonalist theory that Ṣaṇḍa and Amarka taught him, Prahlāda instead made the holy names of Lord Hari the be-all and end-all of his life. Therefore, Prahlāda was a pure devotee. Of this there is no doubt. The truth is that, without careful and impartial investigation, one cannot understand the true meaning of the scriptures.

Nyāyaratna: If this is true, that the Vaiṣṇava religion existed from time immemorial, then what new thing did Caitanya Mahāprabhu teach, that He should be especially honored?

Vaiṣṇava dāsa: The Vaiṣṇava religion is like a lotus flower. It blossoms slowly. First it is a bud. Then it is partly blossomed. Only slowly does it become like a fully-blossomed flower. At the time of the demigod, Brahmā, the impersonalist theory, the practice of devotional service, and the knowledge of the Supreme Personality of Godhead as described in the four essential verses of *Śrīmad-Bhāgavatam* were new sprouts just beginning to grow in the hearts of the living entities. At the time of Prahlāda and the others, the sprout had grown to become a bud. That you can see. At the time of Vyāsa Muni, that bud slowly opened, and at the time of the great Vaiṣṇava *ācāryas*, it became a flower. When Śrīmān Mahāprabhu came to this world, that flower of love became fully blossomed and spread its sweet fragrance to everyone. Śrīmān Mahāprabhu revealed the most confidential secret of the Vaiṣṇava religion: the pure love attained by chanting the Lord's holy names. In this way, He gave the greatest good fortune to the living entities in the material world. The chanting of the holy names of the Lord is such a valuable treasure. Who else but Lord Caitanya revealed the truth of this? Although this truth was certainly described in the scriptures, it had not been revealed to the people in general. Ah, before Lord Caitanya, had the treasure house of the nectar of love of God even been opened in this way?

Nyāyaratna: Well, if the chanting of the holy names is so sweet, why do the learned *paṇḍitas* not like it?

Vaiṣṇava dāsa: In Kali-yuga, the word '*paṇḍita*' no longer means what it once did. In the scriptures, the word '*paṇḍa*' is defined as, 'brilliant intelligence,' and therefore a person who has brilliant intelligence is called a '*paṇḍita*.' Nowadays, anyone who can spout meaningless jargon from the *nyāya-śāstra* or interpret the *smṛti-śāstra* in a way to please the people in general is called a *paṇḍita*. Are such *paṇḍitas* able to understand or teach the truth of religion and the true meaning of the scriptures? Can anyone attain through the meaningless jargon of the *nyāya-śāstra* the spiritual truth, which is to be attained by impartial and careful study of all the scriptures? In truth, only persons who are expert at cheating themselves and others are called *paṇḍita* in the Kali-yuga. These so-called *paṇḍitas* carry on great stormy debates over earthen pots and scraps of cloth. What is reality, what is the relationship between the individual souls and the Supreme, what the real spiritual need of all living entities, and how can that need be fulfilled—these *paṇḍitas* will never have a stormy debate to settle these things. Only when one understands the truths of these things will one be able to know the answer to the question: What is the value of the loving chanting of Lord Hari's holy names?

Nyāyaratna: Well, I'll certainly agree that there are hardly any good *paṇḍitas* nowadays. Still, why is it that the great *brāhmaṇas* who are born in exalted families refuse to accept your Vaiṣṇava religion? The *brāhmaṇa* caste is in the mode of goodness. *Brāhmaṇas* are naturally on the right path and naturally attracted to the highest religious principles. Why, then, are the *brāhmaṇas* so ferociously opposed to the Vaiṣṇava religion?

Vaiṣṇava dāsa: Since you have asked this question, it is right that I give the proper reply. Still, Vaiṣṇavas do not like to criticize others. Look, if you will not feel pain and anger in your heart, and if you desire to know what is the real truth, I can answer your question.

Nyāyaratna: Do it. I have studied the scriptures. I am in favor of peacefulness, self-control, and tolerance. Your words will not be intolerable for me. Please speak straight. I accept what is good and true.

Vaiṣṇava dāsa: Look, Śrī Rāmānuja, Madhva, Viṣṇu Swami, and Nimbarka were all *brāhmaṇas*. They had thousands and thousands of *brāhmaṇa* disciples. In our Bengal, our Mahāprabhu was a *vaidika brāhmaṇa*. Our Nityānanda Prabhu was a *rādhiya brāhmaṇa*. Our Advaita Prabhu was a *rājendra brāhmaṇa*. Our Gosvāmīs and *mahāntas* were mostly *brāhmaṇas*. Thousands and thousands of great souls who wore the *tilaka* markings of great *brāhmaṇa* families took shelter of the Vaiṣṇava religion and preached the pure Vaiṣṇava religion to the people of the world. How can you say that exalted *brāhmaṇas* do not honor the Vaiṣṇava religion? This we know: All the *brāhmaṇas* who honor the Vaiṣṇava religion are exalted *brāhmaṇas*. Only because of bad families, bad association, or bad education, do some *brāhmaṇas* become enemies. Not because their brahminical principles are so great and exalted. They become enemies because they are degraded and unfortunate. The scriptures declare that in Kali-yuga, the number of true *brāhmaṇas* is very few. These few *brāhmaṇas* become Vaiṣṇavas. When he accepts the Vaiṣṇava Gāyatrī, which is the mother of all the *Vedas*, a *brāhmaṇa* becomes an initiated Vaiṣṇava. However, pushed by the faults of Kali-yuga, such a *brāhmaṇa* may then accept another, a non-Vedic initiation. In this way, he loses his status as a Vaiṣṇava. Simply because you see they are few in number, please do not come to the wrong conclusion about the Vaiṣṇava *brāhmaṇas*.

Nyāyaratna: Why do many low-class people embrace the Vaiṣṇava religion?

Vaiṣṇava dāsa: There is no doubt of that. Many low-class people are naturally very humble, and for this reason, the Vaiṣṇavas consider them good candidates for their mercy. No one can become a Vaiṣṇava without first receiving the mercy of the Vaiṣṇavas. Persons who are intoxicated with pride of caste, pride of wealth, or other kinds of pride, cannot be humble. For them, it is very difficult to attain the mercy of the Vaiṣṇavas.

Nyāyaratna: I don't like to know any more about it. I can see that eventually you will quote some hard words from the scriptures. It gives my heart great pain to hear these words, words like these of the *Varāha Purāṇa*: In the Kali-yuga, demons take birth in the families of the *brāhmaṇas*.

I don't like to talk about these things. Now, please say why you have no respect for our Śrī Śaṅkara Swami, who is a shoreless ocean of spiritual knowledge?

Vaiṣṇava dāsa: Why do you say that? We say that Śrī Śaṅkara Swami is an incarnation of Lord Śiva Himself. Śrīmān Mahāprabhu taught us to honor him with the title *ācārya*. The only thing is, we do not accept his Māyāvāda philosophy. The Māyāvāda philosophy is not the religion taught in the *Vedas*. Actually, it is covered Buddhism. In order to give the demons a stable life, by the Supreme Lord's order, the *ācārya* distorted the true meaning of the *Vedas*, *Vedānta*, and *Bhagavad-gītā*, and taught the *advaita-vāda*, the philosophy of an impersonal God. Is the *ācārya* at fault for that? Do people criticize him? Buddha was an incarnation of the Supreme Lord. He preached a philosophy opposed to the *Vedas*. Do the followers of the *Vedas* criticize him?

If someone says, "It is not good for the Supreme Lord and the demigod, Śiva, to act in that way," then I reply, "Why not? They are never cruel or unjust. The Supreme Personality of Godhead, the protector of the universe, and His assistant, Lord Śiva, are both all-knowing and the givers of all good. They are never cruel or unjust. Their actions have a deep purpose the small individual souls have no power to understand. Therefore, They should not be criticized."

Because they are not intelligent enough to understand the purpose of the Lord, people may criticize Him, saying "It is not good for the Supreme Lord to act in this way. He should have acted in that way." Intelligent people never talk like that. Why was the impersonalist philosophy needed then to control the demonic people? Only the all-powerful Lord knows. Why is there a need to create the various life forms and then destroy them at the end? We have not the power to know. These are the pastimes of the Lord. Persons who are devoted to the Lord feel bliss to hear of His pastimes. They are not eager to say the Lord acted wrongly, or to question the virtue of the Lord's actions.

Nyāyaratna: Good. But why do you say that the Māyāvāda philosophy is against the teachings of the *Vedas* and the *Vedānta-sūtra*?

Vaiṣṇava dāsa: If you carefully consider the *Vedas* and the *Vedānta-sūtra*, then please tell me which *mantras* and which *sūtras* support the Māyāvāda conclusion? I will show the proper interpretation of all those *mantras* and *sūtras*. It may seem that some Vedic *mantras* show a dim reflection of the Māyāvāda philosophy. However, when we look at what precedes and follows those *mantras*, in a moment, the Māyāvāda interpretation flees far away.

Nyāyaratna: My brother, I never studied the *Upaniṣads* and the *Vedānta-sūtra*. I can discuss anything about the *nyāya-śāstra*. In that debate, I can turn a clay pot into a piece of cloth and a piece of cloth into a clay pot. I read a little of the *Gītā*, but I did not really enter into it. Here I must stop. Well, I would like to ask one more thing. You are a great *paṇḍita*, so you can give a good answer. Why do the Vaiṣṇavas have faith only in the *prasādam* remnants of Lord Viṣṇu and not in the remnants of the demigods and demigoddesses?

Vaiṣṇava dāsa: I am not a *paṇḍita*. I am a great fool. If I can speak nicely—that is only because of the mercy of my *parāmahāṁsa gurudeva*. Everyone should know that. The ocean of the scriptures has no shore. No one can study all the scriptures. My *gurudeva* churned the ocean of the scriptures and gave me the cream of their final conclusions. I know that what he teaches is the final conclusion of all the scriptures.

The answer to your question is this: The Vaiṣṇavas do not disrespect the *prasādam* remnants of the demigods and demigoddesses. Śrī Kṛṣṇa is the only Supreme God. The other demigods and demigoddesses are His obedience devotees. The Vaiṣṇavas respect the *prasādam* remnants left by the devotees of the Lord. They do not disrespect them. By accepting the *prasādam* remnants left by the devotees, one attains pure devotion to the Lord. The dust of the devotees' feet, the nectarean water that has washed the devotees' feet, and the nectarean food that has touched the devotees' lips—these three are all very wonderful and delightful. They should certainly be accepted. Here is the truth: If an impersonalist worships a demigod and offers food and other things to him, the demigod will not accept the worship, the food, or any other offering, because the person making the offering is contaminated by the impersonalist philosophy. There is abundant proof of that in the scriptures. If you like, I can quote.

The worshipers of the demigods are mostly impersonalists. The demigod *prasādam* they offer destroys devotional service and creates an offense before Bhakti-devī, the goddess of devotion. If a pure Vaiṣṇava offers the *prasādam* tasted by Lord Kṛṣṇa to a demigod or a demigoddess, that demigod or demigoddess happily accepts that *prasādam* and dances with joy. If a Vaiṣṇava then takes that *prasādam*, he becomes filled with happiness. Look, the commands given by the scriptures are most important. It is written in the *yoga-śāstra* that a person practicing *yoga* should not accept the *prasādam* of any demigod. This does not mean that a person practicing *yoga* should disrespect the *prasādam* remnants offered to the demigods. It merely means that renouncing these remnants is helpful for *yoga* meditation. In the same way, if a person is engaged in devotional service accepts *prasādam* remnants offered to any but the Lord He worships, the devotee cannot attain unalloyed devotion to his Lord. This does not mean that he disrespects the *prasādam* remnants offered to the demigods. Please know then that this is ordered by the scriptures and it is meant only to attain a particular goal.

Nyāyaratna: Good. I accept that answer. Why do you reject the animal sacrifices prescribed in the scriptures?

Vaiṣṇava dāsa: The scriptures do not teach that one should kill animals. The scriptures declare: "Don't do violence to any creature." With these words, the *Vedas* prohibit violence to animals. As long as he is in the grip of the modes of passion and ignorance, a man will yearn to associate with women, eat meat, and drink liquor. He does not wait to hear the *Vedas* command him before he does these things.

The purpose of the *Vedas* is this: As long as a man is not situated in the mode of goodness, a man will not be able to renounce killing animals, drinking liquor, and yearning for the touch of a woman. It is to curb these propensities that the scriptures prescribe association with a woman in marriage, killing animals in sacrifice, and drinking liquor at certain ceremonies. In these ways, a man's indulgence in these things is curtailed and at the end, he becomes able to renounce them completely. That is the purpose of the *Vedas*. The *Vedas* do not really teach that one should kill animals.

That is described in these words of *Śrīmad-Bhāgavatam* (11.5.11): In this material world, the conditioned soul is always inclined to sex, meat eating, and intoxication. Therefore, religious scriptures never actually encourage these activities. Although the scriptural injunctions provide for sex through sacred marriage, for meat eating through sacrificial offerings, and for intoxication through the acceptance of ritual cups of wine, such ceremonies are meant for the ultimate purpose of renunciation.

Therefore, the Vaiṣṇavas do not protest if men in the modes of passion and ignorance kill animals in these circumstances. However, men in the mode of goodness should not perform such activities. To be violent to others is the way of the animals.

Śrī Nārada Muni describes the way of the animals in these words (*Śrīmad-Bhāgavatam* 1.13.47): Those who are devoid of hands are prey for those who have hands. Those devoid of legs are prey for the four-legged. The weak are the sustenance of the strong, and the general rule holds that one living being is food for another.

Manu also explains (*Manu-saṁhitā* 5.56): Everyone in material life is attracted to furthering the way of attachment (*pravṛtti-mārga*), but the greatest treasure is to be gained by following the path of detachment (*nivṛtti-mārga*).

Nyāyaratna: Good. Why do the Vaiṣṇavas object to performance of *śrāddha* and other rituals to repay the debts one owes to his ancestors?

Vaiṣṇava dāsa: If men who follow the *karma-kanda* rituals of the *Vedas* perform the *śrāddha* ceremony, the Vaiṣṇavas have no objection. However, the scriptures do say this (*Śrīmad-Bhāgavatam* 11.5.51): Anyone who takes shelter of the lotus feet of Mukunda, the giver of liberation, giving up all kinds of obligation, and has taken to the path in all seriousness, owes neither duties nor obligations to the demigods, sages, general living entities, family members, humankind, or forefathers.

The conclusion, then, is that devotees who have surrendered to the Lord do not need to perform *karma-kanda śrāddha* ceremonies to repay the debts they owe to their ancestors. They worship the Lord, offer the Lord's *prasādam* to their ancestors, and then honor that *prasādam* with their family. That is the *śrāddha* ritual they perform.

Nyāyaratna: When is one qualified to act in that way?

Vaiṣṇava dāsa: On the day when one has faith in the descriptions of Lord Hari and the holy name of Lord Hari, one is counted as a Vaiṣṇava. This is described by the Supreme Lord Himself in these words (*Śrīmad-Bhāgavatam* 11.20.9): As long as one is not displeased by fruitive activity, and as long as one has no faith in hearing about Me, one has to follow the rituals of the *Vedas*.

Nyāyaratna: I am very pleased. When I see your scholarship and sharp intelligence, I have faith in the Vaiṣṇavas. I feel happiness in my heart. Harihara, why should we argue with these people? These people are very great scholars. They are very expert in understanding the scriptures. Whatever we may say to keep our business prosperous, Nimāi Paṇḍita is the greatest philosopher and Vaiṣṇava who ever took birth in the land of Bengal. Of this there is no doubt. Now, let us cross the Ganges. The day is almost ended. Calling out, "Haribol! Haribol!" Nyāyaratna and his companions departed. Singing "Jaya Śacīnandana!," the Vaiṣṇavas danced.

Chapter Eleven

Eternal religion
and byūt-parasta,
or Deity worship.

On the Ganges' western shore is the village of Pāhārpura. That famous village is in the middle of Koladvīpa, which is within Navadvīpa. At the time of Śrīmān Mahāprabhu, there was an especially respectable and influential man named Śrī Mādhava dāsa Caṭṭopādhyāya (also known as Ca'kari Caṭṭopādhyāya). Ca'kari had a son named Śrīla Vaṁśīvadanānanda Ṭhākura. By Lord Mahāprabhu's mercy, Śrī Vaṁśīvadanānanda became very great and powerful. Thinking him an incarnation of Lord Kṛṣṇa's flute, everyone called him Prabhu Vaṁśīvadanānanda. It was well known that Mother Viṣṇupriya was especially merciful to Prabhu Vaṁśīvadanānanda. After Mother Viṣṇupriya disappeared, Vaṁśīvadanānanda moved the Deity form of the Lord from Śrī Māyāpura to Kuliyā Pāhārpura. When his descendants attained the mercy of Mother Śrī Jāhnavī and moved to Śrīpat Baghanapara, the worship of the Deity of Lord Mahāprabhu was continued by the *pūjārīs* living in Malanca in Kuliyā-grāma.

The village of Kuliyā-grāma was situated across the Ganges from the old city of Navadvīpa. In the area of Kuliyā were some famous small hamlets, such as the one named Cināḍāṅgā. A devotee merchant of Cināḍāṅgā once held a great spiritual festival in the temple at Kuliyā Pāhārpura. Many *brāhmaṇa paṇḍitas* and all the Vaiṣṇavas within thirty-two miles of Navadvīpa were invited to that festival. On the day of the festival, the Vaiṣṇavas were coming from all directions. Śrī Ananta dāsa and others came from Śrī Nṛsiṁha-palli. Śrī Gauracandra Bābājī and others came from Śrī Māyāpura. Śrī Nārāyaṇa dāsa Bābājī and others came from Śrī Bilva-puṣkariṇī. Śrī Narahari dāsa and others came from Śrī Modadruma. The *parāmahāṁsa bābājī*, Vaiṣṇava dāsa, and others came from Śrī Godruma. Śrī Śacīnandana dāsa and others came from Śrī Samudrāgar.

The *tilaka* mark of Lord Hari's temple was on their foreheads, *tulasī* beads were around their necks, and all their limbs were resplendent with the marks of Lord Gaura and Lord Nityānanda. In every hand were beads for chanting the holy names of Lord Hari. Everyone loudly chanted: *Hare Kṛṣṇa Hare Kṛṣṇa, Kṛṣṇa Kṛṣṇa Hare Hare, Hare Rāma Hare Rāma, Rāma Rāma Hare Hare.* That was the *mantra* they sang. Some played the *karatālas* and sang: Glorious Lord Gaura dances in the *sankīrtana*!"

Again and again, some danced and sang: *śrī-kṛṣṇa-caitanya prabhu-nityānanda śrī-advaita gadādhara śrīvāsādi-gaura-bhakta-vṛnda.*

Many tears fell from many eyes. Some limbs had hairs standing erect in ecstasy. Some fervently called out, "O Gaura Kiśora! Will Your eternal pastimes ever be seen by our eyes!"

Some Vaiṣṇavas played *mṛdaṅgas* and repeatedly sang the holy names as they walked. The women from Kuliyā who were devotees of Lord Gaura became filled with wonder to see the ecstatic love the Vaiṣṇavas showed. Walking and walking, the Vaiṣṇavas finally came to the temple, which was now a theater where there would be a play about Śrīmān Mahāprabhu. A cloth around his neck, the host merchant fell at the Vaiṣṇavas' feet and spoke many humble words. Then, the Vaiṣṇavas took their seats within the theater. The *pūjārīs* came and placed *prasādam* flower garlands around the Vaiṣṇavas' necks. Then, the play *Śrī Caitanya-maṅgala* began. As they heard the nectarean pastimes of Lord Caitanya, the Vaiṣṇavas manifested different kinds of *sattvika-bhāva* ecstasies.

As everyone was thus plunged into an ocean of transcendental bliss, one of the gatekeepers approached the temple authorities and said that the head mullah of Sātsāika Paraganā had come, was now seated in the courtyard with his associates, and wanted to talk with a Vaiṣṇava *paṇḍita*. The temple authorities informed the assembled *bābājī paṇḍitas*. The nectar of the play was thus interrupted, and so the Vaiṣṇavas became unhappy.

Śrī Kṛṣṇadāsa Bābājī of Madhyadvīpa asked, "What is the mullah's intention?"

Aware of the mullah's intention, one the temple authorities said, "The mullah wishes to talk with the Vaiṣṇavas about the spiritual truth."

He also said that the mullah had no rival among the Mohammedan scholars, he was very earnest about preaching his own religion everywhere, and he was not a fanatic who hated other religions. Also, the emperor at Delhi greatly respected him. The mullah also asked that only one or two Vaiṣṇava *paṇḍitas* engage in the conversation about scripture. He thought in that way, the pure Vaiṣṇava religion would be defeated.

Hearing that an opportunity to preach the Vaiṣṇava religion had now come, the desire to talk with this mullah arose within the hearts of some of the Vaiṣṇavas. Talking among themselves, they decided that Gauracandra dāsa Paṇḍita Bābājī of Śrī Māyāpura, Śrī Vaiṣṇava dāsa Paṇḍita Bābājī of Śrī Godruma, Prema dāsa Bābājī of Jahnu-nagara, and Kali-pavana dāsa Bābājī of Campahaṭṭa would go and talk with the mullah, and when the play *Śrī Caitanya-maṅgala* ended, everyone else would come and join them.

Calling out, "Jaya Nityānanda!" the four *bābājīs* followed the *mahānta* to the outer courtyard. The outer courtyard was very pleasant. It was cool with the shade of a banyan tree. Seeing the Vaiṣṇavas coming, the mullah and his associates greeted them respectfully. Fully aware that all souls are servants of Lord Kṛṣṇa, the Vaiṣṇavas offered *daṇḍavat* obeisances to Lord Vāsudeva residing in the hearts of the mullahs. Then, the Vaiṣṇavas took their seats. It was a very beautiful sight. On one side were fifty white-bearded Mohammedan scholars, nicely dressed and decorated. Behind them, some decorated horses were tethered. On the other side were four humble and effulgent Vaiṣṇavas. Behind them were many Hindus who had come and taken their seats out of curiosity.

The *paṇḍita*, Gauracandra, spoke first, "O noble ones, for what purpose have you remembered us poor people?"

The saintly mullah, Badaruddīn Sāhib, humbly replied, "Salam! Please accept our respects. We have come to ask some questions. The *paṇḍita*, Gauracandra, replied, "As far as I am able, I shall answer your learned questions.

Badaruddīn Sāhib stepped forward and said, "Brothers, in Hindu society, the worship of demigods and demigoddesses has existed for many days. In our holy Koran, I see that Allah is one, not two. He has no form. To make an image of Him and to worship it is a great offense. I asked many *brāhmaṇa paṇḍitas* about this, and they said that although Allah is indeed formless, the mind cannot meditate on a formless thing and therefore, one should create an imaginary form of Allah, and that form should receive our worship and meditation. I am not able to accept these words very happily. Why not? To create an imaginary form like that is the work of Satan. We call that *byūt*. To worship *byūt* is completely forbidden. By that worship, one is pushed far away from pleasing Allah and one becomes worthy of punishment by Him. We have heard that your first preacher,

Caitanyadeva, rejected all the faults of the Hindu religion. Still, He was in favor of this *byūt* worship, or worship of a material thing. What we want to know from the Vaiṣṇavas is: Why, after consulting the scriptures, have you not rejected this *byūt* worship?"

Hearing this question from the mullah, the Vaiṣṇava *paṇḍitas* smiled within their minds. Openly they said, "This saintly *paṇḍita bābājī* will give the answer to you."

Replying with, "As you order," the *paṇḍita*, Gauracandra, said, "He who you call Allah, we call Bhagavān. Both these words refer to the same Supreme Personality of Godhead. He is called by different names in the Koran, the *Purāṇas*, and in different countries and languages. The name that best expresses all the qualities of the Supreme Personality of Godhead should be accepted. That is why we favor the name Bhagavān over Allah, Brahman, Paramātmā, and all others. The word Allah means, 'He who has no superior.' We do not call superiority the best of the Lord's qualities. We say that wonderfulness is the best of His qualities. To be very big is certainly very wonderful. However, the opposite, to be very small, is also very wonderful. Therefore, the name Allah does not reach to the highest limit of the Lord's wonderful qualities. The word Bhagavān, however, refers to all wonderful qualities human beings can know. It puts them all in one word."

"The ultimate of greatness and the ultimate of smallness are only one feature of Bhagavān. That He is the master of all potencies is a second feature of Bhagavān. Whatever a human being thinks is impossible, His inconceivable potency can easily accomplish. It is by the power of His inconceivable potency that He both has a form and does not have a form. If we say that He does not have a form, then we deny His inconceivable potency. By His inconceivable potency, He has a form and He enjoys pastimes with His devotees eternally. Allah, Brahman, and Paramātmā are formless. Therefore, They do not have these wonderful features."

"Bhagavān is all-auspicious and all- famous. His pastimes are sweet like nectar. Bhagavān is sublimely handsome. With spiritual eyes, the liberated souls gaze on His handsomeness. Bhagavān has all knowledge. He is pure and perfect. He is beyond the touch of matter. His form is spiritual. He is beyond the material elements, or *byūt*. Although He is the creator of the material world, Bhagavān is untouched by matter. He is independent. The word Bhagavān means, 'He who has six opulences.'"

"Bhagavān has two features: 1. opulence and 2. sweetness. The feature of sweetness is the best friend of the spirit souls. He is the Lord of our hearts. He is Kṛṣṇa or Caitanya. Therefore, if someone says that the word of an imaginary form of Bhagavān is *byūt* worship, or worship of matter, that is not in opposition to our philosophy. The Vaiṣṇava religion teaches that one should worship the Lord's eternal form (which is perfectly spiritual). According to the Vaiṣṇava philosophy, this kind of worship of the Lord's form is not *byūt* worship. If, in any book, it is said that this kind of worship is *byūt* worship and is forbidden, then that book has no authority to forbid it."

"Everything depends on the faith within the heart. A person whose heart is free from *byūt*, who is beyond the material world, can worship the pure spiritual form of the Lord. You are Mullah Sāhib. You are a great *paṇḍita*. Your heart is certainly free from the touch of matter. But, are the hearts of your neophyte disciples free from the thought of *byūt*? To whatever extent a man is filled with thoughts of *byūt*, to that extent his worship of God is really worship of *byūt*. With his mouth, he says God is formless, and his mind is filled with thoughts of *byūt*. The people in general find it very hard to worship the pure form of the Lord. Only a person who is specially qualified, who is beyond the touch of matter, can rise above thinking of *byūt*. I request that you consider these points."

Mullah: I have considered these points, and I think that the six wonderful qualities of Bhagavān you have described are also ascribed to Allah in the holy Koran. There is no need to debate the etymology of the word Allah as Bhagavān.

Gauracandra: Good. Then you accept that the Supreme Being has opulence and handsomeness. Then it is accepted that He has a handsome form in the spiritual world, which is a place different from the material world. That form of the Lord is the Deity we worship.

Mullah: In our Koran, it is also written that the Supreme has a spiritual form that is greater than the greatest. We accept that. However, when you make a statue of that spiritual form, that statue is material. Therefore, I say that it is *byūt*. Worship of *byūt* is not the same as worship of He who is greater than the greatest. Please say what you think of this.

Gauracandra: In the Vaiṣṇava scriptures, it is said that one should worship the pure and spiritual Deity form of the Lord. Exalted devotees would not worship the Deity form of the Lord if that form were made of earth, or any other material element.

In *Śrīmad-Bhāgavatam* (10.48.13) it is said: A human being who identifies this body made of three elements with his self, who considers the by-products of this body to be his kinsmen, who considers the Deity form of the Lord to be made of earth or other material elements, who goes to the place of pilgrimage simply to take a bath rather than to meet men of transcendental knowledge there, is to be considered as an ass or a cow.

In *Bhagavad-gītā* (9.25) it is said: Those who worship matter remain in the material world.

Therefore, the conclusion of the scriptures is that worship of matter is not allowed. That you can see. However, a certain point should be explained. Human beings are situated on different levels of knowledge and purity. A person situated in pure spiritual knowledge is able to worship the pure spiritual form of the Lord. Persons situated on lower levels of spiritual awareness understand the Lord to a lesser degree, and those who are on the lowest level cannot understand the Lord's spiritual nature at all.

When he meditates on God, a person on the lowest level inevitably imagines that God has a material form with material qualities. To think that the Deity form of the Lord is a statue made of clay is the same as to meditate in the mind on a Supreme that one imagines to have a form made of matter. Actually, for persons on that level of advancement, worship of the Deity form of the Lord is very beneficial. In fact, if there were no Deity worship, the people in general would be in an inauspicious condition. If an ordinary person who is eager to see God were not able to see the Deity form of the Lord, then he would lose hope that he would ever see the Lord.

The followers of religions that forbid Deity worship are on a low level of spiritual advancement. They are materialistic and not interested in worshiping the Lord. Therefore, Deity worship is the foundation of religion. Pure and wise saints gaze on the form of the Supreme Lord. Their hearts purified by devotion, they know that the Deity form of the Lord is pure spirit. As the heart becomes more and more purified by devotion, the worshiper gradually comes to understand that the Deity form of the Lord is a spiritual form reflected within the realm of the material world. Thus, the Deity form is the spiritual form of the Lord, a form that the great saints have arranged to be reflected within the material world.

An advanced devotee can directly perceive that the Deity form is perfectly spiritual. An intermediate devotee thinks that the Deity form is a mental image. At first, a neophyte devotee thinks that the Deity is a statue made of material elements, but as he gradually become pure in heart, he also gradually comes to understand that the Deity is actually made of spirit. Therefore, the Deity form of the Lord should be worshiped by all classes of devotees.

To worship an imaginary form is forbidden. However, to worship the real eternal form of the Lord is very auspicious. Therefore, the worship of the Deity of the Lord is established for all three classes of Vaiṣṇavas. There is nothing wrong in it. On the contrary, it brings the greatest auspiciousness.

In *Śrīmad-Bhāgavatam* (11.14.26) the Supreme Lord Himself declares: When a person purifies his heart by hearing and singing pure songs describing Me, he gradually becomes able to see spirit. He becomes like a person whose eyesight is restored by medicinal ointment.

In the material world, the mind tends to be filled with material thoughts. In that condition, the soul is not able to understand his true spiritual identity, and he is also not able to serve the Supreme Lord, who resides in his heart as the Supersoul. By hearing and chanting the Lord's glories, and by performing other kinds of devotional service, the soul gradually becomes powerful. Then, the bonds of matter that hold him become slackened. As the bondage of matter becomes slackened, the soul becomes stronger and in the course of time, the soul becomes exalted. He can directly see spirit, and he can act on the spiritual platform.

Some say that one should throw far away all that has no relation to the Lord, and one should act only to attain Him. However, one cannot become spiritually strong merely by dry knowledge. How can a conditioned soul get the power to suddenly renounce all that has no direct relation to the Lord? Can a prisoner in jail release himself simply by wishing to be free? The soul imprisoned in the material world has committed an offense to the Supreme Lord. He must find a way to lessen that offense. The spirit soul is by nature an eternal servant of Lord Kṛṣṇa. The root of the soul's offense is that he has forgotten that. Therefore, somehow or other, he should turn his mind to think of the Lord. By gazing at the Deity form of the Lord, hearing the description of the Lord's pastimes, and other devotional activities, the soul gradually revives his original spiritual nature. The more the soul's original nature is revived, the more the soul can see spirit directly. Serving the Deity of the Lord, and hearing and chanting the Lord's glories, are the only way for the neophyte devotee to make spiritual advancement. For this reason, the great saints have established Deity worship in this world.

Mullah: Is it not better to meditate on an imaginary form within the mind than to make an imaginary Deity form out of the material elements?

Gauracandra: They are the same. When the mind is material, it thinks only of material things. You may say that Brahman, the Supreme, is all-pervading. Still, the material mind will think Brahman is like the material element ether, which is also all-pervading. However, if I continue to meditate on Brahman in that way, in the course of time, the real truth about Brahman will be manifested in my heart. Time and space are material. If the mind's meditation is not beyond time and space, then how can the mind meditate on something that is beyond the material world?

Rejecting the Deity form as something made of earth, water, or other material elements, you meditate on an imaginary form of the Lord, a form made of time and space. That is worship of a material form of the Lord, a graven image of the Lord. A material so-called form of the Lord is not needed. The Lord is not material. His form is spiritual. That is His nature. Therefore, a process is given to the conditioned souls by which they can approach the spiritual Supreme Lord. By chanting the Lord's holy names, by narrating His pastimes, and by worshiping His Deity form, one gradually becomes more and more devoted to the Lord. When the worshipper attains pure devotion, he can see the spiritual form of the Supreme Lord. Philosophical speculation and fruitive work will not help one to see the Lord.

Mullah: The Supreme Lord is different from matter. It is said that Satan introduced the worship of material things in order to trap the souls in the material world. Therefore, I think it is not good to worship material things.

Gauracandra: The Supreme Personality of Godhead is one without a rival. No one can possibly compete with Him. Everything in this material world was created by Him and is dependent on Him. The Supreme Lord may be worshiped in many different ways. He is pleased by all these different kinds of worship. It is not that He will become an enemy if someone worships Him in a particular way. He is all-auspicious. If you say that Satan does something, then I say that Satan does not have the power to do anything against the Supreme Lord's will. If Satan exists, then he must be an individual soul dependent on the Supreme Lord.

However, I think that this Satan does not exist. Why not? Because in this material world, nothing can ever be done to thwart the Supreme Lord's will. There is not a single individual soul who is not dependent on the Supreme Lord. You may ask, "What is the origin of sin?" I reply, "The individual soul is by nature a servant of the Supreme Personality of Godhead. Awareness of this fact is knowledge. To forget this fact is ignorance. If an individual spirit soul forgets this fact, then he sows the seed of sins in the field of his heart. A person who always remains a liberated associate of the Lord does not plant the seed of sin in his heart."

Instead of imagining this mythological Satan, one should honestly see the ignorance in his own heart. Therefore, even if one worships the Supreme Lord as present in the material elements, he commits no offense. Therefore, Deity worship is necessary for the neophyte devotee, and it is the source of great auspiciousness for the advanced devotee. Therefore, the idea that Deity worship is not good is only a theory of some thinkers. It is not at all supported by the pure scriptures.

Mullah: Deity worship is not good for attaining love of God. It simply fills the mind with many material ideas.

Gauracandra: By studying the ancient history books, we can see that your conclusion is wrong. Many neophyte devotees begin their spiritual life by worshiping the Deity form of the Lord. As they continue the Deity worship in the association of the devotees, they gradually become advanced, and then they can directly see that the Deity is the spiritual form of the Supreme Lord Himself. Then they become plunged into a great ocean of spiritual love for the Lord. This is the undeniable truth: Association with the devotees of the Lord is the root of all that is good. By associating with spiritually advanced devotees of the Lord, one gradually attains spiritual love for the Lord. When one attains spiritual love for the Lord, the idea that the Deity form is material perishes. As one gradually becomes advanced, he attains great good fortune.

Non-Āryan religions are generally opposed to Deity worship. But look! How many followers of those religions have attained spiritual love for the Lord? They simply spend their time arguing with each other and hating each other. How can they understand loving devotion to the Lord?

Mullah: If one has love for the Lord, then there is no fault in His worshiping the Deity. However, how can the worship of a dog, a cat, a snake, a debauchee, or some other kind of being, be worship of the Supreme Lord? The honorable prophet has specifically forbidden worship of *byūt*.

Gauracandra: The people in general are grateful to God. Whether they sin or not, they have faith in the supremacy of God, and they bow down before the wonders that are displayed in this world. Prompted by their gratitude to God, the ignorant aborigines bow down before the sun, the river, the mountain, or anything that is very big and grand. They offer themselves to these things and they reveal their hearts to them. Although there is certainly a great difference between spiritual love for the Lord and the worship of material things, the bewildered people who show their gratitude to God by bowing down before these material things gradually attain a good result. Therefore, if you see with the eye of reason, you will not blame them for worshipping material things.

If one meditates on a formless all-pervading God, or if, without any spiritual love, one offers *namāz* prayers or other prayers, then how is that different from worshiping a cat? It is our idea that one should do whatever is necessary to arouse one's love for God. If those neophytes are mocked or attacked, then the path of gradual spiritual advancement will be blocked. Dogmatic people refuse to honor the followers of other religions. They mock and attack others who do not worship in the same way they do. They make a great mistake.

Mullah: Should it then be said that everything is God, and the worship of anything is the worship of God? Is the worship of sins worship of God? Is the worship of sinful desires worship of God? Is God pleased by any kind of worship?

Gauracandra: We do not say that everything is God. Rather, God is different from all else. Everything is created by God and dependent on Him. Everything has a relationship with God. By following the thread of that relationship, anything may lead one to become curious about God. Therefore, the Vedic *sūtra* says: "Curiosity pushes one to tastes things."

Therefore, this kind of curiosity gradually pushes one to try to experience what is spirit. You are all great *paṇḍitas*. If you are merciful and generous, you will understand what is the truth of this. We are only poor Vaiṣṇavas. We do not like to enter into debates. If you give permission, we will now hear the musical play, *Śrī Caitanya-maṅgala*.

No one could understand what conclusion the Mullah came to by hearing these arguments. After a short silence, he said, "I am glad to hear your arguments. I will come on another day and ask about something else. Now it is late. We wish to return to our homes."

After speaking these words, the Mullah Sāhib and his followers mounted their horses and left for Sātsāika Paraganā. The *bābājīs* happily called out the holy names of Lord Hari and entered the temple to hear the play, *Śrī Caitanya-maṅgala*.

Chapter Twelve

*Eternal religion
and devotional service
in practice.*

Śrī Navadvīpa-maṇḍala is the best of all holy places in the world. It is a thirty-two mile eight-petal lotus flower. The whorl of that lotus flower is Śrī Antardvīpa. In the center of Antardvīpa is Śrī Māyāpura. To the north of Śrī Māyāpura is Śrī Sīmantadvīpa. In Sīmantadvīpa is a temple of Śrī Sīmantinī devī. To the north of that temple is Lake Bilva-puṣkariṇī, and to the south is Lake Brāhmaṇa-puṣkariṇī. The region that contains Bilva-puṣkariṇī and Brāhmaṇa-puṣkariṇī is called Simuliyā by the people in general. Therefore, the village of Simuliyā-grāma is in the northern part of Śrī Navadvīpa.

At the time of Śrī Mahāprabhu, this place was the home of many, many *paṇḍitas*. This village was the home of Śacī-devī's father, Śrī Nilambara Cakravartī. Not far from his house lived a *vaidika brāhmaṇa* named Vrajanātha Bhaṭṭācārya. By studying in a school at Bilva-puṣkariṇī, in a few days, he had attained great learning in *nyāya-śāstra*, learning that was like a shoreless ocean. All the famous *paṇḍitas* of Bilva-puṣkariṇī, Brahmā-puṣkariṇī, Māyāpura, Godruma, Madhyadvīpa, Āmraghāṭā, Samudragar, Kuliyā, and many other places also were embarrassed and frustrated by Vrajanātha's skill in newer and newer logical arguments.

In the assemblies where the *paṇḍitas* were invited, Vrajanātha Nyāya-pañcānana became like a lion attacking a herd of elephants. Raising newer and newer arguments, he made the *paṇḍitas* burn with anger. Of these *paṇḍitas*, a very hard-hearted logician named Naiyika-Cuḍāmaṇi decided to kill Vrajanātha by casting a spell from the *Tantras*. Day after day, he stayed in the cremation ground of Rudradvipa and chanted *mantras* to kill his foe.

It was a frightening new-moon night. Blinding darkness filled every direction. At midnight, in the cremation ground, Naiyika-Cuḍāmaṇi called out to his worshipable deity, "O mother, only you should be worshipped in the Kali-yuga! I have heard that you are very easily pleased by even a little chanting of your *mantras*, and you easily grant boons. O mother with the terrifying face, your servant has performed great austerities and chanted your *mantra* for many days. Please be merciful this one time. O mother, I have many faults. Still, you are my mother. Please forgive my faults and appear before me."

Again and again screaming, Cuḍāmaṇi offered oblations into the fire and chanted a *mantra* with Nyāya-pañcānana's name. What wonderful power did that *mantra* possess! At that moment, the sky became covered with clouds. A powerful wind blew. A deafening thunder sounded. Again and again, there was lightning. Many grotesque ghosts could be seen. Intoxicated by drinking the sacrificial wine, Cuḍāmaṇi called out, "O mother, please don't delay!"

At that moment, a voice spoke from the sky: "Do not worry. Nyāya-pañcānana will not continue as a logician for many more days. In a few days, he will renounce logical debates. Then he will become silent. He will be your opponent no longer. Be peaceful and go home."

Hearing this voice from the sky, Cuḍāmaṇi became happy. Again and again, he offered *daṇḍavat* obeisances to Lord Śiva, the author of the *Tantras*. Then, he returned home.

Vrajanātha Nyāya-pañcānana became a *dig-vijayī paṇḍita* when he was only twenty-one years old. Day and night, he studied the books of Gaṅgeśopādhyāya. Seeing many faults in Raghunātha (Kāṇābhaṭṭa) Śiromaṇi's commentary, he wrote his own. He never thought about material affairs. Neither would he turn his ear to spiritual life. His whole life was logic, filled with phrases like *ghaṭa, paṭa, avaccheda*, and *vyavaccheda*. Even when he was resting, sleeping, eating, or walking about, his heart was rapt in logic, thinking about the nature of time, reality, solids, liquids, and a host of other things.

One day at sunrise at the Ganges' shore, as he was analyzing the sixteen categories enunciated by Gautama Muni, a new *nyāya* student asked, "O saintly Nyāya-pañcānana, have you heard Nimāi Paṇḍita's analysis of the atomic theory?"

Nyāya-pañcānana roared like a lion, "Who is Nimāi Paṇḍita? Do you speak of Jagannatha Misra's son? What was His argument? Please tell me."

The new student said, "Some days before in Navadvīpa, there was a great person named Nimāi Paṇḍita. He was very expert in considering many different arguments of the *nyāya-śāstra*. He thoroughly embarrassed and defeated Kāṇābhaṭṭa Śiromaṇi. Nimāi Paṇḍita had traveled to the farther shore of the ocean of the *nyāya-śāstras*. Even though He was so learned, in the end, He considered the *nyāya-śāstras* to be insignificant. He came to consider all material knowledge unimportant. He became a *sannyāsī* and traveled from place to place, preaching the chanting of Lord Hari's holy names. The Vaiṣṇavas say

He was the Supreme Personality of Godhead Himself, and they worship Him by chanting the Gaurahari *mantra*. O saintly Nyāya-pañcānana, please take a look at His logical arguments."

After hearing this praise of Nimāi Paṇḍita's logical arguments, Nyāya-pañcānana began to collect some of those famous arguments. It is the nature of a man that when he is very interested in a certain subject, he will honor the great teachers of that subject. Also, people tend not to honor great men while they are alive, but only after they are dead. Thus, after studying Nimāi Paṇḍita's logical arguments, Nyāya-pañcānana held Him in great esteem.

He would say, "O Nimāi Paṇḍita, if only I had been born during Your time! Then I could have been Your student! Then I could have attained great learning! O Nimāi Paṇḍita, please just once enter my heart! You are in truth the Supreme Brahman. If this were not so, then how could these wonderful logical arguments have entered Your intelligence? You are in truth Lord Hari with a fair complexion. How can this not be? You created the most wonderful logical arguments. You destroyed the blinding darkness of ignorance. Now is especially the time of blinding ignorance. You are fair and effulgent. You throw the darkness of ignorance far away. You are Lord Hari Himself. How can this not be? You enchanted the minds of the entire world. With Your logical arguments, You have certainly enchanted my mind."

Again and again speaking words like these, Vrajanātha became like a madman. He called out, "O Nimāi Paṇḍita! O Gaurahari! Please be merciful to me!"

He called out, "When will I be able to make logical arguments like Yours? Please be merciful to me, so I can become a most powerful scholar of the *nyāya-śāstra*!"

Vrajanātha thought, "The worshipers of Gaurahari must be as attracted to Him as I am, because of His great skill in logic. I must see if they have any books about logic written by Him."

Thinking in this way, Vrajanātha decided to associate with the devotees of Lord Gaurāṅga. Thus, Vrajanātha again and again loudly chanted, "Nimāi Paṇḍita! Gaurahari!" and many other holy names of the Lord. He also desired to associate with the devotees of Lord Gaura. These two acts brought him great spiritual merit, just on the verge of bearing fruit.

One day, as he was taking his meal, he asked his paternal grandmother, "O saintly grandmother, did you ever see Gaurahari?"

When she heard the name of Lord Gaurāṅga, Vrajanātha's grandmother began to think of her childhood. She said, "Ah, will the charming form of Gaurāṅga ever again come before my eyes? Who can remain a materialist after seeing Him? When He chanted the holy names of Lord Hari, even the animals, birds, trees, and vines all became stunned, overcome with spiritual love. When I think of Him, tears from my eyes stream over my chest."

Vrajanātha asked, "O saintly grandmother, do you know any stories about Him?"

The grandmother replied, "Yes. When He came to His maternal uncle's house with Mother Śacī, the elderly women of our family served Him the vegetable, *śāka*. Praising the *śāka*, He happily ate it."

Just at that moment, when His grandmother brought him a plate of *śāka*, Vrajanātha said, "*Śāka* is the favorite of the logician, Nimāi Paṇḍita," and he ate it with great relish. No one can describe how much Vrajanātha, who was completely uninterested in spiritual life, became attached to Nimāi Paṇḍita because of Nimāi's great learning in logic. He took a fancy to Nimāi. When he heard Nimāi's name, he became happy. When he gave alms to a beggar, he always said, "Jaya Śacīnandana!" He would visit the *paṇḍita bābājīs* of Śrī Māyāpura, listen to them chant the holy names of Lord Gaurāṅga, and ask them many questions about the Lord's victories in learned debate.

In this way, two or four months passed. Vrajanātha was now a changed man. Previously, it was only the descriptions of Nimāi's learning in logic that pleased him. Now, any talk about Nimāi pleased him. Now, he was no longer interested in logic. The logician, Nimāi, no longer lived in his heart. Now, it was the devotee Nimāi who lived here. When he heard the sounds of *khola* and *karatālas*, his heart danced. When he saw the pure devotees, he bowed down before them in his mind. Declaring that it was the birthplace of Lord Gaurāṅga, he worshiped the land of Navadvīpa. Vrajanātha was now polite and gentle. His opponents in the debating arena could see that his heart had become calm and cool. No longer was he eager to shower them with arrows of logical arguments. Nyāya-Cuḍāmaṇi thought his worshipable deity had made Vrajanātha powerless. Now he felt safe.

One day, in a secluded place, Vrajanātha said to himself, "If Nimāi could abandon the path of logic and turn to the path of devotion, then what is the harm if we do the same? When I was obsessed with logic, I could not hear the name of Nimāi with attention and devotion. Then, the *nyāya-śāstra* had me in its grip. Then, I ignored eating, sleeping, and everything else. Now, I look at the world with different eyes. The arguments of the *nyāya-śāstra* no longer enter my mind. Now, only the name Gaurāṅga enters my mind. Now, when I see the Vaiṣṇavas dancing, I think how beautiful the dancing is. But, I am born in an exalted *vaidika brāhmaṇa* dynasty. My dynasty is honored in society. The Vaiṣṇavas are very respectable people. Still, it is not good that I join them. I worship Lord Gaura only within my thoughts. That is the only proper way for me to act. There are many Vaiṣṇavas at Śrī Māyāpura, at the place where the Kazi broke the drums, and at the place where there are many *sannyāsīs*. When I see how their faces are effulgent, I become happy at heart. Among them, Śrī Raghunātha dāsa Bābājī greatly attracts my mind. I think I should study the *bhakti-śāstras* under his guidance."

"In the *Vedas* it is said (*Bṛhad-āraṇyaka Upaniṣad* 4.5.6): One should always gaze upon, hear about, think of, and meditate on the Supreme Personality of Godhead."

"Although the word *mantavyaḥ* (one should think about Him) here certainly refers to the *nyāya-śāstra*, where by logical analysis, one gradually attains knowledge of the Supreme, I have already spent a long time studying logic. Now, I think it is right for me to do a little more *śrotavyaḥ* (hearing about the Supreme). For a long time, logic was my life and soul. Now I desire to take shelter of Lord Gaurahari's lotus feet. A little after sunset, I will go to see Śrī Raghunātha dāsa Bābājī. I think that is the best thing to do."

The day was ended. The sun was almost invisible. A very gentle breeze blew from the south. In every direction, the birds had gone to their nests. One by one, the stars were visible in the sky. At that time, the Vaiṣṇavas had begun the *ārati* and *kīrtana* in the courtyard of Śrīvāsa's home in Śrī Māyāpura. Vrajanātha slowly entered and sat down under the *bakula* tree in the place in

Śrīvāsa's courtyard where the *khola* was broken. As he listened to the chanting in the *ārati* of Lord Gaurahari, his heart became softened. When the *kīrtana* ended, one by one, the Vaiṣṇavas came and sat under the *bakula* tree also.

When, proclaiming, "Jaya Śacīnandana!" "Jaya Rūpa-Sanātana!" and "Jaya Dāsa Gosvāmī!" elderly Raghunātha dāsa Bābājī Mahāśaya also entered the courtyard, all the elder Vaiṣṇavas greeted him with *daṇḍavat* obeisances. In that situation, Vrajanātha could not avoid also bowing down before him. Seeing the effulgence of Vrajanātha's face, the elderly *bābājī* embraced him and sat down beside him.

He asked, "Bābā, who are you?"

Vrajanātha replied, "I am a person who thirsts for the truth. I have decided to learn the truth from you."

A Vaiṣṇava sitting nearby knew who Vrajanātha was. He said, "He is Vrajanātha Nyāya-pañcānana. In understanding *nyāya-śāstra*, no *paṇḍita* in Śrī Navadvīpa is his equal. Nowadays, he has attained a little faith in Lord Śacīnandana."

Thus hearing the glories of Vrajanātha, the elderly *bābājī* politely said, "Bābā, you are a *paṇḍita*, and we are poor fools. You reside in the holy abode of our Lord Śacīnandana. It is you who should be merciful to us. How can we teach you? It is you who should mercifully tell us about Lord Gaurāṅga, and thus make us cool and peaceful."

As the two of them conversed, all the Vaiṣṇavas gradually left to fulfill their various duties. Only the old *bābājī* and Vrajanātha remained.

Vrajanātha said, "O saintly *bābājī*, I was born as a *brāhmaṇa*. Therefore, I am very proud of my learning. I am so proud that I see the entire world as my possession. I do not know that I should honor saintly persons. How did I become fortunate, that I now have some faith in your saintly character and actions? How can I know that? I wish to ask one or two questions. Please answer them. I do not come to mock or trick you. Please tell me: What is the true goal of life and how may the spirit soul attain it?

When I studied *nyāya-śāstra*, I came to the firm conclusion that the Supreme Lord and the individual spirit soul are different eternally. It is only by the mercy of the Supreme Lord that the individual spirit soul can attain liberation. The Supreme Lord's mercy is then the means by which one attains liberation. By that means, then, one attains the goal of life. Many times I asked the *nyāya-śāstra*, 'What is the true goal of life and how may the spirit soul attain it?,' but the *nyāya-śāstra* gave me no answers. I was always thwarted. Please tell me your idea of what is the goal of life and the way to attain it."

Śrī Raghunātha dāsa Bābājī was very wise. For many days, he had lived at Rādhā-kunda, where he took shelter of Śrī Raghunātha dāsa Gosvāmī's feet. There, he spent every afternoon listening to Lord Gaura's pastimes from Śrī Raghunātha dāsa Gosvāmī's own mouth. Many times, Śrī Raghunātha dāsa Bābājī and Śrī Kṛṣṇadāsa Kavirāja would discuss the spiritual truth, and if any doubt arose among them, they would ask Śrī Raghunātha dāsa Gosvāmī to give the answer. At that time, Śrī Raghunātha dāsa Bābājī was the most prominent of the *paṇḍita bābājīs*. Many times, he and Prema dāsa, the *parāmahāṁsa bābājī* of Śrī Godruma, would discuss the nature of pure spiritual love for the Lord.

Happy to hear Vrajanātha's question, he replied, "O saintly Nyāya-pañcānana, a person who, after studying the *nyāya-śāstra*, is eager to understand the true goal of life and the way to attain it is very fortunate in this world. Why should he not be considered fortunate? *Nyāya-śāstra* is an attempt to understand what is the most important thing. Scholars who understand that grasp the truth of the *nyāya-śāstra*. However, those who study *nyāya-śāstra* only to attain skill in debate do not reap the true fruit of *nyāya*. Their labor is all for nothing. Their lives are wasted. What is attained when one follows the path that leads to the truth is called the true goal of life. The method one adopts to attain that goal is the way of attaining the true goal of life. According to their different qualifications, the individual souls trapped in the material world have differing conceptions of what is the true goal of life. Still, the true goal of life is only one. It is not two."

"According to their different qualifications, the spirit souls proclaim three different goals of life. They are: 1. *bhukti* (material sense gratification), 2. *mukti* (impersonal liberation), and 3. *bhakti* (devotional service). Those who yearn for material pleasures and are bound by the ropes of material *karma* believe that *bhukti* is the true goal of life. The scriptures are a *kāmadhenu* cow that fulfills all desires. Whatever one desires, there is a description somewhere in the scriptures of how to attain it. For those who desire material pleasures, the scriptures give the *karma-kanda* section of the *Vedas*. The residents of the material world generally yearn for material pleasures, so the scriptures give certain specific instructions to them. Those who have material bodies generally think that sense pleasures are the best and most important attainment. The material world is, after all, the abode of material sense pleasures. The material sense pleasures the soul attains from the time of birth until the time of death are called, 'pleasures this world,' and the material sense pleasures one may attain after dying are called, 'pleasures of the next world.'"

"There are many different kinds of pleasure in the next world. In Svargaloka and Indraloka, there are the pleasures of seeing the Apsarās' dancing, drinking heavenly nectar, smelling the flowers and other scented objects in the Nandana gardens, seeing the beauty of Indrapuri and the Nandana gardens, hearing the singing of the Gandharvas and others, and living with the Vidyādharīs. To a lesser degree, these same kinds of material sense pleasure are also available in Tapoloka and Maharloka. In Bhuloka (the earth), the material sense pleasures are gross. As one goes to higher and higher planets, the sense pleasures become more and more subtle. In this way, they are different. Still, they are all material sense pleasures. It is not that any of them are not material sense pleasures. None of these planets are spiritual."

"The subtle body of mind, intelligence, and false ego is a perverted reflection of spirit. In the higher planets, the pleasures are pleasures of the subtle body. All these different kinds of material pleasures are called *bhukti*. The conditioned souls trapped in the circle of *karma* take shelter of karmic activities in order to attain material sense pleasures. That is called their *sādhana*—the means they adopt to attain what they see as the true goal of life."

"In the *Yajur Veda* (2.5.5.) it is said: One who desires to attain Svargaloka should perform the *aśvamedha-yajña*."

"Thus, the *aśvamedha-yajña*, *agniṣṭoma-yajña*, *viśvadeva-bali*, *iṣṭāpūrta*, and *darśa-paurṇamāsī* are some of the ways the scriptures give for the conditioned soul to attain material sense pleasures. In this way, the materialists say that material sense pleasure is the true goal of life. Then, there are other persons who, tortured by the flames of trouble that must accompany life in the material world, know that the fourteen material worlds filled with sense pleasures are all unimportant and unworthy places, and therefore yearn to escape the circle of karmic reactions. These persons think that liberation is the true goal of life. They think that material sense pleasures are the ropes that bind them to the material world."

"Therefore, they say, 'Let those whose desire for material pleasures has not been destroyed follow the *karma-kanda*'s prescription for attaining sense pleasures. Nevertheless, in the *Bhagavad-gītā* (9.21) it is said: *kṣīṇe puṇye martya-lokaṁ viśanti* (When they have thus enjoyed heavenly sense pleasure, they return to this mortal planet again. Thus, through the Vedic principles, they achieve only flickering happiness). In this *śloka* it is seen that material sense pleasure is not eternal. At a certain point, it certainly wanes and perishes. It must perish. It is material. It is not spiritual. One should therefore strive to attain a result that is eternal. Liberation is eternal. Therefore, liberation is the true goal of life for all spirit souls. The fourteen practices that begin with renunciation are the way to attain it. Therefore, they are the way of attaining the true goal of life. Therefore, to understand the true goal of life and the way to attain it, one should study the *jñāna-kanda* portion of the *Vedas*.'"

"The scriptures are like a *kāmadhenu* cow in that they give different attainments to different living entities, according to their different qualifications. Even if a spirit soul attains impersonal liberation, that liberation is not the final goal of life. The highest stage of impersonal liberation is called *nirvāna*, where the individual souls imagine that they cease to exist. However, the spirit souls exist eternally. That is their nature. Therefore, this imaginary *nirvāna* never actually occurs."

"That the individual spirit souls are eternal is confirmed by these words of *Śvetāśvatara Upaniṣad* (6.13): The Supreme Lord is eternal and the living beings are eternal. The Supreme Lord is cognizant and the living beings are cognizant."

"In this way, the Vedic *mantras* affirm that the individual spirit soul exists eternally. It is not possible for something that exists eternally to ever cease to exist. Those who affirm that the individual spirit soul continues to exist even after liberation also affirm that neither *bhukti* (material sense pleasures) nor *mukti* (liberation) are the final, highest goal of life. These are lesser goals. All activities are in relation to a particular goal and a method of attaining that goal. The goal is called *sādhya*, and the means by which one attains it is called *sādhana*. Think of it in this way: goals and ways of attaining them are like links in a chain."

"What at first is considered a goal later becomes a means and something else is the goal. In this way, goals and means are like links in a chain, with each goal being eventually linked into a means for attaining a new goal. Continuing in this way, there is one final goal that does not become the means of attaining another goal. That final goal is *bhakti* (devotional service). Therefore, devotional service is the final goal, because devotional service is the eternal nature of the individual spirit souls. The activities of human beings are all various links in this chain of goals and means. The different kinds of karmic activities are different links in this chain. Following them, the different kinds of philosophical speculation (*jñāna*) are also links in this chain. After the links that are philosophical speculation comes the link that is *bhakti* (devotional service). The goal of fruitive activities (*karma*) is material sense pleasure (*bhukti*). The goal of philosophical speculation (*jñāna*) is impersonal liberation (*mukti*). The goal of devotional service (*bhakti*) is pure love of God (*prema-bhakti*). The final conclusion, then, is that *bhakti* is the final means, and the goal attained by *bhakti* is *bhakti*. Fruitive work (*karma*) and philosophical speculation (*jñāna*) are then only the primary and intermediate links in the chain of means to attain goals. They are not the goal."

Vrajanātha: It is said in the scriptures (*Bṛhad-āraṇyaka Upaniṣad* 4.5.25 and 2.4.24): Who is the seer and who the seen?

It is also said (*Bṛhad-āraṇyaka Upaniṣad* 1.4.10): I am Brahman.

It is also said (*Aitareya Upaniṣad* 1.5.3): Brahman is spiritual truth.

It is also said (*Chāndogya Upaniṣad* 6.8.70): O Svetaketu, you are that.

In these and many other passages of scripture it is not at all seen that devotional service is the final goal. Therefore, how can it be wrong to say that impersonal liberation is the final goal?

Bābājī: I have already said that the goals are different, according to the different desires of the living entities. Those who yearn after material sense pleasures do not accept liberation as the final goal. To these persons, the scriptures advise (*Āpastamba Śrauta-sūtra* 2.1.1): Those who perform the *caturmāsya-yajñas* attain immortality.

There are also many other passages like this. Bābā, is the word *mukti* (liberation) of any use at all? The fruitive workers (*karmīs*) do not aspire for it. They ask, "Why is the word *mukti* (liberation) never mentioned in the *mantras* of the four *Vedas?*" One or two *karmī* philosophers claim that renunciation is only meant for the incompetent, and those are competent should be engaged in fruitive work (*karma*). These instructions are written in the scriptures so that persons situated in the lowest level of spiritual qualification may be steady in their duties. It is not auspicious for the living entities to shirk the duties that fit their spiritual qualification. When a person is steady in the duties for which he is qualified, he easily becomes qualified for the next level of duties. Therefore, the *Vedas* do not criticize being steady in one's duties. Rather, one who criticizes the performance of duties himself falls down.

The souls in this world who have become advanced in spiritual life have all reaped the good results of being steady in their duties. The impersonal path, where one employs philosophical speculation (*jñāna*) to attain liberation, is not revealed to persons qualified only for fruitive work (*karma*). The impersonal path, where one employs philosophical speculation (*jñāna*) to attain liberation, is not praised in the presence of persons qualified only for fruitive work. The Vedic *mantras* praise it only in the presence of persons qualified to follow the impersonal path. As the impersonal path is superior to the path of fruitive work, so the path of devotional service is superior to the impersonal path. By speaking words like *tat tvaṁ asi* (you are that) and *ahaṁ brahmāsmi* (I am Brahman), the Vedic *mantras* make the impersonalist steady in his duty of acting to attain liberation. The *Vedas* are not to be blamed for doing that. Still, the impersonal liberation described there is not the ultimate stage. The final conclusion of the Vedic *mantras* is that the final goal is love of God, and that goal is attained by performing devotional service.

Vrajanātha: Is it possible that great *mahā-vākyas* of the *Vedas* have described only secondary goals and means?

Bābājī: You may call some *mantras mahā-vākyas*, but the *Vedas* themselves do not distinguish any particular *mantras* as better than the others. In order to claim that their doctrine is superior, the impersonalist teachers have labeled some *mantras mahā-vākya*, and all other Vedic *mantras* are subordinate to them. If one wishes to call all the statements of the Vedas *mahā-vākyas*, there is nothing wrong in that. However, if one wishes to label one particular *mantra* the *mahā-vākya*, and all the others ordinary *vākyas*, then one commits an offense to the sacred *Vedas*. In the *Vedas*, there is praise for fruitive work (*karma*), praise for impersonal liberation (*mukti*), and praise for many other goals and means also. Still, one must consider everything as a whole and determine what is the final conclusion of all the *Vedas*. The *Vedas* are like a cow, and the milkman is Lord Kṛṣṇa. It is He who reveals the true purpose of all the *Vedas*.

He explains (*Bhagavad-gītā* 6.46-47): A *yogī* is greater than the ascetic, greater than the empiricist, and greater than the fruitive worker. Therefore, O Arjuna, in all circumstances be a *yogī*. And of all *yogīs*, he who always abides in Me with great faith, worshipping Me in transcendental loving service, is most intimately united with Me in *yoga* and is the highest of all.

In the *Śvetāśvatara Upaniṣad* (6.23) it is also said: Only unto those great souls who have implicit faith in both the Lord and the spiritual master are all the imports of Vedic knowledge automatically revealed.

In the *Gopāla-tāpanī Upaniṣad* (1.14) it is said: Devotional service to Lord Kṛṣṇa is performed when the heart no longer desires any material benefit to be obtained, in this life or the next. This is freedom from the bonds of *karma*.

In the *Bṛhad-āraṇyaka Upaniṣad* (1.4.8) it is said: One should worship the Supreme Lord, considering Him the most dear.

In the *Bṛhad-āraṇyaka Upaṇiṣad* (4.5.6) it is also said: One should gaze on the Supreme Personality of Godhead, hear about Him, think of Him, and meditate upon Him.

One who analyses these statements of the *Vedas* will easily see that devotional service is described in the *Vedas* as the means to attain the goal of life.

Vrajanātha: In the *karma-kanda* section of the *Vedas* it is said that the Supreme Personality of Godhead is the ultimate awarder of the fruits of *karma*. In this way, the *karma-kanda* enjoins one to have faith in devotional service. In the *jñāna-kanda* also, pleasing Lord Hari by engaging in His devotional service is described as one of the four means of attaining the goal. If devotional service is thus one of the means employed to attain sense gratification and impersonal liberation, then how can devotional service be the final goal of life? When sense gratification or impersonal liberation are attained, then the means employed to get them are thrown away. That is what is generally taught. Please give me some clear teaching on this point.

Bābājī: In the *karma-kanda* portion of the *Vedas* it is said that one should engage in devotional service in order to attain sense gratification, and in the *jñāna-kanda* portion of the *Vedas* it is said that to attain impersonal liberation one should engage in devotional service. That is true. Without first pleasing the Supreme Personality of Godhead, no one can attain any result. The Supreme Personality of Godhead is the abode of all potencies. The individual spirit souls and the material worlds are only a small part of the Lord's potencies. The Supreme Lord is not pleased by fruitive work (*karma*) or impersonal speculation (*jñāna*). However, when *karma* and *jñāna* take shelter of devotional service, they can give certain results. Therefore, it is said that in *karma* and *jñāna*, the reflection of devotional service is present. However, the devotional service seen in *karma* and *jñāna* is not pure devotional service. It is merely a reflection of true devotional service, present there to give certain results.

This reflection of devotional service is of two kinds: 1. The reflection of pure devotional service, and 2. The reflection of mixed devotional service. The reflection of pure devotional service I will describe later. The reflection of mixed devotional service is of three kinds: 1. The reflection of devotional service mixed with *karma*, 2. The reflection of devotional service mixed with *jñāna*, and 3. The reflection of devotional service mixed with both *karma* and *jñāna*. At the time of performing a *yajña* one may say, "O Indra, O Sūrya, please be merciful and give me the result of this *yajña*." This is an example of the reflection of devotional service mixed with *karma* (*karma-viddha-bhakty-ābhāsa*). Some philosophers call this reflected devotional service *karma-miśra bhakti* (devotional service mixed with *karma*), and others call it *aropa-siddha bhakti* (artificial devotional service).

Another example is seen in the words, "O Kṛṣṇa, pushed by fear of repeated birth and death, I now approach You. Day after day I chant the Hare Kṛṣṇa *mantra*. Please be merciful and give me impersonal liberation."

Another example is the words, "O Supreme Lord, You are Brahman, and I have fallen into the abyss of *māyā*. Please pick me up and make me one with You."

These two statements are examples of the reflection of devotional service mixed with *jñāna*. Some philosophers call this kind of reflected devotional service *jñāna-miśra bhakti* (devotional service mixed with *jñāna*), and others call it *aropa-siddha bhakti* (artificial devotional service). All these reflections of devotional service are different from pure devotional service.

The devotional service described by the Lord Himself in *Bhagavad-gītā* 6.47 (*śraddhāvān bhajate yo māṁ*) is pure devotional service. It is that kind of devotional service that we adopt as the means to attain the goal of *prema* (pure love of God). *Karma* and *jñāna* are the means to attain sense gratification and impersonal liberation. They are not the means for the individual spirit soul to regain his eternal nature.

After hearing all this, Vrajanātha could not ask any questions. He thought, "It will be good to make the argument for the *nyāya-śāstra* wait for a while as I think about these subtle points. The saintly *bābājī* is especially learned in this topic. In time I will ask him questions and then I will learn what is the truth of this. Now it is night. I should return home."

Vrajanātha then said aloud, "O saintly *bābājī*, I have learned many truths from you today. From time to time, I will return. Please continue to instruct me. You are a very great teacher and I am dependent on your mercy. There is one thing I wish to know. When I hear your reply I will depart. Did Lord Gaurāṅga, the son of Śacī, write any book of His teachings? I would like to have such a book."

Bābājī: Śrī Mahāprabhu did not write any book Himself. By His order, His followers wrote many books. Mahāprabhu personally wrote eight verses, called *Śikṣāṣṭaka*, which are like jewels that the devotees wear around their necks. The teachings in them are very profound. Studying these deep truths, the devotees have written a poem called *Daśa-mūla* (the Ten Roots). In this poem, the goal and the means are briefly described in terms of *sambandha* (the relationship of the living entities and the Supreme), *abhidheya* (the activities of that relationship) and *prayojana* (the final goal of life). You should begin by understanding this poem.

Vrajanātha replied, "As you order. Tomorrow evening, I will return and learn this *Daśa-mūla* from you. You are my *śikṣā-guru* (instructing spiritual master). I offer *daṇḍavat* obeisances to you."

The saintly *bābājī* politely embraced him and said, "Bābā, You purify the community of *brāhmaṇas*. Please come tomorrow evening. That will please me very much."

Chapter Thirteen

Eternal religion and sambandha, abhidheya and prayojana
(Evidence and truth)

The next evening, Vrajanātha sat down under the *bakula* tree facing the courtyard of Śrīvāsa's home. The saintly elderly *bābājī* had developed a kind of paternal love for Vrajanātha. He was waiting for Vrajanātha to come. When Vrajanātha arrived, the *bābājī* at once came out from the courtyard. Embracing Vrajanātha, he took him to his cottage (*bhajana-kuṭira*) in a grove of jasmine vines to one side of Śrīvāsa's courtyard. Touching the dust of the saintly *bābājī*'s feet, Vrajanātha thought that his life had now become successful. He humbly said, "O saintly *bābājī*, please teach me the *Daśa-mūla*, which contains the essence of our Lord Nimāi's teachings."

His heart blossoming with happiness to hear this very appropriate question, the elderly *bābājī* said, "Bābā, I will explain the *Daśa-mūla* to you. You are a *paṇḍita*. Please carefully understand the truths described in these verses. The first verse is this: The *Vedas* teach that Lord Hari is the Supreme Truth. He has all potencies and He is an ocean of the nectar of transcendental mellows. The individual spirit souls, which are His parts and parcels, are divided into groups, some swallowed up by the material energy, and others free from her clutches. Everything that exists is simultaneously one and different from Him. Pure devotional service is the way to attain Lord Hari. The goal of life is to love Him. This Lord Gauracandra personally taught to the living entities."

"In the verses that begin here, Śrīmān Gauracandra teaches ten truths to the faithful souls. Of these, the first verse describes the various kinds of evidence, and the remaining nine verses describe various truths learned from these evidences. First the evidence is given and then the truths that may be learned from that evidence. Evidence is called *pramāṇa*. The verse I have just recited is an introductory verse that contains a summary of the *Daśa-mūla*. The verse that follows it is the first verse of the *Daśa-mūla* proper. In verses two through eight, the relationship (*sambandha*) of the souls and the Lord is revealed. In verse nine, the activities (*abhidheya*) of that relationship are described. In verse ten, the true need of the living entities (*prayojana*) is described."

"The meaning of the introductory, summary verse is this: The word *āmnāyaḥ* means, 'the statements of the *Vedas* as they are understood through the disciplic succession.' The *Vedas*, the *Śrīmad-Bhāgavatam*, and other *smṛti-śāstras* that follow the *Vedas*, as well as direct perception and other kinds of evidence that support the evidence of scriptures are all called *pramāṇa*, or evidence. These evidences support the following definite conclusions: 1. Lord Hari is the Supreme Truth, 2. He has all potencies, 3. He is an ocean of the nectar of transcendental mellows, 4. The liberated and conditioned souls are His parts and parcels, 5. Some souls are imprisoned by the material energy, and others are free from her clutches, 6. The entire material universe, which contains both matter and spirit, is inconceivably, simultaneously one and different from Him, 7. Devotional service is the way to attain Lord Hari, and 8. The goal of life is to love Lord Kṛṣṇa."

After hearing this summary verse, Vrajanātha said, "O saintly *bābājī*, now is not the time for me to ask any questions. After you recite the first verse, I will speak any questions that may arise in my heart."

"Hearing this, the elderly *bābājī* said, "Good. Good. I will recite the first of these *mūla* verses. Please listen carefully. The self-evident *Vedas*, which by Lord Hari's mercy, are obtained from the disciplic succession beginning with the demigod Brahmā, and which are accompanied by other sources of evidence, such as direct perception, are the evidence for the following nine truths. Ordinary logic, called *tarka*, has no power to enter a discussion of these truths."

Vrajanātha: Is there any evidence in the *Vedas* that Brahmā taught his disciples?

Bābājī: Yes, there is. In the *Muṇḍaka Upaniṣad* (1.1.1) it is said: Brahmā, who is the first demigod, the creator of the universe, the protector of the worlds, spoke knowledge of the Supreme, the first of all kinds of knowledge, to his eldest son, Artharva."

There, it is also said (*Muṇḍaka Upaniṣad* 1.2.13): "Brahmā taught him the science of the eternal Supreme Person.

Vrajanātha: Is there any evidence that when they wrote the *smṛti-śāstras* the sages gave the proper interpretations of the *Vedas*?

Bābājī: In *Śrīmad-Bhāgavatam*, which is the crest jewel of all scriptures, the Supreme Personality of Godhead Himself explains (11.14.3): At the time of cosmic annihilation, the *Vedas* became lost. At the beginning of the next creation, I again taught the *Vedas* to the demigod, Brahmā, for the principles of true religion are My very heart. Then, Brahmā repeated this knowledge to his first son, Manu. Then, the seven great sages, whose leader is Bhṛgu, learned this knowledge from Manu."

Vrajanātha: Why is there a Vaiṣṇava disciplic succession?

Bābājī: Misled by impersonalism, many people in the world have left the true path. If the devotees untainted by impersonalism do not have their own disciplic succession, then it will be very difficult to associate with true devotees of the Lord. In the *Padma Purāṇa* it is written: Unless you are initiated by a bona fide spiritual master in disciplic succession, the *mantra* that you might have received is without any effect. The four Vaiṣṇava disciplic successions, beginning from Laksmi-devī, Brahmā, Śiva, and Sanaka-kumara, have purified the entire world.

Of all of these, the disciplic succession from Lord Brahmā is the oldest. The disciplic succession begins with Brahmā and extends even to the present day. The *Vedas*, *Vedāngas*, *Vedānta*, and other scriptures have been passed down unchanged from an ancient time, carefully preserved by the disciplic succession. Nothing has been changed or added to the scriptures under the care of the disciplic succession. Therefore, no one should doubt that the *Vedas* and other scriptures that are accepted by the bona fide disciplic succession are authentic. There is a great need for a bona fide disciplic succession. Therefore, from the earliest time, the great saints have followed the bona fide disciplic succession.

Vrajanātha: Are there complete lists of the disciplic successions?

Bābājī: The lists contain the names of only the most important *ācāryas*. It is their names that are included in the lists.

Vrajanātha: I wish to hear the list of *ācāryas* in the disciplic succession from Brahmā.

Bābājī: Here is the list: Lord Brahmā is the direct disciple of Viṣṇu, the Lord of the spiritual sky. His disciple is Nārada, Nārada's disciple is Vyāsa, and Vyāsa's disciples are Śukadeva Gosvāmī and Madhvācārya. Padmanābha Ācārya is the disciple of Madhvācārya, and Narahari is the disciple of Padmanābha Ācārya. Mādhava is the disciple of Narahari, Akṣobhya is the direct disciple of Mādhava, and Jaya Tīrtha is the disciple of Akṣobhya. Jaya Tīrtha's disciple is Jñānasindhu, and his disciple is Dayānidhi. Vidyānidhi is the disciple of Dayānidhi, and Rājendra is the disciple of Vidyānidhi. Jayadharma is the disciple of Rājendra. Puruṣottama is the disciple of Jayadharma. Śrīmān Lakṣmīpati is the disciple of Vyāsa Tīrtha, who is the disciple of Puruṣottama. And Mādhavendra Puri is the disciple of Lakṣmīpati.

Vrajanātha: In this verse, it is said that the *Vedas* are the only evidence, and direct perception along with the other sources of evidence should be accepted only to help in understanding the *Vedas*. However, *nyāya*, Sāṅkhya, and the other philosophies are also sources of evidence, as are the *Purāṇas*, direct perception, inference, comparison, the *Vedas*, and the Vedic histories (*Itihāsa*). Understanding something by its absence (*anupalabdhi*), circumstantial evidence (*arthapatti*), and probability (*sambhāva*) are all considered different sources of evidence. Why should it be considered that some kinds of evidence are more valuable than others? If direct perception and inference are not considered sources of evidence, then what kind of knowledge will one be able to get? Please explain this so that I may understand.

Bābājī: Direct perception and other sources of evidence like it all depend on the material senses. The material senses of the conditioned soul are subject to four defects: 1. *bhrama* (mistakes), 2. *pramāda* (illusions), 3. *vipralipsā* (cheating), and 4. *karaṇāpāṭava* (sensory inefficiency). How can one attain true knowledge with such faulty instruments? The Supreme Personality of Godhead Himself appeared in the hearts of the great saints and sages as they were rapt in meditation on Him. The Lord then gave them the perfect knowledge that is the *Vedas*. Therefore, without fear, one can accept the *Vedas* as truth.

Vrajanātha: Please explain these four defects: mistakes, illusions, cheating, and sensory inefficiency.

Bābājī: When the imperfect material senses make mistakes in perceiving the world around it, that is called *bhrama*. Seeing a mirage in the desert is an example of such a mistake. The intelligence of the conditioned souls is limited. Therefore, when such a limited intelligence tries to understand the unlimited Supreme Truth, the limited intelligence is bound to be illusioned in many ways. That is called *pramāda*. An example of this is seen when the material intelligence, limited by time and space, questions how the Supreme Person could have created the material world of time and space. Doubt is called *vipralipsā*. The material senses are not very efficient tools for acquiring knowledge. When they make mistakes again and again that is called *karaṇāpāṭava*.

Vrajanātha: Do not sensory perception and other sources of knowledge have any value at all?

Bābājī: Is there a way to understand the material world except with the material senses and other like sources of knowledge? Still, all these sources of knowledge are powerless to understand the spiritual world. For the spiritual world, the *Vedas* are the only source of knowledge. If sense perception and these other sources of evidence confirm the truths revealed in the *Vedas*, they may be accepted.

Vrajanātha: Are the *Bhagavad-gītā*, *Śrīmad-Bhāgavatam*, and other like scriptures not sources of true knowledge?

Bābājī: The *Bhagavad-gītā* has come from the mouth of the Supreme Lord Himself. It is also called the *Gītā Upaniṣad*. It is counted as one of the *Vedas*. Because they are the teachings of Lord Gaurāṅga, the ten verses of *Daśa-mūla* are also one of the *Vedas*. The *Śrīmad-Bhāgavatam* is an anthology of the truths described in the *Vedas*. It is the crest jewel of all sources of knowledge. If they confirm the *Vedas'* teachings, the other *smṛti-śāstras* are also sources of true knowledge. The *tantra-śāstra* is of three kinds: 1. Those in the mode of goodness, 2. Those in passion, and 3. Those in ignorance. Among them, the *Pañcarātras* and other *Tantras* in the mode of goodness expand the confidential portions of the *Vedas'* teachings. The word *tantra* comes from the verbal root *tan* (to expand). Therefore, these *Tantras* are also counted among the sources of true knowledge.

Vrajanātha: The *Vedas* consist of many different books. Among them, which should be accepted and which not? Please tell me.

Bābājī: In the course of time, certain unscrupulous men interpolated many new chapters, *maṇḍalas*, and *mantras* in the text of the *Vedas*. Therefore, it is not that all the parts of the *Vedas* should be accepted. What, in the course of time, the *ācāryas* in the bona fide disciplic succession have accepted—that should be considered the actual *Vedas*. What they have rejected as interpolations should not be accepted.

Vrajanātha: What books of the *Vedas* have the *ācāryas* of the bona fide disciplic successions accepted?

Bābājī: The *ācāryas* have accepted the *Upaniṣads* named *Īśa, Kena, Kaṭha, Praśna, Muṇḍaka, Māṇḍūkya, Taittirīya, Aitareya, Chāndogya, Bṛhad-āraṇyaka* and *Śvetāśvatara*, as well as the *Gopāla-tāpanī Upaniṣad*, the *Nṛsiṁha- tāpanī Upaniṣad* and other like *tāpanī Upaniṣads*, as well as the *Brāhmaṇas, maṇḍalas*, and other portions of the *Ṛg Veda, Yajur Veda, Sāma Veda*, and *Atharva Veda*. The *ācāryas* have accepted all these books as sources of genuine knowledge.

Vrajanātha: You said that material logic has no power to understand spiritual things. What is the proof of that?

Bābājī: In the *Kaṭha Upaniṣad* (1.2.9) it is said: The spiritual truth cannot be understood by material logic.

In the *Vedānta-sūtra* (2.1.11) it is said: Transcendental topics cannot be understood by argument or logic.

In these and other statement of the *Vedas* and *Vedānta*, it is seen that material logic cannot be counted on as a source of true spiritual knowledge. In the *Mahābhārata* (*Bhīṣma-parva* 5.22) it is said: Anything transcendental to material nature is called inconceivable, whereas arguments are all mundane. Since mundane arguments cannot touch transcendental subject matters, one should not try to understand transcendental subject matters through mundane arguments.

In these words of the *Mahābhārata*, the limits of material logic are seen. The conclusion of devotional service is also explained in these words written by Śrīla Rūpa Gosvāmī (*Bhakti-rasāmṛta-sindhu* 1.1.32): For persons who have a natural taste for understanding books like *Bhagavad-gītā* and *Śrīmad-Bhāgavatam*, devotional service is easier than for those simply accustomed to mental speculation and argumentative processes.

Material logic cannot bring a definitive, conclusive understanding. This is described in the following words (*Bhakti-rasāmṛta-sindhu* 1.1.33): A person may become governed by certain convictions derived by his own arguments and decisions. Then another person, who may be a greater logician, will nullify these conclusions and establish another thesis. In this way, the path of argument will never be safe or conclusive.

If this is so, then what is the use of material logic and argument?

Vrajanātha: O saintly *bābājī*, I accept that the self-perfect *Vedas* are the best of all sources of knowledge. If they try to contradict the *Vedas*, the logicians are merely speaking in vain. Now please recite the second verse of the *Daśa-mūla*.

Bābājī: Lord Hari is the only Supreme Truth. Brahmā, Śiva, and Indra bow down before Him. The impersonal Brahman, which is completely untouched by matter, is the effulgence of His transcendental form. The all-pervading Supersoul is His expansion. He is the father of the material universes. He is the lover of Śrī Rādhā. His form is splendid, like a dark monsoon cloud. He is completely spiritual.

Vrajanātha: The *Upaniṣads* teach that the impersonal Brahman is the highest truth and it is beyond the touch of matter. Why, then, does Śrīmān Gaurahari affirm that it is the effulgence of Lord Hari's body? Please explain that to me.

Bābājī: Lord Hari is the Supreme Personality of Godhead, Bhagavān. The word *bhagavān* means, "He who possesses six opulences." In the *Viṣṇu Purāṇa* (6.5.47) it is written: Full wealth, strength, fame, beauty, knowledge and renunciation—these are the six opulences of the Supreme Personality of Godhead.

These six opulences are interrelated, like the limbs of a body. Which of them is the body? Which of them are the limbs? The body is the resting place of the limbs. The tree is the body, and the branches are the limbs. The whole form is the body, and the hands and feet are included among the limbs. The body is the resting place of the limbs. Of the Supreme Lord's opulences, His handsomeness is the body and the other opulences are the limbs. Wealth, strength, and fame are three limbs. The effulgence of fame consists of knowledge and renunciation. Therefore, these two are the effulgence of one of the limbs. They are the opulences of an opulence. They are not direct opulences themselves. Knowledge of changeless spirit and renunciation of matter are the parts of the body of the impersonal Brahman. The impersonal Brahman is the effulgence emanating from the spiritual worlds. The unchanging inactive formless, quality-less Brahman is not the independent highest truth. It is the form of the Supreme Personality of Godhead that is the independent highest truth. The light of a fire is not independent. It is the fire itself that is independent, and the light is merely one of the fire's qualities.

Vrajanātha: In many places in the *Vedas*, after the impersonal Brahman was described, the text declared, "*oṁ śānti. śānti. harih. oṁ.*" In the way, the *Vedas* affirm the superiority of Lord Hari. Who is Lord Hari?

Bābājī: Lord Hari is Rādhā and Kṛṣṇa, who enjoy transcendental pastimes.

Vrajanātha: I will ask about this later. Now please tell me: What kind of expansion of the Supreme Lord (*bhagavān*) is the Supersoul (Paramātmā), the father of the material universes?

Bābājī: Employing the two opulences of wealth and strength, the Supreme Lord created the material world of *māyā*. After creating the world, the Lord expanded Himself as Viṣṇu and entered it. When the Lord expands Himself, each expansion is perfect and complete. This is described in the following words of *Bṛhad-āraṇyaka Upaniṣad* (5.1): The Supreme Personality of Godhead is perfect and complete, and because He is completely perfect, all emanations from Him, such as this phenomenal world, are perfectly equipped as complete wholes. Whatever is produced of the complete whole is also complete in itself. Because He is the complete whole, even though so many complete units emanate from Him, He remains the complete balance.

Therefore, the Supersoul (Paramātmā) is Lord Viṣṇu, who is perfect and complete, who has entered the material world, and who protects the material world. Lord Viṣṇu thus manifests in three forms, as: 1. Kāraṇodakaśāyī Viṣṇu, Kṣīrodakaśāyī Viṣṇu, and Garbhodakaśāyī Viṣṇu. The Kāraṇa Ocean, which is also known as the Virajā River, lies on the boundary that separates the spiritual and material worlds. To that place, Lord Mahā-Viṣṇu goes and reclines on the Kāraṇa Ocean. Thus He is Kāraṇodakaśāyī Viṣṇu. Glancing at her from far away, the Lord employs Māyā-devī to create the material world. The Lord Himself describes this in these words of *Bhagavad-gītā* (9.10): The material nature is working under My direction, O son of Kuntī, and it is producing all moving and unmoving beings.

In the *Vedas* it is said (*Aitareya Upaniṣad* 1.1): The Supreme Personality of Godhead glanced over the material creation.

It is also said (*Aitareya Upaniṣad* 1.1): The Supreme Personality of

Godhead created this entire material world.

The Supreme Lord, whose glance is so powerful, expands Himself as Garbhodakaśāyī Viṣṇu and enters the material world. The particles of light that constitute Lord Mahā-Viṣṇu's glance are the conditioned spirit souls. Into the heart of each conditioned soul, the Lord enters in a form the size of a thumb. That form is called Kṣīrodakaśāyī Viṣṇu, or Hiraṇyagarbha. Thus, the Supreme Personality of Godhead and the individual spirit soul both reside in the heart. This is described in the following words of *Śvetāśvatara Upaniṣad* (4.6): The individual spirit soul and the Supersoul, Supreme Personality of godhead, are like two friendly birds sitting on the same tree.

In this way, the *Śruti-śāstra* explains that the Supreme Personality of Godhead and the individual spirit soul are like two birds. The bird that is the Supreme Personality of Godhead gives the fruits of *karma*, and the bird that is the individual spirit soul tries to enjoy the material world. In *Bhagavad-gītā* (10.41-42), the Supreme Lord declares: Know that all beautiful, glorious, and mighty creations spring from but a spark of My splendor. But what need is there, Arjuna, for all this detailed knowledge? With a single fragment of Myself I pervade and support this entire creation.

Therefore, the Supersoul (Paramātmā), who creates, enters, protects and controls the material world, is an expansion of the Supreme Personality of Godhead (*bhagavān*).

Vrajanātha: I accept that the impersonal Brahman is the effulgence of the Supreme Personality of Godhead's body and that the Supersoul is His expansion. Now please tell me: What is the proof that Lord Kṛṣṇa is the original form of the Supreme Personality of Godhead?

Bābājī: The Supreme Personality of Godhead has all opulence and sweetness eternally. When His opulence is manifested, He is Lord Nārāyaṇa, the master of the spiritual world and the origin of Lord Mahā-Viṣṇu. Thus, when His pastimes of opulence are manifest, He is Lord Nārāyaṇa, and when His pastimes of sweetness are manifest, He is Lord Kṛṣṇa. Lord Kṛṣṇa possesses the highest limit of sweetness. The effulgence of His sweetness is so great that it eclipses all opulence that exists anywhere. Therefore, the conclusion is that Lord Nārāyaṇa and Lord Kṛṣṇa are not different. However, in the spiritual world, the greatest sweetness of transcendental mellows is present in Lord Kṛṣṇa. He is the highest resting place of all transcendental mellows.

This is explained in the following words of the *Ṛg Veda* (1.22.164.31): I have seen a certain *gopa* dressed in colorful garments and accompanied by many beautiful girls as He wanders the pathways in the spiritual world. That same *gopa* again and again enters the material worlds and stays in the hearts of the living beings.

In the *Chāndogya Upaniṣad* (8.13.1) it is said: "To attain Śrī Rādhā, I surrender to Lord Kṛṣṇa. To attain Lord Kṛṣṇa, I surrender to Śrī Rādhā.

These verses describe the liberated souls and their relationship with Lord Kṛṣṇa. In *Śrīmad-Bhāgavatam* (1.3.28) it is said: All of the above-mentioned incarnations are either plenary portions or portions of the plenary portions of the Lord, but Lord Śrī Kṛṣṇa is the original Personality of Godhead.

In the *Bhagavad-gītā* (7.7) Lord Kṛṣṇa Himself declares: O conqueror of wealth (Arjuna), there is no truth superior to Me.

In the *Gopāla-tāpanī Upaniṣad* (1.20) it is said: Lord Kṛṣṇa is the worshipable, all-pervading supreme controller, and although He is one, He manifests in many forms.

Vrajanātha: Lord Kṛṣṇa has an average-sized form. How can He be present everywhere? If we accept that Lord Kṛṣṇa has a form, we must also accept that His form can only stay in one place at a time. Now He must fall under the control of the material modes. No longer can He be supremely independent. How can all these defects be removed from Lord Kṛṣṇa?

Bābājī: Bābā, you are a conditioned soul trapped in the material world of *māyā*. That is why you have all these doubts. As long as it is bound by the ropes of *māyā*, your intelligence will never be able to touch the transcendental reality. When it tries to understand the pure spiritual reality, it will assume that spirit has qualities and forms just like those of matter. When it does this, the intelligence becomes worried that it has followed the wrong path. Then, the intelligence begins to imagine that the Supreme Spirit has no form and no qualities. In this way, the intelligence becomes cheated and cannot understand the truth about the Supreme Spirit.

In truth, the defects you think might affect the ordinary-sized form of

Lord Kṛṣṇa do not have any bearing on His true spiritual form. The idea that the Supreme Spirit is formless, unchanging, and inactive are ideas obtained by looking for the exact opposites of what appears in the material world. These are also qualities of a certain kind. Qualities of another kind are Lord Kṛṣṇa's handsome form, His face blossoming with happiness, His lotus eyes, His lotus feet, which give peacefulness to the devotees, and all His graceful limbs, perfect for enjoying transcendental pastimes. This pure spiritual form of Lord Kṛṣṇa is one feature of the Lord. When these two features, the personal and impersonal, are considered, it is seen that the average-sized form of Lord Kṛṣṇa is the most handsome and pleasing.

This is described in the following words of *Śrī Nārada-pañcarātra*: Lord Kṛṣṇa is supremely independent. His form and qualities are free of any possible flaw. His body is not like the bodies made of matter. His hands, feet, face, belly, and all the other parts of His body are all made of transcendental bliss and nothing else. Lord Kṛṣṇa is not different from His body. He does not reside in a material body that is different from Himself, as the conditioned souls in the material world do. He and His body are one.

Lord Kṛṣṇa's form is eternal and full of knowledge and bliss. His qualities are not material. Nothing about Him is material in even the slightest degree. He is not limited by material time and space. His form is fully present in every place for all time. He is one. His form has all knowledge. The material world is so large it cannot be measured by the conditioned souls. It is natural that a form of average size could never be present everywhere in the material world. However, in the spiritual world, all qualities have limitless power. Therefore, the average-sized form of Lord Kṛṣṇa can be present everywhere. That is actually one of its natural qualities. In the material world, an average-sized form cannot be all-pervading. However, the supremely handsome spiritual form of Lord Kṛṣṇa is certainly all-pervading. The extraordinary qualities of that form are very different from the qualities of material forms. That spiritual form is very glorious.

Can anyone be more glorious than the all-pervading Supreme Spirit? In the material world, everything is limited by time and space. What is the glory of a form that is free from the limits of time and present everywhere? Lord Kṛṣṇa's transcendental abode of Vraja is described in the *Chāndogya Upaniṣad*, which calls it "Brahma-pura." That abode is perfectly spiritual. It has all spiritual wonders. Its activities are all spiritual. Its places are spiritual. Its land and water are spiritual. Its rivers and trees are spiritual. Its sky is spiritual. Its sun, moon, and stars are all spiritual. They have not the slightest drop of any material flaw. Rather, they are filled with spiritual bliss.

O Bābā, the Navadvīpa-Māyāpura where you are sitting now is that same spiritual world. However, because you are trapped in *māyā*'s net, you cannot reach out and touch it. When you attain the mercy of a great saintly person, you will see that everything in this place is spiritual. Then you will be living in the spiritual world of Vraja. When did you get the idea that the average-sized form of Lord Kṛṣṇa could have any flaws? The glory of Lord Kṛṣṇa's average-sized spiritual form is far from what your material intelligence can understand. This has happened because in the past, you committed many impious deeds.

Vrajanātha: O saintly *bābājī*, Śrī Śrī Rādhā-Kṛṣṇa's forms, beauty, features, pastimes, companions, homes, forest groves, and all else are purely spiritual. A wise man will not doubt that. However, in what times and places do They manifest Their forms, abodes, and pastimes?

Bābājī: Śrī Kṛṣṇa is the master of all potencies. He can make any impossible thing possible. There is nothing surprising in this. He is playful and enjoys transcendental pastimes. Whatever He wishes is at once accomplished. He has all powers. If He wishes, He can bring His transcendental form and abode to the material world. There is no doubt of that.

Vrajanātha: The doubt is this. By His own will, Lord Kṛṣṇa appears in the material world. However, the people who see Him tend to think that His transcendental abode is a material place just like other material places, His transcendental form is a material form like the forms of ordinary human beings, and His transcendental pastimes in Vraja are ordinary material activities. Why do they see like that? If it is true that Lord Kṛṣṇa has mercifully appeared within the material world, why do not all people see that His form is spiritual?

Bābājī: One of Lord Kṛṣṇa's limitless transcendental qualities is His mercy to His devotees. Employing His *hlādinī śakti*, He gives His devotees the power to see that everything about Him is spiritual. To His devotees, He reveals everything about His transcendental pastimes. However, the non-devotees' eyes, ears, and other senses, which are contaminated by many offenses, cannot see any difference between the pastimes of the Lord and ordinary historical narratives of human activities.

Vrajanātha: Did not Śrī Kṛṣṇa descend to this material world to show mercy to the people in general?

Bābājī: His descent to this world brings all auspiciousness. When He descends to this world and manifests His transcendental pastimes, the devotees can see that His form and pastimes are purely spiritual. The non-devotees surely see them as material. Still, merely by seeing them, the non-devotees gain great spiritual merit. When this spiritual merit accumulates and becomes very great, they become able to have faith in pure devotional service. Therefore, the Lord's descent to this world brings a great benefit to the conditioned souls.

Vrajanātha: Why are Lord Kṛṣṇa's pastimes not clearly described in every page of the *Vedas*?

Bābājī: On every page, the *Vedas* again and again sing the glories of Lord Kṛṣṇa's pastimes. In some places, they are described directly and in other places, they are only hinted at. When the words of the texts directly refer to Lord Kṛṣṇa, the description is direct. An example of that is the following words of the *Chāndogya Upaniṣad*: To attain Śrī Rādhā, I take shelter of Lord Kṛṣṇa. To attain Lord Kṛṣṇa, I take shelter of Śrī Rādhā.

In these words and the words that follow it in the *Chāndogya Upaniṣad*, the liberated souls and their service to Lord Kṛṣṇa in the different *rasas* is clearly described. When the words only hint at the description of Lord Kṛṣṇa, the description is indirect. In the conversations of Yājñavalkya, Gārgī, and Maitreyī (in the *Bṛhad-āraṇyaka Upaniṣad*), the description of Lord Kṛṣṇa is at first indirect, and then at the end, direct. In some places, the *Vedas* have described Lord Kṛṣṇa's eternal pastimes directly, and in other places, chanting the glories of the impersonal Brahman and the Supersoul, the *Vedas* have described Lord Kṛṣṇa only indirectly. In truth, the *Vedas* have taken a vow to chant the glories of Lord Kṛṣṇa.

Vrajanātha: O saintly *bābājī*, Lord Kṛṣṇa is the Supreme Truth. Of this there is no doubt. However, what is the status of Brahmā, Śiva, Indra, Sūrya,

Gaṇeśa, and the other demigods worshiped in this world? Please tell me. Many *brāhmaṇas* say that Śiva is the Supreme Truth and no one is higher than Him. I was born in the family of such a *brāhmaṇa*, and I have heard and repeated this idea since childhood. What is the truth of this? Please tell me.

Bābājī: Now I will describe to you the relative merits of the ordinary living entities, the demigods and demigoddesses worshiped in this world, and the Supreme Personality of Godhead. Please listen. I will now repeat to you a list of some of Lord Kṛṣṇa's transcendental qualities. They are described in these words of a great philosopher (Śrīla Rūpa Gosvāmī's *Śrī Bhakti-rasāmṛta-sindhu*): Kṛṣṇa, the supreme hero, has the most beautiful transcendental body. This body possesses all good features. It is radiant and very pleasing to the eyes. His body is powerful, strong and youthful. Kṛṣṇa is the linguist of all wonderful languages. He is a truthful and very pleasing speaker. He is expert in speaking and He is very wise, learned, scholar and a genius. Kṛṣṇa is very expert in artistic enjoyment. He is highly cunning, expert, grateful and firmly determined in His vows. He knows how to deal according to time, person and country, and He sees through the scriptures and authoritative books. He is very clean and self-controlled. Lord Kṛṣṇa is steady, His senses are controlled, and He is forgiving, grave, and calm. He is also equal to all. Moreover, He is magnanimous, religious, chivalrous, and kind. He is always respectful to respectable people. Kṛṣṇa is very simple and liberal, He is humble and bashful, and He is the protector of the surrendered soul. He is very happy, and He is always the well-wisher of His devotee. He is auspicious and He is submissive to love. Kṛṣṇa is very influential and famous, and He is the object of attachment for everyone. He is the shelter of the good and the virtuous. He is attractive to the minds of women, and He is worshiped by everyone. He is very, very rich.

Kṛṣṇa is the Supreme, and He is always glorified as the Supreme Lord and controller. Thus, all the previously mentioned transcendental qualities are in Him. The fifty qualities of the Supreme Personality of Godhead above mentioned are as deep as the ocean. In other words, they are difficult to comprehend. These qualities are sometimes very minutely exhibited in living beings, but they are fully manifest in the Supreme Personality of Godhead. Apart from these fifty qualities, there are five other qualities found in the Supreme Personality of

Godhead that are partially present in demigods like Śiva. These qualities are: 1. The Lord is always situated in His original position, 2. He is omniscient, 3. He is always fresh and youthful, 4. He is the concentrated form of eternity, knowledge and bliss, and 5. He is the possessor of all mystic perfection.

There are another five qualities which exist in the Vaikuṇṭha planets in Nārāyaṇa, the Lord of Laksmi. These qualities are present in Kṛṣṇa, but are not present in demigods like Lord Śiva, or in other living entities. These are: 1. Inconceivable supreme power, 2. Generating innumerable universes from the body, 3. Being the original source of all incarnations, 4. Bestowing salvation upon enemies killed and 5. The ability to attract exalted persons who are satisfied in themselves. Although these qualities are present in Nārāyaṇa, the dominating Deity of the Vaikuṇṭha planets, they are even more wonderfully present in Kṛṣṇa.

Apart from these sixty transcendental qualities, Kṛṣṇa has an additional four qualities, which are not manifest even in the personality of Nārāyaṇa. These are: 1. Kṛṣṇa is like an ocean filled with waves of pastimes that evoke wonder within everyone in the three worlds. 2. In His activities of conjugal love, He is always surrounded by His dear devotees who possess unequaled love for Him. 3. He attracts the minds of all three worlds by the melodious vibration of His flute. 4. His personal beauty and opulence are beyond compare. No one is equal to Him, and no one is greater than Him. Thus the Supreme Personality of Godhead astonishes all living entities, both moving and non-moving, within the three worlds. He is so beautiful that He is called Kṛṣṇa.

Above Nārāyaṇa, Kṛṣṇa has four specific transcendental qualities—His wonderful pastimes, an abundance of wonderful associates who are very dear to Him (like the *gopīs*), His wonderful beauty, and the wonderful vibration of His flute. Lord Kṛṣṇa is more exalted than ordinary living beings, and demigods like Lord Śiva. He is even more exalted than His own personal expansion, Nārāyaṇa.

These sixty-four opulences are fully, eternally, and splendidly manifest in Lord Kṛṣṇa, whose pure spiritual form is eternal and full of knowledge and bliss. The last four opulences are present only in the form of Lord Kṛṣṇa. They are not present in even the Lord's pastime incarnations. Now that these four qualities are excluded, the remaining sixty qualities are fully and splendidly manifest in Lord Nārāyaṇa, who is the master of the spiritual sky, and whose form is perfectly spiritual. When the next five opulences are excluded, the remaining fifty-five opulences are present in Lord Śiva and other exalted demigods. Drops of the remaining fifty opulences may be seen in the individual spirit souls.

Śiva, Brahmā, Sūrya, Gaṇeśa, and Indra are partial expansions of the Lord. Although given jurisdiction to rule over certain affairs of the Lord's opulences, they are still individual souls, servants of the Supreme Lord. By their mercy, many people attained pure devotional service. They are rulers over the conditioned souls, and that is why they are objects of worship in the material world. The worship of them gradually leads to worship of the Supreme Lord. If they give to certain souls the gift of pure devotional service to Lord Kṛṣṇa, those souls consider them spiritual masters and worship them eternally. Lord Śiva, who is filled with devotion to the Supreme Personality of Godhead, is considered to be non-different from the Supreme Lord Himself. That is why people addicted to the ideas of impersonalism take shelter of Him and consider Him to be the highest form of the Supreme.

Chapter Fourteen

Eternal religion and sambandha, abhidheya and prayojana
(The Lord's potencies)

When he thought about what he had heard the previous night from the elderly *bābājī*, Vrajanātha became filled with bliss. He thought, "Ah! The teachings of Lord Gaurāṅga are wonderful! When I hear them, my heart becomes filled with nectar. When I hear them from the saintly *bābājī*'s mouth, my thirst to hear them increases more and more. No part of them seems illogical. They seem to be supported by the scriptures. I cannot understand why the *brāhmaṇas* criticize them. I think they criticize because they are impersonalists."

Thinking in this way, Vrajanātha came to Raghunātha dāsa Bābājī's cottage. Seeing the saintly *bābājī*, Vrajanātha offered *daṇḍavat* obeisances. The saintly *bābājī* happily embraced him and made him sit down next to him. With an earnest heart, Vrajanātha said, "O master, I wish to hear the third verse of the *Daśa-mūla*. Please kindly recite it."

The hairs of his body upright with spiritual happiness, the saintly *bābājī* recited: Glory to the Supreme Personality of Godhead, who is never touched by material changes. He is not different from His spiritual potency. He is situated in His own transcendental glory. From Him are manifested His spiritual potency by which all His desires are fulfilled, His potency of the individual spirit souls, and His potency of inanimate matter.

Vrajanātha: The *brāhmaṇas* say that when the Supreme is the impersonal Brahman, He has no potency. It is only when He appears as the Supreme Controller that He has potencies. What do the *Vedas* teach about this?

Bābājī: In every feature of the Lord, His potencies are manifested. The *Vedas* (*Śvetāśvatara Upaniṣad* 6.8) declare: He does not possess bodily form like that of an ordinary living entity. There is no difference between His body and His soul. He is absolute. All His senses are transcendental. Any one of His senses can perform the function of any other sense. Therefore, no one is greater than Him or equal to Him. His potencies are multifarious, and thus His deeds are automatically performed as a natural sequence.

The Lord's *icchā-śakti*, the potency that fulfills all His desires, is described in these words (*Śvetāśvatara Upaniṣad* 1.3): Rapt in meditation, the sages then saw the mysterious potency and transcendental qualities of the Supreme

Personality of Godhead, the original cause, who alone dominates the secondary causes, including time and the individual living entity.

The Lord's *jīva-śakti*, the potency that is the individual spirit souls, is described in these words (*Śvetāśvatara Upaniṣad* 4.5): An unborn man enjoys an unborn red, white, and black woman who bears many children like herself. Another unborn man first enjoys and then forsakes her.

(Note by translators: The unborn woman is the material nature. The colors red, white, and black are the modes of passion, goodness, and ignorance. The many children are the ingredients of the material universes. The first unborn man is the conditioned soul. The second unborn man is the soul who, after trying to enjoy matter, finally renounces the world and attains liberation.)

The Lord's *māyā-śakti*, the potency that is the material world, is described in these words (*Śvetāśvatara Upaniṣad* 4.9): The *Vedas* describe a bewildering variety of hymns, prayers, sacrifices, rituals, vows, austerities, history, and predictions of the future. Simply by studying the *Vedas*, it is very difficult for the conditioned soul, illusioned by *māyā* and trapped in the material world, to understand the Supreme Personality of Godhead, the controller of the illusory potency and the creator of the material universes.

The words *parasya śaktiḥ* (in *Śvetāśvatara Upaniṣad* 6.8) indicate that of all the Lord's potencies, one is the most important. The *Vedas* never say that the Supreme has a feature without potencies. When He has qualities, He is the Supreme Personality of Godhead. When He has no qualities, He is the impersonal Brahman. It is the Lord's most important potency that manifests His feature as impersonal Brahman. In this way, it is seen that the impersonal Brahman does indeed have a potency. That most important potency has been described in the *Vedas* in many places, where it is called by many names, such as *parā-śakti*', *svarūpa-śakti*', and *cit-śakt*'. The impersonalists imagine that the impersonal Brahman has no potencies. The truth is that the impersonal Brahman is beyond the understanding of the impersonalists. The *Vedas* affirm that the Supreme has two features—one with qualities and the other without qualities.

That the impersonal feature of the Lord has potencies is explained in these words of the *Vedas* (Stasvatara Upaniṣad 4.1): Although He has no qualities, by His potencies, the Supreme created the great variety of the material world.

That the personal feature of the Lord has potencies is explained in these words of the *Vedas* (*Śvetāśvatara Upaniṣad* 3.1): Employing His potencies, the Supreme Person created the material world.

In this way, you can see that the Supreme is never bereft of His potencies. The self-manifest Supreme Lord is always accompanied by them. The self-manifest Lord, who is the master of three eternal potencies, is described in this *mantra* of the *Vedas* (*Śvetāśvatara Upaniṣad* 6.16): The Supreme Lord, the creator of this cosmic manifestation, knows every nook and corner of this creation. Although He is the cause of creation, there is no cause for His appearance. He is fully aware of everything. He is the Supersoul, the master of all transcendental qualities, and the master of this cosmic manifestation in regard to bondage of the conditional state of material existence and liberation from that bondage.

The three potencies of the Lord are described in this verse. Here, the word *pradhāna* refers to the Lord's *māyā-śakti*, the word *kṣetrajña* refers to the potency of the individual spirit souls, and the word *kṣetrajña-pati* refers to the Lord's spiritual potency. The idea that when the Supreme manifests His impersonal feature He has no potencies, and when He manifests His personal feature He has potencies, is an idea created in the fertile workshop of the impersonalists' imaginations. In truth, the Lord is always the master of all potencies. When the Lord is situated in His own glory, and when His original, natural condition is manifest, in other words, when He is manifested as the Supreme Person, He is always accompanied by His potencies. Thus, His desires are always fulfilled.

Vrajanātha: If He is always accompanied by His potencies, and if everything is done by His potencies, then How is He independent, and how is it that His desires are always fulfilled?

Bābājī: In the scriptures it is said: The potencies and the master of potencies are not different.

The potencies thus do whatever the master of potencies desires. The duty of the *māyā-śakti* is to manifest the material universes. The duty of the *jīva-śakti* is to manifest the many individual spirit souls. The duty of the *cit-śakti* is to manifest the spiritual world. After assigning these different duties to the *cit-śakti*, *jīva-śakti* and *māyā-śakti*, the Supreme Lord steps back, untouched and unchanged. If these actions are performed because of His desire, how can He remain aloof and unconcerned? If He desires that certain things be done, he will certainly be affected by the result.

When the scriptures say the Lord is not affected, the meaning is that the Lord never undergoes any material change. His material potency is a reflection of His internal, spiritual potency. Whatever the material potency, *māyā*, does may be real, but it does not exist eternally. The changes that *māyā* produces do not last eternally. Whatever changes the Lord may manifest in His desires in His pastimes are all manifested by His spiritual potency, *cit-śakti*. These changes are manifestations of His spiritual love and therefore, they are free of any fault or impurity. They are included within spiritual knowledge. Although it is by His wish that the *māyā-śakti* creates the material world, the Supreme Lord remains perfectly spiritual in His nature. In the great varieties created by His spiritual potency, *cit-śakti*, there is no touch of matter, or *māyā*.

When they hear the descriptions of the great variety manifested by the Lord's spiritual potency, ordinary people, whose intelligence cannot conceive of anything beyond matter, assume that those descriptions must be descriptions of material things. Thus, they are like people who, suffering from jaundice, see everything as yellow, or they are like people who, standing in the shadow of a cloud, cannot see the sun. The root meaning is this: The material potency is a reflection of the spiritual potency. Therefore, the variety manifested in the material world is a reflection of the variety manifested in the spiritual world. To one who looks superficially, they seem to be the same. However, the truth is that they are exact opposites. A mirror's reflection of a man's body seems just like the original body. However, the position of all the various limbs is inverted in the reflection. In the reflection, the right hand is on the left and the left hand is on the right. Therefore, material eyes see the varieties of the spiritual and material worlds to be the same, although spiritual eyes see that they are indeed opposites. Actually, the material variety is a perverted reflection of the spiritual variety.

Superficially, they seem the same but in truth, they are different. Free from material changes, and His every desire at once fulfilled, the Supreme

Personality of Godhead controls the material potency, *māyā*, and gives her various tasks to fulfill.

Vrajanātha: Which of Lord Kṛṣṇa's potencies is Śrī Rādhikā?

Bābājī: Lord Kṛṣṇa is the master of potencies in His perfect, original form. Śrīmati Rādhikā is the potency in its perfect, original form. Śrīmati Rādhikā is the original manifestation of the Lord's internal, spiritual potency. As musk is not different from its fragrance, and as fire is not different from its power to burn, so Rādhā and Kṛṣṇa, who enjoy the nectar of transcendental pastimes together, are eternally different and not different from each other. From the internal potency, Śrī Rādhā, are manifested the three potencies *cit-śakti* (spirit), *jīva-śakti* (the individual souls), and *māyā-śakti* (matter). These three are seen to be three different kinds of *kriya-śakti* (potency of action). The *cit-śakti* is also called *antar antaraṅga-śakti*, and the *jīva-śakti* is also called *taṭasthā-śakti*. The *māyā-śakti* is also called *bahiraṅga-śakti*. Although it is one, the Lord's internal potency assumes these three forms in order to act in these different ways. All the eternal opulences of the internal potency are fully manifested in the *cit-śakti*. An atomic fragment of each of these opulences is present in the *jīva-śakti*, and a perverted reflection of them is present in the *māyā-śakti*. The internal potency is also manifested in three other ways. These three manifestations are called: 1. *hlādinī*, 2. *sandhinī*, and 3. *samvit*. They are described in these words of the *Daśa-mūla*: Glory to Lord Śrī Kṛṣṇa, who enjoys nectarean pastimes in Vraja, who plays in a nectarean ocean of transcendental mellows, who enjoys the feelings of ecstatic love brought by the *hlādinī-śakti*, who tastes the nectar of the confidential love brought by the *samvit-śakti*, and who resides in the pure transcendental abode created by the *sandhinī-śakti*.

Thus, the Lord's internal potency manifests three features: 1. *hlādinī*, 2. *sandhinī* and 3. *samvit*. The *hlādinī-śakti* which in its complete form is Śrī Rādhā, the daughter of Vṛṣabhānu, brings transcendental bliss to Lord Kṛṣṇa. The form of the highest ecstatic love (*mahā-bhāva*) is the very dear and pleasing to Lord Kṛṣṇa. She expands into many other forms. She expands as the eight principal *gopīs* (*aṣṭa-sakhī*), the dear *gopīs* (*priya-sakhī*), the *gopīs* speaking joking words (*narma-sakhī*), the *gopīs* more dear than life (*prāna-sakhī*), and the most dear *gopīs* (*parama-preṣṭha-sakhī*).

These four kinds of *gopīs* are manifested for different kinds of devotional service. These *gopīs* are eternally perfect souls who reside in the spiritual world of Vraja. The *samvit-śakti* manifests the different relationships of the people of Vraja. The *sandhinī-śakti* manifests the land, water, villages, forests, hills like Govardhana Hill, pastime places of Śrī Kṛṣṇa, Śrī Rādhā, Their *gopa* and *gopī* friends, Their servants, the cows, and all the other residents of Vraja, their spiritual forms, and the paraphernalia used in their pastimes. Pushed by the feelings of ecstatic love brought by the *hlādinī-śakti*, Lord Kṛṣṇa is always filled with transcendental bliss. The activities of love are brought by the *samvit-śakti*, activities like Lord Kṛṣṇa attracting the *gopīs* by playing on the flute, His herding the cows, and His *rasa* dance pastimes. To perform all these activities, Lord Kṛṣṇa takes shelter of His *samvit-śakti*. Always swimming in the nectar of transcendental mellows, Lord Kṛṣṇa enjoys pastimes in the land of Vraja, a land manifested by the *sandhinī-śakti*. Of all spiritual abodes, the land of Vraja is the best.

Vrajanātha: You have said that the internal potency is manifested as the *hlādinī*, *samvit*, and *sandhinī* potencies. A tiny fragment of the internal potency is the *jīva-śakti* and a perverted reflection of the internal potency is the *māyā-śakti*. Please tell me how the *hlādinī*, *samvit* and *sandhinī* potencies work in the *jīva-śakti* and *māyā-śakti*.

Bābājī: In the *jīva-śakti*, which is an atomic fragment of the internal potency, a fragmental part of these three potencies is present. There, the *hlādinī-śakti* is manifested as the eternal bliss of the impersonal Brahman, the *samvit-śakti* is manifested as the individual soul's awareness of impersonal Brahman, and the *sandhinī-śakti* is manifested as the atomic spiritual forms of the spirit souls. You wished to know about the individual spirit souls. That is how you should understand them. In the *māyā-śakti*, the *hlādinī-śakti* is manifested as material happiness, the *samvit-śakti* is manifested as material knowledge, and the *sandhinī-śakti* is manifested as the fourteen material worlds and the external material bodies of the conditioned souls.

Vrajanātha: If their activities are so easily explained, why are the Lord's potencies called inconceivable?

Bābājī: When they are considered one by one, each feature is easily understood. However, when all the features are considered together, they are beyond understanding. In the material world, mutually contradictory qualities do not exist together in the same place, for they would negate each other. It is the inconceivable nature of Lord Kṛṣṇa's potency that in the spiritual world, all mutually contradictory qualities exist happily together and the result is very beautiful and pleasing. In Lord Kṛṣṇa, the qualities of having a form and being formless, being all-pervading and having a form present in one place only, being active and inactive, being unborn and being the son of Nanda, being the all-worshipable Supreme Lord and being a *gopa* boy, being all-knowing and having the limited knowledge possessed by a human being, having qualities and having no qualities, being beyond conception and being sweet like nectar, being limited and unlimited, being far away and very near, being completely aloof and also being afraid the *gopīs*' jealous anger, are simultaneously present. The numberless other mutually contradictory qualities happily stay together in Lord Kṛṣṇa's transcendental form, in Śrī Kṛṣṇa's transcendental abode, and in Śrī Kṛṣṇa's transcendental pastimes. That these mutually contradictory qualities help Lord Kṛṣṇa's pastimes, making them more beautiful and pleasing, is beyond human conception. Therefore, it is said that the Lord's potencies are inconceivable.

Vrajanātha: Is this idea supported by the *Vedas*?

Bābājī: This is accepted everywhere in the *Vedas*. In the *Śvetāśvatara Upaniṣad* (3.19) it is said: Learned transcendentalists explain that God is the greatest—the original person. He has no material hands, but He can take anything. He has no material legs, but He can travel faster than anyone. He has no material eyes, but He sees everything. He has no material ears, but He hears everything. He knows everything, but no one knows Him.

In the *Īśa Upaniṣad* (*mantras* 5 and 8) it is said: The Supreme Lord walks and does not walk. He is far away, but He is very near as well. He is within everything, yet He is outside of everything. Such a person must factually know the greatest of all, who is unembodied, omniscient, beyond reproach, without veins, pure and uncontaminated, the self-sufficient philosopher, who has been fulfilling everyone's desires since time immemorial.

Vrajanātha: Is it written in the *Vedas* that by His own will, the Supreme Lord sometimes descends to the material world?

Bābājī: Yes. In many places. In the *Kena Upaniṣad*, in a conversation of Śiva and Uma, it is said that Indra and the demigods became very proud because they had conquered the demons. As the demigods were telling each other how wonderful they were, the Supreme Lord assumed a wonderful form and appeared among them, asked them why they were so proud, and gave them a single blade of grass to burn up with their own power. In this way, the Supreme Personality of Godhead, who has wonderful powers, manifested His form among the demigods.

An example of a *mantra* from that passage is (*Kena Upaniṣad* 3.6): Placing a blade of grass before him, the Supreme Lord said: "Burn this." With all his power, Agni attacked the blade of grass but could not burn it. Returning to the demigods, Agni said: "I do not know who this Yakṣa is."

The hidden meaning of this passage is that the Supreme Lord is a person with an inconceivably handsome form, and who, by His own will, descends to the material world and enjoys pastimes with the individual spirit souls.

Vrajanātha: It is said that the Supreme Lord is an ocean of the nectar of transcendental mellows? Where is this said in the *Vedas*?

Bābājī: In the *Taittirīya Upaniṣad* (2.1) it is clearly said: The Supreme Personality of Godhead is the reservoir of transcendental mellows. When one understands the Supreme Personality of Godhead, the reservoir of pleasure, Kṛṣṇa, he actually becomes transcendentally blissful. Who could breathe without the Lord giving breath? Who could be happy without the Lord giving happiness? It is He who gives transcendental bliss.

Vrajanātha: If He has a form of the nectar of bliss, why can the people of the material world not see Him?

Bābājī: The individual souls imprisoned in the material world are of two kinds. One faces Kṛṣṇa and the other turns his back on Kṛṣṇa. The soul that turns away from Kṛṣṇa cannot see Kṛṣṇa's handsomeness. Instead, he gazes on material sense objects and fixes his mind in thinking of material sense objects. The soul that turns toward Kṛṣṇa turns away from the material world of *māyā*. He is able to see the form of Lord Kṛṣṇa.

In that *Kaṭha Upaniṣad* (2.1.1) it is said: A person eager for material pleasures cannot see the Supreme Personality of Godhead within his heart.

Only a wise man who turns from the world of matter can see the Lord within his heart.

Vrajanātha: The *Vedas* say that the Supreme Personality of Godhead is *raso vai saḥ* (the reservoir of spiritual nectar). How do the *Vedas* describe the Lord's nectarean spiritual form?

Bābājī: In the *Gopāla-tāpanī Upaniṣad* (1.10) it is said: The Supreme Personality of Godhead is a cowherd boy. His eyes are handsome lotus flowers, His complexion a dark monsoon cloud, and His garments are lightning. He has two arms. He is rich in transcendental knowledge. He wears a garland of forest flowers.

Vrajanātha: From this I can understand that the form of Lord Kṛṣṇa is the eternal spiritual form of the Lord in the spiritual world. He is the form of spiritual nectar and He is the shelter of all. He is not attained by impersonal speculation or any other non-devotional means. Those who follow the path of *aṣṭāṅga-yoga* search after the Supersoul, who is His plenary portion. The impersonal Brahman is the effulgence of His transcendental body. He is endowed with all spiritual qualities. He is the highest object of worship in the world. He is not easy to see. He is beyond conception. What method may a human being adopt to understand Him? The *brāhmaṇas* cannot understand Him and neither can the *caṇḍālas*. What method should one adopt to understand Him? It is very difficult to know how to please Him.

Bābājī: In the *Kaṭha Upaniṣad* (2.2.13) it is said: Only saintly persons who can see, within and without, the same Supreme Lord, can actually attain to perfect and eternal peace.

Vrajanātha: Those who can see the Supreme Lord within their hearts attain eternal peace. However, what method should one adopt to see the Lord in this way? That's what I would like to see. That's what I don't understand.

Bābājī: In the *Kaṭha Upaniṣad* (1.2.23) it is also said: The Supreme Lord is not attained by expert explanations, by vast intelligence, nor even by much hearing. He is attained only by one who He Himself chooses. To such a person, He manifests His own form.

In *Śrīmad-Bhāgavatam* (10.14.28) it is said: My Lord, if one is favored by even a slight trace of the mercy of Your lotus feet, he can understand the greatness of Your personality. But those who speculate in order to understand the Supreme Personality of Godhead are unable to know You, even though they continue to study the *Vedas* for many years.

O Bābā, our Lord is very merciful. The Lord of our hearts is Śrī Kṛṣṇa. Simply by studying and understanding the scriptures, one does not attain Him. Simply by being very intelligent or studying from many teachers, one does not attain Him. Only to one who says, "Kṛṣṇa is my Lord," does Lord Kṛṣṇa mercifully reveal His eternal spiritual form of knowledge and bliss. Think about this and you will easily understand it.

Vrajanātha: Is anything written in the *Vedas* about Lord Kṛṣṇa's spiritual abode?

Bābājī: It is described in many places. In some places it is called *paravyoma* (the spiritual sky), in other places *samvyoma* (the great sky), in other places Brahma-gopāla-puri (the city of Lord Gopāla), and in other places Gokula (the world of the *surabhi* cows). It is described in these words of the *Śvetāśvatara Upaniṣad* (4.8): In the eternal spiritual sky, the demigods and the Vedic hymns serve the Supreme Personality of Godhead. What will he who does not know Him do with the Vedic hymns? Those who know Him have attained the goal of life.

In the *Muṇḍaka Upaniṣad* (2.2.1) it is said: The Supreme Personality of Godhead stays in the effulgent spiritual world.

In the *Puruṣa-bodhinī-śruti* it is said: In the spiritual world named Gokula, in the circle of Mathurā, the Supreme Personality of Godhead stays, with Rādhā and Candrāvalī at His sides.

In the *Gopāla-tāpanī Upaniṣad* it is said: In the spiritual sky is the city of Lord Gopāla."

Vrajanātha: *Tantrika brāhmaṇas* say that the potency of Lord Śiva is the *ādya śakti* (original potency). Why do they say that?

Bābājī: The potency of Lord Śiva is the *māyā-śakti*. From *māyā*, the three material modes—goodness, passion and ignorance—are manifested. The *brāhmaṇas* are in the mode of goodness. They purely worship Goddess Māyā, who is the origin of material goodness. Those who are in the mode of passion worship Goddess Māyā as the mother of the mode of passion. Those who have taken shelter of the mode of ignorance worship *māyā* as Goddess Vidyā, the controller of the mode of blinding darkness. In truth, *māyā* is a transformation of the potency of the Supreme Personality of Godhead. *Māyā* is not a separate potency. *Māyā* is a shadow or a reflection of the Supreme Lord's original spiritual potency. *Māyā* imprisons the conditioned souls, and she also sets them free. Persons averse to Lord Kṛṣṇa, she imprisons in the material world and punishes. Persons who are favorably inclined to Lord Kṛṣṇa, she places in the mode of goodness and gives knowledge of Lord Kṛṣṇa. Persons shackled and imprisoned by *māyā* cannot see that *māyā* herself is a reflection of the Supreme Lord's original potency. It is these persons who claim that *māyā* is the *ādya śakti*' (original potency). A person bewildered by *māyā* may reach the right conclusion if he has performed many pious deeds. One who has not performed pious deeds will not.

Vrajanātha: Among the servants of Lord Kṛṣṇa in Gokula is mentioned someone named Durgā-devī. Who is that Durgā?

Bābājī: She is Yogamāyā. She is the seed that grows into the changed forms accepted by the *cit-śakti* (spiritual potency). She stays in the spiritual world and there she is considered identical with the Lord's internal potency. It is by her power that the Lord's spiritual potency is reflected as the material potency, *māyā*. The Durgā of the material world is a maidservant of her, Yogamāyā, who is the Durgā of the spiritual world. This spiritual Durgā assists in Lord Kṛṣṇa's spiritual pastimes. Manifested as Yogamāyā, in the spiritual world, she makes the nectar of Lord Kṛṣṇa's pastimes by convincing the *gopīs* that they are married to others and Kṛṣṇa is their paramour (*parakīya-bhāva*). She also arranges for the Lord's *rasa-līlā* pastimes. This is described in these words of *Śrīmad-Bhāgavatam* (10.29.10): Taking shelter of His Yogamāyā potency, Lord Kṛṣṇa enjoyed the *rasa* dance.

The meaning of these statements is this: Among the many spiritual pastimes arranged by the Lord's internal potency are some activities that seem to be situated in ignorance, although in truth they are not situated in ignorance at all. When these activities that superficially appear to be situated in ignorance are useful to make the nectar of Lord Kṛṣṇa's pastimes sweeter, Yogamāyā arranges that they are manifested. In this way, the nectar of the Lord's pastimes are understood.

Vrajanātha: I wish to understand something about the spiritual abode (*dhāma*) of the Lord. Please be kind and explain this to me: Why do the Vaiṣṇavas use the word Śrīdhāma in relation to Navadvīpa?

Bābājī: Śrī Navadvīpa-dhāma and Śrī Vṛndāvana-dhāma are not different. This Māyāpura is the highest spiritual abode. Śrī Māyāpura is to Navadvīpa what Śrī Gokula is to Vraja. Māyāpura is the holiest place in Navadvīpa. In *Śrīmad-Bhāgavatam* (7.9.38) it is said: O Lord, in the age of Kali, however, You do not assert Yourself. In that age, Your incarnation is hidden.

As the Supreme Lord's incarnation is hidden in the Kali-yuga, so the Supreme Lord's abode, Śrī Navadvīpa, is also hidden. In the age of Kali, there is no holy place like Śrī Navadvīpa. A person who understands the spiritual nature of Śrī Navadvīpa has become qualified to reside in the spiritual world of Vraja. Material eyes see Vraja and Navadvīpa as both material places, made of the five material elements. Only persons who have become fortunate to have their spiritual eyes opened are able to see the truth of these holy abodes.

Vrajanātha: I wish to know the truth about Śrī Navadvīpa-dhāma.

Bābājī: Goloka, Vṛndāvana, and Śvetadvīpa are the names of the innermost places in the spiritual world. In Goloka, the Lord's *svakīya* pastimes are manifested, in Vṛndāvana, the *parakīya* pastimes are manifested, and in Śvetadvīpa, other pastimes are manifested. Gokula, Vṛndāvana, and Śvetadvīpa are not different in nature. Śrī Navadvīpa is therefore not different from Śvetadvīpa and Vṛndāvana. The residents of Śrī Navadvīpa are most fortunate because they are the eternal associates of Lord Gaurāṅga. It is because in past lives they performed many pious deeds that now they are able to reside in Śrī Navadvīpa. The transcendental mellows (*rasa*) that were not revealed in Śrī Vṛndāvana have been revealed in Śrī Navadvīpa. When a person becomes qualified, he is able to taste the sweetness of those mellows.

Vrajanātha: What is the size of Navadvīpa-dhāma?

Bābājī: The circumference of Śrī Navadvīpa is sixteen *krośas* (32 miles). The holy abode of Navadvīpa is an eight-petal lotus flower. Eight of the *dvīpas* form the eight petals, and the island in the middle is the whorl of the lotus. The eight islands that are petals of the lotus are: Sīmantadvīpa,

Godrumadvīpa, Madhyadvīpa, Koladvīpa, Ṛtudvīpa, Jahnudvīpa, Modadruma-dvīpa, and Rudradvīpa. The whorl in the middle of the lotus is Antardvīpa. In the middle of Antardvīpa is Śrī Māyāpura. A soul who performs *sādhana-bhakti* (devotional service in practice) in Navadvīpa-dhāma, or especially in Śrī Māyāpura, quickly attains the perfection of *prema* (pure love of God). In the center of Śrī Navadvīpa is the very holy place of Śrī Jagannātha Miśra's home. The most fortunate devotees are able to see Lord Gaurāṅgadeva enjoying His eternal pastimes in this holy place.

Vrajanātha: Does the Lord's internal potency arrange for Lord Gaurāṅgadeva's pastimes?

Bābājī: As Śrī Kṛṣṇa's pastimes are arranged by the internal potency, so Lord Gaurāṅga's pastimes are arranged in the same way. There is not the slightest difference between Lord Kṛṣṇa and Lord Gaurāṅga. In his notebook, Śrī Svarūpa Dāmodara Gosvāmī explains (Śrī Caitanya-caritāmṛta Adi 1.5): The loving affairs of Śrī Rādhā and Kṛṣṇa are transcendental manifestations of the Lord's internal pleasure-giving potency. Although Rādhā and Kṛṣṇa are one in Their identity, They separated Themselves eternally. Now these two transcendental identities have again united in the form of Śrī Kṛṣṇa Caitanya. I bow down to Him, who has manifested Himself with the sentiment and complexion of Śrīmati Rādhārāṇī, although He is Kṛṣṇa Himself.

Lord Kṛṣṇa and Lord Caitanya are both manifested eternally. No one has the power to say which of Them came first and which second. It cannot be said that Lord Caitanya was manifested first and Śrī Śrī Rādhā-Kṛṣṇa were manifested second. Neither can it be said that Śrī Śrī Rādhā-Kṛṣṇa were manifested first and Lord Caitanya was manifested second. The truth is that Lord Caitanya and Śrī Śrī Rādhā-Kṛṣṇa both exist eternally. All the pastimes of the Supreme are eternal. A person who thinks that of the pastimes of Lord Caitanya and the pastimes of Śrī Śrī Rādhā-Kṛṣṇa, the pastimes of one is more important and the pastimes of the other is less important, does not understand the truth. He does not understand the nectar of the Lord's pastimes.

Vrajanātha: If Śrī Gaurāṅga is the original form of the Supreme Personality of Godhead, then how should one worship Him?

Bābājī: As one worships Lord Kṛṣṇa by chanting the names and *mantras* of Lord Kṛṣṇa, so one should worship Lord Gaura by chanting the names and *mantras* of Lord Gaurāṅga. One may worship Lord Gaura by chanting Kṛṣṇa *mantras*, or for that matter, one may worship Lord Kṛṣṇa by chanting Gaura *mantras*. They are all the same. Anyone who thinks Lord Kṛṣṇa and Lord Gaura are different is a fool. He is a servant of Kali-yuga.

Vrajanātha: If Lord Caitanya is the hidden (*channa*) incarnation described in the Seventh Canto of *Śrīmad-Bhāgavatam*, how are there any *mantras* to worship Him?

Bābājī: The *Tantras* that openly give *mantras* for worshiping the openly-manifested incarnations of the Lord secretly reveal the *mantras* for worshiping the secret, hidden incarnation of the Lord. People whose intelligence is not crooked can understand the presence of these *mantras*.

Vrajanātha: How does one worship the Divine Couple, Śrī Śrī Rādhā-Kṛṣṇa, while one is engaged in worshiping Lord Gaurāṅga?

Bābājī: There are two ways one may worship the Divine Couple, Śrī Śrī Rādhā-Kṛṣṇa, while one is engaged in worshiping Lord Gaurāṅga. These two ways are: 1. *arcanā-mārga* (Deity worship) and 2. *bhajana-mārga* (the practices of devotional service). In the path of *arcanā-mārga*, one worships Gaura-Viṣṇupriyā, and in the path of *bhajana-mārga*, one worships Gaura-Gadādhara.

Vrajanātha: Which potency of Lord Gaurāṅga is Śrī Viṣṇupriyā?

Bābājī: Generally, the devotees say she is the Lord's *bhū-śakti*. But, the truth is that she is *samvit-śakti*, accompanied by the essence of the *hlādinī-śakti*. This means that she is the Goddess of Devotion, Bhakti-devī, and during Lord Gaurāṅga's advent, she comes to help Him preach the glories of the holy name. As the nine islands of Śrī Navadvīpa-dhāma embody the nine kinds of devotional service, so Śrīmati Viṣṇupriyā is also the nine kinds of devotional service personified.

Vrajanātha: Can it be said, then, that Śrī Viṣṇupriyā is the Lord's internal potency?

Bābājī: How can there be any doubt? Is not the internal potency (*svarūpa-śakti*) the same as the *samvit-śakti*, accompanied by the essence of the *hlādinī-śakti*?

Vrajanātha: O master, soon I will learn the proper way to worship Lord Gaura, but now a question has entered my mind. The *cit-śakti, jīva-śakti*, and *māyā-śakti* are manifested from the Lord's internal potency (*svarūpa-śakti*), and the *hlādinī-śakti, samvit-śakti*, and *sandhinī-śakti* are also manifested from the internal potency. All that is done is apparently done by the Lord's potencies. The spiritual world, spiritual bodies, spiritual relationships, and spiritual pastimes are all manifested by the Lord's potencies. Does Lord Kṛṣṇa, the master of all these potencies, do anything Himself?

Bābājī: That is a difficult question. Are you trying to attack an old man with arrows of logical puzzles? The question is simple, and it has a simple answer. Still, it is hard to find a person qualified to understand the simple answer to this question. I will speak. You please try to understand my words. Lord Kṛṣṇa's names, forms, qualities, and pastimes are all manifested by His potencies. Still, Kṛṣṇa's supreme independence and His desires are not manifested by His potencies. They are part of His nature. They are manifested by the Supreme Personality of Godhead alone. Lord Kṛṣṇa can do anything He wishes. He is the shelter of His potencies. Kṛṣṇa is the enjoyer. His potencies are enjoyed by Him. Kṛṣṇa is independent. His potencies are dependent on Him. At every turn, the independent Supreme Personality of Godhead is surrounded by His potencies. Still, He remains always perfect and always independent. Although He is always surrounded by His potencies, He is also always their master. When human beings understand the Supreme, they must do it through the aid of the Lord's potencies. Therefore, it is hard for them to understand that the Supreme Lord is the master of all potencies, and He is actually beyond the influence of His potencies. However, a devotee who has attained love (*prema*) for the Lord can directly see that the Supreme Lord is the master of all potencies and is beyond their influence. Devotional service (*bhakti*) is one of the Lord's potencies and therefore, is feminine in nature. Following the Lord's internal potency, the potency of devotional service can bring one to the position where one can directly perceive the masculine nature of Śrī Kṛṣṇa, the independent, self-willed supreme male.

Vrajanātha: If there is a being beyond the influence of the potencies, that being must be the impersonal Brahman described in the *Upaniṣads*.

Bābājī: The impersonal Brahman described in the *Upaniṣads* has no desires. The *puruṣa* described in the *Upaniṣads* is Lord Kṛṣṇa, the supreme male. He is filled with desires. These two are different in many ways. Impersonal Brahman has no qualities. Kṛṣṇa, completely independent of His potencies, has a host of qualities. They are part of His character as the supreme male, the supreme enjoyer, and the supreme independent being. In truth, Kṛṣṇa and His potencies are not different. The potency that allows us to see Kṛṣṇa is also Kṛṣṇa Himself. Why not? Śrī Rādhā is the most exalted potency. She serves Kṛṣṇa and Kṛṣṇa also serves Her. They worship each other and in this way, they are different from each other.

Vrajanātha: If the fact that Kṛṣṇa has desires and enjoyment are proof of His masculine nature, then how is it that Rādhā has desires, and yet has a feminine nature?

Bābājī: Śrīmatī Rādhā's desires are subordinate to Kṛṣṇa's desires. She never desires anything or does anything that has no relationship with Kṛṣṇa. That is Rādhā's desire. Rādhā is the *pūrṇa-śakti* (complete potency) or *ādya-śakti* (original potency). Kṛṣṇa is the supreme male. He is the master and controller of His potency.

At this point in their conversation, Vrajanātha took permission to depart. After offering *daṇḍavat* obeisances to the saintly *bābājī*, Vrajanātha happily returned to his home in Bilva-puṣkariṇī. Seeing that day by day he was changing, his grandmother said that it was time for him to get married. Vrajanātha would not listen to her. Day and night, he thought about what the saintly *bābājī* was teaching him.

Thinking, "These teachings are very pleasing to my heart. Now I will hear more teachings, teachings that are sweet like nectar," he happily went to Śrīvāsa's courtyard.

Chapter Fifteen

Eternal religion and sambandha, abhidheya and prayojana (The individual spirit souls)

This day, Vrajanātha came a little too early to Śrīvāsa's courtyard. The devotees living in Śrī Godruma had come to Śrīvāsa's courtyard to see the evening *ārati*. Parāmahaṁsa Bābājī Śrī Prema dāsa, Vaiṣṇava dāsa, Advaita dāsa, and all the other devotees had already entered the temple to see the *ārati*. Seeing the residents of Śrī Godruma, Vrajanātha thought, "Now I have their association. My life is now a great success."

Seeing humble, devoted, smiling Vrajanātha, everyone gave him their blessings. When, after a short time, they left, going south to return to Śrī Godruma, the saintly elderly *bābājī* noticed that tears were streaming from Vrajanātha's eyes. Saintly Raghunātha dāsa Bābājī had by this time developed strong affection for Vrajanātha.

He asked Vrajanātha, "Bābā, why are you weeping?"

Vrajanātha humbly replied, "O master, your teachings and association has brought an upheaval in my thoughts. Now, my heart understands how worthless the material world is. My heart yearns to take shelter of Lord Gaura's lotus feet. In my mind there is one question: Who am I in reality, and why do I live in the material world?

Bābājī: Good. With this question, you have made me fortunate. When his auspicious day comes, a soul places this question before all others. When you hear the fifth verse of *Daśa-mūla* and its explanation, doubts will no longer live in your heart: As sparks fly from a blazing fire, or rays of light fly from the sun, so the individual spirit souls come from the Supreme Personality of Godhead, Lord Hari. As the sparks and rays of light are at once different and not different from their source, so the individual souls are different and not different from Lord Hari. Lord Hari is the supreme controller. He is the master of the material world. The illusory potency, *māyā*, is under His control. The individual soul is not like Him. Even when he is liberated, the soul is capable of coming under *māyā*'s control.

Vrajanātha: That is a wonderful conclusion! I wish to hear the evidence the *Vedas* give for it. The words of the Supreme Lord (*Bhagavad-gītā*) are worthy evidence by themselves. However, when they are supported by the words of the *Upaniṣads*, they are more easily accepted by the people in general.

Bābājī: These truths are revealed in many passages of the *Vedas*. I will recite one or two of them. Please listen carefully. In the *Bṛhad-āraṇyaka Upaniṣad* (2.2.20 and 4.3.9) it is said: As tiny sparks fly from a fire, so all individual souls have come from the Supreme. A person has two places: the spiritual world and the place where the spiritual world meets another world. There is also a third place, a place of dreams. Standing between them, the soul sees on one side the spiritual world and on the other side the place of dreaming.

This passage describes the individual souls (*jīva-śakti*), which can reside in either the spiritual or material worlds (*taṭasthā*). In the *Bṛhad-āraṇyaka Upaniṣad* (4.3.18) it is also said: As a large fish in a river may go to one shore or the other, so a person may go to one world or another. He may go to a world where he is awake, or may go to a world made of dreams.

Vrajanātha: How does the *Vedānta* philosophy define the word *taṭasthā*?

Bābājī: The place where a river's water meets the land of the shore is called the *tata*. The *tata* is then the place where water meets the land. What is the nature of this *tata*? It is like the thinnest of threads that runs along the boundary of land and water. A *tata* is like the finest of lines, so small that the gross material eyes cannot even see it. In this example, the spiritual world is like the water and the material world is like the land. The thin line that separates them is the *tata*. That boundary place is the abode of the individual spirit souls. The individual spirit souls are like atomic particles of sunlight. The souls can see both the spiritual world and the material world created by *māyā*. The Lord's spiritual potency, *cit-śakti*, is limitless, and the Lord's material potency, *māyā-śakti*, is gigantic. Standing between them, the individual spirit soul is very tiny. The individual spirit souls are manifested from the *taṭasthā-śakti* of Lord Kṛṣṇa. Therefore, the souls are naturally situated on the boundary (*taṭasthā*) of matter and spirit.

Vrajanātha: What is this *taṭasthā* nature of the individual souls?

Bābājī: Standing between them, the soul can see these two worlds. The *taṭasthā* nature of the souls refers to the fact that they must be under the control of one of these two potencies. The actual place of the *tata* (shore) may change. What was once dry land may be covered with water, and what was once covered by water may again become dry land. If he turns his gaze upon Lord Kṛṣṇa, the soul comes under the shelter of Lord Kṛṣṇa's spiritual potency. But, if he turns away from Kṛṣṇa and turns his gaze to the material potency, *māyā*, then the soul is caught in *māyā*'s trap. That is what is meant by, "the soul's *taṭasthā* nature."

Vrajanātha: Does *māyā* have anything to do with the nature of the spirit souls?

Bābājī: No. The spirit souls are completely spiritual. However, because they are atomic in size, the souls are not very strong. That is why *māyā* can dominate them. However, in the soul's nature, there is not the slightest scent of *māyā*.

Vrajanātha: I heard from my teacher that when it is surrounded by *māyā*, the impersonal Brahman becomes the individual spirit soul. When a small portion of the great sky is surrounded by the walls of a clay pot, it becomes the sky within a pot. In the same way, when the impersonal Brahman is surrounded by *māyā*, it becomes the individual soul. What does this mean?

Bābājī: That is just impersonalism (Māyāvāda). How can *māyā* have the power to touch the Supreme Brahman? If you say that Brahman has no potency, then how can *māyā* even approach Brahman? The *māyā* potency has no independent power. How can she have any effect on Brahman? It cannot be said that the great Brahman becomes covered by *māyā* and is then forced to suffer in different ways. That is not possible. If Brahman's spiritual potency is always awake and vigilant, how can the insignificant *māyā-śakti* defeat her and proceed to create the individual souls from Brahman in this way? The Supreme Brahman is limitless and immeasurable. How can the limitless Brahman be broken into smaller souls in the same way that the great sky is broken into the little skies within a series of clay pots? The idea that *māyā* can have some effect on the Brahman cannot be accepted. *Māyā* has nothing to do with the creation of the individual spirit souls. Although they are atomic in size, the individual spirit souls are superior to *māyā*.

Vrajanātha: At another time, another teacher said that the individual spirit soul is a reflection of Brahman. As the sun is reflected on the water, so the Supreme Brahman, reflected on *māyā*, becomes the individual soul. What does that mean?

Bābājī: That is also impersonalism. Brahman has no limit. Something that is unlimited cannot be reflected anywhere. The *Vedas* do not teach that Brahman is limited. This reflection theory should be rejected.

Vrajanātha: Another time a *dig-vijayī sannyāsī* said that the individual spirit soul does not really exist. The idea of the individual soul is only an illusion. When the illusion is thrown far away, only the undivided Brahman remains. What does that mean?

Bābājī: That is also impersonalism. That idea has no root in the truth. In the *Chāndogya Upaniṣad* (6.2.1) it is said: Brahman is one without a second.

Do these words of the *Vedas* mean that only Brahman, and nothing else, exists? If nothing but Brahman exists, then from where has this illusion come? Who does this illusion bewilder? If you say this illusion bewilders Brahman, then you make Brahman a pathetic being. If you say this illusion bewilders something other than Brahman, then you contradict the idea that only Brahman exists.

Vrajanātha: Another time a *brāhmaṇa paṇḍita* of Navadvīpa said that only the individual soul exists. In a dream, he experiences material happiness and suffering. When he wakes up from the dream, he discovers that he is Brahman. What does this mean?

Bābājī: That is also impersonalism. Brahman has a dream and becomes the individual soul? What proof do they have for that? The scriptures give the examples of mistaking the glittering on a seashell's surface for silver, and mistaking a rope for a snake, but these examples do not prove the impersonalist idea that Brahman alone exists. These words are only a great network of word jugglery meant to bewilder the people in general.

Vrajanātha: The individual soul is not created by *māyā*. That I accept. *Māyā* has the power to dominate the individual soul. That I understand. This is my question: Does the spiritual potency (*cit-śakti*) place the individual soul on the border (*taṭasthā*) of matter and spirit?

Bābājī: No. The *cit-śakti* is the full manifestation of Lord Kṛṣṇa's potency. Whatever she creates is eternally perfect (*nitya-siddha*). The individual spirit souls are not eternally perfect. By engaging in the activities of devotional service (*sādhana*), they may become perfect (*sādhana-siddha*) and thus enjoy spiritual bliss exactly like that enjoyed by the eternally perfect (*nitya-siddha*) beings. The four kinds of *gopī* friends (*sakhī*) of Śrīmatī Rādhārani are eternally perfect beings (*nitya-siddha*). They are manifested from the form of Śrīmati Rādhārani, who is the *cit-śakti* Herself. All the individual spirit souls are manifested from Lord Kṛṣṇa's *jīva-śakti*. The *cit-śakti* is Lord Kṛṣṇa's complete potency (*pūrṇa-śakti*). The individual souls (*jīva-śakti*) are counted among Lord Kṛṣṇa's incomplete potencies (*apūrṇa-śakti*). From the complete potency, complete and perfect things are manifested. From the incomplete potency, all the individual souls, who are atomic fragments of consciousness, are manifested.

Lord Kṛṣṇa manifests different kinds of entities according to the different kinds of potencies He employs to create them. When He is manifested in His *cit-śakti*, He appears as Kṛṣṇa and as Nārāyaṇa, the master of Vaikuṇṭha. When He is manifested in the *jīva-śakti*, He appears as Baladeva, His pastime form (*vilāsa-mūrti*) in Vraja. When He is manifested in the *māyā-śakti*, He appears as the three forms of Kāranodakaśāyī Viṣṇu, Garbhodakaśāyī Viṣṇu and Kṣīrodakaśāyī Viṣṇu. In Vraja, He appears in His original form, as Kṛṣṇa, a form manifested by His complete potency. Appearing as Baladeva, He manifests His *śeṣa-tattva* (nature of Lord Śeṣa). In this way, He manifests the eight kinds of services the eternally liberated associates offer to Him.

Again, in Vaikuṇṭha, He appears as Śeṣa-Saṅkarṣaṇa and manifests the eight kinds of service His eternal associates offer to Lord Nārāyaṇa. Lord Saṅkarṣaṇa incarnates as Mahā-Viṣṇu. He becomes the resting place of the *jīva-śakti* and appears as the Supersoul in the hearts of all the individual souls residing in the material world. All these individual souls are attracted to *māyā*. As long as they do not attain the mercy of the Supreme Personality of Godhead and take shelter of the Lord's spiritual *hlādinī-śakti*, they are defeated by *māyā*. Numberless souls are defeated by *māyā* and cast into Her prison. They are the followers of *māyā*'s three modes. The conclusion is this: The individual souls are manifested by the *jīva-śakti*. They are not manifested by the *cit-śakti*.

Vrajanātha: I have heard that the spiritual world is eternal and that the individual spirit souls are also eternal. How is it possible for eternal things to be born, created, or manifested? If there was a time when they were not manifested, and they only appear at a certain point in time, how can they be eternal?

Bābājī: The time and space present in the spiritual world is different from the time and space you experience now in the material world. In the material world, time has three phases: past, present and future. In the spiritual world, time is not broken in that way. There, time is an eternal present. In the spiritual world, things do not come into being. Everything exists in an eternal present. When we who are living in the world of material time and space try to describe the spiritual world, we tend to say things like, "The individual souls were created," "the individual souls were imprisoned by *māyā*," "the spiritual world was manifested," and "the individual souls are spiritual and were not created by *māyā*." When we talk in these ways, we certainly show how much we are influence by staying in this world of material time. As long as we stay in *māyā*'s prison, we cannot avoid talking in this way. That is why, when we describe the individual souls, or the nature of spirit, we cannot avoid speaking in terms of material time. Therefore, we tend to speak in terms of past and future. Therefore, a person who tries to understand the spiritual world properly tries to speak in terms of an eternal present.

Bābā, logic cannot help us understand these things. Here, logic should be rejected. Then you will be able to see the nature of spirit. When he forgets that he is eternally a servant of Lord Kṛṣṇa, the individual soul enters *māyā*'s prison. Originally, all souls are Vaiṣṇavas. However, they become two groups: 1. *nitya-baddha* (eternally imprisoned by *māyā*) and 2. *nitya-mukta* (eternally liberated).

A human being bewildered by matter cannot describe these things. Still, a saintly devotee can attain the spiritual vision to see these spiritual truths directly. My words are inevitably influenced by matter. I will describe these things as far as I am able. My words will inevitably be imperfect. O Bābā, you will be able to see the pure spiritual truth. However, logic will not help you. Why will logic not help? Because logic is useless in grasping what is beyond the mind's understanding. I know you will not be able to understand this all at once. Still, the more you follow the spiritual path, the more you will be able to see the difference between matter and spirit. Your body is material. All the body's actions are material. But, the truth is that You yourself are not material. You are a tiny particle of conscious spirit. The more you understand that truth, the more you will be able to perceive your own identity and the truth that you are superior to the material world. You will not understand this merely by hearing me tell you about it. As you follow the path of regularly chanting the holy names of Lord Hari, these spiritual truths will gradually spontaneously appear before you. Then, you will understand the spiritual world.

As long as the mind and words are influenced by matter, try as one may, one will not be able to touch the spiritual truth. The *Vedas* (*Taittirīya Upaniṣad* 2.4.1.) explain: The descriptive power of speech fails in the realm of the Absolute Truth and the speculative power of the mind cannot achieve Him.

My advice to you is: Don't ask anyone what they think of these conclusions. Experience them yourself. I can only give a hint about them.

Vrajanātha: I say this: If the individual souls are like sparks from a blazing fire, or atomic particles of sunlight, then what is the function of the *jīva-śakti* potency?

Bābājī: Kṛṣṇa is self-effulgent, like a blazing fire or the sun. Kṛṣṇa is like a blazing fire. In the center of the fire, the *cit-śakti* is present in fullness. In addition to the center, there is also a great expanse illuminated by the fire. In the same way, the Kṛṣṇa-sun illumines a great area with sunlight. The rays of sunlight are particles of His internal potency (*svarūpa-śakti*). Those atomic particles that constitute those rays of sunlight are the individual spirit souls. The internal potency (*svarūpa-śakti*) manifests the Kṛṣṇa-sun planet itself. The sunlight emanating from that planet is manifested by the *cit-śakti*, and the individual particles of light are manifested by the *jīva-śakti*. Therefore, the individual spirit souls are manifested by the *jīva-śakti*. This is described in the following words of the *Śvetāśvatara Upaniṣad* (6.8): The Lord's spiritual potency is manifested in many different ways.

In this way, the Lord's spiritual potency manifests the *jīva-śakti*-sunlight, which shines on the borderline (*tata*) of the spiritual and material worlds. In this way, the eternal individual spirit souls are manifested.

Vrajanātha: A blazing fire is material, the sun is material, and sparks are material. Why are material examples used here to describe the spiritual truth?

Bābājī: I have already explained that when we try to use material words to describe spiritual things, the faults of matter tend to slip into the description. In this situation, we have no choice but to use examples like the fire or the sun. In truth, Lord Kṛṣṇa is much greater than the sun. Lord Kṛṣṇa's circle of spiritual potencies is much greater than the circle of the sun's light. Lord Kṛṣṇa's effulgence is much greater than the sun's light. In this case, certain features that may be similar are considered but in many other ways, the two things being compared are not at all alike. The sun and the sunlight are beautiful and glorious. However, the sun is material and it also burns things to ashes, and has many other such qualities also. These qualities are absent in the spiritual truth. When we say that milk is like water, we mean that as water is a liquid, so milk is also a liquid. We do not mean that milk and water are identical in all respects. If that were so, why would we designate one thing as milk and another as water? Therefore, when we use an example to describe something, the example shows a similarity in only one point. The two things compared are not alike in everything.

Vrajanātha: The individual soul-sunlight is simultaneously one and different from the Kṛṣṇa-sun. How is this possible?

Bābājī: In the material world, when one thing is manifested from another, the thing manifested is either different from or identical with its source. That is the nature of material things. When an egg comes from a bird, the egg and bird are then distinct. The egg does not remain a part of the bird. As long as they are not cut off, the hair and nails of a human body remain part of it. In the world of spirit, the situation is different. When they are emanated from the spiritual sun, the rays of spiritual sunlight remain simultaneously one and different from their source. The rays of light and the atomic particles of which those rays are constituted are not different from the sun that is their origin. In the same way, the sunlight or the *jīva-śakti* and the atomic particles of which that sunlight is composed, the particles of which are the individual spirit souls, are not different from the Kṛṣṇa-sun that is their origin. In this way, the individual spirit souls are not different from Lord Kṛṣṇa. However, the individual souls are all individual persons, and each of them has free will. In this way, they are each eternally different from Lord Kṛṣṇa. In this way, the individual spirit souls are simultaneously one and different from Lord Kṛṣṇa. This is so eternally. In this way the nature of spirit is different from that of matter.

The *paṇḍitas* also give another example from the material world. It is this: There is a large lump of gold, and from that lump a bracelet is fashioned.

Because it is gold, the bracelet is not different from the gold lump. Still, because it is a bracelet, it is also different from the lump of gold. The example here does not hold in all its details, but in one point it holds. The Kṛṣṇa-sun and the individual souls-sunlight are one in the sense that they are both spirit, but they are different in the sense that one is the complete spirit and the other is a tiny particle of spirit. The impersonalists' example of the sky within the clay pot and the great sky expanded everywhere does not properly explain the spiritual truth.

Vrajanātha: If spirit and matter are different, then why are these examples used?

Bābājī: The *nyāya* philosophers like to divide the components of the material world into various categories, and then claim that these divisions are eternal. Matter and spirit are not really different from each other in that way. As I said before, matter is merely a perverted manifestation of spirit. The perverted manifestation and the original pure form from which it has come may share many similar features. The perverted manifestation is certainly different from the original pure form, but still the two share many similarities. Ice is a perverted manifestation of water. Ice is different from water. Still, water and ice may both be cold and may share many other qualities also. There may also be differences. Cold and hot water do not share the quality of coldness. However, they do share the quality of liquidity. Therefore, a perverted manifestation may have many qualities like those present in the pure manifestation that is its origin.

Because matter is a perverted manifestation of spirit, spirit and matter do have some similar qualities. These similar qualities may provide material examples to describe spiritual things. Here, the example of *arundhatī-darśana-nyāya* (showing the position of the star Arundhatī in the sky by using an object on the earth as a point of reference) is relevant. One may say, "If you look between these two branches of this tree, the star in the sky shining there is Arundhatī."

In this way, examples drawn from material things can be used to reveal spiritual truths. Lord Kṛṣṇa's pastimes are perfectly spiritual. They have not even the slightest scent of matter. Lord Kṛṣṇa's Vraja pastimes, which are described in *Śrīmad-Bhāgavatam*, are perfectly spiritual and not material. When they are read to a circle of human hearers, they produce different results according to the qualifications of the different people hearing them. When people very attached to matter hear these pastimes, they enjoy the material poetic language and, as far as they are concerned, think they are hearing descriptions of an ordinary romantic couple. People of an intermediate qualification think in terms of the *arundhatī-darśana-nyāya*. They think these pastimes are examples drawn from the material world to reveal spiritual truths. Persons who are most qualified know that these pastimes are spiritual activities that are far beyond the realm of matter. These persons dive into an ocean of nectarean happiness while hearing these pastimes.

Without speaking examples like these, how can one teach the people about the spiritual truth? The material mind and material words are defeated when they try to describe these things. How will the souls imprisoned in the material world attain an auspicious life? We do not see any way other than by speaking examples like the example of *arundhatī-darśana-nyāya*. Material things are either one or different. Spiritual things are not like that. Lord Kṛṣṇa, His *jīva-śakti* potency and the individual spirit souls manifested from that potency are all inconceivable. You should accept that they are simultaneously one and different.

Vrajanātha: In what ways are the individual spirit soul and the Supreme Personality of Godhead different?

Bābājī: First I will explain how the individual spirit soul and the Supreme Personality of Godhead are eternally one. After that, I will explain how they are eternally different. The Supreme Personality of Godhead is consciousness, a knower, an enjoyer, a thinker, self-manifested, and visible to others. He is also the knower of all fields of activity and He is full of desires. The individual spirit soul is also consciousness, a knower, an enjoyer, a thinker, self-manifested, and visible to others. He is also the knower of a field of activity and he is also full of desires. Because He is the master of all potencies, the Supreme Personality of Godhead has these qualities to the highest degree. On the other hand, the individual spirit soul, possessing only very slight power, has these qualities to a very slight degree. Although they are different in the sense that one is perfect and complete and the other is very small and atomic, the Supreme Personality of Godhead and the individual spirit souls are alike in that they both possess these qualities.

The Supreme Personality of Godhead is the master of all potencies. He is the controller of the *svarūpa-śakti* (internal potency), *jīva-śakti*, and *māyā-śakti*. These potencies are all His obedient maidservants. He is their master. Whatever He wishes, they do. That is the nature of the Supreme Personality of Godhead. He is subordinate to the Lord's other potencies. The word *māyā* is used in the *Daśa-mūla* (in the verse quoted in the beginning of this chapter) to mean not only the Lord's material potency, but also His internal potency (*svarūpa-śakti*). The dictionaries explain: That which measures is called *māyā*.

According to this explanation, the word *māyā* refers to the potency of Lord Kṛṣṇa that manifests the spiritual world, the individual spirit souls, and the material world. Understood in this way, the word *māyā* refers to the Lord's internal potency (*svarūpa-śakti*), not to His material potency. Lord Kṛṣṇa is the master of this *māyā* potency. The individual spirit souls are under the control of the *māyā* potency.

This is described in the following words of the *Śvetāśvatara Upaniṣad* (4.9-10): It is very difficult for the conditioned soul, illusioned by *māyā* and trapped in the material world, to understand the Supreme Personality of Godhead, the controller of the illusory potency and the creator of the material universes. One should know that although *māyā* (illusion) is false, or temporary, the background of *māyā* is the supreme magician, the Personality of Godhead, who is Maheśvara, the Supreme Controller.

In these verses, the word *mayī* refers to Lord Kṛṣṇa, the controller of *māyā*, and the word *prakṛti* refers to His complete potency. This glorious quality (being the controller of *māyā*) belongs to the Supreme Personality of Godhead alone. The individual souls do not possess it. Even the liberated souls cannot attain this quality. In the *Vedānta-sūtra* (4.4.17) it is said: Even after he attains liberation, the individual soul does not have the power to create the material world.

Therefore, the conclusion of *Vedānta-sūtra* is that the individual souls are eternally different from the Supreme Personality of Godhead. The circle of the wise accept this conclusion. This eternal difference is not an imagination.

It is eternally real. The difference between the soul and the Lord will never be destroyed. Therefore, you should know that the statement, "The individual spirit soul is eternally a servant of Lord Kṛṣṇa" is one of the most important teachings of the scriptures.

Vrajanātha: If they are eternally different, then how are they not different? Should we accept the idea that when he attains *nirvāna*, the soul becomes one with the Supreme?

Bābājī: Bābā, it is not like that. At no time does the individual soul become non-different from the Supreme.

Vrajanātha: Then, why do you say that the soul is simultaneously one and different from the Lord?

Bābājī: In the sense that they are both spiritual in nature, Lord Kṛṣṇa and the individual soul are eternally not different. Otherwise, their natures are eternally different. Their oneness is eternal and their difference is also eternal. Their oneness does not refer to the other qualities of their natures. In other qualities, their difference is more prominent. Therefore, if one says that a house is simultaneously, "the property of Devadatta" and "without Devadatta's presence," then even though Devadatta may be absent, the idea that it remains his property is the more important of the two ideas. Now I will give another material example. The sky is a material thing. If some portion of the sky is contained within a clay pot, the existence of the great sky outside the pot remains more important than the sky within the pot. In the same way, the eternal difference between the Supreme Lord and the individual spirit soul is more important than their oneness.

Vrajanātha: Please describe the soul's eternal nature more clearly.

Bābājī: The individual spirit soul is an atomic fragment of consciousness. He has knowledge. He has ego, or a sense of self, and he calls himself by the word, "I." He is an enjoyer, and thinker, and a knower. The soul has an eternal form. That form is spiritual and subtle. That form has hands, feet, eyes, nose, ears, and other limbs, all handsome and graceful, superficially like the limbs of an ordinary material body. That body is made of a spiritual atom. It is very handsome. It is spiritual. That is the eternal form of the individual spirit soul. When the soul is imprisoned by *māyā*, the soul's original spiritual body is covered by two material bodies. One of these bodies is called *liṅga-śarīra* (the subtle body) and the other is called *sthūla-śarīra* (the gross body). The *liṅga-śarīra* covers the atomic spiritual form of the individual spirit soul. From the time the soul is first imprisoned in the material world, until the time he is released, the *liṅga-śarīra* cannot be removed. When the soul takes birth in another body, he enters a different *sthūla-śarīra* (gross body). He does not enter a different *liṅga-śarīra*. He keeps the same *liṅga-śarīra*. The *liṅga-śarīra* is one. On the other hand, the soul periodically leaves one *sthūla-śarīra* and, impelled by his material desires, accepts another *sthūla-śarīra*. Thus, following the path of the five fires described in the *Vedas*, the soul attains a new *sthūla-śarīra*. These five fires, beginning with *citāgni, vṛṣṭyāgni, bhojanāgni*, and *retohavanāgni*, are described in the *Chāndogya Upaniṣad* and the *Vedānta-sūtra*. In this way, one birth follows another. According to the desires he had in his previous births, the soul attains a particular kind of new body. In this way, he attains a certain kind of material nature and a particular status among the castes. According to the way he acts in the *varṇāśrama* system, he gets an appropriate new body at the time of death. Meanwhile his original spiritual form remains covered, first by the *liṅga-śarīra*, and secondly by the *sthūla-śarīra*.

Vrajanātha: What is the difference between the eternal spiritual body and the *liṅga-śarīra*?

Bābājī: The eternal body is an atomic particle of spirit. It has no defects. The soul may properly apply the word "I" to this body alone. The *liṅga-śarīra* is composed of material perversions of the soul's original mind, intelligence and ego.

Vrajanātha: How can mind, intelligence, and ego be material? If they are material, how can they be conscious of anything?

Bābājī: Lord Kṛṣṇa explains in the *Bhagavad-gītā* (7.4-6): Earth, water, fire, air, ether, mind, intelligence and false-ego—altogether these eight comprise My separated material energies. Besides this inferior nature, O mighty-armed Arjuna, there is a superior energy of Mine, which are all living entities, who are struggling with material nature and are sustaining the universe. Of all that is material and all that is spiritual in this world, know for certain that I am both its origin and dissolution.

Look at these words of *Gītā Upaniṣad*. Here two natures: superior (*parā*) and inferior (*aparā*) are described. The superior nature is the *jīva-śakti*, and the inferior nature is the *māyā-śakti*. Because it is a particle of spirit, the *jīva-śakti* is here called "superior." On the other hand, the *māyā-śakti* is made of matter and therefore it is called "inferior." The individual spirit souls are different from the inferior, material potency. The inferior potency has eight elements: the five gross elements and the three subtle elements of mind, intelligence, and false ego. When they are manifested in the material potency, mind, intelligence, and ego are material in nature. These three form a body made of consciousness, but that consciousness is not spiritual, it is material consciousness.

From the material mind, all else is manifested. The mind is thus conscious of material objects and engaged in directing material activities. Thus, the material mind is the root from which material things grow. It is not the root of spiritual things. In the material consciousness is placed the conception of what is good and what is not good. This is called "intelligence." This intelligence is material in nature. From this material intelligence, material ego is manifested. This kind of ego is not spiritual in its nature. When these three material elements (material mind, intelligence, and ego) combine, they form a second body, which is called the *liṅga-śarīra*. The material ego of this material *liṅga-śarīra* then covers the eternal spiritual ego of the individual spirit soul. In the soul's eternal spiritual form, the spiritual ego understands its relationship with the spiritual Kṛṣṇa-sun.

When the soul attains liberation, this original spiritual ego becomes uncovered and is openly manifested. As long as the *liṅga-śarīra* covers the soul's eternal spiritual form, the soul tends to identify itself as matter. At that time, the truth that the soul is spiritual is almost completely lost. The *liṅga-śarīra* is made of subtle matter, and because it is subtle it is easily covered by another body, the *sthūla-śarīra*, which is made of gross matter. When the covering of the *sthūla-śarīra* is in place, the ego identifies with one of the castes or other groups (*varṇas*) of this world. Because they are perverted manifestations of their counterparts in the soul's original spiritual body, the material mind, intelligence, and ego think they are really conscious of the world around them.

Vrajanātha: I understand now that the individual soul has an eternal spiritual form, each limb of which is very graceful and beautiful. When the soul is imprisoned by *māyā*, that original spiritual form is covered by the *liṅga-śarīra*. In this way, the soul's beauty is covered and hidden. Then, the *liṅga-śarīra* is covered by the gross *sthūla-śarīra*. In this way, the soul's original form is completely hidden by a great apparatus of material things. My question is this: Is the liberated soul completely perfect and free of any defect?

Bābājī: Although he is free of defects, the atomic spiritual soul is not perfect. Why not? He is very tiny and very weak. For this reason, one defect may be seen in the individual soul: Because he is so weak, when he comes into contact with the *māyā-śakti*, the soul is easily overpowered and his original form becomes covered. In *Śrīmad-Bhāgavatam* (10.2.32), the demigods speak the following prayer to the Supreme Lord: O lotus-eyed one, those who think they are liberated in this life but do not render devotional service to You must be of impure intelligence. Although they accept severe austerities and penances to rise to the spiritual position, to impersonal Brahman realization, they fall down again because they neglect to worship Your lotus feet.

Therefore, even when he is liberated, the individual spirit soul is not very great and is always imperfect. That is the truth of the individual spirit souls. The *Vedas* declare that the Supreme Personality of Godhead is the controller of *māyā* but on the other hand, the individual spirit souls are so weak that at any moment, they may be overpowered by *māyā*.

Chapter Sixteen

Eternal religion and sambandha, abhidheya and prayojana (The individual souls swallowed by māyā)

Jaiva-dharma

After he had heard the *Daśa-mūla's* teachings about the individual spirit soul, Vrajanātha lay in his bed in his own home and deeply thought, "Who am I? That question was answered. Now I know who I am. I am an atomic particle of light shining from the spiritual sun of Lord Kṛṣṇa. I am atomic in size and therefore, I possess consciousness, a spiritual identity, and a single drop of spiritual bliss. I have a form made of a tiny fragment of spirit. I am very tiny and my form is somewhat like the moderately sized form of Lord Kṛṣṇa. I cannot see my spiritual form. That is my misfortune. That I am now very eager to see this spiritual form means that now I have become fortunate."

"Why did I fall into this unfortunate situation? I must understand that very clearly. Tomorrow, I will place this question before Śrī Gurudeva's feet."

He thought about this again and again. After six hours of the night had passed, the goddess of sleep came like a thief and gradually stole away his wakefulness. Then, as the night was ending, he dreamt that he had renounced the material world and accepted the garments of a Vaiṣṇava.

When his sleep broke, he thought, "Now the Lord will take me from this material life."

He went to the family shrine of Goddess Durgā. His students came, fell at his feet, and requested, "We have come to study logic. Please teach us the book *Kusumāñjali*. That is our wish."

Vrajanātha humbly replied, "Like Nimāi Paṇḍita, I too have closed my books. I have made my mind place its gaze on a different path. Please find another teacher."

One by one, the students left. Then, the matchmaker, Caturbhuja Miśra, visited Vrajanātha's grandmother with a proposal for Vrajanātha's marriage. He said, "Vijaynātha Bhaṭṭācārya comes from a good family. His daughter is very beautiful. She would be good for your grandson. The Bhaṭṭācārya has not yet promised his daughter to anyone."

Hearing this marriage proposal, Vrajanātha's grandmother became very happy. Vrajanātha thought, "What a calamity! Now I have decided to renounce the world. How can any good come from this talking of my marriage?"

With Vrajanātha on one side and his mother, grandmother, and the elderly ladies of the family on the other, there was much talking about it. In that way, the day passed. At sunset, there were clouds, thunder, and rain. That day, Vrajanātha did not go to Māyāpura. The night passed. The next day, there was more talk about the marriage. Vrajanātha could not peacefully take his meals or do anything else.

At sunset, Vrajanātha approached the elderly *bābājī*'s cottages. He offered *daṇḍavat* obeisances. The saintly *bābājī* said, "Last night it rained so you could not come. Now I am very glad to see you."

Vrajanātha replied, "O master, many calamities have fallen upon me. Later I will tell you about them. For now, I will ask this question: The individual soul is pure spirit. Why does the calamity of residing in the material world fall upon him?"

The saintly *bābājī* smiled and recited this verse: Covering them with gross and subtle material forms, chaining them with the modes of nature, and pulling them with the painful ropes of *karma*, *māyā* leads to Svargaloka and to hell the criminal souls who, forgetting their own spiritual welfare, have turned from Kṛṣṇa and become intent on their own happiness.

In Goloka, which is manifested by Lord Baladeva, and in Vaikuṇṭha, which is manifested by Lord Saṅkarṣaṇa, numberless individual souls are eternal associates of the Lord. There, they taste the nectar of worshiping and serving the Lord. They are always inclined to spiritual things. They seek the happiness of worshiping the Lord. They are always eager to serve the Lord. Empowered by the Lord's *jīva-śakti* and *cit-śakti*, they always have great spiritual strength. They never touch *māyā*. They do not even know that a potency called *māyā-śakti* exists. Staying in the middle of the circle of the spiritual world, they are very far away from *māyā*. They always swim in the ocean of pleasure that is worshiping and serving the Lord. They know nothing of suffering, material pleasure, or selfish pleasure. They are eternally liberated. Love for the Lord is their entire life. What are grief, death, and fear they do not know.

When He glances at *māyā*, Lord Kāraṇodakaśāyī Viṣṇu sends numberless atomic spirit souls to the material world. Because they are now on *māyā*'s side, the many creations of *māyā* now enter the pathway of their eyes. These souls have all the qualities of the soul I have already described. However, because they are atomic in size, from the border of matter and spirit (*taṭasthā*) they must place their glance on either the spiritual world or the material world. The individual souls are very weak. How can this not be? These souls did not obtain the spiritual strength that comes from the Lord's mercy, mercy that comes from properly serving Him. That is why these souls develop a desire to enjoy the pleasures that *māyā* offers.

These souls enter *māyā*'s world and there, *māyā* imprisons them for what seems an eternity. When these souls again turn to spiritual life and service to the Lord, they can attain the Lord's mercy, which will give them spiritual strength. Then they can return to the spiritual world. Bābā, I am very unfortunate. I have forgotten that I am eternally a servant of Lord Kṛṣṇa. I have entered *māyā*'s world, and just see how *māyā* keeps me imprisoned. I have forgotten my own spiritual welfare. I am very unfortunate!

Vrajanātha: O master, why did some souls leave the borderline of matter and spirit and enter the world of *māyā*? Why did other souls go to the spiritual world?

Bābājī: Lord Kṛṣṇa's own qualities are present in a very small degree in the individual spirit souls. Because Lord Kṛṣṇa has free will, so the individual souls eternally possess a small quantity of free will also. When that free will is used properly, the individual soul is favorable to Kṛṣṇa and turns toward Him. When the free will is misused, the soul is averse to Kṛṣṇa and turns away from Him. Then, the soul tries to enjoy *māyā*. Puffed up with petty pride, the soul thinks, "I am the enjoyer of matter." Then the pure spiritual form of the soul becomes covered by the five kinds of ignorance that begin with illusion and false ego. Thus, it is the proper or improper use of free will that brings us either liberation or imprisonment in the material world.

Vrajanātha: Lord Kṛṣṇa is supremely merciful. Why then did He make the individual spirit souls so weak that they fall into *māyā*'s world?

Bābājī: As He is merciful, so Kṛṣṇa is also playful. Desiring many different kinds of pastimes with individual spirit souls in many different conditions of life, He created many exalted conditions, which culminate in *mahā-bhāva* great ecstatic spiritual love for the Lord, and He also created, with the help of Śrī Rādhā's expansion, *māyā*, the degraded material conditions of life, which reach their nadir in *ahaṅkāra* (the soul's misidentification with matter). In this way, by the influence of Śrī Rādhā, there is the attainment of limitless transcendental bliss and by the influence of *māyā*, there is a descent into the lower depths. The souls that thus enter *māyā*'s abyss are not interested in their own spiritual well-being. They are averse to Lord Kṛṣṇa and interested in their own selfish pleasure. Thus they go down lower and lower. However, supremely merciful Lord Kṛṣṇa sends His own personal associates from His own spiritual world into the material world to make these souls favorable to Him, and to lift them out of the abyss. In this way, some of the fallen souls gradually become elevated and eventually return to the spiritual world, where they become eternal associates of the Lord.

Vrajanātha: Why must the individual souls suffer so that the Lord can enjoy pastimes like these?

Bābājī: What should be said is this: It is by the great mercy of the Lord that the individual souls have free will. Why not speak in that way? Inanimate matter is very lowly and unimportant because it has no free will. It is because they have free will that the individual souls can become masters of the world of matter. Pain and pleasure are two destinations the mind can attain. What you and I may call pain, another person, who is attached to it, may call pleasure. All material pleasures bring only pain at the end. They do not lead to anything but that. Therefore, a person attached to material pleasures becomes unhappy at the end. When that unhappiness becomes very acute, the soul begins to desire happiness that is not mixed with sufferings. From that desire comes intelligence, and from that intelligence comes the spirit of inquiry. From the spirit of inquiry comes association with saintly persons, from association with saintly persons comes faith in spiritual life, and from faith in spiritual life one becomes gradually elevated. In this way, what began as pain became at the end the giver of auspicious happiness. When it is heated and burnished, impure gold becomes pure. In the same way, when they suffer in *māyā*'s material world, the impure souls averse to Lord Kṛṣṇa and yearning to enjoy *māyā* become purified. That this suffering turns into the giver of happiness is the mercy of Lord Kṛṣṇa. Therefore, those who are far-sighted see that these sufferings of the conditioned souls eventually bring auspicious happiness. Those who are short-sighted cannot see that. They see only sufferings.

Vrajanātha: Although they may bring happiness at the end, for the present, the conditioned souls' sufferings are very painful. Could not the all-powerful Lord invent a different path—one without these sufferings?

Bābājī: Lord Kṛṣṇa enjoys many different kinds of wonderful pastimes. This is one of His wonderful pastimes. A person who is supremely independent can enjoy many different kinds of pastimes, and this may be one of them. Why not? If the Lord has every kind of pastime, then no pastime may be rejected. If one pastime is substituted for another, then still some kind of troubles must be expected. Lord Kṛṣṇa is the supreme person and the creator. Everyone is subject to His will. If one person is subject to the will of another, is there not some difficulty in that? If that difficulty eventually leads to happiness, then it is no difficulty at all. Why do you say it is suffering and difficulty? If to expand Lord Kṛṣṇa's pastimes, the individual souls go through some difficulties, the difficulties are only happiness. Lord Kṛṣṇa's pastimes are naturally full of bliss. If an individual soul of his own free will voluntarily leaves those pastimes and enters the world of *māyā* and accepts the sufferings there, then if anyone is at fault, it is the individual soul. Kṛṣṇa is not at fault.

Vrajanātha: In that situation, what is the harm that Lord Kṛṣṇa does not give the soul free will? Kṛṣṇa knows everything. Therefore, Kṛṣṇa knows if a certain soul will misuse his free will and bring suffering to himself. In that situation, it is cruel of Kṛṣṇa to give such a person free will. Is it not?

Bābājī: Free will is a precious jewel. In the material world, there are many inanimate material objects. None of them were given the jewel of free will. That is why inanimate objects are lowly and unimportant. If he had not been given free will, the individual soul would be lowly and unimportant, just like inanimate objects. The individual soul is a tiny particle of spirit. Whatever qualities spirit has, the soul must also have. Free will is one of the qualities of spirit. Spirit can never be separated from its eternal qualities. Therefore, as a tiny particle of spirit, the soul must have free will. It is because they have free will that the individual souls are superior to inanimate matter and are the masters of the material world.

The souls, who all have free will, are all the dear servants of Lord Kṛṣṇa. When they misuse that free will and enter the world of *māyā*, merciful Kṛṣṇa weeps to see how they are suffering. Eager to deliver them, He follows the individual souls into the material world. Aware that the souls will not see His nectarean pastimes in the material world, He brings His inconceivable pastimes there. Seeing that the conditioned souls do not understand His pastimes, he descends to Navadvīpa and teaches them about His form, qualities, and pastimes, and about His own holy name, which is the best way for spiritual advancement, and He also teaches them by acting the role of His own devotee. Bābā, how can you place the blame on merciful Kṛṣṇa? Even though His mercy is fathomless, you remain unfortunate and very pathetic.

Vrajanātha: Is the *māyā-śakti* then our enemy, and the cause of our misfortune? Kṛṣṇa is all-powerful and all-knowing. If Kṛṣṇa had driven *māyā* far away, then the individual souls would not have to suffer.

Bābājī: *Māyā* is the reflection of the Lord's internal potency. She is a perverted manifestation of the Lord's pure spiritual potency. She purifies the criminal rebellious souls. She gives them a way to reform themselves. *Māyā* is a maidservant of Lord Kṛṣṇa. She punishes the souls averse to Lord Kṛṣṇa. She gives them medicine and cures them. By forgetting, "I am eternally a servant of Lord Kṛṣṇa," the individual souls commit a crime. They are at fault. It is because of this crime that the witch *māyā* punishes them. These criminal souls are sent to the prison that is the world of *māyā*. As it is out of kindness that a king sends a criminal to prison, so it is out of kindness that Lord Kṛṣṇa sends the criminal souls to the prison of the material world, where He has placed *māyā* as the warden.

Vrajanātha: If the material world is a prison, then what are the shackles?

Bābājī: *Māyā*'s shackles are of three kinds: 1. Shackles made of the mode of goodness, 2. Shackles made of the mode of passion, and 3. Shackles made of the mode of ignorance. The criminal souls are bound with these shackles in different appropriate ways. Some souls may be bound with goodness shackles, others with passion shackles, and others with ignorance shackles. All are shackled. There may be golden shackles, silver shackles, or iron shackles. Shackles made of different elements do not cease to be shackles.

Vrajanātha: How can the shackles of *māyā* bind the soul, which is an atomic particle of spirit?

Bābājī: Material things cannot touch spiritual things. When an individual soul gets the idea, "I am the enjoyer of *māyā*," the subtle coverings of material ego is placed around him. Covered in this way by subtle matter, his feet are bound with *māyā*'s shackles. The individual souls covered with material ego in the mode of goodness are the demigods residing in the higher material planets. Their feet are bound with the golden shackles of the mode of goodness. The individual souls covered with material ego in the mode of passion have a nature that is a combination of the natures of the demigods and the human beings. Their feet are bound with the silver shackles of the mode of passion. The individual souls covered with material ego in the mode of ignorance are intoxicated by material pleasures. Their feet are bound with the iron shackles of the mode of ignorance. None of these shackled souls can leave the prison. All are troubled by many kinds of sufferings.

Vrajanātha: What activities are done by the souls in *māyā*'s prison?

Bābājī: First, they do what they can to enjoy material pleasures and second, they do what they can to avoid or negate the sufferings that come from the shackles they wear.

Vrajanātha: Please describe to me the first of these actions.

Bābājī: The *sthūla-śarīra* is the gross material body covering the soul. It has six stages of existence: 1. The birth of the material body, 2. Its growth, 3. Its maintenance, 4. Its transformation, 5. Its dwindling, and 6. Its dissolution. The gross material body undergoes these six changes. Hunger, thirst, and other such urges are also part of the body's nature. Pushed by the desire for material pleasures, the soul within the material body becomes an obedient servant of eating, sleeping, associating with women, and other material activities.

To attain material pleasures, he performs the ten pious rituals that begin with birth and end on the funeral pyre. He performs the eighteen kinds of *yajña* described in the *Vedas*. He hopes, "By following the path of pious deeds (*karma*), I will enjoy with the demigods in Svargaloka. When I again enter the human realm, I will take birth in a *brāhmaṇa*'s home and I will enjoy many kinds of happiness."

Or, the imprisoned soul may follow the impious path. By performing many sins, he enjoys sense pleasures. By the first course of action, one attains Svargaloka and other higher material planets. Then, when his period of enjoyment ends, the soul again attains a human body. By the second course of action, one goes to hell because of his many sins. When his period of suffering ends, the soul again attains a human body. In this way, the soul imprisoned by *māyā* travels on the wheel of *karma*. Day after day, he struggles to enjoy material pleasures and he tastes the fruits of his actions. Thus, beginning at a time he cannot trace, the soul wanders in the material worlds. By performing pious deeds, he briefly enjoys, and by performing sins, he briefly suffers.

Vrajanātha: Now please describe the second kind of action.

Bābājī: Caught in a trap of many needs, the soul in a gross material body suffers. To drive away these sufferings, he acts in many ways. To drive away hunger and thirst, he struggles to get food and drink. So that these things may come easily, he labors to collect money. To drive away the cold, he collects clothing. To stop the thirst for sense pleasures, he becomes married and performs many other activities. To fill the needs and increase the happiness of his family and descendants, he labors hard. When the gross material body is attacked by disease, he must find medicine or other ways to cure it. To protect his property, he enters disputes in the law courts. Tossed about by the six waves—lust, anger, greed, bewilderment, pride, and envy—he engages in fighting, argument, violence to others, tormenting others, robbing others' wealth, cruelty, senseless pride, and a host of other evil deeds. So that he can live independently, he builds his own house and performs other deeds. In this way, the soul in *māyā*'s prison struggles day and night to attain pleasure and stop distress.

Vrajanātha: Had *māyā* only covered the soul with the *liṅga-śarīra* (subtle body), would that not have been enough?

Bābājī: No. With just the *liṅga-śarīra*, no one can perform actions. Therefore, the covering of the *sthūla-śarīra* (gross body) is necessary. Following the results of actions performed by the *sthūla-śarīra*, various desires are created in the *liṅga-śarīra*. Following these desires, (at the time of his next birth) the soul attains an appropriate new *sthūla-śarīra*.

Vrajanātha: What is the relationship between actions and the results they bring? The *mīmāṁsā* philosophers say that God, who awards the results of actions, is only a fiction—that every action produces something called an *apūrva*, and this *apūrva* gives the result of the action. Is this true?

Bābājī: The followers of *karma-mīmāṁsā* do not understand the true conclusion of the *Vedas*. Quickly glancing at the Vedic *yajñas* and other pious deeds, they come to a hasty conclusion. The true conclusion of the *Vedas* they do not grasp.

The *Vedas* explain (*Śvetāśvatara Upaniṣad* 4.6 and *Muṇḍaka Upaniṣad* 3.1.1): The individual spirit soul and the Supersoul, the Supreme Personality of Godhead, are like two friendly birds sitting on the same tree. One of the birds (the individual atomic soul) is eating the fruit of the tree (the sense gratification afforded by the material body), and the other bird (the Supersoul) is not trying to eat these fruits, but is simply watching His friend.

Where is there any mention here of the *mīmāṁsā* philosophers *apūrva*? Any conclusion that denies the existence of God cannot be good.

Vrajanātha: Why did you say that *karma* has no beginning?

Bābājī: Material desire is the root from which all *karma* (fruitive action) grows. Ignorance is the root from which material desires grows. That ignorance did not begin within the boundaries of material time. The ignorance that is the root of the individual soul's *karma* begins at the borderline of matter and spirit (*taṭasthā*). Therefore, the beginning of *karma* occurs outside the framework of material time. In that sense, *karma* has no beginning.

Vrajanātha: What is the difference between *māyā* and ignorance?

Bābājī: *Māyā* is Lord Kṛṣṇa's potency. Using this potency, He created the material world to purify the rebellions souls. *Māyā* has two features, *avidyā* (ignorance) and *pradhāna* (the primordial form of matter). *Avidyā* directs her efforts to the individual souls, and *pradhāna* directs its efforts to inanimate matter. From *pradhāna* the material universes are manifested. From *avidyā* the material desires of the conditioned souls are manifested. *Māyā* also has two other features: *vidyā* (knowledge) and *avidyā* (ignorance). These two direct their efforts to the individual spirit souls. *Avidyā* keeps the souls imprisoned in the material world, and *vidyā* releases them from that prison. When the criminal souls turn toward Lord Kṛṣṇa, the *vidyā* potency acts on them, and when the criminal souls forget Kṛṣṇa, the *avidyā* potency acts. Knowledge of Brahman is a specific feature of *vidyā*. The first phase of *vidyā* is pious deeds, and the concluding phase is understanding the truth. *Avidyā* covers the soul and *vidyā* uncovers him.

Vrajanātha: What does *pradhāna* do?

Bābājī: In the beginning, the Supreme Lord employs time to agitate the material energy. In this way, the *mahat-tattva* is produced. Agitated in this way, *māyā*'s feature called *pradhāna* creates things. From the *mahat-tattva*, the false ego is manifested. When false ego is transformed by ignorance, the sky is manifested. From the sky, air is manifested. From air, fire is manifested. From fire, water is manifested. From water, earth is manifested. In this way, the five material elements, which are called *pañca-mahābhūta*, are manifested.

Now, please hear how the five *tanmātra* are created. When time agitates *avidyā* (ignorance), *jñāna* (knowledge of the impersonal) and *karma* (fruitive action) are manifested from the *mahat-tattva*. From the *karma* thus manifested from the *mahat-tattva*, the modes of goodness and passion are manifested, and from them come *jñāna* (knowledge) and *kriyā* (action). From the *mahat-tattva*, false ego is manifested. From false ego, intelligence is manifested. From intelligence, the quality of sound is perceived in the sky. From sound comes touch. Thus, sound and touch are manifested from the air. From them come *prāṇa* (the life-force), *ojaḥ* (energy) and *bala* (strength). In fire are manifested form, touch, and sound. Then, by the transformation created by time, water is manifested. In water are taste, form, touch and sound. A further transformation brings earth, in which there are fragrance, taste, form, touch and sound.

The all-knowing *puruṣa-avatāra* helps these changes become manifested. False ego has three features: *vaikārikā* (goodness), *taijasa* (passion), and *tāmasa* (ignorance). From false ego in the mode of goodness, material objects are manifested. From false ego in the mode of passion, the ten material senses are manifested. There are two sets of senses: knowledge-acquiring senses and working senses. The knowledge-acquiring senses are: eyes, ears, nose, tongue, and skin. The working senses are: voice, hands, feet, genitals, and rectum.

Even when the gross and subtle elements are assembled together, nothing can happen until the individual soul, the tiny particle of spirit, enters. With a glance, the Supreme Personality of Godhead places the individual soul in the body of gross and subtle elements, and only then does the body begin to move. In this way, the senses manifested by the modes of goodness and passion come into contact with the sense objects which the *pradhāna* has manifested through the mode of ignorance. In this way, *avidyā* and *pradhāna* act. *Māyā* is divided into twenty-four categories: the five great elements, namely earth, water, fire, air and sky; the five *tanmātra*, namely fragrance, form, taste, touch, and sound; the previously described ten knowledge-acquiring and working senses; and in addition to these, mind, heart, intelligence, and false-ego. Altogether these are the twenty-four categories of matter. The conscious individual spirit soul is the twenty-fifth category in the body and the Supreme Personality of Godhead, the Supersoul, is the twenty-sixth.

Vrajanātha: In the human body of seven spans, what part is the subtle body, what part the gross body, and where in the body does the spirit soul reside? Please tell me.

Bābājī: The *sthūla-śarīra* (gross body) consists of the five gross elements (*pañca-mahābhūta*), five sense objects (*pañca- tanmātra*) and the ten senses. The *liṅga-śarīra* (subtle body) consists of the mind, heart, intelligence, and false ego. The individual spirit falsely thinks of this material body in terms of "I" and "mine." In this way, he does not understand how his own welfare is best served. The soul, a tiny fragment of spirit, exists in a dimension beyond time, space, and the other features of the material world. Even though it is a tiny particle, the soul is all-pervading within the material body. As a tiny drop of sandalwood paste cools the entire body, so the soul, situated in one place within the material body, is aware of the pleasures and pains of the body as a whole.

Vrajanātha: If, by his actions (*karma*), the individual soul creates his own pleasures and suffering, what does the Supreme Personality of Godhead do?

Bābājī: The individual soul is the immediate cause, but the Supreme Personality of Godhead is the ultimate cause. By his various actions, the individual soul makes himself qualified to receive various results. However, he does not have the power to simply take them. All results must be given to him by the Supreme Personality of Godhead, the ultimate cause. The Supreme

Personality of Godhead gives the results, and the individual spirit soul receives them.

Vrajanātha: Through what different stages of life do the souls imprisoned by *māyā* pass?

Bābājī: The souls imprisoned by *māyā* in a gross material body pass through five stages of existence. They are: *ācchādita-cetanā* (covered consciousness), *saṅkucita-cetanā* (retracted consciousness), *mukulita-cetanā* (budding consciousness), *vikasita-cetanā* (blossoming consciousness), and *pūrṇa-vikasita-cetanā* (fully blossomed consciousness).

Vrajanātha: Which souls are in the stage of covered consciousness?

Bābājī: The souls who reside in the bodies of trees, grass, and stones are in the stage of covered consciousness. They are close to being unconscious. Forgetting that they are servants of Kṛṣṇa, they have entered deeply into the realm of matter. They have no understanding of spirit. All they know is the six changes of material life. This is the lowest depth to which the soul can fall. Ahalyā, the *yamala-arjuna* trees, and the seven *tāla* trees are some examples the *Purāṇas* give of souls in this stage of existence. Great offenses push souls into that state, and Lord Kṛṣṇa's mercy delivers them.

Vrajanātha: Which souls are in the stage of retracted consciousness?

Bābājī: Animals, birds, snakes, fish, other aquatic creatures, worms, and insects are examples of beings with retracted consciousness. The beings with covered consciousness exist on the verge of being unconscious. The beings with retracted consciousness have their consciousness a little opened. That consciousness is directed toward eating, sleeping, fearing, and bustling to and fro to fulfill a host of desires, arguing with others over property claims, and anger when someone is wronged. However, that consciousness remains unaware of the existence of a world beyond the circle of matter. Monkeys may be mischievous, may give some thought to understanding the way things work by thinking, "This will happen and that will not happen," may plan for the future, and may show signs of gratefulness and other such feelings. Some animals have knowledge of the different properties of various objects. However, the animals do not search to find God. Therefore, their consciousness is said to be retracted.

In the scriptures it is said that the great devotee, Bharata, took birth as a deer and in that condition he was fully aware of the holy names of the Supreme Lord. However, Bharata was a special case. In general, animals do not have spiritual knowledge. Because of offenses, Bharata and Nṛga became animals but then, by the mercy of the Supreme Lord, they again attained an auspicious condition of life.

Vrajanātha: Which souls are in the stage of budding consciousness?

Bābājī: Conditioned souls in human bodies display three stages of consciousness: budding consciousness, blossoming consciousness, and fully blossomed consciousness. There are five kinds of human beings: immoral people, atheists who follow moral principles, people who believe in God and follow moral principles, people engaged in practical devotional service (*sādhana-bhakti*), and people engaged in loving devotional service (*bhāva-bhakti*).

Thus, the categories are: people who because of ignorance or because of improper knowledge become atheists and are immoral; moral atheists; moral people who have a little faith in God; people who, following the rules of the scriptures, engage in *sādhana-bhakti* (devotional service in practice); and the people who have attained love for God and thus engage in *bhāva-bhakti*. Immoral people and moral atheists are situated in the stage of budding consciousness. The people who believe in God and the people engaged in *sādhana-bhakti* are situated in the stage of blossoming consciousness, and the people engaged in *bhāva-bhakti* are situated in the stage of fully blossomed consciousness.

Vrajanātha: For how many days do the souls situated in *bhāva-bhakti* continue to stay in *māyā*'s prison?

Bābājī: This question is answered in the seventh verse of the *Daśa-mūla*. Now it is night. You should go home.

Chapter Seventeen

Eternal religion and sambandha, abhidheya and prayojana (The souls free from māyā's prison)

The grandmother had already made arrangements for Vrajanātha's marriage. That night, she told Vrajanātha all about it. Not giving any reply, Vrajanātha took his meal and went to bed. Again and again thinking about the pure spirit soul, he fell asleep late at night. The old grandmother kept thinking, "How can I make Vrajanātha agree to the marriage?"

At that time, Vrajanātha's cousin, Vāni-Mādhava arrived. The girl in the proposed marriage was Vāni-Mādhava's cousin. Vijaya Vidyāratna had sent Vāni-Mādhava to complete the arrangements for the marriage. Vāni-Mādhava said, "O great aunt, why is there a delay? Please quickly make arrangements for Vrajanātha's marriage."

Vrajanātha's grandmother lamented, "Brother, you are very expert. You convince Vrajanātha to agree to the marriage. I told him about it, but Vrajanātha will not reply."

Vāni-Mādhava was short, with a short neck, dark complexion, and blinking eyes. He started many things, but he did not bring any of them to completion. Hearing the old lady's words, he said, "Nothing can stop me. If you command me, what can I not do? Do you know how expert I am? I can multiply a single coin into a great sum. Well, I will talk to Vrajanātha. Will you not cook me a feast if I succeed?"

The grandmother replied, "Vrajanātha went to bed right after his meal."

Hearing this, Vāni-Mādhava said, "Tomorrow, I will come and take up the task", and left. The next morning came. Vrajanātha was sitting outside the shrine to Goddess Durgā. Seeing Vāni-Mādhava, Vrajanātha said, "Brother, why have you come?"

Vāni-Mādhava replied, "O noble brother, for many days, you studied and taught the *nyāya-śāstra*. You are the son of Haranātha Cūḍāmaṇi. Your name is famous in every country. However, you are the only male in the family. If there are no descendants, how can the family continue? Brother, that is why we all request you: Please get married."

Vrajanātha replied, "Brother, why do you agitate me for no reason? I have taken shelter of Lord Gaurasundara's devotees. Why would I want to marry? When I stay near the Vaiṣṇavas of Śrī Māyāpura, I become filled with happiness. I do not think worldly life is good. I will take *sannyāsa*. I will take shelter of the Vaiṣṇavas' feet. I tell you this confidentially. Please do not reveal it to anyone."

Seeing Vrajanātha's state of mind, Vāni-Mādhava thought, "This will not be an easy path to tread. I will have to trick him."

Cunningly concealing what was in his heart, Vāni-Mādhava said, "I have always helped you. When you were a student, I carried your books. When you take *sannyāsa*, I will carry your *daṇḍa* and waterpot."

Cheaters speak with a forked tongue. To one person, they say one thing, and to another person, they say something different. In this way, they make trouble. From what they say, it is not at once seen what is really in their hearts. Honey sits on their mouths, and poison in their hearts. Hearing Vāni-Mādhava's sweet words, Vrajanātha said, "Brother, I know that for many days you have been my true friend. My grandmother is an old lady. She does not understand anything that is very deep. She wants to push me together with this girl and throw me into the hell of household life. If you can stop her, I will be forever indebted to you."

Vāni-Mādhava said, "Rest easy. No one will do anything against your wishes. Friend, tell me one thing with an open heart, so I will know how to help you. I wish to know: Why do you hate the idea of getting married? Who taught you to become renounced?"

Vrajanātha told Vāni-Mādhava all about how he had become renounced. He also said, "Elderly Raghunātha dāsa Bābājī in Māyāpura is my teacher. Every evening I go to him. He has extinguished the blazing fire of my materialism. He has been very kind to me."

Fashioning a sinister plot in his mind, Vāni-Mādhava thought, "Now I have found his weak point. Now I will construct an expert stratagem. I will turn his weakness against him."

Then, he said aloud, "Brother, in secret I will change your grandmother's mind. But for now, I will go home."

After speaking these words, He first went home and then, by a side road, he quickly went to the entrance of Śrīvāsa's courtyard in Śrī Māyāpura. Sitting under the *bakula* tree, he thought, "These Vaiṣṇavas are plundering all the good things in the world for their own enjoyment! What beautiful homes! What a pleasant garden! What a graceful courtyard! What a beautiful place! One by one, they sit in their *bhajana-kuṭiras*. The Vaiṣṇava sit and chant on *japa* beads. They are like the bulls of religion. They are free of all cares! After bathing in the Ganges, the respectable ladies of the neighborhood bring them gifts of water, fruit, and various kinds of food. The *brāhmaṇas* used to get gifts like that for performing *karma-kanda* rituals. Nowadays, these *bābājīs* enjoy them. O fortunate age of Kali! 'He says he is a devotee of Rāmacandra, but in truth he is a devotee of Kali-yuga.' Now I understand what that old saying means. Alas! I am born in a *brāhmaṇa*'s family in vain! Nowadays, no one gives us fruit! No one gives even water! The Vaiṣṇava says that the followers of *nyāya* are fools for talking so much about clay pots and scraps of cloth. I think they are right, at least about Vrajanātha. Now he has fallen into the hands of these wicked people wearing only loincloths. I am Vāni-Mādhava. I will straighten out my friend. I will straighten out these wicked Vaiṣṇavas too."

Thinking in this way, he entered one of the cottages. By chance, he had entered the cottage of saintly Raghunātha dāsa Bābājī, who was sitting down and chanting the holy names of Lord Hari. A person's nature is easily seen on his face. When the elderly *bābājī* looked, he saw that Kai-yuga personified stood before him in the form of a *brāhmaṇa*'s son.

Vaiṣṇavas naturally think themselves very lowly and fallen. When enemies torment them, they are patient and tolerant. They wish good for all. They don't require that others honor them, although they give honor to everyone else. That is why saintly Raghunātha dāsa Bābājī gave all respect to his guest and politely offered him a place to sit. Vāni-Mādhava was very emphatically not a Vaiṣṇava. He did not understand the proper etiquette of how to approach a Vaiṣṇava. Thinking the elderly *bābājī* to be a *śūdra*, he gave a blessing to him.

The saintly *bābājī* asked him, "Bābā, what is your name? My boy, why have you come here?"

When the elderly *bābājī* used the words *tumi* (you, the young boy) and *āmi* (I, the respectable gentleman), Vāni-Mādhava became angry. Speaking crookedly, Vāni-Mādhava said, "Bābājī! Do you think by wearing a loincloth you are now equal to the *brāhmaṇas*? Ah well, it must be. There is one thing,

I, a respectable gentleman, would like to ask you, O young boy. Do you know a Vrajanātha Pañcānana?"

Bābājī: Please forgive my offense. Please do not find fault with an old man's words. Vrajanātha kindly comes here sometimes.

Vāni-Mādhava: He is not an honest man. He will be humble and polite for two or four days. That is how he will bring you under his control. Then he will be able to make you do what he likes. Seeing the way you act, the Bhaṭṭācāryas of Belapukura have become your bitter enemies. Consulting among themselves, they have sent Vrajanātha to you. You are an old man. You should take care. From time to time, I will come and tell you of their plot. Don't tell anyone about me. If you tell them, it will not be good for you. Now I must go.

After speaking these words, Vāni-Mādhava returned to his own home. After finishing his lunch, Vāni-Mādhava went to Vrajanātha and said, "Brother, today I went to Māyāpura on business. There, I saw an old Vaiṣṇava. Perhaps he was your Raghunātha dāsa Bābājī. As I talked with him, the topic of you came up. He used a very bad word to describe you, a word one should not use for a *brāhmaṇa*. At the end he said, 'I will make Vrajanātha eat the remnants from the plates of thirty-six low-caste people. In that way, I will destroy all the *brāhmaṇas*.' Ha! If *paṇḍitas* like you stay with such people, then no one will ever respect the *brāhmaṇa paṇḍitas*."

Vrajanātha was very surprised to hear all these words of Vāni-Mādhava. There was no knowing why the firm faith he had in the Vaiṣṇavas, and the devotion he had for the elderly *bābājī*, suddenly became doubled. Vrajanātha said, "Brother, today I am very busy. Please go home and in time I will think about what you said."

Vāni-Mādhava went home. Vrajanātha knew well that Vāni-Mādhava was double-hearted. Vrajanātha had been involved in *nyāya* logic, but he did not like dishonesty. Now he could see why Vāni-Mādhava offered to help him take *sannyāsa*. He could understand Vāni-Mādhava's crooked reason for speaking favorably about *sannyāsa*. As he thought about it, he concluded that Vāni-Mādhava must have something to gain from this marriage, and Vāni-Mādhava must have gone to Māyāpura to do something to further his crooked plot.

In his thoughts, Vrajanātha prayed to the Supreme Lord, "O Supreme

Lord, please give me strong faith in my spiritual master and in the Vaiṣṇavas. Let it not diminish because of the misdeeds of cunning men."

As he thought about these things, the day came to an end. With an agitated heart, he went to Śrīvāsa's courtyard at dusk.

After Vāni-Mādhava had left, the saintly elderly *bābājī* thought, "That man is a *brāhmaṇa-rākṣasa*. The scriptures declare: In the Kali-yuga, Rākṣasas take birth in the families of *brāhmaṇas*."

"That man is seen in those words. He has pride of caste, pride even though he has nothing really to be proud about. He hates the Vaiṣṇavas. He is a hypocrite, proudly waving the flag of piety while he sins. All these things are written on his face. His short neck, blinking eyes, and devious words all show what is in his heart. Ah, how pleasant and gentle is Vrajanātha, and how much of a demon is this other fellow! O Lord Kṛṣṇa, O Lord Gaurāṅga, please let me not associate with people like him. Today I will warn Vrajanātha about him."

Vrajanātha entered the cottage. The saintly elderly *bābājī*, his affection for Vrajanātha now doubled, said, "Come in, Bābā. Come in," and embraced Vrajanātha. Tears flowing from his eyes, Vrajanātha kissed the dust of the *bābājī*'s feet. Embarrassed, he could not speak. The saintly *bābājī* said, "This morning a dark-complexioned *brāhmaṇa* came here and spoke some very disturbing words. Do you know him?"

Vrajanātha: O master, you have explained to me that many different kinds of living entities live in this material world. Among all these living entities, some envious beings delight in troubling others. Among these envious beings, my cousin (I am embarrassed to call him my cousin), Vāni-Mādhava, is one of the foremost. If we do not talk about him, that will make me happy. The truth is that to you he speaks bad things about me and to me he speaks bad things about you. He does this so we will think badly of each other and our friendship will break. When you hear his words, did you not form an opinion in your mind?

Bābājī: O Kṛṣṇa! O Gaurāṅga! For a long time, I have served the Vaiṣṇavas. By their mercy, I have a little power to tell who is a Vaiṣṇava and who is not a Vaiṣṇava. I have understood everything. You need not say anything about this.

Vrajanātha: Let us forget all he has said. Please tell me: How is the soul released from *māyā*'s prison?

Bābājī: When you hear the seventh verse of the *Daśa-mūla*, you will find the answer to your question: When a soul wandering from one species to another in the material world sees a Vaiṣṇava filled with the nectar of devotion to Lord Hari, he becomes attracted to follow that Vaiṣṇava. By chanting the holy names of Lord Kṛṣṇa, that soul gradually renounces materialism and in the end, he regains his original spiritual form. In that form, he enjoys the pure and sweet nectar of the spiritual mellows of direct service to Lord Kṛṣṇa.

Vrajanātha: I would like to hear one or two quotes from the *Vedas* as evidence for these truths.

Bābājī: In the *Vedas* it is said (*Muṇḍaka Upaniṣad* 3.1.2 and *Śvetāśvatara Upaniṣad* 4.7): Although the two birds (the Supersoul and the individual soul) are on the same tree, the eating bird (the individual soul) is fully engrossed with anxiety and moroseness as the enjoyer of the fruits of the tree. But if he somehow turns his face to his friend, who is the Lord, and knows His glories, at once the suffering bird becomes free of all anxieties.

Vrajanātha: It is said that when he sees the worshipable Supreme Lord and understands His glory, the individual soul becomes free from anxiety. Do these words describe liberation?

Bābājī: When one is released from *māyā*'s prison, that is called liberation. To attain liberation, one must associate with saintly devotees of the Lord. When he attains liberation, the soul regains its original spiritual glory. That kind of liberation should be sought. In *Śrīmad-Bhāgavatam* (2.10.6) it is said: Liberation is the permanent situation of the form of the living entity after he gives up the changeable gross and subtle material bodies.

When the soul is released from *māyā*'s prison, at that moment he is at once liberated. However, when he is thus situated in his original form, the soul begins to perform an endless series of spiritual activities. The soul's first need is to perform these duties. It may be said that liberation puts an end to a great host of sufferings. However, beyond that, liberation brings with it spiritual bliss.

This is described in the following words of *Chāndogya Upaniṣad* (8.12.3): Then, the soul leaves the material body and goes to the effulgent Supreme Personality of Godhead. The soul then regains his original spiritual form and in that form, he enjoys many pastimes, eating and playing with the Supreme Personality of Godhead.

Vrajanātha: What are the signs that show one has been released from *māyā*'s prison?

Bābājī: Eight signs are described in these words of the *Chāndogya Upaniṣad* (8.7.1): One should seek a soul who is free from sins, old age, death, lamentation, hunger, and thirst, who desires the truth, and whose thoughts are fixed on the truth.

Vrajanātha: In the verse from the *Daśa-mūla* it was said that when he attains the association of a Vaiṣṇava who relishes the nectarean mellows of service to Lord Hari, the soul wandering in the cycle of birth and death can attain auspiciousness. I have a question. By practicing impersonal speculation, *aṣṭāṅga-yoga*, or other auspicious deeds, does one not at the end attain devotional service to Lord Hari?

Bābājī: With His own transcendental mouth, the Supreme Personality of Godhead declares (*Śrīmad-Bhāgavatam* 11.12.1-2): Neither through *aṣṭāṅga-yoga* (the mystic *yoga* system to control the senses), nor through impersonal monism, nor an analytical study of the Absolute Truth, nor through study of the *Vedas*, nor through practice of austerities, nor through charity, nor through acceptance of *sannyāsa*, nor through *yajñas*, nor through chanting Vedic hymns, nor through going on pilgrimages, nor through religious duties and self-control can one attain Me as much as one can by associating with saintly devotees whose good association releases one from all that is inauspicious.

In the *Hari-bhakti-sudhodaya* (8.61) it is said: Association is very important. It acts just like a crystal stone, which will reflect anything which is put before it. If we associate with the flower-like devotees of the Lord, and if our hearts are crystal clear, then certainly the same action will be there.

Therefore, association with saintly devotees brings an auspicious result. When the scriptures say that one should live alone, the meaning is that one should associate only with devotees. If by accident one unknowingly associates with devotees, he attains a great benefit.

In *Śrīmad-Bhāgavatam* (3.23.55) it is said: Association for sense gratification is certainly the path of bondage. But the same type of association, performed with a saintly person, leads to the path of liberation, even if performed without knowledge.

In *Śrīmad-Bhāgavatam* (7.5.32) it is also said: "Unless they smear upon their bodies the dust of the lotus feet of a Vaiṣṇava who is completely freed from material contamination, persons very much inclined toward materialistic life cannot be attached to the lotus feet of the Lord, who is glоried for His uncommon activities. Only by becoming Kṛṣṇa conscious and taking shelter at the lotus feet of the Lord in this way can one be freed from material contamination.

In *Śrīmad-Bhāgavatam* (10.48.31) it is also said: One can take advantage of a place of pilgrimage only after going there. By worshiping a particular demigod, it takes a long time to attain the fulfillment of one's desire, but saintly persons like you, My dear Akrūra, can immediately fulfill all the desires of the devotees.

In *Śrīmad-Bhāgavatam* (10.51.53) it is also said: O my Lord! O infallible Supreme Person! When a person wandering throughout the universes becomes eligible for liberation from material existence, he gets an opportunity to associate with devotees. When he associates with devotees, his attraction for You is awakened. You are the Supreme Personality of Godhead, the highest goal of the supreme devotees and the Lord of the universe.

Vrajanātha: By performing pious deeds one attains the association of saintly devotees. What are these pious deeds? Are they not *karma* (Vedic rituals) and *jñāna* (impersonal speculation)?

Bābājī: The scriptures describe pious deeds. Pious deeds are of two kinds: 1. Pious deeds that bring devotional service, and 2. Pious deeds that bring useless results. Regular and occasional Vedic duties, Saṅkhyā philosophy, and impersonal speculation all bring useless results. Association with saintly devotees and contact with places, times, and things that nurture devotion, bring the result of devotional service. As one accumulates these results, they eventually become so powerful that they bring devotion for Lord Kṛṣṇa. The useless results produced by other pious activities do not accumulate in this way. One enjoys their results and then they are gone.

In this material world, pious activities, such as giving charity, bring material enjoyment as their result. Impersonal speculation and other such activities bring impersonal liberation as their result. These activities do not have the power to give devotional service. Associating with saintly devotees, observing Ekādaśī, Janmāṣṭamī, Gaura-pūrṇimā, and other holy days that instill devotion in persons observing them, worshiping Tulasī-devī, worshiping the Lord in His temple, honoring *mahā-prasādam*, visiting holy places, and seeing and touching the devotees, all bring the result of devotional service.

Vrajanātha: If a person tormented by the troubles of material life flees from material illusion and intelligently takes shelter of Lord Hari's lotus feet, will he not attain devotional service?

Bābājī: If he intelligently understands that his sufferings are all caused by the illusory potency, *māyā*, and that the entire material world is by nature inauspicious, and that his only shelter is the lotus feet of the Supreme Lord, and the association of the Lord's devotees, then he will take shelter of the feet of the devotees who have taken shelter of the lotus feet of the Lord. Taking shelter of their feet is the most effective means to attain devotional service. That is the way one attains the feet of the Supreme Lord. In the beginning, renunciation, and the intelligence to understand what is auspicious and what is not auspicious, are certainly present, but they are of only secondary importance for a person striving for devotional service. Association with saintly devotees is the most important factor in attaining devotional service. Aside from that association, no other means is very important.

Vrajanātha: What is the objection to saying that *karma* (pious deeds), *jñāna* (impersonal speculation), *vairāgya* (renunciation) and *viveka* (the ability to understand what is auspicious and what is not) are secondary means that also help one attain devotional service?

Bābājī: There is an objection. Generally, these means bring results that are trivial and useless. After giving the soul material pleasures, pious deeds go away. Renunciation and the ability to understand what is auspicious and what is not tend to lead to impersonalism. Impersonalism tends to cheat the soul of the opportunity to attain the Lord's lotus feet. One should not trust these means to bring devotional service. Sometimes, these means may take one to devotional service but generally, they do not. On the other hand, association with pure devotees does not bring results that are trivial and temporary. Their association inevitably brings one to pure love of God.

In the *Śrīmad-Bhāgavatam* (3.25.25), the Supreme Lord explains: In the association of pure devotees, discussion of the pastimes and activities of the Supreme Personality of Godhead is very pleasing and satisfying to the ear and heart. By cultivating such knowledge, one gradually becomes advanced on the path of liberation and thereafter, he is freed and his attraction becomes fixed. Then real devotion and devotional service begin.

Vrajanātha: Association with saintly devotees is then the way to attain devotional service. First one hears from the devotees' mouths the descriptions of Lord Hari, and then one attains devotional service. Is that the right sequence?

Bābājī: I will tell you the right sequence. Please listen. A soul wandering from birth to birth in the material world may by destiny attain something that leads to devotional service. In the course of his life, by destiny, a soul may encounter one of the limbs of devotional service. By chance he may fast on Ekādaśī, or see and touch a holy place, receive a pure devotee as a guest, or hear the holy names of Lord Hari, or the descriptions of Him, or songs about Him, from the mouths of saintly devotees who have Lord Hari as their only possession.

If a person performs these activities with a desire to attain material sense pleasures or impersonal liberation, he will not attain devotional service by performing them. However, if an innocent person by chance performs these activities with any motive to use them to attain sense pleasure or impersonal liberation, then these activities will lead him to devotional service. When these devotion-giving pious deeds accumulate after many births, one finally attains faith in pure devotional service. Faith in pure devotional service creates the desire to associate with pure devotees.

By associating with devotees, one gradually becomes engaged in *sādhana* (devotional service in practice) and *bhajana* (worship of the Lord). By performing *bhajana*, one gradually casts all unwanted material desires far away. When material desires are cast far away, one attains pure faith. When faith becomes more and more pure, one gradually attains *ruci* (attraction to the Lord). As one becomes more and more attracted to the beauty of the Lord, the attraction becomes transformed into attachment (*āsakti*) to the Lord. When this attachment becomes fully manifested, one attains ecstatic love (*bhāva* or *rati*) for the Lord. This ecstatic love turns into *rasa* (the nectarean mellows of a relationship with the Lord), which brings *premotpatti* (pure love for the Lord).

Thus, the root of devotional service is seeing and following pure devotees of the Lord. The conclusion, then, is that in the beginning, one associates with devotees. Then one develops faith. Faith is also known as surrender (*śaraṇāpatti*) to the Lord. The first association with the devotees brings attraction to the places, times, things, and persons dear to Lord Hari. The first association with devotees brings with it a faith that becomes manifested as surrender to the Lord. This is seen in the Lord's final teaching in *Bhagavad-gītā* (18.66): Abandon all varieties of religion and just surrender unto Me. I shall deliver you from all sinful reactions. Do not fear.

Here, the word *sarva-dharma* (all varieties of religion) refers to *smārta-dharma* (the rules of the *smṛti-śāstra*), *aṣṭāṅga-yoga*, Saṅkhyā, *jñāna* (impersonal speculation), *vairāgya* (renunciation), and all other such varieties of religion. None of these kinds of religion is able to fulfill the soul's true spiritual needs. Therefore, in the *Gītā* it is written that these religions should be abandoned. In *pravṛtti- śraddhā* (positive faith) one thinks, "I know that Lord Kṛṣṇa, whose form is the perfection of eternity, knowledge, and bliss, and who enjoys pastimes in Vraja, is the spirit souls' only goal. Therefore, completely rejecting material sense gratification, impersonal liberation, and any other non-devotional goal, with unalloyed spiritual love, I now surrender unto Him."

When this kind of faith arises, one becomes the humble follower of a saintly Vaiṣṇava. In this way, one surrenders to a saintly Vaiṣṇava spiritual master.

Vrajanātha: What are the soul's *anarthas* (unwanted things)?

Bābājī: There are four kinds of *anarthas*: 1. *sva-svarūpa-aprāpti* (things that prevent one from reviving one's original spiritual nature), 2. *asat-tṛṣṇā* (thirst for material things), 3. *aparādha* (offenses), and 4. *hṛdaya-daurbalya* (weakness of heart). Forgetting, "I am pure, a particle of spirit, a servant of Lord Kṛṣṇa," the imprisoned soul goes far away from his original nature. That the first *anartha*: *sva-svarūpa-aprāpti*. One may think, "I am material, and these material objects are my property." In this way, one thirsts for happiness in the realm of material things. This is called *asat-tṛṣṇā*. The three kinds of *asat-tṛṣṇā* are: 1. Desire for good children and descendants, 2. Desire for wealth and 3. Desire to reside in Svargaloka. The ten kinds of *aparādhas* (offenses) I will describe later. From *hṛdaya-daurbalya* (weakness of heart) come lamentation and a host of other problems. These four *anarthas* are the natural property of a soul shackled by material ignorance.

By associating with devotees and cultivating Kṛṣṇa consciousness, the soul gradually throws these *anarthas* far away. The path of *yoga*, which consists of the four parts: *pratyāhāra* (withdrawal from sense-objects), *yama* (self-control), *niyama* (restraint), and *vairāgya* (renunciation), is not an easy path to follow. It is filled with problems. It does not easily lead to the final goal. On the other hand, cultivating Kṛṣṇa consciousness in the association of devotees is an easy path to follow. It easily eclipses *anarthas* and materialism. When materialism is eclipsed, the original form of the soul is spontaneously manifested.

Vrajanātha: Should persons free of *anarthas* be called liberated?

Bābājī: Please reflect on these words of *Śrīmad-Bhāgavatam* (6.14.3-5): In this material world there are as many living entities as atoms. Among these living entities, very few are human beings and among them, few are interested in following religious principles. O best of *brāhmaṇas*, Śukadeva Gosvāmī, out of many persons who follow religious principles, only a few desire liberation from the material world. Among many thousands who desire liberation, one may actually achieve liberation, giving up material attachment to society, friendship, love, country, home, wife, and children. And among many thousands of such liberated persons, one who can understand the true meaning of liberation is very rare. O great sage, among many millions who are liberated and perfect in knowledge of liberation, one may be a devotee of Lord Nārāyaṇa, or Kṛṣṇa. Such devotees, who are fully peaceful, are extremely rare.

Only pure devotees are really free of *anarthas*. Such devotees are very rare. One must search among many millions and millions of liberated souls to find one who is a devotee of Lord Kṛṣṇa. Therefore, in this material world, there is no group more difficult to associate with than the devotees of Lord Kṛṣṇa.

Vrajanātha: Does the word Vaiṣṇava refer only to a Vaiṣṇava who has renounced family life?

Bābājī: Vaiṣṇava refers to a pure devotee of Lord Kṛṣṇa. Such a devotee may be either a householder or a *sannyāsī*. He may be a *brāhmaṇa* or a *caṇḍāla* (outcaste). He may be wealthy or poverty-stricken. To the extent that he has pure devotion to Lord Kṛṣṇa, to that extent he is a pure devotee.

Vrajanātha: You have explained that the souls swallowed up by *māyā* are of five kinds. In those five kinds of souls imprisoned by *māyā*, you included the *sādhana-bhaktas* (devotees in the stage of devotional service in practice) and *bhāva-bhaktas* (devotees in the stage of spiritual love). Which devotees are released from *māyā*'s prison?

Bābājī: From the moment he begins to live as a devotee of the Lord, the soul may be said to be released from *māyā*'s prison. However, the final stage of release from *māyā*'s prison is only attained when one attains the final stage of mature devotion to the Lord. Before that, one is situated in the preliminary stage of release from *māyā*'s prison. When the gross (*sthūla-śarīra*) and subtle (*liṅga-śarīra*) material bodies are both finally broken, the soul attains the final stage of release from *māyā*'s prison. By practicing *sādhana-bhakti* (the practical activities of devotional service) one gradually attains *bhāva-bhakti* (spiritual love of God). When *bhāva-bhakti* becomes strong and firm, the soul is able, at the time of leaving the gross body, to leave the subtle body also and be situated in his original spiritual form. Because material life lingers during the stage of *sādhana-bhakti*, and because it is not yet completely removed even in the beginning stages of *bhāva-bhakti*, the *sādhana-bhaktas* and *bhāva-bhaktas* are included among the five kinds of souls swallowed by *māyā*.

The materialists and the impersonalists are certainly to be counted among the souls swallowed by *māyā*. Among the liberated souls, those who have attained liberation by engaging in devotional service to Lord Hari have alone attained the true perfection of liberation. A soul who commits offenses and is therefore imprisoned by *māyā* forgets, "I am a servant of Lord Kṛṣṇa." That forgetfulness is the root from which his offenses grow. Without the mercy of Kṛṣṇa, that soul is not excused from his offense. In the same way, with the mercy of Lord Kṛṣṇa, that soul will not be released from *māyā*'s prison. The impersonalist *sampradāya*'s faith is that by cultivating impersonal speculation, they will attain liberation. That faith is groundless. Without first attaining Lord

Kṛṣṇa's mercy, no one is released from *māyā*'s prison.

In *Śrīmad-Bhāgavatam* (10.2.32-33), the demigods speak these two verses to explain this truth: O lotus eye one, those who think they are liberated in this life but do not render devotional service to You must be of impure intelligence. Although they accept severe austerities and penances to rise to the spiritual position, to impersonal Brahman realization, the fall down again because they neglect to worship Your lotus feet. O Mādhava, Supreme Personality of Godhead, Lord of the goddess of fortune, if devotees completely in love with You sometimes fall from the path of devotion, they do not fall like non-devotees, for You still protect them. Thus, they fearlessly traverse the heads of their opponents and continue to progress in devotional service.

Vrajanātha: What are the different kinds of souls free of *māyā*'s prison?

Bābājī: The souls free from *māyā*'s prison are of two kinds: 1. *nitya-mukta* (the souls who were never placed in *māyā*'s prison), and 2. *baddha-mukta* (the souls who were at one time imprisoned, but now are free). The *nitya-mukta* souls may be divided into two groups: 1. *aiśvarya-gata* (souls who appreciate the Lord's feature of opulence), and 2. *mādhurya-gata* (souls who appreciate the Lord's feature of sweetness). The *aiśvarya-gata nitya-mukta* souls are personal associates of Lord Nārāyaṇa, the master of Vaikuṇṭha. They are particles of spiritual effulgence emanated from Lord Mūla- Saṅkarṣaṇa, who resides in Vaikuṇṭha. The *mādhurya-gata nitya-mukta* souls are personal associates of Lord Kṛṣṇa, the master of Goloka Vṛndāvana. They are particles of spiritual effulgence manifested from Lord Baladeva, who resides in Goloka Vṛndāvana. The *baddha-mukta* souls (who were once imprisoned but now are free) are of three kinds: 1. *aiśvarya-gata* (souls who appreciate the Lord's feature of opulence), 2. *mādhurya-gata* (souls who appreciate the Lord's feature of sweetness), and 3. *brahmajyotir-gata* (souls situated within the Lord's spiritual effulgence).

Souls who, during their period of practicing *sādhana-bhakti*, are attracted to the Lord's opulence become eternal associates of Lord Nārāyaṇa, the master of Vaikuṇṭha. They attain *sālokya-mukti* (the liberation of residing on the same planet as the Lord). Souls who during their period of practicing *sādhana-bhakti* are attracted to the Lord's sweetness, after liberation enjoy the sweetness of direct service to Lord Kṛṣṇa in the eternal spiritual abode of Vṛndāvana, and other like abodes. Souls who during their period of *sādhana* are attracted to become one with the Lord, after liberation attain *brahma-sayujjya-mukti* (the liberation of merging with the Lord). In this way, these souls are completely destroyed.

Vrajanātha: What is the final destination of the soul who is a devotee of Lord Gaura Kiśora (Lord Caitanya)?

Bābājī: Kṛṣṇa and Gaura Kiśora are not different. They are both shelters of the feature of sweetness (*mādhurya-rasa*). They do have one difference. *Mādhurya-rasa* (the Lord's sweetness) has two features: 1. *mādhurya* (sweetness), and 2. *audārya* (mercy). When sweetness is prominent, Lord Kṛṣṇa is manifested. When mercy is prominent, Lord Gaurāṅga is manifested. The spiritual world of Vṛndāvana is divided into two abodes: 1. The abode of Lord Kṛṣṇa, and 2. The abode of Lord Gaura. The eternally perfect and eternally liberated souls who have sweetness first and mercy second reside in Lord Kṛṣṇa's abode. They are Lord Kṛṣṇa's associates. The eternally perfect and eternally liberated souls who have mercy first and sweetness second reside in Lord Gaura's abode. They are Lord Gaura's associates. Some souls manifest two forms and reside in both abodes simultaneously. Other souls manifest only one form and are present in one of the abodes and not in the other.

Souls who, during the time of *sādhana* worship only Lord Gaura, at the time of attaining perfection, go to Lord Gaura's abode and serve Him there. Souls who during the time of *sādhana* worship only Lord Kṛṣṇa, at the time of attaining perfection, go to Lord Kṛṣṇa's abode and serve Him there. Souls who during the time of *sādhana* worship both Lord Kṛṣṇa and Lord Gaura, at the time of attaining perfection, manifest two forms and go to both Lord Kṛṣṇa's abode and Lord Gaura's abode and in their two forms, serve the two Lords simultaneously in both places. This truth—that Lord Gaura and Lord Kṛṣṇa are simultaneously one and different from each other is a very confidential secret.

After hearing these teachings about the souls released from *māyā*'s prison, Vrajanātha, now filled with ecstatic love, fell at the feet of the elderly Vaiṣṇava and stayed there for some minutes. Weeping and weeping, the saintly *bābājī* picked up Vrajanātha and firmly embraced him. A good portion of the night had already passed. Taking leave of the *bābājī*, Vrajanātha returned home.

Traveling on the path, he deeply thought about the soul's final destination.

When he returned home and was taking his meal, he said to his grandmother, "Grandmother, if you wish to continue seeing me, you should stop all this talk of marriage, and you should not allow Vāni-Mādhava to come here. He is my bitter enemy. Tomorrow, I will refuse to talk with him. You also should ignore him."

Vrajanātha's grandmother was intelligent. Thinking about her conversation during the daytime with Vāni-Mādhava and what Vrajanātha has just told her, she decided to stop the marriage. She could see that if too much pressure was placed on him, Vrajanātha would go to Vārāṇasī or Vṛndāvana. That she did not wish. She decided, "What will be, will be."

Chapter Eighteen

Eternal religion and sambandha, abhidheya and prayojana (Simultaneous oneness and difference)

Vāni-Mādhava was a vicious person. Reproached by Vrajanātha, in his mind he plotted how to harm both Vrajanātha and the *bābājīs*. He met with some thugs and together they decided that when he returned from Śrīvāsa's courtyard, Vrajanātha would be attacked at a secluded place near Lakṣmaṇa-ṭilā. Hearing of this plot, Vrajanātha decided to visit the saintly elderly *bābājī* only during the daytime. Also, he would not visit Śrīvāsa's courtyard every day, and when he did, it would be only in the daytime and accompanied by a bodyguard. Vrajanātha had some tenants. Among them was an expert fighter named Harīśa Doma.

Vrajanātha said to Harīśa, "Today a great calamity has fallen upon me. If you help, I may be protected from it."

Harīśa replied, "Sir, I will do whatever you ask. Give the word, and I will kill your enemy."

Vrajanātha said, "Vāni-Mādhava wants to harm me. I am no longer able to visit the Vaiṣṇavas in Śrīvāsa's courtyard. Vāni-Mādhava plans to have me attacked on the road."

Harīśa replied, "Sir, how can he attack you when Harīśa is there? Know that this bamboo club will fall on Vāni-Mādhava Ṭhākura's head. Sir, take me with you whenever you go to Śrīvāsa's courtyard. Who can harm you? I can defeat a hundred fighters."

Accompanied by Harīśa Doma, Vrajanātha would visit Śrīvāsa's courtyard only once every two or four days. He could not stay for long. He could not hear discussions of the spiritual truth. In his heart, he became sad. Ten or twenty days passed in this way and then Vāni-Mādhava died of snakebite. Hearing the news of Vāni-Mādhava's death, the Vaiṣṇava Vrajanātha thought, "Is this the fate of a person who hates Vaiṣṇavas?"

In his mind, he remembered these words of *Śrīmad-Bhāgavatam* (10.1.38): One may die today or after hundreds of years, but death is sure for every living entity.

He thought, "No one lives forever. Everyone must die. What obstacle now stops me from going to Śrīvāsa's courtyard every day?"

That evening at sunset, Vrajanātha went to Śrīvāsa's courtyard and offered *daṇḍavat* obeisances to the saintly *bābājī*. He said, "From today on, I will visit your feet every day. The obstacle Vāni-Mādhava has left this world."

The very merciful *bābājī* was at first silent and thoughtful, unhappy to hear that a person whose spiritual intelligence was not awakened had died. Then he said, "It is said (*Śrī Caitanya-caritāmṛta* Antya 2.163): A person is sure to achieve the results of his fruitive activities.

"The soul must go where Lord Kṛṣṇa sends him. Bābā, are you unhappy at heart?"

Vrajanātha: The only unhappiness in my heart is that for some days I have not heard the nectar of your teachings. That has troubled my heart. I wish to hear the remaining teachings of the *Daśa-mūla*.

Bābājī: I am always ready to teach you. Just tell me how far you have heard and what questions have risen in your mind.

Vrajanātha: What is the name of the pure philosophy Śrī Gaura Kiśora taught to the world? *Advaita-vāda*, *śuddhādvaita-vāda*, *viśiṣṭādvaita-vāda*, and *dvaita- vāda* are the names of the philosophies taught by the previous *ācāryas*. Did Śrī Gaurāṅgadeva accept one of these philosophies, or did He teach a different philosophy? In describing the *sampradāyas*, you said that Śrī Gaurāṅga is in the Brahmā *sampradāya*. Did He teach the *dvaita-vāda* of Śrī Madhvācārya, or did He teach something else?

Bābājī: Bābā, please listen to the eighth verse of the *Daśa-mūla*: The entire spiritual and material creation is manifested from the potency of Lord Hari. The impersonalist idea is an impurity of the Kali-yuga, and it is refuted by the *Vedas*. The pure truth taught by the *Vedas* is the philosophy of *acintya-bhedābheda* (simultaneous oneness and difference). By understanding this truth, one eventually attains the perfection of love for the Supreme Eternal.

The conclusions taught in the *Upaniṣads* are called *Vedānta* (the conclusion of the *Vedas*). Śrīla Vyāsadeva summarized these conclusions in a book of four chapters, a book called the *Brahma-sūtra* or *Vedānta sūtra*. The truly learned people of this world respectfully accept the authority of this book. The general conclusion is that the *Vedānta-sūtra* gives a proper exposition of the truths taught in the *Vedas*.

The different *ācāryas* have each explained *Vedānta-sūtra* in a way to support their conclusions. Śrī Śaṅkarācārya used the *Vedānta-sūtra* to support his philosophy of impersonalism (*vivarta-vāda*). He said that the philosophy of *pariṇāma-vāda* is not correct, for it must lead to the conclusion that Brahman is not the highest. He taught a philosophy called *vivarta-vāda*, which is also called Māyāvāda. To support this philosophy of *vivarta-vāda*, he collected quotations from all the *Vedas*. It seems that the philosophy of *pariṇāma-vāda* must have been popular before his time. By establishing his *vivarta-vāda*, Śrī Śaṅkara suppressed the *pariṇāma-vāda*. Still, the *vivarta-vāda* is only one of many theories.

Displeased with it, Śrī Madhvācārya created the theory of *dvaita-vāda*. He collected quotes from all the *Vedas* to support his theory of *dvaita-vāda*. In the same way, Śrīmad Rāmānujācārya established the *viśiṣṭādvaita-vāda* and collected quotations from the *Vedas* to support it. Śrī Nimbarka Ācārya established his philosophy of *dvaitādvaita-vāda* and he also collected many quotes from the *Vedas* to support it. Śrī Viṣṇu Swami preached the philosophy of *śuddhādvaita-vāda*, which he based on the *Vedānta-sūtra* and the texts of the *Vedas*. The Māyāvāda philosophy preached by Śrī Śaṅkarācārya is opposed to the truths of devotional service. Each with his own philosophy, the four Vaiṣṇava *ācāryas* taught that devotional service is the highest conclusion. Śrīmān Mahāprabhu based His philosophy on all the statements of the *Vedas*. His philosophy is called *acintya-bhedābheda* (simultaneous oneness and difference). This philosophy accepts the basic framework of Madhvācārya's teachings.

Vrajanātha: What is the *pariṇāma-vāda*?

Bābājī: There are two kinds of *pariṇāma-vāda*: *brahma-pariṇāma-vāda* and *śakti-pariṇāma-vāda*. The *brahma-pariṇāma-vāda* teaches that Brahman becomes transformed into the individual souls and the material world. Thus they say that only Brahman exists and to support their idea, they quote these words of the *Chāndogya Upaniṣad* (6.2.1): Brahman is one without a second.

This theory may be called *advaita-vāda* (impersonalism). Look. In this context, *vivarta* and *pariṇāma* are synonyms. On the other hand, the philosophy of *śakti-pariṇāma-vāda* declares that Brahman Himself never becomes transformed. Rather, it is Brahman's inconceivable potency that becomes transformed. The *jīva-śakti* becomes transformed into the individual spirit souls and the *māyā-śakti* becomes transformed into the material world. If this version of *pariṇāma-vāda* is accepted, Brahman does not become transformed. The act of transformation is defined in these words: Transformation is when something appears to be what it is not.

What is transformation? Transformation is when something appears to be different that what it is. Milk becomes transformed into yogurt, but it is still milk in essence. It only appears to be something else. That is transformation. According to the *brahma-parināma-vāda*, the individual spirit souls and the material world are both transformations of Brahman. This idea is not correct. Of this there is no doubt. The impersonal Brahman has no qualities. Therefore, it has nothing that could be transformed into something else, and so could not be said to be the origin of transformations. Therefore, the *brahma-parināma-vāda* theory is not good.

On the other hand, the *śakti-parināma-vāda* does not have these defects. According to *śakti-parināma-vāda*, Brahman is not transformed. Rather, it is Brahman's potency, which can do any impossible thing, that is transformed into the atomic individual souls and into the perverted reflection that is the material world. When Brahman desires, "Let the individual souls come into existence,"numberless souls are manifested from His potency. When Brahman desires, "Let the material world come into existence," material universes without limit are manifested from His potency. These things are not transformations of Brahman.

If someone says, "If Brahman has a desire, then Brahman is transformed. The desire itself is a transformation of the original desireless Brahman. How is it possible that Brahman can be transformed in this way?" I reply, "You are assuming that Brahman's desire is like the desires possessed by the individual spirit souls. That is why you say Brahman's desire is evidence that Brahman becomes transformed. The individual spirit soul is very small and therefore, his desire naturally brings him into contact with Brahman's other potencies. For this reason, the soul's desires are actually transformations. However, Brahman's desires are completely independent. They are part of His intrinsic nature and are not subjected to outside influences. They are at once the same as and different from His potencies. Therefore, Brahman's desires are part of His original nature. They do not involve any transformations.

Ordered by His desires, His potencies act. His potencies then become transformed. The living entity's small intelligence does not have the power to discover these subtle truths unaided. These truths are known only by hearing the testimony of the *Vedas*. Now we may consider the nature of the transformation of the potency. The example of milk being transformed into yogurt is not the only example to show the transformation of potency. Although material analogies cannot give one a complete understanding of spiritual realities, they can help one understand certain aspects of it. Even though it is material in nature, a *cintāmaṇi* jewel is said to produce many other jewels without itself being changed in any way. The spiritual Supreme Personality of Godhead creates in a way like that. The Supreme Personality of Godhead remains completely unchanged after creating, by His desire and with the aid of His inconceivable potency, the numberless individual souls and numberless material universes consisting of fourteen planetary systems.

This explanation that the Supreme is not transformed does not mean that the Supreme exists only as the quality-less impersonal Brahman. The word Brahman means the greatest (*bṛhat*). Therefore, the word Brahman directly refers to the eternal Supreme Personality of Godhead, who is the master of six opulences. If we only say that He is not transformed and do not say anything else about Him, we do not accept His *cit-śakti* (spiritual potency). The truth is that by the power of His inconceivable potency, He is simultaneously the quality-less Brahman, and the Supreme Person who possesses a host of spiritual qualities. Therefore, to say only that He is not transformed means to understand only half of His nature, and thus not to understand Him in full.

The *Vedas* have used the instrumental (by), ablative (from), and locative (in) cases to describe His relationship with the material world. In the *Taittirīya Upaniṣad* 3.11) it is said: Please know that Brahman is He from whom all living beings are born, by whose power they remain alive, and into whom they enter at the end.

When it is said that the living beings are manifested from Brahman, the ablative case is used. When it is said that the living beings live by Brahman's power, the instrumental case is used. When it is said that the living beings enter into Brahman, the locative case is used. In this way, it is said that the Supreme has qualities. This shows that He is the Supreme Person, for it is a person that has qualities.

Śrīla Jīva Gosvāmī describes the Supreme Person in these words: The Absolute Truth is one. Still, by His inconceivable potency, He is manifested in four ways: 1. *svarūpa* (His original form), 2. *tad-rūpa-vaibhāva* (His incarnations), 3. *jīva* (the individual spirit souls), and 4. *pradhāna* (the material energy). These four features are like: 1. The interior of the sun planet, 2. The sun's surface, 3. The sunlight, and 4. The reflection of the sun.

This example of course, explains only a small part of the Lord's nature. His *svarūpa* (original form) is His form of eternity, knowledge, and bliss. His *svarūpa-vaibhāva* (manifestations of His form) are His spiritual abode, name, associates and paraphernalia. The *jīva-śakti* is the abode of the numberless eternally liberated and conditioned individual souls, who are tiny particles of spirit. The *pradhāna* is the material world of subtle and gross material elements. As these four features are eternal, so the oneness of the Absolute Truth is also eternal.

Someone may ask: "How is it possible that the Lord is eternally manifest in these four ways, but still is eternally one? Is it not a contradiction that He is both one and many simultaneously?"

To this, the answer is given: The intelligence of the individual living entities will certainly declare that it is impossible. But why should it not be possible? The intelligence of the individual living entity is very small and limited and, on the other hand, the powers of the Supreme Personality of Godhead are beyond human conception. Therefore, for the Lord, it is not impossible.

Vrajanātha: How do you define *vivarta-vāda*?

Bābājī: In the *Vedas* there is description of transformation (*vivarta*), but that description is not at all like what has become known as the *vivarta-vāda*. Śrī Śaṅkarācārya has used the words *vivarta* and *vivarta-vāda* to mean *māyā-vāda* (the philosophy of impersonalism). The true meaning of the word *vivarta* is given in these words: The word *vivarta* means, "misunderstanding the true nature of a certain thing."

The individual is a tiny particle of spirit. But when he is imprisoned in the gross and subtle material body, he becomes bewildered and thinks, "I am this gross and subtle material body." Thus, he misunderstands his true identity.

"Misunderstanding" is the only definition of *vivarta* given in the *Vedas*. Someone may think, "I am Raghunātha Bhaṭṭācārya, the son of Sanātana Bhaṭṭācārya," and someone else may think, "I am Sādhu Caṇḍāla, the son of Vijaya Caṇḍāla." In this way, the intelligence becomes bewildered. Both of those persons are individual souls, tiny particles of spirit. They are not Raghunātha Bhaṭṭācārya and Sādhu Caṇḍāla. Still, they are bewildered and they think they are identical with the material body. To mistake a rope for a snake or the glistening on a seashell's surface for silver are other examples of misunderstandings (*vivarta*). By all these examples, the *Vedas* teach that one should throw far away the idea that he is identical with the material body.

The Māyāvādīs (impersonalists), however, reject this proper use of the word *vivarta* and teach a funny theory they called *vivarta-vāda*. They say that the idea, "I am the Supreme," is the true idea, and the misconception, or *vivarta*, is the idea, "I am an individual spirit soul." By accepting this kind of *vivarta-vāda*, one will not understand what is the actual truth. The true *vivarta-vāda* does not at all contradict the *śakti-parināma-vāda*. On the other hand, the Māyāvādīs' (impersonalists') *vivarta-vāda* is only an object of laughter. The Māyāvādīs' *vivarta-vāda* is of three kinds: 1. The soul is really Brahman but he becomes bewildered into thinking that he is an individual soul, 2. The idea that the individual souls are reflections of Brahman, and 3. The idea that Brahman takes a nap and dreams that He has become the many individual souls. None of these are the true *vivarta-vāda*. The evidence of the *Vedas* refutes them all.

Vrajanātha: What is this Māyāvāda philosophy? My intelligence does not understand it.

Bābājī: Try to understand it soberly and carefully. The *māyā-śakti* is a perverted reflection of the *svarūpa-śakti* (internal potency). The *māyā-śakti* cannot enter the spiritual world. The *māyā-śakti* is the controller of the material world. Because he is bewildered by ignorance, the soul enters the material world. Spiritual things are real and do have an independent, separate existence.

However, the Māyāvāda theory does not accept the reality of spiritual things. The Māyāvāda theory declares that the individual soul is actually Brahman, and it is only by the influence of *māyā* that he thinks he is different from Brahman. The Māyāvāda theory declares that as long as he is under *māyā*'s influence, the soul thinks he is an individual soul, but when he becomes free of *māyā*'s influence, the soul learns that he is actually Brahman. The Māyāvāda theory declares that when *māyā*'s influence ceases, the individual spirit soul also ceases to exist. In this way, liberation is thought to mean *nirvāna*, or the souls merging into e existence of Brahman. In this way, the Māyāvāda theory does not accept the existence of a pure individual spirit soul, free from *māyā*'s clutches.

The Māyāvāda theory also declares that when He incarnates in the material world, Brahman must take shelter of *māyā* and accept a body made of matter. Brahman thus does not have a spiritual form and must accept a form made of matter. Thus, Brahman accepts the different material forms of His incarnations, descends to the material world, performs very great deeds, leaves His material form behind, and returns to His own abode.

The Māyāvādīs offer one kindness to the Supreme Lord. They say that individual souls and the incarnations of Brahman have one difference. They say that the individual souls are dependent on their past *karma*, are pushed into the gross material body against their will, are carried along by the strong current of their past *karma*, and are forced to suffer old age, death, and rebirth. On the other hand, the Supreme Lord accepts a material body, material identity, material name, material qualities, and other material things voluntarily, by His own will, and by His own will, at a certain time, He abandons those material things and becomes again manifest as pure spiritual consciousness. Although He performs activities, the Lord is not forced to accept the *karmic* results of those actions. All these are the mistaken conclusions of the Māyāvādīs.

Vrajanātha: Do the *Vedas* give any evidence to support the Māyāvāda philosophy?

Bābājī: No. In no place do the *Vedas* teach the Māyāvāda philosophy. Actually, the Māyāvāda philosophy is identical with Buddhism. In the *Padma Purāṇa*, Lord Śiva tells Pārvatī: The Māyāvāda philosophy is impious. It is covered Buddhism. My dear Pārvatī, in the form of a *brāhmaṇa* in Kali-yuga, I teach this imagined Māyāvāda philosophy.

Vrajanātha: O master, why did Lord Śiva, who is the best of Vaiṣṇavas and the leader of the demigods, do such a wicked deed?

Bābājī: Lord Śiva is a *guṇa-avatāra* of the Supreme Personality of Godhead. At one time, the demons had taken to following the path of devotion in order to fulfill their own sinful lusty desires. Seeing this, the merciful Supreme Personality of Godhead, concerned for the benefit of the true sincere devotees decided to deter the demons from following the path of devotion.

With this in mind, He called for Lord Śiva and told him, "O Śiva, that the demons in the mode of ignorance are now preaching the path of pure devotional service is not good for the world. Please write a book to bewilder the demons. Conceal the truth about Me and preach the Māyāvāda, impersonal philosophy. The demons will then leave the path of pure devotional service and take shelter of impersonalism. That will be very pleasing to My genuine pure devotees. Of this there is no doubt."

The great Vaiṣṇava, Śiva, unhappily accepted this order of the Supreme Lord, placing it on his head, and obediently preached the Māyāvāda philosophy. How can there be any fault, then, for Lord Śiva, the spiritual master of the entire world?

Vrajanātha: For the good of all the conditioned souls, the Supreme Personality of Godhead turns the wheel of the material world of birth and death. The Sudarśana *cakra* He holds in His hand brings only good. His order brings only good. The servant's duty is to carry out his master's order. Therefore, the pure Vaiṣṇavas do not blame Lord Śiva for descending as Śaṅkarācārya and preaching the Māyāvāda philosophy. Now I will recite the scriptural evidence for all this. Please listen.

In the *Padma Purāṇa*, the Supreme Lord tells Śiva: "O Śiva, because you worship Me, I will always give My blessings to you. In Kali-yuga, mislead the people in general by propounding imaginary meanings of the *Vedas* to bewilder them. In this way, conceal Me and make people turn away from Me.

In the *Varāha Purāṇa*, the Supreme Lord tells Śiva: "O mighty-armed Śiva, please write books filled with lies and thus bewilder the people. O mighty-armed one, please preach a collection of lies. Place yourself in the forefront and conceal Me.

Vrajanātha: Do any Vedic passages refute the Māyāvāda theory?

Bābājī: All the *Vedas* refute the Māyāvāda theory. Searching through all the *Vedas*, the Māyāvādīs have found four statements to buttress their argument, and these they call *mahā-vākyas* (the great statements of the *Vedas*). These four statements are: (*Chāndogya Upaniṣad* 3.14.1): Everything is Brahman. *Bṛhad-āraṇyaka Upaniṣad* 4.4.19 and *Kaṭha Upaniṣad* 2.1.11: Nothing is different from Brahman. *Aitareya Upaniṣad* 1.5.3: Brahman is consciousness. *Chāndogya Upaniṣad* 6.8.7: O Svetaketu, you are that. *Bṛhad-āraṇyaka Upaniṣad* 1.4.10: I am Brahman.

What does the first of these *mahā-vākyas* teach? It teaches that the material world and the individual souls are all Brahman, that there is nothing but Brahman. What is the nature of Brahman? That is explained in another place in the *Vedas*.

In the *Śvetāśvatara Upaniṣad* (6.8) it is said: The Supreme Lord has nothing to do. Nothing is equal to Him or greater than Him. He acts in different phases by manifesting His parts and parcels, which are all simultaneously differently situated by His unlimited, variegated potencies. Each potency acts quite naturally in sequences, providing Him full knowledge, power, and pastimes.

In these words, Brahman and Brahman's potency are accepted as one. Here it is said that the potency is the property (*svābhāvikī*) of Brahman, and it is also said that the potency is manifested in many different ways (*vividhā*). Because the potency and the master who possesses the potency are not different, it may certainly be said that nothing is different from Brahman. However, when we look at the material world, we can also see that in another sense, Brahman and His potency are certainly different.

In the *Vedas* (*Kaṭha Upaniṣad* 2.13 and *Śvetāśvatara Upaniṣad* 6.10) it is said: The Supreme Lord is eternal and the living beings are eternal. The Supreme Lord is cognizant and the living beings are cognizant. The difference is that the Supreme Lord is supplying the necessities of life for the many other living entities.

In these words of the *Vedas*, variety is accepted as an eternal fact. In the other passages of the *Vedas* (*Śvetāśvatara Upaniṣad* 6.8), the Lord's potency and His knowledge, power, and pastimes are also considered, in one sense, to be different from Him.

Now, let us consider these words of *Aitareya Upaniṣad* (1.5.3): Brahman is consciousness.

Here is it said that Brahman is identical with consciousness. The nature of consciousness is described in these words of *Bṛhad-āraṇyaka Upaniṣad* (4.4.21): A wise man who understands the Supreme falls in love with Him.

Here, the word *prajñā* does not mean merely "consciousness," Here, it means "love and devotion."

Now let us consider these words of *Chāndogya Upaniṣad* (6.8.7): O Svetaketu, you are that.

These words supposedly teach that the Supreme Lord and the individual spirit soul are identical. However, the proper explanation of these words is found in this passage from the *Bṛhad-āraṇyaka Upaniṣad* (3.8.10): He is a miserly man who does not solve the problems of life as a human and who thus quits this world like the cats and dogs, without understanding the science of self-realization.

The words *tat tvaṁ asi* therefore actually mean, "He who has attained devotion to the Lord is a true *brāhmaṇa*.

Now let us consider these words of *Bṛhad-āraṇyaka Upaniṣad* (1.4.10): I am Brahman.

Some thinkers say that the knowledge described in these words does not culminate in devotional service as its final attainment. This idea is criticized by these words of *Śrī Īśopaniṣad* (*mantra* 9): Those who engage in the culture of nescient activities shall enter into the darkest region of ignorance. Worse still are those engaged in the culture of so-called knowledge.

These words mean that persons who are ignorant and do not know that they are pure spirit souls enter into terrible blinding darkness. However, those who, even though they become free from that ignorance, foolishly think that the individual soul is Brahman and not a tiny particle of spirit, enter into an even more terrible blinding darkness of ignorance.

O Bābā, the *Vedas* are like an ocean that has no shore. One should carefully study each *mantra* of each *Upaniṣad* and then one should study the *Upaniṣads* together as a whole. In that way, one will understand the true meaning of the *Vedas*. However, if one only studies a few passages, here and there, the conclusion he gets at the end will be horrible and wrong. Therefore, after carefully studying all the branches of the *Vedas*, Śrīmān Mahāprabhu taught the final conclusion: That the individual spirit souls and the material world are simultaneously, inconceivably one and different from the Supreme Personality of Godhead.

Vrajanātha: Please explain to me more clearly how this philosophy of inconceivable simultaneous oneness and difference is the true teaching of the *Vedas*.

Bābājī: In the *Chāndogya Upaniṣad* (3.14.1) it is said: Everything is Brahman.
In the *Chāndogya Upaniṣad* (7.25.2) it is said: The Supreme Soul is everything. In the *Chāndogya Upaniṣad* (6.2.1) it is said: In the beginning, only the Supreme existed. There was none but Him. In the *Śvetāśvatara Upaniṣad* (5.4) it is said: As the sun shines in all directions—above, below and across—so the glorious Supreme Personality of Godhead rules all creatures.

These passages describe the oneness part of simultaneous oneness and difference. In the *Taittirīya Upaniṣad* (2.1) it is said: One who understands the Supreme, attains the Supreme. In the *Kaṭha Upaniṣad* (1.2.22 and 2.1.4) it is said: A wise man who meditates on the all-pervading Supreme Soul never laments. In the *Taittirīya Aranyaka*, First Anuvāka, it is said: Brahman is limitless, eternal, and all-knowing. A person who knows that Brahman stays both in the spiritual sky and in the hearts of all creatures attains Brahman. He associates with the all-knowing Brahman. All his desires are fulfilled. In the *Śvetāśvatara Upaniṣad* (3.9) it is said: There is no truth superior to that Supreme Person because He is the supermost. He is smaller than the smallest and He is greater than the greatest. He is situated as a silent tree, He illumines the transcendental sky, and as a tree spreads its roots, He spreads His extensive energies.

In the *Śvetāśvatara Upaniṣad* (6.16) it is said: The Supreme Person is fully aware of everything. He is the Supersoul, the master of all transcendental qualities.

In the *Kaṭha Upaniṣad* (2.23) and the *Muṇḍaka Upaniṣad* (3.2.3) it is said: The Supreme Lord is attained only by one who He Himself chooses. To such a person, He manifests His own form. In the *Śvetāśvatara Upaniṣad* (3.19) it is said: Learned transcendentalists explain that God is the greatest, the original person.

In the *Śrī Īśopaniṣad* (*mantra* 8) it is said: "The Supreme Personality of Godhead has been fulfilling everyone's desires since time immemorial. In the *Kena Upaniṣad* (3.6 and 3.10) it is said: I do not understand who this Yakṣa is. In the *Taittirīya Upaniṣad* (2.7) it is said: In the beginning, only the Supreme existed. From Him everything was born. Then He personally appeared within the world. That is why He is called *sukṛta* (the creator). In the *Kaṭha Upaniṣad* (2.13) and the *Śvetāśvatara Upaniṣad* (6.13) it is said: Of all eternal beings, one is the most important. In the *Māṇḍūkya Upaniṣad* (*mantra* 2) it is said: The Supreme soul is the greatest. He is everything. He manifests in four forms. In the *Bṛhad-āraṇyaka Upaniṣad* (2.5.14) it is said: All living beings find that the Supreme Person is sweet like nectar.

In these and countless other passages, the *Vedas* declare that the individual souls are eternally different from the Supreme. Every part of the *Vedas* is beautiful and good. No part should be rejected. That the individual souls are eternally different from the Supreme is the truth. That the individual souls are eternally non-different from the Supreme is also the truth. Both are true simultaneously. All the *Vedas* declare that difference and non difference are both true. This simultaneous difference and non-difference is inconceivable, beyond the power of human intelligence to understand. Applying material logic to understand it will bring only confusion. What the *Vedas* speak is always the truth. The *Vedas'* statements should not be rejected merely because they are beyond the understanding of our tiny human intelligence.

In the *Kaṭha Upaniṣad* (1.2.9) it is said: Ordinary material logic cannot be used to disprove the truths taught by the *Vedas*. In the *Kena Upaniṣad* (2.2) it is said: I do not think, "I do not know anything about the Supreme." Neither do I think, "I know everything about the Supreme."

In these passages, the *Vedas* declare that the Lord's potency is inconceivable. Therefore, material logic is not the proper tool with which to understand the Lord's potency.

In the *Mahābhārata* it is said: The *Purāṇas*, *Manu-saṁhitā*, the *Vedas* with all their limbs, and the science of Vedic medicine are the words of the

Supreme Personality of Godhead. They are His commands. Material logic cannot refute them.

Thus, simultaneous oneness and difference is the pure truth, the conclusion taught by the *Vedas*. When one considers the final goal and need of all individual souls, he will see that there is no conclusion but simultaneous oneness and difference. When one understands this truth of simultaneous oneness and difference, he will see that the difference between the soul and the Supreme is eternal. Without understanding this difference, the individual soul cannot attain the true goal of life: love for the Supreme.

Vrajanātha: What evidence from scripture and logic shows that love for the Supreme is the final goal of life?

Bābājī: The *Vedas* (*Muṇḍaka Upaniṣad* 3.1.4) declare: The Supreme Person is the life of all that lives. One who knows Him is not eager to talk of other things. Such a person loves the Lord, always remembers the Lord's pastimes, and is active in the Lord's service. He is the best of transcendentalists.

In the *Bṛhad-āraṇyaka Upaniṣad* (2.4.5 and 4.5.6) it is said: Every living being loves others not to please them, but to please himself.

These words of *Bṛhad-āraṇyaka Upaniṣad* show that love is the individual soul's primary need and goal. Bābā, love for the Supreme is described in many passages of the *Vedas* and the *Śrīmad-Bhāgavatam*.

It is clearly described in these words of the *Taittirīya Aranyaka*, Seventh Anuvāka: Who could live and who could breathe if he did not find pleasure in his heart? Living in the heart, the Supreme Personality of Godhead gives pleasure to all living beings.

Happiness is a state of being created by love. All spirit souls strive to find pleasure. Persons striving for liberation think liberation will bring them pleasure. That is why they are mad after liberation. Materialists think material sense objects will bring them pleasure. That is why they chase after sense objects. The hope for pleasure pushes the living entity into action. The devotees act so that they can find pleasure in service to Lord Kṛṣṇa. Thus, all living entities are searching for pleasure and for love. For the sake of pleasure and love, they are even willing to give up their bodies. The conclusion is this: Everyone sees pleasure and love as their final goal and their true need. No one will deny it. One may be an atheist, one may be a theist, one may be a proponent of fruitive work (*karma-vādī*), one may be an impersonalist (*jñāna-vādī*), one may be a hedonist (*kāmī*), one may be an ascetic (*niṣkāmī*)—all living entities are searching for pleasure and love. All search for pleasure and love, but not everyone finds it.

The proponents of fruitive work think they will find pleasure and love in Svargaloka. However, the *Bhagavad-gītā* (9.21) says of them: When they have thus enjoyed heavenly sense pleasure, they return to this mortal planet again. Thus, through the Vedic principles, they achieve only flickering happiness.

This means that eventually they must fall down from Svargaloka. In this way, their plan to enjoy becomes frustrated. When a person fails to find true pleasure in the wealth, children, fame, power, and other things available in the world of human beings, he begins to desire the pleasures available in Svargaloka. When he must fall from Svargaloka, he realizes that the pleasures available there are not very valuable. Then, he sees that the pleasures of the human worlds, of Svargaloka, and of the highest material planets, even up to the planet of the demigod, Brahmā, are all temporary. Then, he begins to search for impersonal liberation. When he finally attains impersonal liberation, he sees that there is not real pleasure in that either. Then, he searches for another path to follow. How is it possible to find either pleasure or love in impersonal liberation? If a person's sense of identity is annihilated, how can he enjoy any pleasure? Or, if everything becomes one, how can he enjoy any pleasure? Who will exist to experience the pleasure? If I lose my identity, who will exist to experience Brahman?

The statement, "Pleasure exists in impersonal liberation," has no meaning, for no one exists to experience the pleasure. In impersonal liberation, does pleasure exist, or does it not exist? What is the conclusion? If my personal identity is destroyed, then everything about me is destroyed. What remains of me, that I can experience the attainment of a goal or the fulfillment of a need? In impersonal liberation, I do not exist. I do not exist at all.

If someone says, "In impersonal liberation, I exist as Brahman," then Brahman does not perform any action. Is it not so? If I become Brahman eternally, then there is nothing for me to attain and therefore, I need not perform any action. Therefore, impersonal liberation is not the way to attain pleasure or love. Actually, impersonal liberation does not exist. It is only a trick played on the individual soul. It is a flower imagined to float in the sky. Devotional service is the only method by which the individual souls can attain the true goal of their lives and fulfill their true needs.

The final stage of devotional service is love and pleasure. That love and pleasure are eternal. Pure Kṛṣṇa is eternal, and pure love for Him is also eternal. Therefore, when one accepts the truth of inconceivable oneness and difference, he can attain the eternal perfection of true love. If there is no simultaneous oneness and difference, then the eternal spiritual love that is the soul's true goal and need becomes non-eternal. That non-eternality attacks the love and destroys it. Therefore, all Vedic scriptures confirm that simultaneous inconceivable oneness and difference is the true conclusion. All other conclusions are meaningless speculations.

Plunged into an ocean of bliss as again and again he thought about the meaning of spiritual love, Vrajanātha walked home.

Chapter Nineteen

Eternal religion and sambandha, abhidheya and prayojana (Abhidheya)

After finishing his meal, Vrajanātha went to bed. Again and again in his heart, he thought about simultaneous oneness and difference. He thought, "I used to think that the philosophy of inconceivable simultaneous oneness and difference was only one of many competing philosophies."

As he deeply thought about it, he concluded that no passages of scripture refuted it. Indeed, all the scriptures supported it. Śrī Gaura Kiśora is the Supreme Personality of Godhead Himself: "There cannot be any fault with His profound teachings. I cannot leave the shelter of Lord Gaura Kiśora's lotus feet, which are the abode of spiritual love. Alas! What have I attained thus far? The teaching of inconceivable simultaneous oneness and difference is the truth. That much I know, but by knowing it, what have I attained? The saintly *bābājī* told me that spiritual love is the final goal of life for all souls. The fruitive workers (*karmīs*) and impersonalists (*jñānīs*) are all searching for love, but they do not know what is the pure state of love. One must attain the pure state of love. I will ask the saintly *bābājī* how to attain it. I will hear his conclusion."

Again and again thinking in this way, he gradually fell asleep. It was late at night when Vrajanātha finally fell asleep, and it was late in the morning when he finally awakened. He got up from bed. When he had washed and performed his morning duties, his uncle, Vijaya-kumāra Bhaṭṭācārya Mahāśaya arrived for a visit. Seeing that he had come after many days in Śrī Modadruma, Vrajanātha at once offered *daṇḍavat* obeisances to his uncle.

Vijaya-kumāra was especially learned in *Śrīmad-Bhāgavatam*. By the mercy of Śrīmatī Nārāyaṇī-devī, he had attained great love for Lord Gaurāṅga. Nowadays, he went from place to place, reading aloud from *Śrīmad-Bhāgavatam*. At the village of Denuḍa-grāma, he personally met Śrī Vṛndāvana dāsa Ṭhākura, who advised him to visit Śrī Māyāpura, the inconceivable spiritual abode of the Lord. Vṛndāvana dāsa Ṭhākura told him that soon all the places of Lord Mahāprabhu's pastimes would become hidden and only after four hundred years would they again be openly manifested. He also said that the places of Lord Caitanya's pastimes are not different from Śrī Vṛndāvana, and that only a person who can see the spiritual nature of Śrī Māyāpura and the other places of Lord Caitanya's pastimes has the power to see Vṛndāvana as it truly is.

Hearing these words of Śrī Vṛndāvana dāsa Ṭhākura, who is an incarnation of Śrīla Vyāsadeva, Vijaya-kumāra became very eager to see Śrī Māyāpura. In his mind, he decided to visit his sister and nephew in Bilva-puṣkariṇī and then visit Śrī Māyāpura. In those days, Bilva-puṣkariṇī and Brāhmaṇa-puṣkariṇī touched each other. Nowadays, they are far apart. In those days, the boundary of Bilva-puṣkariṇī was within a mile of holy Śrī Māyāpura. That abandoned village of Bilva-puṣkariṇī now goes by the names Ṭoṭā and Tāraṇavāsa.

Vijaya-kumāra embraced his nephew and said, "Bābā, now I will go to visit Śrī Māyāpura. Please tell your mother that I will return for lunch."

Vrajanātha replied, "Uncle, why are you going to visit Śrī Māyāpura?"

Vijaya-kumāra was not aware of Vrajanātha's present condition, how he had abandoned the study of *nyāya-śāstra* and become an ardent student of *Vedānta*. Therefore, he thought it not appropriate to describe his devotional activities to Vrajanātha. He simply said, "I want to visit someone in Māyāpura."

Aware that his uncle was a devotee of Lord Gaurāṅga and a scholar of *Śrīmad-Bhāgavatam*, and thinking that his uncle must have a spiritual purpose in visiting Śrī Māyāpura, Vrajanātha said, "A very faithful Vaiṣṇava named Śrī Raghunātha dāsa Bābājī Mahāśaya resides in Śrī Māyāpura. Please speak with him when you make your visit."

Hearing Vrajanātha's words, Vijaya-kumāra said, "Bābā, now you have faith in the Vaiṣṇavas? I heard that you had abandoned *nyāya* and turned to *Vedānta*. Now I can understand that you have entered the path of devotional service. I no longer need to conceal things from you. Vṛndāvana dāsa Ṭhākura has ordered me to visit the holy abode of Śrī Māyāpura. In my mind, I have decided to bathe in the Ganges at Śrī Māyāpura-ghāta, see and circumambulate the Yoga-pīṭha, and once roll about in the dust from the Vaiṣṇavas' feet at Śrīvāsa's courtyard."

Vrajanātha said, "Uncle, please be kind and take me with you. I will take permission from mother, and we will both go to Śrī Māyāpura."

After this conversation, Vrajanātha spoke to his mother. Vrajanātha and Vijaya-kumāra then both left for Śrī Māyāpura. With great delight, they both bathed in the Ganges. As they bathed, Vijaya-kumāra said, "Nephew, today I am fortunate. Up until the age of twenty, Lord Śacīnandana showed His mercy to Śrī Gaṅgā-devī by playing in the waters here. By bathing in these waters, I have become very happy."

Melting with happiness to hear these encouraging words, Vrajanātha said, "Today I am fortunate, for today I am able to follow your feet."

After bathing, they both went to Jagannātha Miśra's home. There, they became decorated with streaming tears of great spiritual love. Vijaya-kumāra said, "Those who have taken birth in the land of Lord Gaura but have never touched this most sacred place have taken their birth in vain. That is not just an exaggeration. Look! With material eyes, this looks like another ordinary place, a place of cottages made of leaves. By Lord Gaurāṅga's mercy, what glory do we see now! We see great jeweled palaces, charming gardens, grand archways, and so many other glorious things! Look! How beautiful are the forms of Śrī Gaurāṅga-Viṣṇupriyā in that palace! What beautiful forms!"

Again and again speaking in this way, the uncle and nephew were both overwhelmed, stunned with ecstatic love. For a long time they were both overcome in this way. Finally, some devotees helped them go to Śrīvāsa's courtyard. When they entered it, streams of tears flowed from their eyes. Rolling on the ground in Śrīvāsa's courtyard, they both called out, "O Śrīvāsa! O Advaita! O Nityānanda! O Gadādhara-Gaurāṅga! Please give Your mercy to us. Please take away our false pride. Please give us shelter of Your lotus feet."

Seeing the two *brāhmaṇas* in this devotional mood, the Vaiṣṇavas called out, "Glory to the moon of Māyāpura! Glory to invincible Lord Gaurāṅga! Glory to Lord Nityānanda!" and danced. In a moment, Vrajanātha offered his body at the lotus feet of his worshipable master, Śrī Raghunātha dāsa. The elderly *bābājī* picked him up, embraced him, and said, "Bābā, why have you come at this time, today? Who is the great soul accompanying you?"

Vrajanātha humbly explained everything. The Vaiṣṇavas gave them nice sitting places in the courtyard of the *bakula* tree. Then, Vijaya-kumāra humbly asked saintly Śrī Raghunātha dāsa Bābājī, "O master, what is the real goal and need of all living entities?"

Bābājī: You are both great devotees. You have already attained the goal of life. Still, to show kindness to me, you have asked this question. As far as I know, I will speak. Devotional service to Lord Kṛṣṇa, devotional service that is free of any trace of fruitive work or impersonal speculation, is both the final goal of life and the means to attain the goal of life. In its beginning stage, it is called *sādhana-bhakti* and in its final, perfect stage, it is called *prema-bhakti.*

Vijaya-kumāra: O saintly *bābājī*, what different qualities does devotional service possess?

Bābājī: By Lord Mahāprabhu's order, Śrīla Rūpa Gosvāmī wrote the *Bhakti-rasāmṛta-sindhu*, where the qualities of devotional service are described in these words (1.1.11): One should render transcendental loving service to the Supreme Lord Kṛṣṇa favorably and without desire for material profit or gain through fruitive activities or philosophical speculation. That is called pure devotional service.

In this verse, the direct and indirect qualities of pure devotional service are described. Here, the words *bhaktir uttama* mean, "pure devotional service." Pure devotional service is never mixed with *karma* (fruitive activities) or *jñāna* (impersonal speculation). When the desire for sense gratification is present, devotional service is mixed with fruitive activities. When the desire for impersonal liberation attained through philosophical speculation is present, devotional service is mixed with impersonal speculation. When the desire for sense gratification and impersonal liberation are completely absent, then devotional service is *uttama*, or pure. Pure devotional service brings pure love of God as its result.

What is devotional service? The direct qualities of devotional service are the endeavor to please Kṛṣṇa with the activities of one's body, mind, and words, and also love for Lord Kṛṣṇa within one's heart. The soul has certain powers of his own. However, when one attains the mercy of Lord Kṛṣṇa, and the mercy of a devotee, then Lord Kṛṣṇa manifests His own internal potency (*svarūpa-śakti*). It is then that the true nature of devotional service becomes manifested. In the present condition, the living entity's body, mind, and words are all material. If he works with the power of his own intelligence, his only attainment will be material knowledge and dry renunciation. He will not attain devotional service. However, if Lord Kṛṣṇa's internal potency (*svarūpa-śakti*) becomes manifested, and is even slightly active, then pure devotional service is manifested also.

Lord Kṛṣṇa is the original form of the Supreme Personality of Godhead (Bhagavān). Activities meant to please Him are called devotional service. *Jñāna* (impersonal speculation) and *karma* (fruitive work), which are meant to please Brahman and Paramātmā, are not devotional service. Devotional service should be favorable (*ānukūlya*), meaning that it should be meant to please Lord Kṛṣṇa. If it is not favorable, devotional service cannot reach the perfect stage. The word *ānukūla* means "pleasing to Lord Kṛṣṇa." In the stage of *sādhana-bhakti*, the activities of devotional service are to a certain extent gross and unrefined. In the stage of perfect devotional service, the activities of devotional service are free from connection with the material world. In this way, they are subtle and refined. In both stages, the qualities of devotional service remain the same. Therefore, that devotional service should be favorable (*ānukūlyena*) and directly offered to Lord Kṛṣṇa (*kṛṣṇānuśīlanam*) are the direct qualities of devotional service.

Now that the direct qualities have been described, we will describe the indirect qualities of devotional service. Śrī Rūpa Gosvāmī has mentioned two indirect qualities of devotional service. The first indirect quality is *anyābhilāṣitā-śūnyaṁ* (freedom from other desires), and the second indirect quality is *jñāna-karmādy-anāvṛtam* (freedom from impersonal speculation and fruitive work). In the heart, any desire for something other than devotional service is antagonistic to devotional service. When *jñāna*, *karma*, *yoga*, renunciation, and other things cover the heart, the situation is not favorable for devotional service. Therefore, devotional service is pure when it is freed from these two obstacles, and when it is favorable and directed to Lord Kṛṣṇa.

Vijaya-kumāra: What is the special quality of devotional service? I mean to say, what are its specific characteristics?

Bābājī: Śrīla Rūpa Gosvāmī explains that pure devotional service has six specific characteristics. They are described in these words (*Bhakti-rasāmṛta-sindhu* 1.1.13): There are six characteristics of pure devotional service, which are as follows: 1. Pure devotional service brings immediate relief from all kinds of material distress, 2. Pure devotional service is the beginning of all auspiciousness,

3. Pure devotional service automatically puts one in transcendental pleasure, 4. Pure devotional service is rarely achieved, 5. Those in pure devotional service deride even the conception of liberation, and 6. Pure devotional service is the only means to attract Kṛṣṇa.

Vijaya-kumāra: How does pure devotional service bring immediate relief from all kinds of material distress?

Bābājī: Material distress has three causes: 1. *pāpa* (sins), 2. *pāpa-bīja* (the seeds of sins) and 3. *avidyā* (ignorance). The word *pāpa* (sins) refers to the activities that begin with *pātaka* (sins), *mahā-pātaka* (great sins), and *ati-pātaka* (the greatest sins). When pure devotional service appears in the heart, sinful activities cannot remain there. The desire to commit sins is called *pāpa-bīja* (the seeds of sins). When the heart is purified by performing devotional service, sinful desires cannot stay there. The individual soul's illusions are called *avidyā*. When pure devotional service is performed, the soul thinks, "I am a servant of Lord Kṛṣṇa." When that happens, illusions about the soul's true identity cannot stay.

When the effulgence of Bhakti-devī (the goddess of devotional service) enters the heart, sins, the seeds of sins, and the blinding darkness of ignorance, all perish. Thus, when devotional service arrives, material distress is no longer seen. Therefore, one of the characteristics of devotional service is that it brings immediate relief from all kinds of material distress.

Vijaya-kumāra: How is pure devotional service the beginning of all auspiciousness?

Bābājī: The word auspiciousness means: 1. Love for all living entities, 2. All virtues, and 3. Every kind of happiness. When pure devotional service arises in his heart, a person becomes decorated with these four virtues: 1. humility, 2. mercy, 3. pridelessness, and 4. giving honor to all others. The result of this is that the entire world loves him. Every virtue that exists among the living entities is spontaneously manifested within a person who is a devotee of the Lord. Devotional service also gives every kind of happiness. It gives material sense happiness, the happiness of attaining the quality-less impersonal liberation, all *yogīc* perfections, sense gratification, liberation, and every other kind of happiness. However, the four kinds of devotees do not desire any of these kinds of happiness, for none of them can even approach the eternal bliss attained by engaging in devotional service.

Vijaya-kumāra: Why is it that persons engaged in pure devotional service deride even the conception of impersonal liberation?

Bābājī: When the happiness that comes from pleasing the Lord is even slightly manifested in one's heart, the happinesses obtained from material piety, material sense gratification and impersonal liberation automatically become very insignificant.

Vijaya-kumāra: Why is pure devotional service rarely achieved?

Bābājī: Please try to understand this carefully. By following thousands and thousands of spiritual paths, one will not easily attain devotional service. Lord Hari is not pleased by persons who strive for material sense gratification or impersonal liberation. To them, He will not give devotional service. Therefore, for the followers of these two paths, devotional service is very rarely achieved. By following the path of impersonal speculation, one may attain impersonal liberation, and by performing *yajñas* and other pious deeds, one may easily attain material sense gratification, but by these means, one will never become expert in the *yoga* of devotional service. One may follow thousands and thousands of such paths, but one will not attain devotional service to Lord Hari.

Vijaya-kumāra: How does pure devotional service automatically put one in transcendental pleasure?

Bābājī: Devotional service is filled with spiritual pleasure. It is an ocean of bliss. If all the material pleasures available in the troublesome material world were added to its opposite, the pleasure of merging into the impersonal Brahman, and then multiplied by a hundred thousand million, all that accumulated pleasure would not equal a single drop of the happiness of devotional service. Material sense pleasures are very insignificant, and impersonal Brahman pleasure is very dry. These two kinds of pleasure are very different from spiritual pleasure. Dissimilar things cannot be compared. The pleasure of devotional service is a deep ocean of bliss. Compared to it, the happiness of impersonal liberation is like a mud puddle in a cow's hoofprint. Only persons who have tasted the pleasure of devotional service know what that pleasure is like. They cannot really describe that pleasure to others.

Vijaya-kumāra: How does pure devotional service attract Kṛṣṇa?

Bābājī: When devotional service appears in someone's heart, Lord Kṛṣṇa, who is controlled by love, becomes attracted to enter that heart, along with all His associates. By no other way can Lord Kṛṣṇa be brought under control.

Vijaya-kumāra: If devotional service is as you describe, then why do not all scripture scholars carefully engage in it?

Bābājī: The root of the matter is this: Human intelligence and material logic are limited. Any human being who tries with his limited intelligence to understand Lord Kṛṣṇa and His devotional service, which are far beyond the boundary of the material world, will certainly fail. Lord Kṛṣṇa and devotional service will remain far away from him. On the other hand, a person who, because of past pious deeds, now has a single drop of attraction to Kṛṣṇa can easily understand devotional service. Aside from being fortunate in this way, no one can understand the truth of devotional service.

Vijaya-kumāra: Why is material logic useless in understanding spiritual pleasure?

Bābājī: Material logic has no power to understand spiritual pleasure. In the *Vedas* (*Kaṭha Upaniṣad* 1.2.9) it is said: The Supreme cannot be understood by material logic. In the *Vedānta-sūtra* (2.1.11) it is also said: Transcendental topics cannot be understood by argument or logic.

In this way, it is explained that material logic cannot be used to understand spiritual matters.

Vrajanātha: Is there a stage in between *sādhana-bhakti* (devotional service in practice) and *prema-bhakti* (devotional service in pure love of God)?

Bābājī: Yes. There are three stages: *sādhana-bhakti*, *bhāva-bhakti* (devotional service in ecstasy), and *prema-bhakti*.

Vrajanātha: What distinguishes *sādhana-bhakti* from the others?

Bābājī: The highest stage is *prema-bhakti*. As long as he remains imprisoned by the material senses, the soul's devotional activities are situated in *sādhana-bhakti*.

Vrajanātha: You have explained that *prema-bhakti* is the eternal perfection, the highest stage. How is this highest stage attained?

Bābājī: One cannot attain that eternal perfection by his own efforts. In the beginning, the stage called *sādhana* is manifested in the heart. Until the day when the eternal perfection appears of its own accord, one cannot force its presence. The eternal perfection must come of its own.

Vrajanātha: Please explain more clearly.

Bābājī: Because it is manifested from the Lord's own internal potency (*svarūpa-śakti*), *prema-bhakti* is eternally perfect. It is not manifested in the hearts of souls still imprisoned by matter. With the body, mind, and words, one may endeavor to attain that eternal perfection in his heart, but as long as it is not attained, the devotee is situated in *sādhana-bhakti*.

Vrajanātha: What are the qualities of *sādhana-bhakti*?

Bābājī: The nature of *sādhana-bhakti* is that it is a method of making the mind think of Lord Kṛṣṇa.

Vrajanātha: How many stages are present in *sādhana-bhakti*?

Bābājī: There are two stages: *vaidhī* and *rāgānuga*.

Vrajanātha: What is *vaidhī-sādhana-bhakti*?

Bābājī: *Vaidhī* is of two kinds. When one follows the rules given in the scriptures, his activities are called *vaidhī-pravṛtti*. When, by following the rules given in the scriptures, a person attains devotional service, his activities are called *vaidhī-bhakti*.

Vrajanātha: Later I will ask about *rāgānuga-bhakti*. Now, please tell me: What are the qualities of *vaidhī-bhakti*?

Bābājī: Activities the scriptures say should be performed are called *vaidhī*. Activities the scriptures say should not be performed are called *niṣedha*. To do what should be done and avoid what is forbidden is called *vaidha-dharma*.

Vrajanātha: From your words I have understood that *vaidha* means "following the rules of all the *dharma śāstras* (scriptures)." However, it is very difficult for the living entity to determine from these scriptures exactly what should be done and what is forbidden. Therefore, please briefly summarize the scriptures' rules of what should be done and what is forbidden.

Bābājī: In the *Padma Purāṇa* it is said: Kṛṣṇa is the origin of Lord Viṣṇu. He should always be remembered and never forgotten at any time. All the rules and prohibitions mentioned in the *śāstra* (scriptures) should be the servants of these two principles.

One should always remember Lord Viṣṇu. That is the root of all rules. The duties of *varṇāśrama-dharma* are meant to follow that rule of always remembering Lord Viṣṇu. That is the root of all prohibitions. Avoidance of sin, abandonment of materialism, penance for sins committed in the past, and other like prohibitions are meant to follow this prohibition: that one should never forget Lord Viṣṇu. Therefore, the rules and prohibitions described in the scriptures are the servants of the rule to remember Lord Viṣṇu and the prohibition to never forget Him. Therefore, the rules of *varṇāśrama* and other such rules are meant to enable one to always remember Lord Viṣṇu.

This is described in the following words of *Śrīmad-Bhāgavatam* (11.5.2-3): From the mouth of Brahmā, the brahminical order has come into existence. Similarly, from his arms, the *kṣatriyas* have come, from his waist the *vaiśyas* have come, and from his legs the *śūdras* have come. These four orders and their spiritual counterparts (*brahmācārya*, *gṛhastha*, *vānaprastha*, and *sannyāsa*) combine to make human society complete. If one simply maintains an official position in the four *varṇas* and *āśramas* but does not worship the Supreme Lord, Viṣṇu, he falls down from his puffed-up position into a hellish condition.

Śrīla Rūpa Gosvāmī explains that among the human beings who follow the rules of scripture, some have faith in devotional service. These are the persons qualified to engage in devotional service. These persons are not attracted to following rules for their own sake, and neither are they attracted to renunciation for its own sake. Following the rules of ordinary civilized life and at the same time full of faith in devotional service, they engage in *sādhana-bhakti*. This engagement in *sādhana-bhakti* is the result of many lifetimes of pious deeds. Faithful persons thus engaged in devotional service are divided into three groups: 1. *uttama* (advanced), 2. *madhyama* (intermediate), and 3. *kaniṣṭha* (neophyte).

Vrajanātha: In *Bhagavad-gītā* (7.16) it is said that the devotees are of four kinds: 1. *arta* (the distressed), 2. *jijñāsu* (the inquisitive), 3. *arthārthī* (the desirer of wealth), and 4. *jñānī* (he who is searching for knowledge of the Absolute). How are these persons eligible to engage in devotional service?

Bābājī: When they attain the association of saintly devotees, these four kinds of persons, the *arta*, *jijñāsu*, *arthārthī*, and *jñānī* develop faith in unalloyed devotional service. Then they become qualified to engage in devotional service. Gajendra, Śaunaka Ṛṣi, Dhruva, the four Kumāras, and many others may be cited here as examples of this.

Vrajanātha: Why are the devotees not eager for liberation?

Bābājī: Of the five kinds of liberation— *sālokya* (to live on the same planet as the Lord), *sārṣṭi* (to have the same opulences as the Lord), *sāmīpya* (to have constant association with the Lord), *sārūpya* (to obtain the same bodily features as the Lord) and *sāyujya* (to become one with the Lord)—only *sāyujya* is openly opposed to the principles of devotional service. Therefore, the devotees of Lord Kṛṣṇa never accept *sāyujya* (impersonal) liberation. The other four kinds of liberation— *sālokya*, *sārṣṭi*, *sāmīpya*, and *sārūpya*—are not openly opposed to the principles of devotional service, but some aspects of them are not helpful for developing devotional service. The devotees of Lord Kṛṣṇa do not accept these four kinds of liberation when they are manifested in Vaikuṇṭha, the abode of Lord Nārāyaṇa.

In some situations, spiritual opulence is prominent in these kinds of liberation, and in other situations, loving service is prominent. The devotees reject these kinds of liberation when their final goal is spiritual opulence. In those situations, the devotees say, "Talk of liberation should stay far away."

The devotees' hearts are attracted only to Lord Kṛṣṇa. The devotees' hearts are not enchanted by the mercy of Lord Nārāyaṇa. Why not? Even though Lord Nārāyaṇa and Lord Kṛṣṇa are in the end not different from each other, the highest nectar is present only in the form of Lord Kṛṣṇa.

Vrajanātha: Are persons born in upper-class families in *varṇāśrama* the only persons eligible to engage in devotional service?

Bābājī: Simply by being a human being, one is eligible to engage in devotional service.

Vrajanātha: Persons who follow *varṇāśrama* must follow both the rules of *varṇāśrama* and the rules of devotional service. I see they must follow both sets of rules. On the other hand, persons who do not follow *varṇāśrama* need only follow the rules of pure devotional service. From what I can see, it must be very difficult for the followers of *varṇāśrama* to follow both the rules of *karma*-

kanda and the rules of devotional service. What is the proper understanding of all this?

Bābājī: A person engaged in pure devotional service need only follow the rules of devotional service, even though he may be living within the *varṇāśrama* social system. By following the rules of devotional service, his duty to follow the rules of *karma-kanda* is automatically fulfilled. In the places where they do not oppose devotional service, there is no harm in following the rules of *karma-kanda*. A person engaged in devotional service naturally has no desire to act badly or commit sins. If by accident he commits a sin, he is not required to perform the penance described in the *karma-kanda*. No accidentally-committed sin has the power to stay in a heart where devotional service also stays. A sin that tries to stay there will soon perish. Therefore, such a devotee does not need to perform penance.

Vrajanātha: How does a person engaged in devotional service repay his debts to the demigods and others like them?

Bābājī: Bābā, please reflect on the message of this verse in the Eleventh Canto (*Śrīmad-Bhāgavatam* 11.5.41): Anyone who has completely surrendered unto Kṛṣṇa, Mukunda, giving up all other duties, is no longer a debtor, nor is he obliged to anyone—not the demigods, nor the sages, nor the people in general, nor kinsmen, nor humanity, nor forefathers.

Also, at the end of the *Bhagavad-gītā* (18.66), the Supreme Personality of Godhead declares: Abandon all varieties of religion and just surrender unto Me. I shall deliver you from all sinful reactions. Do not fear.

These words of the *Gītā* mean that a person who engages in unalloyed devotional service is no longer required to follow the rules given in the scriptures describing impersonal liberation (*jñāna-śāstra*) and fruitive work (*karma-śāstra*). Simply by engaging in devotional service, he will attain all perfection. The Supreme Lord also declares (*Bhagavad-gītā* 9.31): My devotee never perishes.

This promise of the Lord stands above all other rules in the scriptures.

After hearing these words, Vrajanātha and Vijaya-kumāra said with one voice, "In our hearts, there is no doubt about devotional service. We know that *jñāna* and *karma* are very insignificant and very unimportant. Without Bhakti-devī's (the goddess of devotion's) mercy, no one an attain auspiciousness.

O master, please be kind to us and describe the different features of pure devotional service. Then our lives will become a success.

Bābājī: Vrajanātha, you have heard the *Daśa-mūla* up to the eighth verse. At another time, please relate these verses to your saintly uncle. My heart blossoms with happiness when I see him. Please listen now to the ninth verse: Hearing about Lord Kṛṣṇa, chanting His glories, remembering Him, bowing down before Him, worshiping Him, serving Him, thinking of Him as a friend, serving His lotus feet, and surrendering everything unto Him are the nine limbs of devotional service. A faithful person who every day worships the Lord by performing these devotional activities attains pure love for Him.

When Lord Kṛṣṇa's spiritual holy name and the descriptions of His form, qualities, and pastimes touch the ear, that activity is called *śravaṇam* (hearing). This hearing is of two kinds: Before one has attained faith in the Lord, one in conversation may hear the qualities of Lord Kṛṣṇa from the mouth of a saintly devotee. That is one kind of hearing. By hearing in this way, one attains faith. When one attains faith, he develops a deep thirst to hear about Lord Kṛṣṇa. Then, again and again, he hears about Lord Kṛṣṇa's holy name and other features. After that, he hears the holy name and qualities of Lord Kṛṣṇa from the mouth of a Vaiṣṇava spiritual master. That is the second kind of hearing.

Hearing is one limb of pure devotional service. At the time of performing *sādhana-bhakti*, one hears from a Vaiṣṇava spiritual master, and when one finally attains perfection, he continues to hear. Hearing is the first limb of devotional service.

When Lord Kṛṣṇa's holy name and the descriptions of His form, qualities, and pastimes touch the tongue, that activity is called *kīrtanaṁ* (chanting). Discussions of Lord Kṛṣṇa, chanting His holy name, attracting everyone by reading aloud the descriptions of Him in the scriptures and singing songs about Him, speaking humble words before Him, proclaiming His glories to others, reciting prayers, and placing humble requests before Him are all counted within the category of chanting. Of all the limbs of devotional service, chanting is said to be the most important.

In Kali-yuga especially, chanting can bring auspiciousness to all souls. This is declared in the scriptures again and again. For example, it is said (*Padma*

Purāṇa, Uttarā-khanda, 72.25): Whatever is achieved by meditation in Satya-yuga, by performance of *yajña* in Tretā-yuga, or by the worship of Kṛṣṇa's lotus feet in Dvāpara-yuga, is obtained in the age of Kali simply by chanting and glorifying Lord Keśava."

No other method is as affective in purifying the heart as *hari-kīrtana* (chanting the glories of Lord Hari). When many devotees chant together, that is called *saṅkīrtana*.

Remembering Lord Kṛṣṇa's name, form, qualities, and pastimes is called *smaraṇaṁ* (remembering). Remembering is of five kinds: 1. When one searches for something, that is called *smaraṇa*. 2. When one withdraws the mind from other things and fixes it on one object, that is called *dhāraṇa*. 3. When one meditates on a particular form, that is called *dhyāna*. 4. When meditation is unbroken and becomes like a flood of nectar, that is called *dhruvānusmṛti*. 5. When only the object of meditation and nothing else is present in the heart, that is called *samādhi*.

Śravaṇam (hearing), *kīrtanaṁ* (chanting), and *smaraṇaṁ* (remembering) are the three most important limbs of devotional service. All the other limbs are included within these three. Of the three limbs of hearing, chanting, and remembering, the most important is chanting, for hearing and remembering are naturally included within it.

In *Śrīmad-Bhāgavatam* (7.5.23) it is said that *pādasevanam* (serving the lotus feet) or *paricaryā* (service) is the fourth limb of devotional service. Serving the Lord's lotus feet should be performed along with hearing, chanting and remembering. When one serves the Lord's lotus feet, one should think oneself worthless and unqualified to serve, and one should think of the object of His service is a person who is eternal and full of knowledge and bliss. To think in these ways is essential. When serving the Lord's lotus feet, one should think that he is seeing the Lord's handsome face, touching Him, circumambulating Him, following Him, and seeing His temple, the Ganges, Jagannātha Puri, Dvārakā, Mathurā, Navadvīpa, and other holy places. Śrīla Rūpa Gosvāmī has eloquently described sixty-four limbs of devotional service. Serving *tulasī* and serving the Lord's devotees are included within this limb of serving the Lord's lotus feet.

The fifth limb is *arcana* (worship). Many things could be said about the qualifications of the worshiper and the activities of worship. If, after being engaged in hearing, chanting, and remembering, one becomes attracted to the path of worship, one should take shelter of the lotus feet of a bona fide spiritual master, accept *mantra dīkṣā* initiation from him, and become engaged in the activities of worship.

Vrajanātha: What is the difference between *nāma* (the holy name) and *mantra*?

Bābājī: The holy name of the Supreme Lord is the life and soul of all *mantras*. By adding the word *namaḥ* (obeisances) and other such words to the Lord's holy names, the sages have given us various *mantras* glorifying the Lord, *mantras* that each possess specific powers. The holy name of the Lord has nothing to do with the material world. To withdraw the mind from thoughts of the material body and other material things, *mantras* containing the Lord's holy names are given. To be able to chant *mantras*, materialistic persons require to accept initiation (*dīkṣā*).

To chant *kṛṣṇa-mantras* there is no need to accept the purificatory processes called *siddha*, *sādhya*, *susiddha*, and *ari*. Initiation into the chanting of *kṛṣṇa-mantras* is very beneficial for the living entity. *kṛṣṇa-mantras* are the most powerful *mantras* in the entire world. When he accepts a *kṛṣṇa-mantra* from a bona fide spiritual master, a qualified person gets strength from Lord Kṛṣṇa Himself. The spiritual master then describes the path of *arcana* (worship) to the inquisitive disciple. I need not describe all of that now.

In brief it may be said that the observance of Śrī Kṛṣṇa-janmāṣṭamī, Kārttika-vrata, Ekādaśī-vrata, Māgha-snāna, and other vows are included in this path of worship. One thing especially should be noted about the path of worshiping Lord Kṛṣṇa: One must worship Lord Kṛṣṇa's devotees along with Lord Kṛṣṇa Himself.

Vandana (offering obeisances) is the sixth limb of devotional service. Although it is included within *pādasevanam*, *kīrtana*, and the other limbs of devotional service, *vandana* is also considered a separate limb. *Vandana* means "offering obeisances." There are two ways to offer obeisances: 1. *ekaṇga-namaskāra* (offering obeisances with one limb) and 2. *aṣṭāṅga-namaskāra* (offering obeisances with eight limbs). To offer obeisances with one hand, with the body completely covered with cloth, directly before, on the left side, or behind the Lord, or very close to the Lord, are all considered offenses.

Dāsya (service) is the seventh limb of devotional service. *Dāsya* means to think, "I am a servant of Lord Kṛṣṇa." The best kind of worship is performed when the worshiper thinks that he is a servant of Lord Kṛṣṇa. Offering obeisances, reciting prayers, offering all of one's actions, serving, offering honor, remembering, hearing about the Lord, and other such activities are included within *dāsya*.

Sākhya (friendship) is the eighth limb of devotional service. *Sākhya* means to act as a friend to Lord Kṛṣṇa. There are two kinds of such friendship: 1. *vaidha*nga (friendship in *vaidhī-bhakti*), and 2. *rāgaṅgā* (friendship in *rāgānuga-bhakti*). Here we will only describe *vaidha*nga friendship. This kind of friendship is possible when the devotee engages in Deity worship. That is called *vaidha-sākhya*.

Ātmā-nivedana (surrendering everything) is the ninth limb of devotional service. To offer the pure soul, the material body, and everything else to Lord Kṛṣṇa is called *ātmā-nivedana*. To act only for Lord Kṛṣṇa's benefit and not for one's own benefit is the special feature of *ātmā-nivedana*. As a cow that is sold to someone does not do anything to protect or maintain herself, so the surrendered soul acts only according to Lord Kṛṣṇa's desires. Such a soul desires whatever Lord Kṛṣṇa desires.

The activities of *ātmā-nivedana* are described in these words (*Śrīmad-Bhāgavatam* 9.4.18-20): "Mahārāja Ambarisa always engaged his mind in meditating upon the lotus feet of Kṛṣṇa, His words in describing the glories of the Lord, his hands in cleansing the Lord's temple, and his ears in hearing the words spoken by Kṛṣṇa or about Kṛṣṇa. He engaged his eyes in seeing the Deity of Kṛṣṇa, Kṛṣṇa's temples, and Kṛṣṇa's places, like Mathurā and Vṛndāvana, he engaged his sense of touch in touching the bodies of the Lord's devotees, he engaged his sense of smell in smelling the fragrance of *tulasī* offered to the Lord, and he engaged his tongue in tasting the Lord's *prasāda*. He engaged his legs in walking to the holy places and temple of the Lord, his head in bowing down before the Lord, and all his desires in serving the Lord, twenty-four hours a day. Indeed, Mahārāja Ambarisa never desired anything for his own sense gratification. He engaged all his senses in devotional service, in various engagements related to the Lord. This is the way to increase attachment for the Lord and be completely free from all material desires.

Filled with bliss to hear all this, Vrajanātha and Vijaya-kumāra offered *daṇḍavat* obeisances to the saintly *bābājī* and said, "O master, you are a personal associate of the Supreme Lord Himself. We are both very fortunate to drink the nectar of your teachings. For so many days, we were uselessly proud of our caste and learning. It is only because of many pious deeds in many past births that now we have attained the shelter of your lotus feet."

Vijaya-kumāra said, "O best of the Lord's devotees, Śrī Vṛndāvana dāsa Ṭhākura instructed me to see the Yoga-pīṭha in the Śrī Māyāpura. It is by his mercy that today I have seen both the Lord's transcendental abode and the Lord's personal associate. Please be merciful and allow that tomorrow evening we may again come to see you."

Hearing the name of Vṛndāvana dāsa Ṭhākura, the elderly *bābājī* at once offered *daṇḍavat* obeisances. He said, "Again and again I offer my respectful obeisances to Vṛndāvana dāsa Ṭhākura, who is Vyāsadeva himself, and who has come to this world to record Lord Caitanya's pastimes."

It was late. Vrajanātha and Vijaya-kumāra returned to Vrajanātha's home.

Chapter Twenty

Eternal religion and sambandha, abhidheya and prayojana (Abhidheya: Vaidha-sādhana-bhakti)

Almost six hours had passed when Vrajanātha and Vijaya-kumāra returned home. Vrajanātha's mother carefully served a delicious lunch to her brother. After lunch, the uncle and nephew conversed very affectionately. To his uncle, Vrajanātha repeated, one by one, all the teachings he had heard from the saintly *bābājī*. Hearing them, Vijaya-kumāra became plunged in an ocean of bliss.

He said to his nephew, "You have become very fortunate! From a great saint you have heard all these descriptions of the spiritual truth. It is always auspicious to hear descriptions of Lord Hari and devotional service, but when these descriptions come from the mouth of a saint, when they enter the ear, they very quickly bring the desired result. Bābā, you are learned in all the scriptures. In the *nyāya-śāstra*, you have no peer. You were born in a family of *vaidika brāhmaṇas*. You are not poverty-stricken. You are wealthy. These advantages are all ornaments decorating you now that you have taken shelter of a Vaiṣṇava's feet and you relish hearing His descriptions of Lord Kṛṣṇa."

Sitting in the house's shrine to Goddess Caṇḍī, the uncle and nephew conversed about spiritual life. In a side room, Vrajanātha's mother privately said to Vijaya-kumāra, "Brother, after many days you have come for a visit. Please try to turn your nephew into a householder. I am afraid to see how Vrajanātha acts. Vrajanātha may never get married. Many matchmakers have offered many matches, but Vrajanātha is stubborn. He refuses to marry. My mother-in-law tried, but she could not convince him.

Hearing all that his sister had to say, Vijaya-kumāra replied, "I will stay for ten or fifteen days. I will think about it and I will tell you what to do. For now, please go to your own part of the house."

When Vrajanātha's mother returned to her rooms, Vijaya-kumāra returned to his spiritual discussions with Vrajanātha. They spent the day in those discussions. The next day, after their meal, Vijaya-kumāra said to Vrajanātha, "This evening, we will go to Śrīvāsa's courtyard. From the mouth of the saintly *bābājī*, we will hear Śrīla Rūpa Gosvāmī's description of the sixty-four limbs of devotional service."

"Vrajanātha, I wish that birth after birth I could associate with saintly devotees like you. If I had not associated with you, I would never have heard such nectarean teachings. Look, the saintly *bābājī* said that the path of *sādhana-bhakti* has two parts: 1. *vaidha-mārga* (devotional service by following the rules and regulations), and 2. *rāga-mārga* (spontaneous devotional service). You and I are qualified to follow the path of *vaidha-mārga*. Later, we will hear about the *rāga-mārga*, but first we should hear about the *vaidha-mārga*. Then we will be able to practice *sādhana-bhakti*."

"After hearing the saintly *bābājī*'s description of the nine processes of devotional service, I do not understand how to begin. Today, I will ask him about that."

The two of them spent the day discussing many things. Then, garlanded with rays of light, the sun approached the western horizon. Again and again exclaiming, "Haribol! Haribol!" our two saintly devotees entered Śrīvāsa's courtyard, offered *daṇḍavat* obeisances to the circle of Vaiṣṇavas, and entered the elderly *bābājī*'s cottage. Seeing the two devotees eager to ask questions, the saintly *bābājī* happily embraced them and offered them sitting places made of banana leaves. The two devotees offered *daṇḍavat* obeisances, sat down, and after some conversation, revealed their questions.

Vijaya-kumāra: O master, we give so you so much trouble. Still, because you are merciful to the devotees, you kindly accept the inconveniences we bring. Today we would like to hear from your mouth Śrīla Rūpa Gosvāmī's description of the sixty-four limbs of devotional service. If you are inclined to be merciful to us, then please kindly describe how we may easily attain pure devotional service.

Smiling, the saintly *bābājī* said, "I will describe to you the sixty-four limbs of devotional service that Śrīla Rūpa Gosvāmī mentions in his book. Here are the first ten of those sixty-four: 1. Accepting the shelter of the lotus feet of a bona fide spiritual master, 2. Becoming initiated by the spiritual master and learning how to discharge devotional service from him, 3. Obeying the orders of the spiritual master with faith and devotion, 4. Following in the footsteps of the great *ācāryas* (teachers), under the direction of the spiritual master, 5. Inquiring from the spiritual master how to advance in Kṛṣṇa consciousness, 6. Being prepared to give up anything material for the satisfaction of the Supreme Personality of Godhead, Śrī Kṛṣṇa (this means that when we are engaged in the devotional service of Kṛṣṇa, we must be prepared to give up something which we may not like to give up, and also we may have to accept something which we may not like to accept), 7. Residing in a sacred place of pilgrimage like Dvārakā or Vṛndāvana, 8. Accepting only what is necessary, or dealing with the material world only as far as necessary, 9. Observing the fasting day on Ekādaśī, and 10. Worshiping sacred trees, like the banyan tree.

The next ten limbs of devotional service are prohibitions that should be carefully followed. They are: 11) One should rigidly give up the company of non-devotees. 12. One should not instruct a person who is not desirous of accepting devotional service. 13. One should not be very enthusiastic about constructing costly temples or monasteries. 14. One should not try to read too many books, nor should one develop the idea of earning his livelihood by lecturing on or professionally reciting *Śrīmad-Bhāgavatam* or *Bhagavad-gītā*. 15. One should not be neglectful in ordinary dealings. 16. One should not be under the spell of lamentation in loss or jubilation in gain. 17. One should not disrespect the demigods. 18. One should not give unnecessary trouble to any living entity. 19. One should carefully avoid the various offenses in chanting the holy name of the Lord, or in worshiping the Deity in the temple. 20. One should be very intolerant toward the blasphemy of the Supreme Personality of Godhead, Kṛṣṇa, or His devotees.

These twenty limbs are the gateway to devotional service. Among them, the first three, beginning with accepting the shelter of the lotus feet of a bona fide spiritual master, are the most important. The next limbs are: 21. One should decorate the body with *tilaka*, which is the sign of the Vaiṣṇavas. 22. In marking such *tilaka*, one may sometimes write Hare Kṛṣṇa on the body. 23. One should accept flowers and garlands that have been offered to the Deity and the spiritual master and put them on one's body. 24. One should learn to dance before the Deity. 25. One should learn to bow down immediately upon seeing the Deity or the spiritual master. 26. As soon as one visits a temple of Lord Kṛṣṇa, one must stand up. 27. When the Deity is being borne for a stroll in the street, a devotee should immediately follow the procession. 28. A devotee must visit a Viṣṇu temple at least once or twice every day, morning and evening. 29. One must circumambulate the temple building at least three times. 30. One must worship the Deity in the temple according to the regulative principles. 31. One must render personal service to the Deities. 32. One must sing. 33. One must perform *sankīrtana*. 34. One must chant. 35. One must offer prayers. 36. One must recite notable prayers. 37. One must taste *mahā-prasāda* (food from the very plate offered before the Deities). 38. One must drink *caraṇāmṛta* (water from the bathing of the Deities, which is offered to guests). 39. One must smell the incense and flowers offered to the Deity. 40. One must touch the lotus feet of the Deity. 41. One must see the Deity with great devotion. 42. One must offer *ārati* at different times. 43. One must hear about the Lord and His pastimes from *Śrīmad-Bhāgavatam*, *Bhagavad-gītā*, and similar books. 44. One must pray to the Deity for His mercy. 45. One should remember the Deity. 46. One should meditate upon the Deity. 47. One should render some voluntary service. 48. One should think of the Lord as one's friend. 49. One should offer everything the Lord. 50. One should offer a favorite article (such as food or a garment). 51. One should take all kinds of risks and perform all endeavors for Kṛṣṇa's benefit. 52. In every condition, one should be a surrendered soul. 53. One should pour water on the *tulasī* tree. 54. One should regularly hear *Śrīmad-Bhāgavatam* and similar literature. 55. One should live in a sacred place, like Mathurā, Vṛndāvana or Dvārakā. 56. One should offer service to Vaiṣṇavas. 57. One should arrange for one's devotional service according to one's means. 58. In the month of Kārttika (October and November), one should make arrangements for special services. 59. During Janmāṣṭamī (the time of Kṛṣṇa's appearance in this world), one should observe a special service. 60. One should do whatever is done with great care and devotion for the Deity. 61. One should relish the pleasure of *Bhāgavatam* reading among devotees and not among scholars. 62. One should associate with devotees who are considered more advanced. 63. One should chant the holy name of the Lord. 64. One should live in the jurisdiction of Mathurā.

Although they had already been mentioned in the list, the last five items are repeated because they are very important. Please know that all these limbs describe how to worship Lord Kṛṣṇa with one's body, senses, and mind. Items twenty-one through forty-nine in the second part describe initiation into the worship of Lord Kṛṣṇa.

Vijaya-kumāra: O master, please explain to us the first item. What does accepting the shelter of the lotus feet of a bona fide spiritual master mean?

Bābājī: The disciple should be qualified to engage in pure devotional service. To learn the science of Kṛṣṇa, the disciple should take shelter of the spiritual master's lotus feet. Any person who has faith is qualified to engage in devotional service. When, after many births of pious deeds, one hears the descriptions of Lord Hari from a saintly devotee's mouth, and from that hearing develops strong faith in Lord Hari, that strong faith is called *śraddhā*. From that *śraddhā* (faith) comes *śaraṇāpatti* (surrender). Faith and surrender are almost the same thing. Devotion to Lord Kṛṣṇa is the most valuable thing in the world.

One should think, "I will do whatever is favorable for devotional service to Lord Kṛṣṇa. I will avoid whatever is not favorable for devotional service to Lord Kṛṣṇa. Lord Kṛṣṇa is my only protector. I am confident that Lord Kṛṣṇa will always protect me. I am very poor and worthless. It is not good that I desire to be independent. I should do whatever Lord Kṛṣṇa desires."

A person who thinks in this way has firm faith. He is qualified to engage in unalloyed devotional service. When a person becomes qualified in this way, he becomes very eager to learn the science of devotional service. To learn it, he accepts the shelter of the lotus feet of a bona fide spiritual master.

The *Vedas* (*Muṇḍaka Upaniṣad* 1.2.12) declare: "To learn transcendental subject matter, one must approach the spiritual master. In doing so, he should carry fuel to burn in sacrifice. The symptom of such a spiritual master is that he is expert in understanding the Vedic conclusion and therefore, he constantly engages in the service of the Supreme Personality of Godhead.

It is also said (*Chāndogya Upaniṣad* 6.14.2): One who approaches a bona fide spiritual master can understand everything about spiritual realization.

The qualifications of a bona fide spiritual master and a bona fide disciple are elaborately described in *Śrī Hari-bhakti-vilāsa*. The gist of that description is this: A person who has faith and a pure character is qualified to be a disciple. A person who is engaged in pure devotional service, who knows the science of devotional service, whose character is saintly, who is honest, straightforward, and sincere, who is not greedy, who is not an impersonalist, and who is expert in performing his spiritual duties is qualified to be a bona fide spiritual master.

A *brāhmaṇa* who has these qualities and who is honored by all others may become a spiritual master of the other castes. In the absence of such a *brāhmaṇa*, a person may become a spiritual master if he is superior to his disciple. The root meaning of these rules is that, regardless of his status in the *varṇāśrama* social system, any person who knows the science of Kṛṣṇa can become a spiritual master. *Brāhmaṇas* who are proud of their high status in the material world may like to accept a spiritual master who is a *brāhmaṇa*, but the truth is that any person who is a pure devotee of the Lord is qualified to be a bona fide spiritual master.

The scriptures describe a time of testing, when the spiritual master and disciple examine each other. That test is to enable the spiritual master to know whether the prospective disciple is truly qualified, and also to enable the prospective disciple to know whether the spiritual master is truly a pure devotee of the Lord. When the disciple has faith that the spiritual master is qualified, the bona fide spiritual master bestows his mercy on the disciple.

There are two kinds of spiritual masters: 1. *dīkṣā-guru* (initiating spiritual master) and 2. *śikṣā-guru* (instructing spiritual master). The *dīkṣā-guru* gives initiation and teaches how to worship the Lord. One may accept only one *dīkṣā-guru*, but one may accept many *śikṣā-gurus*. The *dīkṣā-guru* may also perform the duties of a *śikṣā-guru*.

Vijaya-kumāra: The disciple is not allowed to reject his *dīkṣā-guru*. But if the *dīkṣā-guru* is not qualified to teach, how can he instruct the disciple?

Bābājī: At the time of choosing the spiritual master, the prospective disciple should test to see whether the spiritual master has traveled to the farther shore of the Vedic scriptures and the science of the Supreme Lord. The spiritual master must be qualified to teach all aspects of the spiritual science. The disciple is not allowed to reject his *dīkṣā-guru*. However, there are two circumstances where the disciple must reject his *dīkṣā-guru*. If, at the time of choosing a spiritual master, the disciple did not test to see whether the spiritual master was a Vaiṣṇava and learned in the spiritual science, the disciple may reject the spiritual master. Or, if it is seen that in the course of his activities, the spiritual master does what he should not do, then the disciple may also reject the spiritual master.

Again and again, the scriptures give testimony to prove these points. In the *Nārada-pañcarātra* (quoted in *Hari-bhakti-vilāsa* 1.101) it is said: A spiritual master who speaks wrongly, without logic, and a disciple who hears wrongly, without logic, both go to a terrible hell for a long time that seems not to end.

It is also said (*Mahābhārata*, *Udyoga-parva* 179.25): A spiritual master who is materialistic, who does not know what should be done and what should not be done, and who follows the wrong path, should be rejected."

It is also said (quoted in *Hari-bhakti-vilāsa* 4.144): A person who accepts *mantra* initiation from a non-Vaiṣṇava goes to hell. A person initiated in this way should accept initiation again, this time from a Vaiṣṇava spiritual master.

A second reason for rejecting the spiritual master is this: If, at the time of choosing the spiritual master, the spiritual master was a Vaiṣṇava and learned in the spiritual science but by bad association, the spiritual master became an impersonalist and a hater of Vaiṣṇavas, then that spiritual master should be rejected. If one accepts a spiritual master who is neither an impersonalist nor a hater of Vaiṣṇavas, nor sinful, but is not very learned, then that spiritual master should not be rejected. One should honor that spiritual master. However, with the spiritual master's permission, one should approach another Vaiṣṇava, serve him, and learn from him the spiritual science.

Vijaya-kumāra: What does becoming initiated (*kṛṣṇa-dīkṣā*) by the spiritual master and learning (*kṛṣṇa-śikṣā*) how to discharge devotional service from him mean?

Bābājī: From the spiritual master, one should learn the path of devotional service to Lord Kṛṣṇa and the science of understanding Lord Kṛṣṇa. Applying that knowledge, one should sincerely serve Lord Kṛṣṇa and cultivate Kṛṣṇa consciousness in one's heart. In this way, one should learn the different limbs of worshiping the Lord. At the spiritual master's lotus feet, one should learn *sambandha* (the soul's relationship with Lord Kṛṣṇa), *abhidheya* (devotional service to Lord Kṛṣṇa), and *prayojana* (love for Lord Kṛṣṇa).

Vijaya-kumāra: What does obeying the orders of the spiritual master with faith and devotion mean?

Bābājī: Don't think your spiritual master is an ordinary human being.

Know that he is the embodiment of all the demigods. Never disrespect him. Know that he is a resident of the spiritual world.

Vijaya-kumāra: What does following the footsteps of great *ācāryas* (teachers) under the direction of the spiritual master mean?

Bābājī: Anything at all that makes the mind think of Lord Kṛṣṇa may be considered *sādhana-bhakti*. However, one should follow the path traversed by the great devotees. That path will always be free from sufferings, the cause of all auspiciousness, and free from obstacles. In the *Skanda Purāṇa* it is said: One should follow the path of the great devotees, for that path is free of sufferings and obstacles.

One person by himself cannot determine what is the best path. Therefore, one should follow the devotional path that was walked by the great devotees. In the *Brahma-yāmala* it is said: Devotional service to the Lord that ignores the authorized Vedic literatures like the *Upaniṣads*, *Purāṇas*, *Nārada-pañcarātra*, etc., is simply an unnecessary disturbance in society.

Vijaya-kumāra: How is it that unalloyed devotional service can become an unnecessary disturbance in society? Please explain clearly?

Bābājī: Unalloyed devotional service can be attained only by following the path walked by the previous great devotees. If one creates a new path, he expects to follow it to unalloyed devotional service. Dattātreya, Buddha, and other recent thinkers were not able to understand the truth of pure devotional service. Some taught a philosophy mixed with impersonalism, and others a philosophy mixed with atheism. They taught horrible and ugly philosophies they imagined would lead to unalloyed devotional service to Lord Hari, but in truth did not at all lead to devotional service. Their philosophies became a disturbance to society.

On the other hand, the path of *rāga-mārga* (spontaneous love) does not depend on the rules presented in the authorized Vedic literatures like the *Upaniṣads*, *Purāṇas*, *Nārada-pañcarātra*, etc. Rather, it follows the path walked by the people of Vraja. However, the devotees qualified only to follow the path of *vidhi-mārga* (performing devotional service according to the rules and regulations) must flow the devotional path walked by Dhruva, Prahlāda, Nārada, Vyāsa, Śukadeva, and other great souls. For the devotees on the path of *vidhi-*

bhakti, there is no alternative but to follow the path of the great devotees.

Vijaya-kumāra: What does inquiring from the spiritual master how to advance in Kṛṣṇa consciousness mean?

Bābājī: Persons who are very eager to understand the spiritual truth quickly attain all they desire. "Very eager" here means that they ask saintly devotees to explain the truth of spiritual life.

Vijaya-kumāra: What does being prepared to give up anything material for the satisfaction of the Supreme Personality of Godhead, Kṛṣṇa, mean?

Bābājī: The pleasures attained by eating palatable foods, the pleasures of marriage, and other such pleasures are called material sense pleasures. These pleasures are all obstacles on the path of devotional service. One who renounces them for the sake of worshiping Lord Kṛṣṇa makes easy progress in devotional service. A person attached to material sense pleasures becomes addicted to them in the same way an alcoholic becomes addicted to liquor. Overcome by powerful material desires, he cannot attain pure devotional service. Therefore, one should eat only *prasādam* offered to the Supreme Lord, and then only enough to keep the body fit to engage in devotional service, and one should also fast on Ekādaśī. In this way, one can completely renounce material sense pleasures.

Vijaya-kumāra: What does residing at a sacred place of pilgrimage like Dvārakā or Vṛndāvana mean?

Bābājī: When one lives at the holy places where the Supreme Lord was born or enjoyed pastimes, or at places by the Ganges, or other sacred rivers, one naturally attains faith in devotional service.

Vijaya-kumāra: Is living at Śrī Navadvīpa purifying only because it is by the Ganges, or is there another reason?

Bābājī: Ah! Living within the thirty-two mile area of Śrī Navadvīpa is exactly like living in Śrī Vṛndāvana. This is especially true for Śrī Māyāpura. Seven holy cities are famous for granting liberation. They are: Ayodhya, Mathurā, Māyāpura, Vārāṇasī, Kāñcī, Avantīpura, and Dvārakā. Of them, Māyāpura is the most important. Śrī Mahāprabhu brought the spiritual world of Śvetadvīpa to Māyāpura. Four hundred years after Lord Mahāprabhu's appearance, this land of Māyāpura-Śvetadvīpa will be the most important of all holy places. A person who lives in this place throws all offenses far away and easily attains pure devotional service. Śrī Prabodhānanda Sarasvatī said that this abode of Navadvīpa is not different from Śrī Vṛndāvana. Indeed, he said it was more glorious than Vṛndāvana.

Vijaya-kumāra: What does accepting only what is necessary, or dealing with the material world only as far as necessary, mean?

Bābājī: In the *Nārada Purāṇa* it is written: One should earn and spend money only as far as he truly needs. If one does it too much or too little, he will fall from the spiritual goal.

A person eligible to perform *vaidhī-bhakti* should earn his livelihood by honest means according to *varṇāśrama*. In that way, he will attain auspiciousness. If he becomes greedy for more than he needs, his devotional life will become stunted. If he accepts less than he truly needs, he will gradually become unable to perform devotional activities and in that way, he will also be at fault. As long as one is not able to completely renounce everything, he should collect only as much money as he truly needs for his spiritual life. In this way, he will be able to properly cultivate his Kṛṣṇa consciousness.

Vijaya-kumāra: What does observing the fasting day on Ekādaśī mean?

Bābājī: Pure Ekādaśī is called *hari-vāsara*. One should not observe Ekādaśī when it is interrupted (*viddhā*) by another *tithi*. When there is a Mahā-dvādaśī, that should be observed, and not the Ekādaśī. On the day before Ekādaśī, one should observe celibacy, on the day of Ekādaśī, one should fast completely, avoiding even water, and one should also worship Lord Hari during an all-night vigil. On the day after Ekādaśī, one should continue his observance of celibacy and one should also break his fast at the appropriate time. In this way, one should observe Ekādaśī. During Ekādaśī, one should also fast from *mahā-prasāda* for otherwise, fasting from even water has no meaning. For persons unable to fast completely, certain specific foods may be taken during Ekādaśī. This is described in *Hari-bhakti-vilāsa* in the passage beginning with verse 12.97.

Vijaya-kumāra: What does worshiping sacred trees, like the banyan tree, mean?

Bābājī: In the *Skanda Purāṇa* it is written: "When they are worshiped, meditated on, or bowed down before, the banyan tree, the *tulasī* tree, the *dhātrī* tree, the cows, the earth, the demigods, and the Vaiṣṇavas destroy the sins of the people.

A householder eligible to perform *vaidhī-bhakti* should, in the course of his life, meditate on and bow down before the *aśvattha* and other shade-giving trees, the *dhātrī* and other fruit-giving trees, *tulasī* and other sacred trees, the cows and other animals that do good to the people of the world, the *brāhmaṇas*, who are the teachers of religion and the protectors of true civilization, and the Vaiṣṇava devotees of the Lord. In this way, they should live in this world.

Vijaya-kumāra: What does it mean that one should rigidly give up the company of non-devotees?

Bābājī: When spiritual love arises in the heart, one's devotion to the Lord becomes intense. As long as love does not arise in that way, one must avoid the association of persons opposed to devotional service. Here, the word association means "attachment." When, in the course of ordinary activities, one casually comes into contact with other people—that is not association as meant here. When, by contact with others, one develops a desire to associate with them—that is association. Therefore, association with persons averse to the Supreme Lord should be carefully avoided. When love for the Lord arises within the heart, it is not possible that one will desire to associate with persons averse to the Lord. Therefore, persons who are situated in the stage of *vaidhī-bhakti* should carefully avoid association with persons averse to the Lord. As a very hot summer breeze can wilt vines growing on trees, so association with persons averse to Lord Kṛṣṇa can wilt the vine of devotional service.

Vijaya-kumāra: Who are the non-devotees?

Bābājī: Four kinds of people are averse to Lord Kṛṣṇa. They are: 1. Persons who have no devotion to Lord Kṛṣṇa, 2. Persons addicted to material sense gratification and association with women, 3. Persons whose hearts are polluted by atheism and impersonalism, and 4. Persons dulled by working for material gain. One should stay far away from the company of these four kinds of persons.

Vijaya-kumāra: What does it mean that one should not instruct a person who is not desirous of accepting devotional service?

Bābājī: If, greedy to accumulate money, a spiritual master accepts many disciples, he is greatly at fault. If a spiritual master accepts many disciples, then some of them will likely be unqualified persons who do not have faith in devotional service. To accept such persons as disciples is an offense. Only a person who has faith is fit to be a disciple.

Vijaya-kumāra: What does it mean, that one should not be very enthusiastic about constructing costly temples or monasteries?

Bābājī: Live simply and engage in devotional service to the Lord. Don't be attached to great pomp or activities that require unnecessary endeavor. They will not push the heart to worship the Lord.

Vijaya-kumāra: What does it mean, that one should not try to read too many books, nor should one develop the idea of earning his livelihood by lecturing on or professionally reciting *Śrīmad-Bhāgavatam* or *Bhagavad-gītā*?

Bābājī: The scriptures are like an ocean. If one wants to learn a particular subject, he should carefully study, from beginning to end, the books describing that subject. If one merely reads a little from one book and a little from another, he will not learn the subject properly. Thus, if one does not study them carefully and completely, one will not properly understand the scriptures describing devotional service. One should accept the straightforward, obvious interpretations of the scriptures. One should not struggle to construe obscure, contradictory, opposite meanings from them.

Vijaya-kumāra: What does it mean, that one should not be neglectful in ordinary dealings?

Bābājī: To maintain the material body, one requires food and clothing. If one cannot get these things, he is troubled, and if he loses them, he is also troubled. If he is troubled in these ways, a devotee of the Lord should not become agitated at heart. Rather, he should continue to fix his thoughts on Lord Hari.

Vijaya-kumāra: What does it mean, that one should not be under the spell of lamentation in loss or jubilation in gain?

Bābājī: How is it possible that Lord Kṛṣṇa's spiritual form could appear in a heart overpowered by lamentation, fear, anger, greed, envy, and other vices? A person engaged in *sādhana-bhakti* may feel lamentation, bewilderment, or other inauspicious sentiments, because of being separated from relatives, thwarted in desires, or other problems. However, it is not good to be overpowered by lamentation, bewilderment, and other such inauspicious things. Separation from one's children and other unhappy events inevitably lead to lamentation. However, one should fix his thoughts on Lord Hari and in this way, quickly throw these inauspicious emotions far away. In this way, one should fix his mind on the lotus feet of Lord Hari.

Vijaya-kumāra: What does it mean, that one should not disrespect the demigods? Does this mean that it is right to worship the demigods?

Bābājī: One should have unalloyed devotion to Lord Kṛṣṇa. One should not worship the demigods, thinking them to be independent of Lord Kṛṣṇa. However, when you see other people worshiping the demigods, you should not be disrespectful to the demigods. You should honor the demigods, but always remember that all the demigods worship Lord Kṛṣṇa. As long as the heart remains in the grip of the three material modes, one cannot attain unalloyed devotion to Lord Kṛṣṇa. Only persons overpowered by goodness, passion, and ignorance worship the demigods with the idea that the demigods are equal to Lord Kṛṣṇa. These persons are qualified only to have faith in the demigods. Therefore, one should not disrespect their method of worship. By the mercy of the demigods, these persons will gradually become elevated. Eventually, their hearts will become free of the three material modes.

Vijaya-kumāra: What does it mean, that one should not give unnecessary trouble to any living entity?

Bābājī: Lord Kṛṣṇa is quickly pleased by merciful persons who refrain from bringing suffering to others. Mercy is one of the most important virtues of a Vaiṣṇava.

Vijaya-kumāra: What does it mean, that one should carefully avoid various offenses in chanting the holy name of the Lord, or in worshiping the Deity in the temple?

Bābājī: One should avoid offenses in worshiping the Lord, and one should especially avoid offenses to the holy name. Beginning with riding a palanquin into the Lord's temple and wearing shoes in the Lord's temple, there are thirty-two offenses in worshiping the Lord. Beginning with blaspheming the devotees who have dedicated their lives to preaching the glories of the Lord, there are ten offenses to the holy name. All these offenses should be avoided.

Vijaya-kumāra: What does it mean that one should be very intolerant toward the blasphemy of the Supreme Personality of Godhead, Kṛṣṇa, or His devotees? Does this teaching mean that one should at once verbally attack the blasphemer?

Bābājī: A person who blasphemes Lord Kṛṣṇa or a Vaiṣṇava must be averse to Lord Kṛṣṇa. One should not tolerate their blasphemies. One should react by casting the willingness to associate with them far away.

Vijaya-kumāra: What is the relationship between these first twenty limbs of devotional service with the other limbs?

Bābājī: The next forty-four limbs are actually included in these first twenty limbs. They are described separately in order to give a more detailed explanation. Thirty limbs, beginning with, "One should decorate the body with *tilaka*, which is the sign of the Vaiṣṇavas," and culminating in, "One should offer a favorite article (such as food or a garment)," are included within the path of Deity worship (*arcana-mārga*). These limbs are: 21. One should wear three strands of *tulasī* beads around his neck and decorate his body with twelve *tilaka* markings. These is called, "the sign of the Vaiṣṇavas." 22. To write Hare Kṛṣṇa, other names of Lord Kṛṣṇa, or the names of the Pañca-tattva on the upper part of the body with sandalwood paste, is called, "marking the holy name on the body."

23. That one should accept flowers and garlands that have been offered to the Deity and the spiritual master and put them on one's body is described in these words of *Śrīmad-Bhāgavatam* 11.6.31, where Uddhava tells Lord Kṛṣṇa: My dear Lord, the garlands, scented substances, garments, ornaments, and other such things that have been offered to You may later be used by Your servants. By partaking of these things and eating the remnants of food You have left, we will be able to conquer the illusory energy.

The next limbs of devotional service are: 24. One should learn to dance before the Deity. 25. One should learn to bow down immediately upon seeing the Deity or the spiritual master. 26 As soon as one visits a temple of Lord Kṛṣṇa, one must stand up. 27. When the Deity is being borne for a stroll in the street, a devotee should immediately follow the procession. 28. A devotee must visit a Viṣṇu temple at least once or twice every day, morning and evening.

29. One must circumambulate the temple building at least three times. 30. One must worship the Deity in the temple according to the regulative principles. For these items, no separate explanation is needed. 31. One must render personal service to the Deities is explained in this verse (*Bhakti-rasāmṛta-sindhu* 1.2.61): One should serve the Deity with a parasol, *cāmara*, instrumental music, and many other offerings. This is called worship.

The next items are: 32. One must sing. 33. One must perform *saṅkīrtana*. 34. One must chant. 35. One must offer prayers. 36. One must recite notable prayers. 37. One must taste *mahā-prasāda* (food from the very plate offered before the Deities). 38. One must drink *caraṇāmṛta* (water from the bathing of the Deities, which is offered to guests). 39. One must smell the incense and flowers offered to the Deity. 40. One must touch the lotus feet of the Deity. 41. One must see the Deity with great devotion. 42. One must offer *ārati* at different times. 43. One must hear about the Lord and His pastimes from *Śrīmad-Bhāgavatam*, *Bhagavad-gītā*, and similar books. 44. One must pray to the Deity for His mercy. 45. One should remember the Deity. 46. One should meditate upon the Deity. 47. One should render some voluntary service. 48. One should think of the Lord as one's friend. 49. One should offer everything to the Lord (*ātmā-nivedana*). Here, *ātmā* means the idea of "I" in relation to the material body, and the idea of "mine" in relation to the material body. These two things one should surrender (*nivedana*) to Kṛṣṇa.

Vijaya-kumāra: Please clearly explain these two things: the idea of "I" in relation to the material body and the idea of "mine" in relation to the material body.

Bābājī: Residing in the material body, the conditioned soul thinks, "I am this material body," or "This material body is mine." Both these ideas should be surrendered, offered to Lord Kṛṣṇa. Thus renouncing the ideas, "I am this material body," and "This material body is mine," one should think, "I am a servant of Lord Kṛṣṇa," and "I am dependent on Lord Kṛṣṇa's mercy," and "this material body is a machine that I shall use in Lord Kṛṣṇa's service." To spend one's time within this material body in this way is called *ātmā-nivedana* (offering everything to the Lord).

Vijaya-kumāra: What does it mean, that one should offer a favorite article (such as food or a garment)?

Bābājī: In this material world, many things become dear to a person. To accept the relation that all these things have to Lord Kṛṣṇa is called, "offering a favorite article."

Vijaya-kumāra: What does it mean that one should take all kinds of risks and perform all endeavors for Kṛṣṇa's benefit?

Bābājī: Whatever Vedic or ordinary duties there are in the material world should be performed in such a way that they advance devotional service to Lord Kṛṣṇa. That is performing all endeavors for Kṛṣṇa's benefit.

Vijaya-kumāra: What does it mean that in every condition, one should be a surrendered soul?

Bābājī: To think, "O Lord, I am Yours," and "O Lord, I surrender unto You" is called, "being a surrendered soul."

Vijaya-kumāra: What does it mean, that one should pour water on the *tulasī* tree?

Bābājī: There are nine kinds of service to *tulasī*. They are: 1. Seeing *tulasī*, 2. Touching *tulasī*, 3. Meditating on *tulasī*, 4. Glorifying *tulasī*, 5. Offering obeisances to *tulasī*, 6. Hearing the glories of *tulasī*, 7. Planting *tulasī*, 8. Serving *tulasī*, and 9 Regularly worshiping *tulasī*. In these nine ways, *tulasī* is glorious in the context of service to Lord Kṛṣṇa.

Vijaya-kumāra: What does it mean that one should regularly hear *Śrīmad-Bhāgavatam* and similar literature?

Bābājī: Books that explain the science of devotional service offered to Lord Kṛṣṇa are called *śāstra* (scriptures). Among all scriptures, *Śrīmad-Bhāgavatam* is the best, for it is the essence of the *Vedas* and *Vedānta*. A person who relishes the nectar of *Śrīmad-Bhāgavatam* is no longer attracted to other scriptures.

Vijaya-kumāra: What does it mean, that one should live in a sacred place, like Mathurā, Vṛndāvana, or Dvārakā?

Bābājī: One should hear about, remember, glorify, visit, touch, reside in, and serve Mathurā. In this way, one will attain his spiritual desires.. Know that the same applies to Śrī Māyāpura.

Vijaya-kumāra: What does it mean, that one should offer service to

Vaiṣṇavas?

Bābājī: The Vaiṣṇavas are very dear to the Supreme Lord. By serving the Vaiṣṇavas, one renders devotional service to the Lord. In the scriptures it is said:

Although the *Vedas* mention worship of demigods, the worship of Lord Viṣṇu is topmost, and is ultimately recommended. However, above the worship of Lord Viṣṇu is the rendering of service to Vaiṣṇavas, who are related to Lord Viṣṇu.

Vijaya-kumāra: What does it mean, that one should arrange for one's devotional service according to one's means?

Bābājī: As far as one is able, one should collect various things, offer them to the Deity of the Lord in the temple, and then offer them again to the Vaiṣṇavas. This is called *mahotsava* (a great festival). In the entire world, no festival is better than this.

Vijaya-kumāra: What does it mean that in the month of Kārttika (October and November), one should make arrangements for special services?

Bābājī: The month of Kārttika is also called Ūrja. To render devotional service to Lord Dāmodara by hearing and chanting His glories, and in other ways, also is called Ūrjadara (worship in the month of Kārttika).

Vijaya-kumāra: What does it mean that during Janmāṣṭamī (the time of Kṛṣṇa's appearance in this world), one should observe a special service?

Bābājī: To celebrate a great festival on Lord Kṛṣṇa's appearance day, on the eighth day of the dark fortnight in the month of Bhādra, and again on the full moon day of the month of Phalguṇa, is called Śrī Janma-yātrā (the birth festivals). The surrendered souls should observe these festivals.

Vijaya-kumāra: What does it mean, that one should do whatever is done with great care and devotion for the Deity?

Bābājī: With a heart filled with love and enthusiasm, one should always carefully serve the Deity of the Lord. To a devotee thus engaged, the Lord does not give the pathetic and worthless gift of impersonal liberation. Rather, the Lord gives the great gift of devotional service.

Vijaya-kumāra: What does it mean, that one should relish the pleasure of *Bhāgavatam* reading among devotees and not among outsiders?

Bābājī: *Śrīmad-Bhāgavatam* is the mature fruit of the desire tree of Vedic literatures. One should not taste the sweetness of *Śrīmad-Bhāgavatam* in the company of persons who are not qualified to taste the nectar of transcendental *rasas*. Offenses will result. Therefore, one should read the verses of *Śrīmad-Bhāgavatam* and taste their nectar only with pure devotees, who thirst to taste the nectar of Lord Kṛṣṇa's pastimes, and who have the power to know the sweetness that is in *Śrīmad-Bhāgavatam*. Reciting and hearing *Śrīmad-Bhāgavatam* in the company of non-devotees does not lead to pure devotional service.

Vijaya-kumāra: What does it mean, that one should associate with devotees who are considered more advanced?

Bābājī: One should associate with devotees. If one associates with non-devotees, he will not make progress in devotional service. Devotees yearn to directly serve Lord Kṛṣṇa in His transcendental pastimes. Persons who have that desire are called *bhaktas* (devotees). If we associate with more advanced devotees, then we make progress in devotional service. If we do not, our progress stops. We become like our associates. In the scriptures (*Hari-bhakti-sudhodaya* 8.51) it is written: Association is very important. It acts just like a crystal stone, which will reflect anything which is put before it.

Vijaya-kumāra: What does it mean, that one should chant the holy name of the Lord?

Bābājī: The holy name of the Lord is not material. Rather, it is spiritual, conscious, and full of nectar. It has not the slightest scent of matter. When a living entity desires to serve the Lord, and when he becomes purified by engaging in devotional service, the holy name of the Lord personally appears on his tongue. The holy name of the Lord cannot be understood by the material senses. Therefore, one should always, either alone or in the company of others, chant the holy name of the Lord.

Vijaya-kumāra: By your kindness, I have understood the meaning of the sixty-fourth limb of devotional service—that one should live in the jurisdiction of Mathura. Now, please explain the essence of all these limbs of devotional service.

Bābājī: The last five limbs are the best. By remaining free of offenses and performing these last five items even slightly, one makes wonderful progress in devotional service and attains ecstatic love for the Lord.

Vijaya-kumāra: Please describe whatever else I should know about *sādhana-bhakti.*

Bābājī: Sometimes the scriptures describe many non-devotional benefits to be attained by practicing the different activities of devotional service. These benefits are given to attract materialistic people, who otherwise would have no interest in devotional service. Still, the most important result attained by performing any of the different activities of devotional service is the attainment of attraction and love for Lord Kṛṣṇa. Wise persons who know the truth about devotional service value the different limbs of devotional service and reject materialistic, fruitive activities.

Jñāna (knowledge) and *vairāgya* (renunciation) may give a little help in making a person qualified to enter the temple of devotional service, but still they are not counted among the limbs of devotional service. They make the heart hard, whereas devotional service makes the heart soft and gentle. Therefore, knowledge and renunciation should be accepted only when they come from devotional service. Knowledge and renunciation do not bring devotional service. Devotional service easily gives blessings that knowledge and renunciation can never give. By engaging in *sādhana-bhakti* and worshipping Lord Hari, one attains attraction and love for Lord Hari. At that time, one's attraction for material sense objects disappears.

The aspiring devotee must accept appropriate renunciation (*yukta-vairāgya*) and he also must reject false renunciation (*phalgu-vairāgya*). To accept material things when they have a relationship with Lord Kṛṣṇa is called *yukta-vairāgya* (proper renunciation). To reject, in the hope of attaining impersonal liberation, material things when they have a relationship with Kṛṣṇa is called *phalgu-vairāgya* (false renunciation). One should reject impersonal speculation and false renunciation. To make a show of devotional service in order to attain wealth, disciples, and other material things, is very far from genuine, pure devotional service. Such an artificial show of devotional service is not counted among the limbs of true devotional service.

Material intelligence and other material good qualities are not the distinguishing features of a person qualified to engage in devotional service. Therefore, these material good qualities are not among the limbs of devotional service. Control of the mind, control of the senses, purity, good conduct, and other virtues spontaneously appear in a person who is attached to Lord Kṛṣṇa. Still, these virtues are not counted among the limbs of devotional service. Purity of heart, external cleanliness, austerity, peacefulness, and all other virtues voluntarily take shelter in a devotee of Lord Kṛṣṇa. The devotee does not need to strive to attain them.

I have now described all the limbs of devotional service. By faithfully practicing one or many of these limbs, a person will attain perfection. Thus I have briefly described *vaidhī-sādhana-bhakti.* Think about them in your heart, try to understand them, and try to follow them.

After hearing these instructions, Vrajanātha and Vijaya-kumāra offered *daṇḍavat* obeisances to the lotus feet of their spiritual master. They said, "O master, please be merciful to us. Please deliver us. For a long time we have been drowning in the abyss of false pride.

The *bābājī* said, "Lord Kṛṣṇa will be merciful to you."

It was late. The uncle and nephew left for home.

Chapter Twenty-one

Eternal religion and sambandha, abhidheya and prayojana (Abhidheya: rāgānuga-sādhana-bhakti)

The same wonderful thought arose in the hearts of Vijaya-kumāra and Vrajanātha. With one mind, they decided that they must accept initiation (*dīkṣā*) from the saintly *bābājī*. When he was a child, Vijaya-kumāra was initiated by his family *guru*. Vrajanātha had received Gāyatrī initiation but not initiation into any other *mantras*. From the saintly *bābājī*, they had learned that by chanting a *mantra* given by an impersonalist *guru*, one goes to hell. Therefore, they decided to be properly re-initiated by a Vaiṣṇava spiritual master. If he is initiated by a perfect pure devotee, the disciple very quickly attains perfection by chanting the sacred *mantras*.

Therefore they both decided, "Tomorrow morning we will first bathe in the Ganges and then accept initiation from the worshipable and saintly *bābājī*."

Their hearts fixed in that decision, the next morning, they bathed in the Ganges, decorated their bodies with twelve *tilaka* markings as previously described, and then offered *daṇḍavat* obeisances to the lotus feet of Śrīla Raghunātha dāsa Bābājī. The saintly *bābājī* was a perfect devotee.

Aware of what they were thinking, he asked them, "Why have you come this morning?"

The two of them replied, "O master, we are fallen and worthless. Please be merciful to us."

The saintly *bābājī* took them separately to his cottage and gave them the eighteen-syllable *mantra*. Again and again chanting the *mantra*, the two disciples became maddened with spiritual love. Calling out, "Jaya Gaurāṅga!" they danced.

Seeing the *tulasī* beads on their necks, their splendid sacred threads, their twelve *tilaka* marks, their bright faces, some beginning symptoms of *sāttvikā-bhāva* ecstasy on their bodies, and streams of tears flowing from their eyes, the saintly *bābājī* embraced them and said, "Today you have purified me."

Again and again, the two disciples took the dust of the saintly *bābājī*'s lotus feet and placed it on their heads. Vrajanātha had arranged that many excellent food preparations would be offered to Lord Mahāprabhu. By his arrangement, two servants from his house brought a great abundance of palatable food.

Vijaya-kumāra and Vrajanātha said to the Vaiṣṇavas, "We have brought this food. Please offer it to Lord Mahāprabhu."

The leader of the devotees at Śrīvāsa's courtyard had the *pujāri* cook the food and offer it to the Pañca-tattva Deities. The conchshell sounded. Playing *karatālas* and *mṛdaṅgas*, the Vaiṣṇavas sang as the *bhoga-ārati* was offered to Lord Mahāprabhu. Gradually, many Vaiṣṇavas came. They were all filled with happiness. The *ārati* ended gloriously. A place was arranged before the temple for the Vaiṣṇavas to honor the *prasādam*. Loudly chanting the holy names of Lord Hari, each Vaiṣṇava brought his bowl. At the time of honoring *prasādam*, poetry was read. The Vaiṣṇavas sat down to honor the *prasādam*.

Vrajanātha and Vijaya-kumāra would not sit down and place the *prasādam* in their mouths. The leaders of the *bābājīs* forced them to sit. The *bābājīs* said, "You are householders who have become Vaiṣṇavas. Therefore, by offering *daṇḍavat* obeisances to your feet, we become fortunate."

Vijaya-kumāra and Vrajanātha said, "You are great *sannyāsī* Vaiṣṇavas. Therefore, by accepting the nectarean remnants of the *prasādam* that has touched your lips, we become most fortunate. If we associate with you as equals, it will be an offense on our part."

The Vaiṣṇava *bābājīs* said, "Vaiṣṇavas who are householders or *sannyāsīs* are not different. It is devotion to the Lord that makes one a great Vaiṣṇava."

Conversing in this way, all the Vaiṣṇavas honored the *prasādam*. Hoping to get the remnants of the *prasādam* eaten by their spiritual master, Vijaya-kumāra and Vrajanātha hesitated to honor the *prasādam*. Seeing that they were reluctant to honor the *prasādam*, the Vaiṣṇavas said to Śrīla Raghunātha dāsa Bābājī, "O best of the Vaiṣṇavas, please be merciful to your disciples. They will not honor the *prasādam*."

Hearing this, the elderly *bābājī* placed the remnants of his *prasādam* in his disciples' hands. They accepted them as very valuable things. They said, "We offer obeisances to our spiritual master," and then they began to honor the *prasādam*. As the *prasādam* was honored, many descriptions of the glories of *prasādam* were spoken, as also was the advice, "O devotees, please be careful."

Ah! At that time, the area before Śrīvāsa's courtyard was so beautiful. Then, suddenly, the devotees saw Lord Mahāprabhu and His personal associates honoring the *prasādam* with them, and Śrī Śacī, Sītā, and Mālinī-devī were themselves distributing the *prasādam*. The devotees remembered these lines of Śrī Jagadānanda Paṇḍita's *Prema-vivarta*: Lord Gaura enjoys pastimes in Māyāpura eternally. The power of their transcendental pious deeds enables the Lord's devotees to see these pastimes directly.

As long as these pastimes were present before their eyes, the Vaiṣṇavas were stunned and motionless, like a row of columns. No one was honoring the *prasādam*. After a short while, these pastimes again became invisible. The devotees looked at each other and burst into tears. No one could describe the unprecedented wonderful delicious taste the *prasādam* now had.

Everyone said, "These two young *brāhmaṇas* have attained the mercy of Lord Mahāprabhu. Lord Gaura has again revealed His pastimes at their festival."

Weeping and weeping, Vrajanātha and Vijaya-kumāra said, "We are poor and worthless. One thing we know: It is because of the mercy of our spiritual master and the mercy of the Vaiṣṇavas that we have seen these things."

After honoring *prasādam* and taking permission from the Vaiṣṇavas, Vijaya-kumāra and Vrajanātha returned home. From that day forward, every day they would bathe in the Ganges, offer obeisances to the lotus feet of their spiritual master, see the Deity form of the Lord, circumambulate *tulasī*, and perform many other devotional activities. This they did every day. A day did not pass where they did not learn something new.

On the fourth or fifth evening, after concluding their evening duties at Śrīvāsa's courtyard, seeing the *ārati*, and chanting the holy names in *sankīrtana*, the two of them went to the saintly elderly *bābājī* in his cottage and asked him, "O master, by your mercy, we have been able to understand *sādhana-bhakti*. Now we request you, please be merciful and explain *rāgānuga-bhakti* to these two lowest of persons."

The saintly *bābājī* happily replied, "Lord Gaurāṅga has accepted you two as His devotees. Therefore, I cannot withhold anything from you. Please listen carefully and I will explain *rāgānuga-bhakti* to you. Again and again, I offer my respectful obeisances to Śrīla Rūpa Gosvāmī, who the Supreme Personality of Godhead rescued from the clutches of the Yavanas and who, at *Prayāga-kṣetra*, the Lord taught the science of transcendental mellows. I surrender to the lotus feet of Śrīla Raghunātha dāsa Gosvāmī, who the merciful Supreme Personality of Godhead rescued from the abyss of material life, placed in the hand of Śrīla Svarūpa Dāmodara Gosvāmī, and gave the gift of all spiritual perfections.

"However, before I describe *rāgānuga-bhakti*, I shall first describe the nature of *rāgātmikā-bhakti*.

Vrajanātha: Please tell us what the word *rāga* means. I wish to understand that first.

Bābājī: Materialists fall in love with the objects of the material senses. This love may be called *rāga*. In this way, the eyes become excited when they see beauty and other attractive qualities. In this way, one is attracted to the material sense objects and the mind develops *rāga*, or love for them. When that love (*rāga*) is placed in Lord Kṛṣṇa as its only object—that is called *rāga-bhakti*.

Śrīla Rūpa Gosvāmī explains that when love is focused on a single object of desire, that is called *rāga*. When this kind of love exists in devotional service, then the devotional service is called *rāgātmikā-bhakti*. In brief, when there is a love-filled thirst to attain Lord Kṛṣṇa—that is called *rāgātmikā-bhakti*. As long as this *rāga* has not manifested itself, one is enjoined to follow *vidhi-bhakti*, following the rules and regulations of scripture. Awe, fear, and faith are the three aspects of *vaidhī-bhakti*. An intense desire to meet Lord Kṛṣṇa and associate with Him in His pastimes is the main feature of *rāgātmikā-bhakti*.

Vrajanātha: Who is qualified to perform *rāga-bhakti*?

Bābājī: A person whose faith rests in the rules of the scriptures is qualified to engage in *vaidhī-bhakti*. A person whose faith rests in an intense desire to attain Lord Kṛṣṇa is qualified to engage in *rāgātmikā-bhakti*. Manifested according to their different *rasas* (relationships with Lord Kṛṣṇa), Lord Kṛṣṇa's personal associates in the spiritual world of Vraja with strong faith engage in *rāgātmikā-bhakti*. A person who has a strong desire to love Lord Kṛṣṇa like the residents of Vraja in the spiritual world do, is qualified to engage in *rāgānuga-bhakti*.

Vrajanātha: What are the qualities of this strong desire?

Bābājī: One quality is that when one hears about the sweetness of the love and other emotions manifested by the residents of Vraja in the spiritual world, one yearns to go there. When a person qualified to engage in *vaidhī-bhakti* hears the descriptions of Lord Kṛṣṇa, he calmly thinks about these descriptions, using his intelligence, logic, and the evidence of scripture. However, when a person following the path of *rāgānuga-bhakti* hears these descriptions, he does not carefully consider them in terms of intelligence, logic, and scripture. Instead, he is overcome with the desire to love Kṛṣṇa as the residents of Vraja do.

Vrajanātha: What are the activities of *rāgānuga-bhakti*?

Bābājī: The devotee engaged in *rāgānuga-bhakti* yearns to become one of the residents of Vraja in the spiritual world and there serve Lord Kṛṣṇa directly. He always thinks of that desire. He likes to talk with other devotees about the pastimes of his beloved Kṛṣṇa. He resides in Vraja, either with his external body, or within his thoughts. Yearning to attain the spiritual love that they possess, he becomes a follower of the people of Vraja. He always serves the Lord in two ways. Externally, he performs *sādhana-bhakti*. Internally, he thinks of his original spiritual form, and in that form, he serves the Lord.

Vrajanātha: What is the connection between *rāgānuga-bhakti* and the different limbs of *vaidhī-bhakti*?

Bābājī: A person engaged in *rāgānuga-bhakti* also performs the different activities of *sādhana-bhakti*, such as hearing and chanting the glories of the Lord. However, within his heart, he is a follower of the people of Vraja. In this way, he tastes the nectar of always serving the Lord. At the same time, while serving in this way within his heart, he engages in the activities of *sādhana-bhakti* with his external body.

Vrajanātha: How is *rāgānuga-bhakti* glorious?

Bābājī: By engaging in *rāgānuga-bhakti* one quickly attains what takes a long time to attain by performing sādhana-*bhakti*. *Vaidhī-bhakti* is weak, but *rāgānuga-bhakti* is both independent and very powerful. By following in the footsteps of the people of Vraja, one attains *rāga*. That *rāga* naturally pushes one to engage in the devotional activities of hearing, chanting and remembering the Lord's glories, serving His lotus feet, bowing down before Him, and surrendering everything to Him. When the heart is free of the three material modes, one naturally desires to follow in the footsteps of the people of Vraja. Therefore the attraction to *rāgānuga-bhakti*, or the intense desire to attain *rāgānuga-bhakti* is the inspiration that pushes one to true spiritual life. As there are many different kinds of *rāgātmikā-bhakti*, so there are also many different kinds of *rāgānuga-bhakti*.

Vrajanātha: What are the different kinds of *rāgātmikā-bhakti*?

Bābājī: *Rāgātmikā-bhakti* is of two kinds: 1. *kāma-rūpa* (devotion born from desire) and 2. *sambandha-rūpa* (devotion born of a relationship).

Vrajanātha: Please explain the difference between *kāma-rūpa* and *sambandha-rūpa*.

Bābājī: In the Seventh Canto (*Śrīmad-Bhāgavatam* 7.1.30-31) it is written: Many, many persons have attained liberation simply by thinking of Kṛṣṇa with great attention and giving up sinful activities. This great attention may be due to lusty desires, inimical feelings, fear, affection, or devotional service. I shall now explain how one receives Kṛṣṇa's mercy simply by concentrating one's mind upon Him. My dear King Yudhiṣṭhira, the *gopīs*, by their lusty desires, Kaṁsa by his fear, Śiśupāla and other kings by envy, the Yadus by their familial relationship with Kṛṣṇa, you Pāndavas by your great affection for Kṛṣṇa, and we the general devotees by our devotional service, have obtained the mercy of Kṛṣṇa.

Here, six items are mentioned: Lusty desires, inimical feelings, fear, familial relationships, affection, and devotional service. Among these, inimical feelings and fear are not appropriate sentiments for devotees of the Lord. When it becomes the idea that the Lord is a friend, affection is appropriate in *vaidhī-bhakti*. However, when affection becomes pure love (*prema*), it is no longer within the realm of *sādhana-bhakti*. That kind of love belongs in the path of *rāga*. It has no place in *sādhana-bhakti*.

The word *bhaktyā* in *Bhakti-rasāmṛta-sindhu* (1.2.135) refers to *vaidhī bhakti*. In some situations, the word *bhakti* refers to the *vaidhī-bhakti* performed by the great sages, and in other situations, the word *bhakti* refers to *jñāna-miśra-bhakti* (devotional service mixed with impersonal speculation). Here, the words, "many attained Him" means that because Lord Kṛṣṇa is identical with the impersonal Brahman in the same way that the rays of sunlight are identical with the sun planet, when the impersonalists merge into Brahman, or when Kṛṣṇa's enemies merge into Brahman, they certainly attain Kṛṣṇa. In this way, they become plunged into the happiness of Brahman liberation, which is a perverted reflection of *sārūpya* liberation.

In the *Brahmānda Purāṇa* it is said that they attain Siddhaloka, which is on the farther shore of the ocean of *māyā*. Two different kinds of beings reside in Siddhaloka. They are the impersonalists, who are plunged into Brahman happiness, and the demons killed by Kṛṣṇa. Among those liberated impersonalists, some attain a faint scent of love for Kṛṣṇa (*rāga*). By worshiping Lord Kṛṣṇa's lotus feet, these impersonalists eventually become dear devotees of the Lord. In this way, they attain love (*prema*) for Lord Kṛṣṇa.

As the sun is not different from the rays of sunlight, so Lord Kṛṣṇa is not different from His Brahman effulgence. Therefore, the word *tad-gati* (that attainment) here means Kṛṣṇa-gati (the attainment of Lord Kṛṣṇa). Therefore, the impersonalists and demons who attain *sāyujya* (impersonal) liberation attain Lord Kṛṣṇa's Brahman effulgence. On the other hand, the devotees, who love the Lord, attain direct service to Lord Kṛṣṇa, who is like the sun planet from which the sunlight that is the impersonal Brahman has come. In this way, we have described four of these emotions: inimical feelings, fear, affection, and devotional service. Only lusty desires and familial relationships remain to be described. In the path of *rāga-bhakti*, lusty desires and familial relationships are both very important. Thus, *rāga-bhakti* is of two kinds: 1. lusty desires (*kāma*) and 2. familial relationships (*sambandha*).

Vrajanātha: What is the nature of devotional service with lusty desires?

Bābājī: The word lust means, "The thirst to enjoy," When it is manifested in *rāgātmikā-bhakti*, that thirst to enjoy becomes causeless love for Lord Kṛṣṇa. Thus, it becomes the thirst to enjoy the association of Lord Kṛṣṇa. In this situation, the devotee acts only to please Lord Kṛṣṇa. The devotee does not act for his own happiness. The devotee accepts his own happiness only if it leads to Kṛṣṇa's happiness. This very wonderful unprecedented love is perfectly manifested in the *gopīs* of Vraja. Because it possesses the qualities of wonderful sweetness and playfulness, *paṇḍitas* use the word "lusty desires" (*kāma*) to describe the *gopīs* love (*prema*).

However, the truth is that the *gopīs* "lusty desires" are spiritual and free from the slightest scent of any fault. On the other hand, the lusty desires felt by the souls in *māyā*'s prison are wretched, lowly, and filled with faults. When they saw it, Uddhava and other dear devotees of the Lord yearned to attain the "lusty desires" felt by the *gopīs* of Vraja. The *gopīs*' lusty desire cannot be compared to anything else. It can be compared only to itself. These "lusty desires" in *rāgātmikā-bhakti* exist only in Vraja, and not in any other place. The "lusty desires" that Kubjā manifested in Mathurā are called *kāma-prāya* (resembling lusty desires). Although they bear some resemblance to the *gopīs*' lusty desires, they are different.

Vrajanātha: What is the nature of *rāga-bhakti* with familial relationships?

Bābājī: *Rāga-bhakti* in the *rasa* of familial relationships is manifested when one identifies himself as Kṛṣṇa's parent or other relative. When one thinks, "I am Kṛṣṇa's father," or "I am Kṛṣṇa's mother," or when one thinks of oneself as another kind of relative of Kṛṣṇa—that is called devotional service in the mood of familial relationships. In the Vṛṣṇi dynasty, there are also devotees who identify as Kṛṣṇa's father and mother. Still, devotional service in familial relationships is first manifested in Vraja: in Nanda, in Yaśodā, and in others also.

Pure love for Kṛṣṇa is manifested in these kinds of "lusty desires" and "familial relationships." That is why the eternally liberated souls take shelter of them. In *rāgānuga-bhakti*, these two sentiments are mentioned only briefly. In the practice of devotional service, these two sentiments take two forms: 1. *kāmānuga* (following lusty desires), and 2. *sambandhānuga* (following familial relationships).

Vrajanātha: What are the qualities of *kāmānuga-bhakti* in the practice of *rāgānuga-bhakti*?

Bābājī: When a devotee thirsts to follow the path of *kāma* devotional service—that is called *kāmānuga*. *Kāmānuga-bhakti* is of two kinds: 1. *sambhogecchāmayī* (yearning to enjoy), and 2. *tat-tad bhavecchā-mayī* (yearning to love).

Vrajanātha: What is the nature of *sambhogecchāmayī*?

Bābājī: *Sambhogecchāmayī* means, "the desire to participate in Lord Kṛṣṇa's pastimes (*keli*) with the *gopīs*."

Vrajanātha: What is the nature of *tat-tad bhavecchā-mayī*?

Bābājī: *Tat-tad bhavecchā-mayī* means, "the desire to attain the sweetness of love that the Vraja *gopīs* felt for Lord Kṛṣṇa."

Vrajanātha: How are these two sentiments manifested in the practice of *rāgānuga-bhakti*?

Bābājī: By seeing the sweetness of Lord Kṛṣṇa's Deity form, and by hearing the descriptions of Lord Kṛṣṇa's pastimes, one develops a desire to fall in love with Kṛṣṇa. Devotees who have that desire practice *rāgānuga-bhakti* that is either *kāmānuga* or *sambandhānuga*.

Vrajanātha: Lord Kṛṣṇa is male, and the Vraja *gopīs* are all female. Therefore, I can see that only women are qualified to practice this kind of *rāgānuga-bhakti*. How can men be qualified to attain it?

Bābājī: Each individual soul residing in the material world has an original spiritual form that manifests one of the five *rasas* (relationships with Lord Kṛṣṇa). Four of these *rasas*, namely, *dāsya* (servitorship), *sākhya* (friendship), *vātsalya* (parental love) and *mādhurya* (conjugal love) are present among the people of Vraja. In Vraja, males participate in the *rasas* of *dāsya* (servitorship), *sākhya* (friendship) and the fatherhood portion of *vātsalya* (parental love). In these three *rasas*, males engage in direct service to Lord Kṛṣṇa. However, it is only females who serve the Lord in *mādhurya* (conjugal love), and in the motherhood portion of *vātsalya*. Among both liberated souls and beginners engaged in *sādhana-bhakti*, many souls with external male material bodies have original spiritual forms that are female.

Vrajanātha: How do souls with male external material bodies follow in the footsteps of the Vraja *gopīs*?

Bābājī: In different ways, as they are qualified, they become attracted to the *rasa* of conjugal love (*śṛṅgāra-rasa*). Even though their external material form is male, their original spiritual form, which is female, is always present. According to one's inclination and one's original spiritual form, one is qualified to become the follower of a particular Vraja *gopī*. By following that *gopī*, one's original spiritual form is again openly manifested and in that original form, one serves Lord Kṛṣṇa directly.

In the *Padma Purāṇa* an example is given of souls who, although their external material bodies were male, eventually became *gopīs*. There it is said that when they saw the handsomeness of Lord Rāmacandra, the sages of Daṇḍakāraṇya Forest yearned to attain Him as their husband. When Lord Kṛṣṇa manifested His Gokula pastimes, these same sages were born as women. In those forms, they served Lord Kṛṣṇa in the *rasa* of conjugal love.

Vrajanātha: I have heard that the women of Gokula are eternally liberated souls in the spiritual world who descended to the material world to help Lord Kṛṣṇa's pastimes. Why then does the *Padma Purāṇa* say that these sages were born as *gopīs* in Gokula?

Bābājī: Many eternally liberated souls came to this world to participate in Lord Kṛṣṇa's pastimes. In addition to them, many souls from the material world, who, by engaging in devotional service became qualified to do so, also participated in Lord Kṛṣṇa's pastimes. Worshiping Lord Kṛṣṇa in *kāmānuga-bhakti*, they took birth in Gokula. These *gopīs* are described in *Śrīmad-Bhāgavatam* (10.29.8-11), where it is said that by serving Lord Kṛṣṇa in meditation, they abandoned their external material bodies and regained their original spiritual forms. Many of these *gopīs* had previously been the sages of Daṇḍakāraṇya.

Vrajanātha: Which *gopīs* were eternally liberated and which became liberated by engaging in devotional service?

Bābājī: Śrīmati Rādhikā is Lord Kṛṣṇa's internal potency (*svarūpa-śakti*). She expands into the forms of Her eight close friends (*aṣṭa-sakhī*), and they expand into the forms of other *gopīs* (*sakhīs*). These *gopīs* are all eternally liberated (*nitya-siddha*). These *gopīs* are not manifested by the *jīva-śakti*. Rather, they are manifested by the Lord's internal potency (*svarūpa-śakti*). In addition to these *gopīs*, there are other *gopīs* (also *sakhīs*) who attained liberation by engaging in devotional service (*sādhana-siddha*), and were thus allowed to join Śrīmati Rādhikā's entourage. These *gopīs* are individual souls (*jīva*) who attained liberation by engaging in devotional service (*sādhana-siddha*). By the power of the Lord's *hlādinī-śakti*, they attained *sālokya* liberation and were allowed to associate with Śrī Rādhā, the queen of Vraja.

Devotees who follow the path of *rāgānuga-bhakti* and aspire for *śṛṅgāra-rasa* eventually attain liberation as a result of their devotional service. Thus they are able to join the company of *gopīs* (*sakhīs*). Devotees who follow the path of *vidhi-bhakti* and desire to enjoy Kṛṣṇa, which means they desire that Lord Kṛṣṇa will become their husband, become the Lord's queens at Dvārakā. Devotees who follow the path of *vidhi-bhakti* do not become followers of Śrī Rādhā, the goddess of Vraja. Only devotees who follow the path of *vidhi-bhakti* externally and the path of *rāgānuga-bhakti* internally attain devotional service in the land of Vraja.

Vrajanātha: How does one become purified of the desire to enjoy (*riraṁsa*) Kṛṣṇa, which means the desire that Lord Kṛṣṇa will become one's husband?

Bābājī: These devotees who have accepted the role of Lord Kṛṣṇa's queens should renounce all pride and humbly serve Lord Kṛṣṇa as a wife serves her husband. However, even if they do this, these devotees may not attain the desire to become one of the *gopīs* of Vraja.

Vrajanātha: Please explain this more clearly.

Bābājī: Devotees who aspire to attain Lord Kṛṣṇa as their husband (*svakīya*) become the Lord's queens (*mahiṣī-bhāva*). These devotees cannot taste the *rasa* where Kṛṣṇa is one's paramour (*parakīya*), a *rasa* relished by the Vraja *gopīs*. For this reason, these devotees cannot follow in the footsteps of the *gopīs*. Only by following the path of *rāgānuga-bhakti* and cherishing the idea that Lord Kṛṣṇa is one's paramour (*parakīya*) can one attain the *rasa* of a *gopī* in Vraja.

Vrajanātha: By your mercy, I have understood all this. Now please kindly explain one thing: What is the difference between lust (*kāma*) and love (*prema*)? If there is no difference, why did you use the word *prema-rūpa* (the nature of love)? When I hear it, the word lust (*kāma*) brings pain to my ears.

Bābājī: There is a difference between lust and love. When we say love, we mean an emotion like what is felt in *rāga-bhakti* when the devotee considers Kṛṣṇa a relative in his family (*sambandha*). In that devotional service as a family member, there is no idea of trying to exploit Kṛṣṇa for one's own enjoyment. In devotional service where one relates to Lord Kṛṣṇa as a family member, there is no scope for an amorous relationship. Still, that relationship is undoubtedly based on love (*prema*). However, when this love for Kṛṣṇa is gracefully mixed with the desire to enjoy Kṛṣṇa, the result is devotional service (*bhakti*) performed in the spirit of lust (*kāma*).

In the other *rasas*, lust and devotional service are not mixed together in this way. This combination is present only in the *rasa* of conjugal love. Aside from the Vraja *gopīs*, no one practices this kind of devotional service mixed with lust. In this material world, the word lust means to desire material sense pleasures. However, the lust felt by the *gopīs* is very different from material lust. The lust felt by the *gopīs* is completely pure and faultless. Material lust is a perverted reflection of the *gopīs*' lust.

Though it was directed toward Lord Kṛṣṇa, the lust felt by Kubjā cannot be said to be like the *gopīs*' lust (*sākṣāt-kāma*). Lust to enjoy with the material senses is an emotion that is worthless, wretched, and degraded. On the other hand, lust that is a feature of pure love for Kṛṣṇa is exalted and full of bliss. Because material lust is wretched and degraded, what shall stop you from using the word spiritual lust (*aprākṛta kāma*) to describe the emotion felt by the *gopīs*?

Vrajanātha: Now please explain the aspect of *rāgānuga-bhakti* where one thinks of Kṛṣṇa as one's family member?

Bābājī: Devotional service where one has a family or other kind of relationship with Kṛṣṇa is called *sambandhānuga-bhakti*. This kind of relationship is present in three *rasas*: *dāsya* (servitorship), *sākhya* (friendship) and *vātsalya* (parenthood). In this relationship, one thinks, "I am a servant. Kṛṣṇa is my master," or one thinks, "I am Kṛṣṇa's friend," or one thinks, "I am Kṛṣṇa's father," or one thinks, "I am Kṛṣṇa's mother." These are the thoughts of one in *sambandha*. This *sambandhānuga-bhakti* is manifested in its pure form among the residents of Vraja.

Vrajanātha: How is *rāgānuga-bhakti* cultivated in the *dāsya*, *sākhya*, and *vātsalya rasas*?

Bābājī: A devotee attracted to *dāsya-rasa* (servitorship) should follow in the footsteps of Raktaka, Patraka, and other eternally liberated servitors of the Lord. By emulating the sweetness of their love for the Lord, he will eventually serve Lord Kṛṣṇa directly. A devotee attracted to *sākhya*-rasa (friendship) should follow in the footsteps of Subala and the other friends of the Lord. In this way, he will eventually serve Lord Kṛṣṇa directly. A devotee attracted to *vātsalya*-rasa (parenthood) should follow in the footsteps of Nanda and Yaśodā. In this way, he will eventually serve Lord Kṛṣṇa directly.

Vrajanātha: How does one follow in their footsteps?

Bābājī: The soul's eternal nature gives rise to certain actions. These actions are called *mudrā*. For example, Nanda Mahārāja has a certain eternal nature, and because of that nature, he deals with Kṛṣṇa in a specific way. One should follow in the footsteps of those activities. However, one should not think, "I am Nanda," "I am Subala," or "I am Raktaka." One should only follow in the footsteps of their activities. In that way, one will not commit an offense.

Vrajanātha: What *rasa* should I cultivate in *rāgānuga-bhakti*?

Bābājī: Bābā, look at your own nature. Because of that nature, you have a certain inclination. According to that inclination, you naturally accept a particular *rasa*. You should follow the footsteps of an eternally liberated soul who serves the Lord in that *rasa*. You should closely examine your own inclination. If you are inclined to the path of *rāga-bhakti*, then you should follow your inclination. If you are not inclined to the path of *rāga-bhakti*, then you should follow the path of *vaidhī-bhakti*.

Vijaya-kumāra: Master, I have studied *Śrīmad-Bhāgavatam* for many days. Whenever I hear or read of Lord Kṛṣṇa's pastimes, in my heart I yearn to serve the divine couple as Śrīmatī Lalitā does.

Bābājī: Don't say anything more. You are a *mañjarī* follower of Śrī Lalitā-devī. What service do you think is appropriate for you?

Vijaya-kumāra: In my heart I think Śrī Lalitā has ordered me to string garlands of flowers. I gather many beautiful flowers, make them into garlands, and place them in her beautiful hand. She gives me a smile of mercy, and then she places them around the necks of Śrī Śrī Rādhā-Kṛṣṇa.

Bābājī: May you attain that service. I give you my blessings.

At that moment, Vijaya-kumāra fell, weeping, at his spiritual master's lotus feet. Seeing his emotional state, the saintly *bābājī* said to him, "Bābā, within your heart you should always practice *rāgānuga-bhakti*, and externally you should engage in *vaidhī-bhakti*."

Seeing Vijaya-kumāra's good fortune, Vrajanātha placed these words before his spiritual master's lotus feet: "O master, when I think of Lord Kṛṣṇa's pastimes, I desire to become a follower of Subala."

Bābājī: To what kind of activities do you feel attracted?

Vrajanātha: Subala and I will fetch the calves that have strayed far away. As Kṛṣṇa sits down and plays the flute, by Subala's mercy, I will let the calves drink water, and after I will bring them again to our brother, Kṛṣṇa. That is my desire.

Bābājī: I give you my blessings. May you become a follower of Subala and in that way serve Lord Kṛṣṇa. You are qualified for *sākhya-rasa*.

This was all a great wonder. From that day on, in his heart, Vijaya-kumāra began to think of himself as a maidservant of Śrīmatī Lalitā. Then he began to see the elderly *bābājī* as an incarnation of Śrī Lalitā.

Vijaya-kumāra said, "O master, what more need be done by your mercy?"

The saintly *bābājī* replied, "Nothing more need be done. Only you should know the name, form, and garments of your spiritual body. Come to me in private and I will tell you of them."

Saying, "As you order," Vijaya-kumāra offered *daṇḍavat* obeisances.

From that day on, Vrajanātha saw the elderly *bābājī* as an incarnation of Subala. The *bābājī* said to him, "Come to me and I will tell you the name, form and garments of your spiritual body."

Saying, "As you order," Vrajanātha offered *daṇḍavat* obeisances.

Thinking that their lives had not become perfect, Vrajanātha and Vijaya-kumāra happily followed the path of *rāgānuga-bhakti*. Externally, everything was as before. Externally, Vijaya-kumāra was a male but within his heart, he had become a *gopī*. Meanwhile, within his heart, Vrajanātha had become a cowherd boy.

A good part of the night had already passed. Chanting on *japa* beads the *mantra*: *Hare Kṛṣṇa Hare Kṛṣṇa, Kṛṣṇa Kṛṣṇa Hare Hare / Hare Rāma Hare Rāma, Rāma Rāma Hare Hare* that their spiritual master had given them, the two walked toward Bilva-puṣkariṇī. Almost half the night had passed. The moon rose. The season placed a pleasant situation in every direction.

When they came to Lakṣmaṇa Tila, the two men sat under an *āmalakī* tree.

Vijaya-kumāra asked Vrajanātha, "O Vrajanātha, the desires in our hearts are now fulfilled. Because we have attained the mercy of a great Vaiṣṇava, we will now attain the mercy of Lord Kṛṣṇa. Now we should consider what will happen in the future. Vrajanātha, with an honest heart, please tell me: What will you do? Will you marry, or will you take *parivrājaka sannyāsa*? This request does not come from me. I only ask so I can tell your grandmother."

Vrajanātha: Uncle, I am devoted to you. You are a *paṇḍita* and a Vaiṣṇava. In the absence of my father, you are my guardian. The path that you order, I will follow. I do not wish to become attached to material things and thus forget the spiritual goal of life. Therefore, I do not wish to marry. What do you think?

Vijaya-kumāra: I will not force you. You decide for yourself and tell me.

Vrajanātha: I will ask our spiritual master. I will do whatever he says.

Vijaya-kumāra: Good. Tomorrow we will go and hear what Prabhupāda says about this.

Vrajanātha: Saintly uncle, what do you think? Should I become a householder? Should I not become a *parivrājaka sannyāsī*?

Vijaya-kumāra: Bābā, my conclusion is the same as yours. We are of one mind. Accept *parivrājaka sannyāsa* and extinguish the fire of household life. If you accept household life, your heart will dry up. You will be cheated of the nectar of devotional service. My wish is that you follow whatever Śrī Prabhupāda says about this.

A large part of the night had passed. It was right that they return home. Again and again singing the glories of Lord Hari, the uncle and nephew returned home, honored *prasādam*, and went to sleep.

Chapter Twenty-two

Eternal religion and sambandha, abhidheya and prayojana (The discussion of prayojana begins)

Today is Ekādaśī. Under the *bakula* tree in Śrīvāsa's courtyard, the Vaiṣṇavas are chanting the holy names of the Lord. Some called out, "O Gaurāṅga! O Nityānanda!" and sighed. Our saintly *bābājī* was motionless, plunged in ecstatic love. Who knows what he was thinking? After a few moments he said, "Alas!" and began to weep. "Ah! Where is Rūpa? Where is Sanātana! Where is Raghunātha dāsa Gosvāmī! Where is my life's brother, Kṛṣṇadāsa Kavirāja? I cannot be with them. Today I am all alone. I cannot be happy. The memory of Rādhā-kuṇḍa brings me pain. O my life, now you are leaving me. I pray that Rūpa and Raghunātha show themselves to me and save my life. Even though I am separated from you, still I remain alive. How pathetic is my life."

Again and again speaking in this way, he began to roll about in the dust under the *bakula* tree in Śrīvāsa's courtyard. The assembled Vaiṣṇavas said to him, "Bābājī, be peaceful. Rūpa and Raghunātha are in your heart. Lord Caitanya and Lord Nityānanda are dancing before you."

Saying, "Where? Where?" the *bābājī* jumped up. As he gazed at the Pañca-tattva Deities before him, his grief went far away. He said, "O glorious Māyāpura! Only Māyāpura makes the sadness of Vraja go far away."

Saying these words, he danced for some moments and then sat down in his cottage. At that moment, Vijaya-kumāra and Vrajanātha came and offered *daṇḍavat* obeisances. When he saw them, the *bābājī*'s heart blossomed with happiness. He said, "How is your devotional service progressing?"

Folding their hands, the two disciples humbly said, "O master, your mercy is the be-all and end-all of our lives. In the past, we must have performed many, many pious deeds so that we so easily have attained your fearless lotus feet. Today is Ekādaśī. By your order, we are fasting even from water. We have come to see your sacred feet."

The *bābājī* replied, "You are fortunate. Very soon you will attain *bhāva*."

Vijaya-kumāra asked, "O master, what is *bhāva*? Is there something called *bhāva* that you have not yet taught us?"

Bābājī: Up until now, I have taught you about *sādhana-bhakti*. By practicing *sādhana-bhakti* again and again, one eventually comes to the stage of spiritual perfection. The stage that immediately precedes the perfect stage is called *bhāva* (ecstatic love). The perfect stage is described in these words of the *Daśa-mūla*:

When his *sādhana-bhakti* reaches maturity, the living entity becomes aware of his original spiritual form. Then, by the power of the Lord's *hlādinī-śakti*, the ecstatic love (*bhāva*) of *mādhurya-rasa* becomes manifested. Then, the living entity bears in his heart ecstatic love (*bhāva*) for Śrī Śrī Rādhā-Kṛṣṇa in Vraja. Then, he attains ecstatic love (*prīti*) and bliss. Gradually he attains happiness and good fortune that have no equal anywhere in this world. He enters the Lord's pastimes. There, he attains direct service to the Lord. There is nothing higher than that.

In this verse, the final goal of life (*prayojana*), which is pure love for the Lord, is described. The beginning stage of that pure love is described in the final verse of the *Daśa-mūla*: Who is the Supreme Lord? Who is the individual spirit soul? What is the material world? Considering these questions, a devotee becomes learned in the scriptures. He shuns all offenses, sins, material pious deeds, and aspirations to become one with the Lord and, thinking himself a servant of Lord Hari, in the company of other devotees, he drinks the blissful nectar of Lord Hari's holy name.

What a wonderful poem is the *Daśa-mūla*. In it, the individual souls find the essence of the teachings that have come from Lord Mahāprabhu's sacred mouth.

Vijaya-kumāra: I would like to hear a summary of the *Daśa-mūla's* glories?

Bābājī: Then listen. A person who carefully studies this *Daśa-mūla* becomes free of ignorance. By associating with devotees, he attains spiritual love and bliss.

Vijaya-kumāra: O master, this wonderful *Daśa-mūla* will become the necklace we all wear. Every day, we will recite this *Daśa-mūla* and offer *daṇḍavat* obeisances to Lord Mahāprabhu. Now, please be merciful and explain the clear meaning of these truths.

Bābājī: Pure love of God (*prema*) is like a sun. The pure rays of that *prema*-sun are the spiritual state of *viśuddha-sattva*. The internal nature of *viśuddha-sattva* is called *bhāva*. The *viśuddha-sattva* manifestation called *bhāva* is also called by the names *rati* and *premāṅkura* (the sprouting of love). When the all-enlightening *svarūpa-śakti* (internal potency) is manifested in the activities called *samvit* (knowledge), those activities are called *viśuddha-sattva* (spiritual existence). These are not activities of *māyā* (material illusion).

When the activities of the *samvit-śakti* join with the activities of the *hlādinī-śakti*, the result is the manifestation of *bhāva*. The activities of *samvit-śakti* bring knowledge. The activities of *hlādinī-śakti* bring pleasure. In this way, the activities of the Lord's *svarūpa-śakti* bring knowledge of the Absolute Truth, Śrī Kṛṣṇa. The small knowledge potency (*samvit-śakti*) of the individual souls (*jīva-śakti*) cannot bring understanding of the Absolute Truth. By the mercy of the Supreme Personality of Godhead Himself, or by the mercy of the Lord's devotee, the Lord's *svarūpa-śakti* (internal potency) will appear in a living entity's heart. Then, the *svarūpa-śakti*'s activities of knowledge (*samvit*) can act in the living entity's heart. Then, knowledge of the spiritual world becomes manifested there.

The real form (*svarūpa*) of the spiritual world is the state of spiritual existence (*viśuddha-sattva*). The real form of the material world of *māyā* is gross matter, which is a mixture of the three modes of material goodness, passion, and ignorance. When knowledge of the spiritual world combines with the essence (*sāra*) of the *hlādinī-śakti*, the result is that one is able to relish (*āsvāda*) the pleasures of the spiritual world. When the relishing of the pleasures of the spiritual world reaches its perfection and fullness (*pūrna-svarūpa*), the result is called *prema* (pure love of God). *Prema* is like a sun, and *bhāva* is the rays of that sun. That is the nature of *bhāva*.

The specific nature of *bhāva* is this: *Ruci* (attraction to Kṛṣṇa) makes the living entity's heart melt and become soft (*masṛṇa*). Here, the word *ruci* means, "the desire to attain Kṛṣṇa, the desire to please Kṛṣṇa, and the desire to have a friendly relation with Kṛṣṇa." *Bhāva* is said to be the first manifestation of the splendor of *prema*. The word *masṛṇa* means, "the melting of the heart."

In the *Tantras* it is said that *bhāva* is the first manifestation of *prema*. When *bhāva* appears, the *sāttvikā-bhāvā* ecstatic symptoms, such as the standing erect of the body's hairs, become slightly manifested. In eternally liberated souls, these ecstatic symptoms appear spontaneously. In souls imprisoned in the material world, these ecstatic symptoms appear as activities of the mind, and only gradually do they manifest their original spiritual nature. Although these ecstatic symptoms come of their own accord, they seem to be induced by something external.

The activities of *sāttvikā bhāvā* ecstasy reveal the true nature of Lord Kṛṣṇa and His transcendental pastimes. Manifested among the imprisoned souls as what seems to be an activity of the mind, it seems to bring knowledge of other, non-spiritual truths. The truth is that it enables one to relish spiritual pleasures. In this way, it enables the souls imprisoned in the material world to relish the spiritual pleasures of Lord Kṛṣṇa and Lord Kṛṣṇa's transcendental pastimes.

Vijaya-kumāra: Does *bhāva* manifest any variety?

Bābājī: Yes. *Bhāva* is of two kinds, according to its place or origin. *Bhāva* may come from the practice of *sādhana-bhakti*, or it may come from the mercy of Lord Kṛṣṇa or the mercy of Lord Kṛṣṇa's devotee. Generally, it comes from the practice of *sādhana-bhakti*. It only rarely comes from mercy.

Vijaya-kumāra: What is the nature of *bhāva* produced by the practice of *sādhana-bhakti*?

Bābājī: There are two kinds of *bhāva* created by the practice of *sādhana-bhakti*. One is created by the practice of *vaidhī bhakti* and the other by the practice of *rāgānuga-bhakti*. In the first of these two kinds of *bhāva* created by *sādhana-bhakti*, at the beginning, there is *ruci* (attraction to Kṛṣṇa). From that comes *āsakti* (attachment to Kṛṣṇa). At the end comes *rati* (love for Kṛṣṇa). In the *Purāṇas* and the *nāṭya-śāstra* it is said that *rati* and *bhāva* are symptoms. I also say that they are symptoms. *Vaidhī-bhakti* first creates faith, and from faith attraction to Kṛṣṇa (*ruci*) follows. However, when one practices *rāgānuga-bhakti*, *ruci* appears at once (without any intervening stages).

Vijaya-kumāra: What is the nature of *bhāva* created by the mercy of Lord Kṛṣṇa or Lord Kṛṣṇa's devotee?

Bābājī: When *bhāva* suddenly appears without its recipient having practiced either *vaidhī-bhakti* or *rāgānuga-bhakti*, then *bhāva* is created by the mercy of Lord Kṛṣṇa or Lord Kṛṣṇa's devotee.

Vijaya-kumāra: What is the nature of *bhāva* created by the mercy of Lord Kṛṣṇa?

Bābājī: Lord Kṛṣṇa's mercy is manifested in three ways: 1. *vācika* (by His words), 2. *āloka-dāna* (by a glance), and 3. *hārda* (by the mercy in His heart). Lord Kṛṣṇa may give His mercy to someone by saying, "O king of the *brāhmaṇas*, may devotion to Me, devotion that brings all transcendental bliss and is the crest jewel of all auspicious things, appear within you."

Simply by the Lord's speaking these words, *bhāva* suddenly appears in that *brāhmaṇa*. The aborigines residing in the jungle had never seen Kṛṣṇa before. However, simply by His seeing them, they at once attained *bhāva* because of the compassion in Lord Kṛṣṇa's heart. That is called *āloka-dānaja-bhāva* (*bhāva* created from a glance). When feelings of compassion arise in Lord Kṛṣṇa's heart, they produce the *bhāva* called *hārda*. This *bhāva* is seen in Śukadeva Gosvāmī and other devotees. When He descended to this world, Lord Mahāprabhu granted these three kinds of *bhāva* from mercy on many occasions. Simply by seeing the Lord, many people attained *bhāva*. Jagāi, Mādhāi, and many others attained *bhāva* because of the Lord's words. Śrīla Jīva Gosvāmī attained *bhāva* because of the mercy in Lord Kṛṣṇa's heart.

Vijaya-kumāra: What is the nature of *bhāva* created by the mercy of a devotee of Lord Kṛṣṇa?

Bābājī: Because of the mercy of Śrī Nārada Gosvāmī, auspicious desires appeared in the hearts of Dhruva and Prahlāda. By the mercy of Śrīla Rūpa Gosvāmī, Śrīla Sanātana Gosvāmī, and their associates, the desire to perform devotional service appeared in the hearts of numberless persons.

Vijaya-kumāra: What are the symptoms of *bhāva*'s appearance?

Bābājī: When the seed of ecstatic emotion (*bhāva*) for Kṛṣṇa fructifies, the following nine symptoms are manifest in one's behavior: forgiveness, concern that time should not be wasted, detachment, absence of false prestige, hope, eagerness, a taste for chanting the holy name of the Lord, attachment to descriptions of the transcendental qualities of the Lord, and affection for those places where the Lord resides (a temple or holy place like Vṛndāvana). These are all called *anubhāva*, subordinate signs of ecstatic emotion. They are visible in a person in whose heart the seed of love of God has begun to fructify.

Vijaya-kumāra: What is forgiveness?

Bābājī: Forgiveness is when, even though there is ample reason to become agitated and angry, one is not agitated and angry. This is called forgiveness. Tolerance is a synonym for forgiveness.

Vijaya-kumāra: What is concern that time should not be wasted?

Bābājī: It means not to spend time in useless activities. To always be engaged in devotional service to Lord Hari is called, "concern that time should not be wasted."

Vijaya-kumāra: What is detachment?

Bābājī: To find that one sees no pleasure in so-called material sense pleasures is called detachment.

Vijaya-kumāra: When a person accepts *sannyāsa*, can he claim to have attained detachment?

Bābājī: *Sannyāsa* is a material convention in the material world. When the heart finds its pleasure in the spiritual world, and when the heart finds its pleasure in the material world grow less and less, until finally it disappears almost completely, that is called detachment. A person who is detached from the material world and then accepts *sannyāsa* to remove the obstacles that prevent him from attaining *bhāva* can claim to be a detached Vaiṣṇava. However, a person who accepts *sannyāsa* prematurely, before he has any understanding of the happiness of spiritual life (*bhāva*), is not properly initiated as a *sannyāsī*. He is not a true *sannyāsī*. The Lord's punishment of Chota Haridāsa taught this to the entire world.

Vijaya-kumāra: What is absence of false prestige?

Bābājī: Birth, *varṇa*, *āsrama*, wealth, power, beauty, a high status in society, and many other things make a person proud. To renounce the pride that comes from all these things is called absence of false prestige. In the *Padma Purāṇa* is found the story of a great king who attained devotion to Lord Kṛṣṇa. Renouncing the pride that comes from royal opulence, this king passed his life as a beggar performing *mādhukarī* in the capital city of the king that had been his rival and enemy. He always offered respectful obeisances to everyone, not caring whether they were *brāhmaṇas* or *caṇḍālas*.

Vijaya-kumāra: What is hope?

Bābājī: To engage in devotional service with firm conviction, thinking, "Lord Kṛṣṇa will certainly be merciful to me," is called hope.

Vijaya-kumāra: What is eagerness?

Bābājī: Intense greed to attain what one desires is called eagerness.

Vijaya-kumāra: What is a taste for chanting the holy name of the Lord?

Bābājī: Of all the different activities of devotional service, chanting the holy name of the Lord is the best. When a devotee understands this, he utilizes all of his time chanting the holy names of the Lord. A taste for chanting the holy name of the Lord fulfills all spiritual desires. You will learn more about the holy name separately, at another time.

Vijaya-kumāra: What is attachment to descriptions of the transcendental qualities of the Lord?

Bābājī: In *Śrī Kṛṣṇa-karṇāmṛta* (verse 65) it is written: He is sweeter than sweetness personified. His youthfulness is Kāmadeva himself. He is more restless and playful than restlessness and playfulness personified. Alas, He has stolen my heart. What will I do now?

One may hear again and again of Lord Kṛṣṇa's transcendental qualities, but one's desire to hear them will never be satiated. Rather, one's attachment to hear of them will grow stronger and stronger.

Vijaya-kumāra: What is affection for those places where the Lord resides?

Bābājī: When he circumambulates the holy Navadvīpa, a devotee will ask, "O residents of the Lord's sacred place, where did the Lord take birth? Walking down what pathway did the Lord perform *saṅkīrtana*? Please tell me: where did the Lord enjoy pastimes with the *gopas* in the morning?"

The residents of the holy abode may reply, "In Māyāpura, in a raised *tulasī*-forest, the Lord took birth. In Gaṅgānagara, Simuliyā, Gādigāchā, Mājdīa, and many other villages He performed *saṅkīrtana*."

By drinking with the cup of his ears these nectarean words from the mouth of a resident of the land of Gauḍa, a devotee will manifest ecstatic symptoms, such as shedding tears and the hairs of his body standing erect, as he circumambulates the holy place. This is called, "affection for those places where the Lord resides."

Vijaya-kumāra: When this kind of emotion is present, can we say without doubt that *Kṛṣṇa-rati* (pure love for Kṛṣṇa) is definitely present?

Bābājī: No. When the heart is pure, then *rati* arises within it. The symptoms I have described may appear when other kinds of devotional emotions are manifested. They are not manifested only when there is *rati*.

Vijaya-kumāra: Please be kind and give one or two examples so I may understand.

Bābājī: A person thirsty for impersonal liberation may again and again chant a dim reflection of Lord Hari's holy name (*nāmābhāsa*). Hearing that the holy name has the power to give liberation, he may weep again and again, and may fall down almost unconscious. Still, one should not say that he has attained *Kṛṣṇa-rati* (love for Kṛṣṇa) in the stage of *bhāva* (ecstasy). Such a person does not have sincere love for Lord Kṛṣṇa. Rather, he makes a show of ecstatic symptoms (*bhāvābhāsa*) only because he is greedy to attain his own petty desire.

A person desiring material sense pleasures may worship Goddess Durgā and after the worship, may pray for many things, saying, "Please grant me boons. Please give me wealth." Thinking of how the goddess has the power to fulfill his desires, he may weep and roll on the ground. Still, one cannot say that has attained *bhāva*. Perhaps one can say he has attained a glimpse of *bhāva* (*bhāvābhāsa*), or a mocking imitation of *bhāva* (*bhāva-daurātmya*). *Bhāva* does not appear in a person who is not a pure devotee of Lord Kṛṣṇa. When a person who desires material sense gratification or impersonal liberation manifests a glimpse of *bhāva* (*bhāvābhāsa*), that is not true *bhāva*. Rather, it is only a mocking imitation (*bhāva-daurātmya*) of true *bhāva*. As he stands before the Deity of Lord Kṛṣṇa, such a person may faint and remain unconscious for twenty-one hours. Even then, he does not display true *bhāva*.

Ah, the eternally liberated souls and the souls free from all material desires diligently search for *bhāva*. Still, *bhāva* remains hidden from them. Even after a person performs many devotional activities, Lord Kṛṣṇa does not very quickly or easily give him the gift of *bhāva*. How can pure love (*rati*) for Lord Kṛṣṇa arise in a heart that does not have pure devotion to the Lord, or in a heart crushed by desires for material sense gratification or impersonal liberation?

Vijaya-kumāra: O master, many times it is seen that, when they participate in the chanting of Lord Hari's holy names (*hari-nāma-saṅkīrtana*), persons who thirst for material sense gratification or impersonal liberation may manifest the previously described symptoms of *bhāva*. What shall we call that display?

Bābājī: Only fools think that display to be wonderful. Persons who know the truth of *bhāva* avoid these persons and say that such an outward display is only a glimpse of *bhāva* (*bhāvābhāsa*).

Vijaya-kumāra: What are the different kinds of this glimpse of *bhāva* (*bhāvābhāsa*)?

Bābājī: It is of two kinds: 1. *pratibimba-rati-ābhāsa* (the reflection of ecstatic love), and 2. *chāyā-rati-ābhāsa* (the dim shadow of ecstatic love).

Vijaya-kumāra: What is *pratibimba-rati-ābhāsa*?

Bābājī: A person who desires impersonal liberation may think he can easily attain that liberation by manifesting *bhāva* for Lord Kṛṣṇa. Thus desiring the happiness of impersonal liberation, he puts on a false show of the symptoms of *bhāva*. This is called *pratibimba-rati-ābhāsa*. An impersonalist may think, "Attaining knowledge of impersonal Brahman is the only way to attain impersonal liberation. There is no other way. However, the process by which one attains that impersonal knowledge is very difficult and troublesome. If, by chanting the holy names of Lord Hari, one can easily attain liberation—that must mean that by chanting the holy names one may easily attain knowledge of impersonal Brahman."

Hoping to easily get impersonal liberation, such a person may then make an outward display of ecstatic symptoms, such as shedding tears and standing erect of the bodily hairs. All this is only a glimpse (*ābhāsa*) of true *bhāva*.

Vijaya-kumāra: Why is it called *pratibimba* (a reflection)?

Bābājī: When they engage in chanting the Lord's holy names, or in other devotional activities, persons who thirst after material sense gratification or impersonal liberation may by destiny attain the association of true devotees. When the moon of true *bhāva* arises in the hearts of these true devotees, that moon becomes reflected in the hearts of the hedonist or impersonalist pretenders. That is why their *bhāva* is called *pratibimba* (a reflection). Pure *bhāva* does not appear as long as one thirsts after material sense gratification or impersonal liberation. However, when a person sees pure devotees (*śuddha-bhakta*) of the Lord, the devotees' *bhāva* becomes reflected on him. That is called *pratibimba-rati-ābhāsa* (a reflection of true *bhāva*). *Pratibimba-rati-ābhāsa* does not bring eternal auspiciousness to the soul. As soon as the pretender attains his goal of sense gratification or liberation, his devotional activities stop. Therefore, this *pratibimba-rati-ābhāsa* is said to be one of the offenses against the holy name. It is not praiseworthy.

Vijaya-kumāra: What is *chāyā-rati-ābhāsa* (the dim shadow of ecstatic love)?

Bābājī: An honest neophyte devotee who is not very learned in the science of spiritual life may come into contact with activities, times, places, or persons that are dear to Lord Hari and by this contact, he may attain a small, pleasant, suffering-removing, flickering shadow of true love (*rati*) for the Lord. That is called *chāyā-rati-ābhāsa*. When a person has a small quantity of pure devotion to the Lord, but that devotion is not very strong, then this kind of shadow devotion (*raty-ābhāsa*) is manifested. This shadow of devotion may appear in a person because in the past he performed many pious deeds. This shadow of devotion may gradually bring more and more auspiciousness to the person who obtains it. By the mercy of a pure devotee of Lord Hari, this shadow love can be transformed into genuine pure love for the Lord (*śuddha-bhāva*).

However, if one commits offenses to pure Vaiṣṇavas, this shadow love may gradually diminish, like the waning of the moon in the dark fortnight. This is not said only of the shadow of love. Even pure love (*śuddha-bhāva*) for Lord Kṛṣṇa can be destroyed (*abhāva*) if one commits offenses to Lord Kṛṣṇa's devotees. Or that pure love may gradually become changed into shadow love, or it may be reduced to a lower level of love. If one closely associates with impersonalists, then his love for Kṛṣṇa may also become changed into shadow love, or else one may become an impersonalist himself, and become convinced that he himself is the worshipable Supreme Personality of Godhead. It is because of this bad association that new devotees (*navya-bhakta*) sometimes have impersonalist ideas and think they have become God as they dance in *Kṛṣṇa-kīrtana* or perform other devotional activities. This is sometimes seen.

Unaware of the consequences, new devotees may sometimes associate with impersonalists. From that bad association, many troubles begin. Therefore, new devotees should carefully avoid the association of impersonalists. Sometimes, *bhāva* may suddenly appear in a person who has not performed any devotional activities (*sādhana*). This means that the person involved performed many very good devotional activities in his previous births. Because of certain obstacles, the results of those activities were not immediately manifested. Now that the obstacles are removed, the results are suddenly manifested.

If the highest kind of love (*bhāva*), which is all-powerful and wonderful to everyone, suddenly becomes manifested, it should be said that it was produced by the mercy of Lord Kṛṣṇa. Even if you see some faults in his activities, you should not become the enemy of a person who has natural love (*bhāva*) for the Lord. Why not? A person who has attained love for the Lord has made his life a complete success. A devotee will never commit a sin. However, if it is seen that, somehow or other, a devotee has committed a sin, then one should think of this in two ways: 1. By accident a great soul has somehow committed a sin, but that sin will not stay, 2. This sin is only the reflection of a previous misdeed (*pūrva-pāpabhāsa*). The devotee's spiritual love (*bhāva*) will quickly destroy that sin. Very quickly it will be destroyed. In this way, in one's heart, one should not see the faults of the devotees. To see that devotees have faults is one of the offenses against the holy name.

In the *Nṛsiṁha-Purāṇa* it is written: If a person has completely engaged his mind, body, and activities in the service of the Supreme Godhead, but externally he is found to be engaged in some abominable activities, those abominable activities will surely be very quickly vanquished by the influence of his staunch devotional service. On the full moon there are some spots, which may appear to be pockmarks. Still, the illumination spread by the full moon cannot be checked.

One should not think that this instruction means that the devotees of the Lord are always committing sins. The truth is that when a person has faith in devotional service, he no longer desires to commit sins. However, as long as the material body is present, there may be some accidental slip into a sinful action. Devotional service, however, which is like a blazing fire, at once burns all these sins into ashes and after that, the devotee is cautious not to sin again.

When unalloyed devotional service appears in someone, the ignorance that is the root of sin is flung far away from such a devotee. If it is seen that a person commits sins again and again, one should not be under the misunderstanding that he possesses unalloyed devotion to Lord Kṛṣṇa. Why not? To commit sins with the hope that his devotional activities will nullify his sins is an offense. Devotees do not commit that offense.

Love (*rati*) for Kṛṣṇa makes one desire to please Kṛṣṇa more and more. It is filled with warmth and power. It is sweet like millions of moons.

Hearing these explanations of ecstatic love (*bhāva*), Vrajanātha and Vijaya-kumāra became stunned. Their hearts were filled with love. Even after the *bābājī* had finished speaking, they both remained for a while stunned and silent. Finally, they said, "O master, the nectar of your teachings has brought a flood of love to our burnt-out hearts. Ah, what will we do? Where will we go? We are not able to be steady and calm. We are filled with pride because we were born in *brāhmaṇa* families. In our hearts is not the slightest bit of humbleness. The hope of one day attaining ecstatic love (*bhāva*) for the Lord is very far from us. Our only hope is that you, a personal associate of the Lord, a devotee filled with pure spiritual love (*prema*), may place a single drop of spiritual love (*prema*) in our hearts. Then our lives will become a great success.

Because of our relationship with you, the bird of hope now lives in our hearts. We are very poor and lowly and worthless. You are a great king among the true devotees of the Lord. You are very merciful. Please be merciful to us and explain to us what our duties should be. In my heart, I yearn to renounce the material world and household life and become a servant of your lotus feet."

Then, Vijaya-kumāra took this opportunity to say, "O master, Vrajanātha is still a boy. His mother wishes that he become a householder. However, in his heart, he does not see the same way she does. Please be merciful and say what is to be done."

Bābājī: Lord Kṛṣṇa has given His mercy to you. Your householder life will be Lord Kṛṣṇa's household life, for you will render service to Lord Kṛṣṇa there. Our Lord Mahāprabhu taught the entire world, and the world should follow His teachings. In this material world, there are two kinds of situations: 1. household life, and 2. *sannyāsa*. As long as one is not qualified to become a *sannyāsī*, he should remain as a householder and serve Lord Kṛṣṇa in that *āsrama*.

In the first twenty-four years of His pastimes, the Lord set the example of ideal Vaiṣṇava household life, and in the second twenty-four years of His pastimes, the Lord set the example of ideal Vaiṣṇava *sannyāsa* life. Householders should follow the Lord's example. It is my opinion that for the present, you should act as He did. In your heart, do not think that in the householder *āsrama* you cannot attain the highest stage of pure love for Lord Kṛṣṇa (*Kṛṣṇa-prema*). The devotees who received the greatest mercy from Lord Mahāprabhu were all householders. The Vaiṣṇava *sannyāsīs* offer prayers to these householders and respectfully touch the dust from their lotus feet.

It was late at night. In the company of the Vaiṣṇavas, Vijaya-kumāra and Vrajanātha sang songs glorifying Hari again and again. In that way, they passed the night in Śrīvāsa's courtyard. The next morning, they washed, bathed, performed various duties, sang the holy names with the Vaiṣṇavas, and accepted a *mahā-prasādam* breakfast. In the afternoon, they slowly walked to Bilva-puṣkariṇī. As they thought about it, both uncle and nephew decided that they should serve Lord Kṛṣṇa within the householder *āsrama*. That would be best.

Vijaya-kumāra said to his sister, "Vrajanātha has decided to marry. You make all the arrangements. I will go to Modadruma for a few days. When I hear news that Vrajanātha's wedding day is coming, I will come with all the relatives to celebrate the happy day. Tomorrow, I will send Kaniṣṭha Harinātha to help with the arrangements."

Vrajanātha's mother and grandmother were flooded with bliss. They gave garments and other gifts to Vijaya-kumāra and bade him farewell.

Chapter Twenty-three

Eternal religion and sambandha, abhidheya and prayojana (The discussion of the holy name begins)

Jaiva-dharma

The village of Bilva-puṣkariṇī is very beautiful. The river Ganges flows on its northern and western sides. There, on the shore of the Puṣkariṇī, in a grove of *bilva* trees, is a temple of Lord Śiva. Not far from there is a place called Bhāva-tārana. On one side is Bilva-puṣkariṇī and on the other side is Brāhmaṇa-puṣkariṇī. Between them lies the village called Simuliyā, which on one side borders the town of Navadvīpa. In the middle of Bilva-puṣkariṇī and north of the royal road lies Vrajanātha's house. After traveling a short distance, Vijaya-kumāra returned to his sister.

In his mind, he had decided, "I won't leave until I have learned the truth about the holy name."

Returning to Bilva-puṣkariṇī, he saw his sister and nephew and told them, "I will stay another day or two and then I will go."

That afternoon, two Vaiṣṇavas in the Rāmānuja-sampradāya wearing Śrī-*tilaka* came to the Caṇḍī *maṇḍapa* at Vrajanātha's house. Sitting in the shade of the *panasa* tree before Vrajanātha's house, the two Vaiṣṇavas made a fire with some dried twigs and began to smoke *gañjā*. Vrajanātha's mother was very happy to get the opportunity to show hospitality to some guests. Seeing that they were not eating anything, she brought them different kinds of food. Pleased, they began to cook some *capātīs*. Seeing that the Vaiṣṇavas were peaceful and bright-faced, Vrajanātha and Vijaya-kumāra gradually felt attracted to them. Seeing that Vrajanātha and Vijaya-kumāra wore *tulasī* beads on their necks and twelve *tilaka* marks on their limbs, the two Vaiṣṇavas respectfully greeted them and spread a cloth for them to sit.

As Vrajanātha questioned them, one of the *sannyāsīs* said, "O Mahārāja, we have seen Ayodhyā and now we are going to Navadvīpa. In our hearts, we have decided to see the places of Caitanya Prabhu's pastimes."

Vrajanātha replied, "You are in Śrī Navadvīpa now. Please rest here today and tomorrow see the birthplace of Lord Mahāprabhu and the courtyard of Śrīvāsa. The two *sannyāsīs* then happily recited these words of Lord Kṛṣṇa in the *Bhagavad-gītā* (15.6): Those who reach My supreme abode never return to this material world.

The two *sannyāsīs* said, "Today, we are very fortunate, for we will see holy Śrī Māyāpura, the best of the seven holy cities."

As they sat under the *panasa* tree, the two *sannyāsīs* discussed the *artha-pañcaka* (five topics) of the Rāmānuja-sampradāya. The five topics are: 1. *sva-svarūpa* (the nature of one's own self), 2. *para-svarūpa* (the natures of others), 3. *upāya-svarūpa* (the means for spiritual advancement), 4. *puruṣārtha-svarūpa* (the true goal of life), and 5. *virodhi-svarūpa* (obstacles that prevent one from attaining the true goal of life).

With great attention, Vijaya-kumāra heard and considered the *sannyāsīs*' explanations of these topics and the *tattva-traya* (three truths) of the Śrī-sampradāya. After discussing these points for a long time, Vijaya-kumāra asked, "What is your sampradāya's explanation of the holy name?"

When they heard the two Vaiṣṇava's explanations, Vrajanātha and Vijaya-kumāra did not become very happy. Vrajanātha said, "Uncle, after considering all these points, I have come to the conclusion that only taking shelter of Lord Kṛṣṇa's holy name, and nothing else, brings auspiciousness to the living entities. It was to preach the pure holy name of Lord Kṛṣṇa to the world that Śrī Gaurāṅga, the master of our lives, descended to this world and came to the holy city of Māyāpura. When he was teaching us yesterday, Śrī Gurudeva explained that chanting the holy name is the best of all devotional practices. He also asked us to give special attention to understanding the truth of the holy name. Uncle, let us go there this evening and learn about this."

They spent that afternoon showing hospitality to their guests and talking about many things. When the evening *ārati* ended, the Vaiṣṇavas assembled under the *bakula* tree in Śrīvāsa's courtyard. Chanting the holy names on his *tulasī* beads, saintly elderly Raghunātha dāsa Bābājī sat among them. Vrajanātha and Vijaya-kumāra came and offered *daṇḍavat* obeisances to him.

The saintly *bābājī* embraced them and said, "Are you happy in your devotional service?"

Vijaya-kumāra replied, "O master, by your mercy, everything is auspicious for us. Please be merciful and teach us this evening about the holy name of the Lord."

His face blossoming with happiness, the saintly *bābājī* said, "The Supreme Personality of Godhead has two kinds of names: 1. *mukhya* (primary) and 2. *gauṇa* (secondary). Names that show His relation to the material creation and the material modes of nature are all secondary names. Sṛṣṭi-kartā (the creator of the material world), Jagat-pāta (the maintainer of the material world), Viśva-niyantā (the controller of the material world, Viśva-pālaka (the protector of the material world), and Paramātmā (the Supersoul present everywhere in the material world) are examples of some of these many secondary names.

Some other names, although beyond the touch of the material modes of nature, are also counted among these secondary names. Brahma (Brahman) is an example of these names. When they are chanted, these secondary names bring many different kinds of benefits, but they do not directly or quickly bring the highest spiritual benefit.

The names that describe the Lord as He is manifested in the spiritual world, which is beyond material time and space, and where time is manifested as an eternal present (*nitya-vartamāna*), are names that are all spiritual and primary. Nārāyaṇa, Vāsudeva, Janārdana, Hṛṣīkeśa, Hari, Acyuta, Govinda, Gopāla and Rāma are examples of these primary names. All these primary names are identical with the form of the Supreme Lord Himself, and therefore they exist in the eternal present in the spiritual world. Attracted by devotional service, these holy names dance on the tongues of certain very fortunate souls in the material world. These names have no connection at all with the material world.

When it descends to the material world, the holy name of the Lord, which has all the Lord's powers, destroys the illusions of *māyā*. The individual souls in the material world have the holy name of Lord Hari as their only friend. They have no other true friend. In the *Bṛhan-nāradīya Purāṇa* it is said: The holy name, the holy name, the holy name of Lord Hari is my very life. In this age of quarrel and hypocrisy, the only means of deliverance is the chanting of the holy names of the Lord. There is no other way. There is no other way. There is no other way.

The holy name has limitless power. The holy name uproots all the sins of the conditioned souls burning in a great forest fire of sins. In the *Garuḍa Purāṇa* it is said: If one chants the holy name of the Lord, even in a helpless condition or without desiring to do so, all the reactions of his sinful life depart, just as when a lion roars, all the small animals flee in fear.

A person who takes shelter of the holy name becomes free of all sufferings. The holy name has the power to destroy all sufferings. In the *Skanda Purāṇa* it is said: I offer my respectful obeisances to the limitless Supreme Personality of Godhead. When a person remembers Him or chants His holy names, that person's diseases of the mind or body all run to their extinction.

A person who chants the holy name of Lord Hari purifies his family, friends, and all others. In the *Brahmāṇḍa Purāṇa* it is said: Even if he has committed many great sins, a person who chants the holy name of the Lord, day and night, becomes pure at heart. He purifies all his relatives.

A person who is devoted to the holy name becomes free of all sufferings. In the *Bṛhad-viṣṇu Purāṇa* it is said: "The chanting of Lord Hari's holy name cures all diseases, removes all obstacles, and rescues one from all calamities.

The age of Kali cannot make trouble for a person who loudly chants the holy name of Lord Hari. In the *Bṛhan-nāradīya Purāṇa* it is said: The age of Kali cannot make trouble for a person who always chants, "Hare! Keśava! Govinda! Vāsudeva! Jaganmaya!"

Simply by hearing the holy name of Lord Hari, the residents of hell become delivered. In the *Nṛsiṁha Purāṇa* it is said: "When they began to chant the holy name of Lord Hari, the residents of hell began to develop devotion to Lord Hari. They were carried to the heavenly worlds.

By loudly chanting the holy name, a person destroys his *prārabdha* karmic reactions. In the *Śrīmad-Bhāgavatam* (12.3.44) it is said: Terrified, about to die, a man collapses on his bed. Although his voice is faltering and he is hardly conscious of what he is saying, if he utters the holy name of the Supreme Lord, he can be freed from the reactions of his fruitive work and achieve the supreme destination. But still, people in the age of Kali will not worship the Supreme Lord.

The holy name of Lord Hari is more glorious than all the *Vedas*. In the *Skanda Purāṇa* it is said: My son, don't study the *Ṛg Veda*. Don't study the *Yajur Veda*. Don't study the *Sāma Veda* at all. Simply chant "O Govinda!" Always chant the holy names of Lord Hari.

The holy name of Lord Hari is more glorious than all holy places. In the *Vāmana Purāṇa* it is said: By chanting the holy names of Lord Viṣṇu, a person attains the benefit of visiting hundreds of thousands of millions of sacred pilgrimage places.

Even a glimpse (*nāmābhāsa*) of the holy name is infinitely better than all material pious deeds. In the *Skanda Purāṇa* it is said: Neither giving millions of cows in charity, nor residing at Prayāga by the Ganges for a *kalpa*, nor performing millions of *yajñas*, nor giving a Mount Meru of gold in charity, brings a benefit equal to one hundredth part of the benefit obtained by chanting the holy names of Lord Govinda.

The holy name of Lord Hari gives all benefits. In the *Skanda Purāṇa* it is said: Chanting the holy names of Lord Viṣṇu removes the six troubles of material life, defeats enemies, and is the root of spiritual knowledge.

The holy name of Lord Hari has all powers. In the *Skanda Purāṇa* it is said: Lord Hari has gathered from charity, vows, austerities, pilgrimages, the demigods, the great saints, the *rājasūya* and *aśvamedha yajñas*, and the study of transcendental knowledge, all their powers to bring auspiciousness and remove sins, and placed these powers in His holy names.

The holy name of Lord Hari brings bliss to the entire world. In the *Bhagavad-gītā* (11.36) it is said: O Hṛṣīkeśa, the world becomes joyful upon hearing Your name, and thus everyone becomes attached to You.

The entire world bows down before a person who loudly chants the holy name. In the *Bṛhan-nāradīya Purāṇa* it is said: In every direction, the people bow down to offer respect to the devotees who always chant, "Nārāyaṇa! Jagannātha! Vāsudeva! Janārdana!"

The holy name is the only shelter of the shelterless. In the *Padma Purāṇa* it is said: Even though they may be materialistic, distraught, completely impious, or bereft of knowledge, renunciation, celibacy, and a host of virtues, persons who completely surrender to Lord Viṣṇu and even only once chant His holy name easily attain the supreme spiritual destination that all the pious saints cannot enter.

One should chant the holy name of Lord Hari always and everywhere. In the *Viṣṇu-dharmottara Purāṇa* it is said: A person who is greedy to chant the holy name of Lord Hari does not consider whether the time or place is right for such chanting. He does not accept any restrictions on chanting the holy name.

The holy name easily gives impersonal liberation to those who want it. In the *Varāha Purāṇa*, the Supreme Personality of Godhead declares: A person who always chants, "Nārāyaṇa! Acyuta! Ananta! Vāsudeva! may, if he wishes, merge into My existence."

In the *Garuḍa Purāṇa* it is said: What is the use of Saṅkhyā? What is the use of *yoga*? O king of kings, if you wish to attain impersonal liberation, then you should chant the holy name of Lord Govinda.

The holy name of Lord Hari sends the individual souls to the spiritual world of Vaikuṇṭha. In the *Nandi Purāṇa* it is said: Persons who in the past have committed every possible sin in every possible situation, but who now chant the holy name of the Lord, go to the supreme abode of Lord Viṣṇu.

By chanting the holy name, one pleases the Supreme Personality of Godhead. In the *Bṛhan-nāradīya Purāṇa* it is said: O *brāhmaṇas*, the Supreme Personality of Godhead, who is beyond the touch of the material senses, becomes very pleased with a person who, in spite of hunger, thirst, and many troubles, continues to always chant His holy name.

By chanting the holy name of Lord Hari, one can bring the Supreme Personality of Godhead under one's control. In the *Mahābhārata*, Lord Kṛṣṇa declares: When I was away from Draupadī, she cried with the words, "He Govinda!" This call has put Me in her debt, and that indebtedness is gradually increasing in My heart.

The holy name of Lord Hari gives the final goal of life to the people. In the *Skanda* and *Padma Purāṇas*, it is said: Chanting the holy name of Lord Dāmodara brings the greatest auspiciousness, the greatest wealth, the greatest benefit.

Chanting the holy name of Lord Hari is the best of all devotional activities. In the *Vaiṣṇava-cintāmaṇi* it is said: By working very hard to always remember Lord Viṣṇu, one can destroy all sins. However, one can attain an even greater benefit simply by moving the lips to chant the Lord's holy name.

In the *Viṣṇu-rahasya* it is said: The same result that was obtained in the Satya-yuga by worshiping Lord Hari and in the Tretā-yuga by performing hundreds of sacrifices is obtained in the Kali-yuga simply by chanting the holy name of Lord Govinda.

In *Śrīmad-Bhāgavatam* (12.3.52) it is said: Whatever result was obtained in Satya-yuga by meditating on Viṣṇu, in Tretā-yuga by performing sacrifices, and in Dvāpara-yuga by serving the Lord's lotus feet, can also be obtained in Kali-yuga by chanting the Hare Kṛṣṇa *mahā-mantra*.

O Vijaya-kumāra, think about it and you will see that even the shadow of the holy name of Lord Hari is better than all material pious deeds. And, why not? Pious deeds are only the means to attain an end. Once the end is attained, the means are thrown away. Pious deeds are all material. However, the holy name of Lord Hari is spiritual. The holy name may be the means to attain an end, but when one attains the end, he finds that the holy name itself is also the end. Think about it and you will see that all the different limbs of devotional service take shelter of the holy name of Lord Hari.

Vijaya-kumāra: O master, the holy name of Lord Hari is spiritual. I have faith in that truth. However, so that my faith may be free from doubts, I need to understand how it is that the holy name, which is a series of syllables, is spiritual. Please be merciful and explain.

Bābājī: The scriptures (*Padma Purāṇa*) declare: The holy name of Kṛṣṇa is transcendentally blissful. It bestows all spiritual benedictions, for it is Kṛṣṇa Himself, the reservoir of all pleasure. Kṛṣṇa's name is complete, and it is the form of all transcendental mellows. It is not a material name under any condition, and it is no less powerful than Kṛṣṇa Himself. Since Kṛṣṇa's name is not contaminated by the material qualities, there is no question of its being involved with *māyā*. Kṛṣṇa's name is always liberated and spiritual. It is never conditioned by the laws of material nature. This is because the name of Kṛṣṇa and Kṛṣṇa Himself are identical.

Vijaya-kumāra: How can a name, which is, after all, a series of syllables, be different from other sounds in this material world?

Bābājī: The holy name of Lord Hari does not take its birth in the material world. Only when he is situated in his original spiritual body is the individual soul, who is a tiny particle of spirit, eligible to pronounce the pure holy name of Lord Hari. The material senses of a soul imprisoned in *māyā*'s world have no power to pronounce the pure holy name of Lord Hari. However, by the mercy of the Lord's *hlādinī-śakti*, such a soul can be situated in his original form. Then, the holy name will appear before him. By the mercy of the pure holy name, the holy name enters the devotee's thinking process and then descends to the tongue, if the tongue is purified by devotional service. On that tongue, the holy name dances. The holy name is not a series of material syllables. It only seems to be material syllables when it dances on a tongue made of matter. That is the secret of the holy name.

Vijaya-kumāra: Of the primary names of the Lord, which name is the most sweet?

Bābājī: In the *Śata-nāma-stotra* it is said: One utterance of the name, Viṣṇu, is better than all the *Vedas*. One utterance of the name, Rāma, is equal to a thousand utterances of the name Viṣṇu.

Then, in the *Brahmānda Purāṇa* it is said: The pious results derived from chanting the thousand holy names of Viṣṇu three times can be attained by one repetition of the holy name of Kṛṣṇa.

Therefore, the holy name of Lord Kṛṣṇa is the best. That is why our Lord, Śrī Gaurāṅga, taught the *mantra* that begins, "Hare Kṛṣṇa, Hare Kṛṣṇa". You should always chant that *mantra*.

Vijaya-kumāra: What is the path of chanting the holy name?

Bābājī: Using *tulasī* beads or, in the absence of beads, counting on your fingers, and carefully avoiding offenses, you should always chant the holy name of Lord Hari. By chanting the holy name purely, one attains *prema* (pure love of God). The purpose of counting is to know whether or not the number of names chanted is gradually increasing. *Tulasī* is very dear to Lord Hari. Therefore, touching *tulasī* beads as one chants the holy name brings a better result. When one chants, one should be conscious that the name of Lord Kṛṣṇa is not different from Lord Kṛṣṇa Himself.

Vijaya-kumāra: O master, there are nine processes of devotional service, and sixty four categories of devotional activities. If one constantly chants the holy name, which is only one of the activities of devotional service, how will one find time to perform any other devotional activity?

Bābājī: What is the difficulty? The sixty-four devotional activities are actually included within the nine devotional processes. One may worship the Deity of the Lord, or one may chant the holy name in a solitary place. One can practice the nine processes of devotional service in any situation. In the presence of the Deity, one can purely hear, chant, remember, and in other ways, serve the holy name of Lord Kṛṣṇa. All these activities may be counted together as devotion to the holy name. If one has no opportunity to see the Deity, one may remember the Deity and in this way, in the presence of the Deity, one may practice the nine devotional activities, beginning with hearing and chanting the holy name. If, in the past, one has performed many pious deeds, then he will naturally yearn to chant the holy name. By constantly chanting the holy name, one automatically performs all the activities of the different limbs of devotional service. Of the nine processes of devotional service, beginning with hearing and chanting, chanting the holy name is the most powerful. If one can taste bliss by chanting the holy names, that is enough. It is not that one must perform every devotional activity.

Vijaya-kumāra: What does it mean to always chant the holy name?

Bābājī: Aside for the time when one sleeps, one can chant the holy name throughout the day as one performs various activities. That is called constant chanting of the holy name. One can chant the holy name in any place, at any time, or in any situation. There are no restrictions.

Vijaya-kumāra: Aha! Unless you first give us your mercy, we will never have the power to always chant the holy name in this way. Without your mercy, we do not see any hope that we will ever become true Vaiṣṇavas.

Bābājī: First I will tell you of the different kinds of Vaiṣṇavas. Lord Gaurāṅga, the master of our hearts, told Satyarāja that any person who has once uttered the holy name of Lord Kṛṣṇa should be considered a Vaiṣṇava. Then again, a person who always chants the holy name of Lord Kṛṣṇa is a better Vaiṣṇava. A person, the sight of whom makes the holy name of the Lord appear on others' mouths, is the best Vaiṣṇava. By chanting the holy name of Lord Kṛṣṇa with faith, you will become true Vaiṣṇavas.

Vijaya-kumāra: Please describe to us the pure holy name of Kṛṣṇa and all other things we should know.

Bābājī: When the holy name of Lord Kṛṣṇa appears in a person who has full faith and who practices unalloyed devotional service—that is said to be the true holy name of Lord Kṛṣṇa. When the holy name appears in any other situation, the name is either *nāmābhāsa* (a glimpse of the holy name) or *nāmāparādha* (the holy name chanted with offenses).

Vijaya-kumāra: O master, should we call the holy name the goal (*sādhya*) or the means (*sādhana*) to attain the goal?

Bābājī: When a devotee practices *sādhana-bhakti*, his chanting of the holy name may be said to be the means for attaining the goal (*sādhana*). However, when one practices *bhāva-bhakti* or *prema-bhakti*, his chanting of the holy name is said to be the goal (*sādhya*) itself. In this way, the holy name contracts or expands according to the devotees' stage of spiritual advancement.

Vijaya-kumāra: Is Lord Kṛṣṇa really not different from His name? Or is this not really true?

Bābājī: There is not the slightest difference. However, there is one secret difference: The holy name is more merciful that Lord Kṛṣṇa Himself. If one commits an offense to Him, Lord Kṛṣṇa will not forgive. But if one commits an offense to Lord Kṛṣṇa, or His Holy name, then the holy name will be merciful and forgive. You should carefully understand the offenses to the holy name. Carefully avoiding these offenses, one should chant the holy name. Why should one avoid them? A person who is not free from offenses cannot chant the holy name purely. Tomorrow, you will learn about these offenses.

After thus learning about the true nature and glories of the holy name, Vrajanātha and Vijaya-kumāra respectfully touched the dust of their spiritual master's lotus feet, and then they both returned to Bilva-puṣkariṇī.

Chapter Twenty-four

Eternal religion and sambandha, abhidheya and prayojana (Offenses to the holy name)

That evening, Vrajanātha and Vijaya-kumāra purely chanted 50,000 holy names (twenty-nine rounds) on their *tulasī* beads. Late at night, they finally fell asleep. As they purely chanted the holy name, they both felt the presence of Lord Kṛṣṇa's mercy. The next morning, they told each other all they had felt. They were blissful. They bathed in the Ganges, worshiped Lord Kṛṣṇa, chanted the holy name of Lord Hari, recited the *Daśa-mūla*, studied *Śrīmad-Bhāgavatam*, served the Vaiṣṇavas, honored the Lord's *prasādam*, and performed other devotional activities. In this way, they passed the day.

At dusk, they visited the cottage of the elderly saintly *bābājī* at Śrīvāsa's courtyard. After offering *daṇḍavat* obeisances and sat down. Thinking of what had been proposed during the previous evening's talks, Vijaya-kumāra asked about the offenses to the holy name.

With the cheerfulness that was a part of his nature, the saintly *bābājī* said, "As chanting the holy name is the best of all spiritual activities, so offenses to the holy name are the gravest of sins. When a person takes shelter of the holy name, all his sins flee far away. But, the offenses to the holy name do not flee away so easily.

In the *Padma Purāṇa* it is said: The chanting of Hare Kṛṣṇa is recommended for persons who commit offenses because, if they continue chanting, they will gradually chant offenselessly. Even if, in the beginning, one chants with offenses, one will become free from such offenses by chanting again and again.

Bābā, look! How difficult it is to become free from offenses to the holy name! An intelligent person will strive to chant the holy name without offense. A person who takes great care to avoid offenses is quickly able to chant the pure holy name. A person may display ecstatic symptoms, may shed tears, and the hairs of his body may stand up, but he may still be committing offenses and he may still not chant purely. If they do not take special care, the aspiring devotees will not be able to chant the holy name purely.

Vijaya-kumāra: O master, what is pure chanting of the holy name?

Bābājī: When one does not commit the ten offenses to the holy name, then he chants purely. Chanting purely here does not mean chanting with accurate pronunciation. In the *Padma Purāṇa* it is said: If a devotee once utters the holy name of the Lord, or if it penetrates his mind or enters his ear, which is the channel of aural reception, that holy name will certainly deliver him from material bondage, whether vibrated properly or improperly, with correct or incorrect grammar, and properly joined or vibrated in separate parts. O *brāhmaṇa*, the potency of the holy name is therefore certainly great. However, if one uses the vibration of the holy name for the benefit of the material body, for material wealth and followers, or under the influence of greed or atheism—in other words, if one utters the name with offenses—such chanting will not produce the desired result very soon. Therefore one should diligently avoid offenses in chanting the holy name of the Lord.

Vijaya-kumāra: Now I can see that the aspiring devotee has no alternative but to be aware of the offenses in chanting the holy name. Please be kind and describe those offenses.

Bābājī: There are ten offenses to the holy name. They are described in these words of the *Padma Purāṇa* (*Brahmā-khanda* 25.15-18): 1. Blasphemy of the great saintly persons who are engaged in preaching the Hare Kṛṣṇa *mahā-mantra* is the worst offense at the lotus feet of the holy name. The *nāma-prabhu*, who is identical with Kṛṣṇa, will never tolerate such blasphemous activities, even from one who passes as a great devotee. 2. In this material world, the holy name of Viṣṇu is all-auspicious. Viṣṇu's name, form, qualities, and pastimes are all transcendental absolute knowledge. Therefore, if one tries to separate the Absolute Personality of Godhead from His holy name, or His transcendental form, qualities, and pastimes, thinking them to be material—that is offensive. Similarly, to think the names of demigods such as Lord Śiva to be as good as the name of Lord Viṣṇu is also blasphemous. 3. To consider the spiritual master to be material and therefore, to envy his exalted position. 4. Blasphemy of Vedic literature, such as the four *Vedas* and the *Purāṇas*. 5. To give some interpretation on the holy name of the Lord. 6. To consider the glories of the holy name to be imaginary. 7. To think that since the Hare Kṛṣṇa *mantra* can counteract all sinful reactions, one may therefore go on with his sinful activities and then at the same time chant the Hare Kṛṣṇa *mantra* to neutralize them, is the greatest offense at the lotus feet of *hari-nāma*. One who thinks in this way cannot be purified by any means, such as by austerities or by the various punishments of

Yamarāja. 8. It is a great offense to consider the chanting of the Hare Kṛṣṇa *mantra* to be equal to the performance of religious ceremonies, following austere vows, practicing renunciation, and performing fire sacrifices, which are all materialistic auspicious activities. 9. It is an offense to preach the glories of the holy name to those who will not hear, to those who are atheistic, and to those who have no faith in the chanting of the holy name. 10. That lowest among men who, even after hearing the glories of the transcendental holy name of the Lord, continues in a materialistic concept of life, thinking, "I am this body and everything belonging to this body is mine (*ahaṁ mameti*)", and does not show respect and love for the chanting of the Hare Kṛṣṇa *mahā-mantra* is an offender to the holy name.

Vijaya-kumāra: Please kindly explain each verse separately so that I may understand the offenses.

Bābājī: Two offenses are described in the first verse. The first offense is blasphemy of the great saintly persons who have renounced *karma*, *dharma*, *jñāna* and *yoga*, and have completely taken shelter of the holy name. That is a very great offense. And, why should it not be a great offense? The holy name of Lord Hari will not excuse the blasphemy of great souls who properly preach the glories of the holy name to the world. The holy name is quickly merciful to persons who chant the holy name in the company of the most saintly devotees and who avoid blaspheming devotees attached to the holy name.

Vijaya-kumāra: I can understand the first offense very easily. O master, please explain the second offense.

Bābājī: In the second half of the verse we are discussing, the second offense is described. This offense may be explained in two ways. The first explanation is this: Lord Viṣṇu and Lord Sadā-ṣiva are the leaders of the demigods. To see that Their qualities, names, and other features show that They are both independent of each other is an offense to the holy name. The idea that Lord Viṣṇu may be a supreme controller, but Lord Śiva is also a supreme controller, and he is independent of Lord Viṣṇu, is an idea that leads to *bahvīśvaravāda*, the idea that there are many independent gods. That idea is a great obstruction blocking the path of unalloyed devotional service. The truth is that Lord Śiva and the other demigods have no power independent of Lord Viṣṇu. If one understands in this way, then he does not commit this offense to the holy name.

The second interpretation is this: To think that the name, form, qualities, and pastimes of the all-auspicious (Śiva) Supreme Personality of Godhead are different from the transcendental and eternally perfect spiritual body of the Lord is an offense to the holy name. The truth is that Kṛṣṇa's form, Kṛṣṇa's name, Kṛṣṇa's qualities, and Kṛṣṇa's pastimes, are all spiritual. They are not different from each other. A person who understands this theoretically (*jñāna*) and practically (vi*jñāna*), when he chants the holy name of Lord Kṛṣṇa, does not commit this offense to the holy name. It is with this knowledge that one should chant the holy name of the Lord.

Vijaya-kumāra: I understand the first and second offenses. By your mercy, I have understood that Lord Kṛṣṇa's form is spiritual and not material, that He is not different from His qualities, names, parts and parcels, and all else in relation to Him. A person who takes shelter of the holy name is obliged to learn the truth of matter and spirit by approaching the lotus feet of a bona fide spiritual master. Now. please explain the third offense.

Bābājī: One should have unwavering devotion to the spiritual master who gives one the holy name, for the holy name is the highest of all spiritual activities. A person who disrespects the spiritual master who gives the holy name; a person who thinks that, although his spiritual master may be learned in the scriptures describing the holy name, he is not learned in Vedānta and other philosophies; a person who then thinks he knows more about philosophy than his spiritual master, commits an offense to the holy name. No teacher is superior to the spiritual master who knows the truth of the holy name. Therefore, to think lightly of him is an offense to the holy name.

Vijaya-kumāra: O master, if we are purely devoted to you, then our lives will be auspicious. Now, please be merciful and explain the fourth offense.

Bābājī: In the *śruti-śāstra* it is said that chanting the holy name is the best of all spiritual activities. There, it is said (the *Vedas*, quoted in *Hari-bhakti-vilāsa* 11.510-512): O Lord Viṣṇu, now that we understand the truth, we worship the glory of Your holy name. *Oṁ tat sat oṁ*. I offer my respectful obeisances to the lotus feet of the Supreme Personality of Godhead. To attain liberation, the pure devotees chant and hear His transcendental holy names. As far as they can understand You, the sages in ancient times chanted the glories of You, who are perfect and complete, and who are the father of the *Vedas*. O Lord Viṣṇu, now that we understand the truth, we worship the glory of Your holy name.

In this way, it is seen that all the *Vedas* and all the *Upaniṣads* chant the glories of the holy name. To blaspheme all these scriptures is an offense to the holy name. If one honors the scriptures but blasphemes the parts of the scriptures that teach the glories of the holy name, one commits an offense to the holy name. Because of this offense, one will not feel attracted to the holy name. Fully aware that the holy name is the crest jewel of all the *Vedas*, one should respectfully chant the holy name.

Vijaya-kumāra: O master, your mouth is showering nectar on us! Now, we thirst to learn about the fifth offense.

Bābājī: The fifth offense to the holy name of Lord Hari is to give some interpretation on the holy name of the Lord. In the *Jaimini-saṁhitā* it is said: Persons who give the interpretation that the glories of the holy name as described in the *śrutis*, *smṛtis*, and *Purāṇas* are exaggerations, live always in hell.

In the *Brahma-saṁhitā*, the Supreme Personality of Godhead explains to Brahmā: Any person who, after hearing the descriptions of the various benefits obtained by chanting the holy name, thinks these benefits are exaggerated, I throw into a host of sufferings and torture in many horrible ways.

The scriptures explain that the holy name has all the powers of the Supreme Personality of Godhead Himself. The holy name is perfectly spiritual. Therefore, it has the power to deliver one from the cycle of birth and death.

In the *Viṣṇu-dharma Purāṇa* it is said: My dear king, this word Kṛṣṇa is so auspicious that anyone who chants this holy name immediately gets rid of the resultant actions of sinful activities from many, many births.

In the *Bṛhan-nāradīya Purāṇa* it is said: "O best of the *brāhmaṇas*, chanting Lord Hari's holy names is the only way the people can become free of all sins. I do not see any other way.

In the *Bṛhad-viṣṇu Purāṇa* it is said: A person who chants the holy name of Kṛṣṇa can at once counteract the resultant actions of more sinful activities than he is able to perform.

These descriptions of the holy name's glories are all completely true.

However, when they hear these descriptions, persons who earn their livelihood by performing the rituals of *karma* or teaching the impersonal speculations of *jñāna*, in order to protect their livelihood, say these descriptions are all exaggerations. Their interpretation is this: The scriptures' descriptions of the glories of the holy names are not really true. Exaggerated descriptions of the benefits brought by chanting are given so that the mind may be attracted to the holy name.

Persons who commit this offense do not attain attraction to the holy name. Therefore, with full faith in the words of scripture, you should chant the holy name of Lord Hari. But, you should avoid the company of people who give the interpretation that the glories of the holy name are exaggerated. If somehow you see such a person, you should at once bathe while still wearing all your clothing. That teaching Lord Gaurāṅga has given.

Vijaya-kumāra: O master, it is not easy for householders to chant the holy name purely. And, why not? They are always surrounded by non-devotees who are all offenders to the holy name. *Brāhmaṇa paṇḍitas* like myself find it very hard to have the company of pious devotees. O master, please be merciful and give me the spiritual strength to avoid the company of non-devotees. As I hear the words from your mouth, my faith grows more and more strong. Now, please explain the sixth offense.

Bābājī: The sixth offense is to consider the glories of the holy name to be imaginary. The impersonalists and fruitive workers think that the Supreme is formless and nameless. They think that the sages invented the names Rāma, Kṛṣṇa, and the other names of the Lord to help the people attain perfection. Persons who accept this conclusion are offenders to the holy name. The truth is that the holy name is spiritual and eternal. The holy name appears only on spiritual senses engaged in devotional service. Taking lessons from the bona fide spiritual master and the holy scriptures, you should understand that the holy name is real, spiritual, and eternal. The holy name will not be merciful to you if you think He is imaginary.

Vijaya-kumāra: O master, before we had taken shelter of your lotus feet, which bring freedom from fear, we stayed in the company of fruitive workers and *nyāya* logicians, and we thought as they did. Now, by your mercy, we have thrown those ideas far away. Please be merciful and now explain the seventh offense.

Bābājī: To think that since the Hare Kṛṣṇa *mantra* can counteract all sinful reactions, one may therefore go on with his sinful activities and at the same time chant the Hare Kṛṣṇa *mantra* to neutralize them, is an offense at the lotus feet of *hari-nāma*. A person who commits sins expecting that the holy name will purify him does not become purified even by practicing austerities. And, why not? His action is counted among the offenses to the holy name. Its only atonement is the atonement that removes offenses to the holy name. That is the only way it is removed.

Vijaya-kumāra: O master, in this world, no sin exists that is not destroyed by chanting the holy name. Why then does the holy name not destroy this sin? Why is it counted among the offenses to the holy name?

Bābājī: Bābā, on the day when a living entity purely takes shelter of the holy name, from that day forward, all his sinful reactions, either *prārabdha* (that have already begun to bring suffering) or *aprārabdha* (that will bring suffering in the future), are at once destroyed. Eventually, the holy name gives him *prema* (pure love of God). A person who purely takes shelter of the holy name throws sinful desires far away. He does not even desire the benefits attained by performing material pious deeds. He throws talk of material piety and sin far away. Neither is he attracted to impersonal liberation. Thus, a person who purely chants the holy name does not commit sins.

However, if a person commits offenses while he chants the holy name, his chanting is *nāmābhāsa* (a reflection of the holy name). It is not pure chanting of the holy name. In the stage of *nāmābhāsa*, the chanter's past sins are all destroyed and at present, he is not attracted to sinning. However, some remnant of past sinful habits remains and only gradually is destroyed. If, because of past habits, the chanter accidentally commits some sins, the *nāmābhāsa* (reflection of the holy name) throws that sin far away. However, if a person who takes shelter of the holy name thinks, "The chanting of the holy name destroys all sins. If I commit a sin, then the holy name will destroy that sin," and if he then commits sins expecting to be forgiven, his sinful action is an offense to the holy name.

Vijaya-kumāra: Now, please explain the eighth offense and thus make us happy.

Bābājī: It is a great offense to consider the chanting of the Hare Kṛṣṇa *mantra* to be equal to following the *varṇāśrama-dharma*, giving charity, performing religious ceremonies, following austere vows, practicing renunciation, and performing fire sacrifices, *aṣṭāṅga-yoga*, and other such deeds, which are all materialistic auspicious activities. These and the other pious deeds that are described in the scriptures are all material activities. However, the holy name of the Lord is beyond the world of matter. The pious activities described here are all means to attain certain goals. The final goal is spiritual in nature. All these pious deeds are means. They are not goals. However, the holy name of Hari is a means during the period of *sādhana-bhakti*, and a final goal when the devotee reaps the fruit of his spiritual activities.

Therefore, ordinary material pious activities are not equal to chanting the holy name of Lord Hari. A person who thinks ordinary material pious activities are equal to chanting the holy name of Lord Hari commits an offense to the holy name. Material pious deeds bring only very small and pathetic benefits. A person who prays that the holy name grant him these pathetic material benefits commits an offense to the holy name. And, why not? Such a person thinks material pious deeds are equal to chanting the holy name. A person who knows that material pious deeds bring only small and pathetic results, and who understands that the holy name of Lord Hari is perfectly spiritual, has the knowledge called *abhidheya-jñāna* (knowledge of how one makes spiritual advancement by engaging in devotional service).

Vijaya-kumāra: O master, now I understand that nothing is equal to the holy name of Lord Hari. Now, please explain the ninth offense. My heart thirsts to hear of it.

Bābājī: The *Vedas* teach that the chanting of Lord Hari's holy name is the best of all spiritual activities. A person who has faith in unalloyed devotional service is naturally qualified to chant the holy name of Lord Hari. Persons who have no such faith are naturally averse to spiritual activities. When they hear the holy name, they are not attracted to it. To teach such persons about the holy name is an offense. Chanting the holy name of Lord Hari is the best of all spiritual activities. The holy name brings auspiciousness to everyone. Therefore, the teaching is that it is best to chant the holy name and allow such persons to hear the chanting. However, without first seeing that the recipient is properly qualified, one should not give initiation into the chanting of the holy name. When you become a *parama-bhāgavata* (great devotee of the Lord), then you will have transcendental potency. By the Lord's mercy, you will have the power to give people faith in the holy name. To such persons, you may teach the truth about the holy name of Lord Hari. As long as you remain a *madhyama* Vaiṣṇava (intermediate devotee of the Lord), you should avoid the faithless, the non-devotees, and the persons who hate the Lord.

Vijaya-kumāra: O master, pushed by greed for fame and money, many spiritual masters initiate unqualified persons into the chanting of Lord Hari's holy name. What is the status of these spiritual masters?

Bābājī: They are offenders to the holy name.

Vijaya-kumāra: Please be merciful and explain the tenth offense.

Bābājī: A resident of the material world who is intoxicated with the idea, "I am wealthy and glorious. I have many servants and followers," and who, on some rare occasions, thinks favorably about renunciation, or has a glimpse of spiritual understanding, or hears the glories of the holy name from *paṇḍitas*, but does not earnestly love the holy name as he should, commits an offense to the holy name. To teach these persons, the Lord says in Śrī *Śikṣāṣṭaka* (verse 2): O my Lord, Your holy name alone can render all benediction to living beings, and thus You have hundreds and millions of names like Kṛṣṇa and Govinda. In these transcendental names, You have invested all Your transcendental energies. There are not even hard and fast rules for chanting these names. O my Lord, out of kindness, You enable us to easily approach You by chanting Your holy names but I am so unfortunate that I have no attraction for them.

Bābā, avoid these ten offenses and chant Lord Hari's holy name always. Then the holy name will quickly be merciful to you, give you *prema* (pure love of God), and turn you into a *parama-bhāgavata* (a great devotee of the Lord).

Vijaya-kumāra: O master, now I see that the impersonalists, fruitive workers, and *yogīs* are all offenders to the holy name. When many people gather together to chant the holy name (*saṅkīrtana*), is it right for a pure Vaiṣṇava to join them?

Bābājī: If offenders to the holy name are prominent among the chanters, then it is not right for a true Vaiṣṇava to join them in chanting. However, if the chanters are mostly pure Vaiṣṇavas, or Vaiṣṇavas whose chanting is on the level of *nāmābhāsa* (the reflection of the holy name), then there is no harm. In truth it is good. That chanting brings spiritual happiness. Now it is late at night. Tomorrow you will hear more about *nāmābhāsa*.

Their voices choked with love for the holy name, Vijaya-kumāra and Vrajanātha offered prayers to the saintly *bābājī*, touched the dust from his lotus feet, and, singing the song, *hari haraye namaḥ*, began walking to Bilva-puṣkariṇī.

Chapter Twenty-five

Eternal religion and sambandha, abhidheya and prayojana (Offenses to the holy name)

Jaiva-dharma

The next evening, at dusk, Vijaya-kumāra and Vrajanātha approached the saintly *bābājī* and offered *daṇḍavat* obeisances to him. When it was appropriate, Vijaya-kumāra said, "O master, please be merciful and fully explain *nāmābhāsa* (the reflection of the holy name). We thirst to hear about the holy name."

The saintly *bābājī* replied, "You are very fortunate. To understand the holy name, you should first understand three things: 1. *nāma* (the pure chanting of the holy name), 2. *nāmābhāsa* (the reflection of the holy name) and 3. *nāma-aparādha* (offenses to the holy name). Now I will explain about *nāmābhāsa*. The reflection of the holy name is called *nāmābhāsa*.

Vijaya-kumāra: What kind of reflection is it, and how many kinds of reflections are there?

Bābājī: The word *ābhāsa* has three definitions: 1. *kānti* (light), 2. *chāyā* (shadow) and 3. *pratibimba* (reflection). An effulgent object manifests light, and also creates shadows. In this way, the sun of the holy name manifests as *nāma-chāyā* (the shadow of the holy name) and *nāma-pratibimba* (the reflection of the holy name). The wise speak of *bhakty-ābhāsa* (the partial presence of devotional service), *bhāvābhāsa* (the partial presence of ecstatic love of God), *nāmābhāsa* (the partial presence of the holy name), and *vaiṣṇavābhāsa* (being a Vaiṣṇava in part). Each of these *ābhāsa* is divided into two aspects: *pratibimba* (reflection) and *chāyā* (shadow).

Vijaya-kumāra: How are *bhakty-ābhāsa*, *bhāvābhāsa*, *nāmābhāsa*, and *vaiṣṇavābhāsa* related to each other?

Bābājī: A Vaiṣṇava chants the holy name of Lord Hari. If he chants the holy name with *bhakty-ābhāsa*, then the holy name manifests before him as *nāmābhāsa*, and he himself is a *vaiṣṇavābhāsa*. The words *bhāva* and *bhakti* refer to the same thing. They are called by different names because one is contracted and the other expanded.

Vijaya-kumāra: In what condition of life is one a *vaiṣṇavābhāsa*?

Bābājī: In *Śrīmad-Bhāgavatam* (11.2.47) it is said: A *prākṛta*, or materialistic devotee, does not purposefully study the *śāstra* and try to understand the actual standard of pure devotional service. Consequently, he does not show proper respect to advanced devotees. He may, however, follow the regulative principles learned from his spiritual master, or from his family who worships the Deity. He is to be considered on the material platform, although he is trying to advance in devotional service. Such a person is a *bhakta-prāya* (neophyte devotee), or *bhaktābhāsa*, for he is a little enlightened by Vaiṣṇava philosophy.

The word *sraddhā* (faith) in this verse means *sraddhābhāsa* (the partial presence of faith). And, why not? When faith is directed to the Lord alone and not to the Lord's devotees, such faith is called *chāyā* (shadow) or *pratibimba* (reflection). That is the faith of ordinary materialist people. It is not the spiritual faith of pure devotional service. Because a *bhaktābhāsa* (a person who is partially a devotee) has faith and worship that are material (*prākṛta*) in nature, a *bhaktābhāsa* devotee is also called a *prākṛta-bhakta*, or a *vaiṣṇavābhāsa*. Lord Mahāprabhu said that Hiranya-Govardhana was a *vaiṣṇava-prāya*. The word *vaiṣṇava-prāya* means, "A person who, wearing beads, *tilaka* markings, and other things, looks like a true Vaiṣṇava, although his chanting of the holy name is only *nāmābhāsa*." Such a person is not a true Vaiṣṇava, or a *śuddha* Vaiṣṇava (pure Vaiṣṇava).

Vijaya-kumāra: If an impersonalist accepts the various outward markings of a Vaiṣṇava and chants the holy name, is he then a *vaiṣṇavābhāsa*?

Bābājī: No. They cannot be called *vaiṣṇavābhāsa*. They are offenders. They should be called *vaiṣṇavāparādhi* (offenders to the Vaiṣṇavas). Those who take shelter of *pratibimba-nāmābhāsa* (the reflection of the holy name) and *pratibimba-bhāvābhāsa* (the reflection of ecstatic love for the Lord) may be called *vaiṣṇavābhāsa*. But, it is not right to call the great offenders by the name Vaiṣṇava. They should be called something else.

Vijaya-kumāra: O master, please explain more clearly the nature of the pure chanting of the holy name, so that we may understand it better.

Bābājī: When a person who chants the holy name is *anyābhilāṣitā-śūnyaṁ* (free of all material desires), *jñāna-karmādy-anāvṛtam* (free of impersonalism and fruitive work), and *ānukūlya-bhāva* (favorable to Lord Kṛṣṇa), then his chanting is pure chanting of the holy name. Here, the word *anyābhilāṣa* does not refer to the desire to taste the transcendental bliss that comes when the spiritual holy name is openly manifested.

Anyābhilāṣa here refers to the desire to attain impersonal liberation or freedom from sins as the result of one's chanting of the holy name. If these desires are present, then one's chanting of the holy name will not be pure. If one is not free from the desire to enjoy the so-called benefits obtained by *jñāna* (impersonal speculation) and *karma* (fruitive work), then his chanting of the holy name will not be pure either. If one throws far away all feelings of enmity toward the Lord, and maintains only favorable emotions directed to the Lord, then one's chanting of the holy name will be pure. This way you can see that when one's chanting is free of *nāmāparādha* (offenses to the holy name) and *nāmābhāsa* (the partial manifestation of the holy name), then his chanting is *śuddha-nāma* (the pure chanting of the holy name).

Lord Gauracandra, the purifier of the Kali-yuga, has described this pure chanting in the following words: One should chant the holy name of the Lord in a humble state of mind, thinking oneself lower than the straw in the street. One should be more tolerant than a tree, devoid of all sense of false prestige, and ready to offer all respect to others. In such a state of mind, one can chant the holy name of the Lord constantly.

Vijaya-kumāra: O master, how are *nāmābhāsa* and *nāmāparādha* different?

Bābājī: *Nāmābhāsa* is not *śuddha-nāma* (the pure chanting of the holy name). In one circumstance, the chanting of the holy name is called *nāmābhāsa* and in another circumstance, it is called *nāmāparādha*. When, out of bewilderment and foolishness, one does not chant the holy name purely, his chanting is called *nāmābhāsa*. On the other hand, when a rascal impersonalist who yearns to attain impersonal liberation chants the holy name, or when a hedonist who yearns after material pleasures chants the holy name, their impure chanting is called *nāmāparādha* (offense to the holy name).

I have already described to you the ten offenses. If a sincere person out of ignorance commits these offenses, his chanting is *nāmābhāsa*. This should be understood: As long as one's chanting is *nāmābhāsa* and does not have the nature of *nāmāparādha*, then one may hope that one day he will rise above *nāmābhāsa* and attain *śuddha-nāma* (the pure chanting of the holy name). As long as one is in the stage of *nāmāparādha*, it will not be easy for him to chant the holy name purely. I have already explained how one becomes free from *nāmāparādha* (offenses to the holy name). Aside from that, there is no other method by which one can attain auspiciousness.

Vijaya-kumāra: What should a person whose chanting is *nāmābhāsa* do to turn his *nāmābhāsa* chanting into *śuddha-nāma* (the pure chanting of the holy name)?

Bābājī: By associating with pure devotees, one quickly becomes attracted to pure devotional service. When the holy name dances on the tongue of such a person, that chanting is *śuddha-nāma* (pure chanting of the holy name). However, such a person must scrupulously avoid the association of persons whose chanting is *nāmāparādha*. Why should this be? If he associates with them, he will not be able to chant the holy name purely. Association with saintly devotees is the only way for the individual soul to attain auspiciousness. For this reason, Lord Gauracandra, who is the master of our lives, taught Sanātana Gosvāmī that association with saintly devotees is the root from which devotional service grows. When one associates with saintly devotees and avoids the association of non-devotees and women, he will be able to chant the holy name of Lord Kṛṣṇa properly.

Vijaya-kumāra: O master, does this mean that if a man does not renounce the association of his wife he will not be able to chant the holy name purely?

Bābājī: One should renounce association with women. When a householder Vaiṣṇava associates with his wife and he lives Vaiṣṇava household life in an unattached way—that is not what is meant here by association with women. When a man has a material attachment to a woman, or a woman has a material attachment to a man, that is what is meant here by association with women. A householder may remain in family life, and if he is free from material attachment, he can chant Lord Kṛṣṇa's holy name purely and he can attain the final goal of life.

Vijaya-kumāra: O master, what are the different kinds of *nāmābhāsa*?

Bābājī: In *Śrīmad-Bhāgavatam* (6.2.14) it is said: "One who chants the holy name of the Lord is immediately freed from the reactions of unlimited sins, even if he chants indirectly (to indicate something else), jokingly, for musical entertainment, or even neglectfully. This is accepted by all the learned scholars of the scriptures.

Vijaya-kumāra: O master, what does it mean to chant indirectly (*sāṅketya*)?

Bābājī: At the moment of his death, Ajāmila called for his son, who was named Nārāyaṇa. By speaking the word Nārāyaṇa, which is a name of Lord Kṛṣṇa, Ajāmila attained the benefit brought by chanting the Lord's name indirectly. The *mlecchas* use the words "Ha Rāma! Ha Rāma!" which means "Pig", to show their horror and contempt. However, by chanting Ha Rāma! (O Lord Rāma!), the *mlecchas* chant the Lord's holy name in an indirect way, so that they become free from Yamarāja's grip. *Nāmābhāsa* (the glimpse of the holy name) brings liberation. That is the conclusion of all the scriptures. The holy names of Lord Mukunda (Kṛṣṇa) are not different from the Lord Himself. Therefore, a person who says the word Mukunda touches Lord Mukunda directly. In this way, he easily attains liberation. By following the path of impersonal speculation, one attains liberation only after much difficulty. But by *nāmābhāsa* (the glimpse of the holy name), everyone attains liberation very easily.

Vijaya-kumāra: O master, many arrogant impersonalist scholars, *mlecchas* who are completely ignorant of the truth, and demons who stand opposed to all spiritual goals, attained liberation by jokingly (*pārihāsya*) chanting the holy name. This I have read in many places in the scriptures. Please describe this joking chanting of the holy name.

Bābājī: When a person disrespectfully chants the holy name—that is called *stobha*. As a Vaiṣṇava chants the holy name aloud, a blasphemer may approach and say, "Hey, your Hari Kesta will bring everything to you!" By thus chanting the holy name, even disrespectfully, the blasphemer will eventually attain liberation. That is the power of the holy name.

Vijaya-kumāra: What is chanting the holy name neglectfully (*helana*)?

Bābājī: That is chanting the holy name without honoring it. In the *Prabhāsa-khaṇḍa* it is said: Kṛṣṇa's name is the sweetest of sweet things, the most auspicious of all auspicious things, the transcendental fruit of the vine of all Vedic literature. O best of the Bhṛgus, chanted even once, either with faith or contempt, it delivers the chanter.

In this verse, the word *śraddhayā* means, "with respect," and *helayā* means, "without respect." The words *nara-mātraṁ tārayet* mean that the holy name delivers even the Yavanas.

Vijaya-kumāra: Is it not an offense to chant the holy name without showing respect?

Bābājī: If it is done because of a demonic nature, it is an offense. But, if it is done because of ignorance, it is *nāmābhāsa* (a glimpse of the holy name).

Vijaya-kumāra: Please explain what benefit *nāmābhāsa* brings and what benefit it does not bring?

Bābājī: Sense pleasures (*bhukti*), liberation (*mukti*), and the eighteen yogic perfections are included among the benefits *nāmābhāsa* brings. However, pure love for Lord Kṛṣṇa (*kṛṣṇa-prema*), which is the highest goal of life, is not granted by *nāmābhāsa*. If a person whose chanting is on the level of *nāmābhāsa* associates with a pure devotee (*śuddha-bhakta*), then the chanter can come to the level of a *madhyama* Vaiṣṇava (intermediate devotee). From that status, he can become further elevated, attain pure devotion, chant the holy name purely, and finally attain pure love for Lord Kṛṣṇa (*kṛṣṇa-prema*).

Vijaya-kumāra: O master, in this world there are many devotees who are on the platform of *vaiṣṇavābhāsa*. They have the outward marks of a Vaiṣṇava and they diligently chant the holy name, although their chanting is on the level of *nāmābhāsa*. Even though they chant, after many days, they still do not attain pure love for Lord Kṛṣṇa (*kṛṣṇa-prema*). Why is that?

Bābājī: The reason is confidential. It is this: Persons on the level of *bhakty-ābhāsa* (a glimpse of devotional service) are certainly eligible to eventually attain pure devotional service. However, if such persons mistakenly think impure persons, persons who do not have unalloyed devotion to the Lord, to be great saints, and if by this bad association they eventually associate with impersonalists and other offenders, by that bad association they also become offenders to the pure Vaiṣṇavas. In this way, their path of gradual spiritual advancement becomes checked. Thus, by bad association, they come to accept the doctrines of the impersonalists or other offenders. In this way, they wander far away from pure devotional service and eventually they become offenders. However, if, because of past pious deeds, they are able to shun bad association and remain in the association of good devotees, then they eventually will become pure Vaiṣṇavas.

Vijaya-kumāra: O master, what result is obtained by *nāmāparādha* (offenses to the holy name)?

Bābājī: Even if they were multiplied millions of time, the five sins would not equal an offense to the holy name. You can very easily see the result reaped by offending the holy name.

Vijaya-kumāra: O master, a person who offends the holy name certainly reaps an inauspicious result. Still, does he not also obtain a good result because he has spoken the syllables of the holy name?

Bābājī: The holy name fulfills the chanter's desires, whatever they are. However, to the offensive chanter, the holy name will not give pure love for Lord Kṛṣṇa (*kṛṣṇa-prema*). Eventually, the offensive chanter must taste the result of his offenses. However, a person who, although he commits offenses to the holy name, regularly chants the holy name, will attain the result of his chanting. After some time, his chanting will become a great transcendental pious deed. As that transcendental pious deed grows greater and greater, he will attain the association of saintly devotees who devotedly chant the holy name in a pure way. Thus, by always chanting the holy name, the offender eventually becomes free of his offenses to the holy name. By following this path, even impersonalists gradually become sincere devotees of Lord Hari.

Vijaya-kumāra: By chanting the holy name only once, a person is freed from all sins. Why then should one chant the name always?

Bābājī: Offenders to the holy name have hearts and activities that are always impure. They are naturally averse to the Lord. They are never attracted to saintly persons, holy objects, or holy times. They are naturally attracted to evil persons, evil theories, and evil deeds. However, constant chanting of the holy name turns them away from evil persons and evil deeds. Free from bad association, they come to chant the holy name purely. The holy name then gives them the strength to proceed on the spiritual path.

Vijaya-kumāra: O master, from your saintly mouth flows a nectarean stream of the descriptions of the holy name, a stream that flows through the cave of our ears and into our hearts. Drinking from this stream makes us intoxicated with the nectar of love for the holy name. Now we understand the difference between *nāma* (the pure chanting of the holy name), *nāmābhāsa* (a glimpse of the holy name), and *nāmāparādha* (offensive chanting of the holy name). Now our lives are a success. Please tell us the conclusion of all this. We yearn to hear it.

Bābājī: In Jagadānanda Paṇḍita's *Prema-vivarta*, the conclusion is eloquently taught. Please listen to it.

"O brother, the holy name of Lord Kṛṣṇa does not come from a person who associates with non-devotees. The syllables of the holy name may come from him, but the true holy name does not."

"Sometimes a glimpse of the holy name (*nāmābhāsa*) comes from him. Always offenses to the holy name (*nāmāparādha*) come from him. O my brother, please know that these are all obstacles to the path of devotion to Lord Kṛṣṇa."

"If you wish truly to chant the holy name of Lord Kṛṣṇa, then stay in the association of devotees and keep far away from the desire for sense gratification, impersonal liberation, and *yoga siddhis*."

"Avoid the ten offenses, remain aloof from praise and blame, perform your duties, and chant the holy name of Lord Kṛṣṇa."

"Always accept what is favorable to Lord Kṛṣṇa's devotional service and always reject what is not favorable to Lord Kṛṣṇa's devotional service."

"Avoid impersonal speculation, *yoga*, and fruitive work. Avoid the pretended renunciation practiced by persons who are like monkeys. That so-called renunciation is only a funny comedy played on the stage of the material body."

"Always think, 'Kṛṣṇa is my protector.' By humbly surrendering to Him, you will be free of troubles."

"It is very difficult for a conditioned soul to meet a great saint. That is why Lord Kṛṣṇa came, in the form of a great devotee, to the land of Nadīyā."

"If you are wise, you will take shelter of Lord Gaura's lotus feet. Where is there a saintly guru like Lord Gaura?"

"O *sannyāsī* brother, don't talk or hear gossip when you meet with others."

"O my *sannyāsī* brother, even in dreams, do not talk to women. O my brother, please remember that you have left your wife at home, and now you live in the forest."

"If you wish to keep Lord Gaurāṅga's love, then please keep in your mind the story of Chota Haridāsa."

"Don't eat opulent food. Don't wear opulent clothing. In your heart, always worship Rādhā and Kṛṣṇa."

"Like Haridāsa Ṭhākura, always chant the name of Lord Kṛṣṇa. At every moment of the eight parts of the day, worship Rādhā and Kṛṣṇa in the groves of Vṛndāvana forest."

"To both householder and *sannyāsī*, Lord Gaura Rāya says, 'My brother, do not pass your days without chanting the holy name.'"

"O my brother, there is no need to perform a great variety of many different devotional activities. You need only purely take shelter of Lord Kṛṣṇa's holy name. Pass your life in that way."

"Merciful to the conditioned souls, Lord Kṛṣṇa has descended as His holy name. Merciful to the people in Kali-yuga, Lord Kṛṣṇa has descended as fair-complexioned Lord Gaura."

"Sincerely worship Lord Gaura's devotees. O my brother—that is the way to attain Lord Kṛṣṇa's lotus feet."

"In the company of Lord Gaura's devotees, chant the names of Lord Gaura, chant the Hare Kṛṣṇa *mantra*, and dance again and again."

"O my brother, in this way, you will quickly attain the wealth of love for the holy name, a wealth that our Lord personally came to Nadīyā to deliver."

Hearing Śrī Jagadānanda Paṇḍita's *Prema-vivarta* from the mouth of the elderly saintly *bābājī*, Vijaya-kumāra and Vrajanātha were overcome with spiritual love. For some moments, the saintly *bābājī* fell unconscious. Then, placing his arms around Vijaya-kumāra's and Vrajanātha's necks, he began to sing:

"How powerful is the holy name of Lord Kṛṣṇa!"

"Ablaze with material desires, my heart has become like a desert scorched by the sun. But now, something walks on the pathway of my ears. Now it enters my heart. It is like a peerless shower of nectar."

"That shower of nectar has now left my heart. Now it walks on my tongue.

Assuming the form of a sound, it dances again and again. My voice is choked. My limbs tremble. My feet cannot stay still."

"A torrential stream flows from my eyes. My body is covered with perspiration. The hairs of my body stand erect. I fall unconscious. I think the end of the world has come. My entire body is filled with ecstatic love."

"It greatly troubles me. It showers my heart with nectar. It plunges me into an ocean of love. Now I do not understand anything. It has made me a madman. It has robbed all the wealth I keep in my heart."

"I take shelter of Him, and this is the way He acts. I cannot tell it all. The holy name of Lord Kṛṣṇa is independent. He acts as He likes. If He wishes, He makes me happy. He is the wealth of my happiness."

"The holy name is the budding flower of love. It is the resting place of wonderful nectar. It shows so much power. The budding flower begins to open. It shows a little of its beauty and virtue. Binding me with the ropes of Kṛṣṇa, it steals my heart."

"When it opens fully, that flower carries me to Vraja. It shows me its own form and pastimes. It gives me a perfect spiritual body. It places me by Kṛṣṇa's side. It completely destroys my material body."

"The holy name of Lord Kṛṣṇa is a *cintāmaṇi* jewel. It is the spring from which all nectar flows. It is eternally liberated. It is pure and sweet. If I can die plagued by the troubles brought by the holy name, then I will be happy."

Again and again he sang the glories of the holy name. In this way, half the night passed. Then he stopped. Taking permission from their spiritual master, Vijaya-kumāra and Vrajanātha, now plunged in the nectar of the holy name, returned to their own place.

Chapter Twenty-six

The discussion of rasa begins

Jaiva-dharma

Vijaya-kumāra did not come for almost a month. Knowing the desire of Vrajanātha and Vijaya-kumāra, Vrajanātha's grandmother arranged, with the help of a matchmaker, for a suitable bride. Hearing this news, Vijaya-kumāra sent his brother to Bilva-puṣkariṇī to perform his nephew's auspicious wedding ceremony. The auspicious day of the auspicious ceremony came. Hearing all about the wedding, one day, Vijaya-kumāra came there. His heart was restless for spiritual advancement. He would not talk of material things.

Vrajanātha said to him, "Uncle, why is your heart not peaceful today? Tell me confidentially. By your order, I now wear the shackles of household life. Please tell me what you are thinking about your own self."

Vijaya-kumāra replied, "Bābā, I have decided that at least once I should see Jagannātha Purī. In a few days, I will leave with a group of pilgrims from Jagannātha Purī. Come, let us go to our spiritual master and I will ask his permission."

After lunch, Vrajanātha and Vijaya-kumāra went to Śrī Māyāpur, told everything to saintly Raghunātha dāsa Bābājī, and asked his permission to go on pilgrimage to Jagannātha Purī. With great happiness, the saintly *bābājī* said that nowadays in Jagannātha Purī, at Jagannātha Miśra's home, where Lord Mahāprabhu stayed, resides Śrī Vakreśvara Paṇḍita's disciple, Śrī Gopāla-guru Gosvāmī, whose saintly feet Vijaya-kumāra should see, and whose teachings he should devotedly hear, and around whose neck now rest the teachings of Śrī Svarūpa Dāmodara Gosvāmī.

When Vrajanātha and Vijaya-kumāra returned, Vrajanātha declared that he also wished to go to Jagannātha Purī. Vijaya-kumāra was very glad to hear this. When they both explained all this, it was finally decided that Vrajanātha's grandmother would accompany them.

The month of Jyeṣṭha (May-June) had not yet come when the pilgrims left their homes and entered the path to Jagannātha Purī. Walking and walking, after some days, they came to Dāntana and then Jaleśvara. Eventually they saw the Deity, Śrī Kṣīra-corā Gopīnātha. Then they came to Śrī Virajā-kṣetra. After performing the *nābhi-gāya-kriyā* ritual, they bathed in the Vaitaraṇī River and then went to Cuttack, where they saw the Deity of Śrī Gopāla. Then, they saw a Deity of Lord Śiva in a mango grove. Finally, they came to Jagannātha Purī.

There, the *paṇḍitas* arranged lodgings for each of the pilgrims.

Vijaya-kumāra, Vrajanātha and Vrajanātha's grandmother all stayed at the home of Haracaṇḍi Sāhi. They circumambulated the holy place, bathed in the sea, saw the five famous holy places, and honored the *prasādam* offered to the Lord. Three or four days passed in this way. Then, in the temple, Vijaya-kumāra and Vrajanātha saw a picture of Lord Mahāprabhu, as well as His footprints and fingerprints. Overcome with love, that very day, they went to the home of Kāśi Miśra.

In Kāśi Miśra's home, they saw the stone Gambhīra room and they also saw Lord Mahāprabhu's sandals and other things. On one side was the temple of Śrī Rādhakānta and on the other side was the room of Śrī Gopāla-guru Gosvāmī. Their voices choked with the happiness of spiritual love, Vijaya-kumāra and Vrajanātha fell before Gopāla-guru Gosvāmī's feet.

Gopāla-guru Gosvāmī mercifully glanced at them, embraced them, and asked, "Who are you?"

When Vijaya-kumāra and Vrajanātha told about themselves, tears flowed from the eyes of Gopāla-guru Gosvāmī. When he heard the word Śrī Navadvīpa, he said, "I am fortunate, for today I have seen two residents of the holy abode. Please tell me: How are Raghunātha dāsa and Gauracandra dāsa and the other Vaiṣṇavas in Śrī Māyāpura these days? Ah! Whenever I think of Raghunātha dāsa Bābājī, I also remember my *śikṣā-guru*, Śrīla Raghunātha dāsa Gosvāmī."

Then, Gopāla-guru Gosvāmī called for his disciple, Śrī Dhyānacandra and said to him, "These two great souls should be given *prasādam*."

Going to Dhyānacandra's room, Vrajanātha and Vijaya-kumāra honored the *mahā-prasādam*. After honoring *mahā-prasādam*, the three devotees talked about many things. Learning that Vijaya-kumāra was a scholar of *Śrīmad-Bhāgavatam* and Vrajanātha was a scholar of many scriptures, Dhyānacandra Gosvāmī became very happy. He approached Gopāla-guru Gosvāmī and told him all about it.

Gopāla-guru Gosvāmī merciful said, "These two persons are the great treasure of my heart. Please bring them to see me every day that they stay in Jagannātha Purī."

At that time, Vijaya-kumāra and Vrajanātha said, "O master, Raghunātha dāsa Bābājī Mahāśaya of Śrī Māyāpura has been very merciful to us. He ordered us to take instructions at your lotus feet."

Gopāla-guru Gosvāmī said, "Raghunātha dāsa Bābājī is very learned. You should carefully follow whatever advice he gives. If you wish to study something he has not yet taught you, then you may come tomorrow at midday, honor the Lord's lunch *prasādam*, and the ask questions."

After accepting Gopāla-guru's invitation, the two devotees returned to Haracaṇḍi Sāhi's home. The next day, at the appointed time, the two devotees went to the temple of Śrī Rādhakānta, honored *prasādam*, and then placed some questions before Gopāla-guru Gosvāmī's lotus feet.

They said, "O master, we wish to understand the transcendental *rasas* (relationships with Lord Kṛṣṇa). By hearing the description of the *rasas* of devotional service to Lord Kṛṣṇa from your holy mouth, our lives will become successful. You are the foremost spiritual master of Lord Nimāi Paṇḍita's sampradāya. You stay in Lord Mahāprabhu's home, and you have accepted the seat given by Śrī Svarūpa Dāmodara Gosvāmī. You are the spiritual master of the entire world. When we hear from your mouth about the transcendental *rasas*, whatever little we have learned about the transcendental science will finally bear its proper fruit."

Taking these two disciples to a secluded place, Gopāla-guru Gosvāmī happily said, "May Nimāi Paṇḍita, who is the son of Śrī Śacī-devī and who, descending to this world in the land of Śrī Māyāpura, mercifully delivered the people of Bengal and Orissa, grant transcendental bliss to us. May Śrī Svarūpa Dāmodara Gosvāmī, who pleased Lord Mahāprabhu by describing to Him the sweet mellows of *mādhurya-rasa*, appear in our hearts. May Vakreśvara Paṇḍita, whose dancing made Nimāi Paṇḍita into his submissive servant, and who purified Devānanda Paṇḍita, grant auspiciousness to you."

"The *rasas* cannot be compared to anything else. When the moon of the Supreme Lord's transcendental pastimes directly rises, then the activities of pure devotional service become *bhakti-rasa* (the mellows of devotional service).

Vrajanātha: What pious deeds must one have performed in the past in order that one may attain *rasa*?

Gosvāmī: I cannot answer this question with only a brief explanation. I will explain elaborately. Then you will understand. From your spiritual master, you have heard about *kṛṣṇa-rati* (attachment to Kṛṣṇa), which is also called *sthāyi-bhāva* (steady ecstasy). When that ecstatic love increases, it becomes *kṛṣṇa-bhakti-rasa* (the mellows of devotional service to Lord Kṛṣṇa).

Vrajanātha: Please describe *sthāyi-bhāva* (steady ecstasy) and *sāmagrī* (the ingredients of *rasa*). I have already heard my spiritual master explain what is *bhāva*. I did not hear from him how these things combine to become *rasa*.

Gosvāmī: Generally, *bhāva-bhakti* (ecstatic devotional service) and *kṛṣṇa-rati* (attraction to Lord Kṛṣṇa) appear because of transcendental pious deeds performed in this life, or a previous life. In this way, one attains a condition of life that is filled with bliss. There are four kinds of *sāmagrī* (ingredients of *rasa*). They are: 1. *vibhāva* (special symptoms or causes of ecstasy), 2. *anubhāva* (subsequent ecstasy), 3. *sāttvika-bhāva* (constitutional or existential ecstasy), and 4. *vyabhicārī-bhāva* (aggressive ecstasy), or *sañcāri-bhāva* (continuously existing ecstatic symptoms).

Let me begin by explaining these different *sāmagrīs* (ingredients of *rasa*). *Vibhāva*, which causes one to taste the sweetness of attraction to Kṛṣṇa, is of two kinds: 1. *ālambana* (basic) and 2. *uddīpana* (impelling). *Ālambana* is itself of two kinds: 1. *viṣaya* (the object of love), and 2. *āśrayā* (the reservoir of love). The object of love is the *viṣaya-ālambana*, and the person who possesses the love is the *āśrayā-ālambana*. Thus, the person who is the object of attachment or love is the *rati-viṣaya*, and the person who is attached or who loves is the *rati-āśrayā*. Thus, a devotee who in his heart loves Lord Kṛṣṇa is the *rati-āśrayā*, and Lord Kṛṣṇa, who is the object of His devotee's love, is the *rati-viṣaya*.

Vrajanātha: I have understood that vi*bhāva* is divided into *ālambana* and *uddīpana*. Further, *ālambana* is of two kinds: *viṣaya* and *āśrayā*. Lord Kṛṣṇa is the *viṣaya* and the devotee is the *āśrayā*. This I desire to know: Is there any situation where Lord Kṛṣṇa Himself is the *rati-āśrayā* (a person who loves someone)?

Gosvāmī: Yes. When Lord Kṛṣṇa loves His devotee, then Kṛṣṇa is the *rati-āśrayā* and the devotee is the *rati-viṣaya*.

Vrajanātha: From my spiritual master I have heard the description of Lord Kṛṣṇa's sixty-four qualities. Please tell me what more may be said about Lord Kṛṣṇa.

Gosvāmī: Lord Kṛṣṇa is perfect and complete. He has all transcendental qualities and virtues. When He is in Dvārakā He is perfect. When He is in Mathurā He is more perfect. When He is in Gokula He is most perfect. His transcendental qualities are manifested in this way, in different degrees. In His different pastimes, Lord Kṛṣṇa appears as *dhīrodātta*, *dhīra-lalita*, *dhīra-praśānta*, and *dhīroddhata*. In these four ways, Lord Kṛṣṇa is a hero.

Vrajanātha: What is *dhīrodātta*?

Gosvāmī: As a *dhīrodātta* hero, Lord Kṛṣṇa is very grave, gentle, forgiving, merciful, and virtuous in many ways.

Vrajanātha: What is *dhīra-lalita*?

Gosvāmī: As a *dhīra-lalita* hero Lord Kṛṣṇa is naturally very funny, always in full youthfulness, expert in joking, free from all anxieties, and domesticated and very submissive to His lovers.

Vrajanātha: What is *dhīra-praśānta*?

Gosvāmī: As a *dhīra-praśānta* hero, Lord Kṛṣṇa is very peaceful, forbearing, considerate, and obliging.

Vrajanātha: What is *dhīroddhata*?

Gosvāmī: As a *dhīroddhata* hero, Lord Kṛṣṇa is very envious, proud, easily angered, restless, and complacent.

Vrajanātha: Many of these qualities you have described contradict each other. How is that possible?

Gosvāmī: Lord Kṛṣṇa possesses all powers and opulences without any limit. Therefore, by His inconceivable potencies, it is entirely possible that He possess many mutually contradictory qualities. This is described in the following words of the *Kūrma Purāṇa*: He is not great and He is not small. He is the greatest and He is the smallest. He has no color. His color is dark and the corners of His eyes are red. Because He has all powers and opulences, the Supreme Personality of Godhead possesses contradictory qualities. Even so, there is no fault in this. His contradictory qualities are glories.

In the *Mahā-varāha Purāṇa* it is said: "All the forms of the Supreme Personality of Godhead are eternal and everlasting. Nothing can be given to improve them, for they are perfect. Nothing can be taken from them. They are not material. They are full of transcendental bliss and knowledge. They are filled with all virtues and free from all faults.

In the *Vaiṣṇava-tantra* it is said: The form of the Supreme Personality of Godhead is eternal, full of knowledge, bliss, power, and opulence, and free of the eighteen faults. The eighteen faults are: illusion, fatigue, errors, roughness, material lust, restlessness, pride, envy, violence, disgrace, exhaustion, untruth, anger, hankering, dependence, desire to lord it over the universe, seeing duality, and cheating.

The forms of the Lord's incarnations are all perfect. The form of Lord Kṛṣṇa, who is the source of all incarnations, is supremely perfect. Aside from what has already been said, Lord Kṛṣṇa possesses the eight qualities of a great personality: 1. decorated, 2. enjoying, 3. pleasing, 4. dependable, 5. steady, 6. predominating, 7. a meticulous dresser, and 8. a magnanimous personality. It is said that a person is great if he is decorated with the qualities of being very merciful toward the unfortunate, very powerful, superior, chivalrous, enthusiastic, expert, and truthful.

When a person is always happy and is accustomed to speak smilingly, he is considered to be in the mode of enjoyment. When one's characteristics are very sweet and desirable, his personality is called pleasing. Any person who is reliable in all circumstances is called dependable. A person who is not disturbed even in a situation of reverses is called steady. A person who can affect the mind of everyone is called predominating. A person who is fond of dressing himself is called lalita, or a meticulous dresser. Persons who can give themselves to anyone are called magnanimous.

Although Kṛṣṇa is independent of everyone, out of His causeless mercy, He is dependent upon Garga Ṛṣi for religion instruction, for learning the military art, He is dependent upon Sātyaki, and for good counsel, He is dependent upon His friend, Uddhava

Vrajanātha: Now I have learned how Lord Kṛṣṇa is the hero of *rasas*. Now please describe the devotees who are qualified for the *rasas* and who have attain vi*bhāva*.

Gosvāmī: A person who in his heart has ecstatic love (*bhāva*) for Lord Kṛṣṇa is considered a devotee situated in the *rasas*. The twenty-six qualities of Lord Kṛṣṇa that begin with truthfulness and end with shyness are all present in the devotees of Lord Kṛṣṇa.

Vrajanātha: What are the different kinds of devotees qualified to participate in the *rasas*?

Gosvāmī: The devotees of Kṛṣṇa can be classified into two groups: 1. *sādhaka* (those who are cultivating devotional service in order to enter into the transcendental kingdom), and 2. *siddha* (those who are already in the perfectional stage of devotional service).

Vrajanātha: Who are the *sādhakas*?

Gosvāmī: A person who has reached the stage of attraction for Kṛṣṇa and who is not freed from the material impasse, but who has qualified himself to enter into the kingdom of God is called *sādhaka*. *Sādhaka* means one who is cultivating devotion in Kṛṣṇa consciousness. The description of such a devotee is found in the Eleventh Canto, second chapter, verse 46 of *Śrīmad-Bhāgavatam*: An intermediate or second-class devotee, called *madhyama-adhikārī*, offers his love to the Supreme Personality of Godhead, is a sincere friend to all the devotees of the Lord, shows mercy to ignorant people who are innocent, and disregards those who are envious of the Supreme Personality of Godhead.

Vrajanātha: O master, are not the devotees described in *Śrīmad-Bhāgavatam* (11.2.47) also qualified for the *rasas*? *Śrīmad-Bhāgavatam* (11.2.47): A devotee who faithfully engages in the worship of the Deity in the temple, but does not behave properly toward other devotees or people in general is called a *prākṛta-bhakta*, a materialistic devotee, and is considered to be in the lowest position.

Gosvāmī: If one has not obtained the mercy of a pure devotee and become a pure devotee himself, then he cannot be considered a *sādhaka*. An example of a *sādhaka* cultivating devotional service is Bilvamaṅgala Ṭhākura.

Vrajanātha: Who are the *siddha* devotees?

Gosvāmī: When a devotee is never tired of executing devotional service and is always engaged in Kṛṣṇa conscious activities, constantly relishing the transcendental mellows in relationship with Kṛṣṇa, he is called (*siddha*). There are two kinds of perfect devotees: 1. Those who attained perfection (*samprāpta-siddha*) and 2. Those who were always perfect (*nitya-siddha*).

Vrajanātha: Who are the *samprāpta-siddha* devotees?

Gosvāmī: The perfectional stage can be achieved (*samprāpta-siddha*) in two ways: One may achieve this stage of perfection by gradual progress in devotional service (*sādhana-siddha*), or one may become perfect by the causeless mercy of Kṛṣṇa, even though he has not executed all the details of devotional service (*kṛpā-siddha*).

Vrajanātha: Who are the *nitya-siddha* devotees?

Gosvāmī: Śrīla Rūpa Gosvāmī writes (*Bhakti-rasāmṛta-sindhu* 2.1.290): "Persons who have achieved eternal, blissful life exactly on the level of Śrī Kṛṣṇa and who are able to attract Lord Kṛṣṇa by their transcendental loving service, and who love Lord Kṛṣṇa millions of times more than they love themselves, are called eternally perfect (*nitya-siddha*).

In the *Padma Purāṇa, Uttara-khaṇḍa* it is said: Just as Lord Rāmacandra descends along with Lakṣmaṇa (an incarnation of Saṅkarṣaṇa) and Bhārata (an expansion of Pradyumna), so the members of the Yadu dynasty and the cowherd men of Vṛndāvana also descend with Lord Kṛṣṇa in order to join in the transcendental pastimes of the Lord. When the Supreme Lord returns to His eternal abode, His associates return with Him to their respective places, As such, these ever-liberated Vaiṣṇavas are not bound by the material laws of birth and death.

Vrajanātha: O master, now I can understand the *ālambana* part of *vibhāva*. Please explain the *uddīpana* part.

Gosvāmī: Some things that give impetus (*uddīpana*), or stimulation to ecstatic love of Kṛṣṇa, are His transcendental qualities, His uncommon activities, His smiling features, His apparel and garlands, His flute, His buffalo horn, His leg bells, His conch shell, His footprints, His places of pastimes (such as Vṛndāvana), His favorite plant (*tulasī*), His devotee, and the periodical occasions for remembering Him. One such occasion for remembrance is Ekādaśī.

Vrajanātha: As far as Kṛṣṇa's transcendental qualities are concerned, they can be divided into three groups: qualities pertaining to His transcendental body, qualities pertaining to His transcendental speech, and qualities pertaining to His transcendental mind. Kṛṣṇa's age is considered in three periods: *kaumāra*, *paugaṇḍa*, and *kaiśora*.

These are described in the following words (*Bhakti-rasāmṛta-sindhu* 2.1.309): Kṛṣṇa's age is considered in three periods: from His appearance day to the end of His fifth year is called *kaumāra*, from the beginning of the sixth year up to the end of the tenth year is called *paugaṇḍa*, and from the eleventh to the end of the fifteenth year is called *kaiśora*. After the beginning of the sixteenth year, Kṛṣṇa is called *yauvana*, or a youth, and this continues with no change.

Kṛṣṇa's *paugaṇḍa* age may be divided into three parts. Among His many transcendental qualities manifested in this age, His handsomeness is very prominent. Lord Kṛṣṇa's limbs are graceful and appropriately shaped. This feature is called *saundarya* (handsomeness). Lord Kṛṣṇa is dressed in exquisite garments, decorated with ornaments, and His hair is also decorated. All this is called *prasādhana* (decoration).

There are three kinds of flutes used by Kṛṣṇa. One is called *veṇu*, one is called *muralī*, and the third is called *vaṁśī*. *Veṇu* is very small, not more than six inches long, with six holes for whistling. *Muralī* is about eighteen inches long with a hole at the end and four holes on the body of the flute. This kind of flute produces a very enchanting sound. The *vaṁśī* flute is about fifteen inches long, with nine holes on its body. The right turning conch shell Kṛṣṇa holds in His hand is called Pāñcajanya.

All these *uddīpanas* increase the devotee's attraction and love for Kṛṣṇa and fill the devotee with bliss. The result is that *rati* (attraction) and *sthāyi-bhāva* (continuous ecstasy) turn into *rasa* (the transcendental mellows of a personal relationship with Kṛṣṇa). Come again tomorrow and I will describe *anubhāva* and other things.

The two devotees then took their leave of the Gosvāmī's lotus feet. Again and again thinking about the *rasas*, Vijaya-kumāra and Vrajanātha happily saw the *siddha-bakula* tree and other holy places in Lord Jagannātha's temple. Finally, they returned to their lodgings.

Chapter Twenty-seven

Further consideration of rasas

After the next day's noon *ārati*, the two devotees, thirsting to understand about *rasa*, honored *prasādam* and then went to the Śrī Rādhākānta temple. Śrī Gopāla-guru Gosvāmī honored *mahā-prasādam* and waited for the two inquisitive devotees. Nearby, Śrī Dhyānacandra Gosvāmī was writing a book about the path of devotional service. The features of Gopāla-guru Gosvāmī were very wonderful. He was dressed as a *sannyāsī*. He wore Vaiṣṇava *tilaka*. The holy name of Lord Hari was written on the various limbs of His body. On his neck were four strands of *tulasī* beads. His hands were always on His *japa* beads. He was rapt in meditation, his two eyes half-closed. From time to time, he was decorated with a stream of tears. From time to time, he would call out, "O Gaurāṅga! O Nityānanda!" His body was a little large. His complexion was dark and splendid. He sat on a banana-bark seat. At a little distance were wooden sandals and a coconut shell pitcher of water.

Vijaya-kumāra and Vrajanātha were both learned in many scriptures, were sincere Vaiṣṇavas, and were residents of Śrī Navadvīpa. For these three reasons, everyone at the temple carefully honored them. Vijaya-kumāra and Vrajanātha offered *daṇḍavat* obeisances to Gopāla-guru Gosvāmī, and he respectfully embraced them. In the course of time, Vrajanātha humbly introduced the topic of *rasas*.

The Gosvāmī carefully said, "Today, I will teach you about *anubhāva* and other topics related to the *rasas*. The four *sāmagrīs* (ingredients of *rasa*) are vi*bhāva* (special symptoms or causes of ecstasy), *anubhāva* (subsequent ecstasy), *sāttvika-bhāva* (constitutional or existential ecstasy), and *vyabhicārī-bhāva* (aggressive ecstasy).

Yesterday, I explained about vi*bhāva*. Today I will begin the explanation of *anubhāva*. Please listen. When one is attracted (*rati*) to Kṛṣṇa—that is called vi*bhāva*. When, as a result of that attraction, ecstatic love (*bhāva*) appears in the heart, the result is called *udbhāsvara*. The bodily symptoms manifested by a devotee in expressing that ecstatic love for Kṛṣṇa are called *anubhāva*. Practical examples of *anubhāva* are as follows: dancing, rolling on the ground, singing very loudly, stretching the body, crying loudly, yawning, breathing very heavily, neglecting the presence of others, drooling, laughing like a madman, wheeling the head, and belching.

Vrajanātha: How is it possible that these unusual external symptoms can increase the sweet taste of the *rasas* of *sthāyi-bhāva*? When the devotee relishes the *rasas* in his heart, that taste is manifested externally as these *anubhāvas*. Why then should these *anubhāvas* be considered a *sāmagrī* separate and distinct from the taste of *rasas* in the heart?

Gosvāmī: Bābā, you have learned the *nyāya-śāstra* very well. Until this day, I have not seen anyone raise such a subtle point of logic. When I studied the *rasas*, I also asked this question of Śrīla Paṇḍita Gosvāmī. By my spiritual master's mercy, my doubt was thrown far away. The secret is this: When the heart is agitated by the ecstatic feelings of *vibhāva*, many extraordinary and wonderful feelings (*vaicitrya*) are manifested. These feelings blossom in many different ways in the heart. When these feelings blossom in the heart, they eventually bear fruits of ecstatic symptoms that are manifested in the external body. These fruits are called *udbhāsvara*.

The fruits of ecstatic symptoms are manifested as dancing and in many other ways also. Thus, when the heart dances, then the body dances also. When the heart sings, then the tongue sings also. In this way, you should understand it. Thus, the ecstatic symptoms called *udbhāsvara* are the root from which all this comes. However, the *anubhāvas* do increase the *vibhāvas* within the heart. In this way, the *udbhāsvaras* are manifest in the body. Thus, the *sthāyi-bhāva* and *vibhāva* in the heart manifests the *anubhāvas*, and the *anubhāvas* in turn also have an effect upon the heart.

Because the *anubhāvas* have this effect, they are considered separate *sāmagrīs* (ingredients of *rasa*). When there are singing, yawning, and other such activities, the symptoms are called *śīta*, and where there is dancing and other such activities, they are called *kṣepaṇa*. There are other ecstatic symptoms, such as blossoming of the body, the flowing of blood, and expansion and contraction of the body's joints. However, because these symptoms are very rare, I will not describe them further. However, when He assumed the form of a tortoise and manifested other unusual activities, these symptoms were present on the body of our master, Lord Nimāi Paṇḍita. Still, these symptoms are not seen on the body of a *sādhaka* devotee.

After hearing these confidential explanations from Gopāla-guru

Gosvāmī, the two inquiring devotees were silent for a long time. Then, touching the dust of his lotus feet, they asked, "O master, what are the *sāttvika-bhāvas?*"

Gosvāmī: When a devotee is always intensely affected by love for Kṛṣṇa in a direct relationship with Him, or even a little apart from Him, his status is called *sāttvika-bhāva* (existential ecstatic love). The symptoms originating from such existential ecstatic love are divided into three headings, namely moist (*snigdha*), burnt (*digdha*), and dried-up (*rūkṣa*).

Vrajanātha: What is moist *sāttvika-bhāva?*

Gosvāmī: Moist *sāttvika-bhāva* is divided into two: direct and indirect. When the heart is directly attracted to Lord Kṛṣṇa—that is called *mukhya-snigdha-sāttvika-bhāva* (direct moistened existential ecstatic love). Being stunned and perspiring are some of the symptoms of *mukhya-sāttvika-bhāva.* When the heart is attracted to Lord Kṛṣṇa indirectly, that is called *gauṇa-snigdha-sāttvika-bhāva* (indirect moistened existential ecstatic love). Changing of bodily colors and faltering of the voice are the two symptoms of *gauṇa-snigdha-sāttvika-bhāva.* Aside from direct and indirect moistened existential ecstatic love, *digdha-sāttvika-bhāva* (burnt existential ecstatic love) may also enter the heart. Trembling of the body is the symptom of *digdha-sāttvika-bhāva.* When a non-devotee is filled with wonder and bliss by hearing the description of the great wonder that is Lord Kṛṣṇa's sweetness, the ecstatic symptoms are called 'ruksa' (dried up). Standing of the hairs on the body is the symptom of *rūkṣa-sāttvika-bhāva.*

Vrajanātha: How is *sāttvika-bhāva* created?

Gosvāmī: When the *sādhaka* devotee's vital force of life is in contact with the various external elements, agitation and transformation result. From this agitation, the various ecstatic symptoms, such as becoming stunned, are manifested.

Vrajanātha: What are the different ecstatic symptoms manifested?

Gosvāmī: There are eight symptoms of *sāttvika-bhāva* (existential ecstatic love): becoming stunned, perspiring, standing of the hairs on the body, faltering of the voice, trembling of the body, changing of bodily colors, shedding of tears, and devastation. When the vital force of life is in contact with the earth, one is stunned. When the same force comes into contact with water, there is shedding of tears. When the same force comes into contact with fire, there is perspiration. When the force comes into contact with sky, there is complete devastation. And when that force comes into contact with air, there is trembling, failing of the voice, and standing up of the hairs on the body. In this way, the different ecstatic symptoms are manifested.

These symptoms are sometimes manifested internally and sometimes externally. Sometimes they are called *bhāvas* and sometimes they are called *anubhāvas*. All the *anubhāvas* are manifested externally only. This is not said of the *sāttvika-bhāvas*. For example, in dancing or other such activities, the *bhāva* (ecstatic love) is not manifested directly. The *bhāva* is rather manifested by the intelligence, or the heart. Therefore, the various external symptoms of ecstasy, such as becoming stunned, are considered *anubhāvas*, and are not *sāttvika-bhāvas*. Therefore, the *anubhāvas* and *sāttvika-bhāvas* are different from each other.

Vrajanātha: I desire to understand why the ecstatic symptoms, such as becoming stunned, are manifested.

Gosvāmī: Joy, fear, wonder, lamentation, and hatred create emptiness in the heart that manifests the ecstatic symptom of becoming stunned. Joy, fear, anger, and other emotions combine to moisten the body and thus manifest the ecstatic symptom of perspiration. Wonder, joy, eagerness, fear, and other emotions combine to manifest the ecstatic symptom of the body's hairs standing up. Lamentation, wonder, anger, joy, fear, and other emotions bring the ecstatic symptom of faltering of the voice. Fear, anger, joy, and other emotions bring the ecstatic symptom of trembling of the body. Lamentation, anger, fear, and other emotions bring the ecstatic symptom of changing of bodily colors. Joy, anger, lamentation, and other emotions bring the ecstatic symptom of shedding tears.

When they are produced from joy, the tears are cold, and when they are produced from anger and other such emotions, the tears are hot. Happiness and unhappiness combine to make one fall unconscious and attain other such conditions of life, conditions that are the ecstatic symptom called devastation. These transcendental ecstatic symptoms gradually develop, and in the course of such development, they are sometimes called smoky, sometimes called blazing, sometimes called shining, and sometimes called intensely shining. These are the four kinds.

In dried up *sāttvika-bhāva*, the symptoms are smoky. In moistened *sāttvika-bhāva*, the ecstatic love rises higher and higher. Real love (*rati*) for Lord Kṛṣṇa produces all bliss and wonder. When there is only the semblance of love (*raty-ābhāsa*), the symptoms are dried up. Then there is no wonder.

Vrajanātha: O master, the ecstatic love of *sāttvika-bhāva* brings all good fortune. However, to attain material benefits, many people may make a show of these ecstatic emotions, as if they were acting in a drama. What is the position of these people?

Gosvāmī: Genuine *sāttvika-bhāva* is manifested from genuine pure devotional service. The ecstatic love (*bhāva*) felt by true Vaiṣṇavas is genuine. Aside from this genuine *bhāva*, the other so-called *bhāvas* are divided into four groups: *raty-ābhāsa*, *sattva-ābhāsa*, *niḥsattvā*, and *pratīpa*.

Vrajanātha: What is *raty-ābhāsa*?

Gosvāmī: When they hear the descriptions of Lord Kṛṣṇa, the impersonalists, or the *sannyāsī* followers of Śaṅkarācārya, manifest *raty-ābhāsa*.

Vrajanātha: What is *sattva-ābhāsa*?

Gosvāmī: When they hear about Lord Kṛṣṇa, persons who are naturally soft-hearted may manifest the semblance of joy, wonder, and other ecstatic emotions. The Mīmāṁsaka philosophers and ordinary women may manifest this when they hear about Lord Kṛṣṇa.

Vrajanātha: What is *niḥsattvā-bhāvābhāsa*?

Gosvāmī: Some wicked-hearted persons exhibit artificial ecstatic symptoms as a sort of dramatic show. In this way, they shed tears and perform other actions. These actions are called *niḥsattvā*. In this way, some hard-hearted persons put on an artificial show of crying in ecstatic love. These persons are wicked at heart.

Vrajanātha: What is *pratīpa*?

Gosvāmī: One who acts as Kṛṣṇa's enemy manifests the semblance of the ecstatic emotions like anger and fear. This is called *pratīpa-bhāvābhāsa*.

Vrajanātha: O master, now I have understood *vibhāva*, *anubhāva*, and *sāttvika-bhāva*, and I have also understood the difference between *sāttvika* and *anubhāva*. Now please explain *vyabhicārī-bhāva*.

Gosvāmī: There are thirty-three *vyabhicārīs*. These thirty-three *bhāvas* work to increase the *sthāyi-bhāvas*. That is why they are called *vyabhicārī*. They are manifested in the words, limbs, and thoughts. They are also called *sañcārī-bhāva*. They are like waves in the nectarean ocean of *sthāyi-bhāva*, waves that rise from, and then again disappear into, the ocean of *sthāyi-bhāva*. The thirty-three *vyabhicārī-bhāvas* are: disappointment, lamentation, humility, guilt, fatigue, intoxication, pride, doubt, apprehension, intense emotion, madness, forgetfulness, disease, confusion, death, laziness, inertness, bashfulness, concealment, remembrance, argumentativeness, anxiety, thoughtfulness, endurance, happiness, eagerness, violence, haughtiness, envy, impudence, dizziness, sleepiness, and alertness.

Some of the *sañcārī-bhāvas* are independent (*sva-tantra*) and others are dependent on something else (*para-tantra*). The *para-tantra sañcārī-bhāvas* are of two kinds: superior and inferior. The superior *sañcārī-bhāvas* are themselves of two kinds: direct and indirect. The *sva-tantra sañcārī-bhāvas* are of three kinds: *rati-śūnya* (without attachment to Kṛṣṇa), *rati-anusparśa* (with a touch of attachment to Kṛṣṇa), and *rati-gandha* (with the scent of attachment to Kṛṣṇa). If these *bhāvas* are directed to the wrong object, they are of two kinds: *prātikūlya* (unfavorable) and *anaucitya* (improper). All these *bhāvas* are manifested in four different conditions: 1. *utpatti* (growth), 2. *sandhi* (union), 3. *śābalya* (variety) and 3. *śānti* (peace).

Vrajanātha: *Bhāva-utpatti* is easy to understand. What is *bhāva-sandhi*?

Gosvāmī: When two like or unlike emotions meet, that is called *sandhi*. Desirable laziness and undesirable laziness may both appear simultaneously. This is an example of the meeting of like emotions. Joy and fear may also appear simultaneously. That is an example of the meeting of unlike emotions.

Vrajanātha: What is *bhāva-śābalya*?

Gosvāmī: When two emotions clash, that is called *bhāva-śābalya*. When he heard about Kṛṣṇa, Kaṁsa became simultaneously angry and fearful. That is an example of *bhāva-śābalya*.

Vrajanātha: What is *bhāva-śānti*?

Gosvāmī: When an intense emotion suddenly disappears, that is called *śānti*. When they could not see Kṛṣṇa, the boys of Vraja became anxious but when they heard the sound of Kṛṣṇa's flute from afar, their anxiety was at once pacified. This is an example of the pacification of happiness.

Vrajanātha: If anything else remains to be known about this topic, then please explain it.

Gosvāmī: To these thirty-three *vyabhicārī-bhāvas* may be added the one primary (*mukhya*) *sthāyi-bhāva* and the seven secondary (*gauna*) *sthāyi-bhāvas*. In this way, there are forty-one *bhāvas* that produce ecstatic symptoms on the body and the senses. The activities of the mind are the origin of these *bhāvas*.

Vrajanātha: What are the various *bhāvas* produced in this way?

Gosvāmī: They produce the eight *sāttvika-bhāvas*, the *vibhāvas*, and the *anubhāvas*.

Vrajanātha: Are all these part of the original nature?

Gosvāmī: No. Some are part of the original nature and other come from outside the original nature. The *sthāyi-bhāva* is part of the devotee's original nature, but the *vyabhicārī-bhāvas* mostly come from outside the original nature.

Vrajanātha: Do all devotees possess the same *bhāvas*?

Gosvāmī: No. The devotees have different natures. That is because the nature of the mind and heart is different in each devotee. According to the condition of the heart, the *bhāva* is more or less exalted. The heart may be exalted, lowly, or in an intermediate state. The *bhāvas* are manifested according to the condition of the heart. However, nectar is always liquid and therefore, a devotee's heart is naturally soft and liquid, for it like nectar. Today we will end here. Tomorrow I will describe the *sthāyi-bhāva*.

Vijaya-kumāra and Vrajanātha offered *daṇḍavat* obeisances and took their leave.

Chapter Twenty-eight

Further consideration of rasas, part two

Vrajanātha: O master, I see that *vibhāva*, *anubhāva*, *sāttvika-bhāva*, and *vyabhicārī bhāva* are all *bhāvas*. What is *sthāyi-bhāva*?

Gosvāmī: The one *bhāva* that controls all the other *bhāvas*, both obstructed and unobstructed, and that is the monarch even of Lord Kṛṣṇa Himself, is called *sthāyi-bhāva*. When *kṛṣṇa-rati* (attraction to Kṛṣṇa) takes shelter of a devotee's heart, that attraction is called *sthāyi-bhāva*. Look, among the *sāmagrīs* is vi*bhāva* and, included within vi*bhāva* is *alambana*. However, there is another *bhāva*, a *bhāva* independent of all these others, a *bhāva* that is the origin and the helper of the *rasas*, a *bhāva* that becomes both the enjoyment (*āsvādana*) and the object of enjoyment (*āsvādya*). Please think deeply about this and try to understand how *sthāyi-bhāva* is different from the other *bhāvas*. *Sthāyi-bhāva* is divided in two: primary (*mukhya-rati*) and secondary (*gauna-rati*).

Vrajanātha: What is primary *sthāyi-bhāva*?

Gosvāmī: In the description of *bhāva-bhakti*, you have already heard about *śuddha-sattva-rati*. That is the same as *mukhya-rati*.

Vrajanātha: When I read the *alaṅkāra-śāstra* (books of rhetoric), the love that I understood there was all material. It was very different. The spiritual love that is now described is very different from that material love. Now I understand that only when a person is pure in heart will he attain the nectar (*rasa*) of love for the Supreme Lord. The so-called love written about by the authors of the *alaṅkāra-śāstra* is only the love that appears in the material bodies and material minds of souls imprisoned in the material world. Now I can understand the other kind of love, the love you have described in your explanation of the *rasas*. This pure spiritual love is the be-all and end-all of the pure liberated souls. By the mercy of the *hlādinī-śakti*, this pure love is sometimes experienced even by the conditioned souls imprisoned in the material world. Now I wish to understand the different kinds of pure spiritual love (*śuddha-rati*).

Seeing Vrajanātha's clear grasp of the spiritual truth, Gopāla-guru Gosvāmī, shedding tears of happiness, embraced him and said, "I am very fortunate to have a disciple like you. Please listen. *Mukhya-rati* is of two kinds: *svārtha* (for the sake of one's own self) and *parārtha* (for the sake of the beloved).

Vrajanātha: What is the nature of *svārtha-mukhya-rati*?

Gosvāmī: When no obstacles stop the *bhāva* (*aviruddha-bhāva*), then *svārtha-mukhya-rati* increases. However, when obstacles do stop the *bhāva* (*viruddha-bhāva*), then *svārtha-mukhya-rati* diminishes.

Vrajanātha: What is the nature of *parārtha-mukhya-rati*?

Gosvāmī: Whether obstacles are present or not, *parārtha-mukhya-rati* contracts of its own accord. Aside from these two, there is also another kind of *mukhya-rati*.

Vrajanātha: What is it like? Please tell.

Gosvāmī: This is called *śuddha-mukhya-rati* (pure love). It is divided into five *rasas*: *śānta* (neutrality), *dāsya* (servitude), *sākhya* (friendship), *vātsalya* (parenthood), and *mādhurya* (conjugal love). As sunlight is divided into different colors when it passes through a prism or other such object, so *sthāyi-bhāva* assumes different features according to the different kinds of persons who contain it.

Vrajanātha: Please describe this *śuddha-rati* (pure love).

Gosvāmī: *Śuddha-rati* is of three kinds: *sāmānya* (ordinary), *svaccha* (clear) and *śānta* (peaceful). *Sāmānya-rati* is the love the people in general feel for Lord Kṛṣṇa. When *mukhya-rati* is manifested in different ways in the different kinds of devotees, as light assumes different colors as it passes through colored glass—that kind of *mukhya-rati* is called *svaccha* (clear). In this way, some devotees offer prayers to Kṛṣṇa and call Him master, others joke with Kṛṣṇa and call him friend, still others protect Kṛṣṇa and call him son, and still others meditate on Kṛṣṇa and call Him the Supersoul.

A devotee in *śānta-rati* (neutrality) meditates with a peaceful mind on the unchanging Supreme. *Śuddha-rati* is of two kinds: *kevala* (unmixed) and *saṅkula* (mixed). Among the residents of Vraja, Rasāla and Śrīdāma are examples of devotees whose love for Kṛṣṇa is of one kind only, unmixed with even the slightest scent of any other kind of *rasa*. Their pure love (*śuddha-rati*) is called *kevala* (unmixed). Other devotees, such as Uddhava and Bhīma, have love that is a mixture of different *rasas*. Their pure love (*śuddha-rati*) is called *saṅkula* (mixed).

Vrajanātha: Formerly, I thought there was not *śānta-rati* in Vraja. Now

I see it is slightly present there also. When they consider the different kinds of *rati* (love), books of material rhetoric (*jaḍa-alaṅkāra*) do not accept *śānta-rati* as a genuine kind of love. Here it is seen that *śānta-rati* must be accepted as one kind of love for the Supreme. Now please describe *dāsya-rati* (love in the *rasa* of servitorship).

Gosvāmī: When the devotee thinks, "Kṛṣṇa is the master and I am His servant," he loves Kṛṣṇa in the *dāsya-rasa*. When he is attached to Kṛṣṇa in this way, a devotee is not attracted to or pleased by anything outside this *rasa* of servitorship.

Vrajanātha: What are the qualities of *sākhya-rati* (love in friendship)?

Gosvāmī: When a devotee is firmly convinced that Kṛṣṇa is his equal, his love for Kṛṣṇa is called *sākhya-rati*. In *sākhya-rati*, there are joking, laughing, and other such activities.

Vrajanātha: Please describe the nature of *vātsalya-rati* (parental love).

Gosvāmī: The kindly love that His elders give to Kṛṣṇa is called *vātsalya-rati*. Embracing and fondling Kṛṣṇa, performing auspicious rituals for His benefit, pronouncing blessings upon Him, and affectionately touching His chin, are some of the activities of *vātsalya-rati*.

Vrajanātha: Now kindly describe the qualities of *mādhurya-rati* (conjugal love for Kṛṣṇa).

Gosvāmī: The eight kinds of pleasing activities, beginning with remembering Kṛṣṇa and gazing at Kṛṣṇa, that are performed in the deer-eyed *gopīs*' love for Kṛṣṇa are called the activities of *prīyatā* (love) or *mādhurya-rati* (sweet love). Included in these activities are sidelong glances, moving the eyebrows, speaking sweet words, and speaking joking words. Beginning with *śānta* and extending up to *mādhurya-rati*, the devotees' love, relish, and bliss increase more and more. Thus I have briefly described the five kinds of *mukhya-rati* (primary *rasas*).

Vrajanātha: Now please describe the secondary (*gauna*) spiritual *rasas*.

Gosvāmī: The secondary *rasas* (*gauna-bhāva*), which are part of *alambana*, are: laughter, astonishment, chivalry, lamentation, anger, dread, and ghastliness. In the first six of these *rasas*, the devotee always meditates on Kṛṣṇa. When the devotee attains pure love (*śuddha-rati*), then he finds the material body and material activities to be very distasteful. He is horrified by them. That is the seventh *rasa*, ghastliness. Although these seven *rasas* are different from pure love (*śuddha-rati*), because they are in contact with *parārtha-mukhya-rati* (the primary *rasas*), therefore these seven secondary emotions are included among the *rasas* and the word *rati* (love) is used to described them. For some devotees, one or more of these secondary *rasas* remain a permanent part of their relationship with Kṛṣṇa. But this is not true for every devotee by any means. For most devotees, these secondary *rasas* are manifested only temporarily. In some situations, one or more of these secondary *rasas* become so strong that they eclipse the natural primary *rasas*.

Vrajanātha: In material rhetoric (*alaṅkāra*), eight *rasas*, beginning with conjugal love, laughter, and compassion are described. I can understand how these material *rasas* look beautiful only from the point of view of pathetic material heroes and heroines. These material *rasas* have no bearing on the spiritual *rasas* of Vraja, which are the activities of the pure spirit soul, and thus have nothing to do with the activities of the material mind. The great devotees have divided *sthāyi-bhāva rati* into five primary and seven secondary *rasas*. This is proper. Now please kindly describe *hāsya-rati* (the *rasa* of laughter).

Gosvāmī: Certain unusual words, appearances, or activities cause laughter to appear in the heart. In laughter, the eyes may open wide, and the nostrils, lips, and cheeks may tremble. This laughter is produced by *saṅkoca-bhāva-rati* directed toward Lord Kṛṣṇa.

Vrajanātha: What is the *rasa* of astonishment (*vismaya-rati*)?

Gosvāmī: When one sees something extraordinary, astonishment is manifested in his heart. Some of the symptoms of astonishment are: opening the eyes wide, speaking words of praise, and standing of the body's hairs.

Vrajanātha: What is the *rasa* of chivalry (*utsāha-rati*)?

Gosvāmī: When the heart is determined to perform the noble deeds that are glorified by great saints—that is called chivalry. Promptness, impatience, and enthusiasm are among the symptoms of chivalry.

Vrajanātha: What is the *rasa* of anger (*krodha-rati*)?

Gosvāmī: When actions of an enemy make the heart burst into flames—that is called anger. Harshness, knitting the eyebrows, and redness in the eyes are among the symptoms of anger.

Vrajanātha: What is the *rasa* of dread?

Gosvāmī: When the sight of horrible things makes the heart wish to flee, that is called dread. Hiding oneself, dryness of the heart, and fleeing away are among the symptoms of dread.

Vrajanātha: What is the rasa of ghastliness?

Gosvāmī: When one is averse to abominable things—that is called ghastliness. Spitting, curling the lips, and speaking harsh criticisms are among the symptoms of ghastliness. When this emotion is in relation to Lord Kṛṣṇa, then it is considered one of the spiritual *rasas*. Otherwise, it is merely another material emotion.

Vrajanātha: How many *bhāvas* (emotions) are present in *bhakti-rasa* (the mellows of devotional service)?

Gosvāmī: *Sthāyi-bhāva* has eight *bhāvas*, *sañcārī-bhāva* has thirty-three *bhāvas*, and *sāttvika-bhāva* has eight *bhāvas*. Combined together, there are forty -nine *bhāvas*. When these *bhāvas* are manifested from the three modes of nature and are thus material, they are causes of material happiness and material suffering. When these *bhāvas* help one attain Kṛṣṇa, they are spiritual, beyond the material modes, and filled with bliss, and what seems to be sorrow in them is actually spiritual happiness.

Śrīla Rūpa Gosvāmī explains that Lord Kṛṣṇa and Kṛṣṇa's dear devotees are the two *ālambanas*, or resting places, and therefore the causes of the *rasas* of spiritual love (*rati*). The ecstatic symptoms that begin with being stunned are counted among the effects of *rati* and the ecstatic symptoms that begin with lamentation help the progress of *rati*. When the *rasas* are awakened, these ecstatic symptoms are no longer called cause, effect, and helper. Then they are called *vibhāva*. Because these activities then have an especially sweet taste, the Paṇḍita calls them *vibhāva*.

When dancing and other activities increase the sweetness of *vibhāva*, the *vibhāva* is called *anubhāva*. Spiritual (*sāttvika*) activities bring spiritual results. Thus these actions are called *sāttvika-bhāva*. When these *vibhāvas* bring renunciation and other such emotions, the *bhāva* is called *sañcārī-bhāva*. Readers attracted to poems, plays, and other books describing Lord Kṛṣṇa know that the *vibhāvas* are causes of devotional service. In truth, these activities of *rati* (pure love) are inconceivable. They are very great pastimes of devotional service.

In the *Mahābhārata* and other scriptures it is said that these activities of devotional service are very exalted. They are beyond the touch of ordinary, material logic. In the *Mahābhārata* it is written that these *bhāvas* are beyond the understanding of the material mind, and therefore material logic cannot be employed to understand them. Whatever is beyond the world of matter cannot be understood by the material mind. One who attains sweet love for Lord Kṛṣṇa's form and other features attains *vibhāva*. This *vibhāva* does not remain static. It spontaneously increases, growing greater and greater. *Rati* (love for Kṛṣṇa) enables one to directly perceive Lord Kṛṣṇa, who is the resting place of transcendental sweetness and other virtues. On the other hand, when he directly sees Lord Kṛṣṇa's form and other features, the devotees love Lord Kṛṣṇa more and more. In this way, *vibhāva*, *anubhāva*, *sāttvika-bhāva* and *vyabhicārī-bhāva* all increase *rati*, and *rati* increases them.

Vrajanātha: What is the difference between love for Kṛṣṇa (*kṛṣṇa-rati*) and material love (*viṣayā-rati*). Please kindly explain.

Gosvāmī: Material love is part of the material world. Love for Kṛṣṇa is beyond the material world, and it is also the origin of many wonderful things. Material love is pleasant when the beloved is present and unpleasant when the beloved is absent. When a person loves Kṛṣṇa and Kṛṣṇa is present, then the lover experiences the taste of a certain kind of *rasa*, the *rasa* of *sambhoga-sukha* (the happiness of enjoying with Kṛṣṇa). However, when Kṛṣṇa is absent, the lover experiences the *rasa* of *vipralambha* (separation), which itself produces a specific kind of wonderful transcendental bliss.

In answer to one of Lord Mahāprabhu's questions, Rāmānanda Rāya described (*Śrī Caitanya-caritāmṛta* Madhya 8.194) the wonderful bliss the devotee feels in separation from Kṛṣṇa, a bliss he called *vivarta*. Therefore, what seems here to be suffering is in truth the highest spiritual bliss.

Vrajanātha: Material logicians says that the *rasas* are unimportant. They are only a small portion of what exists. What is the answer to that claim?

Gosvāmī: It is true that the material *rasas* are unimportant. And, why not? In the material *rasas*, material ingredients (*sāmagrī*) may nourish the material *sthāyi-bhāva* (permanent emotions). However, these are only material *rasas*. They are not spiritual. In the state of spiritual perfection, the spiritual *rasas* are eternal, complete, and self-manifest. However, to an inexperienced devotee, the spiritual *rasas* may seem to be material. When the lover is separated from the beloved, the material *rasas* of love do not remain indefinitely. The spiritual *rasa* of love in separation is much more beautiful and glorious than its material counterpart. The great potency, *hlādinī-śakti*, brings transcendental bliss to the *rasa* of spiritual love in separation. That is why the *rasa* of spiritual love in separation is blissful and why it is beyond the power of material logic to understand. Therefore it is said to be inconceivable.

Vrajanātha: How many kinds of spiritual *rasas* are there?

Gosvāmī: Even though the primary *rasas* are five, they are still considered as one. Therefore, adding the seven secondary *rasas*, there are eight *rasas* all together.

Vrajanātha: Please recite the names of these eight *rasas*. The result of my hearing your words is that my desire to hear grows stronger and stronger.

Gosvāmī: Śrīla Rūpa Gosvāmī explains (*Bhakti-rasāmṛta-sindhu* 2.5.115-116): The five primary *rasas*, each more exalted than the preceding one, are: neutrality, servitorship, friendship, parenthood, and conjugal love. The seven secondary *rasas* are: laughter, astonishment, chivalry, lamentation, anger, dread, and ghastliness.

Vrajanātha: In the context of the spiritual *rasas*, what is the proper definition of the word *bhāva*?

Gosvāmī: Considering the truth in their spiritually purified hearts, great *paṇḍitas* have written many books about *rasa* (*rasa-śāstra*), and in these books they have defined the word *bhāva*. I have already explained that *rasa* is of two kinds: 1. *cintya-bhāva* (*bhāva* that can be understood by the material mind), and 2. *acintya-bhāva* (*bhāva* that is inconceivable, beyond the understanding of the material mind). Material logic can be used to understand *cintya-bhāva*. And, why not? The emotions that arise in the heart of a conditioned soul imprisoned in the material world are all material in nature. The conditioned souls' material ideas and emotions about the Supreme Lord are also understandable by the material mind. However, true ideas and emotions directed to the Supreme Lord are inconceivable, beyond the power of the material mind to understand. And, why not? The Supreme Lord is far beyond the touch of matter. Because the Supreme Lord is inconceivable, it is not good to think there can be no *bhāvas* (emotions) in relation to Him. All emotions are possible in relation to the Supreme Lord. But, they are inconceivable, beyond the material mind's understanding.

In your heart, remain rapt in meditation on one of the inconceivable *rasas* in relation to the Lord. Meditate on the appropriate *sthāyi-bhāva* and *sāmagrīs*. Then the eternal and perfect spiritual *rasa* will be manifest to you.

Vrajanātha: O master, what does being rapt in meditation mean?

Gosvāmī: Bābā, contaminated by matter, you have wandered in the circle of *karma* for many births. Meditation is of two kinds: previous meditation (*prāktani*) and present meditation (*ādhunika*). By staying in the material world, your originally pure heart and pure thoughts have both become contaminated. However, by associating with saintly devotees and by performing spiritual pious activities, one can throw far away the contaminated material thoughts and regain his original, natural, spiritual meditation. When this spiritual meditation becomes strong, the inconceivable truth appears in his heart. That is the meaning of being rapt in meditation.

Vrajanātha: Who is qualified to understand the spiritual *rasas*? That, I would like to know.

Gosvāmī: A person who, by constant meditation in this way, finds that the inconceivable spiritual truth is manifested in his heart, is alone qualified to understand the spiritual *rasas*. No one else is qualified to understand the spiritual *rasa*. No one else is qualified.

Śrīla Rūpa Gosvāmī explains (*Bhakti-rasāmṛta-sindhu* 2.5.132): When one transcends the status of ecstatic love and thus becomes situated on the highest platform of pure goodness, one is understood to have cleansed the heart of all material contamination. In that pure stage of life, one can taste this nectar, and this tasting capacity is technically called *rasa*, or transcendental mood.

Vrajanātha: Who is not qualified to thus taste the nectar of the transcendental *rasa*? As it is an offense to give the holy name to an unqualified person, so it must also be an offense to explain the *rasas* to an unqualified person. O master, please be merciful and explain this point to poor and fallen people like myself.

Gosvāmī: Renunciation that has nothing to do with pure devotional service is called *phalgu-vairāgya* (false renunciation). Persons who are in the fire of false renunciation, the dry speculative habit, and who neglect devotional service, are in a lamentable situation. Persons who are attached to the ritualistic ceremonies recommended in the *Vedas*, and to the impersonal Brahman, cannot relish the transcendental pleasure of devotional service. Therefore, devotees who have already tasted the nectar of devotion should be very careful to protect devotional service from such dry speculators, formal ritual elevationists, and impersonal salvationists. Devotees should protect their valuable jewel of spiritual love from the clutches of thieves and burglars. In other words, a pure devotee should not describe devotional service and its different analytical aspects to speculators and false renouncers.

Vrajanātha: I have become very fortunate. I will always honor the order that comes from your saintly mouth.

Vijaya-kumāra: O master, I maintain my family by reading and lecturing on *Śrīmad-Bhāgavatam*. *Śrīmad-Bhāgavatam* is a book describing the *rasas* of devotional service. If a man reads and explains *Śrīmad-Bhāgavatam* to the people in general, in order to earn money, does he commit an offense?

Gosvāmī: Ah! *Śrīmad-Bhāgavatam* is the crest jewel of all scriptures. It is the mature ripened fruit of the tree of Vedic knowledge. In *Śrīmad-Bhāgavatam* (1.1.3), it is said: O expert and thoughtful men, relish *Śrīmad-Bhāgavatam*.

The meaning of these words is that only the expert and thoughtful, who know how to relish the transcendental *rasas*, are qualified to taste the nectar of *Śrīmad-Bhāgavatam*. No one else is qualified. Bābā, give up this profession. You are a person who likes to drink the nectar of the transcendental *rasas*. Don't commit an offense to the *rasas*. In the *Vedas* (*Taittirīya Upaniṣad* 2.7) it is said: The Supreme Lord is *rasa*.

This means that the *rasas* are Lord Kṛṣṇa Himself. There are many other books you could teach to maintain your material body. Teach some other book for that purpose. You should not read *Śrīmad-Bhāgavatam* to the people in general in order to earn money. If you find a person qualified to taste the spiritual *rasas*, then with great bliss, you may read *Śrīmad-Bhāgavatam* to him, but do not accept any salary or any *dakṣiṇa* (donation).

Vrajanātha: O master, today you have saved me from a great offense. What will come from the offense I have already committed?

Gosvāmī: That offense will not stay. With an honest heart, surrender to the *rasas* and take shelter of them. They will certainly forgive you. You need not worry.

Vrajanātha: O master, if need be, I will accept a very lowly profession, but I will not describe the *rasas* to an unqualified person, and I will not accept money for teaching about the *rasas*.

Gosvāmī: Bābā, you are very fortunate. Lord Kṛṣṇa has accepted you as His own devotee. If this were not so, then how could you be so sincere and dedicated to devotional service? Lord Gaura has given all His potencies to you.

Chapter Twenty-nine

Further consideration of the rasas, part three

Vrajanātha and Vijaya-kumāra decided to stay in Jagannātha Purī for *caturmāsya*. After hearing about the *rasas* from the mouth of Śrī Gopāla-guru Gosvāmī, they both decided to follow the path of worshiping the Lord according to the *rasas*. Hearing from him the glories of observing *caturmāsya*, Vrajanātha's grandmother accepted his suggestion to stay in Jagannātha Purī. Every morning and evening, they would all see Lord Jagannātha. They bathed in Narendra-sarovara, and they saw all there was to see in Jagannātha Purī. With devotion, they saw Lord Jagannātha as He was being served.

When he learned of their decision, Śrī Gopāla-guru was very happy. He said, "O Vrajanātha, O Vijaya-kumāra, I love you as a father loves his sons. I am not happy to be separated from you. If you stay here for many days, then I will be happy. It is easy to find a sincere spiritual master, but it is not easy to find a sincere disciple.

Vrajanātha humbly asked, "O master, please explain the features of the different *rasas*. We will consider ourselves fortunate to hear about them from you.

Gosvāmī: Your proposal is excellent. Please hear the words Lord Gauracandra will place in my mouth. First is *śānta-rasa* (neutrality). In this *rasa*, the *sthāyi-bhāva* is *śānta-rati*. The happiness attained in the impersonal Brahman is very slight. The happiness attained in a relationship with the Supreme Person is much greater than that impersonal happiness. The cause of that personal happiness is the direct perception of the Supreme Personality of Godhead's spiritual form.

The *ālambana* (object of worship) in *śānta-rasa* is the four-armed form of Lord Nārāyaṇa. This form of the Lord manifests qualities like supreme power and opulence. In this way, the *viṣaya* and *anubhāva* are manifested in *ālambana*. Peaceful persons situated in *śānta-rasa* are the *āśraya* of *śānta-rati*. *Ātmārāmas* and persons who have faith in the Supreme Personality of Godhead are qualified for *śānta-rasa*. The four sages, headed by Sanaka and Sanandana, are prominent among the *ātmārāmas*. These four sages are boy *sannyāsīs*. At first they were attached to the impersonal Brahman. Later they became attracted to the sweetness of the form of the Supreme Person. They began to worship the Lord's spiritual form.

Persons who are austere and renounced, but who have not yet thrown far away the desire for impersonal liberation, are eligible for *śānta-rasa*. Hearing the important *Upaniṣads*, living in a secluded place, meditating, searching for the truth, study, seeing the universal form, associating with persons engaged in devotional service mixed with impersonal speculation (*jñāna-miśra-bhakti*), and studying the *Upaniṣads* with others of equal scholarship are the *uddīpanās* that inspire this *rasa*. The fragrance of *tulasī* offered to the Supreme Lord's lotus feet, the sound of the conch shell, sacred mountains, sacred forests, sacred places, the Ganges, being free of material desires, and the awareness that time will eventually destroy everything material, are also *uddīpanās* that inspire *śānta-rasa*.

Vrajanātha: What are the *anubhāvas* of this *rasa*?

Gosvāmī: Staring at the tip of the nose, acting like an *avadhūta*, looking for a distance of four hands as one walks, assuming the *jñāna-mudrā* (joining the forefinger and thumb), not hating the enemies of the Supreme Personality of Godhead, being slightly inclined to the devotees who are dear to the Lord, being attracted to the soul's liberation and the end of his residence in the material world, being neutral and aloof, being free of false ego, material possessiveness, and material pride, and feeling a sort of cool-tempered love for the Supreme are included among the *anubhāvas* of *śānta-rasa*. Yawning, swelling of the limbs, teaching about devotional service, bowing down before Lord Hari, and offering prayers to Lord Hari are also included among *anubhāvas*.

Vrajanātha: What are the *sāttvika* ecstatic symptoms in *śānta-rasa*?

Gosvāmī: Devastation (except the aspect of falling to the ground) and being stunned are included among the many ecstatic symptoms in this *rasa*. There are no passionate (*dīpta*) ecstatic symptoms in this *rasa*.

Vrajanātha: What are the *sañcārī-bhāvas* in this *rasa*?

Gosvāmī: Lamentation, patience, joy, thoughtfulness, remembrance, melancholy, eagerness, anxiety, and argumentativeness are seen among the *sañcārī-bhāvas* of *śānta-rasa*.

Vrajanātha: How many are the different kinds of *śānta-rati*?

Gosvāmī: *Sthāyi-bhāva śānta-rati* is of two kinds: 1. *samā* (equipoised) and 2. *sāndrā* (intense). In *samā*, *śānta-rati* is manifested as *asamprajñāta-samādhi*, where the activities of the body are filled with awareness of the Supreme Lord's presence. In *sāndrā*, *śānta-rati* is manifested *nirvikalpa-samādhi*, where all ignorance is destroyed and the direct manifestation of the Supreme Lord's form brings intense bliss. On the basis of these two kinds of *śānta-rati*, there may also be divisions of *pārokṣya* (indirect) and *sākṣāt-kāra-rūpa* (direct) *śānta-rati*. Śukadeva Gosvāmī and Bilvamaṅgala Ṭhākura are examples of two persons who renounced *śānta-rasa* and became expert in tasting the bliss of the *rasas* of direct devotional service. The great scholar Sārvabhauma Bhaṭṭācārya is also an example of that.

Vrajanātha: The books of material rhetoric (*alaṅkāra*) do not accept *śānta-rasa*. Why is that?

Gosvāmī: Peacefulness is far away from all materialistic activities. When spiritual activities are performed, then the peacefulness of *śānta-rasa* gradually becomes manifested. In this way, the spiritual *rasas* become manifested. The Supreme Lord Himself declared, Faith in Me brings peacefulness. Look, how can one attain faith in the Lord without first being situated in *śānta-rati*? Therefore, at the beginning of spiritual life, one must first accept *śānta-rasa*.

Vrajanātha: Now I understand *śānta-bhakti-rasa*. Now, please explain, one by one, the vi*bhāvas* and other aspects of *dāsya-rasa* (servitorship).

Gosvāmī: *Dāsya-rasa* is also called *prīta-bhakti-rasa* by the *paṇḍitas*. *Dāsya-rasa* is of two kinds: 1. *anugrahāya-pātra-dāsya* (the object of mercy), and 2. *lālya-pātra-dāsya* (the object of affection). *Prīta-rasa* is also divided into these two kinds: 1. *sambhrama-prīta* (with pride) and 2. *gaurava-prīta* (with submission).

Vrajanātha: What is *sambhrama-prīta*?

Gosvāmī: Persons who are proud to be servants of Kṛṣṇa have *sambhrama-prīta* for Kṛṣṇa, the son of Nanda. When this *rasa* develops, it is called *sambhrama-prīta-rasa*. In this *rasa*, Kṛṣṇa and Kṛṣṇa's servants are both the *ālambanas*.

Vrajanātha: What form does Kṛṣṇa manifest in this *rasa*?

Gosvāmī: In Gokula, *sambhrama-prīta* Kṛṣṇa has two arms. In the other parts of this *rasa*, He sometimes has two arms and sometimes four arms. In Gokula, Kṛṣṇa is a cowherd boy, has two arms, holds the flute, and is decorated with a peacock feather and other ornaments. When He is manifested outside of Gokula, Kṛṣṇa is decorated with jewels, and His feature is that of *aiśvarya* (power and opulence).

Śrīla Rūpa Gosvāmī (*Bhakti-rasāmṛta-sindhu* 3.2.11-15) explains: Kṛṣṇa possesses the following qualities: 1. Many millions of universes come from the pores of His body, 2. He is an ocean of mercy, 3. He has inconceivable potencies, 4. He is served by all mystic powers, 5. He is the seed from which all incarnations have come. 6. His transcendental qualities attract the hearts of the liberated souls. 7. He is the supreme controller. 8. He is the supreme object of worship. 9. He knows everything. 10. He is determined. 11. He has all wealth. 12. He is tolerant and forgiving. 13. He protects the surrendered souls. 14. He is happy. 15. He is truthful. 16. He is expert. 17. He brings all auspiciousness. 18. He is powerful. 19. He is religious. 20. He sees through the eyes of the scriptures. 21. He is the best friend of the devotee. 2. He is generous. 23. He is glorious. 24. He is grateful. 25. He is the resting place of fame. 26 He is the best. 27. He is powerful. 28. He is controlled by love. In this way, Lord Hari is the *ālambana* (the object of love) for His four kinds of servants.

Vrajanātha: What are these four kinds of servants?

Gosvāmī: The devotees who have taken shelter of *dāsya*-rasa are of four kinds: 1. *praśrita* (who humbly look down when they stand before their master), 2. *ajñānuvarti* (who humbly carry out their master's orders), 3. *viśvasta* (who have full faith in their master), and 4. *prabhu-jñāne-namra-buddhi* (who are humble and very conscious of their master's superiority). These four are also called: 1. *adhikṛta* (those who are qualified), 2. *āśrita* (those who have taken shelter), 3. *pāriṣada* (associates) and 4. *anugata* (followers).

Vrajanātha: Who are the *adhikṛta* servants?

Gosvāmī: Brahmā, Śiva, Indra, and the other demigods and demigoddesses are *adhikṛta* servants and maidservants. By fulfilling various duties in the material world, the eventually become qualified (*adhikṛta*) to serve the Supreme Lord directly.

Vrajanātha: Who are the *āśrita* servants?

Gosvāmī: The three kinds of *āśrita* servants are: 1. *śaraṇāgata* (surrendered souls), 2. *jñānī* (wise philosophers) and 3. *sevā-niṣṭha* (intent on serving). Kaliyā and the kings imprisoned by Jarāsandha are counted among the *śaraṇāgata* servants. Śaunaka and the other sages who have rejected the desire for impersonal liberation and taken shelter of Lord Hari are counted among the *jñānī* servants. Because they were attached to worshiping the Lord from the very beginning of their lives, Candradhvaja, Harihara, Bahulāśva, Ikṣvāku, and Puṇḍarīka are counted among both the *sevā-niṣṭha* and *śaraṇāgata* servants.

Vrajanātha: O master, who are the *pāriṣada* servants?

Gosvāmī: Uddhava, Dāruka, Sātyaki, Śrutadeva, Śatrujit, Nanda (this is another Nanda, not Lord Kṛṣṇa's father), Upananda, and Bhadrā are counted among the parisada servants. Although these persons give advice to Lord Kṛṣṇa, at the appropriate times they also serve Him. Among the Kauravas, Bhisma, Parīkṣit, Vidura and others are counted among the *pāriṣada* servants. Among them all, Uddhava, who is filled with pure love (*prema*), is the best.

Vrajanātha: Who are the *anugata* devotees?

Gosvāmī: The *anugata* devotees, whose hearts are always eager to serve the Lord, are of two kinds: 1. the servants who stay in Dvārakā, and 2. the devotees who stay in Vraja. Sucandra, Maṇḍana, Stambha, and Sutambha are included among the *anugata* devotees in Dvārakā. Raktaka, Patraka, Patrī, Madhukaṇṭha, Madhuvrata, Rasāla, Suvilāsa, Premakanda, Marandaka, Ānanda, Candrahāsa, Pāyoda, Bakula, Rasada, and Śārada are included among the *anugata* servants in Vraja. Raktaka is the best of the *anugata* servants in Vraja.

The *pāriṣada* servants are of three kinds: 1. *dhūrya* (leaders), 2. *dhīra* (philosophers) and 3. *vīra* (heroes). The *āśrita* servants are also of three kinds: 1. *nitya-siddha* (eternally perfect), 2. *siddha* (perfect), and 3. *sādhaka* (aspiring for perfection).

Vrajanātha: What are the *uddīpana* of *dāsya*-rasa?

Gosvāmī: The sound of Kṛṣṇa's flute, the sound of His buffalo horn bugle, His smiling glance, hearing the narration of His glories, His lotus footprints, His bodily limbs as splendid like a new monsoon cloud, and the fragrance of His transcendental body.

Vrajanātha: What are the *anubhāvas* of this *rasa*?

Gosvāmī: To perform one's duties in every situation, to follow orders, to be free of envy, to make friendship with devotees who are sincerely surrendered to Lord Kṛṣṇa, and to have faith in Lord Kṛṣṇa are included among the extraordinary *anubhāvas* of this *rasa*. The *udbhāsvaras* (external symptoms of ecstasy), such as dancing, respect for Lord Kṛṣṇa's personal friends, and renunciation for everything outside the realm of Kṛṣṇa consciousness are also included among these anu*bhāvas*.

Vrajanātha: What are the *sāttvika-vikāras* (ecstatic symptoms) of these three aspects of *pritā-rasa* (*dāsya-rasa*)?

Gosvāmī: In this *rasa*, are many *sāttvika-bhāvas*, among which being stunned is the most prominent.

Vrajanātha: What are the *vyabhicārīs* in this *rasa*?

Gosvāmī: Joy, pride, determination, remorse, melancholy, humility, anxiety, remembrance, misgivings, thoughtfulness, eagerness, fickleness, argumentativeness, passion, shyness, being stunned, illusion, madness, concealment, awakening, dream, exhaustion, disease, and death are the *vyabhicārīs* of this *rasa*. Arrogance, fatigue, fear, forgetfulness, ferocity, anger, envy, and sleep are not present among the *vyabhicārīs* in this *rasa*. When he meets the Lord, the devotee manifests joy, pride, and peacefulness. When he is separated from the Lord, the devotee manifests withering away, disease, and death. The eighteen *bhāvas* that begin with remorse are seen in all circumstances, whether the devotee meets the Lord or is separated from Him.

Vrajanātha: I wish to know what are the *sthāyi-bhāvas* of *pritā-rasa*.

Gosvāmī: The *sthāyi-bhāva* of this *rasa* is the love (*prīti*) that appears in the heart when the heart is filled with awe and trembles at the thought of the master. In *śānta-rasa*, attraction to the Supreme is the only *sthāyi-bhāva*. In *dāsya-rasa*, affection combined with the possessive idea that, "the Lord is mine," is the *sthāyi-bhāva*. This respectful affection gradually grows stronger and stronger until it becomes pure affection (*prema*), love (*sneha*) and intense love (*rāga*).

When it is free from fear and awe, and when it is deep-rooted, this respectful affection (*sambhrama-prīti*) becomes pure affection (*prema*). When that pure affection becomes intense, the heart melts, and the pure affection (*prema*) is called love (*sneha*). In this condition of *sneha*, the devotee cannot bear even a moment's separation from the Lord. When this love (*sneha*) increases to the point where the devotee finds that even his sorrow brings happiness, the love becomes intense love (*rāga*). At this point, the devotee wishes to do whatever pleases Kṛṣṇa, even if the devotee loses his own life in the process.

Adhikṛta and *āśrita* servants experience love up to the stage of *prema*. The *pāriṣada* servants experience love up to the stage of *sneha*. Parīkṣit, Dāruka, Uddhava, and the *anugata* servants in Vraja experience love up to the stage of *rāga*. When *rāga* is manifested, then a small portion of *sākhya-rasa* (friendship) inevitably comes with it.

Paṇḍitas say that in this *rasa* of meeting with Kṛṣṇa is called *yoga* and separation from Kṛṣṇa is called *ayoga*. *Ayoga* is of two kinds: 1. *utkaṇṭhita* (filled with longings), and 2. *viyoga* (tragic). *Yoga* is of three kinds: 1. *siddhi* (perfection), 2. *tuṣṭi* (happiness), and 3. *sthiti* (residence). *Siddhi* is to see Kṛṣṇa after longing to meet Him. *Tuṣṭi* is to see Kṛṣṇa after a long separation. *Sthiti* is to live in the same place with Kṛṣṇa.

Vrajanātha: I understand *sambhrama-prīti* (respectful affection). Now please explain *gaurava-prīti* (love mixed with pride).

Gosvāmī: When he is proud to be able to embrace Kṛṣṇa, the devotee's affection is called *gaurava-prīti*. When the affection present in this *rasa* is increased by the *vibhāvas* and other *bhāvas*, it becomes *gaurava-prīti*. Lord Hari and the servants of Lord Hari are the *ālambanas* of this love. In *gaurava-prīti*, the devotee thinks that Kṛṣṇa is more important, more famous, more intelligent, and stronger than the devotee. The devotee thinks that Kṛṣṇa is his protector and affectionate parent. In this way, Kṛṣṇa becomes the object (*viṣayā*) of the devotee's love.

The affectionate devotees are of two kinds: 1. the devotees who are proud to be younger associates of Kṛṣṇa, and 2. the devotees who are proud to be Kṛṣṇa's sons. Sāraṇa, Gada, and Subhadra are among the devotees who are proud to be younger associates of Kṛṣṇa. Pradyumna, Cārudeṣṇa, and Samba are among the devotees who are proud to be Kṛṣṇa's sons. Śrī Kṛṣṇa's parental affection, gentle smiles, and other activities, are the *uddīpanas* of this love. These affectionate devotees sit on a seat below that of Kṛṣṇa. They respectfully follow behind Kṛṣṇa. They renounce their own wishes and fulfill Kṛṣṇa's wishes. These are the *anubhāvas* of this relationship. The *sañcārīs* and *vyabhicārīs* of this relationship are like those already explained.

Vrajanātha: What does the word *gaurava* mean?

Gosvāmī: The word *gaurava* means, "the situation where the devotee is proud to have Kṛṣṇa as his father or superior (guru)." Love that is mixed with pride to have such a relationship with Kṛṣṇa is called *gaurava-prīti*. That is the *sthāyi-bhāva* of this *rasa*.

Vrajanātha: O master, now I understand the *prīti-rasa* (*dāsya-rasa*). Now, please explain the *rasa* that is called *sākhya-rasa*.

Gosvāmī: In this *rasa*, Kṛṣṇa and His friends are the *ālambanas*. Kṛṣṇa, who is the prince of Vraja, and who holds the flute in His two hands, is the *viṣaya*. Kṛṣṇa's friends are the *āśraya*.

Vrajanātha: I wish to understand the different kinds of friends Kṛṣṇa has, and their qualities and features.

Gosvāmī: Their forms, qualities, and garments are like those of Kṛṣṇa's servants. However, Kṛṣṇa's friends are confident to approach Kṛṣṇa as equals. They are not filled with awe and veneration like Kṛṣṇa's servants. These friends are of two kinds: 1. Friends in Dvārakā and 2. Friends in Vraja.

Arjuna, Bhīma, Draupadī, and Sudāmā Vipra are among the friends in Dvārakā, and the other cities. Among them, Arjuna is the best. The friends in Vraja are always eager to see Kṛṣṇa. Kṛṣṇa is their very life. They are the best of Kṛṣṇa's friends.

In Vraja, Kṛṣṇa has four kinds of friends: 1. *suhṛt* (well-wishers), 2. *sakhā* (friends), 3. *priya-sakhā* (confidential friends) and 4. *priya-narma-vayasya* (intimate friends). Kṛṣṇa's well-wisher friends are a little bit older than Kṛṣṇa and they have some parental affection for Him. Because of their being older than Kṛṣṇa, they always try to protect Him from any harm. As such, they sometimes bear weapons so that they can chastise any mischievous persons who want to harm Kṛṣṇa. Counted among the well-wisher friends are Subhadra, Maṇḍalībhadra, Bhadravardhana, Gobhaṭa, Yakṣa, Indrabhaṭa, Bhadrāṅga, Vīrabhadra, Mahāguṇa, Vijaya, and Balabhadra. Among these friends, Balabhadra and Maṇḍalībhadra are the best.

Friends who are younger than Kṛṣṇa, who are always attached to Him, and who give Him all kinds of service are called ordinary friends, or simply friends. Such ordinary friends are called *sakhās*, and the names of some *sakhās* are Viśāla, Vṛṣabha, Ojasvī, Devaprastha, Varūthapa, Maranda, Kusumāpīḍa, Maṇibandha and Karandhama. Among them, Devaprastha is the best.

The more confidential friends are called *priya-sakhās* and are almost Kṛṣṇa's age. Because of their very confidential friendship, their behavior is only on the basis of pure friendship. Some confidential friends are as follows: Śrīdāmā, Sudāmā, Dāmā, Vasudāmā, Kiṅkiṇi, Stoka-kṛṣṇa, Aṁśu, Bhadrasena, Vilāsī, Puṇḍarīka, Viṭaṅka and Kalaviṅka.

There are other friends who are more confidential than the *suhṛt-sakha* and *priya-sakhā* friends. They are called *priya-narma*, or intimate friends. Counted among the *priya-narma* friends are Subala, Arjuna, Gandharva, Vasanta, and Ujjvala. Among them, Ujjvala, who is always eager to speak joking words, is the best. Among these friends, some are *nitya-siddha* (eternally perfect), others are *sura-cara* (demigods who eventually attained this *rasa*), and others are *sādhaka* (human beings who, by performing devotional service, eventually attained this *rasa*). The friends serve Kṛṣṇa in many different ways. Thus they perform a wonderful variety of different activities.

Vrajanātha: What are the *uddīpanas* of this *rasa*?

Gosvāmī: Kṛṣṇa's age, His beauty, His bugle, His flute, His conch shell, His pleasing attitude, His exceptional joking abilities, His great power, and His playful activities all provoke (*uddīpana*) love in friendship for Him. When Kṛṣṇa is spending His days as a cowherd boy, he is in the *kaumāra* and *paugaṇḍa* ages. In the *paugaṇḍa* age, when Kṛṣṇa appeared in Gokula, He acted as a cowherd boy and then, when He was sixteen, He went to Mathurā.

Vrajanātha: I request that you explain to me the *anubhāvas* of Kṛṣṇa's friends.

Gosvāmī: Kṛṣṇa played with His intimate friends, sometimes by fighting or wrestling with their arms, sometimes by playing ball, and sometimes by playing chess. Sometimes they carried one another on their shoulders and sometimes they exhibited their expertise at whirling logs. And, the cowherd friends used to please Kṛṣṇa by sitting together with Him on couches, or on swings, by lying together on their beds, by joking together, and by swimming in the pool, by playing with the monkeys and other animals, and by dancing, singing, and other activities. All these activities are called *anubhāva*. The *suhṛt* friends used to sit together and advise one another what to do, sometimes inducing one another to be engaged in welfare work. The *sakhā* friends would offer betel nuts to one another, decorate one another's faces with *tilaka*, or smear pulp of *candana* on one another's bodies. The *priya-sakhā* friends wanted to defeat Kṛṣṇa. Sometimes they used to snatch His clothing or snatch away the flowers from His hands. Sometimes they would try to induce one another to decorate His body for Him, and failing this, they were always ready to fight, challenging one another to combat in wrestling. The *priya-narma-sakhā* friends would make arrangements for Kṛṣṇa's *mādhurya-līlā*. Like the servants, these friends also decorated Kṛṣṇa with forest flowers and fanned Him.

Vrajanātha: What are the *sāttvika-bhāvas* and *sañcārī-bhāvas* of this *rasa*?

Gosvāmī: They are like those for *dāsya-rasa*, only a little more.

Vrajanātha: What is the *sthāyi-bhāva* for this *rasa*?

Gosvāmī: Śrīla Rūpa Gosvāmī explains (*Bhakti-rasāmṛta-sindhu* 3.3.105): When there are dealing between Kṛṣṇa and His friends, which are completely devoid of any feelings of respect, and they all treat one another on an equal level, such ecstatic love in friendship is called *sthāyi*.

Vrajanātha: What does the word *viśrambha* mean here?

Gosvāmī: It is said (*Bhakti-rasāmṛta-sindhu* 3.3.106): *Viśrambha* means, "firm confidence that one is equal to his friend."

Vrajanātha: How does this kind of friendship develop?

Gosvāmī: The stages of *sākhya-rasa* are: *prema*, *sneha*, *rāga*, and *praṇaya*.

Vrajanātha: What are the qualities of *praṇaya*?

Gosvāmī: In this kind of love, awe and veneration are completely absent, even in situations where they might be appropriate. *Sākhya-rasa* is very wonderful and unprecedented. *Sākhya-rasa* is very different from either *dāsya-rasa* or *vātsalya-rasa*. Among all the *rasas*, *sākhya-rasa* is especially dear to Kṛṣṇa. And, why not? Kṛṣṇa and His friends have a very close relationship. In some ways, the spiritual ecstasy of *sākhya-rasa* is almost similar to the ecstasy of *mādhurya-rasa*.

Chapter Thirty

Further consideration of the rasas, part four

Jaiva-dharma

Today, after honoring *kicharī prasādam*, Vijaya-kumāra and Vrajanātha saw the *samādhi* of Haridāsa Ṭhākura. Then, they saw the temple of Śrī Ṭoṭā Gopīnātha, and then they went to the temple of Śrī Rādhākānta. There, they offered *daṇḍavat* obeisances to Śrī Gopāla-guru Gosvāmī and then sat down. They discussed many things with Śrī Dhyānacandra Gosvāmī.

Meanwhile, Śrī Gopāla-guru Gosvāmī honored *prasādam* and then also sat down on his seat. Vrajanātha humbly asked him about *vātsalya-bhakti-rasa*. Śrī Gopāla-guru Gosvāmī said, "In *vātsalya-rasa*, Kṛṣṇa is the *viṣaya*, and His elder relatives and superiors are the *āśrayā*. Kṛṣṇa's body is dark and handsome. He has all virtues. He is gentle, a pleasing speaker, honest, sincere, shy, humble, respectful, and generous.

The king and queen of Vraja, Rohiṇī, the elder *gopīs*, Devakī, Kuntī, Vasudeva, and Sāndīpanī Muni are included among the devotees in *vātsalya-rasa*. Nanda and Yaśodā are the best among them. The uddīpanas include Kṛṣṇa's *kaumāra* age and other ages, and His form, garments, childhood, restlessness, talking, joking, and pastimes.

Vrajanātha: What are the *anubhāvas* in this *rasa*?

Gosvāmī: The *anubhāvas* include smelling Kṛṣṇa's head, massaging His limbs, offering blessings to Him, giving orders to Him, caressing Him, protecting Him, and giving good advice to Him. Kissing Him, hugging Him, and calling His name are also included among these activities.

Vrajanātha: What are the *sāttvika* ecstatic symptoms in this *rasa*?

Gosvāmī: The *sāttvika* ecstatic symptoms in this *rasa* include milk flowing from the breasts and the eight ecstatic symptoms that begin with becoming stunned.

Vrajanātha: What are the *vyabhicārī-bhāvas* in this *rasa*?

Gosvāmī: The *vyabhicārīs* in *vātsalya-rasa* are like those in *prīta-rasa* (*dāsya* rasa).

Vrajanātha: What are the *sthāyi-bhāvas* in this *rasa*?

Gosvāmī: The *sthāyi-bhāvas* are mercy and love that is free from awe and veneration. The parental love felt by Yaśodā and other great devotees is naturally very strong. The *sthāyi-bhāva* in this *rasa* proceeds from *prema* to *sneha* and *rāga*. Lord Balarāma's *rasa* is a mixture of *dāsya-rasa* and *vātsalya-rasa*. King

Yudhiṣṭhira's *rasa* is a mixture of *vātsalya*, *dāsya*, and *sākhya*. King Ugrasena's *rasa* is a mixture of *vātsalya* and *sākhya*. The *rasa* of Nakula, Sahadeva, Nārada Muni, and many others, is a mixture of *sākhya* and *dāsya*. The *rasa* of Śiva, Garuḍa, Uddhava, and many others is a mixture of *dāsya* and *sākhya*.

Vrajanātha: O master, now we have heard your description of *vātsalya-rasa*. Please be merciful now and describe *mādhurya-rasa*, the most exalted of the *rasas*. By hearing your description, we will become fortunate.

Gosvāmī: *Mādhurya-rasa* is said to be the most important of the *bhakti-rasas*. A living entity who has taken shelter of the material *rasas* may become devoted to the Supreme Lord and may thus gradually turn from the things of the material world and thus attain renunciation. A person who is not renounced in this way is not qualified to understand the spiritual *rasas*. Therefore, the people in general are not qualified to understand the *mādhurya-rasa*. *Mādhurya-rasa* is very difficult to understand. It is not easy to find a person qualified to understand it. This *rasa* is very confidential. Therefore, it is appropriate to keep it hidden from general view.

Therefore, even though many things could be said about *mādhurya-rasa*, I will describe it only briefly.

Vrajanātha: O master, I am a follower of the cowherd boy, Śrī Subala. Please consider what I am qualified to hear, and tell me only that much.

Gosvāmī: The *priya-narma-sakhā* friends of Kṛṣṇa are to a certain extent aware of the activities of *mādhurya-rasa*. Taking this into consideration, I will tell you what is right for you to hear, and I will not tell you what is not appropriate for you to hear.

Vrajanātha: What are the *ālambanas* of this *rasa*?

Gosvāmī: In this *rasa*, the *viṣaya* is Śrī Kṛṣṇa, the hero whose handsomeness has no equal. The transcendental *āśraya* is the devotees who relish pastimes with Him. Therefore, the Vraja *gopīs* are the *āśraya* in this *rasa*. Of all the dear *gopīs*, Śrī Rādhā is the best. Of the many *uddīpanas* in this *rasa*, the sound of Kṛṣṇa's flute is the first. The *anubhāvas* of this *rasa* include sidelong glances and smiles. All the *sāttvika-bhāvas* are gloriously present in this *rasa*. All the *vyabhicārīs*, except for laziness and ferociousness, are also present in this *rasa*.

Vrajanātha: What are the *sthāyi-bhāvas* of this *rasa*?

Gosvāmī: The appropriate *vibhāvas* act to increase the love present in *mādhurya-rasa*. No *vijātīya* or *svajātīya bhāvas* can break the love that Śrī Rādhā and Śrī Mādhava feel for each other.

Vrajanātha: How many are the different varieties of *mādhurya-rasa*?

Gosvāmī: *Mādhurya-rasa* is of two kinds: 1. *vipralambha* (separation) and *sambhoga* (meeting).

Vrajanātha: What is *vipralambha*?

Gosvāmī: *Vipralambha* is of many kinds, including *pūrva-rāga* (the beginning of love), *māna* (jealous anger), and *pravāsa* (the beloved goes far away).

Vrajanātha: What is *pūrva-rāga*?

Gosvāmī: *Pūrva-rāga* is said to be the situation before the lover's have met.

Vrajanātha: What are *māna* and *pravāsa*?

Gosvāmī: *Māna* is well known. *Pravāsa* is when the lover loses the association of the beloved.

Vrajanātha: What is *sambhoga*?

Gosvāmī: When the two lovers meet and enjoy (*bhoga*) together, that is called *sambhoga*. I will not say anything more about *mādhurya-rasa*. Persons qualified to understand *mādhurya-rasa* should study the confidential description of it in the book *Śrī Ujjvala-nīlamaṇi*.

Vrajanātha: Now please briefly describe the *gauna-bhakti-rasa* (the secondary *rasas* of devotional service).

Gosvāmī: The seven *gauna-rasas* are: laughter, astonishment, chivalry, lamentation, anger, dread, and ghastliness. When one of these secondary *rasas* becomes very powerful, it occupies the place of primary (*mukhya*) *rasas*. In this situation, it seems to be independent of the primary *rasas*. Seemingly independent in this way, the secondary *rasa* then becomes nourished by its own *sthāyi-bhāvas*, *vibhāvas*, and other *bhāvas*. However, the truth is that the five *rasas*, beginning with *śānta-rasa*, are the only primary *rasas*. The seven secondary *rasas*, which begin with *hāsya* (laughter), are considered *vyabhicārīs* in relation to the five primary *rasas*.

Vrajanātha: From my study of rhetoric (*alaṅkāra*), I have learned all these things about the *rasas*. I know all this about the secondary *rasas*, which begin with *hāsya* (laughter). I wish to know how these secondary *rasas* are related to the primary *rasas* of devotional service. Please be merciful and explain this.

Gosvāmī: It is said that among the five *rasas*, some are friends (compatible), and some are enemies (incompatible). The friends of *śānta-rasa* are *dāsya*, ghastliness, *dharma-vīra* (chivalry in performing pious deeds), and astonishment. The friends of astonishment are *dāsya*, *sākhya*, *vātsalya*, and *mādhurya-rasa*. The enemies of *śānta-rasa* are *mādhurya-rasa*, *yuddha-vīra* (chivalry in battle), anger, and dread. The friends of *dāsya-rasa* are ghastliness, *śānta-rasa*, *dharma-vīra* (chivalry in performing pious deeds), and *dāna-vīra* (chivalry in giving charity). The enemies of *dāsya*-rasa are *mādhurya-rasa*, *yuddha-vīra* (chivalry in battle), and anger.

The friends of *sākhya-rasa* are *mādhurya-rasa*, laughter, and *yuddha-vīra* (chivalry in battle). The enemies of *sākhya-rasa* are *vātsalya-rasa*, ghastliness, anger, and dread. The friends of *vātsalya-rasa* are laughter, compassion, and dread. The enemies of *vātsalya-rasa* are *mādhurya-rasa*, *yuddha-vīra* (chivalry in battle), *dāsya-rasa*, and anger. The friends of *mādhurya-rasa* are laughter and *sākhya-rasa*. The enemies of *mādhurya-rasa* are *vātsalya-rasa*, ghastliness, *śānta-rasa*, anger, and dread. The friends of *hāsya-rasa* (laughter) are ghastliness, *mādhurya-rasa*, and *vātsalya-rasa*. The enemies of *hāsya-rasa* are compassion and dread. The friends of *adbhuta-rasa* (astonishment) are chivalry, *śānta-rasa*, *dāsya-rasa*, *sākhya-rasa*, *vātsalya-rasa*, and *mādhurya-rasa*. The enemies of *adbhuta-rasa* are anger and ghastliness.

The friends of *vīra-rasa* (chivalry) are astonishment, laughter, *sākhya-rasa* and *dāsya-rasa*. The enemy of *vīra-rasa* is dread. Some think that *śānta-rasa* is also an enemy of *vīra-rasa*. The friends of *karuṇā-rasa* (compassion) are anger and *vātsalya-rasa*. The enemies of *karuṇā-rasa* are chivalry, laughter, astonishment, and the *sambhoga* (meeting) part of *mādhurya-rasa*. The friends of *raudra-rasa* (anger) are compassion and chivalry. The enemies of *raudra-rasa* are laughter, *mādhurya-rasa*, and dread. The friends of *bhayānaka-rasa* (dread) are ghastliness and compassion. The enemies of *bhayānaka-rasa* are chivalry, *mādhurya-rasa*, laughter, and anger. The friends of *bībhatsa-rasa* (ghastliness) are *śānta-rasa*, laughter, and *dāsya-rasa*. The enemies of *bībhatsa-rasa* are *mādhurya-rasa* and *sākhya-rasa*. All the other *rasas* are closely related.

Vrajanātha: Please explain the result of these *rasas* meeting with each other.

Gosvāmī: When the friendly *rasas* meet, the result is very palatable. It is good when an *aṅga-rasa* (part) meets with an *aṅgī-rasa* (whole). The *rasas* may be primary or secondary. An *aṅga-rasa* should meet with a friendly *aṅga-rasa*.

Vrajanātha: Please explain the difference between *aṅgī* (whole) and *aṅga* (part).

Gosvāmī: Whether it is a primary *rasa* or a secondary *rasa*, when one *rasa* dominates another, the dominating *rasa* is called *aṅgī*. The *aṅga-rasa* (dominated *rasa*) then becomes a *sañcārī-bhāva* that nourishes the *aṅgī-rasa*.

In the *Viṣṇu-dharmottara Purāṇa* is said: When *rasas* meet, the dominating *rasa* becomes the *sthāyi-bhāva* and the others become the *sañcārī-bhāvas*.

Vrajanātha: How is it possible for one of the secondary (*gauna*) *rasas* to become an *aṅgī-rasa* (a dominating *rasa*)

Gosvāmī: Śrīla Rūpa Gosvāmī explains (*Bhakti-rasāmṛta-sindhu* 4.8.45):

Lord Vāmanadeva is actually the Supreme Personality of Godhead, but He appeared to have been born as one of the brothers of Indra. Although Vāmanadeva is sometimes taken as a less important demigod, He is actually the maintainer of Indra, the king of the demigods. Thus, although sometimes Vāmanadeva is considered to be a subordinate demigod, His actual position is that of the supreme whole, the source of the entire demigod system. In the same way, a *rasa* which is actually prominent may sometimes appear to be manifested in a subordinate way, although its actual position is as the main or prominent loving feeling of a devotee.

Vrajanātha: What happens when two inimical *rasas* meet?

Gosvāmī: It becomes like sweet nectar when something salty or sour is mixed in. This mixing of incompatible *rasas* is called *rasābhāsa*.

Vrajanātha: Is the mixing of incompatible *rasas* never good in any situation?

Gosvāmī: Śrīla Rūpa Gosvāmī explains (*Bhakti-rasāmṛta-sindhu* 4.8.63-64):

When an opposing argument is to be refuted, or when remembering something, or when speaking impartially, or in a favorable way one stands between two *rasas*, or when there is a difference of the lover (*āśraya*) and beloved (*viṣaya*), then the meeting of incompatible *rasas* does not produce an unpalatable result.

In this way, it is seen that even though *dāsya-rasa* and *vātsalya-rasa* are enemies, when they are present, at different times, in the relationship of King Yudhiṣṭhira with Lord Kṛṣṇa, there is no incompatibility. Although these two *rasas* are enemies, they are not present simultaneously. Sometimes, when the ecstasy of *bhāva* is very intense, there is no incompatibility when incompatible *rasas* meet.

Śrīla Rūpa Gosvāmī explains (*Bhakti-rasāmṛta-sindhu* 4.8.83): Sometimes, when they are present in very exalted and powerful personalities, many different incompatible *rasas* join to become compatible.

Vrajanātha: I heard from the Vaiṣṇavas that Lord Mahāprabhu was not very happy to hear words contaminated with *rasābhāsa*, and he would not agree to hear songs contaminated with that defect. Now I understand the fault of *rasābhāsa*. Now, please kindly explain the different kinds of *rasābhāsa*.

Gosvāmī: *Rasābhāsa*, or incompatible mixtures of mellows, may be classified as *uparasa* (false expression), *anurasa* (imitation), and *aparasa* (perverted or misrepresented mellows). In this way, there is great, intermediate, or lesser expression of *rasābhāsa*.

Vrajanātha: What is *uparasa*?

Gosvāmī: Pushed by *sthāyi-bhāva*, *vibhāva*, *anubhāva*, and the other *bhāvas*, the twelve *rasas* may become *uparasas*. When *sthāyi-bhāva*, *vibhāva*, or *anubhāva* are manifested in a distorted way, then *uparasa* is manifested.

Vrajanātha: What is *anurasa*?

Gosvāmī: When the twelve secondary *rasas* are manifested, but they have no relation to Kṛṣṇa, then they are *anurasa*. When chivalry and other such *rasas* only approach the borderline of having a relationship with Kṛṣṇa, they are also considered *anurasa*.

Vrajanātha: If these sentiments have no relationship with Kṛṣṇa, then they are not *rasas* at all. They are only material. What is the distinguishing feature of *anurasas* that makes them different from material feelings?

Gosvāmī: *Anurasas* do not have a direct relationship with Kṛṣṇa. Some examples of *anurasas* are the *gopīs*' laughing (*hāsya-rasa*) when they saw a monkey dance and Nārada's astonishment (*adbhuta-rasa*) when he heard two parrots debating *Vedānta* in Bhāṇḍīravana. In these examples, one can see a relationship with Kṛṣṇa, but it is distant. One cannot see a direct relationship with Kṛṣṇa. In such a situation, there is *anurasa*.

Vrajanātha: What is *aparasa*?

Gosvāmī: If Kṛṣṇa becomes the object of His enemy's laughter or other unfavorable sentiments—that is called *aparasa*. When he saw Kṛṣṇa flee from the battlefield, Jarāsandha laughed again and again. That is an example of *aparasa*.

Śrīla Rūpa Gosvāmī explains (*Bhakti-rasāmṛta-sindhu*): Some call these incompatible mellows *tad-ābhāsa* and others call them *rasābhāsa*. But, persons who know the truth about the *rasas* use the word *rasa* to refer to the compatible, pleasing *rasas* only.

After hearing these words, Vijaya-kumāra and Vrajanātha, tears in their eyes and their words choked up, at once fell before the lotus feet of their spiritual master and said, "I offer my respectful obeisances unto my spiritual master, who with the torchlight of knowledge has opened my eyes, which were blinded by the darkness of ignorance."

Filled with the bliss of spiritual love, Śrī Gopāla-guru Gosvāmī embraced the two disciples. With a sincere heart, he blessed them, "May the truth of the *rasas* be manifest before you."

Every day, Vijaya-kumāra and Vrajanātha discussed the spiritual truth with Śrī Dhyānacandra Gosvāmī. They would also accept the *caraṇāmṛta* from Śrī Gopāla-guru Gosvāmī's lotus feet and the nectarean remnants of the *prasādam* food that had touched his lips. Some days they stayed in their own *bhajana-kuṭira*. Other days they would visit Śrī Haridāsa Ṭhākura's *samādhi*. Other days they would visit the temple of Śrī Gopīnātha. Other days they would see the many pure Vaiṣṇavas performing devotional service under the *siddha-bakula* tree. In these ways, the two devotees became plunged in the nectarean ocean of devotional service.

Sometimes they would see the places where Lord Mahāprabhu was overcome with ecstatic love, places described in Śrīla Rūpa Gosvāmī's *Stava-māla*, and Śrīla Raghunātha dāsa Gosvāmī's *Stavāvalī*. Sometimes they would join the pure Vaiṣṇavas in chanting the holy names of Lord Hari. In this way, Vijaya-kumāra and Vrajanātha gradually became advanced in devotional service.

Vijaya-kumāra thought, "Śrī Gopāla-guru Gosvāmī briefly described *mādhurya-rasa* to us. I should hear a more detailed explanation of it from his mouth. Let Vrajanātha remain plunged in his mellows of *sākhya-rasa*. I will go alone and learn all the truths of *mādhurya-rasa*."

By the kind help of Dhyānacandra Gosvāmī, Vijaya-kumāra got a copy of *Śrī Ujjvala-nīlamaṇi*. He studied that book. When any doubts arose, he placed his questions before Śrī Gopāla-guru Gosvāmī.

One afternoon, Vijaya-kumāra and Vrajanātha were sitting by the seashore, looking at the waves, and observing how the wave-filled ocean was like life. Vijaya-kumāra said, "No one could say what would happen next in life. We should learn about the path of *rāga-mārga* (*rāgānuga-bhakti*) from Śrī Gopāla-guru Gosvāmī."

Vrajanātha said, "Śrī Dhyānacandra Gosvāmī has written a book about *rāga-mārga*. I have seen it. If our spiritual master teaches us that book, we will gain a great result. Good. I will make a copy of that book."

After coming to this conclusion, he approached Śrī Dhyānacandra and requested a copy of the book. Śrī Dhyānacandra replied, "I cannot give you a copy. You must first get permission from Śrī Gopāla-guru Gosvāmī."

Then, the two of them approached Śrī Gopāla-guru Gosvāmī and placed their request before him. He said, "Good. Get a copy and then return."

With these words as their permission, Vijaya-kumāra and Vrajanātha got a copy of the book. They thought that at appropriate times they would approach Śrī Gopāla-guru Gosvāmī and learn the book under his guidance.

Śrī Dhyānacandra Gosvāmī was learned in all the scriptures. Especially in the scriptures that describe devotional service to Lord Hari, he had no equal. He was the foremost of Śrī Gopāla-guru Gosvāmī's disciples. Thinking them good candidates for devotional service, he taught Vijaya-kumāra and Vrajanātha everything about the path of devotional service. Again and again, they approached Śrī Gopāla-guru Gosvāmī's holy feet and again and again, Vijaya-kumāra and Vrajanātha had their doubts answered. They learned about Lord Mahāprabhu's daily activities and Lord Kṛṣṇa's daily pastimes. Following these pastimes, they worshiped the Lord during the eight portions of the day.

Chapter Thirty-one

Mādhurya-rasa, part one

Autumn came. After five hours of night, the moon rose. Vijaya-kumāra thought, "I should see Śraddhāvali and Sundarācala. Vijaya-kumāra had studied the method of worshiping the Lord in pure *mādhurya-rasa*. He liked only Lord Kṛṣṇa's pastimes in Vraja and nothing else. He was always rapt in thinking of Lord Kṛṣṇa's pastimes with the *gopīs* in Vraja. He had heard that Lord Mahāprabhu saw Sundarācala as the land of Vraja.

Vijaya-kumāra set out for Sundarācala. He crossed the Balagaṇḍi and began to proceed toward Śraddhāvali. As he walked, he saw gardens on both sides. Finally, Vṛndāvana appeared before him. Plunged in an ocean of spiritual love, Vijaya-kumāra said, "Ah! How fortunate I have become today! Today I can see Vraja-purī, which even Brahmā and the demigods cannot easily attain. Here is a forest garden. Here, in a bower of *mālatī* and *mādhavī* vines, Śrī Kṛṣṇa, the master of my life, is joking with the *gopīs*."

Pushing aside all feelings of awe and veneration, agitated Vijaya-kumāra ran to that place. As he was running, Vijaya-kumāra fainted and fell unconscious to the ground. A gentle breeze blew on Vijaya-kumāra. After a short time, Vijaya-kumāra became conscious again. He looked in one direction and then another. Not seeing the Lord's pastimes, he became unhappy at heart. Eventually, Vijaya-kumāra returned home. He went to bed. He did not tell anyone what he had seen. The sight of Lord Kṛṣṇa's pastimes in Vraja made Vijaya-kumāra's heart blossom with joy.

In his heart Vijaya-kumāra thought, "Today I have seen something very confidential. Tomorrow I will tell my spiritual master."

After a few moments, he remembered that a person who sees the Lord's confidential pastimes should not reveal that fact to anyone. Thinking about this again and again, he gradually fell asleep. When he rose in the morning, he could think of nothing else. He honored *prasādam*, went to the home of Kāśī Miśra and offered *daṇḍavat* obeisances to his spiritual master. His spiritual master respectfully embraced him and asked about his welfare. Vijaya-kumāra kept his eyes on his spiritual master's lotus feet. With a steady heart, he asked about the *mādhurya-rasa*.

Vijaya-kumāra said, "O master, you have been merciful to me without limit. I would like to ask a question about the confidential truths of the splendid *mādhurya-rasa*. I have been reading *Śrī Ujjvala-nīlamaṇi*, and some parts of it I do not understand."

Hearing this, the spiritual master replied, "Bābā, you are a very dear disciple of mine. You may place your questions before me. I will answer as far as I am able."

Vijaya-kumāra said, "O master, it is said that among the five primary *rasas*, the *mādhurya-rasa* is the most confidential. And, why not? *Mādhurya-rasa* eternally possesses all the virtues present in *śānta*, *dāsya*, *sākhya*, and *vātsalya rasas*. *Mādhurya-rasa* is the most wonderful and beautiful of all *rasas*. How can there be any doubt? Persons who follow the path of dry renunciation are completely unqualified to understand the truth of *mādhurya-rasa*. On the other hand, the path followed by the materialists is not a good path to follow. The Vraja *mādhurya-rasa* is completely different from material sexual activities. The *mādhurya-rasa* cannot be understood very easily. If the *mādhurya-rasa* is so wonderful, why it is so much like the affairs of ordinary men and women in the material world?"

Gosvāmī: Bābā Vijaya-kumāra, you know very well that the wonderful variety present in the material world is only a perverted reflection of the wonderful variety present in the spiritual world. The confidential truth here is that in a reflection everything is the reverse of the original. Thus, what is highest in the original is lowest in the reflection, and what is lowest in the original is highest in the reflection. When we look in the mirror, we see our limbs reflected in reverse. That is easy to understand. In the same way, when the shadow of the Supreme Lord's inconceivable potency is reflected in the material world—that reflected image is in reverse. Thus, when the spiritual *rasas* are reflected in the material world—that reflected image is in reverse.

The Absolute Truth has a great variety of unprecedented and wonderful happinesses. The highest stage of those happinesses is the *rasas*. The conditioned souls think of these *rasas* only in terms of their material reflections. Some thinkers claim that the spiritual truth has no variety. These persons try to become one with the Supreme. They think variety exists only in the material world, and in the world of spirit there is no variety. These persons cannot understand the truth about the spiritual world.

However, a person who takes shelter of logic and simple common sense can easily understand the truth. The reality is that the Supreme is the resting place of all *rasas*. Therefore, wonderful variety exists in Him. The great variety of material *rasas* are all reflected from Him. Therefore, by looking at the material *rasas*, we can understand something of the original spiritual *rasa*, which cannot be perceived by the material senses. A great variety of *rasas* exist within the Supreme. That much may be understood. The lowest *rasa* in the spiritual world is the peaceful *rasa* called *śānta-rasa*. Above that is *dāsya-rasa*. Above *dāsya-rasa* is *sākhya-rasa*. Above *sākhya-rasa* is *vātsalya-rasa*. Then, above them all, is *mādhurya-rasa*.

However, when these *rasas* are reflected in the material world, their positions are all inverted. Thus, in the material world, the *mādhurya-rasa* is in the lowest position. Above that is *vātsalya-rasa*. Above *vātsalya-rasa* is *sākhya-rasa*. Above *sākhya-rasa* is *dāsya-rasa*. Then, above them all, is *śānta-rasa*. Those who analyze the different *rasas* in the material world come to the conclusion that *mādhurya-rasa* is the lowest of all. That is why the activities of *mādhurya-rasa* in the material world are very unimportant and are a source of embarrassment.

However, in the spiritual world, the *mādhurya-rasa* is the most pure of all the *rasas*. It is filled with purity, splendor, and wonderful sweetness. In the spiritual world, when Kṛṣṇa, the supreme male, meets with His potencies, who are all female, Their activities are supremely pure. Their activities are the root of spiritual reality. However, the perverted reflection of those activities in the material world is degraded and a source of embarrassment. The truth is that Kṛṣṇa is the only male, and His potencies are all female. Therefore, in this *rasa* in the spiritual world there is nothing that is impious or goes against the teachings of religion.

In the material world, one individual soul is the enjoyer and another individual soul is the enjoyed. In this way, the material *mādhurya-rasa* contradicts the original spiritual reality. That is why the material *mādhurya-rasa* is the resting place of revulsion and embarrassment. The truth is that it is not possible for one individual soul to be the enjoyer of another individual soul. All individual souls are meant to be enjoyed, and Lord Kṛṣṇa is the only enjoyer. It is because it is so much in opposition to the true nature of the individual soul that the material *mādhurya-rasa* is so abominable, repulsive, and embarrassing. How can there be any doubt? Look, consider the nature of a reflection in a mirror. There must be some similarity between the reflected material couples in the material world and their origin in Lord Kṛṣṇa's supreme pure transcendental pastimes. However, the difference between them is that one is the most abominable and the other is the most exalted.

Vijaya-kumāra: O master, now my life is a success. I fully accept your very pleasing conclusion. Now my doubt is destroyed. Now I am able to understand the *mādhurya-rasa* present in the spiritual world. Ah, the very word *mādhurya-rasa* is sweet. It is spiritual and free from the touch of matter. It is the source of supreme transcendental bliss. Who is so unfortunate that he will refer to the happiness of *śānta-rasa* to the sweet happiness of *mādhurya-rasa*? O master, I am very eager to understand the *mādhurya-rasa*. Please be merciful to me.

Gosvāmī: Bābā, please listen carefully and I will speak. In *mādhurya-rasa*, Kṛṣṇa is the *viṣaya* and His beloveds are the *āśraya*. Their meeting is the *ālambana*.

Vijaya-kumāra: What are the features of Kṛṣṇa when He is the *viṣaya* in *mādhurya-rasa*?

Gosvāmī: Ah! That is a very pleasing question. Kṛṣṇa's complexion is the color of a new rain cloud. He is charming. All His features are sweet and charming. He is the strongest. His youthfulness is always new and fresh. He speaks eloquently and sweetly. He is intelligence, glorious, sober and profound, the best, famous, charming to all women, always new and fresh, the enjoyer of incomparable transcendental pastimes, handsome, the most dear, and expert at playing the flute. The supreme male, Kṛṣṇa, has many transcendental qualities like these. The glory of all the Kāmadevas is at once eclipsed by a mere glimpse of the glory of Kṛṣṇa's lotus feet. Lord Kṛṣṇa's sidelong glance enchants the hearts of all. Kṛṣṇa is the great treasure of transcendental pastimes. He is the good fortune attained by the *gopīs*.

Vijaya-kumāra: Kṛṣṇa has a great host of wonderful spiritual qualities. Kṛṣṇa is the only hero of the wonderful and spiritual *mādhurya-rasa*. Now I can fully understand all this. Previously, I studied many scriptures. I had praise only for material logic. Even though I would sometimes meditate on Lord Kṛṣṇa, I did not have firm faith in Him. But now, by your mercy, a little bit of devotion, devotion that is the root of attraction to Kṛṣṇa, has risen in my heart. Now that my heart has become purified by devotion, I have attained the direct perception of Lord Kṛṣṇa. I turned away from Kṛṣṇa, but still, Kṛṣṇa never left my heart. Ah, how merciful He is!

Now I can understand these words (*Bhakti-rasāmṛta-sindhu* 2.5.131-132): Non-devotees cannot understand the transcendental mellows experienced between the devotee and the Lord. In all respects, this is very difficult, but one who has dedicated everything to the lotus feet of Kṛṣṇa can taste the transcendental mellows. When one transcends the status of ecstatic love and thus becomes situated on the highest platform of pure goodness, one is understood to have cleansed the heart of all material contamination. In that pure stage of life, one tastes this nectar, and this tasting capacity is called *rasa*, or transcendental mood.

O master, now I can directly understand that the true *rasas* are the splendid spiritual *rasas* in the heart. The so-called *rasas* in the material world are not the true *rasas*. The true *rasas* are in the spiritual world. Each living being is a tiny particle of spirit, a soul. When the soul becomes rapt in the meditation of devotional service (*bhakti-samādhi*), then the spiritual *rasas* are manifested in him. By the mercy of the spiritual master, one is able to understand both the soul's pure, original, spiritual identity, and the soul's conditioned existence in the material world. One who understands this has no doubts.

Gosvāmī: Bābā Vijaya-kumāra, all you say is true. To further remove any doubts you may still have, I will explain more about the spiritual truth. Tell me: What is the relationship of pure truth and mixed truth?

Vijaya-kumāra: (offering *daṇḍavat* obeisances to his spiritual master's lotus feet) O master, only by your mercy, I will be able to speak properly. If my explanations are faulty, then please be merciful and correct me. That which truly exists is called existence (*sattva*). Thus it is said that there is "true existence of a particular place (sthiti-satta)," "true existence of a form (*rūpa-sattva*)," "true existence of certain qualities (*guṇa sattva*)," and "true existence of certain activities (*kriya-sattva*)."

True existence (*sattva*) has neither beginning nor end. True existence is manifested in an eternal present, uncontaminated by past or future. It is filled with many great wonders and it is perfectly pure in nature. That is pure existence (*śuddha-sattva*). Pure existence is manifested by the Lord's pure spiritual potency (*śuddha-cit-śakti*). The material world of *māyā*, where past and future are manifested, is only a shadow of the original spiritual potency (*cit-śakti*). When that something is seen to begin its existence in the world of *māyā*, that beginning comes from the material mode of passion. When something is seen to come to an end in the material world of *māyā*, that ending comes from the material mode of ignorance. These kinds of existence are all mixed. The pure spirit soul, however, is unmixed, pure existence (*śuddha-sattva*). The form, qualities, and activities of the pure soul are all pure existence (*śuddha-sattva*). However, when the individual spirit soul is imprisoned by *māyā*, the soul's qualities are seen to be mixed with the material modes of passion and ignorance.

Gosvāmī: Bābā, your analysis is very subtle. Now please tell me: How does the living entity's heart become enlightened with pure existence?

Vijaya-kumāra: As long as he remains imprisoned in the material world, the soul does not manifest its original, pure existence. Only with the arising of his brilliant *śuddha-sattva* nature is the soul's original, pure form manifested. The soul's original form is not manifested as a result of impersonal speculation (*jñāna- ceṣṭā*) or fruitive work (*karma-ceṣṭā*). How can one become clean if he washes himself with dirt? Spiritual knowledge is like fire. With the fire of knowledge, one should burn away the contamination of materialism. How does one attain the spiritual happiness that comes from washing away the contamination of matter? By the mercy of Kṛṣṇa and the Vaiṣṇavas one attains devotional service. By engaging in devotional service, one regains his original spiritual identity. When that original identity is regained, the heart becomes effulgent with pure spiritual existence.

Gosvāmī: Bābā, I am very happy to teach a qualified student like you. What other questions do you have?

Vijaya-kumāra: Previously, you said that there are four kinds of heroes:

dhīrodātta, dhīra-lalita, dhīra-praśānta and *dhirodhatta*. Which kind of hero is Kṛṣṇa?

Gosvāmī: Kṛṣṇa is all four of these heroes. If one asks how a personality can be beheld in four quite opposing ways, the answer is that the Lord is the reservoir of all transcendental qualities and activities. Therefore, His different aspects can be analyzed according to the exhibition of His limitless variety of pastimes, and as such there is no contradiction.

Vijaya-kumāra: If you are merciful, then please kindly explain all this. (Speaking these words,) Vijaya-kumāra fell, with tears in his eyes, at the lotus feet of his spiritual master. The saintly Gosvāmī lifted him up, embraced him, and tears flowing from his own eyes, began to speak.

Gosvāmī: In *mādhurya-rasa*, Kṛṣṇa assumes two roles: that of husband and that of paramour.

Vijaya-kumāra: O master, Kṛṣṇa is our eternal husband. How can He be a paramour?

Gosvāmī: This is very confidential. In the realm of spiritual activities, *mādhurya-rasa* is a secretly hidden jewel. Among the many jewels of *mādhurya-rasa*, the jewel where Kṛṣṇa assumes the role of paramour (*parakīya*) is the best, the Kaustubha jewel.

Vijaya-kumāra: The devotees who have taken shelter of *mādhurya-rasa* worship Kṛṣṇa as their husband. What is this secret, that Kṛṣṇa can be a paramour?

Gosvāmī: If the Supreme is impersonal and without qualities, then there is no possibility of a *rasa* with Him. If He is impersonal, the *Veda's* declāration, *raso vai saḥ* (The Supreme Personality of Godhead is the reservoir of transcendental *rasas*), has no meaning. If the Supreme has neither qualities nor happiness, then He cannot have any contact with *rasa*. Only if He has qualities may He have contact with *rasa*.

The *rasas* are manifested in the heart. The *rasas* cannot be manifested in relation to an impersonal quality-less Supreme. They are manifest only in relation to the Supreme Person. In *śānta-rasa*, the Lord's supreme power and opulence are prominent. The *dāsya-rasa*, where the Lord's position as the supreme master is prominent, is above *śānta-rasa*. The *sākhya-rasa*, where the idea that one is the Lord's equal is prominent, is above *dāsya-rasa*. The *vātsalya-rasa*, where the idea that one is the Lord's superior is prominent, is above *sākhya-rasa*. The *mādhurya-rasa* is above the *vātsalya-rasa*. It is above all the other *rasas*.

In *mādhurya-rasa*, *parakīya* is above *svakīya*. These two are based on *ātmā* (myself) and *para* (another person). The one means that one is Kṛṣṇa's, and the other means that one belongs to another. These two opposites are both manifested in relation to the Supreme Person. In one part of Kṛṣṇa's pastimes, *svakīya* love is manifested, and in another part of His pastimes, *parakīya* love is manifested. When the hero and heroine passionately meet, that is the wonderful *parakīya-rasa*. *Parakīya-rasa* is much great then *svakīya-rasa*. The *svakīya-rasa* is dry in comparison, and the *parakīya-rasa* is blossoming with happiness. When Kṛṣṇa is the hero, *parakīya-rasa* is not at all abominable. If an individual soul is the hero, then one can consider whether his actions follow the path of religion or oppose it. If an individual soul is the hero in *parakīya* love, then that is very abominable. Therefore, philosophers affirm that an individual soul who becomes a paramour is very reprehensible.

Śrīla Rūpa Gosvāmī explains that in books of ordinary material rhetoric (*alaṅkāra-śāstra*), it is accepted that a paramour is in an inferior position. This is true for a material paramour, but it is not true for Śrī Kṛṣṇa, the spiritual Supreme Personality of Godhead—the origin of all incarnations.

Vijaya-kumāra: Lord Kṛṣṇa then appears as both husband and paramour. Please first explain His role as husband.

Gosvāmī: When He accepts a girl's hand in marriage, then He is the husband.

Vijaya-kumāra: What is the nature of His role as paramour and His *parakīya-rasa*?

Gosvāmī: When love becomes everything for Him, and when, passionately desiring another's wife, He jumps over the rules of religion, then He is a paramour. When He ignores the religious rules that govern this life and the next and when He has only contempt for the institution of marriage, and when He thus offers Himself to a girl, then Lord Kṛṣṇa enjoys the *parakīya-rasa*. In *parakīya-rasa* there are two kinds of heroines: 1. An unmarried girl and 2. The wife of another.

Vijaya-kumāra: What is the nature of *svakīya-rasa*?

Gosvāmī: When He accepts a girl's hand in marriage, becomes her husband, and protects her, and when she is always faithful to Him, that is *svakīya-rasa*.

Vijaya-kumāra: When does Śrī Kṛṣṇa accept the *svakīya* and *parakīya rasas*?

Gosvāmī: When He marries the queens in Dvārakā, He accepts *svakīya-rasa* and when He becomes the lover of the girls of Vraja, He accepts the *parakīya-rasa*.

Vijaya-kumāra: What is the position of these two kinds of beloveds in Lord Kṛṣṇa's unmanifested pastimes?

Gosvāmī: This is very confidential. You know that Lord Kṛṣṇa's opulences are four quarters. Three-quarters are the spiritual world and one-quarter is the material world. Within that one quarter of the Lord's opulences exist the material universes that have fourteen planetary systems. On the boundary that divides the material and spiritual worlds flows the Virajā River. On the father shore of the Virajā is the spiritual world. The spiritual world is enclosed by a wall of light called the *brahmajyoti*. Beyond that wall may be seen the spiritual sky of Vaikuṇṭha.

In Vaikuṇṭha the Lord's opulence is prominent. There, Lord Nārāyaṇacandra, the king of kings, is served by numberless spiritual opulences. In Vaikuṇṭha, the Lord accepts only the *svakīya-rasa*. There, Śrī, Bhū, Nīlā, and the other wives serve their husband, Lord Nārāyaṇa. Above Vaikuṇṭha is Goloka. In Vaikuṇṭha, the Dvārakā queens serve Kṛṣṇa according to *svakīya-rasa*. In Goloka, the girls of Vraja serve Kṛṣṇa according to their own *rasa*.

Vijaya-kumāra: If Goloka is Lord Kṛṣṇa's highest abode, why is Vraja glorified as the most wonderful place?

Gosvāmī: Vraja, Gokula, Vṛndāvana, and many other places are all situated within Mathurā-maṇḍala. Goloka is the highest abode. When it is manifested within the material world, Goloka is called Mathurā-maṇḍala. They are both the highest abode.

Vijaya-kumāra: How is that possible? I don't understand.

Gosvāmī: It is possible by the power of Lord Kṛṣṇa's inconceivable potency. Lord Kṛṣṇa's inconceivable potency cannot be understood by material thought processes or material logic. The spiritual realm, called Goloka, comes to the material world and is then called Mathurā-maṇḍala. In the Lord's unmanifested pastimes (*aprakaṭa-līlā*), that same world is called Goloka. Lord Kṛṣṇa's transcendental pastimes are eternal. When one is qualified to see pure spirit, then he can see the world of Goloka. Then he sees that the Gokula present in the material world is the same as Goloka in the spiritual world. However, when a person's intelligence is tortured by material ideas, he cannot see that Goloka is the same as Gokula. He sees that they are different. He sees that Gokula is part of the material world.

Vijaya-kumāra: How does one become qualified to see Goloka?

Gosvāmī: Śrī Śukadeva Gosvāmī explains (*Śrīmad-Bhāgavatam* 10.28.14-15):

Kṛṣṇa immediately thought that His devotees in Vṛndāvana should be informed of the spiritual sky and the Vaikuṇṭha planets therein. Thus Kṛṣṇa showed them the eternal, ever-existing spiritual sky, which is unlimited and full of knowledge. Information of the spiritual sky can be had only from great sages and saintly persons who have already surpassed the influence of the three material modes of nature.

Bābā, without Kṛṣṇa's mercy, no one can see Goloka. It was by His mercy that the people of Vraja were able to see Goloka. Goloka is the supreme spiritual abode, far beyond the material world. It contains all wonders. It is eternal and spiritual. It is the home of limitless spiritual pastimes. The spiritual effulgence called *brahmajyoti* is the eternal effulgence emanating from Goloka. The devotees who have completely renounced the material world are able to see Goloka as it is.

Vijaya-kumāra: Are all liberated souls able to see Goloka?

Gosvāmī: Among millions and millions of liberated souls, it is hard to find a single devotee of the Supreme Lord. Persons who follow the path of *aṣṭāṅga-yoga*, or the path of impersonal speculation, may attain liberation but in that kind of liberation, they forget their original spiritual identity in the spiritual world of Vraja. Devotees who are attracted by the Supreme Lord's opulences also cannot see the world of Goloka. Following their hearts, they go to Vaikuṇṭha and there they serve the Supreme Lord in His form of opulence and majesty. Among the devotees who worship Kṛṣṇa according to the *rasas* of Vraja, only those who, by Lord Kṛṣṇa's mercy, are released from *māyā*'s prison are able to see Goloka.

Vijaya-kumāra: Well, if only these few liberated souls can see Goloka, then why is Goloka described in *Śrī Brahma-saṁhitā*, *Hari-vaṁśa*, *Padma Purāṇa*, and other scriptures? Simply by worshiping Him in Vraja, one can easily attain Lord Kṛṣṇa's mercy. Why then do all these scriptures describe Goloka?

Gosvāmī: A *rāsika* devotee who worships Kṛṣṇa according to the *rasas* of Vraja, Lord Kṛṣṇa lifts from the material world and places in Goloka. Such a person can see Goloka in full. Among the pure devotees who worship Kṛṣṇa in Vraja, some very few are able to see Goloka. There are two kinds of devotees: *siddha* (perfect devotees) and *sādhaka* (aspiring devotees). The *sādhaka* devotees are not qualified to see Goloka. The *siddha* devotees are of two kinds: *vastu-siddha* (perfect in reality) and *svarūpa-siddha* (perfect in conception).

The *vastu-siddha* devotees are persons who, by Lord Kṛṣṇa's mercy, are taken directly to Goloka. The *svarūpa-siddha* devotees are persons who, although they are not taken, by Lord Kṛṣṇa's mercy, from the material world and placed in Goloka, can still see the true form of Goloka. There are many kinds of devotees whose eyes of devotional service are gradually opened, by Lord Kṛṣṇa's mercy. Some can see a little of Goloka, some can see more of Goloka, and some can see a great deal of Goloka. According to the degree they have attain Lord Kṛṣṇa's mercy, to that degree they can see Goloka. In the stage of *sādhana*, the devotee can have a brief glimpse of Goloka in Gokula in the material world. When a devotee leaves the stage of *sādhana-bhakti* and attains *bhāva-bhakti*, then he can see Goloka to a greater extent. When a devotee attains the stage of *prema*, then he can see Goloka to a very great extent.

Vijaya-kumāra: O master, what is the difference between Goloka and Vraja?

Gosvāmī: Whatever can be seen in Vraja can also be seen in Goloka. However, persons with different kinds of qualification may see Vraja differently. The truth is that Goloka and Vṛndāvana are not different in anyway. However, there may be differences in different persons' ability to see. A person tightly bound by the mode of ignorance will see Vraja as just another place in the material world. A person influenced by the mode of passion will see Vraja as a pleasant place. A person in the mode of pure goodness will see Vraja more clearly than the others. In this way, different people are more or less able to properly see the land of Vraja.

Vijaya-kumāra: O master, I can understand a little. Please give one or two examples to help me understand. Examples comparing things in the spiritual world to things in the material world are always imperfect. Still, they can be useful, for the nature of one thing can be hinted at by comparing it to another.

Gosvāmī: This is a very difficult topic. If one has a direct spiritual vision, he is forbidden to reveal it to others. If, by Kṛṣṇa's mercy, one is able to see directly, one must keep that revelation always a secret. I will repeat to you what the previous *ācāryas* have taught about this. Anything more than that you will soon see for yourself, by Lord Kṛṣṇa's mercy.

Pure spiritual perception exists in Goloka. Material ideas do not exist there at all. To nourish the *rasas*, the Lord's spiritual potency (*cit-śakti*) manifests all wonderful states of being (*bhāva*). In this way, many ideas and conceptions are manifested. In Goloka, Kṛṣṇa is beginningless. He is never born. Still, to help the Lord's pastimes, the Lord's spiritual potency convinces Nanda and Yaśodā that they are Kṛṣṇa's parents. In this way, the *vātsalya-rasa* is manifested. In *mādhurya-rasa*, the wonderful varieties of *vipralambha* (separation) and *sambhoga* (enjoying pastimes together) are also manifested by the Lord's spiritual potency. In this way, the *parakīya-rasa* and *svakīya-rasa* are manifested in an eternal present (*nitya-vartamāna*).

Look, in this way, many different ideas and beliefs are manifested by Yogamāyā in Vraja. Yogamāyā convinces Yaśodā that Kṛṣṇa was born in her maternity room. Yogamāyā convinces the *gopīs* that they were married to Abhimanyu, Govardhana-gopa, and others. In this way, the *parakīya-rasa* is nourished. These various ideas and beliefs created by Yogamāyā are not really untrue. They are part of the total reality of Goloka. Thus, the different residents of Goloka do indeed see things differently.

Vijaya-kumāra: Should one purify his thoughts by meditating on the Lord's pastimes in the eight periods of the day (*aṣṭakālīya-līlā*), and in this way be able to see the Lord in meditation?

Gosvāmī: It is not like that. One first sees the Lord's pastimes in Vraja, and then one remembers those pastimes of the eight periods of the day. By engaging in devotional service, one obtains Kṛṣṇa's mercy, and then the Lord's pastimes are manifested before one. There is no need to first purify one's thoughts by meditating on the Lord's pastimes.

Vijaya-kumāra: It is said: "One attains perfection that corresponds to his meditation." Does this mean that when one attains perfection, he will obtain what he meditated on during the period of *sādhana-bhakti*? Therefore, one should strive to meditate purely on Goloka.

Gosvāmī: What you say is true. All the ideas and beliefs present in Vraja are pure truths. There is nothing imperfect or wrong with about them. If there were anything untrue about them, they would be faulty. When one perfectly practices *sādhana-bhakti*, he attains perfection. What one purely meditates on during the practice of *sādhana-bhakti*, one directly sees when one attains perfection. Try to perform the duties of *sādhana-bhakti* nicely. Do not try to purify these activities. To purify them is beyond your power. With His inconceivable potency, Lord Kṛṣṇa Himself will purify them. If you try to purify them yourself, you will be pricked by the thorn of material ideas. If Kṛṣṇa is merciful to you, the fruit you pick will not be bitter.

Vijaya-kumāra: Today I have become fortunate. I have one more question. Do the Lord's wives in Dvārakā reside in Vaikuṇṭha? If not, do they reside in Goloka?

Gosvāmī: All bliss is found in Vaikuṇṭha in the spiritual world. There is no attainment higher than Vaikuṇṭha. Dvārakā and all the cities where the Lord resides are manifested in Vaikuṇṭha. Each in her own abode, the Lord's wives in these different cities serve the Lord there. As far as *mādhurya-rasa* is concerned, only the girls in Vraja reside in Goloka. Whatever pastimes were manifested in Vraja in the material world are all manifested in Goloka. Also, in the *Gopāla-tāpanī Upaniṣad* it is seen that Rukmiṇī-devī, following the *svakīya-rasa*, enjoys pastimes in Mathurā Purī in Goloka.

Vijaya-kumāra: O master, the activities of *parakīya-rasa* are manifested in a certain sequence in Vraja in the material world. Are they all manifested in exactly the same sequence in Goloka?

Gosvāmī: They are all exactly the same. They are all spiritual. Only the beliefs created by Yogamāyā are absent. Those beliefs do not remain there. Only the pure spiritual part remains there. I cannot explain that any more clearly. By the power of your devotional activities, you will come to understand what I mean.

Vijaya-kumāra: At the time of cosmic devastation, the entire material world disappears. How then is it possible that the Supreme Lord enjoys pastimes eternally in His abode of Vraja in the material world?

Gosvāmī: The Lord's pastimes in Vraja are eternal in two ways. Traveling in a great circle through the numberless material universes, the Lord manifests all His pastimes, one after another. In this way, the Lord's pastimes are manifested eternally. Also, the Lord's pastimes always exist in the spiritual eternal present (*nitya-vartamāna*), even when they may be invisible to material eyes (*aprakaṭa*).

Vijaya-kumāra: If the Lord openly manifests (*prakaṭa-līlā*) His pastimes in every material universe, does that mean that every universe has its own land of Vraja?

Gosvāmī: Yes, it does. Goloka has the power to manifest itself anywhere. In every material universe, the abode of the Lord's pastimes is manifested. The world of Goloka also manifests itself in the heart of every devotee of the Lord. Why does the land of Mathurā (Mathurā-maṇḍala) continue to exist in the material world, even though the Lord no longer manifests (*prakaṭa*) His pastimes there?

Vijaya-kumāra: The Lord continues to enjoy pastimes there eternally, even though those pastimes cannot be seen by material eyes (*aprakaṭa*). Also, to show mercy to the devotees, the Lord keeps His abode manifested in the material world.

In that way, the day's conversation ended. Again and again thinking of the Lord's pastimes during the eight periods of the day (*aṣṭa-kālīya-sevā*), Vijaya-kumāra returned to his residence.

Chapter Thirty-two

Mādhurya-rasa, part two

Vijaya-kumāra honored *prasādam* and took rest at night. Vrajanātha completed his devotional activities, chanted the holy names of the Lord on his beads, and went to sleep. Vijaya-kumāra did not sleep. He used to think that Goloka was a different place. Now he could understand that Goloka and Gokula are not different. The *parakīya-rasa* has its root in Goloka. However, how could Kṛṣṇa be a paramour? That was his only doubt.

Now, he thought, "Kṛṣṇa is the Absolute Truth. The potency and the master of potencies are not different. If Kṛṣṇa and His potency are not different, then how can Kṛṣṇa be the husband or the paramour of His potency?"

Once, he thought, "Tomorrow I will place this question before my spiritual master, and he will remove my doubt."

Then again, he thought, "It would not be good to ask the master again about Goloka. Still, I must throw this doubt far away."

Thinking very seriously about all this, he fell asleep. Asleep, he dreamed that he met his spiritual master and placed this question before him. In the dream, his spiritual master resolved the doubt.

The spiritual master said, "Bābā, Vijaya-kumāra, Kṛṣṇa's desires are not dependent on the wishes of others, pushed here and there like an elephant prodded with a goad. He eternally desires to conceal His own opulence and divine power and instead, manifest His charming sweetness. He makes His potency exist as a separate entity. Then, His potency manifests Herself as millions and millions of beautiful girls. In this way, His potency serves Him very diligently."

"Kṛṣṇa is not very pleased when His potency serves Him in the mood of opulence. With the wonderful power of His potency, He makes these manifestations of His potency into married girls. Then He becomes their sole paramour. Desiring to enjoy the *parakīya-rasa*, Kṛṣṇa rejects His own natural self-sufficiency (*ātmārāma-dharma*) and enjoys the *rasa* dance and other wonderful pastimes with His potencies, who are all convinced that they are the wives of others. In all these activities, His flute becomes a dear friend. In this way, the *parakīya-rasa* is eternally perfect in the realm of Goloka. It is for this purpose that the pastime forests of Goloka and Vṛndāvana exist."

"Vraja's *rasa-maṇḍala*, Yamunā shore, Govardhana Hill, and other pastime places all exist in Goloka also. In this way, *svakīya-rasa* and *parakīya-rasa* both exist in Goloka. Pure *svakīya-rasa* is splendidly manifested in Vaikuṇṭha. *Svakīya-rasa* and *parakīya-rasa*, which are simultaneously one and different from each other, are both seen in Goloka. Look. This is very wonderful. Although the *parakīya-rasa* in Vraja seems to be material and Kṛṣṇa seems to be an ordinary paramour, the truth is that it is not material, and Kṛṣṇa is not a paramour at all. And, why not? Kṛṣṇa has been enjoying the company of His potencies from a time without beginning. Their relationship is actually the perfection of *svakīya-rasa*, of the love of a husband and wife."

"That His potencies are married to others and Kṛṣṇa is their paramour is only an idea created to nourish the bliss of Their pastimes in Vraja. This same idea also nourishes the Lord's pastimes in Goloka, which is far from the world of matter. In Gokula, which is manifested within the material world, Yogamāyā creates the idea that Kṛṣṇa's potencies are married to others and Kṛṣṇa is their paramour."

Hearing this explanation in his dream, Vijaya-kumāra threw all his doubts far away. He became fully convinced that Goloka beyond the material world and Gokula situated within the material world are indeed the same place. Then, the bliss of the *rasas* of Vraja appeared in his heart. He became firmly convinced of Kṛṣṇa's eternal pastimes in Vraja during the eight periods of the day (*aṣṭa-kālīya*).

Rising the next morning, he thought, "My spiritual master has been merciful to me without any limit."

From that time, he had full faith in his spiritual master's descriptions of the *rasas*.

Vijaya-kumāra honored *prasādam* and, at the appropriate time, shedding tears of love, he fell down before his spiritual master's lotus feet. Filled with spiritual love, the spiritual master picked him up and said, "Bābā, you have attained Lord Kṛṣṇa's mercy. Simply by seeing you, I have become fortunate."

He hugged Vijaya-kumāra and then he began to sing these verses from *Prema-vivarta*: A person who has attained Lord Kṛṣṇa's mercy is the most fortunate person in the entire world. The spiritual love of Goloka is manifest in his heart. He sees Goloka and Gokula. Māyā flees from him.

After singing this song for many minutes, the spiritual master again became aware of the external world. Then, Vijaya-kumāra offered *daṇḍavat* obeisances to him.

Vijaya-kumāra: O master, I do not know anything about Lord Kṛṣṇa's mercy. I only know that everything has come from your mercy. Stopping all efforts to see Goloka directly, I am now content to place my eyes on Gokula. For now, it is good that I try to understand the wonderful variety of *rasas* in Vraja. Now I will return to the original topic we were discussing. O spiritual master, May it be said that the *gopīs* who thought of Kṛṣṇa as their husbands are situated in *svakīya-rasa*?

Gosvāmī: The *gopīs* who thought of Kṛṣṇa as their husband may at that time be situated in *svakīya-rasa*. However, the natural position of the girls in Gokula is *parakīya-rasa*. Although their natural position is not *svakīya-rasa*, because they marry Kṛṣṇa by the Gandharva rite, or another rite, they may for some time be situated in *svakīya-rasa*. This is manifested in the Lord's Gokula pastimes.

Vijaya-kumāra: O master, I have many questions. I shall ask them according to the sequence presented in *Śrī Ujjvala-nīlamaṇi*. Now, I would like to learn about the *nāyakas* (heroes). There are four kinds of *nāyakas*: *anukūla* (friendly) *dakṣiṇā* (sincere), *śaṭha* (deceptive) and *dhṛṣṭa* (arrogant). What is the nature of the *anukūla* hero?

Gosvāmī: A hero who is attached to one heroine and does not desire any other is an *anukūla* hero. Lord Rāmacandra has that kind of love for Sītā. Lord Kṛṣṇa has *anukūla* love for Śrī Rādhikā.

Vijaya-kumāra: I wish to learn how the *anukūla* hero is manifested in the four personality types that begin with *dhīrodātta*. Please be merciful and describe the *dhīrodātta-anukūla* hero.

Gosvāmī: The *dhīrodātta-anukūla* hero is grave, humble, tolerant, merciful, true to His word, averse to praising Himself, modest, and generous at heart. However, the *dhīrodātta-anukūla* hero will renounce these qualities in order to secretly meet with His beloved.

Vijaya-kumāra: What is the *dhīra-lalita-anukūla* hero?

Gosvāmī: The *dhīra-lalita* hero is naturally very funny, always in full youthfulness, expert in joking, and free from all anxieties. If He always enjoys pastimes with the same heroine, the *dhīra-lalita* hero becomes a *dhīra-lalita-anukūla* hero.

Vijaya-kumāra: What is a *dhīra-praśānta-anukūla* hero?

Gosvāmī: A *dhīra-praśānta-anukūla* hero is very peaceful, forbearing, considerate, and obliging.

Vijaya-kumāra: What is a *dhīrodātta-anukūla* hero?

Gosvāmī: A *dhīrodātta-anukūla* hero is very envious, proud, easily angered, restless, and complacent.

Vijaya-kumāra: What is a *dakṣiṇā* hero?

Gosvāmī: The word *dakṣiṇā* means honest. A hero who does not stop feeling respect, awe, and love for His previous beloved, even after He becomes attached to a new beloved, is a *dakṣiṇā* hero. A *dakṣiṇā* hero treats His many beloveds equally.

Vijaya-kumāra: What is a *śaṭha* hero?

Gosvāmī: A hero who is affectionate to His beloved when she is present, but blasphemes her when she is not present, is a *śaṭha* hero.

Vijaya-kumāra: What are the qualities of a *dhṛṣṭa* hero?

Gosvāmī: A *dhṛṣṭa* hero is expert at fearlessly speaking lies, even when His body clearly bears many marks showing how He enjoyed with another beloved.

Vijaya-kumāra: O master, how many different kinds of heroes are there?

Gosvāmī: As far as we are concerned, there is no hero but Kṛṣṇa. In Dvārakā He is perfect. In Mathurā He is more perfect. In Vraja He is most perfect. In each of these places, He is both husband and paramour. In this way He is six (three times two) heroes. In each of these six different situations, He is also the four kinds of heroes that begin with *dhīrodātta*. In that way, he becomes twenty-four (two times three times four) different kinds of heroes.

In each of these twenty-four situations, He is also an *anukūla*, *dakṣiṇā*, *śaṭha* and *dhṛṣṭa* hero. In this way, He becomes ninety-six (two times three times four times four) kinds of heroes. Thus, there are twenty-four *svakīya* heroes and twenty-four *parakīya* heroes. The *svakīya* heroes are less prominent and the *parakīya* heroes are more prominent. In the *rasas* and pastimes of Vraja, the twenty-four kinds of *parakīya* heroes are manifested eternally. In different kinds of pastimes, a different kind of hero is required. In this way, Kṛṣṇa assumes the roles of these different kinds of heroes.

Vijaya-kumāra: O master, now I can understand the different qualities of the hero and heroine. Now I request that you teach me about the hero's different assistants.

Gosvāmī: The hero had five kinds of assistants. They are: *ceṭa* (confidential messenger), *viṭa* (valet), *vidūṣaka* (comedian), *pīṭha-mardaka* (constant companion), and *priya-narma-sakhā* (dear friend). All these assistants are expert at speaking joking words, always bound by ties of strong friendship, an expert judge of time and circumstances, expert, and expert at speaking confidential words to pacify the *gopīs* when they become angry.

Vijaya-kumāra: Who are the *ceṭas*? Please say.

Gosvāmī: The *ceṭas* are expert at arranging Kṛṣṇa's rendezvous with the *gopīs*. The *ceṭas* are naturally bold and arrogant. Bhaṅgura and Bhṛṅgara are prominent among Kṛṣṇa's *ceṭa* companions in Gokula.

Vijaya-kumāra: Who are the *viṭas*? Please say.

Gosvāmī: the *viṭas* are expert in dressing and decorating Kṛṣṇa. They are clever, skilled in conversation, and expert in bringing others under their control. Kaḍāra and Bhāratī-bandha are prominent among the Kṛṣṇa's *viṭa* companions.

Vijaya-kumāra: Who are the *vidūṣakas*? Please say.

Gosvāmī: The *vidūṣakas* are fond of eating, fond of quarreling, and expert at inducing laughter by means of their funny gestures, expert jokes, and funny appearance. Vasanta, Madhu-maṅgala, and many other *gopas* are prominent among Kṛṣṇa's *vidūṣaka* companions.

Vijaya-kumāra: Who are the *pīṭha-mardakas*?

Gosvāmī: The *pīṭha-mardaka* has qualities like those of the hero. He is the hero's constant companion. Śrīdāmā is Kṛṣṇa's *pīṭha-mardaka* companion.

Vijaya-kumāra: What are the qualities of the *priya-narma-sakhā*?

Gosvāmī: The *priya-narma-sakhā* companions have taken shelter of friendship with Kṛṣṇa. They know Kṛṣṇa's closest secrets. Subala and Arjuna are prominent among Kṛṣṇa's *priya-narma-sakhā* friends. The *priya-narma-sakhās* are the best of these five kinds of assistants. Among these five assistants— *ceṭa*, *viṭa*, *vidūṣaka*, *pīṭha-mardaka*, and *priya-narma-sakhā*—the *ceṭas* are in *dāsya-rasa*, the *pīṭha-mardakas* are in *vīra-rasa* (chivalry), and the others are in *sākhya-rasa*. The *ceṭas* are servants, and the other four kinds of assistants are friends.

Vijaya-kumāra: Are there no women among the assistants?

Gosvāmī: Yes. There are. They are the *dūtīs* (messengers).

Vijaya-kumāra: How many different kinds of *dūtīs* are there?

Gosvāmī: There are two kinds of *dūtīs*: *svayaṁ-dūtī* (messengers of their own accord) and *āpta-dūtī* (they who are appointed as messengers). The *svayaṁ-dūtīs* are Kṛṣṇa's sidelong glance and the sound of His flute.

Vijaya-kumāra: Ah! Who are the *āpta-dūtīs*?

Gosvāmī: Vīrā, who is expert at speaking bold and outrageous words, and Vṛndā, who speaks sweetly, are Kṛṣṇa's two *āpta-dūtīs*. The *svayaṁ-dūtīs* and these two *āpta-dūtīs* are extraordinary. In addition, there are many ordinary *dūtīs*, such as Liṅginī, Daiva-jñā, and Śilpa-kāriṇī. It is better that I describe them later, when we discuss the heroines and messengers.

Vijaya-kumāra: Now I understand Śrī Kṛṣṇa's natures, qualities, and other features as a hero. I have also learned that Kṛṣṇa eternally enjoys pastimes as both a husband and a paramour. As a husband, He enjoys pastimes in Dvārakā, and as a paramour, He enjoys pastimes in Vraja. Our Kṛṣṇa is a paramour. Therefore, we must learn about the beautiful girls of Vraja.

Gosvāmī: Almost all of Kṛṣṇa's *gopī* beloveds in Vraja are in the *parakīya-rasa*. And, why not? In *mādhurya-rasa*, nothing is higher than *parakīya*. The *svakīya-rasa* felt by the queens in Dvārakā is dull and stunted in comparison. Therefore, the *parakīya-rasa* gives the most pleasure to Lord Kṛṣṇa.

Vijaya-kumāra: What is the meaning of all this?

Gosvāmī: Lord Śiva, who is expert at understanding the mellows of *mādhurya-rasa*, explains that when women are very contrary or hard to find, or when they are protected by a host of obstacles, then Kāmadeva uses his most powerful weapons. Viṣṇu-gupta also explains that when the hero is forbidden to meet His beloved, or when His doe-eyed beloved is unapproachable, then the hero's heart is very strongly attracted to His beloved.

Look, even though He is always self-satisfied (*ātmārāma*), Kṛṣṇa expanded into as many forms as there were *gopīs* in the *rasa* dance pastime. A *sādhaka* devotee should try to understand the *rasa* dance pastime of the Lord. The instruction is given that if a *sādhaka* devotee desires to attain auspiciousness, then with devotion he should enter into an understanding of the *rasa* dance pastimes. Of course, he should not be so foolish as to try and imitate Lord Kṛṣṇa's activities in the *rasa* dance. The meaning is that the devotee should try to understand how much the *gopīs* love Lord Kṛṣṇa.

Vijaya-kumāra: Please clearly describe the love the *gopīs* feel for Lord Kṛṣṇa.

Gosvāmī: Kṛṣṇa is a *gopa*. He is the son of Nanda. He enjoys pastimes of *mādhurya-rasa* only with the *gopīs*. He does not enjoy these pastimes with other girls. A devotee who is qualified for *mādhurya-rasa*, and who is either a *sādhaka-bhakta* or a *bhāva-bhakta* should worship Kṛṣṇa as the *gopīs* do. In your meditation, you should serve Śrī Śrī Rādhā-Kṛṣṇa as the fortunate *gopīs* of Vraja do. If you cannot think of yourself as a *gopī* married to someone other than Kṛṣṇa, then you will not be able to attain the *parakīya-rasa*. To think that they are married to someone else is the nature of the *gopīs* in Vraja.

Śrīla Rūpa Gosvāmī has written (*Śrī Ujjvala-nīlamaṇi, Kṛṣṇa-vallabhā prakaraṇa* 19): The Vraja *gopīs* never meet with their husband, nor do their husbands even feel jealous, for the *gopīs*' husbands are all creations of Yogamāyā.

The *gopīs*' weddings and husbands are both creations of Yogamāyā. The *gopīs* never had any husband but Kṛṣṇa. Still, in the eternal present (*nitya-vartamāna*) that is the feature of time in the spiritual world, the *gopīs* eternally think that they are married to someone other than Kṛṣṇa. If this were not the case, then the wonderful *rasas* where the beloved is contrary, unattainable, surrounded by obstacles, and forbidden, would not be possible. It is because she refuses to accept *parakīya-rasa* that Goddess Lakṣmī in Vaikuṇṭha cannot become one of Kṛṣṇa's beloveds in the *rasas* of Vraja.

Vijaya-kumāra: How does a *gopī* think herself married to someone other than Kṛṣṇa?

Gosvāmī: A *gopī* thinks, "I was born in a *gopa*'s house. At the appropriate time, I was given in marriage to a certain *gopa*."

Thinking in this way, a *gopī* develops a strong yearning to enjoy pastimes with Kṛṣṇa. In this way, the *gopīs* think they are married to a certain *gopa*, and that they have no children. This is called *gopī-bhāva* (the assumptions of the *gopīs*).

Vijaya-kumāra: How does a male attain this conception?

Gosvāmī: It is only because of the power of *māyā* that a soul residing in the material world imagines that it is male. In the understanding of pure spirit, Kṛṣṇa is the only male and all others are female. In spirit, there is no sign of material male or female. Still, if one intently meditates on this *rasa*, one can become qualified to become a *gopī* in Vraja. A person who yearns to attain the *mādhurya-rasa* will become qualified to become a *gopī* in Vraja. By again and again desiring in this way, one attains that perfection.

Vijaya-kumāra: What is the glory of being a *gopī* married to a *gopa* other than Kṛṣṇa?

Gosvāmī: When the Vraja *gopīs* married to other *gopas* yearn to enjoy pastimes with Kṛṣṇa, then the greatest splendor and the greatest virtues decorate them with the beauty of pure love. Their *rasa* is sweeter than the *rasas* of Lakṣmī and all the goddesses of fortune.

Vijaya-kumāra: How many different kinds of beautiful girls are there in Vraja?

Gosvāmī: There are three kinds: *sādhana-parā* (persons who became *gopīs* by performing *sādhana-bhakti*), *devī* (demigoddesses who became *gopīs*) and *nitya-priyā* (eternally dear *gopīs*).

Vijaya-kumāra: Are the *sādhana-parā gopīs* divided into different groups?

Gosvāmī: The *sādhana-parā gopīs* are divided into *yauthikī* and *ayauthikī*.

Vijaya-kumāra: Who are the *yauthikī gopīs*?

Gosvāmī: Persons who performed *sādhana-bhakti* in order to enter this *rasa* in Vraja become *yauthikī gopīs*. The *yauthikī gopīs* are further subdivided as *muni-gaṇa* sages) and *upaniṣad-gaṇa* (personified *Upaniṣads*).

Vijaya-kumāra: Which sages in this way took birth in Vraja?

Gosvāmī: Some sages found that even after dutifully worshiping Lord

Gopāla, they still could not attain their desired perfection. However, when they were able to personally see the glorious handsomeness of Lord Rāmacandra, they diligently performed *sādhana-bhakti* in order to attain their desire. As a result, they attained ecstatic love (*bhāva*) and then took birth in Vraja as *gopīs*. This is described in the *Padma Purāṇa*. In the *Bṛhad-vāmana Purāṇa* it is said that some of these *gopīs* attained their desired perfection at the beginning of the *rasa* dance.

Vijaya-kumāra: How did the personified *Upaniṣads* take birth as *gopīs*?

Gosvāmī: When they saw the *gopīs*' good fortune, the intelligent *Upaniṣads* became filled with wonder. They faithfully performed austerities and as a result, were born in Vraja as *gopīs* filled with spiritual love (*premavatī*).

Vijaya-kumāra: Who are the *ayauthikī gopīs*?

Gosvāmī: Persons who, seeing the *gopīs*' passionate love for Kṛṣṇa, yearn to become like them, and to attain this end engage in *sādhana-bhakti*, become the *ayauthikī gopīs* (which are divided into two groups: *prācīnā* (elderly) and *navīnā* (young). In this way, one, two, or three of these *gopīs* are born in Vraja. The *prācīnā-ayauthikī gopīs* eventually attain *sālokya-mukti*, and in the spiritual world, they associate with the eternally dear (*nitya-priyā*) *gopīs*. After a lifetime as demigoddesses, human beings, or other kinds of beings, the *prācīnā-ayauthikī gopīs* take birth in Vraja. Eventually, they become *prācīnā gopīs* and at the end, attain the *sālokya-mukti* I have just described.

Vijaya-kumāra: I can understand this description of the *sādhana-parā gopīs*. Now please describe the *devīs*.

Gosvāmī: When Lord Kṛṣṇa took birth as an *aṁśa* incarnation among the demigods in Svargaloka, some eternally dear (*nitya-priyā*) *gopīs* took birth as *aṁśa* incarnations among the demigoddesses to please Him. When Kṛṣṇa took birth in His original form in Gokula, they took birth as daughters of the *gopas*. They became the dear friends (*prāṇa-sakhī*) of the eternally dear (*nitya-priyā*) *gopīs*.

Vijaya-kumāra: O master, when did Lord Kṛṣṇa take birth as an *aṁśa* incarnation among the demigods?

Gosvāmī: Taking birth from Aditi's womb, Lord Kṛṣṇa appeared as the *aṁśa* incarnation Vāmana. The demigods are also *vibhinnāṁśa* manifestations of Lord Kṛṣṇa. Śiva and Brahmā were not born from a mother's womb. Brahmā and Śiva possess fifty of Lord Kṛṣṇa's qualities, as do the ordinary souls. However, Brahmā and Śiva are not counted among the ordinary souls, for they are *vibhinnāṁśas*. In addition to the fifty qualities all individual souls possess, Brahmā and Śiva also possess five other qualities. Therefore, they are called the best of the demigods. Gaṇeśa and Sūrya are also considered on the same level as the millions of Brahmās.

All other demigods are considered to be ordinary individual souls. All the demigods are *vibhinnāṁśas* manifested from Lord Kṛṣṇa. The wives of the demigods are also *vibhinnāṁśas* of the Lord's *cit* potency (spiritual potency). Before Kṛṣṇa's appearance on the earth, Brahmā ordered the demigoddesses to take birth on the earth in order to please Kṛṣṇa. Following Brahmā's order, they took birth in different places in Vraja according to their own inclination and their activities in *sādhana-bhakti*. These demigoddesses who were born in Vraja became dear friends (*prāṇa-sakhī*) of the Lord's eternally dear (*nitya-priyā*) *gopīs*. They yearned to attain the association of Lord Kṛṣṇa.

Vijaya-kumāra: O master, the personified *Upaniṣads* took birth as *gopīs*. Did the goddesses who rule over any other scriptures also take birth in Vraja?

Gosvāmī: In the *Padma Purāṇa, Sṛṣṭi-khaṇḍa*, it is said that Gāyatrī-devī, the mother of the *Vedas*, took birth as a *gopī* and attained Lord Kṛṣṇa's association. It was at that time that she manifested the form of Kāma-Gāyatrī.

Vijaya-kumāra: Is the Kāma-Gāyatrī not beginningless?

Gosvāmī: The Kāma-Gāyatrī is certainly beginningless. However, there is a time when this beginningless Gāyatrī first appeared in the form of the Goddess Gāyatrī, who is the mother of the *Vedas*. Because of her engagement in *sādhana-bhakti*, the Goddess Gāyatrī could understand how fortunate the *Upaniṣads* were to have become *gopīs*. Then, accompanied by the *Gopāla-tāpanī Upaniṣad*, she took birth in Vraja. In this way, it is understood that the Kama-Gāyatrī is eternal, and the Goddess Gāyatrī who is the mother of the *Vedas* is eternally distinct from the Kāma-Gāyatrī.

Vijaya-kumāra: All the *Upaniṣads* took birth as *gopīs* in Vraja. They all accepted the *gopa* hero, Kṛṣṇa, as their husband (*pati*). Following the marriage ritual of the Gandharvas, these *gopīs* then accepted Kṛṣṇa as their husband. This much I understand. However, the *nitya-priyā* (eternally dear) *gopīs* associate with Kṛṣṇa from time without beginning and in that relationship, He is their paramour. Is this relationship created by *māyā*?

Gosvāmī: It may be created by *māyā*, but it is not created by the *māyā* of the material world. The *māyā* of the material world has no power to touch Lord Kṛṣṇa's pastimes. Even though it may be manifested within the material world, Lord Kṛṣṇa's Vraja pastimes are beyond the touch of the material *māyā*. Another name of the Lord's *cit-śakti* (spiritual potency) is Yogamāyā. She arranges Lord Kṛṣṇa's pastimes so that ordinary people influence by *māyā* see them as material. She makes the *nitya-priyā gopīs* of Goloka think they are married to persons other than Kṛṣṇa, and she also brings those *gopīs* to Vraja in the material world. She arranges the *nitya-priyā gopīs*' wedding ceremonies, and she arranges that Kṛṣṇa becomes their paramour. The all-knowing supreme male, Kṛṣṇa, and His all-knowing spiritual potencies voluntarily accept the *rasa* roles Yogamāyā gives Them.

Thus it is seen that this is the best of all *rasas*, Lord Kṛṣṇa is supremely independent, all His desires are at once fulfilled, and His *icchā-śakti* (the potency that fulfills His desires) is supremely glorious. The great glory of this *rasa* is not seen in Vaikuṇṭha, Dvārakā, and other places. When they attain *sālokya* liberation, the *prāna-sakhī gopīs* and the *nitya-priyā gopīs* leave behind any idea that He is their paramour. That is their final attainment.

Vijaya-kumāra: The conclusion is very wonderful. Now I am fully satisfied. O master, please teach me about the *nitya-priyā gopīs*.

Gosvāmī: If you were not qualified to hear these explanations, would Lord Gauracandra make these confidential truths appear in my mouth? Look, all-knowing Śrīla Jīva Gosvāmī kept these truths hidden in his heart, although in some places in his commentaries, in his *Kṛṣṇa-sandarbha*, and in other books, he did reveal them. Śrīla Jīva Gosvāmī was always anxious that if unqualified persons heard these confidential truths, they would take shelter of irreligion. Seeing how the Vaiṣṇavas mostly understood the *rasas* and accepted *rasābhāsa*, Śrīla Jīva Gosvāmī became anxious. For this reason, he took great care not to write anything that would support any false conclusion. You are qualified to hear these things. I do not reveal these truths to unqualified persons. Now I will describe the *nitya-priyā gopīs*.

Vijaya-kumāra: Who are the *nitya-priyā gopīs*? Although I have studied many scriptures, I still yearn to drink the nectarean words that come from my spiritual master's saintly mouth.

Gosvāmī: The *nitya-priyā gopīs* in Vraja, among whom Rādhā and Candrāvalī are the most important, possess transcendental beauty, intelligence, and a host of virtues. In this way, they are like Lord Kṛṣṇa Himself.

They are described in these words *Brahma-saṁhitā* (5.37): I worship Govinda, the primeval Lord, who resides in His own realm, Goloka, with Rādhā, who resembles His own spiritual figure and who embodies the ecstatic potency (*hlādinī*). The companions are Her confidants, who embody the extensions of Her bodily form, and who are imbued and permeated with ever-blissful spiritual *rasa*.

In these words of Brahmā, which are the essence of all the *Vedas*, the *nitya-priyā gopīs* are described. The *nitya-priyā gopīs* are said to be *nitya* (eternal) because they are the Lord's spiritual potency and therefore, they are beyond the limitations of time and space imposed by the material energy. They are an eternal spiritual reality. The word *kalābhiḥ* here may refer to the sixty-four arts practiced by the *nitya-priyā gopīs* in their eternal pastimes. Or, this word may have another meaning.

The commentary of this verse explains: Here, the word *kalābhiḥ* means, "with the potencies, who are expansions of Her form."

What I have explained to you are the opinions of Śrīla Svarūpa Dāmodara Gosvāmī. Please know that these confidential explanations are the great treasure that Śrīla Rūpa Gosvāmī, Śrīla Sanātana Gosvāmī, and Śrīla Jīva Gosvāmī keep hidden in the vaults of their hearts.

Vijaya-kumāra: My ears yearn to hear the names of the *nitya-priyā gopīs*?

Gosvāmī: Rādhā, Candrāvalī, Viśākhā, Lalitā, Śyāmā, Padmā, Śaibyā, Bhadrikā, Tārā, Vicitrā, Gopālī, Dhaniṣṭhā and Pālī are among the names of the *nitya-priyā gopīs* written in the *Skanda Purāṇa*, *Prahlāda-saṁhitā*, and other scriptures. Candrāvalī is also known by the name Somātā. Rādhā is also known by the name Gāndharvā. Khañjanākṣī, Manoramā, Maṅgalā, Vimalā, Līlā,

Kṛṣṇā, Śārī, Viśāradā, Tārāvalī, Cakorākṣī, Śaṅkarī, Kuṁkumā, and many other *gopīs* are also famous in this world.

Vijaya-kumāra: How are these *gopīs* related to each other?

Gosvāmī: All these *gopīs* are *yūtheśvarīs* (leaders of groups of *gopīs*). There are hundreds and hundreds of groups, and in each group there are hundreds of thousands of *gopīs*. From Rādhā to Kuṁkumā, all these groups are *yūtheśvarīs*. Viśākhā, Lalitā, Padmā, and Śaibyā are also mentioned here. Among the *yūtheśvarīs*, eight *gopīs*, headed by Rādhā, are considered the most fortunate. They are called the *pradhāna* (most important) *gopīs*.

Vijaya-kumāra: Viśākhā, Lalitā, Padmā, and Śaibyā are all *pradhāna gopīs*. They are all very expert in making Lord Kṛṣṇa's pastimes especially glorious. Why were they not clearly mentioned as *yūtheśvarīs*?

Gosvāmī: They have all transcendental virtues, and they are certainly very qualified to become *yūtheśvarīs*. However, Lalitā and Viśākhā are so overcome with bliss simply by associating with Śrī Rādhā that they have no desire to become independent *yūtheśvarīs* themselves. Some *gopīs* are followers of Śrīmatī Rādhārāṇī and other *gopīs* are followers of Candrāvalī. This is described in the scriptures.

Vijaya-kumāra: Still, I have heard that Lalitā does indeed have a group. What is it like?

Gosvāmī: Śrīmatī Rādhārāṇī is the foremost of all group leaders. Out of special affection and respect, some *gopīs* are said to belong to Lalitā's group or Viśākhā's group. However Lalitā, Viśākhā, and the other eight principal friends (*aṣṭa-sakhī*) of Rādhā are considered the leaders of different factions in Śrī Rādhā's group. By great good fortune, one may be able to enter Śrīmatī Lalitā's group.

Vijaya-kumāra: O master, in which scriptures are the names of the *gopīs* found?

Gosvāmī: All these names are found in the *Padma Purāṇa*, *Skanda Purāṇa*, and *Bhaviṣya Purāṇa*, *Uttara-khaṇḍa*. In the *sātvata-vaiṣṇava-tantra śāstra*, many other names are also found.

Vijaya-kumāra: *Śrīmad-Bhāgavatam* is the crest jewel of all scriptures in the world. If all these names were found in *Śrīmad-Bhāgavatam*, that would be a source of great bliss.

Gosvāmī: *Śrīmad-Bhāgavatam* is a scripture that teaches the highest truth. It is an ocean filled with the nectar of the spiritual *rasas*. Persons who are expert at relishing the spiritual *rasas* (*rasikā*) can see that all the truths of the *rasas* are described in *Śrīmad-Bhāgavatam*. The name of Śrī Rādhā and the names of all the *gopīs* are secretly written in *Śrīmad-Bhāgavatam*. If you carefully read the verses of the Tenth Canto, you will see them all. To keep unqualified persons far away, Śrīla Śukadeva Gosvāmī described all these things very secretly.

O Bābā Vijaya-kumāra, what will happen if you give *japa* beads to a person who will wear them only as an ornament around his neck? The more the reader is exalted in devotional service, the more he will understand the secrets hidden in *Śrīmad-Bhāgavatam*. Here, the skill of Śrīla Śukadeva Gosvāmī was shown in his power to explain very confidential truths in a way the people in general could not understand. Only a reader qualified to understand these secrets properly has the power to understand them all. The truth is that without taking shelter of the disciplic succession (*guru-paramparā*), no one can understand these truths. A person studying on his own cannot understand them. Carefully study *Ujjvala-nīlamaṇi* and you will become able to see how all the *rasas* are described in *Śrīmad-Bhāgavatam*.

After talking for a long time, they ended the day's conversation about the Lord (*iṣṭagoṣṭhi*). Again and again thinking about the transcendental hero and heroines in the spiritual world, Vijaya-kumāra walked to Haracaṇḍi Sāhi's place. As he thought about the *vidūṣakas*, *pīṭha-mardakas*, and other associates of the Lord, he tasted many different kinds of happiness. As he thought about Kṛṣṇa's flute and the other *svayam-dūtī* messengers, tears came from his eyes. The spiritual love (*bhāva*) of Vraja rising in his heart, Vijaya-kumāra blissfully danced. The pastimes and gardens he saw last night splendidly rose again in his heart.

Chapter Thirty-three

Mādhurya-rasa, part three

Today, Vijaya-kumāra and Vrajanātha bathed in Indrayumna-sarovara, honored *prasādam*, and returned home. After eating, Vrajanātha went to see the *samādhi* of Haridāsa Ṭhākura. Vijaya-kumāra went to the temple of Śrī Rādhākānta and offered obeisances to his spiritual master. At an appropriate time, Vijaya-kumāra asked about Śrī Rādhikā.

Vijaya-kumāra said, "O master, Śrī Rādhā is the be-all and end--all of my life. How can I describe it? When I hear the name, Rādhikā, my heart melts. Even though Śrī Kṛṣṇa is the only goal of my life, still I like to taste only the descriptions of His pastimes with Śrī Rādhā. I do not like to hear descriptions of Śrī Kṛṣṇa if Śrī Rādhā is not included in them. O master, I would like to say that I no longer wish to call myself Vijaya-kumāra Bhaṭṭācārya. I wish to be known as a maidservant protected by Śrī Rādhā. I do not wish to speak the wonderful descriptions of Vraja to materialists. When persons unqualified to understand the transcendental *rasas* (*arasikā*) discuss the glories of Śrī Rādhā, I yearn to flee from that place.

Gosvāmī: You are fortunate. As long as you did not have full faith in the *gopīs*, you were not qualified to understand the pastimes of Rādhā and Kṛṣṇa. Descriptions of those pastimes are far beyond what ordinary human beings can understand. Even the demigoddesses in Devaloka are not qualified to understand them.

O Vijaya-kumāra, I have already described the *gopīs* who are dear to Lord Kṛṣṇa. Among them, Rādhā and Candrāvalī are the most important. Each of them presides over millions and millions of groups of beautiful *gopīs*. At the time of the great *rasa* dance, the *rasa* dance circle is beautiful with many hundreds of millions of beautiful *gopīs*.

Vijaya-kumāra: O master, Candrāvalī may preside over millions and millions of groups of *gopīs*. Still, I wish that the glories of Śrī Rādhā will be the only sweet nectar to flood and purify my contaminated ears. I am your surrendered disciple.

Gosvāmī: Between the two of them—Rādhā and Candrāvalī—it is Rādhā who is the personification of the highest ecstatic love (*mahā-bhāva-svarūpa*). It is She who has the greatest qualities. She is superior to Candrāvalī in every way. Look, the *Gopāla-tapani Upaniṣad* calls Her by the name Gāndharvā, and glorifies Her. In the *Ṛk-pariśiṣṭa* it is said that Lord Mādhava is glorious because Rādhā stands by His side. In the *Padma Purāṇa*, Nārada declares, "As Rādhā is dear to Kṛṣṇa, so Her pond, Rādhā-kuṇḍa is also dear to Him. Of all the *gopīs*, Rādhā is the dearest to Lord Kṛṣṇa." And, why not? What is Rādhā's nature? She is the great *hlādinī-śakti*, the best of Lord Kṛṣṇa's potencies. Rādhā is the essence of the *hlādinī-śakti* (*hlādinī-sāra-bhāva*).

Vijaya-kumāra: These descriptions are very wonderful! What is Śrī Rādhā's nature?

Gosvāmī: My Rādhikā is the most beautiful (*suṣṭhu-kāntā-svarupa*). She is the daughter of King Vṛṣabhānu. She is glorious with the sixteen ornaments. She is also decorated with twelve other kinds of ornaments.

Vijaya-kumāra: What do you mean by the word *suṣṭhu-kāntā-svarupa*?

Gosvāmī: It means that Her form is so beautiful that even the most exquisite garments and ornaments are insignificant in comparison to Her and therefore powerless to make Her any more beautiful. Her hair is gracefully curly, Her face is a blossoming lotus flower, Her large eyes are beautiful, and Her large breasts are wonderfully beautiful. Her waist is slender, Her shoulders are graceful, and Her fingernails shine like a row of jewels. In the three worlds, there is no festival of beauty that compares with Her.

Vijaya-kumāra: What are the sixteen ornaments?

Gosvāmī: The sixteen ornaments are: 1. Her pleasant bath, 2. The glistening jewel decorating the tip of Her nose, 3. Her blue garments, 4. Her belt, 5. Her braids, 6. Her earrings, 7. The sandal paste anointing Her limbs, 8. The flowers placed in Her hair, 9. Her necklace, 10. The lotus flower in Her hand, 11. The betel nuts in Her mouth, 12. The musk dot on Her chin, 13. The mascara around Her eyes, 14. The colorful designs and pictures drawn on Her cheeks, 15. The red *kuṅkuma* on Her lotus feet, and 16. The *tilaka* markings on Her forehead.

Vijaya-kumāra: What are the twelve ornaments.

Gosvāmī: 1. The wonderful jewel that crowns Her head, 2. Her golden earrings, 3. The belt around Her hips, 4. The golden locket around Her neck, 5. Her golden *śalākā* earrings, 6. The bracelets on Her wrists, 7. The ornament on Her neck, 8. The rings on Her fingers, 9. Her pearl necklace, 10. Her armlets,

11. Her ankle bells, and 12. The rings on Her toes are the twelve ornaments decorating Śrī Rādhā's limbs.

Vijaya-kumāra: Please describe the most prominent transcendental qualities of Śrī Rādhā?

Gosvāmī: Like the qualities of Śrī Kṛṣṇa, the qualities of Vṛndāvana's queen, Rādhā, are limitless and cannot truly be counted or listed in full. Among them, these twenty-five may be considered prominent.

· She is very sweet.
· She is always freshly youthful.
· Her eyes are restless.
· She smiles brightly.
· She has beautiful, auspicious lines.
· She makes Kṛṣṇa happy with Her bodily aroma.
· She is very expert in singing.
· Her speech is charming.
· She is very expert in joking and speaking pleasantly.
· She is very humble and meek.
· She is always full of mercy.
· She is cunning.
· She is expert in executing Her duties.
· She is shy.
· She is always respectful.
· She is always calm.
· She is always grave.
· She is expert in enjoying life.
· She is situated at the topmost level of ecstatic love.
· She is the reservoir of loving affairs in Gokula.
· She is the most famous of submissive devotees.
· She is very affectionate to elderly people.
· She is very submissive to the love of Her friends.
· She is the chief *gopī*.
· She always keeps Kṛṣṇa under Her control.

Vijaya-kumāra: I would like to hear an explanation of the fifth quality:

She has beautiful and auspicious lines.

Gosvāmī: The *Varāha-saṁhitā*, *jyoti-śāstra*, *Kāśī-khaṇḍa* of the *Skanda Purāṇa*, *Matsya Purāṇa*, and *Garuda Purāṇa* describe the auspicious lines. These lines are:

(I) On the left foot:

· 1. A barleycorn mark at the root of Her left toe.

· 2. below that toe, a *cakra*.

· 3. below the middle toe, a lotus flower

· 4. below the lotus flower, a banner.

· 5. below the banner, a flag.

· 6. an *urdhva-rekha* line extending from the middle toe to the middle of the sole.

· 7. below the small toe, an elephant goad.

(II) On the right foot:

· 1. at the root of the right big toe, a conch shell.

· 2. on the heel, a fish.

· 3. below the small toe, an altar.

· 4. above the fish, a chariot.

· 5. a mountain.

· 6. an earring

· 7. a club

· 8. the mark of a *śakti* weapon.

(III) On the left hand:

· 1. a long lifeline, beginning at the meeting of the forefinger and middle finger, and extending to below the little finger.

· 2. below that, another line going from below the lifeline to the middle of the space between the forefinger and thumb.

· 3. from below the thumb, a curving line rises from the wrist and goes to the space between the thumb and forefinger.

· 4-8. on the tips of each of the five fingers is a *cakra*.

· 9. below the ring finger is an elephant.

· 10. below the lifeline is a horse.

· 11. below the middle line is a bull.

· 12. below the small finger is an elephant goad.
· 13 a fan.
· 14. a *bilva* Śrī Lakṣmī *bel* fruit tree.
· 15. a *yupa*.
· 16. an arrow.
· 17. a *tomara* weapon.
· 18. a flower garland.
(IV) On the right hand:
· 1-8. In the right hand, like the left, there are three prominent lines, including the lifeline, and on the tips of each finger, a *cakra*.
· 9. below the forefinger, a *cāmara*
· 10. below the small finger, an elephant goad.
· 11. a palace.
· 12. a *dundubhi* drum.
· 13. a lightning bolt.
· 14. two carts.
· 15. an archer's bow.
· 16. a sword.
· 17. a waterpot.

Thus, on the left foot are seven signs, on the right foot are eight signs, on the left hand are eighteen signs, and on the right hand are seventeen signs. Altogether there are fifty auspicious lines.

Vijaya-kumāra: An individual soul may have a drop of some of these qualities, but Śrī Rādhā has them all in perfect fullness.

The demigoddesses may have them slightly more than others. Still, Śrī Rādhā, has them all, and in Her they are all perfectly spiritual, untouched by matter. And, why not? In the material world these qualities are never manifested in purity, perfection, and completeness. Gaurī and other demigoddesses may have these qualities, but in these demigoddesses the qualities are not pure, perfect, or complete.

Vijaya-kumāra: Ah! Śrīmatī Rādhikā's beauty and qualities are inconceivable. Only by Her mercy can one see or understand them.

Gosvāmī: Gazing at Śrī Rādhā's beauty and qualities, even Lord Kṛṣṇa

Himself is bewildered and enchanted. How can I properly describe them with my words?

Vijaya-kumāra: O master, please be merciful and describe Śrī Rādhā's friends (*sakhīs*).

Gosvāmī: Śrī Rādhā's group is the best of all. The girls in Her group are all decorated with all transcendental qualities. Their charming playfulness always attracts Lord Kṛṣṇa.

Vijaya-kumāra: How many different kinds of friends (*sakhīs*) does Śrī Rādhā have?

Gosvāmī: They are of five kinds: 1. *sakhī* (friends), 2. *nitya-sakhī* (eternal friends), 3. *prāna-sakhī* (life friends), 4. *priya-sakhī* (dear friends) and 5. *parama-preṣṭha-sakhī* (most dear friends).

Vijaya-kumāra: Who are the *sakhīs*?

Gosvāmī: The *sakhīs* include Kusumikā, Vṛndā, Dhaniṣṭhā. These *gopīs* are famous among the *sakhīs*.

Vijaya-kumāra: Who are the *nitya-sakhīs*?

Gosvāmī: The *nitya-sakhīs* include Kastūrī, Maṇi-mañjarī, and many others.

Vijaya-kumāra: Who are the *prāna-sakhīs*?

Gosvāmī: The *prāna-sakhīs* include Śaśimukhi, Vāsantī, Lāsikā, and many others. In many ways, they are like the queen of Vṛndāvana Herself.

Vijaya-kumāra: Who are the *priya-sakhīs*?

Gosvāmī: The *priya-sakhīs* include Kuraṅgākṣī, Sumadhyā, Madanālasā, Kamalā, Mādhurī, Muñjakeśī, Kandarpa-sundarī, Mādhavī, Mālatī, Kāma-latā, Śaśī-kāla, and many others.

Vijaya-kumāra: Who are the *parama-preṣṭha-sakhīs*?

Gosvāmī: The *parama-preṣṭha-sakhīs* include Lalitā, Viśākhā, Citrā, Campaka-latā, Tuṅga-vidyā, Indu-lekhā, Raṅgadevī, and Sudevī. These eight are the most important of all the *gopīs*. Therefore, they are called *parama-preṣṭha-sakhīs*. They are situated in the topmost love for Śrī Śrī Rādhā and Kṛṣṇa. Sometimes they show more love to Śrī Kṛṣṇa, and at other times they show more love for Śrī Rādhā.

Vijaya-kumāra: I understand what the word *yūtha* (group) means. What does the word *gaṇa* (sub-group) mean?

Gosvāmī: Every *yūtha* is divided into subgroups, which are called *gaṇas*. For example, Lalitā is a member of Śrī Rādhā's group. However, Lalitā herself has followers, and they are called the members of Lalitā's *gaṇa* (sub-group).

Vijaya-kumāra: That the *gopīs* are married to *gopas* other than Kṛṣṇa is one of the most important characteristics. Still, it does not look good.

Gosvāmī: In this material world, woman and man are only external designations. Because of past material activities, one soul becomes a woman and another soul becomes a man. In the material world of *māyā*, many people are filled with petty or sinful desires. For this reason, the great sages have forbidden, except within the institution of marriage, contact with women.

Writing about the *rasas*, poets have generally avoided describing the love of a woman for a paramour. However, in the Lord's spiritual pastimes, this kind of love is one of the *rasas*. The sexual affairs of men and women in the material world are a perverted reflection of that original *rasas* in the spiritual world. Therefore, material sexual activities are very dull, pathetic, and a breeding ground for a host of anxieties (*kuṇṭha*). Also, the rules of religion place many restrictions on these activities. For these reasons, men in the material world are enjoined to avoid approaching the wives of others. However, if Lord Kṛṣṇa, whose form is eternal and full of knowledge and bliss, is the only male and only hero, and He accepts this activity to increase the sweetness of His spiritual *rasas*, He is never contaminated and He is not to be criticized. He is independent of the material institution of marriage.

When Śrī Kṛṣṇa, who enjoys pastimes in Goloka, came to the material world from Goloka, He took the transcendental *parakīya-rasa* with Him. Therefore, no one should criticize Him for enjoying the *parakīya-rasa* with the *gopīs* who have come from Goloka.

Vijaya-kumāra: What exalted symptoms of love did the *gopīs* from Goloka display?

Gosvāmī: Before the *gopīs*, Lord Kṛṣṇa appears only in His form as the son of Nanda. The non-devotee philosophers are far from understanding the *gopīs*' exalted love for Kṛṣṇa. Even the devotees find it difficult to understand that love. When Kṛṣṇa manifests His form as Nandanandana, His opulence never eclipses His sweetness. One time, as a joke, Kṛṣṇa manifested His four-armed form before the *gopīs*, who were not at all impressed. However, when Śrī Rādhā approached, the four-armed form at once disappeared. Because of the greatness of Rādhā's confidential *parakīya* love, Kṛṣṇa again became two-handed.

Vijaya-kumāra: Now my desires are all fulfilled. O master, please describe the different kinds of heroines (*nāyikās*).

Gosvāmī: There are three kinds of heroines (*nāyikās*): 1. *svakīya*, 2. *parakīya*, 3. *sāmānya*. I have already described the spiritual *svakīya* and *parakīya* heroines. Now I will describe the *sāmānya* heroines. Students of material rhetoric (*alaṅkāra*) explain that the *sāmānya* heroines are prostitutes, interested only in money. If their lover has no good qualities, then they hate him, and if he is virtuous, still they do not really love him. Therefore, their so-called love is only a perverted reflection of love. It is not true love. Sometimes it is said that Kubjā in Mathurā was such a *sāmānya* heroine who does not really love her hero. I do not agree. I place her among the *parakīya* heroines.

Vijaya-kumāra: How did she become qualified to become a *parakīya* heroine?

Gosvāmī: When Kubjā was an ugly, disfigured woman, she never loved any man. However, when she saw Kṛṣṇa and desired to place sandal paste on His limbs, then she thought of Him as her beloved. For this reason, I say that her love is in the *parakīya-rasa*. However, the desire to please only Kṛṣṇa, a desire possessed even by the queens at Dvārakā, was absent in Kubjā. Therefore, her love was inferior to the love of the queens. When she tugged at Kṛṣṇa's upper garment and begged that He enjoy amorous pastimes with her, her love for Him was mixed with her own selfish desires. Therefore, her love is considered *sādhāraṇa* (ordinary).

Vijaya-kumāra: Because Kubjā is considered in the *parakīya-rasa*, I can see that the *svakīya* and *parakīya* heroines are both divided into two sub-groups. How many different sub-groups are there? Please describe them.

Gosvāmī: In the spiritual *rasas*, the *svakīya* and *parakīya* heroines are of three kinds: 1. *mugdhā*, 2. *madhyā*, and 3. *pragalbhā*.

Vijaya-kumāra: O master, when, by your mercy, I think of the spiritual *rasas*, I naturally think of myself as a *gopī* in Vraja. At that time, I do not think of myself as a male in the material world. When I hear of the different kinds of heroines, my heart becomes agitated. And, why not? I do not know what I should do so that some day, I may love the Lord as the *gopīs* do. So that some day I may attain this kind of service to Lord Kṛṣṇa, I now place this question before your holy feet: What is the nature of the *mugdhā* heroines? Please describe them.

Gosvāmī: These are the qualities of the *mugdhā* heroine: She is in the bloom of youth (*nava-yauvanā*), amorous (*kāmini*), contrary in love (*rāti-dane-vāma*), and submissive to her girl friends (*sakhī-vasi-bhuta*). Although externally she is shy to enjoy amorous pastimes, within her heart she secretly and diligently labors to make various arrangements to enjoy with her lover. When her lover offends her, tears flow from her eyes. At that time, she neither speaks sweetly, speaks harshly, nor becomes angry.

Vijaya-kumāra: What are the qualities of the *madhyā* heroine?

Gosvāmī: These are the qualities of the *madhyā* heroine: She is equally amorous and shy, she is in the full bloom of youth, and all her words are touched with a small amount of arrogance. She enjoys amorous pastimes until she faints unconscious. Sometimes her heart is gentle. Sometimes it is hard. Sometimes she is jealous, sometimes peaceful, and sometimes agitated. Sometimes she is both peaceful and agitated (*dhirādhira*).

A heroine who, when her lover offends her, mocks him with crooked words, is called *dhīra-madhyā*. A heroine who in that situation attacks her lover with merciless angry words is called an *adhīra-madhyā* heroine. A heroine who in that situation sheds tears, speaks sweetly, and then also speaks crooked words to mock her lover is called a *dhīrādhīra-madhyā gopī*. In a *madhyā* heroine the natures of the *mugdhā* and *pragalbhā* heroines are mixed together. The *madhyā* heroine is the best of the three kinds of heroines.

Vijaya-kumāra: What are the qualities of the *pragalbhā* heroine?

Gosvāmī: These are the qualities of the *pragalbhā* heroine: She is in the full bloom of youth, blinded with pride, and very eager to enjoy amorous pastimes. She is very passionate. Pushed by the *rasas*, she attacks her lover. Her words and deeds are very passionate. When her jealousy is aroused, she becomes very harsh. The *pragalbhā* heroines are of three kinds: 1. *dhīra*, *adhīra*, and *dhīrādhīra*. The *dhīra pragalbhā* heroine pretends to be disinterested in enjoying with her lover. Externally, she is polite and respectful. She carefully conceals the passion in her heart. The *adhīra pragalbhā* heroine beats her lover with cruel words. The *dhīrādhīra pragalbhā* heroine is like the *dhīrādhīra madhyā* heroine. The *madhyā* and *pragalbhā* heroines are also divided into *jyeṣṭhā* (older) and *kaniṣṭha* (younger). In this way, there are *jyeṣṭhā-madhyā* and *kaniṣṭha-madhyā* heroines and also *jyeṣṭhā-pragalbhā* and *kaniṣṭha pragalbhā* heroines. The difference of *jyeṣṭhā* and *kaniṣṭha* are considered according to the nature of the heroine's love for the hero.

Vijaya-kumāra: O master, how many kinds of heroines are there all together?

Gosvāmī: There are fifteen kinds of heroines. Very young heroines are always *mugdhā*. The three basic kinds of heroines are *mugdhā*, *madhyā*, and *pragalbhā*. The *madhyā* and *pragalbhā* heroines are further divided into *dhīra*, *adhīra*, and *dhīrādhīra*. Thus there are seven kinds of *svakīya* heroines, seven kinds of *parakīya* heroines, and fifteen kinds of heroines in all.

Vijaya-kumāra: What different conditions of life do the heroines experience?

Gosvāmī: The eight different conditions of life are: 1. *abhisārikā* (going to meet her lover), 2. *vāsaka-sajjā* (dressed and decorated to meet her lover), 3. *utkaṇṭhitā* (yearning to meet her lover), 4. *khaṇḍitā* (whose meeting with her lover is broken), 5. *vipralabdhā* (separated from her lover), 6. *kalahāntaritā* (quarreling with her lover), 7. *proṣita-bhartṛkā* (her lover has gone far away), and 8. *svādhīna-bhartṛkā* (she dominates her lover). The previously described fifteen kinds of heroines all experience these eight conditions of life.

Vijaya-kumāra: What is the nature of the *abhisārikā* heroine?

Gosvāmī: A heroine who arranges that her lover meet her, or who goes to meet her lover, is called *abhisārikā*. If, going to meet her lover, she wears white clothing when the moon is bright, she is called *jyotsnā 'bhisārikā*. If, going to meet her lover, she wears dark clothing when the moon is dark, she is called *tamo 'bhisārikā*. She is so shy she seems to hide behind her own body. Silent, nicely decorated, and her head carefully covered, she goes, accompanied by a dear friend, to meet her lover.

Vijaya-kumāra: What is the nature of the *vāsaka-sajjā* heroine?

Gosvāmī: A heroine who, anxious to meet her lover, carefully decorates both her body and the meeting place is called *vāsaka-sajjā*. She yearns to enjoy amorous pastimes, keeps her eyes fixed on the path her lover will walk, discusses with her friends the pastimes of love, and again and again waits for her messenger's return. These are her activities.

Vijaya-kumāra: What is the nature of the *utkaṇṭhitā* heroine?

Gosvāmī: A heroine who is filled with longing and anxiety when her lover is, through no fault of his own, late in coming to the rendezvous, is called *utkaṇṭhitā* by persons learned in the different *bhāvas*. Her heart is feverish, she trembles, she speculates about why her lover has not yet come, she becomes irritated, and she sheds tears. These are her activities. She is not like the *vāsaka-sajjā* heroine. She worries that her lover, now under the control of some other girl, will not come to meet her.

Vijaya-kumāra: What is the nature of the *khaṇḍitā* heroine?

Gosvāmī: When, the time of rendezvous long passed and the night almost over, the lover finally comes, his body bearing the clear marks of his having enjoyed pastimes with some other girl, the heroine is called *khaṇḍitā*. This heroine's activities are anger, long sighs, and silence.

Vijaya-kumāra: What is the nature of the *vipralabdhā* heroine?

Gosvāmī: A heroine who becomes anxious when, somehow or other, her lover does not come to their rendezvous, is called *vipralabdhā*. Unhappy at heart, she laments, weeps, faints, sighs, and performs other such activities.

Vijaya-kumāra: What is the nature of the *kalahāntaritā* heroine?

Gosvāmī: A heroine who will not forgive her lover, even when, surrounded by all her friends, he humbly falls before her feet, and who manifests lamentation, grief, withering, and sighing, is called *kalahāntaritā*.

Vijaya-kumāra: What is the nature of the *proṣita-bhartṛkā* heroine?

Gosvāmī: A heroine whose lover has gone to a faraway place is called *proṣita-bhartṛkā*. She praises the virtues of her lover, is humbler, becomes thin and emaciated, suffers insomnia, and becomes melancholy, restless, stunned, and anxious. Her activities are like that.

Vijaya-kumāra: What is the nature of the *svādhīna-bhartṛkā* heroine?

Gosvāmī: A heroine whose lover always stays with her and is submissive to her is called *svādhīna-bhartṛkā*. Her activities are to enjoy pastimes with him in the forest, in the water, while picking flowers, and in other like situations.

Vijaya-kumāra: The *svādhīna-bhartṛkā* heroine must be very happy.

Gosvāmī: If her lover is completely controlled by his love for her, and if he cannot leave her even for a moment, the *svādhīna-bhartṛkā* heroine is called *mādhavī*. Among the eight kinds of heroines, three kinds—*svādhīna-bhartṛkā*, *vāsaka-sajjā*, and *abhisārikā*—are happy at heart. They are nicely decorated with garments and ornaments. However, the other five kinds of heroines—*kaṇḍhitā, vipralabdhā, utkaṇṭhita, proṣita-bhartṛkā*, and *kalahāntaritā*—do not wear ornaments. A hand resting on their left cheek, they lament.

Vijaya-kumāra: Their love for Kṛṣṇa brings them unhappiness! What does that mean?

Gosvāmī: Love for Kṛṣṇa is spiritual and always blissful. These seeming sufferings are actually included among the wonderful variety of blissful spiritual emotions. In the material world, these emotions are suffering but in the spiritual world, they are different kinds of bliss. A person who has the power to taste spiritual bliss can understand. Other cannot.

Vijaya-kumāra: Among the different kinds of heroines, what are the different degrees of love?

Gosvāmī: According to the intensity of their love for Kṛṣṇa, the heroines are of three kinds: 1. *uttama* (high), 2. *madhyama* (intermediate) and 3. *kaniṣṭha* (low). As the heroines love Him, so Kṛṣṇa loves them in the same degree. This is well known.

Vijaya-kumāra: What is the nature of the *uttama* heroine?

Gosvāmī: The *uttama* heroine is willing to renounce any activity in order to please her lover, even for only a moment. Even if he makes her unhappy, she is never displeased with him. If someone lies that her lover is unhappy, her heart becomes ripped to shreds.

Vijaya-kumāra: What is the nature of a *madhyama* heroine?

Gosvāmī: When she hears that her lover is unhappy, she becomes sad at heart.

Vijaya-kumāra: What is the nature of a *kaniṣṭha* heroine?

Gosvāmī: The *kaniṣṭha* heroine is anxious that obstacles will prevent her from meeting her lover.

Vijaya-kumāra: How many kinds of heroines are there?

Gosvāmī: There are 360 kinds of heroines. The first mentioned fifteen kinds of heroines are each divided according to the next mentioned eight kinds of heroines. In this way (fifteen times eight) there are 120 heroines. These 120 kinds of heroines are each divided according to the last mentioned three kinds of heroines. In this way, there are 360 kinds of heroines.

Vijaya-kumāra: Now I have heard about the heroines. Now I wish to hear about the different kinds of *yūtheśvarīs* (group leaders).

Gosvāmī: According to friends and enemies, the *yūtheśvarīs* are of three kinds: 1. *svapakṣa* (allies), 2. *vipakṣa* (enemies), and 3. *taṭasthā* (neutrals). According to their good fortune, they are of these kinds: 1. *adhika* (great), 2. *samā* (moderate, and 3. *laghvī* (light). They are also of these three kinds: 1. *prakharā* (harsh), 2. *madhyā* (moderate) and 3. *mṛdvī* (sweet). Here, *prakharā* is a synonym for *pragalbhā*.

When the quality of harshness is manifested only very slightly, the *yūtheśvarī* is considered *mṛdvī*. When sweetness and harshness are equally present, she is considered *madhyā*. The *yūtheśvarīs* are also divided into 1. *ātyantikī* (great), and 2. *āpekṣikī* (less). When a *yūtheśvarī* has no equal in any sphere, she is considered *ātyantikī-adhika* (the best of *ātyantikīs*). This refers to Śrī Rādhā alone. She is a *madhyā* and in Vraja, She has no equal.

Vijaya-kumāra: Who are the *āpekṣikī-adhikas* (the second level of the great)?

Gosvāmī: A *yūtheśvarī* who accepts another *yūtheśvarī* as her superior is called *āpekṣikī-adhika*.

Vijaya-kumāra: Who are the *ātyantikī-laghu* (or *ātyantikī āpekṣikī*)?

Gosvāmī: A *yūtheśvarī* who is not inferior to the other heroines is called *ātyantikī-laghu*. In relation to the *ātyantikī-adhika yūtheśvarī* (the greatest *yūtheśvarī*, Śrī Rādhā), all the heroines are *laghu* (inferior). Aside from the *ātyantikī laghus*, all the *yūtheśvarīs* are *adhikas*. Still, the *ātyantikī-adhika yūtheśvarī* (the greatest *yūtheśvarī*, Śrī Rādhā) should never be considered their equal or inferior. Also, the *ātyantikī laghu yūtheśvarīs* should not be considered equal to the *adhika yūtheśvarīs*. There is but one kind of *samā laghu yūtheśvarī*.

Divided according to the qualities of *madhyā*, *adhika*, *prakharā*, and the like, there are twelve kinds of *yūtheśvarīs*. They are: 1. *ātyantikī-adhika*, 2. *samā-laghu*, 3. *adhika-madhyā*, 4. *samā-madhyā*, 5. *laghu-madhyā*, 6. *adhika-prakharā*, 7. *samā- prakharā*, 8. *laghu-prakharā*, 9. *adhika-mṛdvī*, 10. *samā-mṛdvī*, 11. *laghu-mṛdvī*, and 12. *ātyantikī-laghu*.

Vijaya-kumāra: I wish to hear about the different kinds of duties (messengers)?

Gosvāmī: The heroines thirsting for association with Kṛṣṇa need the help of the *dūtīs*. The *dūtīs* are of two kinds: 1. *svayam-dūtī* (messengers who act on their own initiative), and 2. *āpta-dūtī* (messengers given a specific order).

Vijaya-kumāra: What is the nature of the *svayam-dūtī* messengers?

Gosvāmī: When great enthusiasm breaks apart any shyness she may have possessed, and, bewildered with love, she openly declares her love for the hero—that is a *svayam-dūtī* messenger. These messengers are three kinds: 1. *kāyika* (bodily gestures), 2. *vācika* (words), and 3. *cakṣuṣā* (glances).

Vijaya-kumāra: What is the nature of the *vācika* (words) messenger?

Gosvāmī: Hints (*vyaṅga*) expressed in words are of two kinds: 1. *śabda-vyaṅga* (the hint is present in the sound of the words), and 2. *artha-vyaṅga* (the hint is present in the meaning of the words). Sometimes the hints are directly related to Kṛṣṇa and at other times the hints pretend to be about some other topic.

Vijaya-kumāra: What are the hints directly related to Kṛṣṇa?

Gosvāmī: They are of two kinds: 1. Hints to Kṛṣṇa Himself and 2. Hints spoken on some pretext.

Vijaya-kumāra: What are hints to Kṛṣṇa Himself?

Gosvāmī: Speaking proudly, lamenting, and begging are some of the many ways that hints may be expressed before Kṛṣṇa Himself.

Vijaya-kumāra: What is the hint in the form of a lament?

Gosvāmī: A lament expressed by the sound of the words (*śabda-vyaṅga*) is one kind of lament hint, and a lament expressed by the meaning of the words (*artha-vyaṅga*) is another kind of lament hint. You studied rhetoric (*alaṅkāra*). I need not give many examples.

Vijaya-kumāra: Yes. That is good. What is the nature of a hint in the form of begging?

Gosvāmī: Begging is of two kinds: 1. begging for oneself, and 2. begging on behalf of another person. Then begging may again be divided into these two kinds: Begging expressed by the sound of the words (*śabda-vyaṅga*), and 2. begging expressed by the meaning of the words (*artha-vyaṅga*). The begging described here is all hints. When the begging is for oneself, the heroine tells her own story. When the begging is on behalf of another person, the speaker tells another's story.

Vijaya-kumāra: I understand these direct hints. In them, the heroine may directly accuse Kṛṣṇa of something. These hints are also *śabda-vyaṅga* (according to the sound) and *artha-vyaṅga* (according to the meaning). Many poets have expertly placed such clever hints in the mouths of actors and actresses. Now, please explain *vyapadeśa* (a pretext).

Gosvāmī: In the *alaṅkāra-śāstra* it is said the *vyapadeśa* and *apadeśa* are synonyms. *Apadeśa* means to indicate one thing while speaking of another. In this way, one speaks words that clearly mean one thing while hinting a request to serve Kṛṣṇa in a certain way. This is called *vyapadeśa*. *Vyapadeśa* should be spoken by a messenger (*dūtī*).

Vijaya-kumāra: *Vyapadeśa* is then a kind of trick where a request has a hidden meaning. Now, please describe *puruṣa-viṣaya-gata-vyaṅga* (the hint of talking about something before one's eyes).

Gosvāmī: When one thinks, "Kṛṣṇa has heard, but He did not hear," and when Kṛṣṇa changes the subject, talking instead about some nearby animal of something else—that is the hint called *puruṣa-viṣaya-gata-vyaṅga*. This hint is of two kinds: 1. *śabda* (sounds) and 2. *artha* (meaning).

Vijaya-kumāra: By your mercy, I understand everything. Now please describe the hints given by bodily gestures.

Gosvāmī: Gesturing with the fingers, moving quickly on some pretext, covering the body out of fear and shyness, scratching the ground with one's foot, scratching the ear, making a gesture of applying *tilaka*, dressing in a certain way, moving the eyebrows, embracing a *gopī* friend, hitting a *gopī* friend, biting one's lips, playing with one's necklace, making one's ornaments tinkle, moving one's shoulders, writing the name Kṛṣṇa, and twining a vine around a tree are all included among the hints given by bodily gestures.

Vijaya-kumāra: Now, please describe the hints given by the eyes.

Gosvāmī: Laughing and smiling with the eyes, half-closing the eyes, moving the eyes, looking in the distance, crooked glances, glancing with the left eye, and sidelong glances are some of the hints given by the eyes.

Vijaya-kumāra: Now I understand the *svayam-dūtīs*. You have only given some hints but that is good enough. There are limitless kinds of such messengers. Now, please describe the *āpta-dūtīs*.

Gosvāmī: The messenger who is a beautiful Vraja *gopī*, who is affectionate and eloquent, and who one can trust to faithfully keep a secret, even to the end of life, is this kind of messenger (*āpta-dūtī*).

Vijaya-kumāra: How many kinds of *āpta-dūtīs* are there?

Gosvāmī: The *apta-dutis* are of three kinds: 1. *amitārthā*, 2. *nisṛṣṭārthā*, and 3. *pātra-hāri*. A messenger who, understanding the meaning of various hints and signs, brings the lovers together, is called an *amitārthā-dūtī*. A messenger who uses the persuasive power of her eloquent words to bring the lovers together is called a *nisṛṣṭārthā-dūtī*. A messenger who carries letters is called a *pātra-hāri-dūtī*.

Vijaya-kumāra: Are there any other *āpta-dūtīs*?

Gosvāmī: The *śilpa-kāriṇī* (artists), *daiva-jñā* (astrologers), *liṅgiṇī* (*brāhmaṇa* girls), *paricārikā* (maidservants), *dhātreyī* (nursemaids), *vana-devī* (goddesses of the forest), *sakhīs* (*gopī* friends), and many others are also counted among the *āpta-dūtīs*. The *śilpa-kāriṇīs* include girls who use their skill at drawing pictures to arrange for the meeting of the lovers. The *daiva-jñās* use their knowledge of astrology to arrange the lovers' meeting. The *liṅgiṇīs* dress in the garments of *brāhmaṇa* ascetics, like Paurṇamāsī. There are many *paricārikā* messengers, such as Lavaṅga-mañjarī and Bhānumatī. The *dhātreyīs* are the women who had been nursemaids to Rādhā and the other *gopīs*. The *vana-devī* is the goddesses of Vṛndāvana (forest). The *sakhīs* have already been described. They also become messengers. These girls carry messages, either direct and clear messages or messages filled with hints and suggestions, hints that may be either *śabda-vyaṅga* or *artha-vyaṅga*, both of which I have already described.

In this situation, the may be *vyapadeśa* (statements with a hidden meaning), *artha-mūla*, *praśaṁsa* (words of praise), *ākṣepa* (words of lamentation), and many other kinds of words also.

After hearing all these explanations, Vijaya-kumāra offered respectful obeisances to his spiritual master's lotus feet and then took his leave. Thinking and thinking of all these descriptions, he walked home.

Chapter Thirty-four

Mādhurya-rasa,
part four

Quickly honoring *prasādam*, and then walking by seacoast, Vijaya-kumāra went to Kāśī Miśra's home. As he looked at the waves in the ocean, the thought of the ocean of *rasas* entered his heart.

He thought, "Ah! This ocean reminds me of ecstatic love (*bhāva*) for Lord Kṛṣṇa. Even a material thing can remind one of spiritual love. This ocean is like the ocean of *rasas* my spiritual master described. Some day, I will throw this gross and subtle material body far away, I will attain the form of a *mañjarī*, I will go to the shore of the ocean of *rasas*, and I will taste the sweetness of the *rasas*. Lord Kṛṣṇa, who is dark like a monsoon cloud, is the only master of my life. Śrī Vṛṣabhānu-nandinī (Śrī Rādhā), who stays by His side, is the queen of my life."

"This ocean is like the ecstatic love Śrī Rādhā and Kṛṣṇa feel for each other. Their *rasas* and *bhāvas* are an ocean garlanded with waves. When *bhāva* arises, then there are wonderful waves in this ocean. Then, I am a *sakhī* (*gopī*) standing on the shore. Then, I float in the ocean of *prema-rasa* (the *rasas* of spiritual love). Lord Kṛṣṇa is the ocean of *rasas*. Kṛṣṇa is dark like the ocean. Śrī Rādhā is the waves of love (*prema*) in that ocean of Kṛṣṇa. She is beautiful, with a fair complexion. The many great waves in that ocean are Her friends (*sakhīs*). The smaller waves are Her maidservants (*paricārikās*). I am very far from them all. I am a maidservant of Rādhā's maidservants."

Thinking and thinking in this way, Vijaya-kumāra fell unconscious. Soon he regained consciousness. Slowly, he approached his spiritual master and offered *daṇḍavat* obeisances to his lotus feet. Humbly, he sat down.

Gopāla-guru Gosvāmī embraced him and said, "O Vijaya-kumāra, is everything well with you?"

Vijaya-kumāra replied, "O master, your mercy is the root of all auspiciousness. I am a follower of the *sakhīs* (*gopī* friends of Śrī Rādhā). Therefore, I want to clearly understand about the different kinds of *sakhīs*.

Gosvāmī: O Vijaya-kumāra, to properly glorify the *sakhīs* is beyond the power of the individual souls. You are a follower of Śrīla Rūpa Gosvāmī, so you can understand all this. The beautiful girls of Vraja who are *sakhīs* are expert in manifesting many (*vistāriṇī*) pastimes of love (*prema-līlā*). They are great reservoirs filled with faith in Vraja's divine youthful couple. A person who wishes to clearly understand them is certainly very fortunate. When describing the different groups of *gopīs*, I have already described the different kinds of *sakhīs*, namely the *sakhīs* who are *adhikā*, *samā*, and *laghvī*, and the *sakhīs* who are *prakharā*, *madhyā*, *mṛdvī*. I explained all these divisions yesterday.

Here is the evidence for them, from Śrīla Rūpa Gosvāmī (*Ujjvala-nīlamaṇi, Sakhī-prakaraṇa*, 3-5): In the matters of spiritual love, good fortune and spiritual virtues, and in other matters also, the *sakhīs* are divided into three groups: 1. *adhikā*, 2. *samā*, and 3. *laghu*. A *prakharā-sakhī* speaks heavy words that are difficult to counter. A *mṛdvī-sakhī* does not speak harshly at all. A *samā-sakhī* stands midway between the *prakharā* and *mṛdvī sakhī*. The *sakhīs* may be divided into different types, beginning with the *ātyantikādhika*. In each group of *sakhīs*, the leader is *ātyantikādhika*. Some of the *ātyantikādhika sakhīs* are *prakharā*, some are *madhyā*, and some are *mṛdvī*.

Vijaya-kumāra: The *yūtheśvarī* is the leader of a particular group. You have already described how the *yūtheśvarīs* are *ātyantika*, and how they are divided into three kinds: *prakharā*, *madhyā*, and *mṛdvī*. In this way, they are either *ātyantikādhika prakharā*, *ātyantikādhika madhyā*, or *ātyantikādhika mṛdvī*. This you have already explained. Now please describe the different kinds of *sakhīs*.

Gosvāmī: In each group, the *yūtheśvarī* is the only *ātyantikādhika sakhī*. The other *sakhīs* are all *āpekṣika-adhikā*, *āpekṣika-samā*, or *āpekṣika-laghvī*. Then again, these are also divided into *prakharā*, *madhyā*, and *mṛdvī*. In this way the three groups are multiplied by three to bring nine groups altogether. They are: *āpekṣika-adhikā prakharā*, 2. *āpekṣika-adhikā madhyā*, 3. *āpekṣika-adhikā mṛdvī*, 4. *āpekṣika-samā prakharā*, 5. *āpekṣika-samā madhyā*, 6. *āpekṣika-samā mṛdvī* and 9. *āpekṣika-laghvī mṛdvī*.

The *ātyantika laghvī* is of two kinds: 1. *ātyantika-laghvī*, and 2. *samā-laghvī*. These two are added to the preceding nine, and to them added the *yūtheśvarī*. In this way, there are twelve types of heroines in each group.

Vijaya-kumāra: O master, which famous *gopīs* are examples of each of these different kinds of *sakhīs*?

Gosvāmī: Lalitā and many other *sakhīs* in Śrī Rādhā's group are *āpekṣika-adhikā prakharā sakhīs*. Viśākhā and many other *sakhīs* in the same group are *āpekṣika-adhikā madhyā sakhīs*. Citrā, Mādhurīka and many other *sakhīs* in that group are *āpekṣika-adhikā mṛdvī sakhīs*. However, Lalitā, and the other *aṣṭa-sakhīs* (eight closest friends of Śrī Rādhā) are all *āpekṣika laghvī* when compared to Śrī Rādhā Herself.

Vijaya-kumāra: Are the *āpekṣika-laghvī prakharā sakhīs* and the other groups of *sakhīs* like them further divided into other kinds of *sakhīs*?

Gosvāmī: The *laghvī prakharā sakhīs* are of two kinds: 1. *vāmā* (left wing), and 2. *dakṣiṇā* (right wing).

Vijaya-kumāra: What are the qualities of *vāmā-sakhīs*?

Gosvāmī: They are always very proud. If there is some slackening in the respect shown to them, they become angry. They are not submissive to their lover. Such a *sakhī* is called *vāmā*. In Rādhā's group, Lalitā and many others are considered *vāmā-prakharā-sakhīs*.

Vijaya-kumāra: What are the qualities of the *dakṣiṇā-sakhīs*?

Gosvāmī: These heroines cannot tolerate pride. These heroines speak sweetly to their lover and they are conquered by His sweet words to them. Such a *sakhī* is called *dakṣiṇā*. In Śrī Rādhā's group. Tungavidyā and many others are *dakṣiṇā-prakharā-sakhīs*.

Vijaya-kumāra: Who are the *ātyantika-sakhīs*?

Gosvāmī: These *sakhīs* are always sweet. They are less important than the other *sakhīs*. Kusumika and many others are said to be *ātyantika-laghvī-sakhīs*.

Vijaya-kumāra: How do the *sakhīs* carry messages?

Gosvāmī: The *sakhīs* bring the hero, who has come a great distance, to meet the heroine. That is the message they carry.

Vijaya-kumāra: Are the *sakhīs* ever heroines?

Gosvāmī: The *yūtheśvarīs* are heroines eternally. The *āpekṣika-adhikā-prakharās*, *āpekṣika-adhikā-madhyās*, and *āpekṣika-adhikā-mṛdvīs* may be either heroines or *sakhīs*. They have both natures. When *gopīs* of an inferior status are present, they may assume the role of heroine. When a *gopī* of superior status is present, they assume the role of *sakhī*. The *gopīs* of inferior status consider them heroines, and the *gopīs* of superior status consider them *sakhīs*. Therefore they are called 'nāyikā-praya' (almost heroines).

The *āpekṣika-prakharā*, *āpekṣika-madhyā*, and *āpekṣika-mṛdvīs* also play double roles. They become *sakhīs* when superior *gopīs* are present, and heroines when inferior *gopīs* are present. The *āpekṣika-prakharā*, *āpekṣika-madhyā*, and *āpekṣika-mṛdvīs* are most often *sakhīs*. Because the *yūtheśvarī* and the previously described three classes of *gopīs* are superior to them, the *ātyantika-laghvī gopīs* are considered here as a fifth category. They are always *sakhīs*. In the presence of the *yūtheśvarī*, the *āpekṣika gopīs* are all *sakhīs* and *dūtīs* (messengers). Then they are not heroines. The *ātyantika-laghvī gopīs* are always *sakhīs*. They are never heroines, and they are never *dūtīs*.

Vijaya-kumāra: Who are the *sakhīs* that act as *dūtīs*?

Gosvāmī: The *yūtheśvarī* are always heroines. Everyone always honors them. They do not carry messages. However, the *yūtheśvarī* entrusts to her favorite *sakhī* the task of carrying messages. However, when one of her *sakhīs* becomes the object of the hero's love, the *yūtheśvarī* will become a *gauna* (secondary) kind of messenger on her behalf. Here, *gauna* means that the *yūtheśvarī* does not come and go for long distances carrying messages. This kind of carrying messages is of two kinds: 1. When Kṛṣṇa is present, and 2. When Kṛṣṇa is not present.

Vijaya-kumāra: In what different ways are messages carried when Kṛṣṇa is present?

Gosvāmī: These messages are of two kinds: 1. Hints, and 2. Direct statements.

Vijaya-kumāra: What are the hints?

Gosvāmī: When, by a sidelong glance, an eyebrow movement, a movement of the forefinger or another part of the body, or another kind of hint, a *sakhī* sends Kṛṣṇa to the heroine, that is called the message in the form of a hint.

Vijaya-kumāra: What are the direct statements?

Gosvāmī: When, either directly to Lord Kṛṣṇa or secretly behind his back, the messenger speaks appropriate words—that is called a message in the form of a direct statement.

Vijaya-kumāra: What are the messages when Kṛṣṇa is absent?

Gosvāmī: Here, one *sakhī* brings another *sakhī* to Kṛṣṇa. There are many ways a message can be carried in this way. These are all considered carrying a message when Kṛṣṇa is not present.

Vijaya-kumāra: What are messages carried for the *nāyikā-prāya* (almost heroine)?

Gosvāmī: When an *āpekṣika-adhikā-prakharā*, *āpekṣika-adhikā-madhyā*, or *āpekṣika-adhikā-mṛdvī* carries a message for a *gopī* of inferior status, this is called, carrying a message for a *nāyikā-prāya*. The *samā-sakhīs* and *madhyā-sakhīs* are naturally friends. Their friendship is mostly sweet and for the most part, they have no difference between them. *Paṇḍitas* who are learned in the science of spiritual love (*prema*) can understand all this.

Vijaya-kumāra: What is 'a message carried by a *sakhī-prāya* (one who is almost a *sakhī*)?

Gosvāmī: These are messages carried by a *laghu-prakharā*, *laghu-madhyā*, or *laghu-mṛdvī gopī*. When they are engaged in carrying messages, they are called *sakhī-prāya* (almost *sakhī*).

Vijaya-kumāra: What is a *nitya-sakhī* (always a *sakhī*)?

Gosvāmī: *Gopīs* who only wish to be a *sakhī* and never desire to become a heroine are called *nitya-sakhī*. The *nitya-sakhīs* are of two kinds: 1. *ātyantika laghvī* and 2. *āpekṣika laghvī*.

Vijaya-kumāra: Do the *sakhīs* eternally possess certain specific qualities, like the quality of being *prakharā* (harsh), qualities that they always manifest and never abandon?

Gosvāmī: Although certain qualities are part of the eternal nature of each *gopī*, sometimes, according to time, place, and circumstances, the *gopīs* manifest other qualities, even qualities that are the opposite of their ordinary nature. An example of this is Lalitā's attempt to calm Rādhā's jealous anger.

Vijaya-kumāra: It seems to me that Rādhā takes great care to arrange the meeting of Lord Kṛṣṇa with her friends.

Gosvāmī: O Vijaya-kumāra, I can say something about that. When a *sakhī* sent with a message meets Kṛṣṇa in a secluded place, and He requests that she enjoy with Him, she will not agree. She will not break the trust of the *gopī* friend who sent her with the message.

Vijaya-kumāra: What are the *sakhīs*' activities?

Gosvāmī: The *sakhīs* have sixteen kinds of activities: 1. To praise the virtues of the hero before the heroine, and to praise the virtues of the heroine before the hero. 2. To make the hero and heroine attached to each other. 3. To arrange for the rendezvous of the hero and heroine. 4. To give the heroine to Kṛṣṇa. 5. To speak eloquent jokes. 6. To give consolation. 7. To decorate the heroine in her room. 8. To reveal to the hero the love in the heroine's heart, and to reveal to the heroine the love in the hero's heart. 9. To hide faults. 10. To teach the heroine how to deceive her husband and other superiors. 11. To bring the hero and heroine together at the appropriate time. 12. To fan with a *cāmara* and perform other such services. 13. To approach the hero or heroine when it is appropriate. 14. To carry a message. 15. To save the heroine's life, and 16. To be careful and diligent in everything. Many examples could be given to illustrate each of these. What more shall I say:

Vijaya-kumāra: O master, I understand these brief explanations. Later I will see the examples given in the book *Ujjvala-nīlamaṇi*. Now I have learned a great deal. O master, now I would like to learn about the *sakhīs*' affection for each other and love for Lord Kṛṣṇa.

Gosvāmī: The *sakhīs* are of two kinds: 1. The *sakhīs* whose love for Kṛṣṇa and their own *yūtheśvarī* is not equal, and 2. The *sakhīs* who love Kṛṣṇa and their own *yūtheśvarī* equally.

Vijaya-kumāra: What *sakhīs* have love for Kṛṣṇa and their own *yūtheśvarī* that is not equal.

Gosvāmī: These *gopīs*, who are called *asama-sneha sakhīs* are of two kinds. Some love their *yūtheśvarī* more than they love Kṛṣṇa. Others think, "I am a maidservant of Kṛṣṇa." These *gopīs* will not leave their group to join another. Still, they love Kṛṣṇa more than they love their *yūtheśvarī*. A *gopī* who is proud to serve her *yūtheśvarī*, and who loves her *yūtheśvarī* more than Kṛṣṇa, is called *sakhī-snehādhika*.

Vijaya-kumāra: Who are they?

Gosvāmī: Among the five kinds of *sakhīs* I have already described, those who are simply called *sakhīs* love Kṛṣṇa more (*kṛṣṇa-snehādhika*). The previously described *nitya-sakhīs* and *prāna-sakhīs* love their *yūtheśvarī* more (*sakhī- snehādhika*).

Vijaya-kumāra: Who are the *gopīs* that love Kṛṣṇa and their *yūtheśvarī* equally?

Gosvāmī: The *gopīs* that love Kṛṣṇa and their *yūtheśvarī* equally are called *sama-sneha*.

Vijaya-kumāra: Of these *sakhīs*, who are the best?

Gosvāmī: The *sakhīs* who love Rādhā and Kṛṣṇa equally, and who think, "I am a follower of Rādhā," are the best of all. They are called *priya-sakhīs* and *parama-preṣṭha-sakhīs*.

Vijaya-kumāra: O master, please describe the rivalries of the different groups of *sakhīs*.

Gosvāmī: All the groups of Vraja *gopīs* are divided in four ways: 1, *sva-pakṣa* (one's own group), 2, *suhṛt-pakṣa* (friends), 3, *taṭasthā-pakṣa* (neutral parties), and 4, *prati-pakṣa* (enemies). The *gopī* groups associate with the *suhṛt-pakṣas* and *taṭasthā-pakṣas*, and they avoid the *prati-pakṣas*. In this way there is exchange of *rasas*.

Vijaya-kumāra: Please describe the *sva-pakṣa*, *prati-pakṣa*, and the others.

Gosvāmī: The *sva-pakṣa* I have already explained. Now I will explain how the *suhṛt-pakṣas* and the other groups differ. The *suhṛt-pakṣas* are of two kinds: 1, *iṣṭā-sādhikā* (friends pushed together to do something favorable) and *aniṣṭā-sādhikā* (friends pushed together to do something unfavorable). The *taṭasthā-pakṣa* is friendly to both the *sva-pakṣa* and the *prati-pakṣa*.

Vijaya-kumāra: Please describe the *prati-pakṣas*.

Gosvāmī: The *vipakṣas* are enemies. They destroy what is good and bring what is evil. The *vipakṣas* manifest trickery, malice, restlessness, envy, spite, mercilessness, pride and a host of other such qualities.

Vijaya-kumāra: How is pride manifested?

Gosvāmī: False-ego, self-importance, arrogance, mocking, conceit, and haughtiness are the six manifestations of pride.

Vijaya-kumāra: What is the nature of false-ego?

Gosvāmī: When one praises the *sva-pakṣa* and reviles the *prati-pakṣa*—that is false-ego.

Vijaya-kumāra: What is self-importance?

Gosvāmī: When one explains how one's own group has the most exalted spiritual love—that is self importance.

Vijaya-kumāra: What is arrogance?

Gosvāmī: When one is convinced that one's own group enjoys the most exalted spiritual pastimes—that is arrogance.

Vijaya-kumāra: What is mocking?

Gosvāmī: When one laughs at the other group—that is mocking.

Vijaya-kumāra: What is conceit?

Gosvāmī: When pride improves one's devotional service—that is conceit in this context.

Vijaya-kumāra: What is haughtiness?

Gosvāmī: To openly declare one's own superiority is called haughtiness. To criticize other *sakhīs* and speak sarcastically about them is also haughtiness.

Vijaya-kumāra: Do the *yūtheśvarīs* show malice directly?

Gosvāmī: No. The *yūtheśvarīs* always keep their gravity and decorum. They do not openly express malice. Even if a *prakharā-sakhī* speaks maliciously in her presence, the *yūtheśvarī* continues to speak pleasantly.

Vijaya-kumāra: O master, the *yūtheśvarīs* in the Lord's Vraja pastimes are all eternally perfect. They are one of the Lord's potencies. What does it mean that malice and other inauspicious qualities are present among them? Seeing these qualities, non-devotee philosophers will criticize the Lord's Vraja pastimes. They will say, "If malice and other inauspicious qualities are present in the spiritual world, then why do the devotees criticize or renounce the material world?"

O master, I am a resident of holy Navadvīpa where, by the will of Lord Kṛṣṇa Caitanya, many materialists may be seen. Some are followers of *karma-kanda*. Some are barren logicians. Some are impersonalists. In this way, there are many offenders. They condemn the Lord's pastimes. They claim that the Lord's pastimes are material and are filled with imperfections.

Gosvāmī: Persons who cannot understand the Lord's spiritual *rasas* (arasikā) claim that it is not right for the Lord's personal associates to manifest malice or other seemingly inauspicious qualities. When one is at last able to understand the spiritual truth, then one can see Vraja's *mādhurya-rasa*, which is the dear friend of Lord Kṛṣṇa, the Lord who destroys all sins and whose transcendental form enchants a multitude of Kāmadevas. Malice and other seemingly inauspicious emotions felt by Lord Kṛṣṇa's personal associates are meant to enhance Lord Kṛṣṇa's transcendental pleasure when the associates are in His company. Apart from these pastimes with Kṛṣṇa, these seemingly inauspicious qualities are not manifested. At that time, there is only love.

Vijaya-kumāra: O master, I am a tiny creature. These confidential truths do not easily enter my heart. Please be merciful and explain it very simply and clearly. That will be auspicious for me.

Gosvāmī: The *rasas* of spiritual love (*prema-rasa*) are like a great ocean of milk. However, material logic is bitter like cow's urine. One who can understand the spiritual *rasas* obtains an auspicious life. And, why not? It is after a person performs many pious deeds that Bhakti-devī (the goddess of devotional service) places the fruit of the *hlādinī-śakti* in his heart. Thus, a person who shuns the study of material logic obtains the final truth. On the other hand, persons who use material logic to understand the truth cannot understand the spiritual truth, which is inconceivable, being beyond the understanding of the material mind. The so-called truth they accept is filled with misconceptions.

However, you are a fortunate soul. Therefore, by the grace of Bhakti-devī, you understand everything. However, to make the truth very clear, I must answer your question. You are not a material logician, nor a follower of *karma-kanda*, nor a follower of *jñāna-kanda*, nor a doubter. You are a sincere devotee engaged in *vaidhī-bhakti* devotional service. I will explain the truth to you. I have no objection.

You asked two kinds of questions. One kind of question takes shelter of dry material logic. The other kind of question may be satisfied by faith in devotional service. You should not answer the question posed by the impersonalist. Why not? Because they have no faith in the actual truth and thus they will not believe what is the true answer. Without taking shelter of the Lord's *cit-śakti* (spiritual potency), a soul imprisoned by *māyā* cannot understand the inconceivable spiritual truth merely by using the instrument of material logic in a great series of debates. That is the fate of persons who have no faith in the Supreme Personality of Godhead. Many different kinds of persons engage in devotional service. Persons who are qualified to understand the *mādhurya-rasa* can understand all these truths from their spiritual master.

O Vijaya-kumāra, the Lord's pastimes and *rasas* in Vṛndāvana are very wonderful. The Lord's *mādhurya-rasa* is very different from the amorous pastimes of the material world. By studying *Śrīmad-Bhāgavatam's* five-chapter description of the Lord's *rasa* dance, a devotee will uproot the desire that grows in his heart. What disease grows in the heart of the souls imprisoned by *māyā*? The disease is material lust.

A soul who has taken shelter of the subtle material body, consisting of mind, intelligence, and false ego, who is filled with material desires, who identifies with the gross material body made of seven elements, beginning with flesh, and who thinks it is a man or a woman, does not have the power to throw material lust far away very easily. Only by hearing about the Lord's Vraja pastimes will that soul be able to throw material lust far away. In the end, such a person is able to see the great wonder that is the Lord's *mādhurya-rasa* pastimes in Vṛndāvana.

When He throws the impersonalists philosophy far away, then the spiritual *mādhurya-rasa* is eternally manifest before him. When he understands the lesser importance of the Lord's majestic feature in Vaikuṇṭha, the soul can understand the supreme glory of the Lord's eternal and splendid *rasas*. Then, the soul is filled with intense transcendental bliss. Then, the dry happiness of impersonalism and the dull pleasures of the material world become very unimportant for him. Then, he is filled with a bliss that is perfect and complete.

This perfect and complete bliss is manifest in many places and in many ways. In some *bhāvas*, it is manifested as affection and other such emotions, and in other places, it is manifested as malice and other so-called inauspicious emotions. Material malice and material inauspicious emotions are all abominable. These spiritual emotions are not like them. They are all various transformations of spiritual bliss. They are like waves in the great ocean of the spiritual *rasas*. They make that ocean glorious.

The conclusion of Śrīla Rūpa Gosvāmī is that these different *rasas* show the wonderful variety of ecstatic (*bhāva*). In the *sva-pakṣa*, these *bhāvas* are all the same. In the *suhṛt-pakṣa*, the *bhāvas* are slightly different. In the *taṭasthā-pakṣa*, the *bhāvas* are slightly similar. In the *vipakṣa*, the *bhāvas* are completely different. Look. When the *bhāvas* are not compatible, the situation is not pleasant. In that situation, the supremely blissful *rasas* produce malice and other seemingly inauspicious emotions.

Vijaya-kumāra: Why do *sva-pakṣas* and *vipakṣas* exist?

Gosvāmī: When two heroines have the same nature, *sva-pakṣa* and *vipakṣa* are manifested. In this way, friends and enemies are manifested from the spiritual *rasas*. The purpose of these emotions is to increase the sweetness of the Lord's spiritual *mādhurya-rasa*.

Vijaya-kumāra: Are Rādhā and Candrāvalī equally powerful?

Gosvāmī: No. No. Śrī Rādhā is full of the highest ecstatic love. She is the essence of the *hlādinī-śakti*. Candrāvalī is manifested from a tiny particle of Śrī Rādhā's transcendental form. Still, in order to increase the *prema-rasa* (loving pastimes) of Śrī Rādhā, Candrāvalī is manifested as if she were Rādhā's equal and rival (*vipakṣa*). Look, it is not possible for these two *yūtheśvarīs* to be completely alike. If these two seem sometimes to be equals, it is only an accident, like the path of a bookworm accidentally forming the shape of a certain letter of the alphabet. In truth, the *sva-pakṣas* and *vipakṣa* are needed to make the *rasas* glorious.

Vijaya-kumāra: O master, no I have no doubts. The nectar of your words flows into my ears and enters my heart, where it destroys all the bitterness that was there. In my heart, I can now understand the transformations of *mādhurya-rasa*. Lord Kṛṣṇa is eternal and full of knowledge and bliss. He is the only hero (*nāyakā*).

I meditate on His form, qualities, and activities. He is *dhīrodātta, dhīra-lalita, dhīra-śānta,* and *dhīroddhata*. His qualities are *anukūla, dakṣiṇa, śaṭha,* and *dhṛṣṭa*. He is always served by His *ceṭa, viṭa, vidūṣaka, pīṭha-mardda,* and *priya-narma-sakhā* companions. He likes to play the flute. Lord Kṛṣṇa, who enjoys the *mādhurya-rasa*, is manifest in my heart. I have also understood the descriptions of the beautiful girls of Vraja, who have taken shelter of the *mādhurya-rasa*. They are heroines (*nāyikā*).

The heroines are of two kinds: 1. *svakīya*, and 2. *parakīya*. The best *rasa* is that of the *parakīya* heroines in Vraja. These heroines are of three kinds:

1, *sādhana-para*, 2, *devī*, and 3, *nitya-priya*. Divided into many, many different groups, the girls of Vraja serve Lord Kṛṣṇa. There are many millions and millions of such girls of Vraja, each of them subordinate to one of the many, many *yūtheśvarīs*.

Rādhā and Candrāvalī are the most important of the *yūtheśvarīs*. There are five kinds of *sakhīs*: 1 *sakhī*, 2 *nitya-sakhī*, 3 *prāna-sakhī*, 4 *priya-sakhī*, and 5 *parama-preṣṭha-sakhī*. In Rādhā's group, the eight *sakhīs*, headed by Lalitā, are *parama-preṣṭha-sakhīs*. These eight *sakhīs*, headed by Lalitā, are qualified to become *yūtheśvarīs* themselves, but they do not form separate groups, for they prefer to remain followers of Śrī Rādhā. Still, many other girls of Vraja consider themselves followers of these eight *sakhīs*.

The heroines are divided in different ways: as *mugdhā*, *madhya*, and *pragalbhā*; as *dhīra*, *adhīra*, and *dhīrādhīra*; and as *kanyā*, *svakīya* and *parakīya*. In this way, there are fifteen different kinds of heroines. The heroines have eight different conditions of life, which begin with *abhisārikā*. The heroines are also divided into *uttama*, *madhyama* and *kaniṣṭha*. In this way, there are 360 (fifteen times eight times three) different kinds of heroines.

Knowledge of the friendship and other emotions felt by the *yūtheśvarīs* is now also present in my heart. Knowledge of the messengers and *sakhīs* is now also manifested in my heart. Now I am able to understand the shelter in whom the *rasas* rest. Now I understand the *viṣaya* and *āśraya* and, included within them, the *vibhāva* and *ālambana*. Tomorrow, I will take shelter of your lotus feet and learn from you about the *uddīpanas*. Lord Kṛṣṇa has been very kind to me, to give me such a kind spiritual master. Tomorrow, I will be very well nourished by drinking the nectarean words that flow from your mouth.

Śrī Gopāla-guru Gosvāmī embraced Vijaya-kumāra and said, "Bābā. I am very fortunate to have you as a disciple. You like to ask many questions and Lord Caitanya Himself has placed all the answers in my mouth."

The two of them wept tears of love. After that, they were both stunned and motionless. Seeing how fortunate Vijaya-kumāra had become, Dhyānacandra and the other great souls there became plunged into great transcendental bliss. At that moment, some pure Vaiṣṇavas came to visit the Śrī Rādhākānta temple.

They began to sing this song of Caṇḍīdāsa: O friend, who did I hear pronounce the name Śyāma? That name entered my ears. Then, it traveled to my heart. Now my life-breath trembles. I do not know why the name Śyāma is so sweet. My mouth cannot renounce saying it. I say it again and again. My senses are all overwhelmed. What will become of me? If this name makes my senses burn with fever, what would happen if the bearer of this name were to touch my limbs? If I were to see this person with my eyes, how could I continue on the religious path? In my heart, I decide to forget Him but He will not be forgotten. What will I do? Considering the fate of a saintly young girl in danger of destroying her family, the *brāhmaṇa*, Caṇḍīdāsa speaks these words.

Accompanied by *karatālas* and *mṛdaṅga*, everyone sang this song. An hour and a half passed in this way. Everyone was plunged in spiritual love (*prema*). When the spiritual bliss was a little broken, Vijaya-kumāra offered *daṇḍavat* obeisances to Śrī Gopāla-guru Gosvāmī and the other Vaiṣṇavas, respectfully bade them farewell, and began walking to Haracaṇḍi Sāhi's house.

Chapter Thirty-five

Mādhurya-rasa, part five

Again and again Kṛṣṇa appeared in his thoughts. Vijaya-kumāra's heart was attracted to Kṛṣṇa. His ordinary dealings were now chaotic. He ate a little of what food was around and then ran like a madman to his spiritual master, and then fell down before his lotus feet.

Gopāla-guru Gosvāmī carefully picked him up and embraced him. Vijaya-kumāra said, "O master, I wish to learn about the *uddīpanas* in *mādhurya-rasa.*"

Then, the saintly Gosvāmī carefully spoke.

Gosvāmī: The qualities, names, activities, decorations, and other things directly and indirectly related to Kṛṣṇa and His beloved *gopīs* are the *uddīpanas* in *mādhurya-rasa*.

Vijaya-kumāra: Please describe these qualities.

Gosvāmī: The qualities are of three kinds: 1. mental, 2. verbal, and 3. physical.

Vijaya-kumāra: What are the mental qualities?

Gosvāmī: Gratefulness, forgiveness, and kindness are included among the many mental qualities.

Vijaya-kumāra: What are the verbal qualities?

Gosvāmī: The verbal qualities are words that delight the ear.

Vijaya-kumāra: What are the physical qualities?

Gosvāmī: Youthfulness, splendor, charm, beauty, delight, sweetness, and gentleness are included among the physical qualities. Four kinds of youthfulness take shelter of *mādhurya-rasa*. They are: 1 *vayaḥ-sandhi*, 2 *navya-vayasā*, 3 *vyakta-vayasā* and 4 *pūrṇa-vayasā*.

Vijaya-kumāra: What is *vayaḥ-sandhi*?

Gosvāmī: The point where *bālya* and *yauvana* meet is called *vayaḥ-sandhi*. It is also called *prathama-paugaṇḍa*. When *paugaṇḍa* arises, that is *vayaḥ-sandhi*. Here, *bālya* and *paugaṇḍa* are synonyms. The sweetness of the *gopīs*' *vayaḥ-sandhi* age is an *uddīpana* that inspires Lord Kṛṣṇa.

Vijaya-kumāra: What is *navya-vayasā*?

Gosvāmī: It is the beginning of *yauvana*. In this age, the *gopīs* smile gently, their eyes are restless, their hearts are beginning to become agitated, and their breasts are beginning to manifest.

Vijaya-kumāra: What is *vyakta-vayasā*?

As this question was spoken, the Śrī Vaiṣṇava and a *paṇḍita sannyāsī* from the Śaṅkara-maṭha came to see the Deity. The Śrī Vaiṣṇava considered himself a male servant of the Lord, and the Śaṅkara *sannyāsī* was plunged in dry meditation on impersonal Brahman. Neither of them were qualified to hear about the Vraja *gopīs*. It is forbidden to discuss *mādhurya-rasa* with persons firmly convinced of their material malehood.

Gopāla-guru Gosvāmī and Vijaya-kumāra at once stopped their conversation and made small talk about other things. After a short while, the two guests left to see the *siddha-bakula* tree. Gently smiling, Vijaya-kumāra repeated his question.

Gosvāmī: When the breasts are clearly manifested, three folds of skin are manifested on the waist, and all the limbs are splendid, then the age is said to be *vyakta-vayasā*.

Vijaya-kumāra: What is *pūrṇa-vayasā*?

Gosvāmī: When the hips are large, the waist slender, all the limbs splendid with extraordinary beauty, the breasts large, and the thighs like banana trees, the age is called *pūrṇa-vayasā*.

Vijaya-kumāra: Now I understand these different ages. Now please describe form.

Gosvāmī: When the form is so splendid and glorious that it seems to be decorated even when it is not—that is called splendor. When all the limbs are beautiful, that is called splendor.

Vijaya-kumāra: What is charm?

Gosvāmī: When all the limbs shine with a splendor like the splendor of pearls—that is called charm.

Vijaya-kumāra: What is beauty?

Gosvāmī: When each limb is shaped in the most appropriate way, and when all the limbs are combined together in the most beautiful way—that is called beauty.

Vijaya-kumāra: What is delight?

Gosvāmī: When one's wonderful qualities make those who are nearby also wonderful in the same way—that is called delight.

Vijaya-kumāra: What is sweetness?

Gosvāmī: When the body's beauty is so great that it cannot be described, that is sweetness.

Vijaya-kumāra: What is gentleness?

Gosvāmī: When the body is so soft and delicate it cannot tolerate even the slightest touch—that is called gentleness. Gentleness is of three kinds: 1 great, 2 intermediate, and 3 less.

Vijaya-kumāra: O master, now I understand all these qualities. Now, please describe the names.

Gosvāmī: Transcendental names, such as the name Rādhā-Kṛṣṇa, are the birthplace of the *rasas* and *bhāvas*.

Vijaya-kumāra: I understand. Now please describe the activities.

Gosvāmī: The activities are of two kinds: 1 *anubhāva* and 2 *līlā*. *Anubhāva* was already described after *vibhāva*.

Vijaya-kumāra: Please describe *līlā*.

Gosvāmī: Beautiful pastimes, dancing, playing the flute, milking the cows, herding the cows from the hill, and other such activities are all called *līlā*.

Vijaya-kumāra: What are beautiful pastimes?

Gosvāmī: The *rasa* dance, and playing games with a ball, are included among the numberless beautiful pastimes that charm the heart.

Vijaya-kumāra: What are the decorations?

Gosvāmī: Garments, ornaments, garlands, and ointments are the four kinds of decorations.

Vijaya-kumāra: What are the things directly related to Kṛṣṇa and the *gopīs*?

Gosvāmī: Two kinds of things are directly related to Kṛṣṇa and the *gopīs*. They are: 1. Things touching and 2. Things nearby.

Vijaya-kumāra: What are the things touching?

Gosvāmī: The sound of the flute, the sound of the buffalo horn bugle, singing, fragrance, tinkling of the ornaments, footprints, sound of the *vīṇā*, and artistic skill are included among the things touching.

Vijaya-kumāra: What is the sound of the flute?

Gosvāmī: From Kṛṣṇa's mouth, nectarean flute music flows. That music is the best of the *uddīpanas*.

Vijaya-kumāra: Please be kind and describe the things nearby.

Gosvāmī: Flower remnants, peacock feathers, mineral dyes from the hills, the cows, the stick, the flute, the buffalo horn bugle, the sight of Kṛṣṇa's dear associates, the dust raised by the cows, Vṛndāvana, the living entities and things that have their shelter in Vṛndāvana, Govardhana Hill, the Yamunā, and the *rasa* dance arena are included among the things nearby.

Vijaya-kumāra: Who are the living entities that have taken shelter in Vṛndāvana?

Gosvāmī: Many birds, bees, deer, forest groves, vines, *tulasī* plants, *karnikā* flowers, and *kadamba* trees have taken shelter of Vṛndāvana.

Vijaya-kumāra: What are the things indirectly related to Kṛṣṇa and the *gopīs*?

Gosvāmī: The moonlight, clouds, lightning, springtime, autumn, full moon, breeze, and birds are included among what is indirectly related.

After hearing about all these *uddīpanas*, Vijaya-kumāra was silent for a moment. Pushed by the *uddīpanas*, ecstatic love arose in his heart. Then, the *anubhāvas* became manifested on his body.

With a choked voice, Vijaya-kumāra said, "O master, please describe the *anubhāvas*. When describing His *līlās*, you said they were part of Lord Kṛṣṇa's activities. When I understand the *anubhāvas*, I will be able to know the full outline of Kṛṣṇa's activities."

Gosvāmī: The *anubhāvas* are of three kinds: 1. *alaṅkāra*, 2. *udbhāsvara*, and 3. *vācika*.

Vijaya-kumāra: What are the *alaṅkāras*?

Gosvāmī: In their *yauvana* age, the beautiful girls of Vraja manifest twenty kinds of *alaṅkāra* (ornaments). With these ornaments, they conquer their beloved. These ornaments are:

Ornaments manifested from the body: 1. *bhāva*, 2. *hāva* 3. *helā*.

Ornaments manifested spontaneously: 4. *śobhā*, 5. *kānti*, 6. *dīpti*, 7. *mādhurya*, 8. *pragalbhatā*, 9. *audārya*, 10. *dhairya*.

Natural ornaments: 11. *līlā*, 12. *vilāsa*, 13. *vicchitti*, 14. *vibhrama*, 15. *kila-*

kiñcita, 16. *moṭṭāyita*, 17. *kuṭṭāmita*, 18. *vivvoka*, 19. *lalita* and 20. *vikṛta*.

Vijaya-kumāra: What is *bhāva* in this context?

Gosvāmī: When the heart is steady in *mādhurya-rasa*, that state is called *rati*. The first manifestation of *rati* is called *bhāva*. When the heart is steady in *rati*, that state is called *sattva*. When the heart becomes agitated with ecstatic love—that is called *bhāva*.

Vijaya-kumāra: O master, what is *hāva*?

Gosvāmī: To tilt the neck, move the eyes or eyebrows, or give other hints of love is called *hāva*.

Vijaya-kumāra: What is *helā*?

Gosvāmī: When the amorous hints of *hāva* are more openly expressed, that is called *helā*.

Vijaya-kumāra: What is *śobhā*?

Gosvāmī: The beauty that amorous pastimes use to decorate the limbs is called *śobhā*.

Vijaya-kumāra: What is *kānti*?

Gosvāmī: When amorous desires are satisfied, the splendor then manifested is called *kānti*.

Vijaya-kumāra: What is *dīpti*?

Gosvāmī: When youthfulness, enjoyment, place, time, virtues, and other such things bring a great and glorious splendor, that splendor is called *dīpti*.

Vijaya-kumāra: What is *mādhurya*?

Gosvāmī: The delicate grace and exquisite dexterity that is maintained by the *gopīs* under all circumstances as they execute all endeavors for Kṛṣṇa's happiness is called *mādhurya*.

Vijaya-kumāra: What is *pragalbhatā*?

Gosvāmī: To be self-assured and free from doubt is called *pragalbhatā*. This brings great splendor to every limb.

Vijaya-kumāra: What is *audārya*?

Gosvāmī: To be humble in every situation is called *audārya*.

Vijaya-kumāra: What is *dhairya*?

Gosvāmī: When the mind is exalted, that is called *dhairya*.

Vijaya-kumāra: What is *līlā*?

Gosvāmī: To imitate the beloved's graceful garments and actions is called *līlā*.

Vijaya-kumāra: What is *vilāsa*?

Gosvāmī: When walking, staying still, sitting, the mouth, the eyes, and many other things are all employed to give amorous hints to the beloved—that is called *vilāsa*.

Vijaya-kumāra: What is *vicchitti*?

Gosvāmī: If there is great beauty, even though the ornaments are few, that is called *vicchitti*. In the opinion of some scholars of *rasa*, when the lover commits an offense, the *sakhīs* carefully decorates Him, and in spite of all efforts, the girl remains angry, her condition is called *vicchitti*.

Vijaya-kumāra: What is *vibhrama*?

Gosvāmī: When, at the time of going to meet her beloved, a girl is so bewildered with amorous desire that she decorates herself with necklace, garland, and other ornaments in the wrong way—that is called *vibhrama*.

Vijaya-kumāra: what is *kila-kiñcita*?

Gosvāmī: Pride, desire, weeping, laughing, envy, fear, and anger, when they are manifested as symptoms of happiness when one meets the beloved, are called *kila-kiñcita*.

Vijaya-kumāra: What is *moṭṭāyita*?

Gosvāmī: When, by remembering the beloved or receiving news of him, the lover feels love and then desire—that is called *moṭṭāyita*.

Vijaya-kumāra: What is *kuṭṭāmita*?

Gosvāmī: When the lover touches the beloved's breast, and the beloved, although actually pleased, puts on an outward show of anger—that is called *kuṭṭāmita*.

Vijaya-kumāra: What is *vivvoka*?

Gosvāmī: When pride and jealousy make the beloved insult the lover—that is called *vivvoka*.

Vijaya-kumāra: What is *lalita*?

Gosvāmī: When the movements of the body and the eyebrows show softness—that is called *lalita*.

Vijaya-kumāra: What is *vikṛta*?

Gosvāmī: When shyness, pride, and anger are expressed not by words but by actions, that is called *vikṛta*. In this way, twenty ornaments are manifested from the body and mind. Some scholars of *rasa* add two more ornaments—*maughdya* and *cakita*—to this list.

Vijaya-kumāra: What is *maughdya*?

Gosvāmī: When, even though she already knows the answer, the beloved, as if she didn't already know, asks the lover anyway, that is called *maugdhya*.

Vijaya-kumāra: What is *cakita*?

Gosvāmī: When, even though there is no reason to fear, the beloved tells her lover that she is very afraid, that is called *cakita*.

Vijaya-kumāra: O master, thus I have heard about these *alaṅkāras* (ornaments). Now please teach me about the *udbhāsvaras*.

Gosvāmī: When the ecstatic love present in the heart is splendidly manifested in the body—that is called *udbhāsvara*. When, in *mādhurya-rasa*, the belt, bodice, and braids become loosened, the limbs are agitated, the mouth is opened wide and, with dilated nostrils, there is heavy breathing—that is called *udbhāsvara*.

Vijaya-kumāra: All these *udbhāsvaras* could easily have been included within *moṭṭāyita* and *vilāsa*.

Gosvāmī: They have a different kind of glory. Therefore, they are considered separately.

Vijaya-kumāra: O master, now please describe the verbal *anubhāvas*.

Gosvāmī: *Ālāpa, vilāpa, saṁlāpa, pralāpa, anulāpa, apalāpa, sandeśa, atideśa, apadeśa, upadeśa, nirdeśa*, and *vyapadeśa* are the twelve verbal *anubhāvas*.

Vijaya-kumāra: What is *ālāpa*?

Gosvāmī: When one speaks pleasing, flattering words, that is called *ālāpa*.

Vijaya-kumāra: What is *vilāpa*?

Gosvāmī: When one laments, that is called *vilāpa*.

Vijaya-kumāra: What is *saṁlāpa*?

Gosvāmī: Pleasing conversations are called *saṁlāpa*.

Vijaya-kumāra: What is *pralāpa*?

Gosvāmī: Meaningless words are called *pralāpa.*

Vijaya-kumāra: What is *anulāpa?*

Gosvāmī: Repeating the same thing over and over is called *anulāpa.*

Vijaya-kumāra: What is *apalāpa?*

Gosvāmī: To explain something a second time is called *apalāpa.*

Vijaya-kumāra: What is *sandeśa?*

Gosvāmī: To send a letter to a beloved in a faraway place is called *sandeśa.*

Vijaya-kumāra: What is *atideśa?*

Gosvāmī: To say, "His words are my words," is called *atideśa.*

Vijaya-kumāra: What is *apadeśa?*

Gosvāmī: While speaking about one thing to reveal another is called *apadeśa.*

Vijaya-kumāra: What is *upadeśa?*

Gosvāmī: To give instruction is called *upadeśa.*

Vijaya-kumāra: What is *nirdeśa?*

Gosvāmī: To affirm, "I am that person," is called *nirdeśa.*

Vijaya-kumāra: What is *vyapadeśa?*

Gosvāmī: To misrepresent one's true desire is called *vyapadeśa.* All these *anubhāvas* are present in all the *rasas.* However, they are famous for making the *mādhurya-rasa* sweet.

Vijaya-kumāra: O master, why are these *rasa anubhāvas* considered separately?

Gosvāmī: When the *ālambanas* and *uddīpanas* enter the heart, *bhāva* is manifested. Then, the symptoms called *anubhāvas* are manifested on the body. If all the *anubhāvas* were not discussed separately, then it would not be possible to see their natures clearly.

Vijaya-kumāra: Now please describe the *sāttvika-bhāvas* in *mādhurya-rasa.*

Gosvāmī: The eight *sāttvika-bhāvas,* beginning with being stunned and perspiring, which I had previously described, are also present in *mādhurya-rasa.* However, in this *rasa,* they are manifested in a different way.

Vijaya-kumāra: How is it different?

Gosvāmī: Look at the Lord's Vraja pastimes. Being stunned comes from joy, fear, wonder, melancholy, and anger. Perspiration comes from joy, fear, and anger. Standing up of the body's hairs comes from wonder, joy, and fear. Choking up of the voice comes from melancholy, wonder, anger, and fear. Trembling of the body comes from fear, joy, and anger. Becoming pale comes from fear, joy, and anger. Shedding tears comes from joy, anger, and melancholy. Devastation comes from either happiness or distress.

Vijaya-kumāra: Are these *sāttvika* ecstatic symptoms manifested differently in *mādhurya-rasa*?

Gosvāmī: Yes. They are. When before I described the *sāttvika-bhāvas*, I explained that they were manifested as either *dhūmāyitā* (smoky), *jvalitā* (blazing), *dīpta* (shining), or *uddīpta* (bright shining). In *mādhurya-rasa* these *bhāvas* are manifested only in two ways, as either *uddīpta* (brightly shining) or *sūddīpta* (brilliantly shining).

Vijaya-kumāra: O master, please be kind to me. Please describe the *vyabhicārī-bhāvas* in *mādhurya-rasa* and make me happy.

Gosvāmī: The thirty-three *vyabhicārī-bhāvas*, or *sañcārī-bhāvas*, which begin with *nirveda* (disappointment), and which I have previously described to you, are almost all present in *mādhurya-rasa*. Only *augrya* (violence) and *ālasya* (laziness) are not present in this *rasa*. In *mādhurya-rasa*, these *sañcārī-bhāvas* are very wonderful.

Vijaya-kumāra: What is the most wonderful thing about them in this situation?

Gosvāmī: The love for Kṛṣṇa (*kṛṣṇa-prema*) that Kṛṣṇa's friends and superiors feel for Him in *sākhya-rasa* and the other *rasas*, becomes *sañcārī-bhāva* in *mādhurya-rasa*. In other words, what was *sthāyi-bhāva* in the other *rasas* becomes *sañcārī-bhāva* or *vyabhicārī-bhāva* in *mādhurya-rasa*.

Vijaya-kumāra: What else is wonderful in this situation?

Gosvāmī: The *vyabhicārī-bhāvas* are not considered direct ingredients of *mādhurya-rasa*. Even the *vyabhicārīs* that begin with *maraṇa* (death) are not direct ingredients. Instead of being ingredients, the *vyabhicārī-bhāvas* are considered the qualities of *mādhurya-rasa*. The *vyabhicārī-bhāvas* are the qualities, and *mādhurya-rasa* is the possessor of the qualities. That is the proper conclusion.

Vijaya-kumāra: How are the *vyabhicārī-bhāvas* manifested in this *rasa*?

Gosvāmī: *Nirveda* (disappointment) is born from suffering, unpleasantness, envy, melancholy, calamity, and offense.

Vijaya-kumāra: From what is *dainya* (humility) born?

Gosvāmī: *Dainya* is born from unhappiness, fear and offense.

Vijaya-kumāra: From what is *glāni* (guilt) born?

Gosvāmī: *Glāni* is born from fatigue, anxiety, and attraction.

Vijaya-kumāra: From what is *śrama* (fatigue) born?

Gosvāmī: Śrama is born from losing one's way, dancing, and attraction.

Vijaya-kumāra: From what is *mada* (intoxication) born?

Gosvāmī: *Mada* is born from drinking liquor. In this way, one becomes jubilant and one also loses one's power of discrimination.

Vijaya-kumāra: From what is *garva* (pride) born?

Gosvāmī: *Garva* is born from good fortune, beauty, virtue, and obtaining what is the best of all.

Vijaya-kumāra: From what is *śaṅkā* (apprehension) born?

Gosvāmī: *Śaṅkā* is born from theft, offense, cruelty to others, lightning, fearsome creatures, and fearsome sounds.

Vijaya-kumāra: From what is *āvega* (intense emotion) born?

Gosvāmī: *Āvega* is born from seeing the object of love, hearing about the object of love, seeing what is not loved, and hearing about what is not loved. The heart becomes bewildered by these intense emotions.

Vijaya-kumāra: From what is *unmāda* (madness) born?

Gosvāmī: *Unmāda* is born from intense bliss or separation from the beloved.

Vijaya-kumāra: From what is *apasmṛti* (forgetfulness) born?

Gosvāmī: *Apasmṛti* is born from unhappiness, which upsets the body and the mind.

Vijaya-kumāra: From what is *vyādhi* (disease) born?

Gosvāmī: *Vyādhi* is born from fever and other such causes. It is also born from anxiety, intense emotion, and other feelings.

Vijaya-kumāra: From what is *moha* (confusion) born?

Gosvāmī: *Moha* is bewilderment of the mind. *Moha* is born from joy, separation, and sorrow.

Vijaya-kumāra: From what is *mṛtyu* (death) born?

Gosvāmī: *Mṛtyu* is not directly manifested in *mādhurya-rasa*. Sometimes there is the desire for death.

Vijaya-kumāra: From what is *ālasya* (laziness) born?

Gosvāmī: *Ālasya* is not directly manifested in *mādhurya-rasa*. When a strong person pretends that he is not strong, that is called *ālasya*. *Ālasya* does not exist in devotional service to Lord Kṛṣṇa. However, it is seen indirectly, as the opposite of true devotional service.

Vijaya-kumāra: From what is *jāḍya* (inertness) born?

Gosvāmī: *Jāḍya* is born from hearing about the beloved, seeing the beloved, seeing what is unpleasant, and separation from the beloved.

Vijaya-kumāra: From what is *vrīḍā* (bashfulness) born?

Gosvāmī: *Vrīḍā* is born from first meeting, doing what should not be done, words of praise, and words of insult.

Vijaya-kumāra: From what is *avahitthā* (concealment) born?

Gosvāmī: *Avahitthā*, or concealment, is born from treachery, shyness, cleverness, fear, and respect.

Vijaya-kumāra: From what is *smṛti* (remembrance) born?

Gosvāmī: *Smṛti* is firm belief based on previous direct perception.

Vijaya-kumāra: From what is *vitarka* (argumentativeness) born?

Gosvāmī: *Vitarka* is born from melancholy or doubt.

Vijaya-kumāra: From what is *cintā* (anxiety) born?

Gosvāmī: *Cintā* is born from failing to attain what one desires, or attaining what one does not desire.

Vijaya-kumāra: From what is *mati* (thoughtfulness) born?

Gosvāmī: *Mati* is giving thought to understand something.

Vijaya-kumāra: From what is *dhṛti* (endurance) born?

Gosvāmī: *Dhṛti* is steadiness of the mind. It is born from the absence of suffering and the attainment of the best thing.

Vijaya-kumāra: From what is *harṣa* (happiness) born?

Gosvāmī: When, because of seeing or attaining the object of one's desires, one is pleased, that is called *harṣa*.

Vijaya-kumāra: From what is *autsukya* (eagerness) born?

Gosvāmī: *Autsukya* is born from the desire to see or attain the beloved.

Vijaya-kumāra: From what is *augrya* (violence) born?

Gosvāmī: Violence is called *augrya*. As I have already said, it is not manifested in *mādhurya-rasa*.

Vijaya-kumāra: From what is *amarṣa* (haughtiness) born?

Gosvāmī: Inability to tolerate disrespect and insult is called *amarṣa*.

Vijaya-kumāra: From what is *asūyā* (envy) born?

Gosvāmī: *Asūyā* is hatred of another person's good fortune. It comes from good fortune and virtue.

Vijaya-kumāra: From what is *cāpalya* (impudence) born?

Gosvāmī: Lightness of the mind is called *cāpalya*. It is born from attraction and revulsion.

Vijaya-kumāra: From what is *nidrā* (dizziness) born?

Gosvāmī: *Nidrā* is born from exhaustion.

Vijaya-kumāra: What is *supti* (sleepiness)?

Gosvāmī: *Supti* is sleepiness.

Vijaya-kumāra: What is *bodha* (alertness)?

Gosvāmī: *Bodha* is the opposite of sleepiness.

O Bābā Vijaya-kumāra, all these *vyabhicārīs* are manifested in four ways: 1. *utpatti*, 2. *sandhi*, 3. *śābalya* and 4. *śānti*. When two *bhāvas* join together, that is called *bhāva-sandhi*. When two different manifestations of one kind of *bhāva* join together, that is called *svarūpa-sandhi*. When different kinds of *bhāvas* join together, that is called *bhinna-sandhi*. When many different *bhāvas* are mixed together, that is called '*bhāva-śābalya*. When a *bhāva* disappears, that is called *bhāva-śānti*.

Thus hearing about the *vibhāvas*, *anubhāvas*, *sāttvika-bhāvas*, and *vyabhicārī-bhāvas* of *mādhurya-rasa*, Vijaya-kumāra could understand the *sāmagrīs* (ingredients) of this *rasa*. His heart became plunged in *prema* (pure love). Still, he thought he had no *prema*.

Falling at His spiritual master's lotus feet, and weeping and weeping, he said, "O master, why is my heart not plunged in *prema*? Please be merciful and tell me."

Gopāla-guru Gosvāmī replied, "Come tomorrow and I will teach you about *prema*. You have understood the *sāmagrīs* (ingredients) of *prema*. But *prema* is still not openly manifested in your heart. The *prema* that is the same as *sthāyi-bhāva* you have heard from me in a general way. When you hear how *prema* is manifested in *mādhurya-rasa*, you will attain all perfection."

After speaking these words, Gopāla-guru Gosvāmī embraced Vijaya-kumāra. Vijaya-kumāra offered *daṇḍavat* obeisances and then he returned to his own residence.

Chapter Thirty-six

Mādhurya-rasa, part six

Today, Vijaya-kumāra came at the appointed time and offered *daṇḍavat* obeisances to Śrī Gopāla-guru Gosvāmī. Seeing that today Vijaya-kumāra was very eager to learn about *sthāyi-bhāva*, the spiritual master began to speak.

Gosvāmī: The *sthāyi-bhāva* of *mādhurya-rasa* is *mādhurya-rati*.

Vijaya-kumāra: What causes *mādhurya-rati* to become manifested?

Gosvāmī: *Mādhurya-rati* is manifested from *abhiyoga*, *viṣaya*, *sambandha*, *abhimāna*, *tadīya-viśeṣa*, *upamā*, and *svabhāva*. Each item in this list is better than the preceding item. In this way, the *rati* that is manifested from *svabhāva* is the best of the *ratis*.

Vijaya-kumāra: What is *abhiyoga*?

Gosvāmī: To openly reveal one's love (*bhāva*) is called *abhiyoga*. One may make the revelation personally, or another person may do it.

Vijaya-kumāra: What is *viṣaya*?

Gosvāmī: The five *viṣayas* are sound, touch, form, taste, and fragrance.

Vijaya-kumāra: What is *sambandha*?

Gosvāmī: The four glorious *sambandhas* are family, beauty, virtue, and pastimes.

Vijaya-kumāra: What is *abhimāna*?

Gosvāmī: When, given the choice of many beautiful and pleasing objects, a person conclusively chooses one and one alone, demanding, "I want that one," that is called *abhimāna*.

Vijaya-kumāra: What is *tadīya-viśeṣa*?

Gosvāmī: The *tadīya-viśeṣas* are footprints, the land of the cows, and dear friends. In this context, the land of the cows is the land of Vṛndāvana, and the dear friends are the devotees who love Kṛṣṇa deeply.

Vijaya-kumāra: What is *upamā*?

Gosvāmī: When one thing is somewhat like another, that is called *upamā*.

Vijaya-kumāra: What is *svabhāva*?

Gosvāmī: The nature that manifests spontaneously, without any external cause, is called *svabhāva*. *Svabhāva* is of two kinds: *nisarga* and *svarūpa*.

Vijaya-kumāra: What is *nisarga*?

Gosvāmī: A habit born from repetition is called *nisarga*. Qualities, form, and hearing are included among the causes of *nisarga*. The meaning here is that when the soul again and again acts in a certain way, after many births, he develops a habit, which is called *nisarga*. Therefore, if, when hearing about Lord Kṛṣṇa's qualities and form, a person suddenly and passionately falls in love (*bhāva*) with Kṛṣṇa, that love is caused not by the immediate circumstances, but by repeated past devotional activities (*nisarga*).

Vijaya-kumāra: What is *svarūpa*?

Gosvāmī: What is unborn, beginningless, and self-perfect is called *svarūpa*. *Svarūpa* is of three kinds: 1 *kṛṣṇa-niṣṭhā* (faith in Kṛṣṇa), *lalanā-niṣṭhā* (faith in the *gopīs*), and *ubhaya-niṣṭhā* (faith in both Kṛṣṇa and the *gopīs*). Persons of demonic nature do not attain *kṛṣṇa-niṣṭhā*. On the other hand, persons of godly nature easily attain it. Persons who are spiritual enlightened can attain *lalanā-niṣṭhā*. Sometimes, even without seeing or hearing of Kṛṣṇa's form and other features, a person suddenly develops intense love for Him. When one has both *kṛṣṇa-niṣṭhā* and *lalanā-niṣṭhā*—that is called *ubhaya-niṣṭhā*.

Vijaya-kumāra: Is every aspect of *mādhurya-rasa* manifested from the seven causes—*abhiyoga*, *viṣaya*, *sambandha*, *abhimāna*, *tadīya-viśeṣa*, *upamā*, and *svabhāva*?

Gosvāmī: The beautiful girls of Gokula love Kṛṣṇa with a love that is part of their own nature (*svabhāva*), a love that is naturally perfect (*svarūpa-siddha*), a love that is not caused by the seven causes that begin with *abhiyoga*. Rather, their love is caused by various pastimes. However, for the *sādhana-siddha* (who attained perfection by engaging in *sādhana-bhakti*) and *nisarga-siddha-sādhaka* (who are still striving to attain perfection) devotees, the seven causes that begin with *abhiyoga* do indeed inspire love for Kṛṣṇa.

Vijaya-kumāra: One or two examples here would be very pleasing to the heart.

Gosvāmī: This kind of love is attained by practicing *rāgānuga-bhakti*. It cannot be attained by *vaidhī-bhakti*. This kind of love stays far away from a person who practices *vaidhī-bhakti*. When a devotee engaged in *sādhana-bhakti* sees the loving service that the beautiful girls of Vraja offer to Lord Kṛṣṇa, and when that devotee yearns to serve Kṛṣṇa in the same way, then the previously mentioned causes, with *priya-jana* (the dear friends of Kṛṣṇa) especially prominent and now numbering only six because *svabhāva* is not present here, become the causes of his ecstatic love for Kṛṣṇa. In this way, the devotee gradually attains *rati* (spiritual love). When the devotee attains the stage of *sādhana-siddha*, then he may attain *lalanā-niṣṭhā*.

Vijaya-kumāra: What are the different kinds of *rati*?

Gosvāmī: There are three kinds of *rati*: 1 *sādhāraṇi* (ordinary), 2 *samañjasā* (proper) and 3 *samarthā* (perfect). Kubjā is an example of *sādhāraṇi-rati*. She yearned for her own person enjoyment in Kṛṣṇa's company. Therefore, her love is of an inferior nature. The Dvārakā queens' love is *samañjasā* (proper). And, why not? They enjoyed Kṛṣṇa's company within the religious institution of marriage. The love of the Gokula goddesses, the *gopīs*, is *samarthā*. It exists in a plane above the ordinary activities of the world and the ordinary rules of religion. This *samarthā* love is not improper (*asamañjasā*). Rather, because is has the power to bring the highest goal of life, it is the most proper (*ati-samañjasā*). *Sādhāraṇi* love is like a jewel, *samañjasā* love is like a *cintāmaṇi* jewel, and *samarthā* love, which has no equal, is like a Kaustubha jewel.

Vijaya-kumāra: (weeping and weeping) What a wonderful description this is! I wish to learn more about *sādhāraṇi-rati*.

Gosvāmī: When, by directly seeing Kṛṣṇa, a person yearns to enjoy in His company, and in this way feels a love that is not yet very intense, that love is called *sādhāraṇi*. Because that love is not yet very intense, the desire for one's own enjoyment is still present within it. When the desire for personal enjoyment becomes dwarfed, then what remains to dwarf the growth of real love?

Vijaya-kumāra: What is *samañjasā-rati*?

Gosvāmī: When, by hearing the qualities of Kṛṣṇa, a girl yearns to become His wife, her intense love is called *samañjasā*. Still, in this love, there is sometimes the desire for personal enjoyment. However, without this desire, the wife will not be under Kṛṣṇa's dominion.

Vijaya-kumāra: What is *samarthā* love?

Gosvāmī: In *rati* the desire for enjoyment is always present. In *sādhāraṇi-rati* and *samañjasā-rati*, the devotee desires her personal enjoyment. When the desire for enjoyment is completely free for the desire for one's own personal enjoyment, and one desires only the enjoyment of the beloved, that kind of love is called *samarthā*.

Vijaya-kumāra: What is that like? Please explain and make it more clearly understood.

Gosvāmī: The desire for enjoyment is of two kinds. One kind is the desire that the beloved will please my own senses. The other kind is the desire that I will please the senses of my beloved. The first kind of desire is called *kāma* (lust). And, why not? In that situation one is eager only for his own happiness. In the second kind of desire one is eager for the happiness and well-being of the beloved. That desire is the desire of love (*prema*). In *sādhāraṇi* love, the desire for personal enjoyment is strong. In *samañjasā* love, that desire is not strong. In *samarthā* love, the desire for enjoyment is of a different nature. It is, as I have already said, the desire that the beloved should enjoy.

Vijaya-kumāra: In loving affairs, the touch of the beloved inevitably brings pleasure. How is it possible that in *samarthā* love, this pleasure is not desired?

Gosvāmī: That desire is inevitably difficult to stop. Still, in *samarthā* love, that desire of the heart is very weak. In this kind of love, the desire to please the beloved is very strong. That desire then embraces the desire for personal enjoyment and in that embrace, both desires become one. Because this is the strongest (*samarthā*) of all kinds of love, it is called *samarthā*.

Vijaya-kumāra: What are the glories of *samarthā* love?

Gosvāmī: Among the seven previously described causes, beginning with *abhiyoga*, *sambandha* may be manifested, or *tadīya-viśeṣa* may be manifested, or *svarūpa* may be manifested, and in this way, *samarthā* love may come into being. Or, forgetting all these, this very powerful love may come into being by itself.

Vijaya-kumāra: How do the desire for personal enjoyment and the desire that the beloved should enjoy join and become a single desire?

Gosvāmī: The beautiful girls of Vraja love Kṛṣṇa with *samarthā* love. They desire only for His happiness. When they associate with Kṛṣṇa, they certainly experience their own happiness. However, they accept only those activities that bring happiness to Kṛṣṇa. Thus, the desire for personal enjoyment and the desire only to please Kṛṣṇa meet in the waves of sublime and wonderful pastimes. In that condition, the desire for personal enjoyment does not exist apart from the desire to please Kṛṣṇa. In this way, the desire for personal enjoyment ceases to exist.

Vijaya-kumāra: Aha! How wonderful is this love! I yearn to hear of its highest glories.

Gosvāmī: When this love (*rati*) matures, it reaches the stage called *mahā-bhāva*. All the liberated souls seek this stage of love. The five kinds of devotees attain it to the degree they are able.

Vijaya-kumāra: O master, I request that you explain the different stages of this love.

Gosvāmī: It is said (*Ujjvala-nīlamaṇi, Sthāyi-bhāva-prakarana*): When *rati* becomes very intense, it is called *prema*. As *prema* gradually manifests its sweetness, it is called *sneha*, *māna*, *pranaya*, *rāga*, *anurāga*, and *bhāva*."

Vijaya-kumāra: O master, please give an example.

Gosvāmī: As there is a progression in sweetness from sugarcane plant, to sugarcane juice, to molasses, to gur, to sugar granules, and to rock candy, so there is a progression in love from *rati* to *prema*, to *sneha*, to *māna*, to *pranaya*, to *rāga*, to *anurāga*, and finally to *bhāva*. The word *bhāva* in this progression refers to *mahā-bhāva*.

Vijaya-kumāra: Why are so many different stages with so many different names grouped under the general heading of *prema*?

Gosvāmī: The six kinds of love, which begin with *sneha*, are all different pastime stages of *prema*. The *paṇḍitas* who are learned in this matter call them all by the name *prema*. In this way, *prema* is manifested.

Vijaya-kumāra: What are the different kinds of *prema*?

Gosvāmī: There are three kinds of prema: 1. *prauḍha* (mature), 2. *madhya* (intermediate) and 3. *manda* (slow).

Vijaya-kumāra: What is *prauḍha-prema*?

Gosvāmī: When the lover is anguished to think her delay may worry her beloved—that is *prauḍha-prema*.

Vijaya-kumāra: What is *madhya-prema*?

Gosvāmī: When the lover is not concerned about the beloved's anguish—

that is *madhya-prema.*

Vijaya-kumāra: What is *manda-prema?*

Gosvāmī: When the lover neither cares nor does not care, that is *manda-prema.* This kind of love can inspire one to create obstacles to stop the exalted love of a rival.

O Vijaya-kumāra, *prauḍha, madhya* and *manda* are thus the three divisions of *prema.* They can also be described in these words: When the lover cannot tolerate the beloved's suffering—that is *prauḍha-prema.* When the lover can tolerate the beloved's suffering—that is *madhya-prema.* When the lover forgets whether the beloved suffers or not—that is *manda-prema.*

Vijaya-kumāra: Now I understand *prema.* What are the characteristics of *sneha?*

Gosvāmī: When it reaches its highest state, *prema* is like a brilliant lamp. This is known as *cit-prema* (spiritual love). When it makes the heart melt, this spiritual prema is called *sneha.* The by-product of *sneha* is that the lover never becomes satiated or disinterested, even if the lover sees the beloved at every moment.

Vijaya-kumāra: Are there different kinds of *sneha*, some better and some lesser?

Gosvāmī: In the lowest kind of *sneha*, the lover's heart melts at the touch of the beloved. In the intermediate kind of *sneha*, the lover's heart melts at the sight of the beloved. In the best kind of *sneha*, the lover's heart melts simply by hearing of the beloved.

Vijaya-kumāra: What are the other different kinds of *sneha?*

Gosvāmī: *Sneha* is also of two kinds: 1. *ghṛta-sneha* (ghee-like love) and *madhu-sneha* (honey love).

Vijaya-kumāra: What is *ghṛta-sneha?*

Gosvāmī: When love is very respectful (*ādara-māyā*) it is called *ghṛta-sneha.* When *ghṛta-sneha* is mixed with *madhu-sneha*, the result is very palatable. *Ghṛta-sneha* is by nature cool. When the respect (*ādara*) is increased (*ghani-bhuta*), this love becomes more intense. It is called *ghṛta-sneha* because it has the qualities of *ghṛta* (ghee).

Vijaya-kumāra: What is respect (*ādara*)?

Gosvāmī: Respect (*ādara*) comes from honoring others (*gaurava*). In this way, respect and honor are interdependent. When love (*rati*) is manifested with them, it is called in this context *sneha*.

Vijaya-kumāra: What is *gaurava* (honor).

Gosvāmī: When one thinks of a person as a *guru*, that is called *gaurava*. From *gaurava* is manifested *sambhrama* (esteem). This is all said to be included within *ādara* (respect). *Ādara* and *gaurava* are interdependent.

Vijaya-kumāra: What is *madhu-sneha*?

Gosvāmī: When the lover thinks, "The beloved is my property," then that is called *madhu-sneha*. Many different *rasas* meet in this sweet love. This love is passionate and therefore it brings warmth. Because this love is sweet (*mādhura*), there it is called *madhu-sneha*.

Vijaya-kumāra: What does it mean to think, "The beloved is my property?"

Gosvāmī: Love is manifested in two ways. In one way, the lover thinks, "I am the property of my beloved." In the other way, the lover thinks, "My beloved is the property of me." In *ghṛta-sneha*, the idea, "I am the property of my beloved," is prominent. In *madhu-sneha*, the idea, "My beloved is the property of me," is prominent. Candrāvalī possesses *ghṛta-sneha*. Rādhā possesses *madhu-sneha*.

Vijaya-kumāra: (after offering *daṇḍavat* obeisances to his spiritual master). What is *māna*?

Gosvāmī: When *sneha* becomes exalted and manifests a new kind of sweetness, the lover manifests various crooked dealings with the beloved. That is called *māna*.

Vijaya-kumāra: What are the different kinds of *māna*?

Gosvāmī: There are two kinds of *māna*: 1 *udātta* and 2 *lalitā*.

Vijaya-kumāra: What is *udātta-māna*?

Gosvāmī: It is of two kinds. In one kind, the lover is straightforward, open, and free of diplomacy. In the other kind, the lover engages in concealment and crooked diplomacy. *Udātta-māna* is manifested in *ghṛta-sneha*.

Vijaya-kumāra: What is *lalitā-māna*? I cannot say why, but somehow I feel attracted to it.

Gosvāmī: *Lalitā-māna* is of two kinds. In *kauṭilya-lalitā-māna* there is independence and crookedness. In *narma-lalitā-māna* there are joking words. Both kinds of *lalitā-māna* are manifested in *madhu-sneha*.

Vijaya-kumāra: What is *praṇaya*?

Gosvāmī: When the lover trusts the beloved and feels one at heart with the beloved—that is called *praṇaya*.

Vijaya-kumāra: What does trust (*viśrambha*) mean in this situation?

Gosvāmī: The real nature of *praṇaya* is trust, which is called *viśrambha*. *Viśrambha* is of two kinds: 1. *maitra* and 2. *sakhya*. *Viśrambha* means "firm trust." This trust is not merely the secondary cause of *praṇaya*. It is the original cause of it, the very ingredient of which it is made.

Vijaya-kumāra: What is *maitra-viśrambha*?

Gosvāmī: When *viśrambha* is joined with humility—that is called *maitra*.

Vijaya-kumāra: What is *sakhya-viśrambha*?

Gosvāmī: When the lover is free from all fear, and convinced that the beloved is completely under the lover's control, that is called *sakhya-viśrambha*.

Vijaya-kumāra: Please clearly explain how *praṇaya*, *sneha*, and *māna* are related to each other.

Gosvāmī: In some situations, *sneha* gives birth to *praṇaya*, and from *praṇaya*, *māna* is manifested. In other situations, *sneha* gives birth to *māna* and from *māna*, *praṇaya* is manifested. Therefore, *māna* and *praṇaya* may assume both roles of either cause or effect.

Viśrambha requires a separate explanation. *Udātta* and *lalitā* exist in both *maitra* and *sakhya*. However, in *sakhya*, they are also called *su-maitra* and *su-sakhya*.

Vijaya-kumāra: What is *rāga*?

Gosvāmī: When *praṇaya* becomes exalted, even great suffering is considered happiness. That stage of *praṇaya* is called *rāga*.

Vijaya-kumāra: What are the different kinds of *rāga*?

Gosvāmī: There are two kinds: 1. *nīlimā-rāga* and 2. *raktimā-rāga*.

Vijaya-kumāra: How many kinds of *nīlimā-rāga* are there?

Gosvāmī: There are two kinds of *nīlimā-rāga*: 1. *nīlī-rāga* and 2. *śyāma-rāga*.

Vijaya-kumāra: What is *nīlī-rāga*?

Gosvāmī: In this *rāga* there is no possibility of loss or destruction. Externally, there is a great display of the glory and love concealed within the heart. That is *nīlī-rāga*. Candrāvalī manifests this *rāga* before Lord Kṛṣṇa.

Vijaya-kumāra: What is *śyāma-rāga*?

Gosvāmī: When the beloved's delay makes the worried lover water the forest plants with a stream of tears—that is called *śyāma-rāga*.

Vijaya-kumāra: How many kinds of *raktimā-rāga* are there?"

Gosvāmī: *Raktimā-rāga* is of two kinds: 1. *kusumbha* and 2. *mañjiṣṭhā*.

Vijaya-kumāra: What is *kusumbha-rāga*?

Gosvāmī: When the other *rāgas* manifest their beauty and glory—that is called *kusumbha-rāga*'. *Kusumbha-rāga* rests in a particular object. When it mixes with *mañjiṣṭhā-rāga*, it produces withering and melancholy in a *gopī* who loves Kṛṣṇa (*kṛṣṇa-praṇayī*).

Vijaya-kumāra: What is *mañjiṣṭhā-rāga*?

Gosvāmī: The eternal, unchanging, unalloyed, eternally very glorious love that Śrī Śrī Rādhā and Mādhava feel for each other is called *mañjiṣṭhā-rāga*. The final conclusion is that *ghṛta*, *sneha*, *udātta*, *maitra*, *su-maitra*, *nīlimā*, and other such *bhāvas* that have been described here are manifested in Candrāvalī and by the queens, headed by Rukmiṇī.

On the other hand, *madhu*, *sneha*, *lalitā*, *sakhya*, *su-sākhya*, *raktimā*, and other such *bhāvas* are manifested in Śrī Rādhā. Sometimes they are also seen in Satyabhāmā. I have already explained that the beautiful girls of Vraja are divided into many rival (*sva-pakṣa* and *vipakṣa*) groups. In this way, there is much dissension among them. When they relate to the other *bhāvas*, these create many different features. Only *paṇḍitas* who are learned in this particular topic can understand all this. In other words, I will not give a more elaborate explanation of it.

Vijaya-kumāra: To which *bhāvas* does the phrase, "the other *bhāvas*" refer?

Gosvāmī: It refers to *sthāyi-mādhura-bhāva*, the thirty-three *vyabhicārī-*

bhāvas, and the seven *bhāvas* that begin with *hāsya*. Thus, it refers to forty-one *bhāvas*. These are the other *bhāvas* referred to here.

Vijaya-kumāra: Now I understand *rāga*. Please explain *anurāga*.

Gosvāmī: The *rāga* that is always newer and newer and makes the beloved newer and newer at every moment is called *anurāga*.

Vijaya-kumāra: What is the glorious wonder that this *rāga* manifests?

Gosvāmī: It brings the lover under the beloved's control and the beloved under the lover's control. It creates *prema-vaicittya*. It makes one yearn to take birth even as a very lowly being (if that birth is within the holy abode is Śrī Vṛndāvana). It is limitless and most exalted. It makes Kṛṣṇa present even when the devotee is separated from Him.

Vijaya-kumāra: I can easily understand how *anurāga* brings the lover and beloved under each other's control, and how it makes one yearn to take birth as a tree or other lowly being (within the holy abode of Śrī Vṛndāvana). But, O master what is *prema-vaicittya*?

Gosvāmī: *Prema-vaicittya* is the love the devotee feels in separation from Kṛṣṇa. You will learn about that later.

Vijaya-kumāra: Now please describe *mahā-bhāva*.

Gosvāmī: O Vijaya-kumāra, I am a very insignificant person. I am not really qualified to describe the wonders of the *rasas* of Vraja. Whatever Śrīla Rūpa Gosvāmī and Śrīla Paṇḍita Gosvāmī have mercifully taught me, I will now reveal to you. Please consider it their mercy upon you.

Vijaya-kumāra: O master, I, the asker of questions, am very fallen and unintelligent. Please explain *mahā-bhāva* so that even my heart can understand it.

Gosvāmī: Śrī Rādhā is the *āśrayā* of *anurāga* and Lord Kṛṣṇa is the *viṣaya*. Śrī Kṛṣṇa, who is the son of Nanda, is the *viṣaya* in *mādhurya-rasa*. Śrī Rādhā is the *āśrayā*. *Anurāga* is the *sthāyi-bhāva*. When that *anurāga* reaches its highest, most glorious stage, it is called *mahā-bhāva*.

Vijaya-kumāra: Aha! *Mahā-bhāva*! *Mahā-bhāva*! Today I can understand something of *mahā-bhāva*. The highest point of all the *bhāvas* is *mahā-bhāva*. Please place on my ears an example of *mahā-bhāva*.

Gosvāmī: O Vijaya-kumāra, you are very fortunate. The following verse is an example of *mahā-bhāva*: Vṛndā-devī said to Lord Kṛṣṇa: O regal elephant, who wanders in the jungles and mountains, Your amorous pastimes have shaken away Rādhā's sadness in separation from You. With the red color of ever-new love, the artist of Your amorous pastimes paints a glorious picture in the palace of the world.

Vijaya-kumāra: Where does *mahā-bhāva* reside?

Gosvāmī: *Mahā-bhāva* does not reside in the Dvārakā queens. It resides only in the *gopīs*, the goddesses of Vraja.

Vijaya-kumāra: What does all this mean?

Gosvāmī: When the lover and beloved are bound by ties of marriage, the relationship is *svakīya-rasa*, and the love is *samañjasā*. In this situation, *samarthā* love, which brings the possibility of *mahā-bhāva*, is not present. In Vraja, although *svakīya-rasa* is also present, *parakīya-rasa* predominates. In the highest stage of *parakīya-rasa*, *samarthā* love, *mahā-bhāva* is manifested.

Vijaya-kumāra: How many are the different kinds of *mahā-bhāva*?

Gosvāmī: When it appears, *mahā-bhāva* floods the heart with nectar. *Mahā-bhāva* is of two kinds: 1. *rūḍha* and 2. *adhirūḍha*.

Vijaya-kumāra: What is *rūḍha mahā bhāva*?

Gosvāmī: When all the *sāttvika-bhāvas* shine very brightly, that is *rūḍha mahā-bhāva*.

Vijaya-kumāra: Please describe the *anubhāvas* in *mahā-bhāva*.

Gosvāmī: Inability to tolerate the eye's natural activity of blinking, agitating the hearts of those nearby, thinking a *kalpa* to be as long as a moment, worrying that Kṛṣṇa may be suffering, even when it is obvious that He is happy, forgetting everything, thinking a moment to be as long as a *kalpa*, and although they are not bewildered, they forget everything about themselves. These anu*bhāvas* are present in both meeting the beloved (*sambhoga*) and separation from the beloved (*vipralambha*).

Vijaya-kumāra: What is the inability to tolerate the eye's natural activity of blinking?

Gosvāmī: In this *bhāva*, the feeling of separation (*vipralambha*) is present in meeting (*sambhoga*). Here, the lover is unable to tolerate even a brief moment's separation from the beloved. At Kurukṣetra, the Vraja *gopīs* cursed the creator, Brahmā, for creating eyelashes that impeded their always seeing Kṛṣṇa. And, why not? The blinking of their eyelashes became an obstacle that stopped them from seeing Kṛṣṇa for a moment.

Vijaya-kumāra: What does it mean—agitating the hearts of those nearby?

Gosvāmī: When they saw the *gopīs*' ecstatic love, the kings and queens present at Kurukṣetra felt deeply moved at heart.

Vijaya-kumāra: What is thinking a *kalpa* to be as long as a moment?

Gosvāmī: The *rasa* dance lasted for an entire night of Brahmā. Still, the *gopīs* thought it lasted for only a moment.

Vijaya-kumāra: What does it mean—worrying that Kṛṣṇa may be suffering, even when it is obvious that He is happy?

Gosvāmī: In *Śrīmad-Bhāgavatam* (10.31.19), the *gopīs* worry that Kṛṣṇa will suffer if He places His lotus feet on their hard breasts.

Vijaya-kumāra: What does it mean—although they are not bewildered, they forget everything about themselves'?

Gosvāmī: Because Kṛṣṇa is always present before them, they are not bewildered. However, when Kṛṣṇa is present, they forget everything about their own bodies and about everything else in the material world.

Vijaya-kumāra: What is thinking a moment to be as long as a *kalpa*?

Gosvāmī: Kṛṣṇa said to Uddhava: "When I was with the *gopīs* in Vṛndāvana, all the nights seemed to pass like half a moment. But now that I am separated from them, every night seems like a *kalpa*." This is an example of thinking a moment to be as long as a *kalpa*?

Vijaya-kumāra: Now I understand the *rūḍha-bhāvas*. Please describe the *adhirūḍha-bhāvas*.

Gosvāmī: When these *rūḍha-bhāva anubhāvas* I have just described become very wonderful, they become the *adhirūḍha-bhāvas*.

Vijaya-kumāra: How many kinds of *adhirūḍha-bhāva* are there?

Gosvāmī: There are two kinds: 1. *modana* and 2. *mādana*.

Vijaya-kumāra: What is *modana*?

Gosvāmī: When Rādhā and Kṛṣṇa both feel *adhirūḍha-bhāva*, and when They both manifest all the *sāttvika-bhāvas* with the most brilliant glory, that is called *modana*. In *modana-bhāva*, Rādhā and Kṛṣṇa both become very agitated. This condition is the highest good fortune of spiritual love manifested among the *gopī* lovers of Lord Kṛṣṇa.

Vijaya-kumāra: Where does *modana-bhāva* reside?

Gosvāmī: *Modana-bhāva* does not reside outside of Śrī Rādhā's group. *Modana-bhāva* is manifested in the very dear pastimes of the *hlādinī-śakti*. When the lovers are separated, *modana* gives birth to *mohana*. When there is great distress because of separation, the *sāttvika-bhāvas* are very brilliantly manifest.

Vijaya-kumāra: Please describe the *anubhāvas* of *mohana*?

Gosvāmī: Embraced by His beloved, Kṛṣṇa falls unconscious. Although she suffers unbearably, a *gopī* still thinks only of how Kṛṣṇa will be happy. Thirsting for the touch of Kṛṣṇa, a *gopī* becomes mad and decides to commit suicide, thus filling the spiritual and material worlds with anxiety and making the nearby animals weep. *Mohana-bhāva* is possible in Śrī Rādhā, the queen of Vṛndāvana. These *mohana vyabhicārī-bhāvas* are not present in anyone but Rādhā.

Vijaya-kumāra: O master, if you think it is right, then please describe *divyonmāda* (transcendental madness).

Gosvāmī: When it enters a certain indescribable state, *mohana-bhāva* becomes like a bewildered condition. This very surprising and wonderful state is called *divyonmāda*. This state has many different divisions, such as *udghūrṇā* (agitation) and *citra-jalpa* (surprising talk).

Vijaya-kumāra: What is *udghūrṇā*?

Gosvāmī: Many different kinds of activities can be called *udghūrṇā*. When Kṛṣṇa went to Mathurā, Śrī Rādhā manifested *udghūrṇā*.

Vijaya-kumāra: What is *citra-jalpa*?

Gosvāmī: Seeing one of the beloved's friends, with wonderful anger, the lover harshly expresses her anxiety and longing. This is called *citra-jalpa*.

Vijaya-kumāra: What are the different kinds of *citra-jalpa*?

Gosvāmī: The ten kinds of *citra-jalpa* are: 1. *prajalpa*, 2. *parijapita*, 3. *vijalpa*, 4. *ujjalpa*, 5. *sañjalpa*, 6. *avajalpa*, 7. *abhijalpa*, 8. *ājalpa*, 9. *pratijalpa*, and 10. *sujalpa*. All these different kinds of *citra-jalpa* are manifested in the

Bhramara-gītā chapter of *Śrīmad-Bhāgavatam's* Tenth Canto.

Vijaya-kumāra: What is *prajalpa*?

Gosvāmī: *Citra-jalpa* has numberless wonderful forms. Therefore, it is very difficult to describe it with any kind of completeness. When the lover spitefully, maliciously, and passionately insults the beloved—that is called *prajalpa*.

Vijaya-kumāra: What is *parijalpita*?

Gosvāmī: When the lover claims that the beloved, who is the master of her heart, is merciless, crooked, and fickle—that is called *parijalpita*.

Vijaya-kumāra: What is *vijalpa*?

Gosvāmī: When, in the heart, one honors and loves Kṛṣṇa, although externally one casts spiteful glances and speaks spiteful words—that is called *vijalpa*.

Vijaya-kumāra: What is *ujjalpa*?

Gosvāmī: When the lover angrily, arrogantly, and spitefully insults Kṛṣṇa, calling Him a rake and a rogue—that is called *ujjalpa*.

Vijaya-kumāra: What is *sañjalpa*?

Gosvāmī: When the lover mocks Kṛṣṇa with many sarcastic words and asserts that Kṛṣṇa is ungrateful—that is called *sañjalpa*.

Vijaya-kumāra: What is *avajalpa*?

Gosvāmī: When the lover says that because Kṛṣṇa is harsh, lusty, and crooked, she is afraid of what loving Kṛṣṇa may bring—that is called *avajalpa*.

Vijaya-kumāra: What is *abhijalpa*?

Gosvāmī: When the lover says, "It is foolish and useless to fall in love with Kṛṣṇa. He is so cruel, he tortures even the innocent birds," these crooked words are called *abhijalpa*.

Vijaya-kumāra: What is *ajalpa*?

Gosvāmī: When the lover, filled with disgust, declares, "Kṛṣṇa is crooked and deceptive. He only gives us pain. We should stop talking of Him and instead talk about something else, something more pleasant," that is called *ajalpa*.

Vijaya-kumāra: What is *pratijalpa*?

Gosvāmī: When the lover declares, "Kṛṣṇa is a highwayman in loving affairs. He is a rake who likes to enjoy pastimes with many girls. Therefore, he should not come anywhere near me," that is called *pratijalpa*.

Vijaya-kumāra: What is *sujalpa*?

Gosvāmī: When the lover sincerely, deeply, humbly, and restlessly asks many questions about Kṛṣṇa—that is called *sujalpa*.

Vijaya-kumāra: O master, am I qualified to understand *madana*?

Gosvāmī: When the most exalted love of the *hlādinī-śakti*, a love that is the best of all the *bhāvas*, is splendidly manifested—that is called *madana*. *Madana-bhāva* is eternally manifested in Śrī Rādhā.

Vijaya-kumāra: Does envy exist in *madana-bhāva*?

Gosvāmī: Envy is very prominent in *madana-bhāva*. It is seen that even inanimate objects are envied. Again, sometimes, it is seen that words of praise are offered to all who have a relationship with Kṛṣṇa. Words describing envy of Kṛṣṇa's flute and words praising the Pulinda girls may be cited as examples here.

Vijaya-kumāra: At what stage is *madana* seen?

Gosvāmī: The wonderful *madana-bhāva* is manifested when the lovers meet and enjoy pastimes together. *Madana-bhāva* is manifest in thousands of ways in the eternal pastimes.

Vijaya-kumāra: O master, do the great sages give a description of *madana-bhāva*?

Gosvāmī: *Madana-rasa* is limitless. Even Lord Kṛṣṇa Himself could not understand everything about the spiritual *madana-rasa*. The great sage, Śukadeva Gosvāmī, found himself unable to describe it completely. The *rasa-ācārya*, Bhārata Muni, and many others were also unable to properly describe *madana-rasa*.

Vijaya-kumāra: What wonderful things have I heard! Even Lord Kṛṣṇa Himself, the enjoyer of *madana-rasa*, cannot understand it completely. Why is that?

Gosvāmī: Lord Kṛṣṇa is *rasa* personified. He is limitless, all-knowing, and all-powerful. Nothing is unknown by Him, unattainable for Him, or impossible for Him to do. He is inconceivably and simultaneously one and different from the *rasas*. He is each *rasa* and He is all *rasas*. He accepts each *rasa*. In this way, He is *ātmārāma* (the enjoyer of the spiritual *rasas*). Nothing in the *rasas* is apart from Him. He is present in all the *rasas* simultaneously.

Aside from Kṛṣṇa's own (*ātmā*) *rasa*, there is also the *rasa* of others (*parā*). Both these kinds of *rasas* bring the experience of the happiness of spiritual pastimes. When the *rasa* of others (*parā*) is manifest in its highest stage, it is called *parakīya-rasa*. This highest stage is manifested in all its glory in the land of Vṛndāvana. When the *ātmā-rasa* (*svakīya-rasa*) is completely unknown, and only *parakīya-rasa* is known, that is the highest stage of *madana-rasa*. In this way, *madana-rasa* is purely manifested in the Lord's *aprakaṭa* (invisible to material eyes) pastimes in Goloka. It is also manifested in the land of Vraja, situated in the material world.

Vijaya-kumāra: O master, your mercy to me has no limit. I request that you please give a summary of the whole *mādhurya-rasa*.

Gosvāmī: The various *bhāvas* manifested by the Vraja *gopīs* are all spiritual, beyond the touch of the material world. They are beyond the understanding of material logic. Therefore, the human intelligence cannot describe them completely. I have heard in the scriptures that Śrī Rādhā's *rāga* (love) for Kṛṣṇa was manifested even in Her *pūrva-rāga* (the beginnings of love). From this *rāga* came the *anurāga*, *sneha*. From that came *māna* and *praṇaya*. These topics cannot be understood completely. In *sādhāraṇi-rati* is manifested *dhūmāyitā*. *Sneha*, *māna*, *praṇaya*, *rāga* and *anurāga* are manifested in *samañjasā-rati*. From that comes splendid *dīpta-rati*. Then, are manifested *rūḍha*, *uddīpta*, *modana*, and *sudīpta-rati*. Please know that this is merely a general summary. And, why not? There may be exceptions according to time, place, and object. *Sādhāraṇi-rati* culminates in *prema*. *Samañjasā-rati* culminates in *anurāga*. *Samarthā-rati* culminates in *mahā-bhāva*.

Vijaya-kumāra: What is the extent of *rati* in *sākhya-rasa*?

Gosvāmī: The highest stage of the *narma-sakhās* is *anurāga*. However, Subala and some others among them attain *mahā-bhāva*.

Vijaya-kumāra: You have already described *sthāyi-bhāva*. *Sthāyi-bhāva* culminates in *mahā-bhāva*. Why are different *rasas* seen in *sthāyi-bhāva*, even though it has only one nature?

Gosvāmī: *Sthāyi-bhāva* is manifested in the different *rasas*. The secret activities of *sthāyi-bhāva* are not openly manifested. When there is contact with the *sāmagrīs*, then the different *rasas* may be seen. The appropriate *sāmagrīs* are manifested in *sthāyi-bhāva*.

Vijaya-kumāra: Are *svakīya-rasa* and *parakīya-rasa* both eternally manifested in *mādhurya-rasa*?

Gosvāmī: Yes. *Svakīya* and *parakīya* are both eternal. The difference between them is not merely a material designation. If the difference between them were material, the *mādhurya-rasa* and the other *rasas* would all be material in nature. The *rasas* are eternal and they are manifested eternally. In the *rasas*, there are *ruci* (attraction to Kṛṣṇa), *bhajana* (service to Kṛṣṇa), and *prāpti* (attainment of Kṛṣṇa). *Svakīya-rasa* is also present in Vraja. In that *rasa*, the devotee thinks of Kṛṣṇa as her husband. In that *rasa*, *ruci*, *sādhana* (spiritual practice), *bhajana*, and *prāpti* are all manifested. The *svakīya-rasa* manifest in Dvārakā is the same as that of Vaikuṇṭha. However, please know that the *svakīya-rasa* of Vraja is different from the *rasas* of Goloka. In other words, Lord Kṛṣṇa, the master of Vraja, resides in the highest portion of the Vaikuṇṭha world.

With great love, Vijaya-kumāra offered *daṇḍavat* obeisances and returned to his residence.

Chapter Thirty-seven

Śṛṅgāra-rasa (Mādhurya-rasa)

Jaiva-dharma

Again and again relishing the sweetness of the *bhāvas*, Vijaya-kumāra offered *daṇḍavat* obeisances to his spiritual master's lotus feet. He asked, "O master, I have understood *vibhāva*, *anubhāva*, *sāttvika-bhāva*, and *vyabhicārī-bhāva*. I have also understood *sthāyi-bhāva*. However, the *rasa* that comes from the meeting of the *sthāyi-bhāva* with the previously described four ingredients has not yet manifested within me. Why is that?"

Gosvāmī: O Vijaya-kumāra, you should understand about the *rasa* called *śṛṅgāra-rasa*. Only then will you be able to understand the sweetness of *sthāyi-bhāva*.

Vijaya-kumāra: What is *śṛṅgāra-rasa*?

Gosvāmī: When *mādhurya-rasa* becomes very beautiful, it is called *śṛṅgāra-rasa*. This *rasa* is of two kinds: 1. *vipralambha* (separation) and 2. *sambhoga* (enjoyment).

Vijaya-kumāra: I wish to learn about *vipralambha*.

Gosvāmī: Whether they meet or not, the two youthful lovers yearn to embrace and enjoy many pastimes. When these desires remain unfulfilled, their love (*bhāva*) becomes very great. This most intense emotional state, which makes the happiness of meeting all the greater, is called *vipralambha*. The word *vipralambha* means parting (*virāha*) or separation (*viyoga*).

Vijaya-kumāra: How does *vipralambha* make the happiness of *sambhoga* (meeting) greater?

Gosvāmī: When a red cloth is placed again into red dye, the cloth is made even redder. In the same way, *vipralambha* increases the enjoyment of the lovers when they finally meet. Without *vipralambha*, the enjoyment of *sambhoga* does not become increased.

Vijaya-kumāra: What are the different kinds of *vipralambha*?

Gosvāmī: There are four kinds of *vipralambha*: 1. *pūrva-rāga*, 2. *māna*, 3. *prema-vaicittya*, and 4. *pravāsa*.

Vijaya-kumāra: What is *pūrva-rāga*?

Gosvāmī: Before the young lovers meet, they may somehow see each other, hear of each other, or in some other way come to know of each other. When, by these activities, they become attracted to each other and begin to fall in love—that is called *pūrva-rāga*.

Vijaya-kumāra: What are the different ways they may see each other?

Gosvāmī: The lover may see Kṛṣṇa directly, see a picture of Him, or see Him in a dream. These ways of seeing Him are called *darśana.*

Vijaya-kumāra: What are the different ways they may hear of each other?

Gosvāmī: They may hear from the mouth of a poet reciting prayers, from the mouth of a *gopī* friend, from the mouth of a *gopī* messenger, from a song, or in some other way. That is called *śravaṇa.*

Vijaya-kumāra: What causes them to be attracted and fall in love (*rati*).

Gosvāmī: I have already described the many causes of *rati*, causes that begin with *abhiyoga.* These are said to be the causes in *pūrva-rāga* also.

Vijaya-kumāra: Who attains *pūrva-rāga* first: Kṛṣṇa or the *gopīs*?

Gosvāmī: This may be considered in different ways. In the material world, women are shy and posses other feminine qualities. For this reason, it is the man who pursues the woman. However, it is also said that women are naturally more attracted to the affairs of love and therefore, doe-eyed women feel *pūrva-rāga* first. In the *Bhakti-śāstra* it is said that the devotee feels *pūrva-rāga* first, and the Supreme Personality of Godhead feels *pūrva-rāga* afterward. Therefore, it is said that the Vraja *gopīs* feel *pūrva-rāga* most intensely, and they feel it first.

Vijaya-kumāra: What are the *vyabhicārī-bhāvas* in *pūrva-rāga*?

Gosvāmī: Included among the *vyabhicārī-bhāvas* in *pūrva-rāga* are: disease, doubt, envy, fatigue, disappointment, eagerness, humility, anxiety, dizziness, alertness, lamentation, inertness, madness, confusion, and death.

Vijaya-kumāra: How many different kinds of *pūrva-rāga* are there?

Gosvāmī: There are three kinds of *pūrva-rāga*: 1. *prauḍhā*, 2. *samañjasā* and 3. *sādhāraṇa.*

Vijaya-kumāra: What is *prauḍhā-pūrva-rāga*?

Gosvāmī: When it is manifested in *samarthā-rati*, *pūrva-rāga* is manifested as *prauḍhā-pūrva-rāga.* In this kind of *pūrva-rāga*, yearning, death, and other conditions of life are manifested. The *vyabhicārī-bhāvas* are filled with yearnings.

Vijaya-kumāra: Please describe these different conditions of life.

Gosvāmī: It is said in the *Ujjvala-nīlamaṇi*: Yearning, anxiety, wakefulness, emaciation, being stunned, bewilderment, disease, madness, illusion, and death are the ten conditions present in *pūrva-rāga*.

Vijaya-kumāra: What is yearning?

Gosvāmī: Yearning is an intense desire to attain the beloved. In it, eagerness, restlessness, moving to and fro, sighing, and other such symptoms are manifested.

Vijaya-kumāra: What is anxiety?

Gosvāmī: Anxiety is when the mind is restless. In this condition, there are deep sighs, restlessness, being stunned, worry, tears, becoming pale, perspiring, and other such symptoms.

Vijaya-kumāra: What is wakefulness?

Gosvāmī: Wakefulness is when sleep is destroyed. In this condition, there are being stunned, being withered, being angry, and other such symptoms.

Vijaya-kumāra: What is emaciation?

Gosvāmī: Emaciation is when the body becomes very thin. In this condition, there is weakness, giddiness, and other such symptoms. In some texts, the word *vilāpa* (lamentation) is read here.

Vijaya-kumāra: What is being stunned?

Gosvāmī: Inability to see any difference between what is desirable and what is not desirable, failure to answer questions, and the inability to see or hear are present when one is stunned. Inarticulate sounds made suddenly and for no reason, inertness, long sighs, and bewilderment are also included among the symptoms here.

Vijaya-kumāra: What is bewilderment?

Gosvāmī: The state of being deeply upset and thus unable to cope is called bewilderment. In this condition, there is disappointment, melancholy, envy, and loss of discrimination.

Vijaya-kumāra: What is disease?

Gosvāmī: Disease is when, because of being unable to attain the beloved, one become pale and feverish. In that condition, one yearns for coolness, one is bewildered, one sighs, and one falls to the ground.

Vijaya-kumāra: What is madness?

Gosvāmī: When, in every place, every condition, and every time one is bewildered and says things are other than they actually are—that is called madness. Hatred of the beloved, sighing, blinking of the eyes, and separation from the beloved are included in madness.

Vijaya-kumāra: What is illusion?

Gosvāmī: When the mind acts in a contrary, improper way—that is called illusion. Being motionless and fainting occur in illusion.

Vijaya-kumāra: What is death?

Gosvāmī: When, in spite of all efforts to make Him return, the beloved does not return, the lover, tormented by love, yearns for her own death. She bequeaths to her friends all her favorite things: the bumblebees, the gentle breeze, the moonlight, and the *kadamba* flowers. This is the *anubhāva*.

Vijaya-kumāra: What is *samañjasa-pūrva-rāga*?

Gosvāmī: *Samañjasa-pūrva-rāga* is manifested in *samañjasa-rati*. In it are manifested desire, thoughtfulness, remembrance, glorifying the beloved's virtues, passion, lamentation, madness, disease, being stunned, and death.

Vijaya-kumāra: In this context, what is desire?

Gosvāmī: To yearn for the touch of the beloved is called desire. To attain this desire, the lover decorates herself with ornaments and reveals her passion.

Vijaya-kumāra: In this context, what is thoughtfulness?

Gosvāmī: To think of different ways to attain the beloved is called thoughtfulness. In this situation, the lover carefully arranges the bed, sighs, and anxiously looks to see the beloved's arrival.

Vijaya-kumāra: In this context what is remembrance?

Gosvāmī: To think of the beloved and things in relation to Him is called remembrance. In this situation, the lover trembles, has a seizure where she loses control of her limbs, weeps, sighs, and performs other like activities.

Vijaya-kumāra: What is glorifying the beloved's virtues?

Gosvāmī: To praise the beloved's handsomeness and other virtues is called glorifying the beloved's virtues. In this situation, the *anubhāvas* include trembling, standing up of the body's hair, and choking of the voice. In this situation, anxiety, mad lamentation, disease, being stunned, and death are manifested in *samañjasa-pūrva-rāga* as they are also in *samañjasa-rati*.

Vijaya-kumāra: O master, please describe *sādhāraṇa-pūrva-rāga*.

Gosvāmī: *Sādhāraṇa-pūrva-rāga* is like *sādhāraṇa-rati*. In it are manifested the six conditions, beginning with lamentation, only their manifestation is softer. The situation is natural, so there is no need to give any examples. In this *pūrva-rāga*, the lovers send love letters, garlands, and other things to be placed in each other's hands.

Vijaya-kumāra: What are the love letters?

Gosvāmī: Love letters are of two kinds: 1. Those that are not written with words, and 2. Those that are written with words. Because in them, the author reveals His or Her love, they are called love letters.

Vijaya-kumāra: What are the love letters that are not written with words?

Gosvāmī: Without drawing any words, the author may use her fingernail to draw a half moon on a red flower petal or leaf. That is called a letter written without any words.

Vijaya-kumāra: What is a love letter that is written with words?

Gosvāmī: When the lover personally writes with His or Her own hand verses in the *prākṛta* language—that is called a love letter that is written with words. The ink for the letter may be red hingula, musk, or black ashes and water. The pages of the letter are extraordinarily large flower petals. The stamp to seal the letter is made of *kuṅkuma*. Lotus fibers are the strings to tie the pages together.

Vijaya-kumāra: What is the sequence of events in *pūrva-rāga*?

Gosvāmī: First, there is the sight of something pleasing to the eye. Then, there is thinking of what one has seen. Then, there is attachment, then yearning, then loss of sleep, then becoming emaciated, then renouncing all else, then destruction of shyness, then madness, then falling unconscious, and then death. These are the stages of love. These stages are manifested in both the hero and the heroine. However, they are manifested first in the heroines and only later in Kṛṣṇa.

Vijaya-kumāra: What is jealous anger?

Gosvāmī: When the lovers meet, but the heroine will not allow her lover to touch her—that is called jealous anger. Disgust, anxiety, restlessness, arrogance, envy, concealment, loss, and worry are included among the *sañcārī*-

bhāvas in jealous anger.

Vijaya-kumāra: Where does jealous anger rest?

Gosvāmī: Jealous anger rests in *praṇaya* (love). Before *praṇaya* exists, jealous anger cannot be said truly to exist. If it exists at all, it is very stunted. Jealous anger is of two kinds: 1. With a cause, and 2. Without a cause.

Vijaya-kumāra: What is jealous anger with a cause?

Gosvāmī: When the beloved gives His affection to a rival, and the lover feels jealous anger mixed with love (*praṇaya*), that is called jealous anger with a cause. The ancient sages affirm that without *sneha*, fear is not possible, and without *praṇaya*, jealous anger is not possible. Therefore, when jealous anger is manifested, this reveals the love felt by the hero and heroine. A girl who sincerely loves her beloved cannot bear the idea of a rival for her beloved's affections. When the Dvārakā queens heard that Kṛṣṇa had given a *parijāta* flower to Rukmiṇī, jealous anger arose only in the heart of Satyabhāmā, and not in the heart of any other queen.

Vijaya-kumāra: In what different ways is the rival (*vipakṣa*) discovered?

Gosvāmī: There are three ways: 1. The lover hears about her rival, 2. She suspects the rival's existence, and 3. She sees the rival in a dream.

Vijaya-kumāra: What is hearing about the rival?

Gosvāmī: The lover may hear from the mouth of one of her friends, from the mouth of a parrot, or from the mouth of someone else. In these ways, she hears about her rival.

Vijaya-kumāra: How does she suspect her rival's existence?

Gosvāmī: She may see the marks of amorous enjoyment, hear the name of her rival accidentally spoken, or see her rival in a dream. In these ways, she may suspect the existence of a rival. On the limbs of her beloved, she may see various signs of His having enjoyed with another girl. That is called. "seeing the marks of enjoyment." Her beloved may accidentally speak the name of a rival. That is called, "hearing the name of her rival accidentally spoken." These things make the heroine so sad that she wishes she were dead. In a dream, the lover may see Kṛṣṇa and a rival beloved. This is called, "seeing the rival in a dream."

Vijaya-kumāra: What is directly seeing the rival?

Gosvāmī: The girl may directly see her beloved enjoying pastimes with a rival. That is called, "directly seeing the rival."

Vijaya-kumāra: What is jealous anger without a cause?

Gosvāmī: When there is no real cause, but there is only a flimsy reflection of a cause, and the heroin takes shelter of *praṇaya* (love), the result is jealous anger without a cause. Jealous anger with a cause is itself a transformation of *praṇaya*. When the pastimes of *praṇaya* are manifested, one by-product is the creation of jealous anger without a cause. This kind of jealous anger is called *praṇaya-māna*. The ancient *paṇḍitas* declare that spiritual love moves in a crooked way, like the movements of a snake. That is why the heroine manifests these two kinds of jealous anger, anger with and without a cause. This *rasa* has many *vyabhicārī-bhāvas*. Among them, concealment is the most important.

Vijaya-kumāra: How does the beloved pacify jealous anger without a cause?

Gosvāmī: Jealous anger without a cause will be pacified spontaneously. No effort is needed to pacify it. In the course of joking and other such pastimes, it will go away. Jealous anger with a cause will be pacified when there is conciliation, quarrel, giving a gift, and bowing down to offer respects. Jealous anger may also be pacified by shedding tears, by joking pastimes, or in other ways also.

Vijaya-kumāra: What is conciliation?

Gosvāmī: Speaking affectionate words is called conciliation.

Vijaya-kumāra: What is quarrel?

Gosvāmī: Quarrel is of two kinds: 1. crookedly praising one's own glories, and 2. using a friend to criticize the beloved.

Vijaya-kumāra: What is giving a gift?

Gosvāmī: When, on some pretext, an ornament or other gift is given to the jealous beloved—that is called giving a gift.

Vijaya-kumāra: What is bowing down to offer respects?

Gosvāmī: When the lover humbly falls at the feet of the jealous beloved—that is called bowing down to offer respects.

Vijaya-kumāra: What is *upekṣā*?

Gosvāmī: When, seeing that neither conciliation nor any other means will pacify His jealous beloved, and so the lover simply remains silent, that is called *upekṣā*. Some scholars say that *upekṣā* here means that by speaking joking words, the lover pacifies His jealous beloved.

Vijaya-kumāra: You used the word *rasāntara*. What does that word mean?

Gosvāmī: To speak words that bring sudden fear to the jealous beloved is called *rasāntara*. *Rasāntara* is of two kinds: 1. *yādṛcchika* and 2. *buddhi-pūrvaka*. When it occurs accidentally, it is called *yādṛcchika*. When it happens because of the lover's great intelligence, it is called *buddhi-pūrvaka*.

Vijaya-kumāra: In what other ways can the lover break His beloved's jealous anger?

Gosvāmī: One way is to play the flute at an appropriate time and place. There are also other ways to remove the jealous anger of the Vraja *gopīs*. A small amount of jealous anger may be easily pacified. A moderate amount of jealous anger may require some effort. Intense jealous anger is difficult to pacify, even with great effort. When a *gopī* expresses her jealous anger at Kṛṣṇa, she may say, "O crooked one, O crest-jewel of the malicious, O king of cheaters, O king of the deceivers, O best of the wicked, O great demon, O hard-hearted one, O shameless one, O rake whose playing is a host of sins, O lecher who hunts out the *gopīs*, O thief of beautiful girls' hearts, O destroyer of the *gopīs*' piety, O rake who mocks the saintly *gopīs*, O king of the debauchers, O great darkness of sins, O thief of the *gopīs*' garments, O highwayman who lurks in the valley of Govardhana Hill!"

Vijaya-kumāra: What is *prema-vaicittya*?

Gosvāmī: When, even though her beloved is present before her, a girl suffers, mistakenly thinking He is far away, that is called *prema-vaicitya*. When she is so overwhelmed with intense love that her mind mistakenly thinks her beloved is far away, that is called *vaicittya*.

Vijaya-kumāra: What is *pravāsa*?

Gosvāmī: When, although previously they were together, the hero and heroine now stay in different countries, different towns, different *rasas*, or different localities—that is called *pravāsa*. The *vyabhicārīs* of the *pravāsa* separation are all the *vyabhicārīs* of *śṛṅgāra-rasa*, except for joy, pride, passion, and shyness. *Pravāsa* is of two kinds: 1. *buddhi-pūrvaka* and 2. *abuddhi-pūrvaka*.

Vijaya-kumāra: What is *buddhi-pūrvaka pravāsa*?

Gosvāmī: When the beloved goes far away to perform a specific duty—that is called *buddhi-pūrvaka pravāsa*. Kṛṣṇa's duty in this situation is to give pleasure to His devotees. This kind of *pravāsa* is of two kinds: 1. Going a short distance, and 2. Going far away. When the journey is far away, it is of three kinds: 1. Future, 2. Present, and 3. Past. When the journey is far away, the lovers exchange letters.

Vijaya-kumāra: What is *abuddhi-pūrvaka pravāsa*?

Gosvāmī: When fate forces the beloved to live far away—that is called *abuddhi-pūrvaka pravāsa*. In the grip of the demigods or other forces, the lovers are forced into many different situations. Anxiety, sleeplessness, agitation, being emaciated, bodily limbs becoming discolored, wild talking, disease, madness, bewilderment, and death are the ten conditions of life in this kind of *pravāsa*. When Kṛṣṇa goes far away, all these ten conditions of life are manifested. O Vijaya-kumāra, these different kinds of spiritual love (*prema*) and these ten conditions of life can be understood only by mercy. Without mercy, they cannot be understood.

Vijaya-kumāra: When my heart thinks about this description of separation, it says that separation is not an end in itself. Rather, it is meant to increase the ocean of pleasure the lovers feel when they meet. Although a soul imprisoned by *māyā* will prefer the ocean of happiness obtained in meeting and think it better than the *rasa* of separation still, the *rasas* of separation is eternally manifested. The Lord's pastimes would not be so wonderful if it were absent.

Chapter Thirty-eight

Śṛṅgāra-rasa, part two

Folding his palms, Vijaya-kumāra asked his spiritual master about *sambhoga* (enjoyment in meeting).

Gosvāmī: Śrī Kṛṣṇa's pastimes are of two kinds: 1. *prakaṭa* (manifested and 2. *aprakaṭa* (unmanifested). The separation from Kṛṣṇa I described occurs in the *prakaṭa* pastimes. In Vṛndāvana, Kṛṣṇa eternally enjoys the *rasa* dance and other pastimes with the *gopīs*. Therefore, because these pastimes are eternal, Kṛṣṇa and the *gopīs* are never separated. In the *Mathurā-mahātmya* it is said that Kṛṣṇa eternally enjoys pastimes with the *gopas* and *gopīs*. There, the verb *krīḍati* (enjoys pastimes), which is in the present tense, affirms that Lord Kṛṣṇa eternally enjoys pastimes in Vṛndāvana. Therefore, in Goloka or in Vṛndāvana, in Lord Kṛṣṇa's *aprakaṭa* (unmanifested) pastimes, Kṛṣṇa and the *gopīs* always enjoy together. Kṛṣṇa never goes to a faraway place. There is no separation. Gazing at each other, embracing and enjoying many pastimes, Kṛṣṇa eternally enjoys (*sambhoga*) with the *gopīs*. This enjoyment (*sambhoga*) is of two kinds: 1. *mukhya* (primary) and 2. *gauna* (secondary).

Vijaya-kumāra: What is *mukhya-sambhoga*?

Gosvāmī: When Kṛṣṇa and the *gopīs* enjoy while they are awake, that is called *mukhya-sambhoga*. *Mukhya-sambhoga* is of four kinds. The *sambhoga* that occurs soon after the *pūrva-rāga* is called *saṅkṣipta* (brief). The *sambhoga* that occurs after jealous anger is called *saṅkīrṇa* (narrow). The *sambhoga* that occurs after a nearby *pravāsa* (journey) is called *sampanna* (fortunate). The *sambhoga* that occurs after a faraway journey is called *samṛddhimān* (opulent).

Vijaya-kumāra: What is *saṅkṣipta-sambhoga*?

Gosvāmī: When fear, shyness, and other such emotions keep the meeting brief—that is called *saṅkṣipta-sambhoga*.

Vijaya-kumāra: What is *saṅkīrṇa-sambhoga*?

Gosvāmī: When the lovers worry that an unpleasant obstacle may thwart their pastimes and therefore, Their enjoyment becomes like drinking hot sugarcane juice—that is called *sakirna-sambhoga*.

Vijaya-kumāra: What is *sampanna-sambhoga*?

Gosvāmī: When, after a long journey, the lover meets His beloved, Their enjoyment is called *sampanna-sambhoga*. This *sambhoga* is of two kinds: 1. *āgati* and 2. *prādurbhāva*. An ordinary meeting is called *āgati*. When the two passionate lovers accidentally and suddenly come face-to-face, that is called *prādurbhāva*. *Prādurbhāva* brings a great festival of the best transcendental happiness.

Vijaya-kumāra: What is *samṛddhimān-sambhoga*?

Gosvāmī: This is when the young lovers have a rare opportunity to see each other. And, why not? Because they are under the control of others, this does not always happen. Now that they are free from the control of others, they can enjoy without any obstacles. This is called *samṛddhimān-sambhoga*. This *sambhoga* is of two kinds: 1. concealed and 2. openly manifested. I need not describe them now.

Vijaya-kumāra: What is *gauna-sambhoga*?

Gosvāmī: When one enjoys pastimes with Kṛṣṇa in a dream—that is called *gauna-sambhoga*. These dreams are of two kinds: 1. *sāmānya* (general) and 2. *viśeṣa* (specific). This *gauna-sambhoga* is of two kinds. When the *vyabhicārī-bhāva* sleep is prominent, it is *sāmānya-gauna-sambhoga*. *Viśeṣa-gauna-sambhoga* is when one awakens from the dream and sees that the waking reality is exactly the same as the dream. Thus, the meeting with Kṛṣṇa in the waking state is exactly like the meeting with Him in the dream. This *rasa* is filled with the yearnings of love. The four divisions of *saṅkṣipta*, *saṅkīrṇa*, *sampanna*, and *samṛddhimān* also exist in *gauna-sambhoga*.

Vijaya-kumāra: Dreams aren't real. How can *samṛddhimān-sambhoga* occur in a dream?

Gosvāmī: In the spiritual world, waking and dreaming are the same. Ūṣā and Aniruddha met in a dream. In the same way Kṛṣṇa and His beloved *gopīs* can meet in Their dreams. Perfected devotees (*siddha-bhakta*) sometimes have very wonderful dreams and when they awaken, they attain an ornament or something else that they first saw in the dream.

These dreams are of two kinds: 1. Being asleep when one is dreaming, and 2. Dreaming when one is awake. The *gopīs*' dreams, which are filled with spiritual love, are in the fifth condition of life, far beyond the *yogīs*' *samādhi*, which is in the fourth condition of life. Thus, the *gopīs*' dreams are not at all like material dreams, which are born from the mode of passion. This means that the *gopīs*' dreams are not material and are not impelled by the material modes of nature. Rather, they are eternal spiritual reality. Therefore, Lord Kṛṣṇa can certainly enjoy wonderful pastimes with the *gopīs* in their dreams.

Vijaya-kumāra: Please describe *viśeṣa-gauna-sambhoga*.

Gosvāmī: The following are all the activities of *viśeṣa-gauna sambhoga* (special situations of meeting): seeing, talking, touching, blocking the path, putting an obstacle on the path, pastimes in a house, pastimes in Vṛndāvana forest, pastimes in the Yamunā's waters, pastimes in a boat, pastimes of stealing flowers, pastimes at a *ghāta* (the *dāna-keli* pastime), playing hide-and-seek in the forest, drinking *madhu* nectar, Kṛṣṇa disguising Himself as a woman, pretending to be asleep, gambling with dice, tugging at garments, kissing, embracing, scratching with fingernails, drinking the nectar of each other's *bimba* fruit lips, and enjoying amorous pastimes.

Vijaya-kumāra: O master, playful pastimes (*līlā-vilāsa*) is one thing, meeting (*samprayoga*) is another thing. Of the two, which brings the most happiness?

Gosvāmī: Playful pastimes (*līlā-vilāsa*) bring more happiness than meeting (*samprayoga*).

Vijaya-kumāra: With what affectionate names do the *gopīs* address Kṛṣṇa?

Gosvāmī: The *gopīs* address Kṛṣṇa with the following affectionate names: Gokulānanda (O bliss of Gokula), Govinda (O pleasure of the cows, land and senses), Goṣṭhendra-kula-candra (O moon born from the king of Vraja), Prāṇeśvara (O master of our lives), Sundarottaṁsa (O crown of all handsome men), Nāgara-śiromaṇi (O crest-jewel of amorous heroes), Vṛndāvana-candra (O moon of Vṛndāvana), Gokula-rājā (O king of Gokula), and Manohara (O enchanter of our hearts). There are many other names also.

Vijaya-kumāra: O master, Lord Kṛṣṇa's pastimes are of two kinds: 1. *prakaṭa* (manifested) and 2. *aprakaṭa* (unmanifested). Still, all His pastimes are the same spiritual reality. What are the different kinds of His *prakaṭa* pastimes in Vraja?

Gosvāmī: The Lord's *prakaṭa* pastimes in Vraja are of two kinds: 1. *nitya* (regular) and 2. *naimittika* (for some special occasion). The Lord's *aṣṭakālīya-līlā* (pastimes in the eight periods of the day) in Vraja are His *nitya* pastimes.

Other pastimes, like His killing Putanā and other demons, and His going far away on a journey, are His *naimittika* pastimes.

Vijaya-kumāra: O master, I wish to learn about the Lord's *nitya* pastimes.

Gosvāmī: O Vijaya-kumāra, would you like to hear the description given by the ancient sages, or would you like to hear the description given by the Six Gosvāmīs?

Vijaya-kumāra: I would like to hear the descriptions given by the ancient sages.

Gosvāmī: It is said: The eight periods of the day are: 1. The end of night, 2. The early morning, 3. The late morning, 4. Midday, 5. The afternoon, 6. Sunset, 7. Evening, and 8. Night. Midday and night last for six *muhūrtas* each. Evening and the other periods last for three *muhūrtas* each.

Two *daṇḍas* (twenty-four minutes) equal one *muhūrta* (forty -eight minutes). In the *Sanat-kumāra Saṁhitā*, Lord Sadāśiva described Lord Kṛṣṇa's pastimes in these eight periods of the day.

Vijaya-kumāra: O master, am I qualified to hear these words of Lord Sadāśiva, the spiritual master of the universe?

Gosvāmī: Please listen. Lord Sadāśiva said (*Śrī Sanat-kumāra Saṁhitā* 183-188): Thinking of Him as their paramour, with hidden love, the *gopīs* please their beloved Kṛṣṇa. One should think of oneself as a beautiful young *gopī* girl who is expert in various arts, pleasing to Lord Kṛṣṇa, reluctant to directly enjoy with Lord Kṛṣṇa, even if He were personally to invite you, a follower of Śrī Rādhā, always devoted to Her service, more affectionate to Śrī Rādhā than to Lord Kṛṣṇa Himself, every day carefully and affectionately arranging the meeting of Śrī Śrī Rādhā-Kṛṣṇa, and becoming happy to see Them pleased by your service. Thinking of oneself in this way, one should serve Śrī Śrī Rādhā-Kṛṣṇa from the early morning of *brāhma-muhūrta* to the end of night.

Vijaya-kumāra: what are the pastimes at the end of night?

Gosvāmī: Śrī Vṛndā-devī said (*Śrī Sanat-kumāra Saṁhitā* 196-201): In the middle of beautiful Vṛndāvana forest, which is decorated with fifty groves, in a grove of *kalpa-vṛkṣa* trees, in a glittering jewel palace, on a graceful bed, the sleeping, tightly embracing Divine Couple were awakened by birds following my command. Their firm embrace broken, the Divine Couple became unhappy at the thought of Their impending separation. They had no wish to rise even slightly from Their bed. Awakened by the cheerful words of many parrots and other birds, Śrī Śrī Rādhā-Kṛṣṇa rose from Their bed. Seeing that the divine couple had happily risen from bed, the *gopīs* entered and served Them in ways appropriate to that time. When the female parrots spoke, the Divine Couple rose from Their bed. Very anxious, They returned to Their homes.

Vijaya-kumāra: What are the pastimes in the early morning?

Gosvāmī: There, it is said (*Śrī Sanat-kumāra Saṁhitā* 202-218): Wakened by His mother in the early morning, Lord Kṛṣṇa rose from bed. Then, He and Balarāma brushed Their teeth. With His mother's permission, Lord Kṛṣṇa eagerly went to the barn to milk the cows. Then, Śrī Rādhā, wakened by the elder *gopīs*, also rose from Her bed.

Śrī Rādhā rose, brushed Her teeth, anointed Herself with fragrant oils, and then went to the bathing room, where Lalitā and the other *gopīs* bathed Her. Then, She went to the decorating room, where Her friends decorated Her with garlands, scents, oils, and many glittering ornaments. Then, after first speaking to Rādhā's mother-in-law, Yaśodā called Rādhā and Her friends to cook breakfast for Lord Kṛṣṇa.

Śrī Nārada said: O goddess, why did Yaśodā call Śrī Rādhā to cook, when Rohiṇī and so many other expert cooks were present in her home?

Śrī Vṛndā-devī said: The great sage, Durvāsa, gave Rādhā a boon that She would be the best of cooks. This I heard from the mouth of Kātyāyanī.

Durvāsa said to Rādhā: O goddess, by my mercy, whatever You cook will be more delicious than nectar. It will increase the life of whoever eats it.

That is why, every day, Yaśodā calls Rādhā to cook. Yaśodā thinks, "Eager to eat this delicious food, my son will live a very long life."

Receiving permission from Her mother-in-law, Rādhā becomes very happy. Accompanied by a host of friends, She goes to Kṛṣṇa's home to cook. Meanwhile, Lord Kṛṣṇa milked some cows and had the other boys milk the others. Then, called by His father, He and His friends returned home. Then, the servants happily massaged Lord Kṛṣṇa, bathed Him, dressed Him in clean garments, garlanded Him, and anointed His body with sandal paste. Then, the servants gathered Lord Kṛṣṇa's hair from His forehead to His neck and tied it in a topknot. They made the moon of His forehead splendid with *tilaka* and curling locks of hair.

They decorated Lord Kṛṣṇa with armlets and bracelets. They made His hands splendid with jeweled rings. They placed a necklace of pearls across His chest and decorated His ears with shark-shaped earrings.

Again and again called by His mother, Lord Kṛṣṇa, holding His mother's hand, finally followed Balarāma into the breakfast room. Accompanied by His mother and His friends, Lord Kṛṣṇa ate a breakfast feast of many different kinds of food. He told many jokes, laughing, and made His friends laugh. Then, the servants brought betel nuts. After sharing them with His friends and chewing some Himself, Lord Kṛṣṇa rested for a moment on a splendid bed.

Vijaya-kumāra: Please describe the pastimes of the late morning.

Gosvāmī: It is said (*Śrī Sanat-kumāra Saṁhitā* 220-223): When, dressed as a cowherd boy, Lord Kṛṣṇa followed the cows to the pasture, all the people of Vraja affectionately followed Him on the path. Bowing down before His father and mother, casting sidelong glances at His *gopī* beloveds, and dealing appropriately with all the others, Lord Kṛṣṇa sent them all back. Then, He again proceeded to the forest.

Lord Kṛṣṇa entered the forest, played for a while with His friends, and then slipped away with two or three especially close friends. Eager to see His beloved, Lord Kṛṣṇa happily went to meet Her.

Vijaya-kumāra: Please describe the pastimes of midday:

Gosvāmī: It is said (*Śrī Sanat-kumāra Saṁhitā* 223-262): When She saw that Lord Kṛṣṇa had gone to the forest, Śrī Rādhā returned to Her home. Then, on the pretext of gathering flowers and other things for the worship of the sun-god and other purposes, Śrī Rādhā tricked Her superiors and, yearning to meet Her beloved, went to the forest.

Finally meeting after a great effort, the Divine Couple enjoyed many happy pastimes in the forest, with Their associates. Sometimes, Rādhā and Kṛṣṇa enjoy pastimes on a swing hanging from a tree branch and pushed by the *gopīs*. Sometimes, Rādhā steals the flute from Lord Kṛṣṇa's hand. Sometimes, the *gopīs* hide and make Him search after them. Sometimes, they tease and scold Him. Sometimes, they joke with Him and make Him laugh. In these ways, they charm Lord Kṛṣṇa and steal His heart.

Sometimes, Lord Kṛṣṇa happily enters the forest in the beautiful springtime, and with a sprinkler, sprinkles the *gopīs* with water mixed with sandal, kuṅkuma, and other colorful scents. The *gopīs* respond by sprinkling Him. Then, Rādhā and Kṛṣṇa sprinkle each other, again and again.

O *brāhmaṇa*, in the forest groves, the Divine Couple enjoy many different pastimes with Their associates, pastimes appropriate to the different times and seasons.

O best of sages, sometimes They become tired. Then, sitting on a splendid throne under a tree, They drink nectar. Intoxicated by drinking nectar, Their eyes become closed with sleepiness. Holding hands, They are attacked by Kāmadeva's arrows. Desiring to enjoy, They place Their lotus feet in a forest grove. There, They enjoy pastimes like two regal elephants. Intoxicated by drinking nectar, and their eyes closed with sleepiness, the *gopīs* enter the nearby forest groves. Expanding into many different forms, all-powerful Lord Kṛṣṇa approaches each *gopī* individually.

As an elephant king enjoys with His many wives, so Lord Kṛṣṇa enjoys with the *gopīs*. Then, Lord Kṛṣṇa, His beloved Rādhā, and all the *gopīs* enter a lake.

Śrī Nārada said: O Vṛndā-devī, if His pastimes of sweetness are like this, then when does Lord Kṛṣṇa manifest His pastimes of opulence? Please cut apart my doubt?

Śrī Vṛndā-devī said: O sage, the powerful potency of the pastimes of sweetness is one of Lord Hari's potencies. With that potency, Lord Hari enjoys pastimes with the *gopīs*. When, in His original form, Lord Kṛṣṇa enjoys pastimes with Śrī Rādhā, He manifests the potency of His pastimes of sweetness. At that time, He does not manifest the potency of His pastimes of opulence.

Accompanied by Their *gopī* friends, the Divine Couple enjoy pastimes of splashing each other in the water. Then, They are decorated with splendid garments, ornaments, garlands, and sandal paste. Then, in a jeweled cottage by the lake shore, the Divine Couple eat a snack of delicious fruit and roots carefully prepared by me. After Their snack, Lord Hari and His beloved recline on a couch of flowers. There, two or three *gopīs* serve Them.

Served by the *gopīs* who offer Him betel nuts, fan Him, and massage His lotus feet, Lord Kṛṣṇa, His thoughts fixed on His beloved, becomes filled with happiness. As Lord Kṛṣṇa sleeps, Śrī Rādhā and Her associates happily eat the remnants of His meal. After eating, Śrī Rādhā goes to the bed to gaze on Her beloved's lotus face, just as a *cakorī* bird gazes at the moon. The *gopīs* there give Her the remnants of betel nuts chewed by Lord Kṛṣṇa. Some She chews and some She gives to Her friends.

Eager to hear what the *gopīs* said, Lord Kṛṣṇa only pretends to be asleep as He lies under the covers. As they playfully joke about their beloved Hari, they can gradually understand that He is only pretending to sleep. Seeing the signs of wakefulness on Lord Kṛṣṇa's face, they look at each other and suddenly become silent, out of embarrassment.

Suddenly pulling the blanket from His limbs and exclaiming, "My, You must have had a pleasant sleep!" they laughed and make Lord Kṛṣṇa laugh also.

O best of sages, in this way, the Divine Couple enjoy a pleasant nap and a host of happy joking words.

Sitting on a splendid throne and surrounded by Their associates, the Divine Couple gamble at dice, with garlands, kisses, and embraces as the winner's prize.

Joking with words of love, Rādhā and Kṛṣṇa gamble with dice. Defeated by His beloved, Lord Kṛṣṇa slowly pronounces, "I have lost."

Taking the necklace and other prizes, Śrī Rādhā strikes Lord Kṛṣṇa with a lotus flower.

O Nārada, His unhappiness showing on His face, Lord Kṛṣṇa feels as if He has lost a great treasure. "O goddess, You have defeated Me," He says. "Please take the winner's prize."

To see Rādhā's crooked raised eyebrows and hear Her words of rebuke, Lord Kṛṣṇa declares, "Now I will give You the kiss and the other prizes." Then, He gives Her all the prizes. Then, hearing the parrots calling, Rādhā and Kṛṣṇa bathe and decide to return to Their homes.

Taking leave of His beloved, Lord Kṛṣṇa returns to the cows. Accompanied by Her friends, Śrī Rādhā goes to the temple of the sun-god. Lord Kṛṣṇa goes a short distance, disguises Himself as a *brāhmaṇa* and then goes to the temple of the sun-god. Requested by the *gopīs*, the disguised Kṛṣṇa worships the sun-god. Lord Kṛṣṇa then recites a host of imaginary Vedic prayers, prayers made up on the spot and filled with a host of errors.

Finally understanding that this person is their beloved Kṛṣṇa, the intelligent *gopīs* became plunged in an ocean of bliss. Intoxicated with bliss, they do not know who they are, or who anyone else is.

O sage, in this way, the Divine Couple and Their associates pass six hours enjoying many pastimes. Finally, the *gopīs* return to their homes and Lord Kṛṣṇa returns to the cows.

Vijaya-kumāra: What are the afternoon pastimes?

Gosvāmī: It is said (*Śrī Sanat-kumāra Saṁhitā* 263-270): Meeting with His *gopa* friends, taking the cows with Him, and attracting everyone with the music of His flute, Lord Kṛṣṇa returns to Vraja village. Hearing the sound of Kṛṣṇa's flute and seeing the sky filled with the dust raised by the cows, King Nanda and all the men and women and children of Vraja stop all they were doing and run to see Kṛṣṇa.

Śrī Rādhā, bathed and decorated, comes, bringing many delicious food preparations for Her beloved. She and Her friends are all eager to see Kṛṣṇa. On the royal road at the entrance to Vraja village, Lord Kṛṣṇa meets all the people of Vraja, one after another. He meets them with embraces, glances, and smiling. He bows before the elder *gopas* and He honors them with His words.

O Śrī Nārada, Lord Kṛṣṇa prostrates His entire body to show respect to His parents and to Rohiṇī-devī. From the corner of His eye, He shyly glances at His *gopī* beloveds. Then, in the ways proper for each, all the people of Vraja worship Lord Kṛṣṇa. Then, Lord Kṛṣṇa takes the cows into the barn.

Requested by His parents, Lord Kṛṣṇa goes home with mother Yaśodā. Requested by her, He bathes and then He eats and drinks, and then He goes to milk the cows.

Vijaya-kumāra: What are the sunset pastimes?

Gosvāmī: It is said (*Śrī Sanat-kumāra Saṁhitā* 271-272): After milking some of the cows, having the other *gopas* milk the other cows, and allowing the calves to also drink some of the milk, Lord Kṛṣṇa, accompanied by His father and by servants carrying the milk, returns home.

Then, accompanied by Lord Balarāma, the *gopa* boys, and the boys' mothers, Lord Kṛṣṇa eats a feast of many different kinds of food, foods to be chewed, licked, or consumed in other ways.

Vijaya-kumāra: What are the evening pastimes?

Gosvāmī: It is said (*Śrī Sanat-kumāra Saṁhitā* 273-277): On Mother Yaśodā's request, Śrī Rādhā and Her friends had cooked this feast. After enjoying the feast in the company of His father and the others, Lord Kṛṣṇa praises it with many words. Then, accompanied by the poets and reciters, Lord Kṛṣṇa goes to the assembly house.

Then, Mother Yaśodā gives abundant remnants from the feast to the *gopīs* who had brought it in the first place. Mother Yaśodā gives them the remnants from Lord Kṛṣṇa's plate. The *gopīs* take it and in a secluded place present it before Śrī Rādhā. Then, Śrī Rādhā and Her friends honor Lord Kṛṣṇa's remnants. Then, to prepare for Her meeting with Lord Kṛṣṇa, the *gopīs* decorate joyful Rādhā.

Vijaya-kumāra: O master, I yearn to hear the pastimes of night.

Gosvāmī: Śrī Vṛndā-devī described them in these words (*Śrī Sanat-kumāra Saṁhitā* 278-285): One of the *gopīs* has already made arrangements for Śrī Rādhā's secret meeting with Lord Kṛṣṇa by the Yamunā's shore. Accompanied by Her friends and dressed in garments suitable for a bright or dark night, Śrī Rādhā goes to a jeweled palace in a *kalpa-vṛkṣa* grove.

Meanwhile, Lord Kṛṣṇa sees many festive ceremonies and hears many beautiful poems and songs. Then, Lord Kṛṣṇa pleases the artists and performers with many valuable gifts and then, called by His mother, He goes to bed. When, after giving Him a night-time snack, mother Yaśodā leaves the bedroom, unseen by anyone, Lord Kṛṣṇa leaves His home and goes to meet His beloved.

Meeting in the forest groves, Śrī Śrī Rādhā and Kṛṣṇa enjoy singing, dancing, and many other pastimes. After enjoying pastimes for seven-and-a-half hours of the night, Lord Kṛṣṇa becomes sleepy. Accompanied by five or six *gopīs* and unseen by the others, He enters another forest. Served by Their dear *gopī* friends, the Divine Couple sleeps there on a beautiful pastime bed made of unstemmed flowers.

O Vijaya-kumāra, These are the *aṣṭa-kālīya* pastimes. They have all the *sāmagrīs* (ingredients) of the *rasas*. All these pastimes have been described in the books of the ancient sages. In every time, place, and situation, you should mediate on these pastimes and engage in devotional service.

Hearing these pastimes, the learned *paṇḍita*, Vijaya-kumāra, became plunged into the nectar of ecstatic love. Streams of tears flowed from his eyes. The hairs of his body stood up. He spoke one or two broken words in a choked voice. He fell before Śrī Gopāla-guru Gosvāmī's lotus feet, offering obeisances for a long time. Then, he rose up and slowly walked home. Day and night, these words about the *rasas* stayed in his heart.

Chapter Thirty-nine

Entering the Lord's pastimes

Now, Vijaya-kumāra was always eager to hear about these pastimes. He did not like to hear about anything else. When he went to see Lord Jagannātha, Vijaya-kumāra could not remain peaceful and composed. For many days now, he had studied the *rasas*. He had learned about *mādhurya-rasa*, *sthāyi-bhāva*, *vibhāva*, *anubhāva*, *sāttvika-bhāva*, and *vyabhicārī-bhāva*. One by one, the different kinds of ecstatic love entered his heart. They would bring him great delight, and then they would go away. Some days passed in this way. He did not understand how the presence of ecstatic love had changed him.

One day, with tears in his eyes, he fell down before His spiritual master's lotus feet and said, "O master, by your mercy, I have learned everything. However, I am not able to make spiritual advancement. I have not attained *sthāyi-bhāva* and I have not entered Lord Kṛṣṇa's pastimes. Please teach me what I should do."

Seeing how his disciple was rapt in ecstatic love, Gopāla-guru Gosvāmī was very pleased. In his heart, he thought, "Love for Kṛṣṇa (*kṛṣṇa-prema*) is such that its happiness brings distress, and its distress brings happiness."

Then, he openly said, "I will tell you how to enter Lord Kṛṣṇa's pastimes."

Vijaya-kumāra: How can I enter them?

Gosvāmī: Śrīla Raghunātha dāsa Gosvāmī has revealed the way in these words (*Manaḥ-śikṣā* 2): Mind don't do the pious and impious deeds described in the *Vedas*. Intently serve Śrī Śrī Rādhā-Kṛṣṇa in Vraja. Always remember that Lord Caitanya is Lord Kṛṣṇa, the son of Mahārāja Nanda, and my spiritual master is most dear to Lord Mukunda.

The purport of this verse is as follows: Don't perform the pious and impious deeds described in the *Vedas*. Reject this part of the *Vedas* and instead earnestly engage in *rāgānuga-bhakti*. Again and again, serve Śrī Śrī Rādhā-Kṛṣṇa in Vraja. Serve the Lord according to the *rasas* of Vraja. If you ask, "Who will teach me how to serve the Lord according to the *rasas* of Vraja?" then I will tell you. Please listen. Śrīdhāma Navadvīpa, where Lord Caitanya appeared in Śacī-devī's womb, is a manifestation of Vṛndāvana. Lord Caitanya is Kṛṣṇa Himself, Kṛṣṇa the son of Nandīśvara's king. Lord Caitanya is not different from Kṛṣṇa. Thinking that Lord Kṛṣṇa has descended to Navadvīpa to enjoy pastimes as Lord Caitanya, one should not reject the worship of Lord Kṛṣṇa as the amorous hero of Vraja and instead worship Lord Caitanya as the amorous hero of the young girls in Navadvīpa. Lord Caitanya is Lord Kṛṣṇa Himself. Still, one should not criticize the devotees who worship Him with different *mantras* and meditate on Him separately. In the path of the *rasas*, one should worship only Kṛṣṇa, the beloved of Rādhā, and Lord Caitanya one should worship as the spiritual master of the *rasas* of Vraja. One should meditate on Lord Caitanya's pastimes and on Lord Kṛṣṇa's *aṣṭa-kālīya* pastimes. One should not think that one's spiritual master is not a *sakhī* or a *yūtheśvarī* in Vraja. By worshiping in this way, one will be able to enter Lord Kṛṣṇa's pastimes in Vraja.

Vijaya-kumāra: O master, I understand that one should reject other scriptures and other paths, worship Lord Caitanya and serve one's spiritual master, aware that the spiritual master is a *sakhī* in Lord Kṛṣṇa's pastimes. How can one make his heart steady and determined to follow this path?

Gosvāmī: Two things should be understood: 1. *upāsya-pariṣkṛti* (the worshiper) and 2. *upāsaka-pariṣkṛti* (the object of worship). You have learned about the *rasas*. Therefore, you have learned about *upāsya-pariṣkṛti*. The *upāsaka-pariṣkṛti* has eleven *bhāvas*. Almost all of them you have already learned. Only one remains for you to learn.

Vijaya-kumāra: Please describe these eleven *bhāvas*.

Gosvāmī: These eleven *bhāvas* are: 1. *sambandha* (relationship), 2. *vayasa* (age), 3. *nāma* (name), 4. *rūpa* (form), 5. *yūtha* (group), 6. *veṣa* (garments), 7. *ājñā* (command), 8. *vāsa* (residence), 9. *sevā* (service), 10. *parākāṣṭhā-śvāsa* (highest aspiration) and 11. *pālya-dāsī-bhāva* (the nature of a maidservant).

Vijaya-kumāra: What is *sambandha*?

Gosvāmī: *Sambandha* is the foundation of spiritual attainments. When one has a relationship with Kṛṣṇa, then the *bhāvas* are manifested. The final goal one attains is based on the relationship. Souls who address Kṛṣṇa as master become servants of Kṛṣṇa. Souls who address Kṛṣṇa as friend become friends of Kṛṣṇa. Souls who address Kṛṣṇa as son become the mother or father of Kṛṣṇa. Souls who address Kṛṣṇa as husband become queens at Dvārakā. In Vraja, there is no *śānta-rasa*, and *dāsya-rasa* is curtailed. Each devotee attains a relationship according to his own natural inclination. You are naturally attracted to *parakīya-*

rasa. Therefore, you are a follower of Vraja's queen. In your relationship, you say, "I am a maidservant of Śrī Rādhā's maidservant. She is the controller of my life. Kṛṣṇa is the controller of Rādhā's life and therefore, Kṛṣṇa, the beloved of Rādhā, is the controller of my life also."

Vijaya-kumāra: I have heard that the great *ācārya*, Śrīla Jīva Gosvāmī, preferred *svakīya-rasa*. Is that true?

Gosvāmī: Not one of the true followers of Lord Caitanya Mahāprabhu rejected the pure *parakīya-rasa*. Who can be a better teacher of this *rasa* than Śrīla Svarūpa Dāmodara Gosvāmī? He taught the truth of the pure *parakīya-rasa*. Śrīla Jīva Gosvāmī, Śrīla Rūpa Gosvāmī, and Śrīla Sanātana Gosvāmī all accepted his teachings in this matter. In his own personal devotional service, Śrīla Jīva Gosvāmī did not accept *svakīya-rasa*. However, he did explain that even in Vraja, some devotees manifest a scent of *svakīya-rasa*. When *samarthā-rati* carries a scent of *samañjasā-rati*, then *svakīya-rasa* is present in Vraja. Therefore, when a slight sense of *svakīya-rasa* is present, the devotee may be called a worshiper in *svakīya-rasa*. Śrīla Jīva Gosvāmī has two kinds of disciples. One group of his disciples was situated in pure *parakīya-rasa*. Another group of his disciples were situated in *parakīya-rasa* mixed with *svakīya-rasa*. According to the different inclinations of his different disciples, he gave different appropriate instructions. This he clearly explained when he wrote the words: "What I have written is appropriate for devotees who are inclined in a certain way."

Vijaya-kumāra: Now I clearly understand that the pure Gauḍīya Vaiṣṇava philosophy teaches the pure *parakīya-rasa*. Now that I understand *sambandha*, please describe *vayasa*.

Gosvāmī: When you attain your relationship with Kṛṣṇa, you will have a wonderful form. In your case, it will be the form of a beautiful girl in Vraja. That form will be manifested in a specific age that is appropriate to your service. The age from ten to sixteen years is called *paugaṇḍa*. That is generally the appropriate age in this situation. Therefore, in your spiritual form, your age begins at ten and, as you make advancement in service, it increases up to the age of sixteen. That is called *vayaḥ-sandhi*. *Bālya* (childhood), *paugaṇḍa* (pre-adolescence) and *vṛddha* (old age) do not exist among the beautiful girls of Vraja. Therefore, you should know that your spiritual form is situated in the *paugaṇḍa* age.

Vijaya-kumāra: O master, what is name? I have already received a name. Please clearly explain name to me.

Gosvāmī: You naturally become the follower of a maidservant friend of Śrī Rādhā. That friend's name is your name. Examining your nature, your spiritual master gives you a name. Please know that is your name eternally. The beautiful girls of Vraja will delight in addressing you by that name.

Vijaya-kumāra: O master, please explain *rūpa*.

Gosvāmī: Your spiritual master reveals to you the nature of the beautiful and youthful *paugaṇḍa* age form that, according to your own inclination, is your own form. You have an inconceivable beautiful spiritual form. If that were not so, then how could you be a maidservant of Śrī Rādhā?

Vijaya-kumāra: Please clearly describe *yūtha*.

Gosvāmī: Śrī Rādhā is your *yūtheśvarī*. You belong to a *gaṇa* (sub-group) presided over by one of Śrī Rādhā's eight closest friends (*aṣṭa-sakhī*). Your spiritual master has placed you in Lalitā's *gaṇa*. Therefore, following Lalitā's orders, you will serve your *yūtheśvarī* (Śrī Rādhā) and playful Lord Kṛṣṇa, who enjoys pastimes with Her.

Vijaya-kumāra: O master, who are the devotees that follow Candrāvalī as their *yūtheśvarī*?

Gosvāmī: After many births, a soul will become fortunate and desire to be a follower of a *yūtheśvarī*. A soul who has all good fortune enters the group led by Śrī Rādhā. The *gopīs* led by Candrāvalī strive to increase the bliss that Śrī Rādhā and Lord Kṛṣṇa enjoy in Their pastimes. Therefore, the rival groups, called *pakṣa*, and *vipakṣa*, make the taste of *rasa* sweeter. In truth, Śrī Rādhā is the only real *yūtheśvarī*. Because She enjoys wonderful pastimes with Kṛṣṇa, She is glorious and a soul who serves Her becomes glorious also.

Vijaya-kumāra: Please explain *veṣa*.

Gosvāmī: Your spiritual master describes to you your garments, personal qualities, and the skills you have to perform various kinds of service.

Vijaya-kumāra: Please describe *ājñā*.

Gosvāmī: *Ājñā* are of two kinds: 1. *nitya* (regular) and 2. *naimittika* (occasional). A merciful *sakhī* orders you to engage in a certain regular (*nitya*) service. This service you should diligently execute during the eight periods of the day. Any other service she may give you is *naimittika* service. That also you should execute diligently.

Vijaya-kumāra: What is *vāsa*?

Gosvāmī: Your eternal residence in Vraja is called *vāsa*. You will take birth as a certain *gopī* in a certain village within the land of Vraja. Within that village, you will be married to a certain *gopa*. However, you will be attracted by the sound of Kṛṣṇa's flute. You will be the follower of a certain *sakhī*. Her cottage at Rādhā-kuṇḍa will be your residence also. In this way, your eternal nature is situated in *parakīya-rasa*.

Vijaya-kumāra: Please describe *sevā*.

Gosvāmī: You are a follower of Śrī Rādhā. Your service is to serve Her. If, when she sends you with a message, and you meet Kṛṣṇa in a secluded place and Kṛṣṇa expresses His love for you and proposes that you enjoy with Him, you should not accept His proposal. You are Rādhā's maidservant and without Her permission, you cannot serve Kṛṣṇa. You are not independent. Although you love Rādhā and Kṛṣṇa both, your love and service to Rādhā is more important to you than your love and service to Kṛṣṇa. That is the explanation of the word *sevā*. Your service is to serve Śrī Rādhā throughout the eight periods of the day. Following the descriptions in Śrīla Svarūpa Dāmodara's *kaḍacā* (notebook), Śrīla Raghunātha dāsa Gosvāmī describes these services in his poem, *Vilāpa-kusumāñjali*.

Vijaya-kumāra: What is *parākāṣṭhā-śvāsa*?

Gosvāmī: In the following two verses (*Vilāpa-kusumāñjali* 102 and 100), Śrīla Raghunātha dāsa Gosvāmī describes *parākāṣṭhā-śvāsa*: O Rādhā, for me, somehow, the present moment is flooded by a nectarean ocean of many hopes. If You do not give Your mercy, then of what use to me are this life, the land of Vraja, and Śrī Kṛṣṇa, the enemy of Baka? O Lord Kṛṣṇa, O nectarean moon of Gokula, O Lord, whose cheerful face is a lotus flower, O sweetly smiling one, O Lord melting with compassion, so that I may serve You both with love, please lead me to the place where Your beloved enjoys pastimes with You.

Vijaya-kumāra: Please describe *pālya-dāsī-bhāva*.

Gosvāmī: In the following words of *Vraja-vilāsa-stava* (text 29) Śrīla

Raghunātha dāsa Gosvāmī describes *pālya-dāsī-bhāva*: Flooded with the nectar of intense love for her two friends (Śrī Śrī Rādhā-Kṛṣṇa), who are more dear to her than her own life, affectionately arrogant in Their presence, and daily arranging for Their rendezvous, Lalitā-devī expertly teaches her friend, Rādhā, the art of jealous anger. I pray that Lalitā-devī will one day accept me as one of her associates.

Vijaya-kumāra: How should such a *pālya-dāsī* (maidservant) act in relation to the other *gopīs* who are companions of Śrī Lalitā?

Gosvāmī: Śrīla Raghunātha dāsa Gosvāmī studied all the *rasa-śāstras* under Śrīla Svarūpa Dāmodara Gosvāmī. Śrīla Raghunātha dāsa Gosvāmī has written (*Vraja-vilāsa-stava*, text 38): By offering Her betel nuts, by massaging Her feet, by bringing Her water, by arranging for Her secret meeting with Lord Kṛṣṇa, and by performing many other services, many *gopī* maidservants affectionately please Śrī Rādhā, the great queen of Vṛndāvana forest. When the Divine Couple enjoy the presence of the great *gopīs*, for whom Śrī Rādhā is dearer than life, I take shelter of these *gopī* maidservants, who have Śrīmati Rūpa-mañjarī as their leader.

Vijaya-kumāra: What is the nature of the other prominent *sakhīs*?

Gosvāmī: Śrīla Raghunātha dāsa Gosvāmī gives this hint about their nature (*Vraja-vilāsa-stava* text 30): Viśākhā-devī is the person who makes the youthful Divine Couple enjoy affectionate and playful joking pastimes. Her sweet transcendental singing eclipses the voices of the cuckoos. I pray that Viśākhā-devī may become pleased with me and accept me as her student.

Vijaya-kumāra: What is the nature of the *vipakṣa* (rival) *gopīs*?

Gosvāmī: Śrīla Raghunātha dāsa Gosvāmī describes them. Please hear this description (*Vraja-vilāsa-stava*, text 41): In order to increase the splendid and nectarean jealous love of Śrīmati Rādhārani, who sometimes becomes proud of Her own good fortune, Lord Kṛṣṇa briefly enjoys pastimes with other *gopīs*, who blossoms with many amorous desires. Let us offer our respectful obeisances to these *gopīs*, who must have performed many great pious activities in their previous births in order to play this role in the Lord's pastimes.

That is how you should think about the rival groups of *gopīs* (*pakṣa* and *vipakṣa*). However, when they are serving the Lord directly in the spiritual world, there may be a situation where mocking *gopī* rivals is appropriate. This direct service in the spiritual world is described in Śrīla Raghunātha dāsa Gosvāmī's *Śrī Vilāpa-kusumāñjali*. The proper way to relate to the other liberated associates of the Lord is described in Śrīla Raghunātha dāsa Gosvāmī's *Śrī Vraja-vilāsa-stava*. The Divine Couple's pastimes are seen in Śrīla Raghunātha dāsa Gosvāmī's *Śrī Viśākhānanda-stotram* and other prayers.

You should see the *aṣṭa-kālīya* pastimes in those poems. The proper method of worship (*paddhati*) is seen in Śrīla Raghunātha dāsa Gosvāmī's *Śrī Manaḥ-śikṣā*. By following that method of worship, you will become rapt in meditation on the Divine Couple's pastimes. Ecstatic love (*bhāva*) is seen in Śrīla Raghunātha dāsa Gosvāmī's *Śrī Svaniyama-daśaka-stotram*. You should carefully observe the vows described in that poem. Śrīla Rūpa Gosvāmī described the *rasas* in his books. Lord Caitanya gave that task to him. However, Śrīla Rūpa Gosvāmī did not describe how an aspiring devotee can enter into these *rasas*. That, Śrīla Raghunātha dāsa Gosvāmī, following the teachings in Śrīla Svarūpa Dāmodara's *kaḍacā*, described. Lord Caitanya gave these specific tasks to these devotees, and they all followed His order.

Vijaya-kumāra: Please describe the tasks Lord Mahāprabhu ordered these devotees to perform.

Gosvāmī: The Lord ordered Śrīla Svarūpa Dāmodara Gosvāmī to describe the method of worship according to the *rasas*. Following that order, Śrīla Svarūpa Dāmodara Gosvāmī wrote his *kaḍacā*, which is divided into two parts, one part describing the internal path (*antaḥ-panthā*) of worship according to the *rasas*, and the other part describing the external path (*bahiḥ-panthā*) of worship according to the *rasas*. The internal path he placed around the neck of Śrīla Raghunātha dāsa Gosvāmī, who described that path in his writings. The external path Śrīla Svarūpa Dāmodara Gosvāmī gave to Śrīla Vakreśvara Paṇḍita. That teaching is the great treasure of this temple. That treasure I have given to Śrīla Dhyānacandra Gosvāmī, and he has written that treasure into a book. You already have a copy of that book.

Lord Mahāprabhu ordered Lord Nityānanda and Lord Advaita to preach the glories of the holy name, and He also gave Them the power to do it. Lord Mahāprabhu gave Śrīla Rūpa Gosvāmī the order to write books about the *rasas*, and He also gave him the power to do it. Lord Mahāprabhu gave Śrīla Sanātana Gosvāmī the order to write about *vaidhī-bhakti* and the relationship between *vaidhī-bhakti* and *rāga-bhakti*. The Lord also gave Śrīla Sanātana Gosvāmī the order to write about the Lord's *prākṛta* and *aprākṛta* pastimes in Gokula. Lord Nityānanda Prabhu and Śrīla Sanātana Gosvāmī gave Śrīla Jīva Gosvāmī the order to write books about *sambandha, abhidheya* and *prayojana*, and they also gave him the power to do it. All of these great devotees fulfilled the orders they were given.

Vijaya-kumāra: O master, what task was given to Śrīla Rāmānanda Rāya?

Gosvāmī: Lord Mahāprabhu gave Śrīla Rāmānanda Rāya the task of expanding the *rasas*. Śrīla Rāmānanda Rāya used Śrīla Rūpa Gosvāmī as his instrument in fulfilling this task.

Vijaya-kumāra: O master, what task was given to Śrīla Sārvabhauma Bhaṭṭācārya?

Gosvāmī: To Śrīla Sārvabhauma Bhaṭṭācārya, He gave the task of explaining philosophy. Śrīla Sārvabhauma Bhaṭṭācārya executed that task by having one of his disciples teach Śrīla Jīva Gosvāmī.

Vijaya-kumāra: What task did the Lord give to the great devotees in Bengal?

Gosvāmī: To the great devotees in Bengal, the Lord gave the task to teaching the truth about Lord Caitanya and showing the people how to have faith in Lord Caitanya's descriptions of *kṛṣṇa-rasa*. These devotees fulfilled that order by writing many books glorifying the *rasas*.

Vijaya-kumāra: What task was given to Śrīla Raghunātha dāsa Gosvāmī?

Gosvāmī: To him was given the task of preaching the glories of *Śrīmad-Bhāgavatam*.

Vijaya-kumāra: What task was given to Śrīla Gopāla Bhaṭṭa Gosvāmī?

Gosvāmī: To Śrīla Gopāla Bhaṭṭa Gosvāmī was given the task of stopping perverted misinterpretations of pure *śṛṅgāra-rasa* and also stopping the tendency not to have faith in *vaidhī-bhakti*.

Vijaya-kumāra: Śrīla Prabodhānanda Sarasvatī was the uncle and spiritual master of Śrīla Gopāla Bhaṭṭa Gosvāmī. What task was given to him?

Gosvāmī: To Śrīla Prabodhānanda Sarasvatī was given the task of showing the world that the path of the *rasas* and *anubhāvas* in Vraja is the highest of all paths.

Hearing all this, Vijaya-kumāra thought himself to be very fortunate.

Chapter Forty

The greatest good fortune

Jaiva-dharma

Vijaya-kumāra decided that by hearing about the Lord's pastimes in Vraja, one gradually attains the greatest good fortune. Thinking in this way, he posed a question.

Vijaya-kumāra: O master, I would like to know how many stages there are between first hearing about the Lord and finally attaining the greatest good fortune.

Gosvāmī: There are five stages: 1. *śravaṇa-daśā* (hearing), 2. *varaṇa-daśā* (desiring), 3. *smaraṇa-daśā* (remembering), 4. *bhāvapāñā-daśā* (attaining ecstasy) and 5. *prema-sampatti-daśā* (the greatest good fortune of spiritual love).

Vijaya-kumāra: Please describe *śravaṇa-daśā*.

Gosvāmī: When he attains faith in hearing about Kṛṣṇa (*kṛṣṇa-kathā*), a soul throws materialism (*bahirmukha-dāsa*) far away. In that stage, the soul yearns to hear about Kṛṣṇa. Such a soul intently hears about Kṛṣṇa from an exalted devotee.

This is described in *Śrīmad-Bhāgavatam* (4.29.40): My dear king, in the place where pure devotees live, following the rules and regulations and thus purely conscious, and engaged with great eagerness in hearing and chanting the glories of the Supreme Personality of Godhead, in that place, if one gets a chance to hear their constant flow of nectar, which is exactly like the waves of a river, one will forget the necessities of life—namely hunger, and thirst—and become immune to all kinds of fear, lamentation, and illusion.

Vijaya-kumāra: Sometimes, the people hear about Kṛṣṇa from materialists. What is the result of that hearing?

Gosvāmī: One may hear about Kṛṣṇa from a materialist, or one may hear about Kṛṣṇa from a devotee. These two kinds of hearing are different in many ways. By hearing about Kṛṣṇa from a materialist, the hearer does not gradually attain faith. On the other hand, by hearing about Kṛṣṇa from a devotee who is eager to engage in devotional service, the hearer attains spiritual piety. In some future birth, spiritual faith will rise within him. When he attains this faith, a soul is eager to hear the glories of Kṛṣṇa only from the mouths of great devotees. This stage is called *śravaṇa-daśā*. *Śravaṇa-daśā* is of two kinds: 1. *krama-śuddha-śravaṇa-daśā* and 2. *krama-hīna-śravaṇa-daśā*.

Vijaya-kumāra: What is *krama-hīna-śravaṇa-daśā*?

Gosvāmī: When the hearing is done without determination, and when it does not touch Lord Kṛṣṇa's pastimes, it is called *krama-hīna*. If there is no touch of Lord Kṛṣṇa's pastimes, the *rasas* will not become manifested.

Vijaya-kumāra: What is *krama-śuddha-śravaṇa-daśā*?

Gosvāmī: When hearing is done with great determination, and when it touches on Lord Kṛṣṇa's pastimes, then the *rasas* will become manifested. Hearing about Lord Kṛṣṇa's *aṣṭa-kālīya nitya-līlā* (regular pastimes in the eight periods of the day), and His birth pastime and other *naimittika-līlā* (occasional pastimes) is called *krama-śuddha-śravaṇa-daśā*. To properly engage in devotional service, one must perform *krama-śuddha-śravaṇa-daśā*. By again and again engaging in *krama-śuddha-śravaṇa-daśā*, and hearing the Lord's pastimes, one perceives how sweet the Lord's pastimes are. At that time, the activities of *rāgānuga-bhakti* rise in the heart of the hearer.

Then, the hearer thinks in his heart, "Aha! Subala has such wonderful ecstatic love! I should serve Kṛṣṇa in *sākhya-rasa*, as Subala does." This kind of activity is called *lobha* (greedy desire). To thus worship Kṛṣṇa by greedily following the liberated residents of Vraja is called *rāgānuga-bhakti*. I have given an example in *sākhya-rasa*. *Rāgānuga-bhakti* exists in the four *rasas* that begin with *dāsya-rasa*. By the mercy of Lord Caitanya, who is the master of our lives, you have become qualified for *śṛṅgāra-rasa*. Seeing the beautiful *gopīs* of Vraja, you have yearned to become like them. That yearning will lead you to the path of fulfilling that yearning. In truth, this is revealed in the conversation of the spiritual master and the disciple. That is *śravaṇa-daśā*.

Vijaya-kumāra: How does one attain the perfection of *śravaṇa-daśā*?

Gosvāmī: When one understands that Lord Kṛṣṇa's pastimes are eternal, and when one declares that they are pure and spiritual, one's heart will become enchanted by them. Then, one will become agitated with an intense desire to enter those pastimes. When he sees that the disciple is qualified, the spiritual master will show him the eleven *bhāvas* described in the scriptures. When the disciple's heart is passionately devoted to the Lord's pastimes—that is the perfection of *śravaṇa-daśā*. When he is greatly agitated in this way, the disciple attains *varaṇa-daśā*.

Vijaya-kumāra: O master, what is *varaṇa-daśā?*

Gosvāmī: Bound with the shackles of the eleven *bhāvas*, the heart becomes passionately attached to the Lord's pastimes. Weeping, the disciple falls before his spiritual master's feet. Then, the spiritual master's original form as a *sakhī* is manifested and the disciple manifests his original form as a *gopī* maidservant. This disciple is agitated to engage in devotional service as a *gopī*. By serving the spiritual master, the disciple attains the supreme goal of his life and becomes a beautiful girl in Vraja.

The disciple speaks these words (Śrīla Raghunātha dāsa Gosvāmī's *Śrī Prema-marandākhya-stava-rāja* 11-12): Taking a straw in his mouth, this person offers respectful obeisances unto you. This person is very unhappy. Please bring him to life by sprinkling him with the nectar of service to you. O *gopī* friend of Śrī Rādhā, as merciful Lord Kṛṣṇa never rejects a surrendered soul, even a soul who has performed many misdeeds, in the same way, I request that you please do not reject a person like me.

This state is called *varaṇa-daśā*. Then, in his form as a *sakhī*, the spiritual master gives to his disciple residence in Vraja and orders him to take shelter of Lord Kṛṣṇa's holy name and meditate on Lord Kṛṣṇa's pastimes. Then, the spiritual master gives encouragement, saying, "Soon you will attain what your heart desires."

Vijaya-kumāra: What is *smaraṇa-daśā?*

Gosvāmī: Śrīla Rūpa Gosvāmī gives this description (*Bhakti-rasāmṛta-sindhu* 1.2.150-152): Always meditating on Kṛṣṇa as the object of one's love, and always engaged in hearing and chanting His glories, a devotees should always live in the land of Vraja. Desiring to become like them, the *sādhaka* and *siddha* devotees should follow in the footsteps of the liberated residents of Vraja. In this way, the wise understand the activities of *vaidhī-bhakti*, which begin with hearing and chanting.

After hearing these three verses, Vijaya-kumāra asked, "What do the words *kuryād vāsaṁ vraje sadā* (a devotee should always live in the land of Vraja) mean?

Gosvāmī: Śrīla Jīva Gosvāmī explains: To place one's body in the circle of Vraja means to place it in the circle of the Lord's pastimes. If one is not able to place his physical body in Vraja, one can meditate on living in Vraja. By this meditation, one attains the final goal. Then one becomes the follower of a particular *sakhī*, one serves that *sakhī* in the forest, and one always meditates on that *sakhī* and her particular kind of love for Lord Kṛṣṇa. Thus you should engage your gross material body in the activities of *vaidhī-bhakti*, which begins with hearing and chanting, and also, with the eleven *bhāvas*, you should meditate on the pastimes of a liberated *sakhī* in Vraja. In this way, you should engage in devotional service. Thus you should engage your material body in the activities of *vaidhī-bhakti*. When your spiritual body becomes manifest, you will become averse to all that is not related to Vraja.

Vijaya-kumāra: Please clearly describe this path.

Gosvāmī: The word *vraja-vāsa* means, "to avoid the company of materialists." One should chant a certain prescribed number of holy names of Lord Hari and also meditate on the Lord's *aṣṭa-kālīya* pastimes. Do not think of your material body as an enemy. Rather, use it and everything in relationship with it in favorable service to the Lord.

Vijaya-kumāra: (after deep thought) O master, these descriptions are very pleasing to my heart. How can I make my heart determined to follow this path?

Gosvāmī: When it attains *rāgānuga-bhakti*, the heart will be determined. And, why not? If there is even a slight scent of *rāgānuga-bhakti*, then one will be inclined to Vraja. Then, one will no longer be attracted to material things. If you are worried that you will stray from the path, then at first proceed gradually. When you become steady, you will not be able to stray from the path.

Vijaya-kumāra: Please describe this gradual path.

Gosvāmī: Every day, for a certain amount of time, one should, avoiding all material interruptions, chant the holy name with sincere love. The time spent in this way should be gradually increased. When one finally spends all his time in this way, he will attain very wonderful love for the Lord. At that time, one will dread any external thing that may come to interrupt these activities.

Vijaya-kumāra: For how many days should one practice in this way?

Gosvāmī: Until one is free from all material obstacles, or until material obstacles no longer arise in one's meditation.

Vijaya-kumāra: What does it mean, "to remember the holy name with love?" Please clearly explain.

Gosvāmī: In the beginning, one joyfully chants the holy name. That joy leads one to think, "The holy name is mine." From that feeling of possessiveness, one attains love for the holy name. Gradually, pure ecstatic love (*bhāva*) becomes manifested. This is called *bhāvapāñā-daśā*. At the stage of *smaraṇa-daśā*, love is merely an external imposition. However, in the stage of *bhāvapāñā-daśā*, genuine, pure love is manifested. In this way, the devotee finally attains *prema*, the highest love. This is called *upāsanā-niṣṭhā*. There is also another path, which is called *upāsya-niṣṭhā*.

Vijaya-kumāra: What is *upāsya-niṣṭhā*?

Gosvāmī: If one wholeheartedly yearns to attain *prema*, he should honor this advice given by Śrīla Raghunātha dāsa Gosvāmī (*Manaḥ-śikṣā* text 3): Mind, listen to me! If you desire to reside in Vraja, birth after birth, and if you desire to directly serve the youthful Divine Couple, then with great love always remember and bow down before Śrīla Svarūpa Dāmodara Gosvāmī, Śrīla Rūpa Gosvāmī, his elder brother, Śrīla Sanātana Gosvāmī, and all their associates and followers.

Vijaya-kumāra: How does one gradually become purified by meditating on the Lord's *aṣṭa-kālīya* pastimes?

Gosvāmī: Please consider what Śrīla Rūpa Gosvāmī has said (*Ujjvala-nīlamaṇi, Gauṇa-sambhoga-prakarana*) about the great wonder of the *rasas* manifested in the Lord's *aṣṭa-kālīya* pastimes: Because it is shoreless, peerless, and unfathomable, I merely stand on the shore of the ocean of *rasa* and touch only one drop of its sweetness.

Why should this not be so? The ocean of *rasa* is spiritual, wonderful, all-pervading, and shoreless. If one tries to describe that spiritual ocean of *rasa* with words, his words will inevitably be both impure and incomplete. Even if the Supreme Lord Himself describes it, the hearers and readers, still bearing the faults that the material world impresses on them, will not be able to understand it perfectly. Therefore, because the ocean of *rasa* cannot e fathomed, one can merely stand at its shore and understand only a single drop of it.

Vijaya-kumāra: O master, if this is so, then how can I have any conception at all of the spiritual *rasas*?

Gosvāmī: The *mādhurya-rasa* is shoreless, peerless, and unfathomable. Lord Kṛṣṇa's pastimes are like that. However, Lord Kṛṣṇa has two transcendental qualities that give us hope: He is all-powerful, and He can do whatever He likes. Therefore, even though the ocean of *rasa* is peerless, shoreless, and unfathomable, Lord Kṛṣṇa can shrink it so that it fits within the material world. The material world is indeed a very small place. Still, if Kṛṣṇa wishes, He can bring His supremely glorious *rasas* to the small and insignificant material world. In this way, He mercifully descends to the material world and He takes His spiritual and eternal *rasas* and pastimes with Him.

When He descends to the material world, Kṛṣṇa brings with Him His own spiritual world of Mathurā-maṇḍala, which is beyond the touch of matter. One cannot ask how the Lord does all this. Why not? All this is done by His inconceivable potency. Even the demigods and other exalted beings are not intelligent enough to understand how it is done. In this way, the Lord manifested His Vraja pastimes, which are the best of all pastimes, and which are beyond the touch of matter. I do not lament merely because I cannot understand them perfectly or completely.

Vijaya-kumāra: If the Lord's *prakaṭa* (manifested) and *aprakaṭa* (unmanifested) pastimes are the same pastimes, then why are the *aprakaṭa* pastimes considered superior?

Gosvāmī: These two kinds of pastimes are identical. Of this there is no doubt. They are both perfect, complete, glorious and beyond the touch of matter. However, the *prakaṭa* pastimes can be seen and remembered by conditioned souls imprisoned in the material world, but the *aprakaṭa* pastimes can be seen only by purified souls who are in mature devotional service and who have attained the stage of *bhāvapāñā-daśā*.

O Vijaya-kumāra, to you I can disclose this secret. And why not? You are qualified to hear it. By practicing *smaraṇa-daśā* for a long time, one eventually becomes qualified for *bhāvapāñā-daśā*. During *smaraṇa-daśā*, one begins to become cleansed of material contamination, but that cleansing is not complete until one attains *bhāvapāñā-daśā*. By following *smaraṇa-daśā*, one attains pure *sādhana-bhakti*. In this way, by the Lord's mercy, pure devotional service is manifested in the devotee's heart. That pure devotion attracts Kṛṣṇa. In this way, by Lord Kṛṣṇa's mercy, the devotee advances beyond *smaraṇa-daśā.*

This is described by the Supreme Lord Himself in these words (*Śrīmad-Bhāgavatam* 11.14.26): When a diseased eye is treated with medicinal ointment, it gradually recovers its power to see. Similarly, as a conscious living entity cleanses himself of material contamination by hearing and chanting the pious narrations of My glories, he regains his ability to see Me, the Absolute Truth, in My subtle spiritual form.

This is also described in the following words of *Brahma-saṁhitā* (5.38): I worship the primeval Lord, Govinda, who is always seen by the devotee whose eyes are anointed with the pulp of love. He is seen in His eternal form of Śyāmāsundara, situated within the heart of the devotee.

A person who has attained the stage of *bhāvapāñā-daśā* attains spiritual vision and thus can see his spiritual master as a *sakhī* and *yūtheśvarī*. He can also see Lord Kṛṣṇa, the master of Goloka. Still, until his *liṅga-śarīra* (subtle material body) is at last dissolved, he does not attain *sampatti-daśā* (the greatest good fortune) and he does not see Kṛṣṇa at every moment. When he attains *bhāvapāñā-daśā*, the pure soul has complete control over his gross and subtle material bodies. However, only when he attains Lord Kṛṣṇa's complete and full mercy will the soul attain the final spiritual goal, where the soul completely breaks off all relationship with the material world of five elements. *Bhāvapāñā-daśā* is also called *svarūpa-siddhi*, and *sampatti-daśā* is also called *vastu-siddhi.*

Vijaya-kumāra: When one attains *vastu-siddhi*, in what way will he see Lord Kṛṣṇa's name, form, qualities, pastimes, and abode?

Gosvāmī: I cannot answer. When I myself attain *vastu-siddhi*, I will be able to see and tell. When you attain *sampatti-siddhi*, you will certainly be able to understand. You will understand without any struggle. And, why not? You will see it all before your eyes. You will not need to ask questions. Even what the soul sees at the stage of *svarūpa-siddhi* or *bhāvapāñā-daśā*, an ordinary person cannot understand. And, why not? Even if he hears, when a person in *bhāvapāñā-daśā* describes what he sees, an ordinary person will not understand the description.

The nature of a soul situated in *svarūpa-siddhi* is described by Śrīla

Rūpa Gosvāmī in these words (*Bhakti-rasāmṛta-sindhu* 1.3.29 and 1.4.12): If a person is completely detached from material enjoyment and has developed pure ecstatic devotion, even if he is sometimes accidentally found not living up to the standard of devotional service, one should not be envious of him. Only the most fortunate persons can achieve such success in life. Those who are simply academic students of the Vedic scriptures cannot appreciate how such a development takes place.

Vijaya-kumāra: If this is so, then why do the *Brahma-saṁhitā* and other scriptures try to describe the world of Goloka?

Gosvāmī: When, by the Lord's mercy, they attain the stage of *svarūpa-siddhi*, Brahmā and the demigods speak many prayers to describe what they have seen. However, ordinary persons who are less spiritually advanced cannot understand these prayers very well. Still, there is no need for the devotees to understand all these points. By Lord Kṛṣṇa's mercy, His *prakaṭa* pastimes are manifested, and you can worship Him. By doing that, you will attain all perfection. Within a short time, you will attain great spiritual faith, and then the spiritual world of Goloka will be manifested before you. Gokula is the same as Goloka. And, why not? Gokula and Goloka are not different places. That spiritual realm is not seen by the eyes of materialists. Materialists do not attain the stage of *svarūpa-siddhi*. Only persons who are qualified can see these spiritual truths.

Please Kṛṣṇa by engaging in His devotional service. Follow Kṛṣṇa's commands. By following Kṛṣṇa's commands, you will gradually attain His mercy. Then, your vision will be revived and perfect.

Vijaya-kumāra had no longer any doubts. He followed the eleven *bhāvas*. He meditated on Lord Kṛṣṇa's handsome form and pastimes. Staying in a cottage by the seashore, he always tasted the sweetness of pure spiritual love (*prema*). Meanwhile, Vrajanātha's mother fell sick with cholera and died. Vrajanātha and his grandmother returned home.

In Vrajanātha's pure heart was manifested pure love (*prema*) in *sākhya-rasa*. He passed his days staying among the Vaiṣṇavas by the Ganges shore at Śrīdhāma Navadvīpa. Vijaya-kumāra renounced household life and accepted the *kaupīna* of a *sannyāsī*. He lived by taking a little *mahā-prasādam* he obtained by *mādhukarī* begging. During the eight periods of the day, he meditated on Śrī Śrī Rādhā-Kṛṣṇa. At night, he briefly slept. He honored a little *prasādam*. While he was awake, he served the Divine Couple in ways appropriate to the particular time of day. On *japa* beads, he always chanted the holy names of Lord Hari. Sometimes he danced, sometimes he wept, and sometimes he smiled to see the waves in the ocean.

Who can understand the symptoms of his devotional life? He accepted the name Nimāi dāsa Bābājī. He would neither hear nor speak gossip. He was very humble. His actions were pure. He was fixed in devotional service. When someone offered him *mahā-prasādam* or cloth for his *kaupīna*, he accepted only what he actually needed. He never accepted more than that. When he chanted the holy names of Lord Hari, tears would stream from his eyes, his voice would become choked, and the hairs of his body would stand erect. After only a few days, he became perfect in devotional service. He obtained Lord Kṛṣṇa's mercy and thus he became qualified to enter the Lord's *aprakaṭa* pastimes. Like Haridāsa Ṭhākura, when he died, his material body was placed in a tomb by the seashore.

Gaura-premānanda Hari Hari bol!

Bearing with him the mercy of his spiritual master, Lord Kṛṣṇa, and the Vaiṣṇavas, a poor person named Bhaktivinoda labored greatly to write this book.

This book, Jaiva-dharma, written in the Bengali language, was completed by the Ganges' shore at Surabhī-kuñja in Godruma, at Navadvīpa, on the full moon day of the month of Māgha in the 410th year after Lord Caitanya's appearance in this world.

Persons who yearn to attain the lotus feet of Lord Gaura, the deliverer of the Kali-yuga, will have faith in this book.

I place a curse on any person who does not have even the smallest particle of faith, but still reads this book.

Persons who speak the theory of dry impersonal liberation cannot understand Kṛṣṇa. Only faithful persons can purely understand Lord Kṛṣṇa's pastimes in Vraja.